Long Cycles: Prosperit

Dennis Smith

August 1988

LONG CYCLES

Prosperity and War in the Modern Age

JOSHUA S. GOLDSTEIN

Yale University Press: New Haven and London

Set in Times Roman type by
Keystone Typesetting, Orwigsburg, Pa.
Printed in the United States of America by
Edwards Brothers, Inc., Ann Arbor, Mich.

Library of Congress Cataloging-in-Publication Data

Goldstein, Joshua S., 1952–
    Long cycles: Prosperity and war in the modern age.

    Revision of thesis (Ph.D.)—Massachusetts
Institute of Technology.
    Bibliography: p.
    Includes index.
    1. Long waves (Economics)   2. Business cycles.
I. Title.
HB3729.G64   1988   338.5'42   87–10723
ISBN 0–300–03994–8 (alk. paper)
ISBN 0–300–04112–8 (pbk.: alk. paper)

10   9   8   7   6   5   4   3   2   1

The author gratefully acknowledges permission to
reproduce the following: Table 6.1 appeared originally
in Jack S. Levy, "Series of General Wars," *World
Politics* 37, no. 3 (April 1985), © 1985 by Princeton
University Press; reprinted by permission of Princeton
University Press. Figure 13.8 appeared originally in
S. H. Steinberg, *The Thirty Years' War and the
Conflict for European Hegemony, 1600–1660,* © 1966
by S. H. Steinberg; reprinted by permission of W. W.
Norton & Company.

For my teachers

Generally, operations of war require . . . 100,000 mailed troops. . . . [E]xpenditures . . . will amount to one thousand pieces of gold a day. After this money is in hand, 100,000 troops may be raised. . . .

Where the army is, prices are high; when prices rise the wealth of the people is exhausted. When wealth is exhausted the peasantry will be afflicted with urgent exactions. With strength thus depleted and wealth consumed the households in the central plains will be utterly impoverished and seven-tenths of their wealth dissipated.

—Sun Tzu, *The Art of War* (ca. 400 B.C.)

CONTENTS

LIST OF FIGURES

LIST OF TABLES

PREFACE

As this book goes to press, the connection between economics and war is a "hot topic." Both the American and Soviet economies, struggling under the burden of large military expenditures, are facing major obstacles to sustained prosperity. In the United States, these take the form of massive debts and government and trade deficits. The Reagan administration military buildup has slowed substantially for reasons of cost, but the price tag for 1980–85 will be with us for some years to come. In the Soviet Union, economic growth has been extremely sluggish in recent years, partly as a result of central planners' allocation of investment to the military rather than consumption and other sectors.

This, however, is not a book about current events. It explains neither how to solve the debt problem, nor when the next war will break out, nor even how to get rich playing long cycles on the stock market. It does, I hope, offer new perspectives and insights for thinking about current issues in light of longer-term historical processes.

The roots of this book go back to two experiences I had in 1970. First, my high-school social studies class heard a lecture by Professor Robert North of Stanford's political science department, who described how researchers were using quantitative analyses and computers to better understand conflict, escalation, and war. I found the idea irresistible and went on to work with Professor North during a good part of the next decade. Second, as a freshman at Stanford I took a seminar from Pierre Noyes, a theoretical physicist, on "the terrestrial revolution." This seminar dealt with long-term social evolution on planet Earth and introduced me to Marxist traditions, among other things.

Later in the 1970s I had the good fortune to work with the late Professor William Linvill, head of the Stanford Department of Engineering-Economic Systems. Professor Linvill showed me how to look at economics from a broad social perspective and how to bring numbers to life and play with them. As I complete this book, I look back gratefully to the contributions of these three teachers in particular.

The book itself is a revised version of my Ph.D. thesis, completed at the MIT Department of Political Science under the supervision of Hayward R. Alker, Jr. Without Professor Alker's intellectual and practical support over the past four years, the book could never have taken form.

Past research on long cycles has the reputation of being at best a well-meaning effort in a field where scientifically valid results are impossible and at worst an exercise in astrology and mysticism. Why has there been such a hostile reception to long cycles among the established academic disciplines, especially economics? I think the answer has to do with a paradigm shift required to take long cycles seriously. Long cycles require thinking on a new time scale, looking at history differently, thinking about the connections of economics and politics in new ways.

I first became interested in long cycles because of the fascinating theoretical questions raised in the past debates on this topic—debates reviewed in Part One of the book. Different schools of research have created different theories of long cycles; notably, Marxists and non-Marxists have seen reality through different lenses. As I dug into the long cycle debates, I realized that many of the central theoretical questions could not be answered without new empirical research. My empirical analyses are reported in Part Two of the book. I have included my data base as a resource for others interested in historical issues of political economy. In so doing, I hope to encourage others to give greater attention to long-term historical processes. I have also provided a bibliography of about 670 works referred to in the book. The bibliography is a resource for further work in the field, particularly to help those interested in long cycles to become familiar with works in a variety of traditions.

My research on long cycles has benefited from the advice and suggestions of many people. Randall Forsberg shared her thoughts extensively on the relevance of the project to security issues. W. Dean Burnham, Manus Midlarsky, and Bruce Russett offered many constructive ideas after reading earlier drafts. Others who contributed helpful ideas include Richard Ashley, Francis Beer, Suzanne Berger, Albert Bergesen, Lincoln Bloomfield, Peter Brecke, Christopher Chase-Dunn, Nazli Choucri, Lee Farris, Jay Forrester, John Freeman, Avram Goldstein, Dora Goldstein, Harold Guetzkow, Nancy Hodes, Robert Keohane, Charles Kindleberger, Joseph Klesner, Edward Kolodziej, Peter LeMieux, Jack Levy, Cathie Martin, George Modelski, Steve Moss, Robert North, Pierre Noyes, Kate Rooney, Andra Rose, Steve Rosenstone, Peter Senge, Drorah Setel, David Singer, William Stanley, Sally Zierler, Dina Zinnes, and the editors of the *International Studies Quarterly*. I also benefited from comments by faculty and students at several universities where I presented parts of this work—MIT, Indiana University at Bloomington, University of Illinois at Champaign-Urbana, Boston University, Syracuse University, University of California at Los Angeles, University of Southern California, and Yale University.

Travel funds provided by the National Science Foundation, the MIT Department of Political Science, and Hayward Alker, Jr., allowed me to present papers about my work at three conferences. Computer funds were provided by the MIT Department of Political Science. The book is based on work supported under a National Science Foundation Graduate Fellowship. Any opinions, findings, conclusions or recommendations expressed herein are mine and do not necessarily reflect the views of the National Science Foundation.

In summarizing theoretical debates I review, condense, and organize many scholarly works as I search for the "big picture." Although I have tried to make the "small pictures" accurate as well, in such a process I have probably misunderstood or miscommunicated particular points in certain works or categorized others' work in ways they might not have done themselves. To any such misrepresented colleagues I apologize in advance.

CHAPTER ONE

World System and World Views

In 1983 President Ronald Reagan, in a speech to the American Legion, accused the American peace movement of making "the same old mistake" British prime minister Neville Chamberlain had made before World War II—trying to "wage peace by weakening the free."

The next day, the Soviet Novosti news agency commented that "as usual, [Reagan] seems not to be well-versed in history." The real mistake of the 1930s, according to Novosti, had been committed by Western governments that had equated the peace and anti-Nazi movements in their countries with socialism and communism, while ignoring the threat from fascism. It is President Reagan, according to Novosti, who repeats the same old mistake "when he insists that the current peace movement is communist-inspired."[1]

Political leadership in today's world is dominated by the generation that came of age in World War II; and the "lessons of history" for this generation tend to be the lessons of World War II and the forty years since. These "lessons" underlie the practice of world politics today, especially superpower deterrence, in fundamental ways.

But world history is more than the history of one generation. World politics today grows out of many centuries of evolution and is rooted directly in the development of the Eurocentric world system over the past five centuries. This book examines the dynamics of that integrated world system of politics and economics, centered in Europe, as it developed between the sixteenth and twentieth centuries.

The *world system,* as a useful and appropriate concept with relevance to contemporary world politics, is the first of four themes that intersect in the book. The second theme is the close connection between *economics and politics* at the international level. A third theme is the concept of *social cycles,* for which the book seeks to develop an appropriate definition and framework—drawing on both quantitative and qualitative approaches. And the fourth theme is the interplay of revolutionary, liberal, and conservative *world views* that shape the ways in which different research schools see the first three themes (the world system, political economy, and social cycles).

1. *Boston Globe,* 24 Aug. 1983, p. 1; 25 Aug. 1983, p. 9.

1

The style of this work is *adductive*. The goal is to develop a *plausible* account that is both internally consistent˙ and largely consistent with empirical evidence. The adduced long cycle theory lies somewhere between proven "fact" and ungrounded speculation. It is a first cut at a comprehensive treatment of long cycles and a starting point for future work (which will undoubtedly force revisions in the theory). The work is intended to be "definitive" in its comprehensive treatment of the subject of long cycles; but the state of knowledge resulting from my study is still quite preliminary.

The World System

My first theme is the world system as a meaningful unit of analysis. A world level of analysis is distinct from an international one. The international level consists of the interactions of separable units—sovereign nation-states—while the world level consists of a single, holistic system whose parts are mutually constitutive rather than separable.[2]

The most important features of the world system for this book are its political and economic structure and dynamics. The world system is characterized *economically* by the unequal geographical division of labor between the core (secondary producers of manufactured goods) and the periphery (primary producers of raw materials). *Politically* the system is characterized by the systematic use of violence both to maintain and to change the power relationships in the system. Those power relationships include both the dominance of the core over the periphery and the struggle for dominance of one political unit over others within the core (hegemony).

The pattern of regional division of labor between primary and secondary producers—along with the violently enforced dominance of the core over the periphery—traces back to early societies and empires. In the ancient city-state on a river, peasants upstream produced food, which was shipped downstream to the city at low cost using the river as an energy source. The city in turn shipped (lighter-weight) weapons and luxury goods upstream to the local warriors who suppressed the peasants. In later, larger, Mediterranean empires, a similar pattern occurred, with oar-driven slave boats bringing food and raw materials to the metropolis from the peripheral regions along the coast.

With the advent of the sailing ship in fifteenth-century Portugal, a few individuals could move a large cargo efficiently almost anywhere in the world, using the wind as their energy source and the ocean as their medium. This, with the addition of shipborne cannons,[3] allowed the Europeans to dominate trade globally and laid the basis for a truly world system of politics and economics. The core of the world system consisted of the most developed European countries, and the periphery was

2. The world system perspective thus, in my opinion, goes beyond the level of analysis labeled as "international" by Waltz (1959) or Singer (1961). In addition to the individual, national, and international levels, the world system constitutes a fourth level of analysis (see North 1985: chap. 12).

3. See Cipolla (1965).

wherever their sailing ships (and later steamships along with railroads to the interior) could take them. European monarchs thus concentrated economic surplus from large areas, using that surplus, among other things, to fund the making of wars on each other. These wars brought about the consolidation of the nation-state system in Europe beginning about five centuries ago.

This book is about the economic and political core of the world system. It focuses on the most advanced, largest economies at the center of the world economy, which generally are also the military great powers at the center of world politics.[4] It does not, except in passing, deal with relations between the core and periphery of the world system or the issues of underdevelopment in the periphery, of global exploitation, or of violence and war in the periphery, although these areas contain many interesting and important questions. The world system has been a Eurocentric one,[5] and this book, focusing on the core, will be Eurocentric as well.

Immanuel Wallerstein (1974, 1980) sparked the current world system debates with his Marxist interpretation of the development of the "modern world-system" in sixteenth- to eighteenth-century Europe. Capitalism has been a "world-economy" from the outset, Wallerstein (1974:86) argues, with a division of labor between world regions.[6] Manufactured goods are produced mainly in the core and raw materials mainly in the periphery; between them are intermediate producing regions called the "semi-periphery." Each of these three zones has its own form of production, its own historical mode of labor (slaves, serfs, and wageworkers, respectively), and its own modes of political control (Wallerstein 1974:87).[7]

Wallerstein (1974:38) states that three things were necessary for the creation of a capitalist world-economy: (1) the expansion of the geographic size of the "world" (led by the Portuguese sailing ships),[8] (2) the differentiation of labor by product and zone, and (3) the creation of strong state machineries in the core states.

Core and peripheral areas are not unchanging, according to Wallerstein, nor are they homogeneous. An area such as North America, which began outside the world-economy, could become incorporated into the periphery and later become part of the core. Within the core, there is constant competition and conflict between rival states and elites, and within states there is conflict between classes. The overall structure of

4. I will not distinguish separate economic and military definitions of the core.

5. The core eventually expanded to include the United States, Soviet Union, and Japan. The present configuration of core and periphery is global, dividing the industrialized north from the impoverished south.

6. Wallerstein's neo-Marxist approach differs from traditional Marxist approaches in its stress on international class divisions rather than on domestic class divisions within industrialized countries.

7. Bergesen (1980:124) notes that all three zones constitute "one mode of production [capitalism]. To make the *slavery* that harvests cotton which is then spun into cloth by British *wage* earners into two modes of production denies the obvious connection."

8. A "world-system" in Wallerstein's usage need not include every area of the globe. Rather it implies a system that is (1) international (though this does not negate the strong dynamics operating at the national and subnational levels), and (2) the dominant system in the world. Wallerstein's (1974:301) "world-economy" does not encompass certain "external arenas" that are not integrated into the world-economy, for example, Russia until the 18th or 19th c. These differ from the "peripheral" areas that are integral to the world-economy.

the world-system remains the same, however, despite this "game of musical chairs" (Hopkins and Wallerstein 1979:485).

My approach to the world system in many ways flows out of Wallerstein's but is not a Marxist interpretation. It does not see capitalism as the essential defining characteristic of the world system, and it sees politics as coequal with economics even over the long run, not as arising ultimately from economic forces.[9] I have focused on the core countries rather than the periphery and have given war a central place in the analysis. In both these ways my approach reflects "realist" rather than neo-Marxist conceptions of the world system.[10] But in other respects this study draws more on Marxist than realist conceptions, and despite the differences in my approach from Wallerstein's many of my conclusions converge with his.

Economics and Politics

I will develop in this book the theme of interconnection between economics and politics in the core of the world system.[11] On the *economic* level, I focus on the economies of the core countries as they developed over five centuries. Whereas most economic histories of Europe stress secular economic growth (and technological advances as a driving force of that growth), I will stress the different phases—expansion and stagnation—along the way as these economies developed. The economy of Europe did not develop in one continuous forward motion but in phases marked by accelerated growth or by stagnation, by high or low inflation. The long-term ups and downs of national economies are not autonomous but synchronous throughout the core. Synchrony spreads to larger and larger regions of the world over the centuries as the core expands (see chapter 9).[12]

9. Politics is, however, constrained by economic forces and certainly not autonomous from economics.

10. In neo-Marxist approaches, the unequal relationship between core and periphery is the primary contradiction (to use Mao's terminology), and relationships within the core are secondary. In my approach, contradictions *within* the core itself are central to the development of the world system, and I give the periphery less attention. Also, Marxists generally treat war as an outcome of deeper socioeconomic forces rather than as a driving force in itself. My approach gives war a central role in the development of the system. The system of war among great power nation-states strongly influences both economic development and class relationships.

11. I will emphasize politics at the international level (primarily war) and will delve only slightly into domestic politics. Likewise in economics the emphasis will be on the world economy as a whole rather than the domestic economies of each country. While this approach is consistent with the level of analysis of this study, it goes against both traditional Marxist approaches (stressing class struggle within core countries) and contemporary "comparative politics" (stressing domestic factors and comparisons among countries).

12. Jozsef Nyilas (1976:14–16), a Hungarian Marxist, says of the past two centuries: "The production and thus the very existence of each nation of the world . . . depend, more or less, on other nations' production." The world division of labor represents "the socialization of production of the highest order, reaching over frontiers and tending increasingly to integrate the independent economies of their units into a uniform whole—a world economy." Even today, with the split between socialist and capitalist economies, the "world-economy remains . . . as a peculiar antagonistic unity of the two existing socioeconomic systems."

Lwy 1983

On the *political* level, the core experiences structural shifts over time, from greater hegemony (a hierarchical structure in which one nation is firmly on top) toward greater competition (a flatter hierarchy in which nations are vying for position). Ultimately, the position of nations in such a system has been decided by resort to war. In studying wars among the core countries, I rely on Levy's (1983a) quantitative data set on wars in the "great power system" since 1495 as well as his definitions of countries that belonged to that system (a membership that changes over time). "Great power wars" (wars between two or more great powers) have occurred sixty-four times between 1495 and 1975 according to Levy's count. These sixty-four wars are particularly important in this study.[13]

Although no country has yet exerted complete control in the sense of an embracing empire, a few countries have at times gained ascendancy within the core. At other times the structure of the core has not centered so strongly on one country, being more multipolar and competitive. A *hegemonic* power is a core state that commands an unrivaled position of economic and military superiority among the core states and is thus able largely to shape the operation of the international system. The position of the Netherlands in the seventeenth century, of Great Britain in the nineteenth century, and of the United States in the mid-twentieth century are commonly cited as such cases. Other countries have made concerted drives for world dominance but have failed (for example, Napoleon's France and Hitler's Germany).

The economic and political processes of the core are closely intertwined. There is a strong historical connection between economic long waves and bouts of severe[14] great power wars. And the struggle for hegemony is as much an economic as a political phenomenon. The strongest economic units can support the most powerful political and military capabilities and hence gain position in the world order. Conversely, political and military position are used to further a country's economic enrichment.

Social Cycles

The third theme of the book—and the immediate object of study—is the attempt to understand long cycles in social life, cycles that take longer than a generation to complete. The very word *cycle* seems to ring alarm bells for many social scientists. They presume it to mean something mechanistic or even mystical, beyond scientific inquiry, and unproven if not unprovable. Social systems,

13. Violence within the core cannot be claimed to be either more important or more pervasive than in (or against) the periphery, but this book limits the focus to the core as the locus of forces that drive the development of the world system. Galtung (1980:70) distinguishes four types of violence: (1) revolutionary violence directed against exploitation (vertical violence from below); (2) counterrevolutionary violence (vertical violence from above); (3) horizontal violence between equals over some incompatible goals; and (4) random violence "related neither to interests nor to goals." This book focuses on the third type (horizontal violence between the core states).

14. The "severity" of war is a term borrowed from Singer and Small's (1972) approach (which Levy also uses) and refers to battle fatalities.

unlike the physical world, are not only enormously complex but self-directing and continually evolving. The word *cycle,* for some, evokes images of clockwork mechanisms exhibiting strict periodicity and regularity of a type ill-suited for describing social processes.[15]

One of the challenges of this book is to develop appropriate definitions and methodologies for the study of social cycles. In the physical sciences, the interval of time making up a cycle can be treated as a fixed, constant, and measurable number, a frequency. In the social sciences, however, the length of a phase can vary, and the appropriate emphasis is on a regularly recurring sequence rather than a fixed periodicity. As Part Two tries to show, it is possible to define, measure, and analyze long cycles using "cycle time" rather than periodicity.

In the physical world, cycles are central to the structuring of mass/energy throughout the universe at every level; but every level also manifests noncyclical, irreversible change in time. Electromagnetic radiation, a basic form of mass/energy in the universe, contains a cyclical component (wave nature) as well as a forward or linear component (particle nature), and I find these two kinds of motion to be very basic to systems at all levels. Doran (1971:2) writes of social change:

Historical continuity and change manifest themselves in two basic forms: as a *cyclical repetition* of events, which gives the appearance of novelty but in fact reasserts the fundamental similarity and uniformity of events; and as a long-term *linear evolution or progression of events,* which . . . represents the emergence of new ideas and problem-contexts.

My approach acknowledges the importance of both repetitive and evolutionary change. The image of a *spiral* embodies both types of motion—cyclical and linear. The end point of a long cycle is not the same as its beginning. Long cycles are not a mechanical process but a repetition of themes, processes, and relationships along the path of an evolving social system. The world system itself is not only changing through time in a quantitative sense but also passing through qualitative stages of development over time. I will thus combine repetition and evolution, cycles and stages, continuity and change, in tracing the development of the core of the world system over five centuries.

The cyclical view of social change seems to gain adherents during stagnant phases of social growth (see chapter 2). Historian E. H. Carr describes the cyclical approach as "the characteristic ideology of a society in decline."[16] Van der Zwan (1980:199) agrees that "in the face of a crisis there is a psychological inclination to look for security. The concept of recurrent movements . . . seems to offer an element of continuity."

Cycles of many lengths are woven into social life. Braudel (1972:892) refers to a

15. This is one reason many writers have adopted the terminology of *waves* rather than *cycles.* But neither wave nor cycle conveys an inherently mechanistic implication, in my view. Both terms can refer either to physical periodicity or to a non-periodic repeating sequence (see chap. 8). In this book, the term *long wave* will be reserved for the economic cycle of about 50 years' duration, and the term *long cycle* will refer to the more general class of social cycles longer than about 20 years.

16. Carr (1975) quoted in Eklund (1980).

"web of vibrations which makes up the economic world." In existing research on all long cycles (real or imagined), the greatest interest lies in two clusters: (1) economic cycles of roughly 50 years' duration (long waves), and (2) longer cycles of hegemony and hegemonic war.[17] These two cycles are the subject of this book.[18] The long wave (roughly 50 years) will be taken up in chapters 2–4 and 8–12 and the hegemony cycle (roughly 150 years) in chapters 5–6 and 13–14.

Long waves (or Kondratieff cycles) are defined by alternating economic phases— an *expansion phase* (for which I will often use the more convenient term *upswing*) and a *stagnation phase* (which I will often call the *downswing*).[19] These economic phase periods are not uniform in length or quality. The transition point from an expansion phase to a stagnation phase is called a *peak,* and that from stagnation to expansion is a *trough.*[20] The long wave, which repeats roughly every fifty years, is synchronous across national borders, indicating that the alternating phases are a systemic-level phenomenon.

Hegemony cycles are ultimately defined by a special set of wars that I call *hegemonic wars* (see chapter 13). These wars mark the end of a long period of hegemonic decline and rivalry and the rise of a new hegemony in the world system. Shifts between hegemony and rivalry in the core follow a cyclical pattern but on a longer time scale than the long wave. Hegemonic war is followed by strong hegemony (as one country emerges from war in the strongest position), followed by the weakening of hegemony, increasing competition, and ultimately another hegemonic war. This sequence, which I call the *hegemony cycle,* takes on the order of a century and a half to complete. Thus several economic long waves occur within one hegemony cycle. But the hegemonic wars, dating the long hegemony cycle, do not seem to be tightly synchronized with the shorter ups and downs of the long wave.

Superficially, the long wave is an economic phenomenon, and the hegemony cycle is a political one. But in fact the long wave contains key political elements (war plays a central role), and the hegemony cycle contains economic elements (economic hegemony and competition).

17. Cycles of different lengths are not mutually exclusive: the hegemony cycle contains long waves, and the long wave contains shorter economic fluctuations.

18. They should be distinguished from other postulated cycles that will be treated only superficially if at all:

1. Business (or "trade" or "Juglar") cycles, about 5 years long (see also Macrae 1981 on "political business cycles" of 4–5 years, based on the frequency of elections in democratic countries).

2. "Kitchin" cycles, about 10 years long, thought to be based on depreciation of short-term capital investments.

3. "Kuznets" cycles ("building cycles" or "long swings") about 20 years long, based on waves of migration and the associated construction booms.

4. Very long cycles. Forrester (1981a:5) refers to an S-shaped "life cycle of economic development" lasting over 200 years. Earl Cook (1972) identifies four long logistic curves of energy and materials use and human population over the past million years—of which Forrester's curve would be the fourth. Taagepera (1978, 1979) describes "life cycles" of empires often spanning many centuries.

19. The stagnation phase does not always show actual decline, however, but only a lower rate of growth than the upswing phase.

20. The dates of these transition points define the historical dating of the long wave phases (see chap. 8).

The long wave has been historically realized in nine cycles between the years 1495 and 1945.[21] The same period has seen three hegemony cycles. These cycles have been not fixed and mechanical but irregular and evolutionary through time. They do not allow us to predict the future, but they can help us to understand the dynamics of international politics in its deep context and to understand better how the "lessons of history" apply to today's world.

Revolutionary, Liberal, and Conservative World Views

In the first part of the book I review, compare, and integrate various bodies of literature relevant to the study of long cycles. The existing literature on long cycles consists of disconnected fragments of theory and evidence, with no consensus on what a long cycle is, how to measure and identify it, or how to account for it theoretically. The book's first task is to make sense of these past studies, to compare them, and to account for differences and similarities among them.

As an ordering principal for that review, I distinguish three *world views*—revolutionary, liberal, and conservative—that shape different perspectives, approaches, and epistemologies. They are the lenses through which people see the world and the frameworks within which theories of that world are built.

The three world views shape the outlines of the major theoretical traditions in the long wave debate (see chapters 2 and 3) and in the war/hegemony debate (chapters 5 and 6). The different research schools rooted in each world view have different vocabularies, theoretical frameworks, methodologies, and results—and communication among them is problematical. I will try to interpret between them without being wedded to one particular school or world view. The three world views are only approximate ideal types. They should be seen not as a rigid framework but as a tool for understanding the long cycle field and its development from a philosophy of science perspective (see chapter 7). I will not try to give a definitive or full explanation of each world view.

Theoretical and empirical work from six research schools (three on long waves and three on hegemony cycles) will be drawn on in an effort to find both agreements and differences between them. Despite the major differences among the theories of different research schools, many areas of convergence can be found. I call this approach *triangulation* in the sense of locating the object of study by taking bearings from different angles.[22]

The idea of triangulation is shown schematically in figure 1.1. In the center is the

21. While most past work on long waves has referred only to the industrial period of history (the 19th and 20th c.), this book extends the analysis back to around 1500—the starting point for Wallerstein's (1974) "modern world-system" and Levy's (1983a) "great power system."

22. Alker and Biersteker (1984) use a triangular framework to structure their summary of the international relations field. They argue that "alternative approaches to International Relations theorizing . . . should be taken seriously . . . . There are genuine insights to be gained from any of the major traditions which are hard to appreciate until their genuine vantage points and learned achievements are better appreciated."

Figure 1.1. The Triangulation of World Views

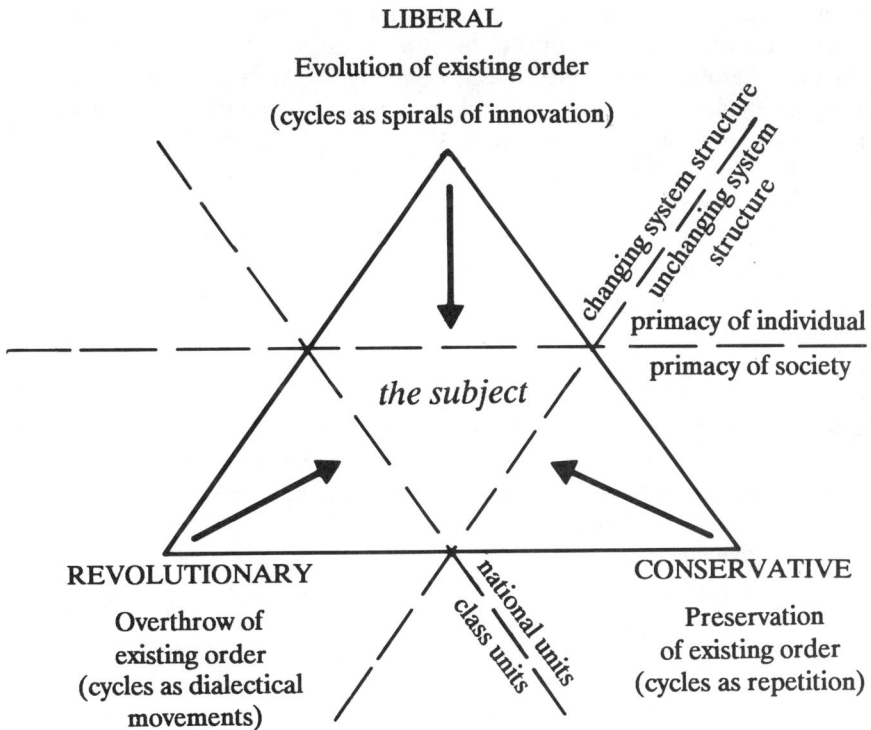

LIBERAL

Evolution of existing order

(cycles as spirals of innovation)

changing system structure   *unchanging system structure*

the subject

primacy of individual

primacy of society

REVOLUTIONARY

Overthrow of
existing order
(cycles as dialectical
movements)

class units   *national units*

CONSERVATIVE

Preservation
of existing order
(cycles as repetition)

subject being studied—long cycles. Each of the three world views represents an angle from which this reality is seen—conditioning the thematic questions asked, the types of data examined, the methodologies used, the theories postulated, and the conclusions drawn.

The conservative approach centers thematically on the "preservation of the established order" and is "opposed to change or innovation."[23] Conservative theories tend to portray the world as a relatively timeless and unchanging structure and hence see cycles as repetition—a regular repetition of the same rhythms over time.

The liberal approach centers thematically on the evolution of the existing order. Continual progress, brought about through human innovation, leads to greater freedom (material and political) for the individual. Liberal theories portray cycles as upward spirals leading to higher stages of social evolution.

23. Webster's Collegiate Dictionary, S. V. "conservative."

The revolutionary approach centers thematically on the overthrow of the existing order and on its internal contradictions, which inevitably produce crises. Cycles are seen as dialectical movements—the product of internal contradictions that drive the system in which they are found toward its own negation and transformation.

Figure 1.1 also indicates some distinguishing aspects that separate each world view from the other two (dotted lines). Conservatives tend to see the structure of society as essentially fixed; liberals and revolutionaries tend to see that structure as changing (in an evolutionary or revolutionary manner). Liberals see the important driving force of society as residing in the individual person; revolutionaries and conservatives see society as more important than the individual.[24] For revolutionaries, the social class is the key actor in world affairs; for conservatives and liberals, it is the nation. Finally, revolutionaries tend to see economics as shaping politics, conservatives see politics as shaping economics, and liberals tend to see the two as autonomous.

World Views and International Economics

Benjamin Ward (1979:viii, 461–62) structures his overview of economic theories around these three world views (a term he also uses).[25] He argues that these (and only these) three distinctive world views have shaped the study of economics; that each builds its own framework of reference within which its theories and their variants are judged; and that communication among them is problematical. The "shift from one world view to another is really like shifting from one world to another."

The *liberal* tradition, according to Ward (1979a:3, 8, 9), first reached maturity in the eighteenth century and currently is the "ideological heart of the belief system" of almost all practicing U.S. economists. It is embodied in the economic and political structures of the most advanced industrialized countries, in the principles of affluence, social openness, and concern for public welfare. Free markets as opposed to bureaucracies are supported by liberalism (Ward, 1979a:25–26), as markets sum up the actions of individual people and individual deals: "The market captures the essence of the liberal notion that what counts is not nations but individuals and that big changes are made up of a large number of small ones." Ward (1979a:102) sums up the liberal view of human nature as hedonism (seeking pleasure, avoiding pain), rationalism (making deliberate choices), and atomism (the essential separateness of human beings).

Ward's (1979:175) *radical* world view is defined by two qualities—a "commitment to the wretched of the earth" and a belief that human wretchedness is unnecessary and yet "cannot be eliminated within the framework of existing society." Capitalist society, with its "constant contrasts between extremes of deprivation and

24. See n. 27, below.
25. Ward uses the term *radical* rather than *revolutionary,* which I prefer. My triangular scheme was developed independently of Ward's, which I was not yet aware of. I took the term *world view* from Thomas Kuhn (1970:111). Ward, although Kuhnian in flavor, does not cite Kuhn. Readers interested in explorations of economic issues from each of the three world views will enjoy Ward's book.

wealth,'' makes the best case for the radical world view. And radical theory is not just ''academic'' but explicitly a tool for developing successful strategies to change the world. According to Ward (1979:175), radical thought is centered on political economy, because ''material deprivation is at the heart of most of the misery in the world today.'' Radical thought has been in the process of developing for at least two centuries, although its concern with practical change means that contemporary affairs are of greatest interest. Radical thought is currently at a ''relatively low ebb'' in U.S. economics departments[26] but is surging in the third world and is firmly rooted in the socialist countries, according to Ward.

Ward (1979:325) argues that the *conservative* world view is even more under-represented in U.S. economics departments than the radical view, although conservatives have played a major role in the reevaluation of Keynesian economics and the emergence of public choice theory in recent years. The conservative tradition rests on four points, according to Ward (1979:326): rejection of utopian and mechanistic solutions to social problems; recognition of the individual person as the primary element in society;[27] emphasis on the family as the most important social unit; and belief that government must provide order if society is to function effectively. Ward (1979c:20) points to ancient China and Venice as examples of successful, durable societies based on conservative principles. Finally, Ward (1979c:33) stresses the centrality of property rights in the conservative economic view. Property rights must be exclusive, transferable, well defined, enforceable, and not prohibitively expensive to define, enforce, and transfer.

Moving from Ward's general economic distinctions to international economics in particular, the three world views may be seen as shaping the traditions of Marxist theories of imperialism, liberal free trade theory, and conservative mercantilism, respectively. With respect to international trade, the Marxist perspective sees trade as an exploitative relationship benefiting the capitalists of the core countries. In the liberal view, free trade benefits all parties involved, since each uses its comparative advantage for maximum efficiency. The conservative mercantilist view holds that trade should be used to build up national wealth to compete more effectively with other nations.

World Views and International Politics

As with economic theories, so too in the study of world politics, different world views generate different explanations and areas of focus (see Thompson, ed., 1983). For example, Wallerstein's (1974) interpretation, discussed earlier in this chapter, is

26. A number of journals, however, do publish Marxist economic thought, and radical political economy is still alive, though not dominant, in the United States.

27. In my view, the paramount importance of the individual is more a liberal than a conservative belief. It traces back to classical liberalism in the 18th c., when it was a rather radical, antimonarchist idea. Two hundred years later, and in contrast to today's socialist radicalism, the same belief looks rather conservative. Ward's version of ''conservatism'' resembles libertarianism, which he calls the ''pure breed'' of conservatism. Milton Friedman's views are included in Ward's ''conservative'' grouping, but Friedman (1962) himself calls those views ''liberal'' in the classical sense.

a Marxist elaboration in which the world system is inherently structured by capitalism and defined by global class divisions between core and periphery.

Conservative scholars of international relations, by contrast, see world politics as a balance of power system made up of roughly equal, autonomous states. In this view, the division between core and periphery is much less important than the balance of power among core states. While revolutionary approaches see the modern world system as a phase in the development of human society through successive modes of production, conservative approaches see the balance of power system as more or less timeless and eternal.

Liberal approaches to the world system tend, like revolutionary ones, to see the system as evolving (developing) over time but see the political and economic elements of the system as largely independent of each other. Revolutionaries, by contrast, tend to see economic factors as shaping political ones internationally as well as domestically,[28] while conservatives tend to see power politics as dominant over economics. These distinctions will be discussed further in chapters 5 and 6.

Methodological Issues

As these four themes indicate, I undertake in this book a macro analysis of social dynamics over relatively long historical periods. Such an inquiry is fraught with difficulties. It is not clear that *scientifically* meaningful statements can be made about macrohistorical processes that are historically unique,[29] especially if one believes, as I do, that the future is indeterminate (see Popper 1957; Fischer 1970). But in my view we should not give up on trying to understand an important subject just because it presents difficulties for "scientific" study. Rather, we should use as much "scientific" apparatus as is useful and as much "interpretive" apparatus as is appropriate and proceed with caution, tentatively.

This book is full of numbers. There are two dangers here. First, some people may be scared off by the numbers. Many scholars in the social sciences and humanities have little interest in statistics and certainly doubt that a statistical analysis could help them understand the historical political economy of the world system. For that group, I have tried to boil down numerical data into summary and graphic form, with verbal explanations, so that no knowledge of statistics is necessary to follow my arguments and conclusions.

The second danger comes from those who believe in "hard" social science methodologies (behavioralism, statistical inference, formal models, and so forth). Because this book contains a lot of numbers, this group may expect it to conform to harder scientific standards than is in fact the case. To this group, I stress that my study addresses a "universe" (the world), not a "sample"—and hence the spirit behind my statistics is descriptive rather than inferential.

---

28. This view is crystallized in Lenin's (1917) theory of imperialism as an outgrowth of finance capitalism.

29. There is only one planet Earth and one world system passing through historical time once.

By combining quantitative analysis with historical interpretation, I walk a thin line between two opposing tendencies. Yet I believe that both approaches are needed in order to understand a social reality containing both generalizable patterns and historical singularities.

This book works in both a deductive and an inductive manner in building a theory of long cycles. But more importantly it stresses an "adductive" approach (Fischer 1970) that "tries out" possible answers to relevant questions, checking whether they can be made consistent both with empirical evidence and with the tentative answers to other questions. Each tentative answer affects the next questions asked.

The idea of a world system, for example, is both an assumption and a hypothesis in this book. I assume, provisionally, that there has been a world system since around 1495. In this context, I study historical data in search of long cycles at the world level and ultimately find an international synchrony in long-term price movements back to 1495. This synchrony of political-economic forces across national entities corroborates and strengthens the original assumption that a world system exists. The logic is partially circular and does not exclude the possibility that another study, in another theoretical framework, would select, view, and interpret the data differently, also corroborating its own framework.[30]

I begin by wondering, "What if there are long cycles in world politics and economics?"—a question raised repeatedly in the social sciences in recent years. I then show what a *consistent* long cycle theory would have to look like and what it would imply in terms of how we could interpret historical and present social realities. I do not seek to convince the reader that my theory of long cycles is *necessarily true*—only that it is plausible, that it might be true, that if true it would have interesting and important ramifications, and that it is an advance over previous long cycle theories.

This study, then, proceeds as though piecing together a jigsaw puzzle (drawing on induction, deduction, intuition, and common sense), without requiring that all the pieces fit or that there be only one correct solution to the puzzle. There will always be missing pieces and pieces that do not fit well, but in some solutions more pieces will fit than in others. The iterative process of building theory and sifting evidence gradually narrows the possible solutions, but the book never arrives at a single, complete, or final answer to the questions regarding long cycles. We are left with an impressionist painting rather than a photograph.

A Preview

I have discussed up to now in this chapter the themes of the book and its general approach to the study of long cycles. It might help the reader for me also to outline the book in summary form.

The book is organized in three parts. Part One reviews the past work—both

---

30. See chap. 7 on competing research programs.

theoretical and empirical—on long economic and political cycles. Part Two presents a quantitative analysis of long waves, using historical time-series data, and develops a rough theoretical model of the long wave. Part Three discusses the hegemony cycle and its historical connection with the long wave and draws out some implications of long cycles for the present and future.

Part One: Debates

Part One reviews, organizes, and synthesizes the past work on long cycles, a task complicated by the nature of the existing literature. The past work is scattered among various disciplines, approaches, and languages and has never been adequately cataloged, reviewed, or integrated into one framework. In particular, there has been a divide between the economic and political disciplinary territories, so that instead of one debate on long political-economic cycles, there have been two debates—one on economic cycles and one on political cycles. Within each of these, there have been subdebates, the structures of which I will investigate.

In the economic long wave debate, although many scholars have examined long waves over the past sixty years, little agreement has been reached on the central questions:

1. Do long waves of approximately fifty years' duration exist in the economies of the core countries, synchronized internationally and across different economic variables?[31]
2. If so, what causes these long waves, and which variables are central to them?

The overall empirical evidence for long waves is still quite mixed, but surprising consensus is found on the dating of price phases. Drawing on the existing literature, I develop a consensual *base dating scheme* covering 1495–1975.

The debate on long waves has proceeded in two rounds of activity, centered in the 1930s and 1970s–1980s respectively—times of stagnation in the world economy. In the first round of the debate, four theoretical schools emerged in accounting for the causal dynamics of the long wave. These focused on capital investment, innovation, capitalist crises, and war, respectively, as the driving force of the long wave. In the second round of the debate, the "war" school withered away,[32] but the other three schools (reflecting three world views) continue to define the contours of the debate today. No theory has gained broad acceptance, and no consensus has been reached on the central issues of the debate. Each research school continues in its own framework but understands only with difficulty what another research school has learned; this impedes the cumulation of knowledge in the long wave field.

The debate on hegemony cycles has followed a somewhat parallel development. Out of several different roots in the 1940s and 1950s, the debate has coalesced around three main research schools, again corresponding roughly with the three world

31. Prices, production, trade, wages, interest rates, and so on.
32. Discussion of war cycles became a separate debate as the disciplinary boundaries between economics and politics were more sharply drawn after World War II.

views. As in the long wave debate, these three schools have difficulty communicating effectively with each other and building on each other's work.

Part One uses these difficulties in knowledge cumulation to explore the philosophy of science aspects of long cycle research. The difficulties of knowledge cumulation in the long cycle field are attributed to the character of the long cycle research community—a fragmented community that crosses but never fully bridges the borders of ideology, language, nationality, and discipline. Part One reviews the past empirical evidence for long waves and concludes by codifying the alternative hypotheses put forward by different scholars in the debate.

Part Two: Analysis

Part Two uses empirical analysis to address several outstanding questions in the long wave debate:

1. Can long waves be found in historical data?
2. In which economic or political variables can they be found?
3. Are they synchronous across countries?
4. How early in history can they be found?
5. Do wars play a role in economic long waves? What is the connection between the economic and political aspects of long waves?

In order to test my long wave base dating scheme against a variety of economic data, I compiled a set of fifty-five economic time series—price series, production series, and a handful of series on investment, trade, innovation, and wages. The data cover, in various segments, the period since 1495 and come from a variety of core countries. I analyze these time series data to find out whether the data follow the long wave patterns defined by the base dating scheme. I develop a statistical methodology to determine whether growth rates in expansion phases are in fact higher than in stagnation phases.

The results of this analysis show that long waves in prices can be identified over the entire period from 1495 to the present and that severity levels of great power wars are also strongly correlated with the long wave base dating scheme, at least since the seventeenth century. Much more severe wars occur during upswing phases than downswings. Long waves in production can be identified,[33] but the synchrony between production and prices is lagged. Trends in production seem to lead war and price trends by about ten to fifteen years.[34]

Using the relationships among production, war, and prices that emerge from the analysis, I develop a new theory of long waves, in which wars play a crucial role in relation to economic growth. Growth creates the economic surplus required to

33. In the period since about 1800 for which data are available.
34. This allows a new interpretation of the previously anomalous "stagflation" of the 1970s, which lies between the end of the production expansion phase around 1968 and the end of the price expansion phase around 1980 (making it structurally analogous to the post–World-War-I inflation of the early 1920s).

sustain major wars among core powers. But these large-scale wars drain surplus and disrupt long-term economic growth.

Two data appendixes at the end of the book provide additional materials related to the data analysis in Part Two. Appendix A lists the sources of, and other notes on, each of the fifty-five economic time series. Appendix B reproduces the economic and war data used in the empirical analysis; these have been pieced together from about thirty sources and are listed here in a standardized format suitable for use by other researchers.

Part Three: History

Part Three turns from quantitative analysis to qualitative interpretation in elucidating a structural history of the core of the world system. Structural history emphasizes long-term social processes rather than day-to-day events, people, and narratives. This part of the book builds a reinterpretation of European political-economic history around hegemony cycles and long waves.

Three hegemony cycles (and the beginning of a fourth) structure the past five centuries. These cycles are delineated by three periods of very large *hegemonic wars,* ending in 1648, 1815, and 1945 respectively. These datings in turn correspond roughly with other changes in war and politics discussed in chapter 13. Part Three considers each of the three hegemony cycles from 1495 to 1945 in succession, tracing out the historical instantiation of both hegemony cycles and long waves within each hegemonic era.

Each hegemony cycle begins with a period of strong hegemony following a hegemonic war (the Netherlands after 1648, Britain after 1815, and the United States after 1945).[35] The predominance of one core country over the others erodes, however, and the system moves toward a more multipolar, competitive power structure, eventually resolving the question of hegemonic succession with another hegemonic war. This hegemony cycle takes one to two centuries to complete and encompasses several long waves. Long waves and hegemony cycles do not appear to be tightly synchronized or linked. The long wave affects all countries in synchrony, while the hegemony cycle concerns the *relative* rise and decline of nations. Nonetheless the two cycles intersect in the same political-economic arenas.

The book ends by drawing on this historical analysis to consider the relevance of past history to present-day world politics and to the future. Projection of cyclical patterns into the future is problematical, especially with the various anomalies and conflicting interpretations concerning the period since World War II.[36] But with appropriate caution, it is possible to make a rough projection that can offer new

35. The starting date of 1495 was not, apparently, also the start of a hegemony cycle. Braudel (1984:77), for instance, dates a parallel longer cycle in prices as beginning around 1350. In this framework, used in chap. 13, the hegemonic decline of Venice was already well under way by 1495.

36. The advent of Keynesian economics, the permanent war economy, nuclear weapons, and the transition from the European states system to a global bipolar order all mark the current era (since 1945) as different in important ways from those that preceded it.

insights into possible futures. The cyclical projection as a baseline for thinking about the future results in different interpretations of trends than the more common linear or static modes of projection. The long cycle perspective points to useful historical precedents—past periods in which dynamics might be similar to those of the present or near future.

The specific interpretation and projection put forward in this book is tentative and open to revision but seems to fit best the available evidence. The world is currently moving from a period of strong hegemony following hegemonic war (the 1950s and 1960s) to one of declining hegemony (a process that may stretch out over many decades to come). In terms of the long wave, we are in a period of stagnation in production, war, and prices.

Looking to the future, my projection suggests that reinvigorated world economic growth could occur somewhere around 1995 to 2020. A period of increasing war could be expected sometime around 2000–2030 and an inflationary phase around 2010–35. While these dates are extremely rough, the sequence suggests that, structurally, the early decades of the twenty-first century may see a dangerous combination of economic expansion and declining hegemony. Such a period would not resemble any part of the period 1945–85 but would most resemble the buildup to World War I around 1893–1914.

To return to the theme with which this chapter started, this suggests a "lesson of history" missed by both President Reagan and his Soviet critics—the importance of the period before 1914, not 1939, as a precedent. The pre-1914 period showed that an arms race in which both sides seek deterrence through a "balance of terror" can lead to a catastrophic war.

In the concluding sections of the book I speculate about change and continuity in the world system in the twentieth and twenty-first centuries. If the system of international power politics continues to operate as it has over the past five centuries, the world will drift closer to another hegemonic war, and the early twenty-first century will be a very dangerous time. Only major changes in the nature of world politics can temper these dangers. Some of these changes have already occurred with the advent of nuclear war; others are beginning to develop in such areas as the information revolution, the conquest of space, and the development of new international regimes. Evolving patterns of international relations are bringing a globalization in which the only security is common security. The next world order will have to be built around this common security, not power politics, if the cycle of great power war is finally to be broken.

Part One: DEBATES

CHAPTER TWO

The Long Wave Debate 1: Roots

The period of the long wave (Kondratieff cycle) debate from the time of Nikolai Kondratieff in the 1920s through the trailing off of interest in long waves in the 1950s constitutes what I call the first round of the debate.[1] It then died down in the 1950s and 1960s (an expansion phase in the world economy) but sprang to life again with the second round in the 1970s and 1980s (a stagnation phase). Interest in long waves in both rounds reflected contemporary problems in the world economy for which the long wave seemed to give a plausible explanation.

What is the basic idea of a long wave? There is no single answer to this—different scholars have adopted different definitions—but most would agree on a definition based on alternating phases of rapid expansion and stagnation in the world economy, taking about fifty years per cycle.[2] These phases have been synchronous across the major core countries and across different economic variables.[3]

The scope of long waves is a subject of divided opinion. They are variously claimed to exist in at least price series and at most a wide range of economic and social variables and to extend over at least the period from about 1790 to 1925[4] and at most the longer period from around 1500 (or even earlier) to the present. My study adopts the latter, broad approach covering the past five centuries and a variety of economic variables. Note that throughout I will use the year 1790 as shorthand to refer to the transition from preindustrial to industrial times.[5]

Liberal economists have, on the whole, been critical of long waves. Paul Samuelson is quoted as calling them ''science fiction'' (*Business Week* 1982), and the *Citibank Monthly Economic Letter* in 1978 defined long waves as ''a myth perpetuated by people who—sharing the apocalyptic visions of Plato, Marx, Toynbee and

1. The publication of Kondratieff's (pronounced and sometimes written ''Kondratyev'') seminal article, ''The Long Waves in Economic Life,'' in English in 1935 (9 years after its German appearance) marked the high point of interest in the first round of the debate, about 50 years ago.

2. The long wave is generally conceived of as one of several economic movements ranging from shorter ''business cycles'' to longer ''secular trends.''

3. I will later suggest a lagged synchrony, rather than simple synchrony, among economic variables (chap. 8).

4. The period covered by Kondratieff's studies.

5. The year 1790 is the starting date of Kondratieff's studies, which were explicitly limited to industrial times.

Figure 2.1. The Long Wave Debate in Round One

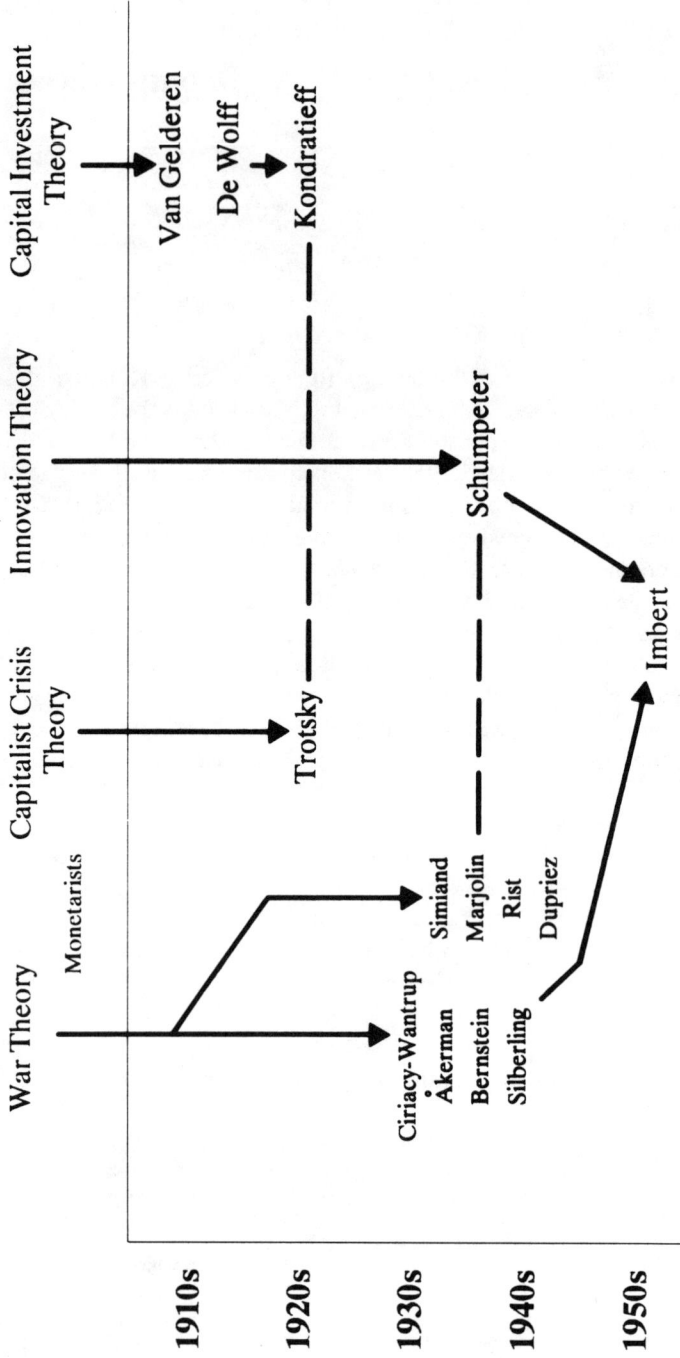

others—believe that there is a mystical pattern of history that permits true believers to divine the future.''[6]

The study of long waves has generated heated controversy, contradiction, and irresolution for over sixty years without making much progress in "cumulating knowledge." Knowledge cumulation implies an established body of knowledge in the field, the frontiers of which may be expanded by ongoing research. In the long wave field there is no such body of knowledge, and no consensus exists on the central issues: the existence of long waves, their scope, and their causal dynamics. Instead, isolated research traditions create "pockets" of theory that are accepted only within their own tradition.[7]

As Kitwood (1984:164) notes, "No clear means have yet been devised for classifying the major long-wave theorists." The past work on long waves has never been adequately cataloged, much less integrated into a unified framework. These chapters will try to pull together the disparate literatures of past work in this field, to make sense of them, to make the debate accessible, and to provide a framework in which the theoretical and empirical questions surrounding the long wave can be addressed in a logical and orderly manner.

The long wave debate has proceeded on two tracks—empirical and theoretical. Kuznets (1940:267) described both as necessary for establishing the existence of long waves: "First a demonstration that fluctuations of that approximate duration recur, with fair simultaneity, in the movements of various significant aspects of economic life . . . ; and second, an indication of what . . . factors . . . account for such recurrent fluctuations." In the past, empirical and theoretical work on long waves has not been well integrated. On the empirical side a number of studies have used quantitative data to try to prove or disprove the existence of long waves. These studies present little theoretical material and rarely attempt to test different theories against each other. On the theoretical side there is a much greater body of work, much of it quite speculative, that puts forward theories of the long wave with little grounding in empirical data. I therefore separate for review purposes the theoretical and empirical works. Chapters 2 and 3 review the theoretical debate, while chapter 4 presents the past empirical work.

Four Theories

The first round of the long wave debate was dominated by four theories, associated respectively with Nikolai Kondratieff, Leon Trotsky, Joseph Schumpeter, and a group of mostly European scholars. Figure 2.1 illustrates

---

6. Cited in Gordon (1980:9). Dupriez (1978:200), who is sympathetic to long wave theories, suggests that English and American economists have looked askance at the long wave mainly because of its association with the "simplistic and circumstantial" approach of Kondratieff and certain others. He criticizes this as "throwing the baby away with the bath."

7. Along the way, the debate over long waves has become entangled in other feuds—between Marxists and non-Marxists, between economists and political scientists, and between advocates of different empirical and theoretical approaches to social science.

the structure of the debate among these four theories before 1960—and hence provides a "road map" for this chapter. The four approaches may be summarized as follows:

1. The *capital investment theory* argues that long waves arise from the massive investment in, and depreciation of, such long-lived capital goods as railroads, canals, and factories. During an economic upswing, overinvestment in capital goods occurs; this causes a downswing in which excess capital is depreciated. The depreciation of capital on the downswing opens the way for a new period of massive investment, again overshooting as the upswing continues. Key variables are capital investment and production.

2. The *innovation theory* argues that long waves arise from clusters of innovations at particular times and in particular economic sectors. These clusters of related innovations create a new "leading sector" of the economy that grows rapidly and drives a general economic upswing. While that upswing continues, radical innovations are discouraged since existing investments in existing technologies are bringing good returns. However, the initial innovations eventually bring diminishing returns, and the economy slows down and slides into a downswing. The downswing encourages innovations, but there is a time lag before these can be developed. Key variables are inventions and innovations, production, and employment.

3. The *capitalist crisis theory* argues that long waves, defined by recurring major crises in capitalism, arise from the tendency of the rate of profit to decline. The recovery from such crises is not endogenous to the capitalist economy, but results from exogenous factors (such as imperial expansion, the discovery of new natural resources, or the suppression of labor movements) that intervene to restore favorable long-term conditions of accumulation.[8] The rate of profit increases, allowing a new upswing—but the next crisis follows inevitably. Key variables are the profit rate, class struggle, and production.

4. The *war theory* argues that the economic long wave results from, or is closely connected with, major wars. The effects of recurring major wars—primarily inflationary effects—act as periodic shocks to the world economy and create long waves. Key variables are prices and war incidence and size. A related group (monetarists) in the early decades of the debate developed a parallel theory in which gold production rather than war (or sometimes combined with war) affected prices. In both the war and gold versions, the economic long wave is mainly a monetary phenomenon.

While these schools shape the main lines of the debate, hybrid theories combine them in interesting ways. The work of Gaston Imbert in the 1950s contains an interesting synthesis of war and innovation explanations.

After the 1950s, the war school no longer played a role in the economic debate, reflecting the strong disciplinary border separating politics from economics in the

8. The outcome of a crisis is not predetermined but depends on class struggle and concrete historical conditions.

1950s and 1960s.[9] In political science and sociology it became a debate of its own, which I will take up in chapters 5 and 6.

Each of the three remaining schools was to form the seed of a research tradition over the subsequent decades, however. The three research schools growing out of the theories of Kondratieff, Trotsky, and Schumpeter, respectively, shape the lines of debate on long waves today (see chapter 3).

These three theories roughly reflect the three world views of chapter 1 (conservative, revolutionary, and liberal). The revolutionary world view is expressed in the "capitalist crisis theory" of Trotsky, which stresses qualitative change, stages of development, and indeterminacy of outcome. The liberal world view is represented in the "innovation theory" of Schumpeter and stresses evolutionary progress through human inventiveness. The conservative world view underlies Kondratieff's "capital investment theory," stressing quantitative change and repetition within a stable system structure.[10]

Nikolai Kondratieff: Capital Investment

Kondratieff, a Russian Marxist economist, ran an institute in Moscow in the 1920s concerned with the study of all types of business cycles in the capitalist economies. Kondratieff was not the first to entertain the idea of long-term cycles of about fifty years' duration.[11] But he was the first to marshal substantial empirical evidence for the idea and spark a sustained debate on the topic.

Kondratieff's principal interest in long waves was empirical, not theoretical; indeed in his most widely read article ([1926] 1935:115) he stated that he "had no intention of laying the foundations for an appropriate theory of long waves" but only of demonstrating their existence empirically. This he tried to do by accumulating data on a variety of economic variables from different countries and examining long-term moving averages in the series. Some of these synchronous long waves in moving averages of various indicators are shown in figure 2.2.[12]

Kondratieff could not, however, hold to a purely empirical position in the face of theoretical attacks from his critics in the Soviet Union. In 1928 he elaborated a *theory* of long waves in a book that included responses from some of his critics (see Kondratieff [1928] 1984).

Kondratieff's theoretical explanation centered on capital investment—the wearing

9. The arguments of the war school still occasionally resurface (e.g., Craig and Watt 1985); see chapter 5.

10. Kondratieff, himself a Marxist, hardly embodies the conservative world view. Yet his long wave theory, with its endogenous self-repeating and nonevolutionary cycles, is a conservative variant. Within the Marxist debate, Kondratieff's was a more "conservative" Marxism and Trotsky's a more "revolutionary" Marxism (see below).

11. Notable earlier work included that of Van Gelderen (1913). The early works are summarized briefly by Barr (1979) and discussed by Tinbergen (1981).

12. The figure shows the most promising series, not a random sample.

Figure 2.2. Kondratieff's Long Waves

Chart 1. Index Numbers of Commodity Prices *(1901-10 = 100)*

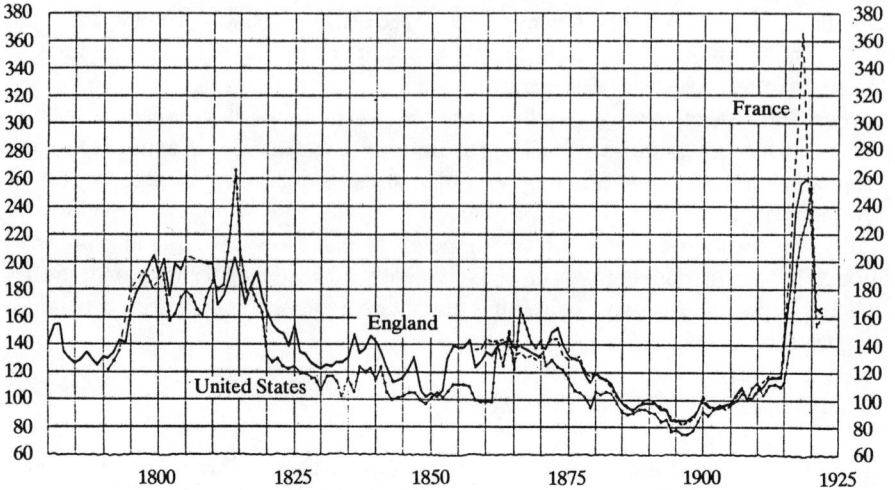

Chart 2. Quotations of Interest-Bearing Securities

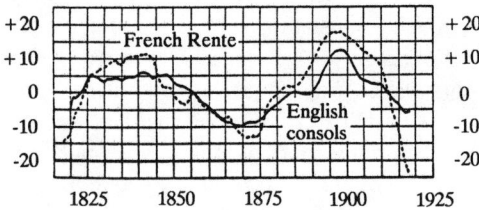

Chart 3. Wages in England

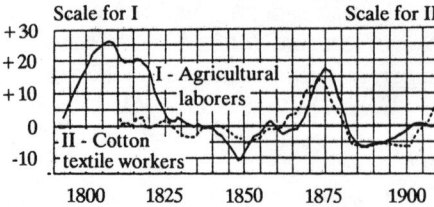

Chart 4. French Foreign Trade

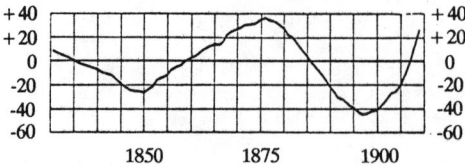

Chart 5. Consumption of Coal in France and Production of Coal, Pig Iron, and Lead in England

Coal production and coal consumption

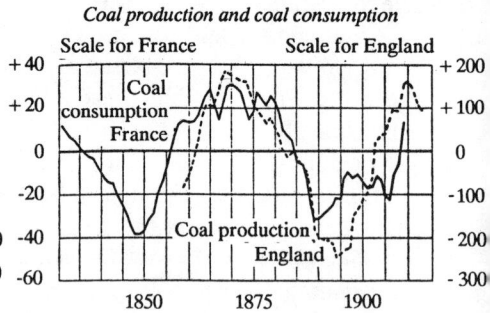

Pig iron and lead production in England

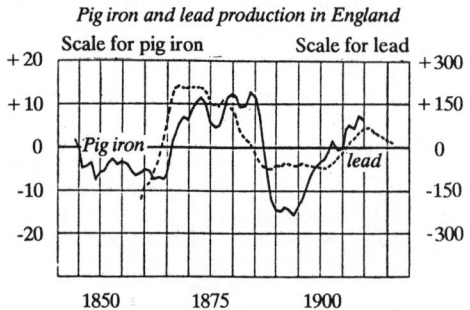

Copyright: President & Fellows of Harvard College
Note: All graphs except prices represent moving averages
Source: Kondratieff ([1926] 1935: 106-9).

26

out of capital equipment and its concentrated replacement in waves of massive investment using savings accumulated during an economic downswing:

Marx affirmed that the material basis for [seven-to-eleven-year business cycles] was the material wear and tear, replacement, and increase in . . . machines with a service life lasting ten years, one may assume that the material basis for the long cycles is the wear and tear, replacement, and increase in those basic capital goods requiring a long period of time and tremendous investments for their production. *The replacement and expansion of the fund of these goods does not take place smoothly but in spurts, and the long waves in economic conditions are another expression of that* (Kondratieff [1928] 1984:93; italics in original).

Thus increased construction of basic capital goods is the central feature of the upswing phase.

This increased construction requires the availability of capital for investment (p. 94). But "the investment of capital in big and expensive projects increases the demand for capital," which eventually raises the price of capital (p. 96). The high price of capital dampens investment and—notwithstanding long time lags—leads to the end of the upswing and the beginning of a downswing. In the downswing phase investment decreases, capital becomes cheaper, and hence "conditions favorable to an upswing are again created" (p. 97).

Kondratieff, under attack from Marxists around him, elaborated his theory within a traditional Marxist framework. He stressed that his analysis applied only to capitalist systems (p. 25) and only to industrial capitalism since the late eighteenth century (p. 32). He was careful to build on the work of Marx himself. Marx's view of short-term (seven to eleven years) business cycles with their recurrent crises stressed two points, according to Kondratieff: "First, that they are periodic; second, that they are organically inherent in the capitalist system" (p. 28). These quotations from Marx were a defense against Kondratieff's most prominent critic, Bolshevik activist-theorist Leon Trotsky, who saw Kondratieff's theories as far too conservative.

Leon Trotsky: Capitalist Crisis

Trotsky's first work on long waves, in 1921, was done independently and in igno-rance of (rather than in response to) either Kondratieff's or J. Van Gelderen's (1913) work. From 1923 through the late 1920s in Moscow, however, Trotsky and Kondra-tieff engaged in a running debate on long waves.

Trotsky's initial idea, which remained central to his approach, characterized long waves as historical periods of accelerated and retarded growth in the development of capitalism (see fig. 2.3). Trotsky pointed to five "different and distinct periods" from 1781 to 1921—two periods of stagnation alternating with two of rapid growth, the fifth period, since 1914, being "the period of the destruction of capitalist economy."[13] These phases arose from "a process of adaptation" as capitalism reacted to events in the "superstructure": "It will depend upon great historical events—crises, revolutions, etc., whether the period will become one of accelerated

13. Speech of 1921 quoted in Day (1976:69).

Figure 2.3. Trotsky's Curve of Capitalist Development

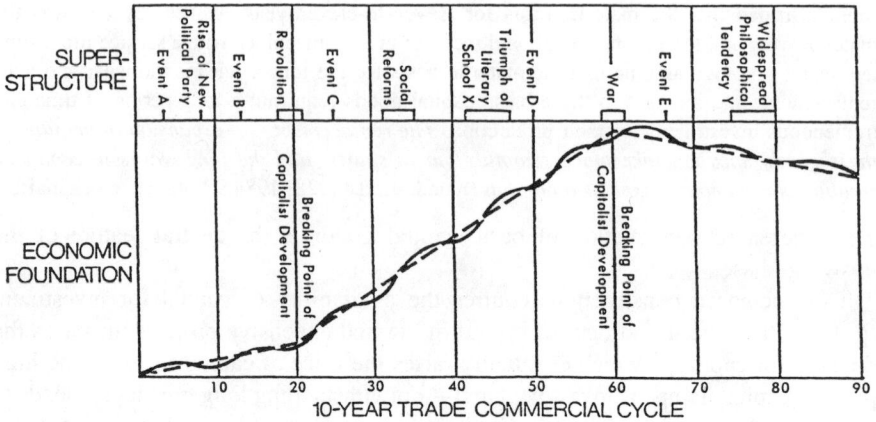

Source: Trotsky ([1923] 1973: 278)   (Pathfinder Press).

growth, stability, or decline. This is a cardinal trait of the process of capitalistic development."[14] Thus Trotsky claimed that long waves are not organically inherent in capitalism but result from the effects of factors exogenous to the capitalist system.

In 1923, responding specifically to Kondratieff, Trotsky elaborated his view of long waves as "epochs of capitalist development" (1923:275). He called Kondratieff's formulation of long waves, as cycles inherent to capitalism, a "symmetrically stylized construction" in which the "rigidly lawful rhythm" of shorter business cycles was extended to long-term periods—a case of an "obviously false generalization from a formal analogy" (p. 276).

Trotsky stressed that long-wave periods are not internal to the laws of capitalism:

As regards the large segments of the capitalist curve of development (fifty years) which Professor Kondratiev incautiously proposes to designate also as cycles, their character and duration are determined not by the internal interplay of capitalist forces but by those external conditions through whose channel capitalist development flows. The acquisition by capitalism of new countries and continents, the discovery of new natural resources, and, in the wake of these, such major facts of "superstructural" order as wars and revolutions, determine the character and the replacement of ascending, stagnating, or declining epochs of capitalist development (p. 277).

Trotsky thus anticipated the neo-Marxists of some decades later in ascribing "relative autonomy"[15] to the "superstructure" of society. Trotsky agreed that Marxism "looks for the causes of changes in social superstructure in the changes of

14. Speech of 1921 quoted in Kuznets (1930:262).
15. Not his phrase, but used by Day (1976:71) in describing his position.

the economic foundation'' but argued that ''economics is decisive only in the *last analysis*'' (p. 277; italics in original).[16]

The Kondratieff-Trotsky Debate

Kondratieff's response to Trotsky's argument was that Trotsky ''takes an idealist point of view.''[17] New markets and resources are drawn into the capitalist system ''not by accident, but in face of the existing economic preconditions.'' That is, the internal dynamics of capitalism shape the long wave, which in turn shapes the superstructural factors such as innovation and war that Trotsky called ''external.'' Specifically, Kondratieff argued that ''during the recession . . . an unusually large number of important discoveries and inventions in the technique of production and communication are made, which, however, are usually applied on a large scale only at the beginning of the next long upswing'' ([1926] 1935:111). Likewise, ''the most disastrous and extensive wars and revolutions occur'' on the upswing of the long wave (p. 111), because long-term economic expansion aggravates the international struggle for markets and raw materials while domestically sharpening the struggle over the distribution of the fruits of that economic growth ([1928] 1984:95). Wars, revolutions, and innovations are thus products, not causes, of the long wave.[18]

In asserting that long waves are self-generating and inherent in capitalism ([1926] 1935:115), Kondratieff conceded to Trotsky only that ''each new cycle takes place under new concrete-historical conditions, at a new level in the development of productive forces, and hence is by no means a simple repetition of the preceding cycle'' ([1928] 1984:99). On this question of distinct historical periods, Kondratieff responded to Trotsky's criticism by arguing that ''crossing through different stages, capitalism remains capitalism and maintains its basic features and regularities.''[19] Kondratieff stated that Trotsky, ''while not denying the existence of long waves in economic conditions, refused to recognize their patterned, cyclical character'' (p. 31.)

Trotsky's argument with Kondratieff thus centered on two related points: first, whether the long wave upswings and downswings are *cyclical* or just historical periods, and second, whether long upswings and downswings are generated *internally* to the capitalist economy or by external forces.

The Kondratieff-Trotsky debate reflects deeper divisions within Marxism that predate and underlie the question of long waves. The argument between Kondratieff

---

16. Trotsky begins his 1923 article with a quotation from Engels that begins: ''In judging the events . . . of day-to-day history, it will never be possible for anyone to go right back to the final economic causes.''

17. Quoted in Day (1976:78). Among other forums, Trotsky and Kondratieff debated long waves at a 1926 conference on the world economy in Moscow.

18. Kondratieff suggests, however, that although wars and revolutions are primarily an effect of the long wave, they also play a lesser role in *causing* the downturn by increasing nonproductive consumption, destroying existing capital plant, and increasing the demand for capital ([1928] 1984:96). See chap. 12.

19. Quoted in Day (1976:79).

and Trotsky parallels in important ways the debate between Karl Kautsky and Lenin (see Willoughby 1979), that is, between socialism and communism as competing Marxist traditions. Kautsky, a leading socialist theoretician, was a primary object of Lenin's (1917) attack. Kautsky argued that imperialism should be seen as a "policy" rather than a necessary phase or stage in the development of capitalism, a view that was "diametrically opposed" to Lenin's concept of imperialism as a stage of development based on the ascendancy of monopoly finance capitalism (Lenin 1917:238).

In Kautsky's view, international monopoly capitalism, through the internationalization of capital, opened the possibility for stable peace under capitalism without any inherent necessity for imperialism or war (Lenin 1917:225).[20] Lenin called this a "stupid little fable about 'peaceful' ultra-imperialism" (p. 243) and considered Kautsky an apologist for capitalism. In Lenin's view, monopoly capitalism was inextricably linked with imperialist expansion and wars among the capitalist powers.[21]

Kondratieff's theory of long waves, rightly or wrongly, was too closely associated with the approach of the socialist Kautsky to be acceptable to the Bolsheviks, including Trotsky. Kondratieff's work on long waves followed that of J. Van Gelderen (1913), a Dutch *socialist*.[22] Kondratieff's approach also closely paralleled that of Sam De Wolff,[23] another Dutch socialist, whose work on long waves (1924) appeared in a book published in honor of Karl Kautsky! Finally, Kautsky himself had given some discussion to long waves and, like Kondratieff, had stressed increases of capital investment on the upswing (although he thought them caused by gold discoveries).

The key issue in the Lenin-Kautsky and Trotsky-Kondratieff debates is the stability of capitalism—a central question in the Marxist approach. Kautsky viewed capitalism as relatively stable and could conceive of a capitalist world free of imperialism and war. He downplayed the development of "stages" of capitalism (imperialism being a final stage) in favor of a more static view in which imperialism and war were merely "policies." Lenin, by contrast, saw capitalism in dynamic and rapid development toward its own (dialectical) self-negation.

The Kondratieff-Trotsky long wave debate also revolved around the question of the stability of capitalism. Do "universal crises" threaten the survival of capitalism (as Trotsky thought), or are they only a phase of a more stable capitalist dynamic (as

20. Lenin argues that Kautsky, by defining imperialism in terms of territorial annexations, stresses only the political aspect of imperialism and misses the economic aspect (p. 239).

21. As a German Socialist Kautsky supported Germany's participation in World War I (which Lenin opposed), hoping to protect German socialism, which was then strong, from being defeated by Russian absolutism.

22. Trotsky, by contrast, originally developed his work independently and in ignorance of Van Gelderen's work, which was published only in Dutch, according to Kuznets (1930:261).

23. De Wolff's 1924 and 1929 publications follow (in content and timing) Kondratieff's 1922 and 1928 publications, respectively, but other scholars cite him as Kondratieff's predecessor. Imbert (1959:38) cites De Wolff's work in 1913, well before Kondratieff's work.

Kondratieff argued)? Kondratieff, like Kautsky, presented a picture of capitalism as more stable over the long term than either Trotsky or Lenin saw it. This parallel between Kondratieff's approach and that of the hated Kautsky may help to explain the very negative reception given to Kondratieff by his fellow Soviet Marxists.[24]

The issue of the stability of capitalism—central to this debate—came to a head with the deepening crisis of the capitalist economies in the West after 1929. Kondratieff's theory implied that the Great Depression might not be the "final crisis of capitalism" and that the capitalist economy might recover and begin growing again of its own internal dynamic. Although history would later prove this correct, in 1930 (under Stalin) Kondratieff was officially repudiated, arrested, and subsequently died in a Siberian prison camp. This, along with the exile and assassination of Trotsky, ended the Marxist discussion on long waves for the time being. Kondratieff has not been "rehabilitated" in the Soviet Union since that time.[25]

The Trotsky-Kondratieff debate exemplifies the fact that Marxism is not a monolithic entity but contains its own subdebates and divisions. Although both are Marxists, Kondratieff presents a more conservative and Trotsky a more revolutionary interpretation of capitalist dynamics.

Joseph Schumpeter: Innovation

As the debate on long waves was suppressed in Marxist circles after 1930, it began to catch on among some Western liberal economists, who found the concept of long-term capitalist stability more appealing than had Stalin and Trotsky.[26] Joseph Schumpeter was foremost in resurrecting Kondratieff and naming the long wave after him.[27] Schumpeter ([1934] 1951) argued that the depression of the 1930s resembled previous depressions around 1825 and 1873.

Schumpeter (1939) attempted to build a unified, although tentative, theory of business cycles (both short and long), based primarily on the concepts of innovation and of "leading sectors" of the economy. Innovation, in Schumpeter's view, consists not just of inventions but of any "change in the method of supplying commodities" (p. 84).[28] Innovations "turn existing factors of production to new uses" without being a direct consequence of any one of them (p. 86). Schumpeter

24. Further discussion of the Russian debate may be found in Kuznets 1930; Garvy 1943; Day 1976; and Barr 1979.

25. However, a long wave conference sponsored by the International Institute for Applied Systems Analysis (IIASA) in 1985 did bring participants from Eastern Europe and the Soviet Union (and one from China), so interest in long waves may now be reviving in communist countries.

26. The majority, however, never accepted long waves.

27. Ehrensaft (1980:69), from the point of view of the (Schumpeterian) innovation school, finds it "paradoxical" that Kondratieff's theory of long waves, "whose theoretical base derived from Marx," should find its principal advocate in Schumpeter, who opposed Marxism. But I find this no mystery. Schumpeter particularly opposed the communism of Trotsky, Lenin, and Stalin. The resurrection of Kondratieff was directed against Stalin, not Marx.

28. This includes the introduction of new commodities, technological changes in the production of commodities already in use, the opening up of new markets or sources of supply, new business organizations (such as department stores), or improved methods of work.

called innovation "the outstanding fact in the economic history of capitalist society" and designated the "changes in the economic process brought about by innovation . . . by the term Economic Evolution" (p. 86). Innovations result from the rise to leadership of particular individuals and the emergence of new firms (pp. 94–96). Schumpeter saw clusters of innovations as driving the irregular rhythms of business cycles of various lengths.[29]

In the case of the long wave, major innovations bring to the fore a new "leading sector" of the economy, supplanting the previously dominant industry or group of industries. The new leading sector drives a powerful expansion of the economy until it runs into diminishing returns and is eventually supplanted by another new leading sector. Each of the long wave upswings, then, is associated with a particular historical technological basis. Schumpeter identified these as: (1) the industrial revolution (1780s–1842); (2) the age of steam and steel (1842–97); and (3) electricity, chemistry, and motors (1898–).[30] Simon Kuznets (1940:261) elaborated these (with Schumpeter's advice) as the Industrial Revolution Kondratieff (cotton textiles, iron, steam power), the Bourgeois Kondratieff (railroads), and the Neo-Mercantilist Kondratieff (electricity, automobiles). Each of these periods began with an upswing and ended with a long downswing.[31]

Schumpeter's approach is grounded in a "liberal" framework. The key force in economic change is the individual (the individual entrepreneur who develops an innovation). The long economic cycle represents forward steps in an evolving system—"Economic Evolution," as Schumpeter calls it.

Nonetheless, many liberal economists rejected Schumpeter's long wave theory. Among the critics, Kuznets (1940:258–63) argued that entrepreneurs would not simply disappear while an innovation was being imitated and built but would "turn to new feats and thus initiate an uprush in another industry." Thus innovations would be conceived of not as "bunching" together but as "flowing in a continuous stream." The economy might move forward in a "jerky" sort of evolution but not with a cyclical character, according to Kuznets.

Johan Åkerman, Norman Silberling, and Others: War

Johan Åkerman, a Swedish economist, was among the first to argue (1932:79) that war rather than capital investment, capitalist crises, or innovation is the central cause of the long wave. The long wave is "a problem which goes far beyond the bounds of

29. Schumpeter's theory is not strictly periodic for any inherent reason. However, long cycles gain some regularity through their connection to shorter business cycles. "There is a theoretically indefinite number of fluctuations present . . . at any time" (p. 168), but for simplicity Schumpeter limited his analysis to three types of cycles: short (40 months), middle (10 years), and long (60 years). These three types tend to group in integral numbers (three short cycles in a middle cycle and six middle cycles in a long one), since the upswing or downswing of a longer cycle is initiated in the short term by a peaking or troughing of a shorter cycle. The deepest depressions in Schumpeter's study (1825–30, 1873–78, and 1929–34) were marked by synchronous depression phases among all three types of cycles (p. 173).

30. No ending date was clear as of 1939.

31. A fourth cycle, from the 1940s on, is often associated with the automobile, plastics, and electronics sectors.

economics.''[32] Åkerman noted that long wave upswings have "culminated in general inflation during a war period" (p. 87–88). The end of the war period in turn is followed by a "deflation crisis" and a downswing period of falling prices ending with a crisis of credit institutions. In 1944 Åkerman wrote:

We can draw the conclusion that it is the *frequency of wars—i.e. a political* phenomenon—that introduces the periodical element in the secular economic changes. The 'enigma of the long waves' in econometrics is thus in a first approximation nothing but a mirror of the enigma of the periodicity of wars.''[33]

Thus what I call the *war theory* of long waves holds that recurrent major wars are central to economic long waves.[34]

Albert Rose, in a brief article in 1941, most concisely stated the response of the war school to Schumpeter's innovation theory:

Modern war may be *the innovation* par excellence in the Schumpeterian system, and as such, the dominant cause of long waves in economic activity. Professor Schumpeter, of course, has virtually disregarded [this possibility] by means of the inadequate declaration that war is an external factor of declining significance to the cyclical processes of the capitalistic economy.

It is significant . . . that Kondratieff's three long waves are centered upon major wars, while at the same time, those innovations which 'carry' Schumpeter's three Kondratieff waves reached their large-scale commercial application in the depths of the reaction from these major wars (p. 105).

Upswings "seem related in some fashion to the three major wars since 1787," according to Rose, and the three long downswings contained depressions (1820–25, 1873–78, and 1929–34) that might have been caused by the petering-out of postwar demands.

E. M. Bernstein (1940:524–27) studied "the economic disturbances initiated by war." He noted that "the whole level of demand, the propensity to consume, is raised by war" due to the heavy expenditure for war goods. At the same time, "the volume of production is certain to decline" in an extended war because of labor shortages, blockades of raw materials or export markets, shortages of foreign exchange, and/or the depletion of capital equipment resulting from the precedence given to war goods. For a belligerent country the initial effect of war may be a quick economic upswing initiated by war spending; but within a few years the economy will slow down due to the limitations on production. To summarize Bernstein's argument, during war periods consumption rises and production falls, leading to a

32. The "traditional answer" explaining long-term price trends, namely gold production, was unsatisfactory to Åkerman (1932:83). Rather, he saw gold production as a dependent variable in that mine owners will increase production when prices of goods are low (i.e., the price of gold is high). Åkerman (1932:86) also considered the argument that long waves arise from waves of population growth caused by birth rate increases after major wars. This explanation elucidates the "interdependence between economics and politics," but unfortunately is not well empirically supported, Åkerman concludes.

33. Åkerman (1944:125), quoted in Eklund (1980), emphasis in original.

34. Since these theories deal with war, they might seem more appropriate for chaps. 5 and 6. But these are economists seeking to explain economic cycles, not scholars of war cycles per se.

higher ratio of demand to supply and hence to higher prices. This inflationary jolt will tend to become globalized particularly in the event of prolonged wars involving the world's major powers and underlies the long wave price upswing.

Norman Silberling (1943:47) also subscribed to the war theory of long waves. Most long wave movements, Silberling argued, "have resulted from specific factors in the nature of exceptionally serious breakdowns in business activity and interruption of trade relations. Invariably such unusual interruptions in the progress of economic development have occurred following major wars." Silberling's analysis was limited to American economic history rather than that of the world system. Seeking to "examine the relationships between political disturbance and economic disturbance," Silberling examined the effects of wars on the U.S. economy (p. 50). "[E]very war that has directly involved American participation," Silberling noted, "has been marked by a more or less violent general rise in prices" (p. 51). But these inflationary periods do not correlate with changes in production or other physical measures, Silberling reported. The long wave is a price wave only and as such can be explained as a product of the timing of wars (pp. 53–55).

The connection of war and prices is evident in the history of the U.S. wholesale price index (see fig. 2.4).[35] Each sharp upsurge in the price index corresponds with a U.S. war: the War of 1812 (and Napoleonic Wars in Europe); the Civil War; World War I; and World War II followed by the Korean and Vietnam wars.

Silberling summarized the economic effects of wars as follows: Major wars spark a sudden and powerful increase in demand,[36] while the growth of supply cannot keep up.[37] This triggers the strong wartime inflation characteristic of each long wave upswing. War also creates long-term disequilibrium, leading to a dampening of growth over the decades following the war—that is, the long wave downswing phase (pp. 58–66).[38]

Silberling's comments on Kondratieff show that he was unaware of the debates within Marxism, both on whether long waves were inherent or exogenous to capitalism and on whether long waves caused the fluctuations in major wars or vice versa. Silberling saw Kondratieff as a "Marxist" who "attributes to the dynamics of capitalism most of the things that happen in the world" (p. 57). Silberling by contrast saw long waves not as inherent in capitalism but as "unnecessary and harmful" fluctuations whose removal would not be incompatible with continued capitalism

35. Not taken from Silberling but from Senge (1975), who does not mention war in discussing this graph (war is not part of Senge's "world" of economic dynamics).

36. "The Government enters the markets supplied with virtually unlimited funds and bids against the private consumer or business firm; the result is naturally a swift and more or less cumulative spiral of price advances" (p. 59).

37. The drafting of men from the labor force brings about a substitution of less highly trained workers. Faster depreciation and inadequate replacement of equipment occur. The expansion of agriculture and mining, to serve the urgent demand for food and minerals for war needs, is a slow process. Meanwhile, supplies of materials from abroad may be curtailed, leading to production bottlenecks.

38. This is true especially in agriculture, mining, and transportation, where wartime overexpansion leads to inflated fixed costs in the postwar period, according to Silberling.

Figure 2.4. U.S. Wholesale Prices

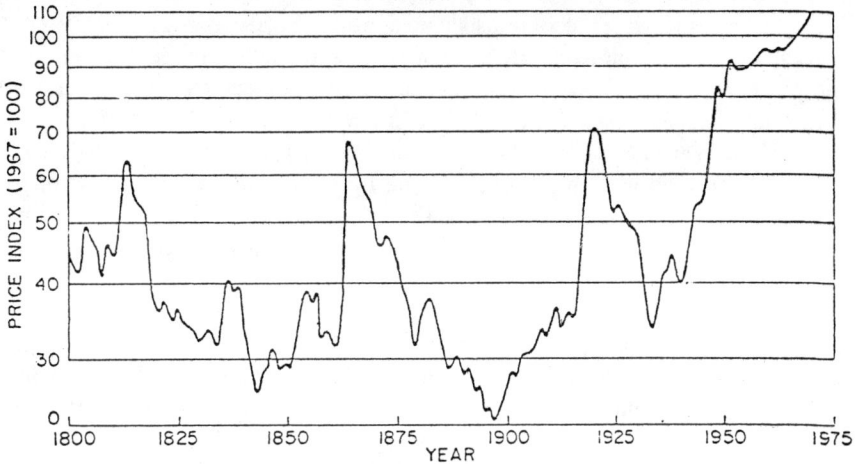

Note: The price data are derived by combining two time series for wholesale prices, one from 1800 to 1890 (series E52) and one from 1890 to 1970 (series E23). Data are from U.S. Department of Commerce, Bureau of the Census, *Historical Statistics* (1975 ed.).

Source: Senge (1982: 9).

(long-term progress, the maintenance of a high degree of individual initiative, and a legal framework of private property). Silberling was apparently unaware of the parallels between his theory (long waves exogenous to capitalism and caused by wars and other political factors) and that of Trotsky!

Tinbergen and Polak (1950:137) followed a similar line to that of Silberling in explaining the connection of war and inflation. "[A]ll the most pronounced instances of inflation in history have occurred in or shortly after great wars," they wrote. Other scholars also pursued the war-inflation link. A 543-year time series showing wheat prices in Europe and America, 1400–1942 (Valley Camp Coal Company 1942), indicated that periods of sharp price increases have historically accompanied periods of war since about 1562.[39]

Siegfried von Ciriacy-Wantrup (1936) was another scholar who connected wars with long waves. Frank G. Dickinson (1940:334) argued along similar lines that "the stimulus to investment of the shift from peace to war and back again . . . largely explains the long cycle." Thus the war theory had a number of proponents during the

39. This graph is not accompanied by the time series data, so I could not analyze the latter. Earl Hamilton (1977:13) cites data for grain prices in Frankfurt am Main and Leipzig (rather than the Strasbourg prices in the above) suggesting that grain prices actually fell during the Thirty Years' War, but he finds these data fragmentary and the interpretation suspect. Hamilton suggests, however, that a clear upward pressure on prices in Spain was evident only beginning with the War of the Spanish Succession (1702–11) and that even then inflation was less than 10%. Hamilton (1947:217) concludes that in 17th-c. Spain "wars had little effect upon commodity prices." My analysis of two of Hamilton's Spanish price series (chap. 9) failed to find long waves.

first round of the debate. After World War II, however, as the gap between economics and politics widened, this school died out as an explanation of long waves.[40]

Kuznets and other liberal economists who opposed the idea of long waves used the
war argument to discount Kondratieff's long waves as existing not in production and
other physical series but only in price and other monetary series "necessarily
dominated by the price peaks of the Napoleonic wars, of the 1870s (not unconnected
with the Civil War in this country), and of the World War" (Kuznets 1940:267).

Closely connected with the war school and from the same period is a set of long
wave theories concerned with long waves as exogenously caused *monetary* phenomena. These theories focus on gold production or the release of gold stocks during
war as the exogenous force that drives monetary long waves.[41] Gustav Cassel
([1918] 1932), the first central figure in the "monetarist" group, argued that gold
production, by changing the amount of money in circulation, drives long-term price
fluctuations (the quantity theory of money). Marcel Lenoir (1913) had made a
somewhat similar argument. Others in this tradition include Simiand (1932a, b),
Marjolin (1937, 1938, 1941a, b), Rist (1938), and Dupriez (1947, 1951, 1959).

The long wave debate in the 1930s and 1940s was thus dominated by the argument
between Schumpeter's "innovation" approach and the war school (and monetarists), of which Åkerman and Silberling provide the best examples. The innovation
school argued that long waves are inherent in capitalism and arise from the development of new innovations driving each new upswing. The war school (and in parallel,
the monetarists) replied that long waves were economic reflections of "external"
events, namely wars (and/or gold production), and did not arise from internal
economic causes. This debate among liberal economists thus parallels the Kondratieff-Trotsky debate on this point.

Gaston Imbert: Innovation and War

Gaston Imbert (1956) provides the first example of what I call a "hybrid" theory,
one that combines two theoretical schools in trying to account for long waves.
Imbert, writing in the 1950s as interest in long waves was diminishing, integrated the
war and innovation theories that had dominated the 1930s and 1940s.[42]

Imbert is noteworthy also as the first person to study in depth the question of long
waves in the preindustrial age, claiming to identify long waves all the way back to the

40. The debate on war cycles became focused on longer-term cycles than the long wave, despite several
unsuccessful attempts to link these longer cycles with long waves (see chap. 6). Some work continues to
look at war and inflation (e.g., Thompson and Zuk 1982). Passing reference is occasionally made to the
"sharp spikes in the price level . . . associated with wars" (Warsh 1984:73). Craig and Watt (1985) come
closest to resurrecting the war school of Kondratieff cycles by restating the connection of war with long
waves, an observation they support with graphs of battle deaths from Lewis F. Richardson's data.

41. Much of this literature is in French (see Marjolin, 1941b:1) and has not been translated into English,
and this group has no real following in the current debate. I have not called it a separate school because of
its theoretical affinity with the war school.

42. Imbert built on Hansen's ([1932] 1971:98) theory that "the up swing of the long wave tends to
produce wars, and prolonged wars in turn tend, through the resulting upheaval in prices, to initiate the
down-swing movement."

Figure 2.5. Imbert's Theoretical Long Wave Scheme

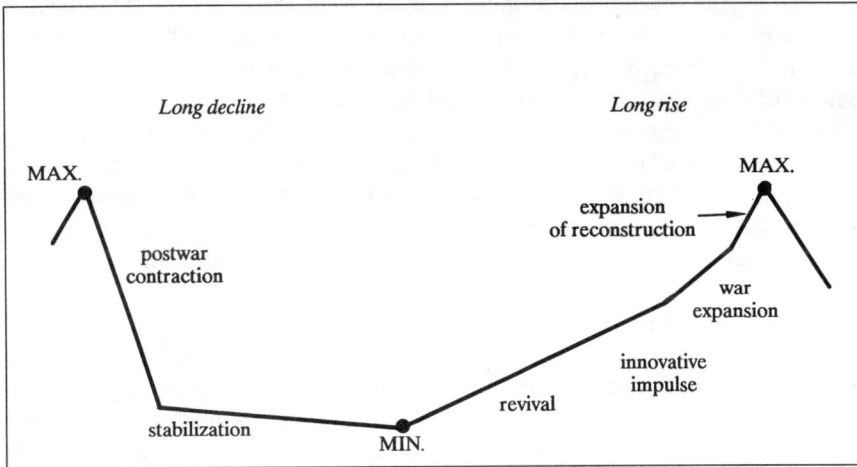

Source: Imbert, 1956, p. 477.

thirteenth century. In this respect he differs from almost all the long wave scholars discussed above, who date long waves only from the late eighteenth century (the industrial age).[43] This distinction will be considered further in chapter 4.

Imbert's theory is represented schematically in figure 2.5. Beginning at the trough of the long wave is a long economic recovery based on increased innovation. Production increases precede price increases. "Dynamic industries" lead the economic progress during the rising phase, incorporating innovations that allow expansion to continue despite the relative rigidity of factors of production (p. 480). Thus the expansion phase is based on innovation.

But economic expansion, according to Imbert (like Kondratieff), leads to war:

The economic impulse of the long rising phase produces progressively the causes that engender . . . the period of war. The rise in economic activity, the strain on markets, the boom fever, the needs of the capitalist economies for raw materials, leads the economically dominant countries to a political and colonial expansion. . . . The unfolding of the rising phase creates an increasing competition between the capitalist countries which dispute the zones of colonial influence. . . . Finally the general tension provokes a war between the economically dominant countries (pp. 484–85; my translation).

This rising tension in international relations disrupts economic stability, bringing higher state expenditures on armaments and the military, heavier taxes, and state competition (against entrepreneurs) for loans. Arms expenditures gradually take precedence over public works (the two having roughly the same immediate effect on the economy). While innovative industries find more and more rigidities and obstacles to their dynamism, the economy becomes increasingly dependent on the "dope"

43. Simiand (1932a:17), like Imbert, claimed that long waves can be found since the 16th c.

of war spending. Military service absorbs part of the work force and helps maintain full employment. "The result of these measures is an augmentation of production, unless an invasion deprives the country of a part of its means, but the equilibrium of the economy is destroyed" (p. 486). "The total national revenue increases in general without the country necessarily being enriched" (p. 486).

Similar effects extend to neutral countries, where industries at first develop in response to increased demands from the belligerent countries for raw materials, war goods, and general consumption goods (as well as to fill neutral countries' import demands that had been met by the belligerents). Payments in precious metals from the belligerents augment the credit possibilities for the neutrals, creating a war boom (p. 486).[44]

But despite short-term "boom" effects, war lays the groundwork for the long wave stagnation phase. War " 'consumes' part of the human capital as it destroys physical capital. It destroys some of the combatants, the civilian population, brings epidemics and illness. It leaves behind a mass of invalids, misfits, and wounded people who increase considerably the expenses of the State" (p. 487). Thus "the causes created by the conflict . . . produce the reversal of the long [expansion] tendency and lead to the long decline of economic activity" (p. 487). Imbert (pp. 488–90) listed five causal links between the war economy and the ensuing economic stagnation phase:

1. War drains precious metal reserves of belligerents, forcing them to abandon the convertibility of currency and to print large quantities of paper money. Currency depreciates, prices rise, and gold accumulates in the neutral countries.
2. War creates disequilibrium in the system of production (sudden rise in demand, destruction caused by war), leading to stagnation after the brief postwar reconstruction boom.
3. War creates rigidities in economic production due to the control and direction of the economy by the state.
4. War brings an exceptional level of mortality among combatants and civilians. After the war, marriages and births boom. The addition of young children to the population (along with war invalids) at the same time the working population is reduced increases the load on the economy.
5. The trauma of war shapes the psychological atmosphere of the stagnation phase. The war generation remembers this painful experience and guards the peace. "Moreover, the financial and economic conditions of the declining phase make the explosion of a general conflict impossible."

The stagnation phase, according to Imbert, is characterized internationally by the absence of major conflicts among the economically dominant countries and domestically by the rise of "order," "reaction," and conservatism. "The economic

---

44. However, if they depend on raw materials from a country involved in the war (or depend on maritime imports that are disrupted), they may suffer depressive effects.

difficulties of the decline bring about insurrections and revolutions'' as well (p. 493). According to Imbert, the stagnation phase continues until the economy stabilizes itself on a nonwar basis with minimal state control, laying the basis for the next expansion phase.

Imbert considered himself to be following in the Schumpeterian tradition, and his theory seems opposite to Trotsky's in its view of capitalism. In Trotsky's theory capitalism tends inherently toward stagnation and crisis and can expand only with the intervention of external forces (including war). In Imbert's theory, capitalism tends inherently toward expansion (if government lets entrepreneurs do their job) and declines because of the intervention of war.

Imbert thus shows that the basic elements of the innovation and war approaches can be combined in a single framework. One major weakness with Imbert's theory is that it works poorly for the most recent expansion phase, which (if one accepts most economic datings) *began* with a major war (World War II). Imbert suggests that after 1929 the capitalist economy progressively gave way to ''new economic structures'' tending towards the formation of a new economic system in which the place of long waves is unclear. I will discuss the anomalous aspects of World War II further in chapter 11.

CHAPTER THREE

The Long Wave Debate 2:
The Current Debate

T he debate on economic long waves resumed after the lull of the 1950s and 1960s;[1] figure 3.1 shows the evolution of the long wave debate up through the mid-1980s. By around 1980 the debate had coalesced into three research schools (shown by dotted boxes), descended from the approaches of Kondratieff, Trotsky, and Schumpeter, respectively. The left side of the figure indicates that war and hegemony have been fenced off from the long wave debate as the disciplinary divide between economics and political science hardened in the 1950s and 1960s.[2]

The "capitalist crisis" school is led by Belgian Trotskyist Ernest Mandel. The "capital investment" school is dominated by Jay Forrester and his team of System Dynamics modelers at MIT. The "innovation" school is centered around Gerhard Mensch in West Germany and Christopher Freeman in Sussex, England. The synthetic work of Dutch scholar Jacob Van Duijn, and the less well known Marxist-innovation synthesis of Alfred Kleinknecht in West Germany, connect the innovation school with both the capital investment and the capitalist crisis schools. This chapter will discuss each of the three current schools of research in turn, then turn to the hybrid theories spanning research schools.

The Capitalist Crisis School

Ernest Mandel

The Marxist debate on long waves lay dormant from the time of Kondratieff's arrest in 1930 until the mid-1970s, when the Belgian Trotskyist scholar Ernest Mandel (1975, 1980, 1981) reformulated a Marxist long wave theory. Mandel builds explicitly on Trotsky's approach. He argues (1980:1) that the rejection of long waves "prevented most Marxists from foreseeing important turning points in recent economic history"—the upturn of capitalism in the 1940s and its downturn in the 1970s—and hence weakened Marxism.

1. The second round of the long wave debate began in 1975 with the publications of Ernest Mandel and W. W. Rostow.
2. The group centered around Wallerstein linking long waves with war and hegemony will be reviewed in chap. 6.

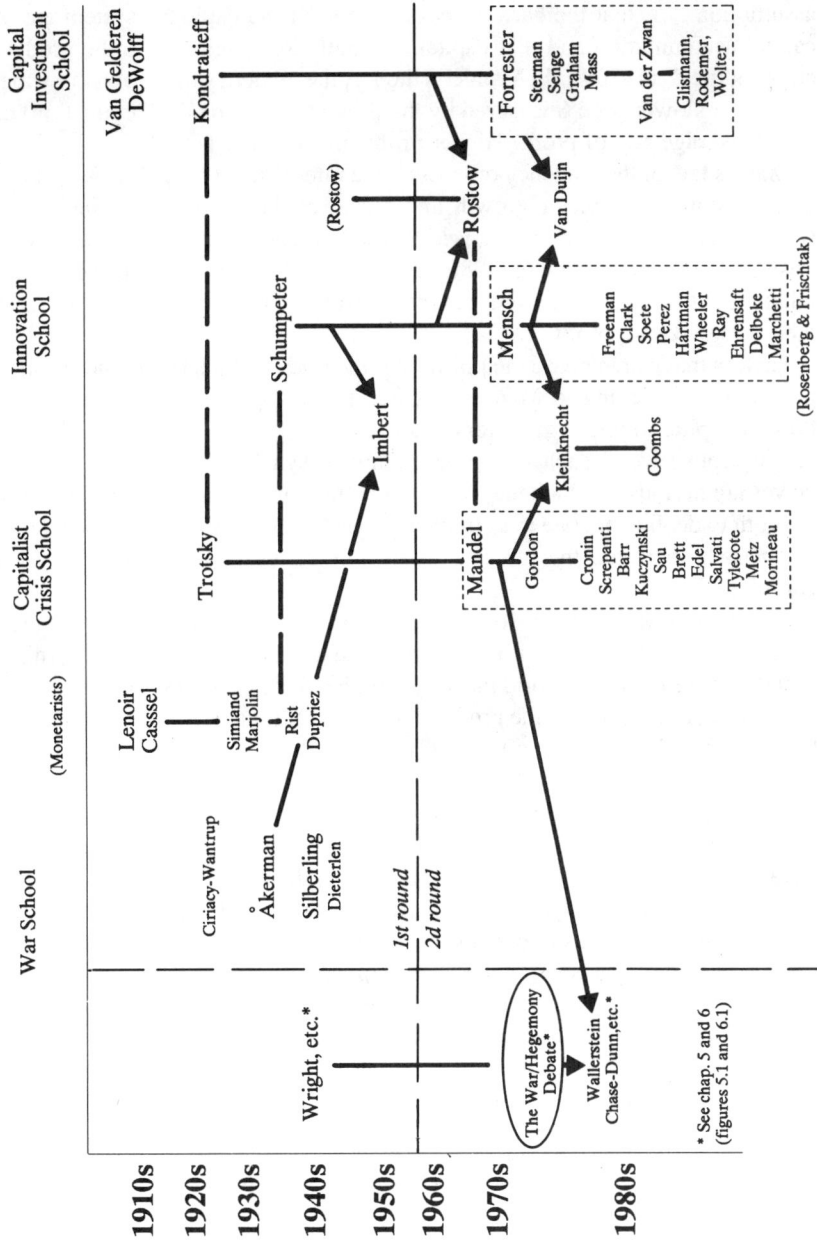

Figure 3.1. Structure of the Long Wave Debate

Mandel stresses that a Marxist theory of long waves should measure production, profits, and (since production serves a world market) exports.[3] He starts "from the assumption . . . that the basic laws of motion of the capitalist system are those of capital accumulation and that capital accumulation originates in the production of commodities" (1980:8). In Mandel's theory, the tendency of the economy to grow at a faster or slower pace (measured by the growth of commodity production) depends on the average rate of profit. Higher profits mean faster growth.

Marx's law of the tendency of the average rate of profit to decline would indicate a general slowing down of growth and hence explain the downswing of the long wave—the onset of capitalist crises. How then can the upswing, the resolution of crisis, be explained? Mandel (1980:21, 28), like Trotsky, argues that recovery is not inherent in the capitalist system but results from exogenous forces acting to increase the average rate of profit.

Factors that can increase the profit rate (the rate at which economic surplus can be generated), according to Mandel, include technological changes and shifts in the flow of capital to different sectors and countries. A sudden upturn in the profit rate results from several such factors operating in synchrony: "Thus, expansive long waves are periods in which the forces counteracting the tendency of the average rate of profit to decline operate in a strong and synchronized way. Depressive long waves are periods in which the forces . . . are fewer, weaker, and decisively less synchronized" (p. 15).

Mandel delineates the historical factors behind each long wave upswing as follows:[4] (1) the revolution of 1848 and the discovery of gold in California, which broadened the capitalist world market, stimulated industrialization and technological innovation, and increased the productivity of labor (and hence the rate of profit);[5] (2) the growth of imperialism after 1893; and (3) the historical defeat suffered by the international working class in the 1930s and 1940s (fascism, war, cold war, McCarthyism), which increased the rate of surplus value extracted from labor; while cheap Middle East oil, state-guaranteed profits from the armaments sector, and advances in telecommunications also increased the profit rate.

Class struggle ("working class militancy and radicalization"), according to Mandel, intensifies late in the expansionary phase, when the working class has been strengthened and expanded. During the depressive phase and early in the expansion (when workers still carry the scar of years of unemployment), by contrast, the interests of capitalists tend to prevail over those of workers. Figure 3.2 shows

3. Mandel seems to contrast his theory with Rostow's, which emphasizes prices (see below). Most Marxists see prices and monetary variables as reflecting "exchange relations" rather than "production relations." Only the latter are seen as fundamental driving forces in social development.

4. Why these upturns occurred "at certain turning points can be explained only in the light of concrete historical analysis of a given period of capitalist development" and "cannot be deduced from the operation of 'capital in general' " (Mandel 1980:16, 21).

5. At the same time, changes in transportation and telecommunications (the steamship, the telegraph, and extensive railroad construction) and changes in credit and trade caused an increase in the rate of turnover of capital.

Figure 3.2. Mandel's Long Waves in Class Struggle

Note: Graph represents European class struggle and economic growth.
Source: Mandel (1980: 50).   Copyright Cambridge University Press. Reprinted by permission.

Mandel's schematic graph correlating class struggle and economic growth in Europe from 1871 to 1974.[6]

Mandel (1980:50, 52) argues that class struggle plays a central role in producing long waves, through a "relatively autonomous long-term cycle of class struggle."[7] Thus, "the outcome of the depressive long wave is not predetermined (it depends on the outcome of class struggles between living social forces)." Here again, Mandel parallels Trotsky.

Mandel sees technological change as an effect rather than a cause of the long wave (this responds to the competing procapitalist "innovation" school). He argues that investment in new technologies is held back during periods of low growth when profit expectations are low; then, as the expansionary phase begins, massive investment takes place in new technologies (using the backlog of unapplied inventions from the downswing period).[8]

Each of the last few upturns, in Mandel's view, has been more difficult to achieve (particularly since the Russian revolution). The upturn since the 1940s occurred only through massive public and private debt[9] and the "artificial stimuli of permanent inflation, growing state intervention, permanent rearmament, etc." (p. 76). Mandel

6. The horizontal axis on this figure is not a linear scale (for reasons unknown to me), and the measurement unit of class struggle (vertical axis) is undefined.

7. Again, like Trotsky, Mandel sees superstructural events as important: "No Marxist would deny that the subjective factor in history . . . is in its turn determined by socioeconomic factors. But it is determined in a long-term sense" (p. 51).

8. Here Mandel seems to have adopted Kondratieff's approach, making common ground against those who see innovation as an inherent driving force in capitalism.

9. "Without the permanent debt explosion of the last thirty years . . . there never could have been any new long wave of expansion" (p. 75).

sees the downturn since 1968 as the last of the long waves. Capitalism can no longer recover since a massive change in the rate of surplus value extraction is not possible with today's stronger and better-organized working class.[10] Mandel concludes that the only way to avoid economic ruin is through "socialism . . . on a broad international scale" (p. 123).[11]

Other Marxist Theories

After Mandel, a number of other Marxist scholars began to write on long waves. I will summarize several of these to convey the scope and flavor of current Marxist scholarship in this field.

David Gordon (1978, 1980) develops a Marxist theory of long waves as *endogenous* to capitalist development—explicitly in contrast to Trotsky and Mandel (Gordon 1978:26). Gordon argues that "a full set of integrated institutions is necessary for individual capitalist-accumulation to continue (p. 27)."[12] "The interdependencies among the individual institutions create a combined social structure with a *unified* internal structure of its own." This he calls the "social structure of accumulation" (1980:17, 12).

The general tendency toward crisis in the capitalist economy (declining rate of profit) combines with a "relatively independent dynamic at the level of the social structure of accumulation": "When either the economy begins to stagnate or institutional contradictions within the social structure of accumulation begin to 'erupt,' accumulation in general *and* the social structure of accumulation are *both* likely to begin to dissolve" (p. 19). This creates what Marx called a "universal crisis." While short-term downswings can be resolved "within the context of prevailing social relationships," universal crises require a restructuring of social relationships (p. 20).[13]

Gordon sees the long wave as a "succession of qualitatively differentiable social structures of accumulation" (p. 22). When the internal contradictions of capitalism give rise to crisis, "individual accumulation cannot resume until the social basis for accumulation is reconstituted" (p. 25). The crisis under one social structure of

10. A drive to break the strength of the working class in today's context (in contrast to the 1920s and 1930s) "would imply a radical curtailment of the democratic freedoms" of the Western industrialized countries, which would be "impossible in the short run" (pp. 113, 115).

11. Mandel's call to arms is weakened, however, by his own evidence and that of Cronin (see below) that working-class militancy peaks near the crest, not the trough, of the cycle.

12. For Gordon, stable accumulation of capital requires stability in internal corporate structure, competition, class struggle, labor management, the monetary system, and the state (limiting the claims of personal political rights on capitalists' rights of property); as well as stable access to raw materials, to intermediate products, and to reliable supplies of labor; a supportive structure of family, schools, and other institutions; a structured social foundation for final consumer demand; a financial structure assuring access to external funding for investment; and a structure of administrative management to manage the circulation of commodities (record keeping, market research, advertising).

13. See also Gordon, Weisskopf, and Bowles (1983) on the relationship of the business cycle and the long wave.

accumulation creates, through class struggle, the institutional changes that allow the next upswing.[14]

Gordon's theory also incorporates capital investment but (unlike Kondratieff) not as a central cause. Each new stage of accumulation requires a physical foundation based on new systems of natural and intermediate supply, transportation, and communication—causing a bunching of infrastructural investments at the beginning of a stage of accumulation.[15] These long-term investments may help stabilize the timing of long waves (1978:31).[16] Investment bursts do not *cause* the upturn, however.

Gordon's theory resembles Trotsky-Mandel in locating the cause of long waves in the social "superstructure" and in seeing long waves as qualitative stages of development rather than endogenously generated cycles. And, like Trotsky and Mandel, Gordon (1978:28, 32) sees capitalism as fundamentally unstable: "Capitalist economies are incapable of permanent prosperity and stability." He agrees that the stagnation phase results from the tendency of profits to decline under capitalism. But Gordon differs in seeing capitalism as able to endogenously move from the downswing to the upswing as well: "Crises can . . . eliminate the problems which might originally have provoked the crisis. . . . [T]he process of crisis will force the system into a new set of institutional relationships" (p. 28).[17]

Mandel (1980:51–52) opposes Gordon's idea "that resolution of the long-term crisis of accumulation is as endogenous to the system as is [its] generation." He says of Gordon's approach that although it seems to break with "economism"[18] by introducing the "social conditions of accumulation," in fact it "sees the outcome of the depressive long wave as predetermined by the processes of capital accumulation and labor organization in the previous period. 'Economism' and straightforward economic determinism are back with a vengeance."

James Cronin (1980:101) does not share the neo-Marxist distaste for "economism." Cronin seeks a "properly materialist rendering of the past," emphasizing "the impact of economic change on social and political movements."[19] Cronin

14. Thus, "long cycles of class struggle 'cause' the burst of new activity at the beginning of long waves" (1978:31).

15. Gordon (1980:31) adds that "infrastructural costs" of "world-market control" (e.g., transport, colonial, and military costs) follow the same timing, tending to cluster at the beginning of a stage of accumulation.

16. Here Gordon's theory draws on Kondratieff's approach.

17. Gordon (1978:26; 1984:123) has a good grasp of the previous long wave debate, including Trotsky, Kondratieff, and Schumpeter. However, he confuses the debate by referring to long waves as "long swings"—a term usually reserved for 20-year "Kuznets" (construction/migration) cycles. Edel (1983) and Glissman, Rodemer, and Wolter (1983) have followed Gordon's usage.

18. Economism is "the devil that latter-day Marxists of the Althusser-Poulantzas school relentlessly try to exorcise." Economism refers to the view that economic factors determine superstructural (political, social, cultural) ones.

19. Cronin (1980:101) stresses that "the baser aspects of things, the social relations and techniques surrounding production and reproduction, affect belief and behavior." He criticizes the tendency "among contemporary Marxist historians . . . to treat economic forces like the Deists treated the creator: the divine presence set everything moving and then retired; in like manner, the mode of production calls forth an

(1978) therefore seeks to explain the incidence of strikes [20] as an outcome of the economic long wave. In the British labor movement from 1871 to the present, Cronin finds that sudden upsurges of labor militancy have taken place during long phases of prosperity.[21] By contrast, the labor movement has been much less successful during long downswings.[22]

Cronin (1980:109) concludes that economic conditions determine the behavior and success of the labor movement. Long waves "lie behind the discontinuous course of social struggle; they determine its form and content, and guarantee its expression." Cronin thus sees class struggle as economically determined, in contrast to the "relatively autonomous" class struggle dynamic of Mandel and Gordon. Yet all agree on the timing—working class militancy increases (and succeeds) on the upswing, especially near the crest, of the long wave.

Ernesto Screpanti (1984:509), like Cronin, notes "a correlation between long economic cycles and recurring explosions of social strife." But while Cronin portrays class struggle as an outcome of the long wave, Screpanti considers it a cause. Economic growth depends upon the "capitalists' attitude toward investment expenditure," which in turn depends on "strong psychological, social, and political—in a word, extra-economic—influences" (pp. 521–22). A higher "degree of workers' militancy" will discourage investment (p. 523), while a decrease in workers' militancy triggers the upturn and continues into the upswing phase. Late in the upswing phase, however, worker militancy eventually explodes again. This shakes the confidence of capitalists, reducing investment and hence growth. Lower growth decreases the gains workers can make, "workers begin to realize they have lost the game," and militancy decreases again (p. 536).

Kenneth Barr (1980:87) focuses on the individual capitalist enterprise, arguing that "the business activity of an enterprise is . . . both a manifestation and a motor force of long waves." He examines the English cotton-spinning industry during a single long wave, 1789 to 1849, following a single firm through each phase.[23] The upswing brought higher profits, mechanization, and specialization. The "transition phase" brought uneven growth, a contraction of profits, and an "explosion of working class political action"[24] lasting through the downswing. The downswing

---

array of class forces that face each other and do battle through culture and politics, but with little further attention to economic considerations narrowly or broadly conceived."

20. Strikes are "a better indicator of working-class attitudes and behavior than any other as yet available" (p. 1194).

21. For example, "at the height of the speculative boom that preceded the Great Depression of 1873–1896," major trade union membership quadrupled in four years. The years 1910 to 1913 (near the crest of the next long upswing) saw "another dramatic explosion of both union membership and strikes" (1980:106). The 1968–72 period (the next long wave peak) again saw "a strike wave of massive proportions and enormous success" (p. 108). Although workers are more needy during downswings, according to Cronin, more can be won from capitalists during the upswing. "Clearly, workers have learned to press their grievances at the hour most advantageous to themselves and are no longer governed by the cries of their bellies" (p. 103).

22. For instance, "the entire working class was defeated in the General Strike of 1926" (1980:107).

23. He dates the expansion phase in 1789–1810, a "transition period" in 1811–17, and the period of "forced growth" in 1818–49.

24. This timing agrees with Mandel and Cronin.

phase brought "a sharp and persistent decline" in profit margins; wage cutting; integration and reorganization of the industry; increasing investment in fixed capital;[25] and attempts to consolidate markets in an oligopolistic fashion (pp. 87–91).

In other recent Marxist scholarship, *Thomas Kuczynski* (1978:80) argues that falling profits cause the long downswing, which in turn stimulates new methods of production, leading to the upswing. Basic innovations, which are new productive forces, require changes in the relations of production (remaining within the capitalist framework), according to Kuczynski. *Ranjit Sau* (1982:574), an Indian Marxist, discusses the current world downswing in terms of the long wave and notes the downturn in profit rates in the major capitalist economies beginning in the late 1960s. *E. A. Brett* (1983:chap. 4) discusses long waves in the context of a more general Marxist theory of crises in capitalism, which stresses the disequilibrium inherent in capitalism and attributes crises to declining profits.

Matthew Edel (1983:117, 119) argues that energy policy is crucial in the upturn of the long wave. "Questions of the types and quantities of energy to be supplied must be settled at least partially before a new investment boom can occur." *Michele Salvati* (1983:204) applies Kalecki's (1943) Marxist theory of political business cycles to the long wave,[26] arguing that political power shifts between "the capitalists" and "the masses" in the course of the long wave. *Andrew Tylecote* (1984:703) ties economic growth phases to the "degree of inequality . . . in the world-economy. To simplify heroically, fast growth leads to increased inequality, which leads to slower growth, which leads to increased equality."

Other recent Marxist long wave research, most of it preliminary, includes *Jan Reijnders* (1984), a German working on removal of long-term trends in identifying long waves; Swiss scholars *Ulrich Pfister* and *Christian Suter* (1985) and *Volker Bornschier* (1985) working on long waves in international financial crises and the role of cultural consensus in long waves, respectively; and *Peter Grimes* (1985), an American studying the role of global inequality.

The Capital Investment School

This research school elaborates a capital investment theory much like that of Kondratieff. It developed rather independently of the Marxist capitalist crisis school and contains fewer internal debates.

Jay Forrester & Co.

The capital investment theory was recreated in the late 1970s by the System Dynamics National Model Project under Jay Forrester at MIT.[27] Forrester and his

---

25. This timing does not agree with Kondratieff's theory.

26. Salvati distinguishes Kalecki's theory from current non-Marxist theories of the electoral business cycle (see Macrae 1981 on the latter).

27. Forrester (1976, 1977, 1978, 1979, 1981a, b, 1982, 1985); Forrester et al. (1984); Mass and Senge (1981); Senge (1982); Graham and Senge (1980); Mass (1975); Sterman (1983a, b, 1985, 1986); Sterman and Meadows (1985); and *Business Week* (1982).

Figure 3.3. Forrester's Long Waves in Capital

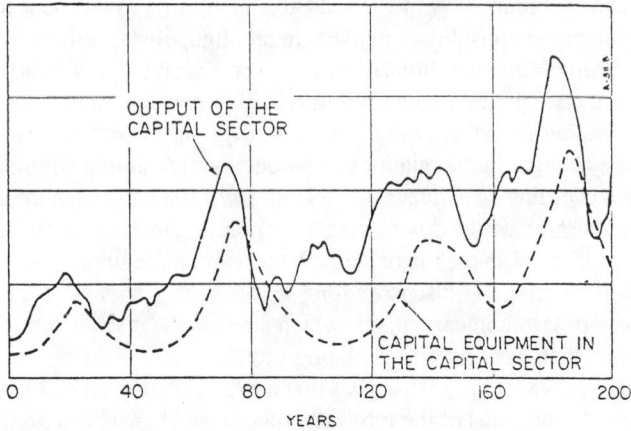

OUTPUT OF THE
CAPITAL SECTOR

CAPITAL EQUIPMENT IN
THE CAPITAL SECTOR

0   40   80   120   160   200

YEARS

Note: Graph represents long waves generated in the capital-equipment sector of
    the model.
Reprinted from Jay W. Forrester, "Information Sources for Modeling the
National Economy." Journal of the American Statistical Society 75,
no. 371, 1980:555-74.

colleagues developed a computer model of the U.S. economy (Forrester, Mass, and
Ryan 1976) and found that the model generated cycles of about fifty years' length
(see fig. 3.3). After initially suspecting an error in the model, they eventually came
across the existing literature on Kondratieff cycles and formulated a theory of why
the economy as modeled would give rise to such cycles (Forrester 1978:6).

This theory sees long waves as "primarily a consequence of capital overexpansion
and decline" rather than of basic innovation (Senge 1982:15).[28] The long wave
upswing brings "an overbuilding of the capital sectors during which they grow
beyond the capital output rate needed for long-term equilibrium" (Forrester
1981a:9). This is largely because in the early stages of the upswing capital investment takes place at a rate determined by the rebuilding of the economy from the
depression rather than at the slower rate needed in the long term for depreciation of
the existing capital stock.[29] Eventually, "capital plant throughout the economy
exceeds the level justified by the marginal productivity of capital," and "the overexpansion is ended by a great depression during which excess capital plant is
physically worn out and is financially depreciated on the account books" (Forrester
1981a:11). During the depression, capital investment is very low until the old capital

28. Forrester (1981a:9) notes that capital investment since 1800 "has been concentrated in periods of
economic excitement lasting about three decades." Between these were depressions in the 1830s, 1890s,
and 1930s.
29. Senge (1982:13) argues that long wave upswings in this model first generate employment but then
displace employment. The initial employment created by renewed economic growth is later counteracted
by the overexpansion of the capital-producing sector, which "begins to push capital into the rest of the
economy, thereby displacing further employment."

plant is cleared out and "the economic stage has been cleared for a new era of rebuilding" (Forrester 1981a:9).

This tendency to overbuild capital stock is amplified by what Sterman (1983a:3) calls the " 'self-ordering' of capital by the capital sector of the economy: the dependence of capital-producing industries, in the aggregate, on their own output." This helps to explain the long span of the cycle and the difficulty of recovering smoothly from long-term overinvestment. Without this self-ordering of capital, the fifty-year cycle would be only a twenty-year cycle, according to Sterman.

Innovation, while not central, plays a role in the model. Forrester (1978:10) picks up the "leading sector" concept, reasoning that "each major expansion of the long wave grows around a highly integrated and mutually supporting combination of technologies." Each such combination, because it embodies a massive long-term capital commitment, "rejects incompatible innovations." Thus during the last half of an upswing, "radical innovation remains outside the circle of acceptance" (p. 10). During the early depression phase, "the process of using up and wearing out the old technology runs its course" (p. 11), so although innovations continue to be created, they are stored up and left dormant. As the depression draws to an end, "accumulated new ideas are tried and developed," and innovation surges with the emergence of a new combination of technologies.[30]

The theory of Forrester's school follows that of Kondratieff in two important respects: (1) it sees long waves as endogenously generated within a fixed system structure,[31] and (2) it explains the long wave with a capital investment theory. Forrester's general approach is "conservative" in stressing the management of social systems (which he conceives as "multi-loop nonlinear feedback systems" in which actions can have unexpected consequences). Forrester's computer models aim to enhance corporate and social management.[32] While Trotskyists see the resolution of the long wave in class revolution and Schumpeterians (see below) see the resolution in technical innovation, Forrester's approach implies that what is really needed is better management.

Wassily Leontief criticizes Forrester's long wave model because "the whole structure of the economy changes" over the long time periods covered by long waves (see *Business Week* 1982).[33] Forrester (1982) responds that the model is based on

30. Forrester (1982:7) calls the depression period "a technological 'window of opportunity' when the old technology has faltered and new technology can most easily enter." Forrester's innovation theory parallels that of the Schumpeterian "innovation school" (see below) but sees clusters of innovations as an effect rather than a cause of long waves. The system dynamics model "can generate the long wave without any technological change" (Sterman 1983b).

31. I consider this theory conservative in assuming a fixed rather than evolutionary social structure.

32. "Until recently, those responsible for managing corporations and countries have not been able to test policy changes in the laboratory before trying them full-scale in the real system. Now, however, computer simulation models are becoming laboratories for analyzing social and corporate policy alternatives quickly and at low cost before new policies are committed to full-scale use" (Forrester 1971:2).

33. Forrester's theory has been rejected by most liberal economists, who differ with his entire epistemology. Forrester's dynamic modeling uses deductive reasoning (positing a theory and then seeing what data it generates) rather than the inductive reasoning of most of liberal economics (econometrics: applying standards of statistical assessment to build theory from data).

"five fundamental processes" that "have changed very little": (1) the use of capital equipment for production; (2) the ten-to-forty-year life of capital plant; (3) the processes existing for the expansion of credit; (4) the lifetime of people; and (5) the influence of recent trends on the speculative attitudes of people. The Forrester-Leontief debate illustrates the different perspectives of the conservative and liberal world views.

Other Capital Investment Theorists

While Forrester's group dominates the current capital investment school, several other scholars have recently proposed capital investment theories as well.

A. *Van der Zwan* (1980:201) proposes an "overinvestment hypothesis" of the long wave. He stresses the role of technologically advanced leading industries—these are where overcapacity occurs, and these industries shape the prospects for recovery from a prolonged depression (p. 205). As regards the current economic downswing, van der Zwan argues that "control of production capacity, especially within the advanced sector of the economy, is a prerequisite for a more lasting improvement of investment expectations" (p. 220).

West Germans *Hans Glismann, Horst Rodemer,* and *Frank Wolter* (1983:139–42) elucidate mechanisms whereby changes in capital investment affect upswings and downswings in production and employment. In their theory, the long wave is caused by changes in investment activity, which reacts to incentives. Long lags result from "institutional sluggishness in reacting to market signals." Glismann et al. argue that labor cost developments and governmental activities (taxes, transfers, and consumption) are "the central agents in long waves" since they affect the incentives for investment. Their approach "is basically endogenous, as was Schumpeter's" (and Kondratieff's and Forrester's). But they contrast it with Schumpeter's theory in that they see investment incentives as central causes of the long wave, while Schumpeter sees them as effects, and in that Schumpeter sees clusters of innovations as central causes, while Glismann et al. see them as effects. This point parallels Forrester's approach.

The Innovation School

The third research school in the current round of the long wave debate—the innovation school—follows in the tradition of Schumpeter.

Gerhard Mensch

Gerhard Mensch, the first central figure in this group, writes that the common factor in depressions recurring every fifty years is "the economic stagnation of . . . the then predominant technologies" (1979:5). This stagnation, which Mensch calls a "stalemate in technology," results from a failure to bring about new innovations in production and is overcome by the emergence of new innovations.[34] "There was

34. The innovation process, according to Mensch, is an attribute not only of capitalism but also of socialist economies.

Figure 3.4. Mensch's Metamorphosis Model

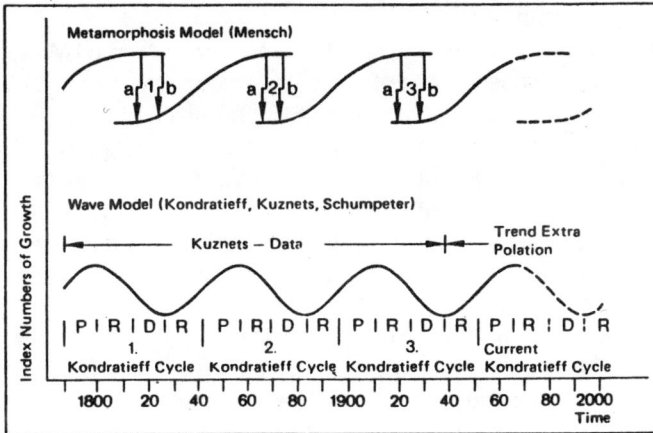

Source: Mensch (1979: 73). From Mensch's *Stalemate In Technology: Innovations Overcome The Depression,* Copyright 1975 by Umschau Verlag, Frankfurt. Reprinted by permission from the Ballinger Publishing Company.

only a limited interest in implementing basic innovations during the prosperous phases . . . ; in contrast to this attitude, the tendency to innovate was very marked during the critical periods of technological stalemate'' (p. 130). Mensch's central thesis (a restatement of Schumpeter) is that "basic innovations occur in clusters" (p. 11). Innovations include both "basic innovations, which establish new branches of industry, and radical improvement innovations, which rejuvenate existing branches" (p. xvii).

According to Mensch, new products follow "life cycles" in which the market at first accepts them hesitantly, then rushes to acquire them, then eventually loses interest (p. 52)—the more basic the innovation, the longer the life cycle. A new product eventually saturates the market, and refinements in subsequent years bring diminishing returns (p. 63). The saturation of the market, supplier concentration,[35] and diminishing returns on improvements combine to set the stage for technological stalemate, according to Mensch. But stagnation in turn eventually stimulates innovation and leads to new growth in new economic sectors. Mensch predicts that the present technological stalemate will break with a cluster of innovations in 1984–94,[36] which will stimulate a new long-term upswing (p. 197).

Mensch proposes that the economy has "evolved through a series of intermittent innovative impulses that take the form of successive S-shaped cycles" (p. 73). Mensch calls this the "metamorphosis" model, as distinct from a "wave" model (see fig. 3.4). It parallels the approach of Trotsky and Mandel (and W. W. Rostow,

35. Concentration of economic firms, through mergers, "increases the market power of suppliers and allows them to . . . slow down the rate of quality improvements."
36. That decade, Mensch predicts, will achieve two-thirds of all basic innovations to be achieved in 1950–2000.

see below) in its stress on qualitatively different phases of development but differs in its formulation of innovation as an outgrowth of stagnation and hence as endogenous to the economic long wave.[37]

In 1981 Mensch, Charles Coutinho, and Klaus Kaasch elaborated Mensch's model in terms of "phases of extensive and of recessive structural change in the economy" (p. 283). In expansion phases, extensive structural change occurs—innovations diffuse through new or modernized sectors, and capital stocks (fixed plant and equipment) rise in value, inducing owners to invest in "more of the same." In stagnation phases, recessive structural change occurs—the diffusion of innovations slows down, and the valuation of that capital falls, causing a shift of investment into alternative types of capital goods. This explains the rise in the innovation rate on the downswing.[38]

Mensch's work has been criticized, mainly for inadequate empirical evidence of increased innovation on the downswing. Mansfield (1983:144), for instance, concludes that "evidence does not persuade me that the number of major technological innovations conforms to long waves of the sort indicated by Mensch's data . . . . The hypothesis that severe depressions trigger and accelerate innovations is also questionable."

Christopher Freeman & Co.

Christopher Freeman, John Clark, and Luc Soete (1982) build on the theories of Schumpeter and Mensch.[39] They argue that "the upswing of the long waves involves a simultaneous or near-simultaneous explosive burst of growth of one or several major new industries and technologies" (Freeman, Clark, and Soete 1982:80). The upswing builds momentum through economies of scale and generates high employment, especially in the early stages when "standardized plant and machinery is not yet available" and the industry is hence fairly labor intensive (p. 75).[40] Eventually, however, the new industry matures, as profits deriving from the innovation are reduced by competition and high labor costs. A process of concentration and cost cutting ensues, with lower employment being generated per unit of investment.[41] As profits decline, unemployment grows and labor force willingness to cooperate with technical innovation decreases. Intense efforts at productivity improvement thus prove less effective than during the expansionary phase, and the economy heads into a period of stagnation and depression.

---

37. Note also Mensch's rejection of the Marxist term *developed* in favor of the liberal word *evolved*.

38. Mensch et al. (p. 281) work within a generally Schumpeterian framework but disagree with Schumpeter's "heroic interpretation of the causes of discontinuity" (sudden jumps caused by individual innovative entrepreneurs).

39. Clark, Freeman, and Soete (1981) call themselves "neo-Schumpeterian." See also Freeman (1979, 1981).

40. At the peak of the boom, demand for labor stimulates significant flows of immigration into the leading industrial countries and the entry of new groups into the labor force.

41. High labor costs, resulting from both the general expansion of the boom period and from shortages of certain essential skill categories in that expansion, continue even beyond the peak of the upswing.

Freeman et al., in contrast to Mensch, argue that deep depressions inhibit, rather than stimulate, new basic innovations. While they "do not rule out the possibility of some form of bunching of basic innovations or inventions," they attribute such bunching to scientific and technological breakthroughs and periods of strong demand, including booms and wars (Clark, Freeman, and Soete 1981:321). They (Freeman, Clark, and Soete 1982:81) therefore stress that "the role of public policy is crucial" in leading the way out of a depression by stimulating an increase in the general level of profitability.[42] As for the economic situation in 1982, Freeman et al. conclude that technology policies, while not a cure-all, "are a vital ingredient of any strategy" against stagflation (p. 200).[43]

Freeman's associate,[44] Venezuelan scholar *Carlota Perez* (1983:358), starts from a "Schumpeterian view" of innovation in the long wave but sees long waves as "not a strictly economic phenomenon, but rather the manifestation, measurable in economic terms, of the harmonious or disharmonious behaviour of the *total* socioeconomic and institutional system (on the national and international levels)." Whereas Schumpeter had assumed that social and institutional conditions are exogenous to the economic system, Perez proposes that capitalism contains two "subsystems": one "techno-economic" and the other social and institutional (p. 359). While short business cycles are explainable within the former subsystem alone, long waves involve both subsystems and are seen as "successive phases in the evolution of the total system" or "successive modes of development" (p. 360). Each phase in this evolution of economic life is marked by a "technological style . . . based on a constellation of interrelated innovations" (pp. 358, 360). A technological style generates a "dynamic complementarity" of economic and social/institutional factors that sustains the long upswing until the technological style approaches the "limits of its potential," culminating in a "structural crisis." Such a crisis indicates "a breakdown in the complementarity between the . . . economic subsystem and the . . . socio-institutional framework" and "forces the restructuring of the socio-institutional framework" to correct this. Perez does not mention the striking similarity between her theory and that of David Gordon (above), in the capitalist crisis school. She argues that her model is "consistent" with Forrester's capital investment theory—excess capital capacity occurring in the old technological style—as well as with Mensch's, Van Duijn's, and Freeman et al.'s innovation approaches (Perez 1983:8).[45]

---

42. Their view of the exogenous causation of long upswings parallels that of Trotsky and Mandel.

43. Clark (1980) examines the economic effects of technical change, particularly on employment. He notes that the economic lifetime of a certain "vintage" of equipment may be less than its physical lifetime if newer models are more cost-effective. Clark builds a computer model of this process and draws conclusions generally supportive of Mensch's view of innovation.

44. As Freeman (1983:6) notes, his research group has no specific program on long waves. Since they are policy oriented, historical research on long waves remains "a hobby of a few highly motivated and interested individuals, unfortunately without formal financial backing."

45. Tylecote (1984:705) elaborates on Freeman's theory of the diffusion of innovations, paralleling Perez, from a Marxist perspective. Clusters of technical and organizational innovations, constituting a

Other Innovation Theorists

Several other authors working on long waves within the general framework of the Schumpeterian innovation approach may be mentioned.

Raymond S. Hartman and *David R. Wheeler* (1979:65–66) examine waves of innovation and of infrastructural development in British and American economic experience. Like Mensch, they find downswings "characterized by significant innovative activity" (as indicated by patents) and by high levels of infrastructural expansion as measured by miles of canals, railroads, highway, and aviation routes.

George F. Ray's (1980a, b; 1983a, b) approach parallels Mensch's but focuses on energy as a central element in the innovations associated with each upswing. The steam engine was developed to pump water from coal mines and in turn burned coal; the railway boom depended on the locomotive, built to haul coal and also fueled by coal; the generation of electricity drove the third upswing; and oil tied together the developments in transportation in the fourth upswing (motor vehicles, air transport, and expanded shipping fleets).

Philip Ehrensaft (1980:75–79) argues that waves of clustered basic innovations in North American agriculture closely follow the long wave. On the downswing phase, farmers adopt new technologies in an effort to increase production in order to maintain revenues in the face of declining prices. Ehrensaft argues that downswings in agriculture correspond with upswings in the general economy. Like Freeman et al., Ehrensaft argues that long waves call for "a degree of state intervention surpassing that of the neo-Keynesian system"—in order to bring about "collective action to direct resources towards innovative sectors."

Jos Delbeke (1982a, b) studies production trends in nineteenth-century Belgium. Like Van Duijn (see chapter 4), Delbeke dates the long wave according to a sequence of shorter business cycles. He attempts to identify leading sectors in Belgium on this basis.

Cesare Marchetti (1983:331), who is associated with the International Institute for Applied Systems Analysis (IIASA) in Vienna, argues that the growth of a particular technology, such as motor vehicles, follows an S curve.[46] In the case of automobiles, Marchetti shows that "market saturation . . . comes practically at the same time all over the world" (p. 333), because the later a country started producing cars, the faster its growth. Thus, exports cannot be used to compensate for saturated domestic markets (p. 334), and the resulting global overcapacity leads to the long wave downswing. The fifty-year timing of long waves derives from the time required for a new technology to reach world market saturation (p. 336). Marchetti predicts a rush of innovations between 1984 and 2002, providing the "seeds of the next boom"

---

new technological "style," appear in the leading country or countries; but their diffusion is held up by institutional rigidities and the unfavorable economic climate of the downswing. Institutional changes eventually come about, leading to faster diffusion of the "style" and hence a new upswing.

46. Marchetti argues that a set of innovations, like a species in a habitat, grows as if filling an ecological niche left by the dying-off of the previous population (earlier technologies).

(p. 337), and suggests nuclear energy as the "new primary energy source" in the next upswing. His prescriptions for government policy include helping entrepreneurs by "giving them money, making them heroes, and perhaps detaxing them" (p. 341).[47]

A critical review of innovation theories by *Nathan Rosenberg* and *Claudio R. Frischtak* (1983, 1984), however, concludes that "an adequate or even plausible theory of long cycles, based primarily on technological determinants, does not presently exist" (1984:8). Such a theory, they argue, would have to fulfill four interconnected requirements: (1) causality—in particular, the relationship between growth and innovation;[48] (2) timing[49]—since major innovations vary in terms of their rate of diffusion and how long they remain important, temporal regularity can come only from macroeconomic effects on the timing of innovation; (3) linkages— "the mechanisms through which particular changes in technology exercise *sizable* changes in the performance of the macroeconomy" (p. 16); and (4) repetition—not only that innovations create long waves but that such waves repeat themselves (p. 18).

Hybrid Theories

The hybrid theories of W. W. Rostow and Jacob Van Duijn combine innovation and capital investment theories, while Alfred Kleinknecht's theory combines Schumpeterian innovation with a Marxist approach (see fig. 3.1).

W. W. Rostow

In his first work on long waves, W. W. Rostow (1948) criticized some of the assumptions of the innovation and capital investment schools. He objected that Schumpeter's theory was vague regarding which variables (prices, production, and so forth) follow long waves and that Schumpeter "adduces no intrinsic reason" for the cycle. The actual scale and consequence of innovations historically "are demonstrably inadequate to explain the central phenomena," according to Rostow (p. 29).[50] He was equally skeptical about Kondratieff's concept of self-generating economic cycles. Rostow preferred the concept of "trend periods" rather than "cycles" (p. 7). A trend period is a period of time during which a coordinated trend (up, flat, down) affects such economic variables as economic expansion, commodity prices, interest rates, real wages, and terms of trade.[51]

In 1975 and 1978, however, Rostow pulled together his own long wave theory and

47. Other recent long wave innovation theorists include *Giarini* (1984) and *Erickson* (1985).
48. Forrester and Kondratieff postulate a causality opposite to that of Schumpeter.
49. "It is not enough to argue that the introduction of new technologies generates cyclical instability. It is necessary to demonstrate why technological innovation leads to cycles of four-and-a-half to six decades in length" (1984:11).
50. These criticisms were typical of the liberal economists of the era.
51. This conception of cyclicality is closer to Trotsky's than to Schumpeter's or Kondratieff's.

applied it to the world economy from 1790 to 1976.[52] He reviewed the long wave literature and concluded that "the phenomena identified but not explained by Kondratieff have still not been brought within the framework of 'an appropriate theory of long waves'" (1975a:729). Rostow offered his own theory as such a framework.

From the innovation approach, Rostow incorporates the leading sectors concept, arguing that different economic sectors grow at different rates: "Old sectors may be declining, others may be stagnant, others may be moving forward at about the average rate . . . but there will be one or more leading sectors, reflecting the introduction of major new technologies, moving ahead more rapidly than the average" (1978:104). Historically, Rostow delineates the "classic sequence of such great leading sectors" as "cotton textiles; railroads and iron; steel, chemicals, and electricity; and the automobile industry" (see fig. 3.5).

From the capital investment approach Rostow (1978:107) incorporates the idea of capital over- and underinvestment. He attributes heavy investment in each new leading sector and the tendency over time to overshoot the appropriate long-term level of investment to three factors that distort the assessment of future profitability in the sector: (1) investors look at current profitability rather than rational long-term assessments; (2) investors rarely take into account that the same factors motivating them to invest also motivate others to act in the same direction; and (3) capital markets suffer from a psychological follow-the-leader tendency. The same factors that cause an overinvestment then bring about, in reaction, an underinvestment. These characteristics lie behind both the short cyclical fluctuations of the economy and the long trend periods, according to Rostow.[53]

Through 1935, Rostow's dating of upswings and downswings corresponds generally with that of Kondratieff and other scholars.[54] But, because of his emphasis on prices, Rostow calls 1935–51 an upswing (high inflation), 1951–72 a downswing (low inflation),[55] and the period starting in 1972 an upswing (high inflation). Rostow thus explains the high inflation of the 1970s as the start of a new long wave upswing phase. This is directly opposite to the majority of scholars, Mandel in particular, who see the 1970s as a stagnation phase rather than an upswing.[56] Rostow (1978:298)

52. As noted above, this helped (along with Mandel's work) to reinvigorate the long wave debate in 1975. See also Gayer, Rostow, and Schwartz (1975).

53. Rostow embraces two other elements in building his long wave theory. First, fluctuations in migration rates cause "accelerated investment in transport, housing, and urban infrastructure" (1978: 103). This migration/construction theory pertains to shorter cycles (about 20 years) discussed by Simon Kuznets, and I will not include them in this discussion of long waves. Second, "phases of agricultural and raw-material scarcity or abundance" play a central role. During Rostow's upswing phases, prices of primary commodities (food and raw materials) tend to rise, along with prices in general; interest rates are high; agriculture expands rapidly; and income distribution shifts in favor of agriculture and profits at the expense of urban real wages. During downswings, price and interest trends are downward, income distribution shifts toward urban real wages, and profits are under pressure.

54. The question of alternative dating schemes will be taken up in chap. 4.

55. The period 1951–1972 is noted as sharing only some of the characteristics of previous price-decrease periods.

56. These scholars were generally interested more in production, and less in prices, than Rostow.

Figure 3.5. Rostow's British Sectoral Growth Patterns

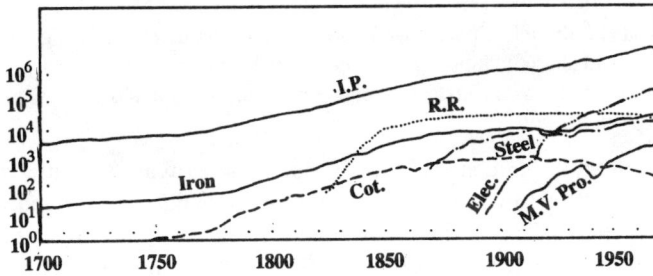

Note: Graph represents aggregate and sectoral growth patterns for Britain, 1700-1972.
I.P. = Industrial production. R.R. = Railroad mileage. Cot. = Raw cotton consumption.
Iron, Steel, Elec., and M.V. Pro. = Production of iron, steel, electricity and motor vehicles,
respectively.

Source: W.W. Rostow, *The World Economy, History and Prospect*, p. 107, Copyright (c) 1978. By
permission of the University of Texas Press.

projects the 1980s as the "fifth Kondratieff upswing," while Mandel (1980) foresees
the 1980s as the fourth Kondratieff downswing.

Rostow's dating has received considerable attention, but little support, from other
long wave scholars.[57] Dupriez (1978:203–7) opposes Rostow's dating and concurs
with Mandel, describing 1945–74 as a rising phase (and 1974 as the point of
downturn), despite assuming that the pricing system (Rostow's key indicator) and
credit system are "central to the long waves." Dupriez argues that the "logarithmic
growth" prevailing before 1974 "has been broken" by unprecedented structural
unemployment and exhaustion of natural resources, which emerged as prime concerns in the early 1970s. These nonmonetary features were characteristic of previous
downturns, including 1818, 1872, and 1920. In addition, Dupriez points to major
changes in the monetary system around 1974. "The [1974] downturn stood in the
center of monetary crises and reforms" (including the liquidation of the gold standard), which parallels past downturns.[58] As regards prices, Dupriez admits the
sudden upsurge in prices in 1974 was "anomalous." Nonetheless, from 1974
onward, Dupriez argues, "price relations became obviously of the type conducive to
economic recession and reorganization" even though inflation continued. "Something of the same sort had happened around 1872, but not to the same extent," he
concludes.

Wallerstein (1979:669–70) also opposes Rostow's dating. He suggests a more
complex explanation to reconcile "stagflation" with Mandel's dating. He links

---

57. Wallerstein (1979) reviews the Mandel-Rostow debate.
58. The introduction of the gold standard in England in 1818, the liquidation of the silver standard in
1874, and a general upheaval of currency parities after 1920.

"stagflation" to even longer price waves ("logistics," see below), in which the period after 1815 was "one long deflationary B phase" and the period beginning in the 1970s was an A phase.

It would follow that Kondratieff B phases *within* logistical B phases showed a high correlation between stagnation and sharp deflation. But Kondratieff B phases within logistical A phases (the latter being in crude terms the sixteenth, eighteenth, and twentieth centuries) might well show the inverse phenomenon.[59]

In my own reading, the evidence of the past decade goes against Rostow's dating. In Wallerstein's (1979:669) words, "the present phase is not yet over and we have yet to see if in the 1980's the price inflation will not break." Inflation did in fact break (at least in the United States) the following year. At this writing, for five years (1982–86) U.S. inflation has not exceeded 4 percent annually. Meanwhile, production, employment, and debt have continued to indicate stagnation in long-term growth.[60] Thus Mandel's dating seems preferable to Rostow's.

Rostow's work has not been well integrated into the current long wave debate, probably because of his unusual dating scheme.[61] Since the downturn in the world economy was the apparent factor that triggered the new round of interest in long waves, it is logical that those scholars would not take seriously a dating scheme that portrays the world economy as beginning an upswing just then.

Jacob Van Duijn

Jacob Van Duijn (1979, 1981, 1983), like Rostow, integrates the innovation and capital investment theories[62]—but without Rostow's dating scheme. Van Duijn (1983) provides perhaps the most widely accepted current synthesis of non-Marxist approaches to the economic long wave. Van Duijn's (1981:19) theory integrates innovation and capital investment as follows:

[B]asic innovations will give rise to new industrial sectors. These sectors develop according to the familiar S-shaped life cycle pattern. [Van Duijn, like Rostow, begins with the idea of S curves of growth.] New sectors require their own infrastructure. . . . [E]xcess accumulation

59. Note that my review of Wallerstein's own long cycle theory follows in chap. 6. In my view Wallerstein's approach here is a more "conservative" Marxist interpretation (like Kondratieff and unlike Trotsky-Mandel). Logistic cycles lend stable structure to the world political economy over very long periods. Even phenomena that seem to represent sharp changes in the system (stagflation) are not really new. Wallerstein (1979:670) notes that both Rostow and Mandel "seem to feel that the years from here to 2000 A.D. will mark the definitive turning point towards a new era. Rostow is filled with liberal optimism" and Mandel with socialist enthusiasm. Wallerstein prefers Mandel's analysis to Rostow's, but "the preoccupation with the present forces Mandel (as it does Rostow) to concentrate on what's new rather than what's old, on what has changed rather than on what has remained the same" (p. 672).

60. As of 1986, U.S. production growth remains sluggish. 1985 GNP growth was back to 2.2%, typical of the 1980s, after a one-year spurt to 6.6% in 1984 (election year?), and the economy has been unable to shake massive trade and budget deficits.

61. He does not seem to attend the same conferences and publish in the same places as the other long wave scholars, although he continues to work in the field.

62. See Van Duijn (1983:chap. 8) in particular.

of physical stock will eventually occur. The levelling off of demand in the innovation-incorporating sectors will accentuate the overexpansion of the capital sector. The combined effect of those two forces is a long-wave downturn . . . . A long-wave decline means a period of depressed investment. A recovery sets in when replacement investment picks up . . . . The stimulus of investment demand will change the overall economic outlook, setting the scene for a new burst of innovations.

Van Duijn (1981; 1983) rejects Mensch's theory that downswings stimulate innovations, arguing instead that while ''process'' innovations will be stimulated by downswings, the more important ''product'' innovations will be held back until the upswing: ''Ultimately, . . . innovators need to be convinced that they are tapping new growth markets. That conviction becomes easier during recovery than in the midst of a depression'' (1981:29). According to Van Duijn (1981:25), different types of innovations cluster at different phases of the long wave as follows (my synopsis):

Phase*:	R	P	S	D
Product innovations:				
in existing industries	most			most
in new industries	most			
Process innovations:				
in existing industries		some	some	most
in basic sectors	some	most	some	

*R=recovery; P=prosperity; S=recession; D=depression

Thus it is only the *product innovations* that cluster in the late downswing and early upswing period.

Alfred Kleinknecht

Alfred Kleinknecht incorporates the idea of innovation as driving the long wave within a ''capitalist crisis'' framework. Kleinknecht (1981a:688) argues that Mandel's exogenously induced upswings ''seem to be more or less historically unique, if not purely accidental'' and proposes instead an endogenous theory of long waves based on technological innovation, where the ''basic renewal in production technology . . . [is] itself a result of low profitability and of sharper competition'':

If Mandel assumed as a precondition for the achievement of a ''technological revolution'' an extraordinary increase in the average profit rate, we must here assume the exact opposite, namely the exploration of new spheres of economic endeavor through basic innovations as an expression of deteriorating valorization of capital within the existing areas (p. 707).[63]

63. Mandel (1980:25) had argued that ''large-scale innovation does not take place during the long wave of relative stagnation . . . because profit expectations are mediocre. Precisely for that reason, once the sharp upsurge in the rate of profit starts, capital finds a reserve of unapplied or only marginally applied inventions and therefore has the material wherewithal for an upsurge in the rate of technological innovation.''

Thus while Mandel sees innovations as clustering in the early upswing, Kleinknecht puts them in the downswing.

Kleinknecht also finds fault with certain aspects of the innovation theory, however. In explaining the lack of basic innovations during upswings, Kleinknecht (p. 704) finds Mensch's blaming of "directive mistakes by management" unsatisfactory. He argues that actions leading into technological stagnation are not mistakes but "rational on the basis of the single firm." Carrying out a basic innovation involves heavy expenditure in research and development and heavy risks. Increasing such expenditures would be unwise for the individual firm as long as money can be made more quickly and safely with established products. "This means that during periods of prosperity it is rational to restrict innovations within existing industrial lines" (p. 705).[64]

Rod Coombs (1981, 1984) follows in Kleinknecht's footsteps in integrating the innovation and capitalist crisis schools, in particular Freeman and Mandel: "[S]ome aspects of technical change at the lower turning point of the wave can be seen as endogenous to the mechanism, . . . without sacrificing the essentially political and nondeterminist character of the lower turning point" (1984:675–76).

Preindustrial Times

The hybrid theories conclude my discussion of long wave schools. Several other points of interest in the long wave debates remain to be noted. First, almost all scholars of long waves (Marxist and non-Marxist) have concentrated on the period since the late eighteenth century, since the industrial revolution.[65] But a few scholars claim to find long waves in earlier centuries.[66] This possibility raises thorny issues for Marxists—if long waves are seen as a necessary product of capitalism, then they should date back only to the beginning of capitalism (or even, as many argued, industrial capitalism). The traditional Marxist answer (held by both Kondratieff and Trotsky) is that long waves exist only in the era of industrial capitalism. But Wallerstein's "world-system" approach claims that a "capitalist world-economy" has existed since the early sixteenth century and that long waves may be found throughout that period.[67] Wallerstein (1984a) argues that an appropriately conceived long wave framework can be used for the pre-1800 as well as post-1800 period. While the world economy was "less structured and less commodified" before 1800, this change has been a secular trend over centuries, not a sudden shift in 1800, Wallerstein argues.[68]

64. Here Kleinknecht parallels Mandel rather than Mensch.

65. Some are explicit in limiting long waves to the industrial period, while others simply ignore earlier times.

66. Imbert (1959) even claims to identify five long cycles of about 50 years' length (the third is shorter and weaker), dating from 1286 to 1510.

67. Imbert's long waves going back to the 13th c. would predate even Wallerstein's version of capitalism.

68. Nonetheless there were differences in the pre-1800 period, when economies were directly based on agriculture and crises arose from poor harvests, as compared with the industrially based economies after 1800, when harvests played a lesser role (Wallerstein 1984a).

Fernand Braudel (1972) describes long waves in fifteenth-to-seventeenth-century Europe.[69] Braudel (1984:75) argues that price waves were roughly synchronous across Europe, indicating an integrated network of markets, as early as the fifteenth century. He (1984:87) reviews the research indicating an inverse correlation of real wages to long-term price trends.[70] During economic expansion phases, wages fall behind prices, and real wages drop: "The progress made by the upper reaches of the economy . . . were paid for by the hardship of the mass of people . . . [and] the downturn at superstructural level actually led to an improvement in living standards for the masses." Braudel (1972:897–99) also notes that crusades and outbreaks of anti-Semitism in preindustrial Europe occurred during economic stagnation phases in this preindustrial era.[71]

Michel Morineau (1984) discusses long waves in grain harvests and grain prices in France in the sixteenth to eighteenth century. Morineau argues that war and technological innovation play a role in long waves in that era.[72]

Rainer Metz (1984b) claims to show "long waves" in grain prices from the fifteenth to eighteenth centuries, but his "waves" are quite irregular and do not match the long waves described by other scholars (see chapter 4).

A separate but related debate among Marxists regarding this early period concerns longer cycles of several hundred years' duration, sometimes called "logistics" (or "secular cycles"), which apparently span the precapitalist and capitalist eras. Wallerstein (1984a) identifies these logistics, "even more strongly than the Kondratieffs," as price movements. He suggests that what is "exogenous" to the long wave for Mandel "is clearly endogenous to the longer 'logistic.' "[73] Nicole Bousquet (1979:503) notes that "from the point of view of a world economy, the origins of which could date back only to the first half of the sixteenth century, the presence of such logistics [predating 1500] is a bit embarrassing [my translation]." The rise of the capitalist world economy should have broken their dynamic, Bousquet argues, but this did not happen. Albert Bergesen (1983a:78) likewise worries that "the fact that [logistics] appear to begin within the feudal era and carry over into the period of the capitalist world-economy presents questions of whether they represent the dynamics of feudalism or capitalism, or both." Hopkins and Wallerstein (1979:488) write that "one question that is blurred in the literature concerns the kinds of economic systems within which these very long cyclical rhythms are said to occur."[74]

---

69. These cycles seem to follow on the earlier waves of (non-Marxist) Imbert (1959), whom Braudel cites.

70. Braudel cites Phelps-Brown and Hopkins ([1956] 1962), from whose data I draw similar conclusions in chapter 10. See also Von Tunzelman (1979) and Flinn (1974) on wages.

71. I wondered whether witch trials might follow a similar pattern. But data on witch trials in Southwest Germany in 1500–1700 (Midelfort 1972:201–30) showed no clear pattern when summed by economic phase period (the base dating scheme from chap. 4, below, was used). Data for England in 1560–1680 (Macfarlane 1970:26) showed one major concentration of witch trials, on the upswing phase of 1575–94. No long cycle was evident.

72. In a rare occurrence, Morineau cites Åkerman, the early theorists of the war school.

73. Wallerstein offers this as a resolution of the debate between Mandel and Gordon over endogeneity in the long wave.

74. See also Cameron (1973) and Hart (1945) on logistics.

Popularizations

With the deepening economic stagnation in the United States around 1980 the long wave began to receive more public attention. Various communities became interested in long waves, generally for reasons relating to their own interests.[75]

Some members of the business community see the long wave as showing the importance of investment in new technologies (see *Business Week* 1982). Whatever set of industries emerges as a new leading sector in the next upswing (electronics, biogenetics, computers?) may be extremely profitable.

High-technology entrepreneurs use the long wave to call for increased public assistance to their industries. Craig Volland (1983:76), president of a Missouri consulting firm, writes in *High Technology* magazine that new technologies[76] could overcome the resource limitations of the previous "hydrocarbon era" and spur a new Kondratieff upswing.[77] "It is critical that policies for long-term economic recovery encourage new technologies . . . and not subsidize the further growth of conventional hydrocarbon-based technologies," writes Volland.

The innovation theory of long waves has been taken up by "reform-oriented circles of the labor movement" in West Germany, according to Kleinknecht (1981a: 709). "Slogans like 'policy of innovations support' . . . could take on ideological importance (as possible cures to the crises of capitalism) similar to the 'Keynesian economics' of the past."

An article in *Science* magazine (Dickson 1983) suggests that the long wave calls for "increased support for basic research" to lay the groundwork for technological innovation and hence economic recovery.

One book (Shuman and Rosenau 1972) attempting to popularize the Kondratieff wave for the general public (including effects on politics, foreign trade, war, women's liberation, and so forth) made the mistake of predicting a "golden period" of economic prosperity, balanced federal budgets, and an end to inflation in the 1970s! It did not become a best-seller. Responsive to changing conditions, Beckman (1983) wrote a similar popularization a decade later based on the theme of how-to-profit-from-the-depression.

Weather Cycles

My review of the theoretical debates on long waves would not be complete without mention of what I call "crackpot theories." All manner of cycles have been "discovered" at one time or another, covering every aspect of society (economic, political, spiritual, cultural, and so on). Many of these are

75. Even the Central Intelligence Agency wrote a staff report on long waves (Levy-Pascal 1976).
76. "Electronics and telecommunications, dependent on ubiquitous silicon, and genetic engineering, based on an endless supply of low-paid and easy-to-please microbes."
77. Elsewhere, Volland (1985) reviews Kondratieff ([1928] 1984).

theories based on metaphysical or mystical ideas, usually elaborated with little regard for empirical evidence, and are responsible in part for the bad reputation of the cycles field.

Theories of long waves as driven by weather cycles generally fall in this category. For example, Raymond Wheeler (1943) attempts to tie both war and economic cycles to alternations in world climate (hot/cold and wet/dry). Wheeler's theory rests on racist assumptions about differences in productivity between peoples living in warmer and colder regions of the world, which he extrapolates to cover warmer and colder periods in history.

I do not dismiss weather cycles out of hand, however. A fifty-year weather cycle in the preindustrial period could plausibly affect harvests, hence economic surplus, and hence also the capacity to wage war.[78] Nevertheless, I find no evidence of such a cycle in weather, in sunspots (which affect weather), or in the record of tree-ring growth.[79]

78. Recently, Danish researchers have tried to tie long waves to climate. Petersen (1986) argues that Goldstein's (1985) emphasis on war in long waves should be rejected in favor of climatological explanations. He cites Danish climatologist Christian Vibe, who claims to find climate cycles of 1395, 698, 116, 58, 30, and 10 years. I find these arguments unconvincing.

79. Rainfall and temperature data for several countries (from Mitchell 1980) were examined in a preliminary search for correlation with economic phase periods without success. Huntington (1914:117) gives annual Arizona tree-ring growth data in which he claims to find cycles of 11, 21, and 150 years—but not 50 years. Stetson (1947:chap. 14) claims a correlation of sunspots and short business cycles, but not long waves.

CHAPTER FOUR

The Long Wave Debate 3: Empirical Arguments

In this chapter I review the past empirical evidence for long waves, comparing and sifting evidence presented by adherents of different theoretical schools. This combined with the preceding theoretical discussions will facilitate sorting out the alternative hypotheses of different schools and subschools and their respective strengths in chapter 7.

What Variables to Include?

I have organized my review of empirical evidence around the different variables of interest. From the theoretical discussions of chapters 2 and 3, the relevant variables and time span of the long wave can be identified.[1] The time span of interest is maximally 1495 to the present, with distinction between the preindustrial and industrial periods (before and after about 1790).[2] There are seven basic variables of interest:

1. *Prices:* Are there synchronous long price waves in the core countries? How early can they be found, and in what countries? These questions interest almost all long wave scholars since prices are the most readily available economic data and since all schools posit long waves of prices.
2. *Production:* Are there alternating phases of fast and slow growth in core countries' production? In what countries and time periods can they be found? These questions are central to the capitalist crisis school as well as to certain liberal critics who see long waves as ''only price waves.''
3. *Innovation and Invention:* Are waves or clusters of innovations synchronous with long waves? Are they directly or inversely correlated with economic growth phases? These questions are central to the innovation school.
4. *Capital Investment:* Do spurts of capital investment correlate with the early

---

1. A few ''outliers'' beyond this domain are ignored.
2. Again, I use 1790 as shorthand to refer to the transition to industrial economies. Note that for production (except for scanty data on harvests), innovation, and capital investment, virtually no data are available for the preindustrial period and that the temporal scope under discussion begins around 1790.

upswing of the long wave? The correlation of investment levels with long waves is of particular concern to the capital investment school.

5. *Trade:* Do levels of exports or other indicators of international trade follow the long wave phases? Trade concerns some members of the capitalist crisis school who see capitalism as production for a world market.

6. *Real Wages and Working-Class Behavior:* Do real wages fluctuate with the long wave? Do strikes and other worker protests follow long wave phases? These questions concern the capitalist crisis school.

7. *War:* Do major wars tend to occur at one point in the long wave? Does the timing of major wars correlate with long wave phases? These questions concern the war school and the participants in the debates discussed below in chapter 5.

These seven variables encompass the essential variables of interest to all schools. But the choice of what variables one examines depends on one's theoretical approach to long waves and the world view that underlies it. Marxists tend to be concerned with the means of production and the accumulation of surplus as well as with class struggle—and hence try to measure the total growth of production, the overall rate of profit, the unemployment rate, and such indicators of working-class behavior as strikes. Monetary variables, representing exchange relations rather than production relations, are of much less interest to Marxists. Neo-Schumpeterians try to measure the rate of innovation, invention, or the diffusion of innovations. Capital investment theorists are interested in such variables as total investment in capital plant. The differences in variables of interest to different theoretical schools contribute to the difficulty in cumulating results across schools (see chapter 7).

Of all the questions concerning the scope of the long wave, the central issue is whether long waves exist only in *prices* and other monetary variables (for example, interest rates) or also in *production* and other "real" variables (for example, employment, capital investment, volume of trade). Most long wave studies have treated prices and production as moving in synchrony, particularly since periods of marked depression have generally combined both stagnant production and falling prices.[3] But in recent decades, production and prices seem less synchronous, especially with the stagflation (high inflation combined with stagnation of production and employment) of the 1970s. This has led to somewhat divergent interpretations of the long wave.[4] I will take up this puzzle directly in my analysis in Part Two.

All variables are not equally accessible to investigation. Price data are relatively plentiful, while data on innovations and worker protests are much scantier and less reliable. Prices have one big advantage over all other variables—the availability and consistency of data.

In the preindustrial age (which makes up more than half of the total period of my

3. This assumption of synchrony is taken for granted in many long wave theories. My reinterpretation is given in chap. 10.

4. As noted earlier, Rostow's long wave dating based on prices opposes most other datings based on production.

study) prices are virtually the only good economic data available.[5] Economic historians have been able to dig up annual or monthly price series in quite a few cases from records kept by institutions that made regular purchases. In some cases they have pieced a number of these series together to make an overall price index for a region or country. However, for production variables (as well as employment, investment, innovation, and so forth) there are no comparable data sources. No one kept central records on the total production of a region or country in the preindustrial period. The very concept of a "national product" (GNP) is a twentieth-century creation. Economic historians have reconstructed some national production totals, but only back to the late eighteenth century at best.

Methodologies

In addition to focusing on different variables, scholars have used different methodologies to study long waves. Almost all empirical studies, however, actually use one or more of just six basic methodologies:[6]

1. *Visual inspection* of time series or intermittent data or the synthesis of qualitative economic histories are used to establish historical datings of upswing and downswing periods in particular variables or in national or international economies.
2. *Moving averages*[7] are used to bring out underlying long wave movements in long time series. This method attempts to eliminate short business cycles by using long-term (for example, nine-year) moving averages.
3. Growth rates are calculated[8] for economic variables within predefined historical *phase periods*. Growth rates are compared between upswing and downswing phases to show alternating behavior in successive phases.
4. *Trend deviations* are used to bring out long-term movements around an underlying secular trend. The form of the underlying curve must be specified.[9]
5. Long waves are analyzed in terms of the shorter *business cycles* they contain.[10]
6. *Spectral analysis* and related statistical techniques[11] use sophisticated statistical routines to search for regular fixed periodicities (not irregular periods, as the above methods allow) in time series data.

5. With a few exceptions (see chap. 8).

6. Discussed further in chap. 8.

7. A moving average at a given point in time is the average value of data for a certain number of years on either side.

8. The nontrivial question of how to calculate those growth rates is discussed in chap. 8.

9. First the form of the trend equation is given and estimates are calculated from the data to find the coefficients in that equation that best fit the long-term curve. Then the residuals—the difference between the fitted curve and the actual data at a given time—are graphed or otherwise analyzed to find long waves.

10. The characteristics of business cycles (e.g., growth from one peak or trough to the next) on the long wave expansion phase are compared with those on the stagnation phase.

11. Spectral analysis creates a function in which the degree of correlation of a sine wave to the time series data is expressed in relation to the wavelength of the sine wave. Cross-spectral analysis concerns the correlation among more than one series conceived as sine waves. Fourier analysis breaks a time series down into a set of sine waves of different wavelengths whose sum best approximates the series.

The Dating Game

All of these methods,[12] applied to all the variables of interest, have one goal in common—to identify or validate the dates of long wave phases. A *dating scheme,* delineating the turning points between phase periods, defines a long wave pattern historically. The general aim of empirical studies is to show either how such a dating scheme may be derived from data or how data support the claim of alternating phases embodied in the dating scheme.

A comparison of dating schemes can show whether scholars are talking about very different cycles or essentially the same cycles with slight variations in the dating of turning points. I will compare the dating schemes arrived at by thirty-three long wave scholars and demonstrate a strong consensus around a single basic dating of long wave phases.

As a framework of reference with which to compare these dating schemes, I will use a *base dating scheme* that I developed by splicing together four scholars' datings.[13] The base dating scheme uses the dates of Braudel (1972:896) for the phases of the European economy from 1495 to 1650.[14] It then uses Frank's (1978) dates of the phases of development of the British economy from 1650 to 1790.[15] From 1790 to 1917, the dates of Kondratieff ([1926] 1935) are used,[16] and from 1917 on, those of Mandel (1980).[17]

The dates of the base dating scheme are:

	1st wave	2d	3d	4th	5th	6th	
Peak	(1495) 1529	1559	1595	1650	1720	1762	
Trough	1509	1539	1575	1621	1689	1747	1790

	7th	8th	9th	10th
Peak	1814	1872	1917	1968[18]
Trough	1790	1848	1893	1940

12. With the possible exception of spectral analysis.

13. This base dating scheme will also form the starting point for my own empirical analysis (see chap. 8). All four sources of this dating lean toward a Marxist or material interpretation of economic history. However, the dates through the 1920s derive mainly from prices, while Mandel's dates are explicitly based on production. In chap. 10, when it becomes clear that prices and production are not synchronous, I revise Mandel's last date to reconcile prices and production.

14. Although Braudel does not call these long waves, he later (1984:80) makes clear that this was his intention, stating that the Kondratieff wave predates 1790 by hundreds of years and is a cycle defined by prices (Imbert, whom Braudel cites, also relies on prices). Braudel gives troughs of 1539 and 1575 without dating the peak between them. Imbert (1959:196–201) finds this cycle nonexistent in data from France, Strasbourg, Germany, or Italy but evident in data from England (peaking at 1556/58) and Spain (peaking at 1562). I chose 1559 for this peak.

15. This is used in lieu of an explicitly international measure. There is a 20-year gap between the end of Braudel's account in 1650 and the beginning of Frank's in 1670. I included this period with the following downswing based on Imbert's (1959) dating of this downswing phase from 1650 to 1685/88.

16. I used the middle year of the range of years Kondratieff gave for each turning point.

17. Mandel lists 1940 as the trough for the United States and 1948 for Europe. I used 1940, since the United States was the leading world economy. Bieshaar and Kleinknecht (1984:290) test both dates (actually 1939 and 1948) and find the earlier date to be "the more realistic demarcation point."

18. The 1968 turning point is modified to 1980 in chap. 10.

Dating Schemes for the Industrial Age

Kondratieff ([1926] 1935) put forward an overall dating scheme for the world economy based on a variety of price and production series since the late eighteenth century:

Peak	1810/17	1870/75	1914/20
Trough	1787/93	1844/51	1890/96

These are the three long waves around which the literature has centered (along with a fourth, more recent, wave), and these dates are used in my base dating scheme for the period 1790–1917.

Mandel[19] provides four sets of dates of long waves based on the growth of industrial production and trade:

British industrial production:
Peak	1827	1876	1914	1968
Trough		1848	1894	1939

United States industrial production:
Peak		1874	1914	1968
Trough		1849	1894	1939[20]

German (and then West German) industrial production:
Peak		1875	1914	1968
Trough	1850	1898	1939	

World trade:
Peak	1820	1870	1913	1968
Trough	1840	1891	1938	

Mandel's dates correspond closely with Kondratieff's through 1913 (after which Mandel's own dates are used in the base dating scheme).

Imbert (1959:47) gives the following dates for upswing and downswing phases of prices:

France:
Peak	1817	1872	1926	(1954+)
Trough	(1787)	1851	1896	1935

United States:
Peak	1814	1865	1920	(1954+)
Trough	(1791)	1849	1896	1932

19. Mandel (1975:141–42) summarized by Eklund (1980:413).
20. In Mandel's later book, on which my base dating scheme is based, this upswing is dated from 1940.

Germany:

Peak	1808	1873	1925	(1954+)
Trough	(1792)	1849	1895	1933

England (based on *Sauerbeck*):

Peak	1810	1873	1920	(1954+)
Trough	1786/89	1849	1896	1933

Belgium (based on *Loots*):

Peak		1873	1929
Trough	1852	1895	1934

Italy (based on *Loots*):

Peak		1926
Trough	1897	1934

Imbert (1959:38) also lists the dating schemes of several other long wave scholars. *Simiand*'s (1932b) dates for prices and production in France are:

Peak	1815/20	1875	1928/29
Trough	late 18th c.	1850	1896/97

Those of *Dupriez* (1947 2:24) for wholesale prices in the major countries are:

Peak	1808/14	1872/73	1920	
Trough	1789/92	1846/51	1895/96	1939[21]

For *Van Gelderen* [Fedder] (1913:268), the following dates are given for general economic movements of major countries:

Peak		1873	(1913+)
Trough	1850	1895

For *De Wolff* (1924:21), the long wave dating is:

Peak	1825	1873/74	1913
Trough	1849/50	1896	

Hansen's (1941:30) dating of general economic movements is:

Peak	1815	1873	1920/21
Trough	1787	1843	1897

21. Van Duijn (1983:163) notes Dupriez's (1978) continuation, with 1939/46 as the trough and 1974 as the next peak.

The dating of *Woytinsky* (1931:5, 10) based on Spiethoff's study of major countries is:

Peak	1822	1873	1920
Trough	1842	1894	

That of *Ciriacy-Wantrup* (1936) representing general economic movements in major countries is:

Peak		1815	1875	1913
Trough	1792	1842	1895	

Åkerman's (1932:87) dating for general economic movements is:

Peak	1817	1873	1920
Trough	1848	1896	

Imbert continues with closely corresponding dating schemes from *Wicksell, Estey, Edie, Marjolin, Rouquet La Garrigue, Lescure,* and *Sirol* (Imbert, 1959:38).

Schumpeter's (1939) dating for general economic movement does not specify the upper turning points but is anchored by the lower turning points, which match the general dating scheme as follows:

Trough	1787	1842	1897

Kuznets (1940) elaborates Schumpeter's scheme with the advice and consent of Schumpeter:[22]

Peak		1814	1870	1925
Trough	1787	1843	1898	

Burns and *Mitchell* (1946) give the following dates based on prices:

United States:				
Peak		1814	1864	1920
Trough	1789	1843	1896	1932

22. Kuznets's full scheme has four phases in each cycle: prosperity, recession, depression, and recovery.

Great Britain:

Peak		1813	1873	1920
Trough	1789	1849	1896	1933

France:

Peak		1820?	1872	1926
Trough		1851	1896	1935

Germany:

Peak		1808	1873	1923
Trough	1793	1849	1895	1933

Rostow (1978) generally follows the base dating until World War II, where his emphasis on prices leads him away from dating schemes based on production (see chapter 3):

Peak		1815	1873	1920	1951
Trough	1790	1848	1896	1935	1972

Van Duijn (1983:155), who focuses on world industrial production, finds the evidence unconvincing for Kondratieff's first long wave but dates the subsequent waves in rough synchrony with other schemes:[23]

Peak		1872	1929	1973
Trough	1845	1892	1948

Ischboldin[24] bases dates for long waves in Europe and in North America on prices. He finds long waves of about fifty years' duration only since 1815, arguing that before then only longer-term phases can be found:

North America:

Peak		1812	1865	1929	(?)
Trough	1790	1843	1897	1939

Europe:

Peak	(1650)	1815	1873	1920	(?)
Trough	(1500)	(1721)	1848	1896	1938

After 1815 there is a one-to-one correspondence between Ischboldin's long waves and the base dating scheme.

---

23. Like Kuznets, Van Duijn adopts a four-phase dating scheme, of which I have indicated only the transitions between upswings and downswings.

24. Ischboldin (1967:319–22) discussed in Baqir (1981).

Cole (1938:107) gives the following dating scheme for long-term movements in wholesale commodity prices in the United States:

Peak	1720		1778?		1814/19	(1860)
Trough		1744		1789		1843

Again there is one-to-one correspondence with the base dating scheme, although one date (1778) differs by fifteen years.[25]

Dupriez (1951:247–48) dates trends in gold holdings and currency issue in six countries (Great Britain, France, Germany, Belgium, the Netherlands, and the United States) as follows:

Peak		1818		1873		1913
Trough	1791		1844		1898	

These dates also match the base dating scheme quite closely.

Dating Schemes for the Preindustrial Age

For the preindustrial age, scholars rely more on qualitative data and price histories and reach more tentative conclusions, but again they demonstrate surprising consensus.

Braudel (1972:896) states that economic historians agree on the following periodization of upswings and downswings in the European economy:

Peak	1483		1529		(1559)		1595		1650
Trough		1460		1509		1539		1575	1621

These are the dates used in the first century and a half of the base dating scheme shown above.

Imbert's (1959:181–200) price datings since 1495 are:[26]

25. The date 1860 precedes Kondratieff's peak of 1872, but Cole's study covers only the period through 1860.

26. Imbert (1956) identifies five long waves between 1286 and 1510—predating the period of this study but of interest in terms of historical continuity. These waves are found in French wheat prices (p. 224–25), various British commodity prices (p. 225–30), and, for the last two cycles, prices in Flanders (p. 230–31), Strasbourg (p. 232) and Spain (p. 232–33). The following dating is from the French series:

Rising	*Declining*
1286–1313/16	1313/16–1335/38
1335/38–1349/70 (stayed high)	1370–1380/86
1380/86–1391/93	1391/93–1410/12
1410/12–1421/39 (stayed high)	1439–1450/70
1450/70–1482/83	1482/83–1509/10

These very early long waves seem to join well with my base dating scheme, since Imbert's last wave corresponds with the first wave of the base dating scheme (from Braudel).

England:

Peak	(1480/90)	1530	1556/58	1597	1649	1710
Trough		1507	1540	1569/71	1617/20	1685/88	1732/43

The fit to the base dating for 1495–1650 is excellent,[27] and the fit after 1650 is good.

France:

Peak		1530	—	1595	1650	1712
Trough	1510	1539	—	1612	1671	1733

The dating matches that for England, although Imbert is unable to identify the third English cycle in the French data.

Spain:

Peak		1530	1562	1601/05
Trough	1510	1540/55	1594	1618

These continue to match the English dates roughly.

Germany:

Peak		(1535)	(1570)	1590	1620	1700
Trough	1505	(1546)	(1580)	1605	1670	1720/30

These dates correspond in a one-to-one manner with the base dating scheme, but the particular turning points deviate more than in most dating schemes.

Moving to the late preindustrial period (about 1650–1790), *Frank* dates the phases of development of the British economy. These dates were used in the base dating:

Peak	(pre-1670)	1720	1762
Trough		1689	1747	1790

Baehrel (1961:50–51, 83–86) dates economic phases of grain prices in Provence:

Peak		1594	1655	1725	1785
Trough	1573	1625	1689	1754

Baehrel's dating corresponds closely with the base dating through 1650 but diverges by about 1750.[28]

---

27. As it should be; Braudel, from whom that part of the base dating scheme derives, cites Imbert as a main source.

28. See also Baehrel, below, in section on preindustrial prices.

Wagemann (1931:368) gives the following dates for the expansion and stagnation phases of the world economy in the late preindustrial and industrial periods:

Peak	1720	1763	1815	1873	1920	
Trough	1690	1730	1790	1845	1895	(1931+)

These dates correspond closely with those of Frank and Kondratieff (except for a difference in dating one trough, which Wagemann puts at 1730 while Frank suggests 1747) and indicate a continuity to the dating of the long wave between the preindustrial and industrial eras.

Mauro (1964:313) elaborates upswings and downswings in world trade, particularly between the core and periphery (Europe and the Americas), and taking account of wars and production of precious metal in the periphery. His dates are:

Peak	1590	1640	(1670)	1720	1775	1815	1873
Trough	1620	(1660)	1690	1730	1792	1850	

This dating corresponds roughly, in a one-to-one manner, with the base dating scheme except for the addition of an extra cycle by Mauro, which I have indicated in parentheses.

In addition to the above dating schemes, there are occasional "stray" dating schemes in which a scholar claims to identify "long waves" substantially different in length or timing from those defined by the consensus of above datings. *Metz*[29] provides one example of such datings. For example, Metz's dating of "long waves" for wheat prices in Cologne hardly corresponds with the base dating:

Metz:							
Peak	1494	1534	1591	1636	1703	1762	
Trough	1518	1569	1613	1680	1724	1780	
Base dating:							
Peak	(1495) 1529	1559	1595	1650	1720	1762	
Trough	1509	1539	1575	1621	1689	1747	1790

Leaving aside one or two "stray" dating schemes, however, there is a remarkable consensus on dating among thirty-three scholars from all theoretical schools of the long wave debate.

Past Empirical Work

Given the agreement on dating phases, what is the evidence for long waves in each of the economic variables of interest: prices, production,

29. Metz (1983:216–17; 1984b:614–17), Irsigler and Metz (1984).

innovation, and other variables? The latter (for which little past empirical work is available) include capital investment, wages and worker protests, trade, and war.[30] A summary of the empirical studies showing each researcher's theoretical orientation, methodology, variables, time period, countries of analysis, and summary results appears in table 4.1, which may be a useful guide to the following pages.

Prices in the Industrial Period

Kondratieff ([1926] 1935) uses moving averages and trend deviation to show long waves in time series data on wholesale prices, interest rates, wages, foreign trade, and production—mainly for Great Britain, France, and the United States. The results for non-price series will be discussed in a later section.

Kondratieff identifies long waves in prices by graphing price series and their moving averages.[31] Some of these were shown in chapter 2 at the top of figure 2.2. The methodology for prices differs from that used for production and other "nonstationary" time series[32] (see below) in that the latter also involve trend deviation.

Kondratieff's use of long-term moving averages has been criticized. Slutsky (1937) shows that a statistical effect (the Yule-Slutsky effect) arising from long-term smoothing of the type done by Kondratieff shifts the spectra of the series toward the longer wavelengths. As Garvy (1943:219) notes, "In many series, [shorter] cyclical swings of particularly large amplitude influence moving averages strongly enough to produce the illusion of major cycles." These methodological criticisms, however, apply mostly to Kondratieff's study of non-price series (see below), while his price waves have been more widely accepted.

Gordon (1978:24) presents data on U.S. price changes averaged by long wave phase periods, basing the dates of turning points on the peaks and troughs of short price cycles (business cycles) derived from the National Bureau of Economic Research (NBER) (Burns and Mitchell 1946:432). The average annual percent change in prices in each period is:

1800–1814 (upswing)	+1.7%
1815–1843 (downswing)	−1.9%
1844–1864 (up)	+0.9%
1865–1896 (down)	−1.4%
1897–1920 (up)	+5.8%
1920–1940 (down)	−1.5%

These results support the idea of long waves in prices.

Van Ewijk (1982) uses spectral analysis to search for long waves in several price and production series from Britain, France, the United States, and Germany from the late eighteenth century. By limiting his time frame to 1770–1930, Van Ewijk excludes the anomalous price behavior since World War II. Despite some meth-

---

30. War, however, is reserved for chaps. 5 and 6.
31. Nine-year moving averages are used in order to eliminate the effects of shorter business cycles.
32. Series with an underlying long-term secular trend.

Table 4.1. Summary of Empirical Long Wave Studies

Prices since 1790

Author Year	School Method.	Variables Countries	Time span Find waves?
Kondratieff 1920s	CI MA	Commodity prices Major capitalist countries	ca. 1790-1922 yes
Gordon 1978	CC BC	Prices U.S.	1800-1940 yes
Van Ewijk 1982	? SA	Prices Britain, France, U.S., Germany	1770-1977 only to 1930
Cleary and Hobbs 1983	? VI	Price, prod., innov., invest., employ. U.S., Britain	ca.1756-1979 mostly prices

Prices before 1790

Author Year	School Method.	Variable Countries	Time span Find waves?
Imbert 1959	I/W VI	Agricultural prices mainly Various European countries	1286-1954 yes
Baehrel 1961	? MA	Grain prices and harvests Southern France	1573-1789 yes, and correlate
Margairaz 1984	? VI	Wheat prices France by region	1756-1870 yes
Grenier 1984	? SA	Prices France	1500-1790 no
Metz and Irsigler 1983-84	CC? MA/SA	Prices and other variables Germany, England	ca. 1530-1950 yes(irregular)

Production

Author Year	School Method.	Variables Countries	Time span Find waves?
Kondratieff 1920s	CI TD/MA	Production, trade, etc. Major capitalist countries	ca. 1790-1922 yes
Oparin 1920s	CC? TD/MA	Prices, wages, trade Major capitalist countries	ca. 1790-1922 prices only
Isard 1942	? VI	Various commodity production U.S.	ca. 1825-1934 no
Burns and Mitchell 1946	? BC	Short business cycles U.S.	ca. 1860-1940 no
Mandel 1975	CC PP	Industrial output, trade U.S., Britain, Germany	c.a. 1830-1967 yes
Gordon 1978	CC PP	Industrial production World	1865-1938 yes
Gordon 1978	CC BC	National growth US, Britain, Germany	1848-1940 yes
Kleinknecht 1981a	CC/I PP	National production Ger., Italy, Brit., Swed., Den., Nor.	ca. 1850-1969 yes
Bieshaar and Kleinknecht 1984	CC/I PP	National production 11 national series	ca. 1890-1980 weakly yes

Author Year	School Method.	Variables Countries	Time span Find waves?
Kuczynski 1982, 1978	CC PP	Industrial production, agri. prod., exports World	1830-1980 yes
Screpanti 1984	CC PP	Industrial production France, OECD countrie	ca. 1846-1970 yes
Van der Zwan 1980	CI TD/PP	Production, national income, trade U.S., U.K., Germany, world	ca. 1850-1940 no
Van Duijn 1980	I/CI BC	Industrial production U.S., Britain, France Germany, world	ca. 1790-1973 yes (?)
Delbeke 1982	I BC	Industrial production Belgium	1831-1913 yes (?)
Kuczynski 1978	CC SA	Production, exports, innovation World	1850-1976 weakly yes?
Van Ewijk 1982	? SA	GNP, industrial prod., invest., trade Britain, France, U.S.	ca. 1800-1977 no

Innovation

Author Year	School Method.	Variables Countries	Time span Find waves?
Mensch 1979	I VI	Innovations (list 1) World	ca. 1850-1950 yes
Clark and Freeman 1981	I VI	Innovations (list 2) World	ca. 1850-1950 no
Van Duijn 1981	I/CI PP	Innovations (list 3) World	1921-1957 yes (?)
Kleinknecht 1981b	I/CC VI	Innovations (list 4) World	ca. 1860-1970 yes
Hartman and Wheeler 1979	? PP	Patents Britain, U.S.	ca. 1800-1974 Brit. only
Kuczynski 1978	CC PP	Basic innovations World	1878-1955 yes

Other Variables

Author Year	School Method.	Variables Countries	Time span Find waves?
Dupriez 1951	? PP	Central bank note issue Britain, France, Ger., Bel., Neth., U.S.	1791-1939 yes
Gordon et al. 1983	CC BC	Labor costs U.S.	1890-1981 yes
Sau 1982	CC VI	Profit rates U.S., Britain, France, Germany, Japan	1960-1975 peak ca. 1967

Note: Theoretical schools: CI = Capital investment; I = Innovation; CC = Capitalist crisis; W = War.
Methodologies: VI = Visual inspection; MA = Moving averages; PP = Phase period growth rates; TD = Trend deviation; BC = Business cycle analysis; SA = Spectral analysis.

Figure 4.1. Van Ewijk's Spectra of Price Series

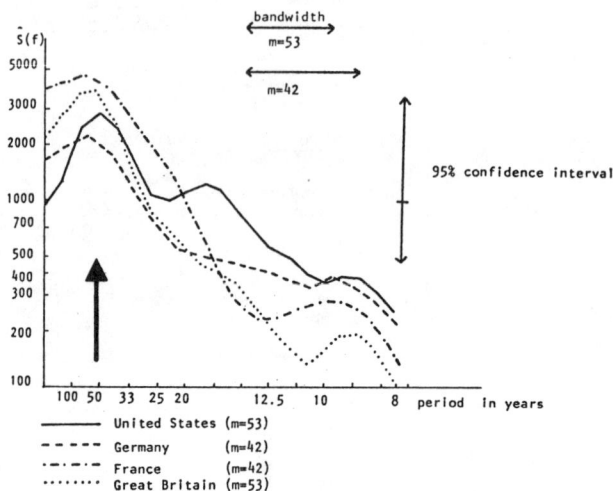

Note: Graph represents sample spectra of price series for Great Britain, France, Germany and the United States, 1770-1930. Only the spectral estimates for the low-frequency bands (0 to 0.125 cycles per year) are shown.

Source: Van Ewijk, *KYKLOS* (1982: 481) by permission of *KYKLOS*.

odological problems,[33] Van Ewijk does find long waves in the price data. As shown in figure 4.1, prices in all four countries show a peak in their spectra around fifty to sixty years.[34] Van Ewijk (1982:482) finds "no trace" of a long wave in price spectra in the longer period extended to 1977 rather than 1930 (from 1770). This is attributed to either nonstationarity or perhaps changes in the long wave since 1930.

Cleary and *Hobbs* (1983) use mainly visual inspection to weigh the empirical evidence for long waves.[35] They examine data on prices and on various indicators of production, innovation, capital formation, and unemployment mainly for the United States and Great Britain. They conclude:

The strongest empirical evidence in favour of the long-wave hypothesis undoubtedly comes from price series. Supporting evidence can also be found in the behaviour of long-term interest rates, world energy production and innovation. Limited and not very convincing evidence can be seen in world industrial production, U.S. mineral production, unemployment and investment (p. 180).

33. Inadequate degrees of freedom, which Van Ewijk says can only be resolved by waiting one or two centuries.

34. "As could be expected, given the relatively short series, the spectral peaks are small relative to the 95% confidence interval. However, both from the stability of the location of these 'long wave' peaks, when the number of lags is varied, and from the great international similarity, it may be concluded that these peaks are a real trace of a long wave in prices" (Van Ewijk 1982:482).

35. "While not disputing the value of statistical analysis techniques, in this paper we are asking the readers to use their eyes and trust their own judgement" (p. 165).

The above empirical results generally converge in showing fairly strong evidence for long waves in prices in the major economies since around 1790 (at least up through the 1930s), despite a variety of methodological and theoretical approaches.

Prices in the Preindustrial Period

Imbert ([1956] 1959) has done the most detailed work on preindustrial prices. He discusses the various statistical approaches to the identification of long waves in time series data and adopts "direct observation of the raw data" as his method for identifying long waves (1959:45).

As mentioned above, Imbert dates long waves from about 1500 to 1790 in a variety of European countries. In addition to the national datings discussed above, he dates long waves in a variety of specific (mostly agricultural) commodities in this period (p. 198–201). These datings follow fairly closely a one-to-one correspondence with his English dates and with the base dating scheme.[36] From these price histories Imbert concludes that internationally synchronized long waves of prices date back through the entire period to 1495 and before. Only the third downswing of 1557–70, which appears in the English data, is not found in some countries (and appears only weakly in others).

Baehrel (1961) identifies phases of increasing and decreasing grain prices in southern France from 1573 to 1789. She builds on the work of Imbert in identifying preindustrial price waves and uses a methodology similar to his, relying on inspection of time series data.

Baehrel claims that these price waves correlate inversely with long-term fluctuations in harvests during that period, as seen in harvest data smoothed by moving averages.[37] For Galignan harvest data I have reconstructed the following table based on Baehrel's dating of price phases (p. 98):[38]

Turning point in prices	Change in harvest level from previous turning point
1573 (trough)	
1594 (peak)	−30% (approximately)
1625 (trough)	+60% (approximately)
1655 (peak)	−20% (approximately)
1689 (trough)	? (−15% to +5%?)
1725 (peak)	−25% (approximately)
1754 (trough)	+5% (approximately)
1785 (peak)	? (about zero?)

36. The series include grain prices at Avenel (1510–1733), wheat and grain prices at Paris (1531–1745), grain prices at Grenoble (the third cycle of 1557–97 is not found), wheat prices at Strasbourg and Bale (1595–1730, earlier periods showing only longer-term movements), prices of wheat, oats, butter, and cheese in Flanders (1585–1733), and prices on the Amsterdam stock exchange (1620–1734).

37. Harvests really belong with production, below, rather than prices, but since this is the only study of preindustrial production I have not made it a separate section, particularly since Baehrel connects harvests with prices.

38. Baehrel's own analysis uses different transition dates to show harvest phases than for her earlier price analysis.

As mentioned earlier, Baehrel deviates from my base dating scheme after 1725. The changes in harvest for the last two phase periods can be roughly recalculated from Baehrel's data using the base dating scheme (derived from Frank's dates) as follows:

Turning point in prices	Change in harvest level from previous turning point
1747 (trough)	+2% (approximately)
1762 (peak)	−20% (approximately)
(1782)	+20%? (data fragmentary)

Thus Baehrel's harvest data seem to correlate more closely with the base dating scheme than with her own price phases when the two diverge (a minor victory for the base dating scheme).

Baehrel's conclusion (p. 100) that downswing phases in harvests correlate with upswing phases in prices (and vice versa) should be treated cautiously because of the poor quality of data. Her analysis also leaves open the questions of whether harvest waves *cause* price waves, whether a third factor such as war affects trends in both harvests and prices,[39] and whether long waves in harvests are connected with later long waves in industrial economies.

Margairaz (1984:673) investigates the variations in long-term movements of wheat prices among different regions of France from 1756 to 1870 (before and after the start of the industrial age). She finds prices rising from 1756 to 1812 (an up-down-up on the base dating scheme), with the intermediate downswing appearing after 1770 except in the southern regions. The next downswing, from 1812 to 1850/52, appears in twenty-eight of thirty-one regions, and the timing of the turning points corresponds between regions. Thus, "there exist[s] a real interdependence of long regional fluctuations" of prices in that era.

Grenier (1984) applies spectral analysis to French price series from about 1500 to 1790. Although he finds long-term movements ranging up to thirty years (p. 435), Grenier's spectra do not show peaks in the long wave range (pp. 443–44). He concludes that one can find regular price movements but not cycles involving a continuity of motion (p. 438).[40]

Metz (1983, 1984b) and Irsigler and Metz (1984) apply a combination of trend deviation and spectral methods to analyze preindustrial economic data. Metz proposes a new method for defining and then eliminating a secular trend and finding long waves in the residual data. Metz's (1983:185) method for eliminating the long-term

---

39. See later chapters on war. Major European wars will be shown plausibly both to depress harvests (destruction caused by war) and to raise prices. Baehrel (1961:101–2), rejects weather cycles as a cause of the harvest/price waves.

40. Grenier suggests (p. 442) dropping the idea of "long cycle" (with fixed periodicity as searched for by spectral analysis), in favor of "long phases" (where the alternation of upswing and downswing is not systematic). See chap. 8.

trend uses complex statistical filters though which the time series data are passed and which damp out the long wavelength spectral frequencies (longer than sixty years).[41]

Metz (1983:181) analyzes nine German and English economic time series.[42] He concludes that only agrarian prices show cycle lengths typical of "Kondratieff" cycles in the spectral analysis (p. 204). I note that only German wheat and rye prices (1561–1934) show even a rough correspondence with the base dating scheme (p. 216).[43] Metz (1984b:601) conducts a similar analysis for twelve preindustrial (northern European) time series on prices, money, and metal. He concludes that in the preindustrial series analyzed, "in all series concerning the agrarian sector, long waves could be shown" (p. 629).

Irsigler and Metz (1984:385) examine series for prices and agrarian production in preindustrial times (and for production indicators and capital investment in industrial times). Only the consumer price index for western Brabant (1410–1700) matches the base dating scheme reasonably well. Thus in each study Metz claims to identify "long waves" that are synchronous across countries and variables,[44] but as noted above these do not correspond in most cases with the timing of other scholars' long waves (Metz 1983:216–17; 1984b:614–17; Irsigler and Metz 1984).

To recap the evidence for long waves in preindustrial prices, then, there is agreement among those using a visual inspection methodology as to the existence and dates of cycles in agricultural prices. Those using spectral analysis, however, are generally unable to identify those same cycles statistically.[45]

Production in the Industrial Period

The evidence for long waves in production[46] and related "real" variables cover only the industrial period since around 1790.

Kondratieff claims to show long waves in a number of production series, although there are others in which he does not find long waves.[47] Long waves that do appear in series seem to be closely correlated among the different series, including those from different countries. For example, 1893 to 1917[48] shows a rising trend in curves for

---

41. Unfortunately, Metz's "trend" is even more complicated than was Kondratieff's (discussed below). The "detrended" series may show long-term oscillations, but these are difficult to interpret.

42. Four agricultural price series from the preindustrial period and five production, wage, or investment series from the industrial period.

43. All the other series that exhibit long-term oscillations called long waves by Metz are quite irregular and vary in length. "It would . . . be wrong to emphasize the importance of the different datings of the upswings and downswings," says Metz (1984b:613). But the datings show Metz to be describing different long-term movements than those discussed by other scholars of the long wave.

44. Some do appear to be synchronous.

45. This indicates the divergence of the approaches requiring fixed periodicities from those requiring only an alternating sequence of historical phases of variable length.

46. Production series include overall production indexes (national product), indexes of industrial production, and production series for particular industries.

47. Eklund (1980:396) points out that Kondratieff found long waves in only 11 of the 21 production and consumption series analyzed.

48. A period of rising English, French, and U.S. prices.

English wages, French foreign trade, and French and British production of coal, iron, and lead (see fig. 2.2). The preceding period, 1872 to 1893, shows declining trends in these curves. From this evidence Kondratieff concludes that long waves exist across the entire economy and are international.

Kondratieff's empirical work on production (and other nonprice) series has been strongly criticized. Garvy (1943:209) notes that in the Russian criticisms of Kondratieff's work, "the methodological part of Kondratieff's work in particular attracted the attention of his critics." Foremost among the methodological criticisms have been those directed against Kondratieff's use of trend curves.[49] Kondratieff's method is first to fit a long-term trend to a series and then to use moving averages to bring out long waves in the residuals (the fluctuations around the trend curve). But "when he eliminated the trend, Kondratieff failed to formulate clearly what the trend stands for" (Garvy 1943:209). The equations Kondratieff uses for these long-term trend curves (as fitted to the data) appear in table 4.2 and include rather elaborate (often cubic) functions. This casts doubt on the theoretical meaning and parsimony of the resulting long waves, which cannot be seen as simple variations in production growth rates.

Oparin, a leading contemporary and critic of Kondratieff, illustrated his objections to Kondratieff's trend curves by extending some of Kondratieff's series forward to the 1920s and fitting new trend curves to them. The latter differed considerably from Kondratieff's and showed long waves with a different timing and amplitude. Many of Kondratieff's contemporaries thus concluded that long waves "were definitely established only for series including the price element" (Garvy 1943:210–11).

In the 1920s Oparin conducted his own analysis of long time series data to test Kondratieff's conclusions. He found that "long waves can be observed only in the movement of prices and of the long-term interest rates. The long waves immediately disappear from wage and foreign trade series when changes in the price level are eliminated" (quoted in Garvy 1943:211).

Other of Kondratieff's Russian critics arrived at a similar conclusion (Garvy 1943:211). In 1928 Gerzstein asserted that movements of prices and production do not coincide and thus that Kondratieff's price waves do not represent production phases. Gerzstein, using qualitative economic history, argued that great development of productive forces took place on Kondratieff's (price) downswing periods, at least as much as on the upswings. Garvy himself (1943:217) arrives at the same conclusion regarding Kondratieff's long waves in production series: "Even the few production series which Kondratieff considered as demonstrative of long cycles fail, upon closer examination, to support his conclusions."[50] Snyder (1934) likewise finds long waves in prices but not in production (Barr 1979:704).

49. This criticism applies only to Kondratieff's work with real series, which have a secular trend, not with prices. Garvy (1943:211) notes that Kondratieff's *data* did not come under criticism by and large.

50. The central problem, Garvy (1943:218) agrees, is in Kondratieff's trend deviation methodology for these series: "Less arbitrariness in the choice of the period to which the trend was fitted, and more adequate trend formulas, would have yielded, for nearly all series, deviations of a different shape."

Table 4.2. Kondratieff's Trend Equations

(Long waves are found in deviations from these trends)

Commodity prices (England, France, U.S.): (no secular trend)

Quotations of English consols: $y = 112.57 + .26x - .012x^2 - .0002x^3$

Quotations of French rente: $y = 78.99 + .23x$

Wages in English cotton industry: $y = 64.128 + 1.053x + .0099x^2 - .00023x^3$

Wages in English agriculture: $y = 91.587 + .454x$

English foreign trade: $y = 10 (1.0293 + .0096x - .00006x^2)$ [a]

French foreign trade: $y = 146.39 + 3.46x + .006x^2$

English coal production: $y = 10 (3.6614 + .0063x - .000094x^2)$ [a]

French mineral fuel consumption: $y = 539.21 + 16.9x + .1326x^2 + .00026x^3$

English pig iron production: $y = 193.3 + 2.28x - .0556x^2$

English lead production: $y = 10 (0.0278 - .0166x - .00012x^2)$ [a]

French savings bank liabilities: $y = 1133.9 + 57.227x + .7704x^2$

English commodity prices on a gold base: $y = 139.0 - 1.113x - .0028x^2 + .000196x^3$

Source: Kondratieff ([1928] 1984: 110-135)
a. In these equations 10 is raised to the power of the expression shown

Walter Isard (1942a:156) reexamines some of Kondratieff's production variables for the United States. He "accepts the existence of the Kondratieff cycle in the price data . . . [but] can find no evidence of Kondratieff cycles in other data." Isard traces pig iron production (a variable in which Kondratieff claimed to find long waves) for the United States and finds "no evidence whatsoever of Kondratieff's long waves." Similar results obtain for coal production, lead output, cotton acreage, and the number of spindles in the cotton industry (also variables used by Kondratieff). Isard suggests Kondratieff's results (for iron and coal) may be an artifact of failing to carry the data sets back far enough in time.

Burns and *Mitchell* (1946:432) also criticize Kondratieff's approach to identifying long waves in production. They agree that wholesale prices tended historically to move in long upward or downward periods that correspond closely with Kondratieff's dating. But they question whether these price movements reflect overall economic growth as defined by their own NBER indicators.[51] Burns and Mitchell examine the shorter business cycles in the NBER data, asking whether those occurring during Kondratieff's (price) upswing differ from those during the downswing.[52] They find the business cycles to be similar during the two long wave phases, a negative result for the idea of long waves in production.

Klas Eklund (1980:398–99) says that by the end of the first wave of debate on long

51. Burns and Mitchell note that Kondratieff's data cover only 2 ½ long waves (since 1790) and that the NBER data go back only to the 1850s or 1870s, making a meaningful assessment of 50-year cycles impossible.
52. If a long wave exists, then "the position that an individual business cycle occupies in a 'long cycle' determines whether [the business cycle] is a mild movement . . . or a convulsive fluctuation" (p. 383).

waves, "a consensus of opinion seemed to emerge among economists, according to which the long waves were a monetary phenomenon, found in certain price and value series, but not in the entire economic sphere—or in the social and political spheres—the way Kondratieff had claimed." The view that "came to dominate among economists," according to Eklund, was that "long waves were a monetary phenomenon, exogenously determined" by wars and other noneconomic phenomena.

This did not end the debate on long waves in production, however. In the second round of interest in long waves, a number of new studies of this question have emerged, mostly from the capitalist crisis school.

Mandel's growth rates by phases for world trade and for industrial production in Great Britain, Germany, and the United States (Mandel 1980:3; from 1975:141) are reprinted in table 4.3. Growth rates clearly alternate between successive phases. Although his turning points for each variable correspond roughly with the base dating (the last part of which comes from Mandel), there is a slight problem with Mandel's practice of dating each variable's turning points on the basis of its own local peaks and troughs. Long waves should be defined as synchronous across variables and countries. It is easy to show alternating growth rates in successive phases by defining those phases as starting at some local peak (or trough) in the series and ending at some later local trough (or peak). But its ad hoc nature makes this a weak approach. The stronger test, which Mandel does not make, is whether growth rates alternate when a single dating scheme is imposed on all the countries and variables at once. Nonetheless, the turning points of Mandel's different series are close enough to each other that the degree of bias seems to be small.

Gordon (1978:24), also from the capitalist crisis school, presents data on physical output in the "advanced countries." Like Mandel, he presents average growth rates

Table 4.3. Mandel's Statistical Evidence for Long Waves

	Years	Percent		Percent for 1947–1966	Percent for 1967–1975
Annual compound rate of growth in world trade (at constant prices)	1820–1840	2.7	Annual compound growth of industrial output after World War II		
	1840–1870	5.5			
	1870–1890	2.2			
	1891–1913	3.7	United States	5.0	1.9
	1914–1937	0.4	Original EEC six	8.9	4.6
	1938–1967	4.8	Japan	9.6	7.9[c]
Annual compound rate of growth of industrial output in Britain	1827–1847	3.2	Britain	2.9	2.0
	1848–1875	4.55[a]			
	1876–1893	1.2			
	1894–1913	2.2			
	1914–1938	2.0			
	1939–1967	3.0			
Annual compound rate of growth of industrial output in Germany (after 1945: FRG)	1850–1874	4.5[b]			
	1875–1892	2.5			
	1893–1913	4.3			
	1914–1938	2.2			
	1939–1967	3.9			
Annual compound rate of growth of industrial output in the United States	1849–1873	5.4			
	1874–1893	4.9			
	1894–1913	5.9			
	1914–1938	2.0			
	1939–1967	5.2			

[a] Dr. J. J. Van Duijn, *De Lange Golf in de Economie* (Assen, 1979), p. 213, contests this figure. He appears to be right.
[b] R. Devleeshouwer ("Le Consulat et l'Empire, Période de 'takeoff' pour l'économie belge?" in *Revue de l'Histoire Moderne et Contemporaine*, *XVII*, 1970) gives the following annual compound rates of growth for the Belgian economy: 1858–1873: 6%; 1873–1893: 0.5%; 1893–1913: 4%.
[c] This was down to 7% for the 1967–79 period, and it will continue to slide down. *The Economist* (May 24, 1980) puts the annual rate of growth of Japan's GNP at 4.1% for the 1973–1979 period and estimates that it will decline to 3.5% for the 1979–1985 period.
Source: Mandel (1980: 3). Copyright Cambridge University Press. Reprinted by permission.

for each long wave phase using world production data from Dupriez (1947 2:567).[53] For comparison I include my base dating of phases:

Phase	Gordon Dating (Years)	Average annual growth in production per capita (%)	Base dating scheme Corresponding phases (Years)
U	1865–1882	2.58	1848–1872
D	1880–1894	0.89	1872–1893
U	1895–1913	1.75	1893–1917
D	1913–1938	0.66	1917–1940

As with Mandel, Gordon selects the best local turning points based on the series itself. This problem is somewhat worse for Gordon than Mandel: he does not show largely convergent dating for a number of series, nor do his dates follow the base dating as closely (the first date differs by seventeen years).

Gordon supports these results using a different methodology—analysis of shorter business cycles (p. 26). He compares the ratio of total "expansion months" (short cycle trough to peak) to "contraction months" in business cycles on long wave upswing phases against those on downswing phases:

Phase	Years	Ratio of expansion to contraction months U.S.	Great Britain	Germany
U	1848–1873	1.80	2.71	1.61
D	1873–1895	0.86	0.76	0.79
U	1895–1913	1.14	1.62	1.33
D	1919–1940	0.67	1.36	1.82

The methodological problem of ad hoc turning points recurs as above.[54] The differences do, nonetheless, seem fairly strong between the periods—and these periods now match the base dating scheme fairly closely.

Gordon's conclusions contradict those of Burns and Mitchell (discussed above), although Gordon uses Burns and Mitchell's general methodology and business cycle datings. This is one of several examples of different results produced by different schools.

Kleinknecht (1981a:689, 692–93) explicitly follows Mandel's methodology and examines data from additional countries. He gives the following estimates of average annual growth rates of real national product (constant prices) within long wave phases, using data from Mitchell (1980:779ff.):

53. "Annual cumulative rates of growth in physical output per capita, adjusting production indices for price changes and aggregating across countries" (p. 24).

54. The dates used for each country actually differ slightly from those shown above, based on the local turning points in the country's business cycles. War years are excluded, and certain other ad hoc adjustments are made.

Phase	Germany Years	(%)	Italy Years	(%)	Great Britain Years	(%)
U	1850–1873	2.77	1861–1873	0.91	1850–1873	3.02
D	1874–1893	1.92	1874–1893	0.68	1874–1893	1.42
U	1894–1913	2.95	1894–1913	2.48	1894–1913	2.01
D	1913–1938	1.77	1920–1938	1.83	1914–1938	0.75
U			1951–1969	6.50	1950–1969	2.74

Phase	Sweden Years	(%)	Denmark Years	(%)	Norway Years	(%)
U	1861–1873	3.29	1870–1873	4.46	1865–1873	2.30
D	1874–1893	1.55	1874–1893	2.63	1874–1893	1.50
U	1894–1913	3.61	1894–1913	3.87	1894–1913	2.67
D	1914–1938	2.60	1914–1938	2.88	(1914–1929	2.96
U			1950–1969	3.92	1930–1938	2.60)

Thus, except for the unusual dating for Norway since 1914 (enclosed in parentheses)—and acknowledging some minor discrepancies in turning points and the omission of World War II years—these data give further support to the alternation of higher and lower production growth rates on long wave upswings and downswings. The ad hoc selection of turning points for each series remains, however.

Bieshaar and *Kleinknecht* (1984) measure average growth rates for eleven national production series within predefined historical phase periods (using Mandel's datings) by fitting a trend line to logged data within the period.[55] The predefined phase periods minimize the ad hoc dating problem, but the mixed results show at best long waves only since 1890 (less than two waves) and not for Great Britain.

Kuczynski (1982:28) calculates the average annual growth rates of capitalist world industry as follows:

Phase	Kuczynski's dating Years	Average annual growth of world industry (%)	Corresponding dating from base scheme Years
D	(1830)–1847	4.16[a]	1814–1848
U	1847–1872	4.31	1848–1872
D	1872–1894	2.77	1872–1893
U	1894–1913	4.67	1893–1917
D	1913–1939	2.13	1917–1940
U	1939–1973	4.72	1940–1968
D	1973–(1980)	3.10 (unfinished)	1968–

[a]Kuczynski says too high because early downswing depression years around 1825 excluded.

55. The trend lines are constrained to intersect at turning points, and the methodology is rather complex.

Kuczynski (1978:86) gives the following average growth rates for the world economy (in constant prices). For each variable, the starting date of the long wave phase and the growth rate for that phase are shown:

Phase	Total production Year	(%)	Industrial production Year	(%)	Industrial share of total Year	(%)	Agricultural production Year	(%)	Total exports Year	(%)
U	1850	2.3	1850	4.8	1850	2.2	1850	2.0	1850	5.7
D	1867	1.7	1867	3.3	1870	0.5	1881	1.2	1867	3.1
U	1894	2.8	1897	4.5	1897	1.4	1895	2.1	1894	3.5
D	1914	2.5	1914	2.3	1914	0.6	1916	1.2	1914	0.6
U	1951	4.5	1951	5.6	1951	1.1	1951		1950	
D	1967	3.5	1970	3.4	1967	0.5	$\left\{2.4\right\}$		$\left\{7.1\right\}$	
	(1977)		(1977)		(1977)		(1977)		(1977)	

The dates are based on cluster analysis (grouping together years with similar data), so once again a bias is introduced by ad hoc dating of turning points for each series.

Screpanti (1984) continues in the same vein after reviewing the contributions of Mandel, Gordon, and Kleinknecht. Screpanti tabulates average annual compound growth rates of industrial output based on the data of Maddison (1977), for France, and for 16 OECD countries as a whole:[56]

Phase	France Years	(%)	16 OECD Countries Years	(%)
U	1846–1878	1.3		
D	1878–1894	0.9	1870–1894	2.1
U	1894–1914	1.5	1894–1913	2.8
D	1914–1938	1.0	1914–1950	1.9
U	1939–1967	3.7	1950–1970	4.9

From these results, and those of Mandel, Rostow, Kleinknecht, Gordon, Kondratieff, Dupriez, and Imbert, Screpanti concludes that "long waves in the growth rate of industrial output occurred in many advanced capitalist countries" and that "the timing of the long cycle is practically uniform throughout the center of the world capitalist system" (p. 519). He does, however, call attention to the "vagueness" of turning point datings that reflect both differences of opinion and actual differences in turning points between countries.

To summarize, six scholars—all from the capitalist crisis school of the theoretical debate—have attempted to show alternating patterns of rapid and slower growth in overall (national) production on alternating long wave phases. The results have been

56. The French figures apparently derive from another study by Gordon, Edwards, and Reich (1982).

consistently positive across a range of countries and data sources, although weakened somewhat by problems in dating turning points.

Other scholars from different theoretical schools have applied other methodologies to the production question with varied results. *Van der Zwan* (1980:192–97) analyzes time series data for production in the United States, United Kingdom, Germany, and the world and for U.K. income and world trade in primary products, covering various ranges of years around 1850–1940. He combines trend deviation and phase period methodologies—first fitting a time series to a long-term growth curve, then estimating the growth rates of the deviations from this curve in each long wave phase period.[57] Van der Zwan does not find significant differences in the growth rates across phases, however.[58] "The period 1874–1913 can be described nearly perfectly as one of constant growth" rather than stagnation followed by expansion. Van der Zwan's findings contradict those of the six capitalist crisis scholars just discussed, despite some methodological similarities.

Van Duijn (1980:224), however, disputes Van der Zwan's conclusions[59] and argues for a "business cycle" methodology for measuring long waves in production (see also Van Duijn 1979; 1983:165ff.). He divides a time series into short business cycles and defines the long wave as a group of four to six (typically five) such cycles (1980:226). Growth rates for each business cycle are determined by the difference from the peak of one business cycle to the peak of the next.[60] Van Duijn uses four long wave phases—prosperity, recession, depression, and recovery—but these phases are not always consistent with my base dating scheme,[61] and the dates of

---

57. The phase periods are predefined by price movements.

58. For example, he gives the following growth rates for U.S. production (index of production of manufactures), as estimated by linear trends in logged data:

Phase	Years	(%)
U	1861–1873	6.02
D	1874–1894	5.42
U	1896–1913	5.28

The British series are "completely inconsistent with the alleged long wave" (p. 193). German data, as well as world production and trade data, could support the long wave hypothesis but with "negligible" magnitude (p. 194).

59. Van Duijn (1980:224–26) criticizes both the quality of historical data and Van der Zwan's trend deviation method, which assumes a simple growth curve as the underlying trend about which production varies. Van Duijn would prefer an S curve as the underlying trend. Van Duijn echoes the early critics of Kondratieff in arguing that "the pattern of residuals is very sensitive to the trend assumptions one makes." Finally, Van Duijn objects to using price phases as a priori time periods in which to compare production growth rates. He argues that prices are not central to or even necessarily correlated with the long wave (as shown by the different histories of prices and production in the 20th c.).

60. Like Kondratieff's, this methodology aims to eliminate the effect of short business cycles on the measurement of long waves. It has the disadvantage of using only one (not necessarily representative) data point in each cycle (see chap. 8).

61. The "recession" phase sometimes falls late in the base dating upswing and sometimes early in the downswing, while "recovery" sometimes comes late in the downswing and sometimes early in the upswing. World War I is treated as a separate "war" phase, but World War II is included with "recovery."

Table 4.4. Results of Van Duijn's Analysis

*	Phase	Start of business cycle					Growth of Industrial Production Annual % Growth Rates				
		Brit.	Fr.	Ger.	U.S.	World	Brit.	Fr.	Ger.	U.S.	World
D	Prosperity	1782					4.8				
U	Prosperity	1792					2.4				
	(War)	1802					2.1				
	Recession	1815	1815				3.9	1.4			
D	Depression	1825	1824				3.7	0.5			
	Recovery	1836	1836				3.3	2.3			
	Prosperity	1845	1847	1850			3.3	2.8	3.4		
U	Prosperity	1857	1856	1857			2.1	0.6	3.9		
	Recession	1866	1866	1866	1864		3.6	2.1	5.9	6.2	
D	Depression	1873	1872	1872	1873	1873	2.0	1.9	1.2	5.8	3.1
	Recovery	1883	1882	1882	1882	1883	1.3	0.4	5.0	4.0	3.3
U	Prosperity	1890	1890	1890	1895	1892	1.3	1.6	3.8	6.4	4.2
	Prosperity	1903	1903	1903	1903	1903	2.6	3.5	4.4	5.3	4.0
	(War)	1913	1913	1913	1913	1913	-1.4	-6.7	{1.1}	3.1	{2.8}
D	Recession	1920	1920	1920	1920	1920	1.7	8.1		4.8	
	Depression	1929	1929	1929	1929	1929	2.7	-2.6	3.0	0.4	1.4
	Recovery	1937	1937	1937	1937	1937	0.8	0.3	...	5.0	2.9
U	Prosperity	1948	1948		1948	1950		6.6	15.4	4.4	
	Prosperity		1957	1957	1957			6.1	5.8	5.3	
D	Recession		1966	1966	1966			5.8	5.2	3.9	
	Depression		1973	1973	1973						

Source: These results have been reformatted from Van Duijn (1980: 228-230). Data sources vary; world production excluding USSR is from Lewis (1952). * = Grouping of Van Duijn's short cycles into my base dating scheme. Boxes indicate Van Duijn's "prosperity" phases.

business cycle turning points (which define long wave turning points in this approach) vary from country to country.

Van Duijn's (1980:228–30) results are summarized in table 4.4. I have grouped the business cycles by the base dating scheme as well as by Van Duijn's phases. Van Duijn concludes that the long wave in industrial production can be found (p. 231–32),[62] but my reading of his results is more skeptical. There is little apparent difference between growth on the (base dating) upswing phases and that on the downswings. Even using Van Duijn's own categorization of phases, the growth rates

---

62. He qualifies this with a series of ad hoc adjustments, taking into account the different courses of the business cycle and the long wave in different countries.

during "prosperity" phases (marked in boxes on table 4.4) are not higher than in the other phases for any of the four countries.[63]

Van Duijn later (1983:156–57) gives the following growth rates of industrial production by phases, as summarized by Thompson (1984:15a):[64]

Phase	Years	Great Britain (%)	U.S. (%)	Germany (%)	France (%)	Japan (%)
U	1840s–1870s	3.0	6.2	4.3	1.7	
D	1870s–1890s	1.7	4.7	2.9	1.3	
U	1890s–1913	2.0	5.3	4.1	2.5	2.4
	1920–1929	2.8	4.8	?	8.1	3.4
D	1929–1948	2.1	3.1	?	−0.9	−0.2
U	1948–1973	3.2	4.7	9.1	6.1	9.4

Van Duijn's methodology, variables, countries, and results resemble those of Gordon (1978:26), yet Van Duijn (1980; 1983) does not cite Gordon—another illustration of the problematical communication between schools.

Delbeke (1982b) follows Van Duijn in criticizing the use of trend deviation methods and in using a business-cycle methodology.[65] He tries to identify leading sectors in Belgian economic development (1831–1913) based on production growth rates analyzed by industry. Delbeke (p. 21) gives the following figures for the average annual growth of Belgian industrial production as a whole (as with Van Duijn I have separated the base dating scheme periods):

Phase[a]	Delbeke's phase	Start of business cycle	Growth rate (%)
D	(Depression)	1831	5.6
	Recovery	1837	1.0
U	Prosperity	1847	3.6
	Prosperity	1858	4.2
	Recession	1866	3.0
D	Depression	1875	1.3
	Recovery	1884	2.1
U	Prosperity	1893	3.3
	Prosperity	1900	3.4
	(Recession)	1908	3.5
D	Depression	1913	

[a]Dating of upswings and downswings by base dating scheme.

63. For the world total, the boxed growth rates are higher, but those data cover only 77 years (and only one prosperity period, 1892–1913).

64. Note that World War I years (but not World War II) are omitted and that the 1920s, a downswing in the base dating scheme, shows high growth and is included with the upswing here. Years vary between countries on the first three turning points. Japanese data are for total (not industrial) production.

65. "The long wave, in fact, can only be observed through the business cycles" (Delbeke, p. 19).

Delbeke's results, like Van Duijn's, are inconsistent, and he resorts to various ad hoc interpretations in order to reconcile them with the long wave theory.

Kuczynski (1978) (from the capitalist crisis school) uses spectral analysis to look for long waves in world agricultural production, total exports, inventions, innovations, industrial production, and total production for 1850–1976.[66] Kuczynski's results "seem to corroborate" the hypothesis of a long wave in these data (p. 81). The sixty-year cycle has a large bandwidth, however, due to the shortness of the time series. Also, Kuczynski notes that long waves account for only about one-sixth to one-fourth of the residual variance in production and trade series, and a much smaller porportion in the innovation and invention series. Kuczynski concludes that "we cannot exclude the possibility that the 60-year-cycle . . . is a random cycle" (p. 82).

Van Ewijk (1982), who claimed to show long waves in prices using spectral analysis (see above), applies the same methodology to real variables (British industrial production, GNP, investment, exports, and imports; French industrial production; and U.S. GNP) in the period since about 1800.[67] His results are even more negative than Kuczynski's: "With respect . . . to real economic variables, the analysis yields not even a trace of a long wave" (p. 495). Cross-spectral analysis indicates that "price-movements correspond badly to movements in industrial production" (p. 490).

Several works on production variables are methodological "outliers" from the main body of empirical work. *Metz's* (1984a) "long waves" in production variables parallel his price waves, discussed earlier. These are irregular, smoothed, upward and downward trends that do not match the long waves of other scholars. *Bossier* and *Huge* (1981) look for long waves in Belgian real variables—industrial production, zinc and lead production, railroad traffic—from 1840 to 1978. They use a trend deviation methodology that involves three filters for stationarity and, depending on the filter used, find different cycles, none of which exceeds twenty-four years in length. *Keen* (1965) uses a method similar to Kondratieff's—trend deviation filters plus moving averages—for Japanese real variables from 1890 to 1938.[68]

Sterman (1984:35–37), from Forrester's group, compares historical data on U.S. GNP against the simulation produced by the system dynamics model (see fig. 4.2). While the model does indeed generate regular long waves of production, the historical data do not match this pattern very closely (my conclusion, not Sterman's).

To summarize, the empirical studies of long waves in production fall into two groups, generally dividing the Marxist capitalist crisis approaches from the other schools. In the former group, six scholars applied the same methodology—estimating growth rates by phase period—and found consistent results showing alternating growth patterns on successive long wave phases. Among the second group of

66. Data are listed in Kuczynski (1980:309–12).

67. Because of nonstationarity in the real series (p. 477), the residuals from a loglinear trend were used (p. 478).

68. Keen tries to find the sequence of leads and lags among variables to infer possible causality; however, his study is flawed by the problems discussed above with trend deviations and moving averages plus the problem of an extremely short time span.

Figure 4.2. Sterman's Actual and Simulated U.S. GNP

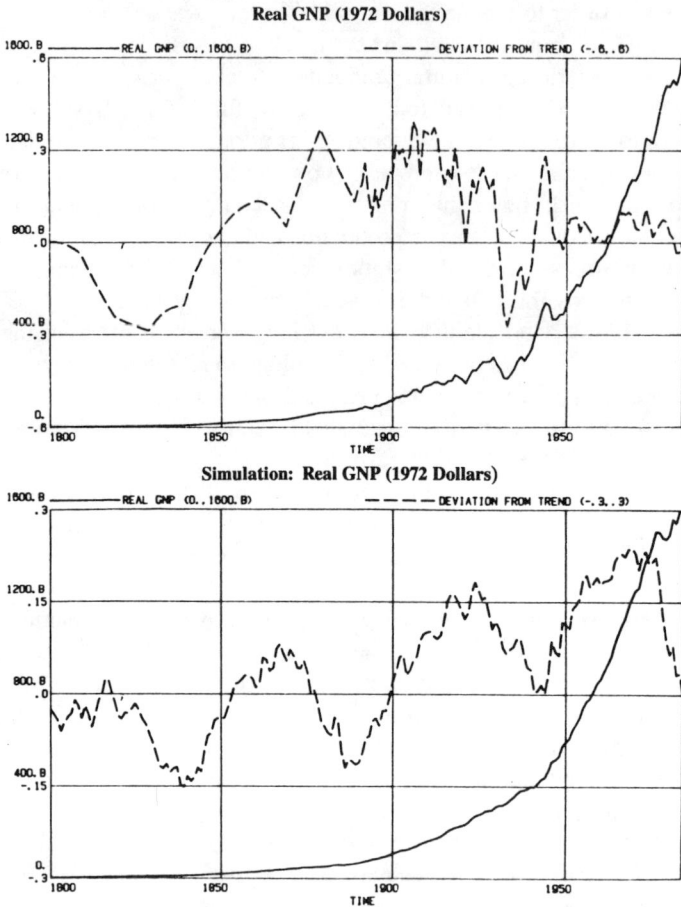

Real GNP (1972 Dollars)

Simulation: Real GNP (1972 Dollars)

Source: Sterman (1986: 90,92)

studies, however, only weak support for long waves in production variables was found. This contrasts sharply with the strong support for long waves in *prices* found by some of those same researchers.[69]

Innovation

There is no consensus on how to measure innovation.[70] Studies rely either on such proxy variables as patent applications (whose meaning may not be clear) or on lists of

69. Eklund's (1980:412) review of empirical studies concludes that "wave-like fluctuations in prices . . . have been found—but these are quite compatible with explanations based exclusively on exogenous factors. In physical time series of production . . . there has been no evidence of long waves."
70. Innovation generally is taken to mean putting an invention or discovery into commercial application, sometimes many years after the initial invention or discovery.

Figure 4.3. Mensch's Swells of Basic Innovations

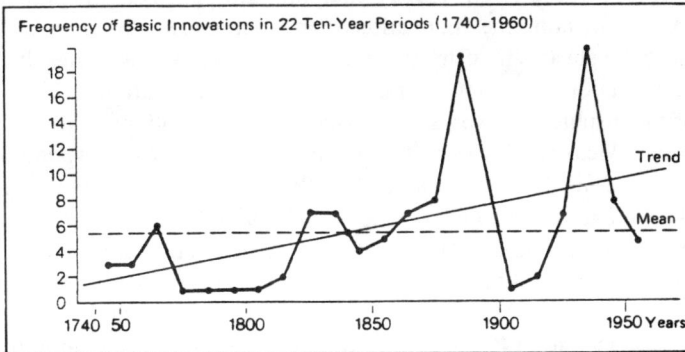

Source: Mensch (1979: 130). From Mensch's *Stalemate In Technology: Innovations Overcome The Depression*, Copyright 1975 by Umschau Verlag, Frankfurt. Reprinted by permission from the Ballinger Publishing Company.

innovations put together by authors based on their own criteria. The different methods of counting innovations (and "basic" innovations as a subset) account for the different results of various researchers. After deciding what to count, most studies have tried to calculate the annual innovation rate during successive long wave phases. But, as with studies reviewed above, there are problems defining and dating phase periods (inconsistent or ad hoc datings).

As discussed in chapter 3, the innovation school contains an important subdebate between scholars who correlate innovative surges with the long wave downswing phase (for example, Mensch) and those who correlate innovative surges with the early upswing phase (for example, Freeman et al.). The empirical evidence bearing on this debate comes from Mensch and Freeman (innovation school), Van Duijn and Kleinknecht (hybrid theories), and Hartman/Wheeler and Kuczynski (outside the innovation school).

Mensch (1979:123) presents data on the frequency of innovations dated according to when the newly discovered material or technique is put into production (or the new product marketed) for the first time. These are graphed in figure 4.3. Mensch concludes that "there are innovative surges in which swarms of technical innovations do emerge in close formation. However, in between these surges, there are long dry spells in which there is scarcely any movement in the basic innovative process" (p. 119). He dates periods of "technology stalemate" around 1825, 1873, and 1929 (p. 4) and swarms of innovation around pre-1787, 1815–27, 1871–85, and 1926–38 (p. 132).[71] Thus Mensch's evidence supports the hypothesis that innovation rises on

71. These correspond in the base dating scheme with the downswings of 1762–90, 1814–48, 1872–93, and 1917–40.

the stagnation phase of the long wave. Other researchers, however, have questioned Mensch's methods and findings.[72]

Clark, Freeman, and *Soete* (1981) examine U.S. patents, "significant inventions" in Great Britain, the innovations corresponding to those inventions, and innovations in the plastics industry specifically. These data show some clustering but with no clear relationship to the overall level of economic activity.

Much of the dispute revolves around what list of innovations to use. Clark et al. (1981) criticize Mensch's list of forty-one inventions and the corresponding innovations taken from Jewkes, Sawers, and Stillerman's list of sixty-one inventions (p. 313). They point to the "high degree of ambiguity" in dating innovations based on arbitrary and subjective standards. Their own dating of the same set of innovations (developed after first resolving differences among themselves!) differs substantially from Mensch's. Whereas Mensch's data seemed to show that during the depression lead times from invention to innovation were reduced (the acceleration hypothesis) and more innovations occurred (the bunching hypothesis), Clark et al. find no support for these conclusions in their revised data (p. 316). While some bunching did occur in the 1930s, they note, most innovations fall in the period of recovery, and the rest do not seem to have been induced by economic conditions.

There are two ways to resolve the Freeman-Mensch dispute on what innovations to include, suggests Kleinknecht (1981b). The size of the sample can be increased by including more cases of basic innovations (as Van Duijn does)—but this does not guarantee a reduction in selection bias. Or, as Kleinknecht does, one can "evaluate other random samples from independent sources."

Van Duijn (1981:24–30) tests Mensch's innovation hypothesis with an expanded set of cases—eighty "major innovations that shaped the lives of 13 twentieth-century growth sectors." The list is based on the judgments of "various experts." Van Duijn finds that "a simple match between long-wave phase and innovation life cycle phase does not exist." Innovations between 1921 and 1957 are grouped as follows:

Phase	Years	Innovations
Recession	1921–1929	5
Depression	1930–1937	11
Recovery	1938–1948	15
Prosperity	1949–1957	9

Van Duijn, in contrast to Mensch, emphasizes the "recovery phase as the period during which major product innovations are most likely to be introduced" (p. 30). Van Duijn's 1983 study likewise finds the evidence unsupportive of Mensch's

72. Mansfield (1983:141) criticizes Mensch's dating of innovations (e.g., the diesel locomotive innovation in 1934 rather than Mansfield's suggestion of 1913) and his distinction of "basic" from other innovations. "For example, Mensch does not include the electronic computer or the birth control pill as basic innovations, but does include the zipper. Moreover, the reasons for excluding the many important, but not basic, innovations are not obvious."

depression-trigger explanation and somewhat supportive of the opposite recovery-stimulus explanation.

Kleinknecht (1981b) tests Mensch's hypothesis against a list of innovations derived from a second (independent) source.[73] Kleinknecht groups the 120 cases into three categories: scientific instruments, improvement and process innovations, and product innovations. He hypothesizes that improvement and process innovations cluster on the upswing and product innovations cluster on the downswing. Relying on visual inspection of the data and simple statistical tests, Kleinknecht finds support for this hypothesis. The evidence "confirms the depression-trigger hypothesis" of Mensch as applied to product innovations (basic innovations) but "does not contradict the prosperity-pull position" of Freeman for the less basic "improvement and process" innovations (Kleinknecht 1981b:303).

Hartman and *Wheeler* (1979:60–65) investigate innovation in Britain and the United States for 1760–1974 and 1873–1974, respectively.[74] Annual patent data support the hypothesis that "downswing periods . . . are all characterized by significant innovative activity":

	Great Britain		United States	
		Increase in		Increase in
	Starting	patents sealed	Starting	patent applications
Phase	date	(%)	date	(%)
D	1760	438		
U	1790	56		
D	1813	472		
U	1849	51		
D	1873	341	1873	120
U	1896	20	1896	52
D	1920	40	1917	8
U	1938		1940	50
			1974	

However, this correlation seems to apply only to British, not American, patents.

Kuczynski (1978:86) calculates the average annual rates for basic innovations from 1878 to 1955, developed from his own list of innovations:

Phase	Period starting date	Annual innovations
D	1878	1.48
U	1899	0.13
D	1922	1.48
U	1943	(0.69)
	(1956)	

73. Mahdavi (1972), who investigated innovations for reasons unconnected with long waves and whose list may therefore be less biased than those of Mensch and Van Duijn.

74. They also study indicators of infrastructural development, including the length of canals, railroads, highways, and air routes opened and the number of commercial vehicles. These data on infrastructure are too spotty to be of much use, however.

Although there is an ad hoc dating problem,[75] Kuczynski's dates correspond *roughly* to the base dating scheme, which supports the idea of increased innovation on downswing phases.

Kuczynski (1978) also investigates the temporal relationship of innovation and production (as well as trade) using cross-spectral analysis (spectral analysis between two time series). Kuczynski claims that industrial production leads in the long wave sequence and that innovation follows.[76] "It is obvious that industrial production predominates over all the other economic activities" (p. 82).[77]

To summarize, the empirical evidence for long waves in innovation is mixed. Several studies (Mensch, Kleinknecht, Hartman and Wheeler, and Kuczynski) show innovation clustering on the downswing, but others (Freeman, Clark, and Soete; Van Duijn) question these findings and the data and methods behind them.

Other Variables

Several empirical studies have examined other variables, although most attention has been on prices, production, and innovation. Several of the variables of interest listed at the beginning of this chapter—capital investment, wages and protests, and trade—have been addressed by almost no empirical work, and only spotty evidence can be found.[78]

Two studies of production—Cleary and Hobbs, and Van Ewijk—also include *capital investment* data, but neither finds long waves in either capital investment or production.

Kondratieff and Oparin look at *wages*—disagreeing on the presence of long waves. Little has been done since then. The study of long waves of protest has been more interpretive than quantitative and has not used wage data.

Trade is touched on by several scholars, but none distinguishes patterns in trade from those in production. Kondratieff, Mandel, and Kuczynski find long waves in both production and trade, while Oparin, Van der Zwan, and Van Ewijk find long waves in neither production nor trade.

75. As with Kuczynski's production analysis, above, the same data are used both to determine turning points and then to estimate growth rates between those points. Kuczynski's datings are based on cluster analysis, in which similar years are grouped together.

76. His long wave sequence begins with changes in the ratio of industrial to total production, followed by changes in the level of industrial production, in the export/production ratio and the export level, in innovation and invention, and finally in the level of agricultural production and the ratio of agricultural to total production. My own reading of Kuczynski's evidence leaves me skeptical of these claims, although as I will show in chapter 10, I arrive at certain similar results when using Kuczynski's data.

77. Kuczynski suggests that "one could say—in contrast to Mensch—that economic recessions *generate* innovating activities, and innovating activities *generate* inventive activities." However, because of methodological difficulties, Kuczynski says only that the empirical data do not conflict with such an interpretation. Kuczynski's timing actually supports that of Mensch; but he sees economic downswings as causing innovation upswings, rather than innovation upswings causing economic upswings (the two are not incompatible). While the liberal innovation school sees innovation (individual human creativity) as driving economic evolution, Kuczynski's Marxist argument stresses that economic/social conditions shape individual creativity.

78. A few empirical studies connecting the last variable, war, with long waves will be reviewed in chap. 5.

Several other empirical studies have been made of less common variables. Dupriez (1951:247) measures the connection between *central bank note issue* and long waves. For six countries—Great Britain, France, Germany, Belgium, the Netherlands, and the United States—he gives the following data on the annual increment of the note issue:

Phase	Starting date	Growth rate (%)
U	1791	5.15
D	1818	1.18
U	1843/44	6.97
D	1873	1.83
U	1898	4.30
D	1913	(stationary?)

Gordon, Weisskopf, and Bowles (1983) use the short business cycle methodology to study U.S. *labor costs* as a long wave variable. They classify business cycles as either "reproductive" cycles, in which the business cycle recession cuts labor costs and restores profits, or "nonreproductive" cycles, in which labor costs rise during the business cycle recession (p. 154). Gordon et al.'s results "indicate alternating periods of nonreproductive and reproductive cycles," with nonreproductive periods in 1890 to 1903, 1926 to 1937, and 1969 to the present. These periods correspond roughly (but only roughly) with the downswings of the base dating scheme. The results (with datings based on NBER business cycles except for minor ad hoc adjustments) are as follows:

Business cycle recession (peak→trough) Years	Average annual change in labor costs[a] (%)	Business cycle recession (peak→trough) Years	Average annual change in labor costs (%)
1890–1891	0.78	1926–1928	0.97
1892–1894	4.54	1929–1933	0.15
1895–1897	2.30	1937–1939	−1.32
1899–1901	0.58	1944–1947	−1.60
1903–1905	−3.48	1948–1950	−0.54
1907–1909	−5.91	1953–1955	−1.77
1910–1912	−1.61	1957–1959	−0.56
1913–1915	−7.97	1960–1962	−0.34
1919–1922[b]	−4.96	1969–1971	0.16
1923–1925	−4.02	1973–1976	0.10
		1979–1981	0.39

[a]Labor cost data source not indicated.
[b]Changed from NBER dating of business cycle.

Gordon et al.'s dating diverges from the long wave base dating scheme (as does Gordon's, discussed above), and they make ad hoc adjustments to the NBER data. But overall their results provide some evidence of long waves in labor costs.

Sau (1982:574–75), although not addressing long waves primarily, attempts to relate *profits* to the long wave in a Marxist framework. His study, however, is limited to a single turning point in the period since 1960. The data show gross profit rates peaking out as a percentage of assets in 1965 (United States), 1966 (Great Britain), and 1969 (France, West Germany, and Japan). This would support the (Marxist) declining rate of profit theory of the onset of economic decline.

Conclusions Regarding the Empirical Evidence

Quantitative empirical studies of long waves over the past sixty years have produced some areas of convergent results and other areas of unresolved dispute.

The overall dating schemes of researchers associated with all theoretical schools of the long wave debate showed very strong convergence. With few exceptions, dating schemes of thirty-three scholars showed a one-to-one correspondence with my base dating scheme, despite minor differences in dating particular turning points. With regard to price data since 1790, there was strong consensus on the existence of long waves, manifested as higher and lower inflation rates in successive historical periods. Only the conceptualization of the long wave in terms of fixed periodicities yielded weak or negative results in the post-1790 period. For prices before 1790, the results are similar but less conclusive, partly because of the smaller number of studies and the lower quality of data.

In the production variables (since 1790), by contrast, there is a strong division between the results of different theoretical schools. Studies by six Marxists, using similar methodologies based on phase-period growth rates, all found that production (especially industrial production) consistently grows more rapidly on long wave upswings. However, studies by scholars from other theoretical schools using different methodologies either failed to confirm this finding or provided only weak evidence in its support.

As regards innovation, there was modest (and disputed) evidence of a clustering of basic innovations on the economic downswing. Several other variables—labor costs, profit rates, and central bank note issue—showed some evidence of alternating growth rates on successive long wave phases.

These results will be taken up further in chapter 7, which (among other tasks) will sort out the theoretical and empirical arguments of the long wave debate from a philosophy of science perspective, framing the alternative hypotheses of different researchers. The process of sifting, weighing, and testing long wave hypotheses will then lead into Part Two (chapters 8–12), in which I will present my statistical analyses of time series data in support of the development of a long wave theory. First, however, I will take up the separate but related debate on cycles of war and hegemony.

CHAPTER FIVE

The War/Hegemony Debate 1: Roots

As I noted in chapter 3, war was discussed less often as the long wave debate moved into its second round after the 1950s. But the debate on war cycles, although separated from that of economic cycles, continued in a separate research community with its disciplinary center in political science.[1] I will review in this chapter and the next the debates on long cycles of war and related political phenomena.

This chapter could be called the "Quincy Wright chapter" in that it explores three strands of research that trace back to Wright's work in the early 1940s. These strands of research are illustrated in figure 5.1.

The first strand (at the left) concerns fifty-year cycles in war and politics correlated with long waves. Because of the disciplinary border between politics and economics, these studies have not been well integrated in the long wave debate and remain a scattered collection of research projects. The second strand of research concerns the statistical search for periodicity in war data. This line is a self-proclaimed dead-end, currently inactive. The third strand concerns longer cycles of very large wars that take more than a hundred years,[2] which I call hegemony cycles. Toynbee integrated Wright's idea of hundred-year war cycles with Dehio's framework of long cycles of hegemonic challenge and succession. Organski's "power transition" theory (an offshoot of post-World War II realism) became joined with this theoretical framework and gave rise to the current "war/hegemony debate," which I will review in chapter 6.[3]

Quincy Wright

Wright (1942) occupies a position with respect to war cycles similar to that of Kondratieff with respect to long economic cycles. Like Kondratieff,

1. As with long waves, however, the war cycle theorists were always a minority within the discipline.
2. These longer cycles were originally conceived as composed of two long waves of war, one more severe and one less severe, totaling about 100 years. In the recent war/hegemony debate, however (see chap. 6), the longer cycles are being theoretically decoupled from long waves; and my interpretation (chap. 13) sees them as about 150 years long and not closely tied to long waves.
3. Farrar's 1977 synthesis best captures the essence of the hegemony cycle strand originating with Wright's work and will close this chapter.

Figure 5.1. An Overview of the War/Hegemony Debate

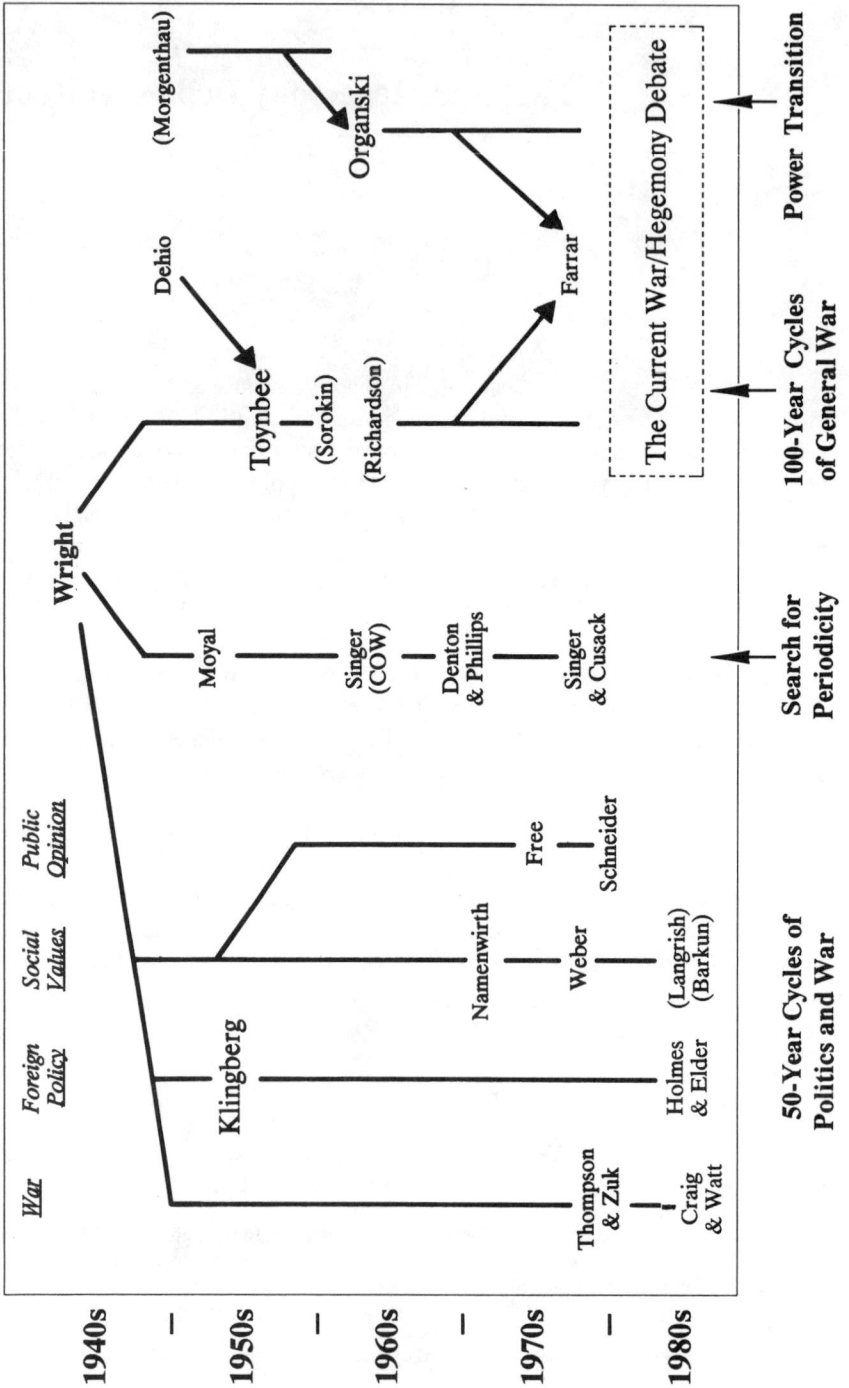

| War | Foreign Policy | Social Values | Public Opinion | | Search for Periodicity | 100-Year Cycles of General War | Power Transition |

50-Year Cycles of Politics and War

he advances tentative hypotheses of what might cause such a phenomenon but mainly presents the evidence descriptively rather than theoretically.

Wright (1942:227) studies "fluctuations in the intensity of war" and concludes that "There appears to have been a tendency in the last three centuries for concentrations of warfare to occur in approximately fifty-year oscillations, each alternating period of concentration being more severe" (p. 227). Wright defines these concentrations as follows:[4]

*War of the Spanish Succession (1701–14)
 Concentration of wars around the Seven Years' War (1756–63)
*Napoleonic wars (1795–1815)
 Concentration of wars around 1853–71[5]
*The World War (1914–18, renewed in 1939)
     *More severe war concentration

He concludes that "in the modern period of world-civilization fluctuations of war and peace have tended to become stabilized at about fifty years" (p. 378). These fifty-year concentrations of war are synchronous with Kondratieff's long waves.[6]

Wright is aware of Kondratieff's argument that economic long waves, endogenous to the world economy, determine the timing of wars and revolutions rather than that wars determine the timing of long waves, as Trotsky held.[7] But Wright (1942:1273) finds available evidence insufficient to judge the direction of causality. Nonetheless, Wright's speculations on the possible causes of war cycles point toward causes arising from political factors rather than reflecting economic cycles.

Wright tentatively suggests three factors that might contribute to war cycles:[8] psychological factors, economic factors, and the embedding of these factors in an international system that tends toward war:

Fluctuations in the intensity of war in the history of a state would tend to assume a definite periodicity if the international system exerted a persistent pressure toward war and if the economic and technological period necessary to recover from a severe war and to prepare for another were identical with the psychological and political period necessary to efface the anti-war sentiment after such a war and to restore national morale (p. 231).

4. It seems to me that the Thirty Years' War (1618–48) could well be added at the beginning of the list, about 50 years before the War of the Spanish Succession.

5. Crimean War (1853–56), War of Italian Unification (1859), Austro-Prussian War (1866), and Franco-Prussian War (1870–71).

6. The war periods correspond with the long wave expansion phases of 1689–1720, 1747–62, 1790–1814, 1848–72, and 1893–1917 (the renewal of war in 1939 comes just at the start of the long wave expansion phase, out of line with the previous wars near the end of expansion phases).

7. Wright seems to have been unaware of his contemporaries, Silberling and Åkerman, from the war school of the long wave debate (see chap. 2). Thus, already in the 1940s the disciplinary boundaries seem to have been formidable. Wright's student, Frank L. Klingberg, who studied 50-year cycles, had not heard of Åkerman or Silberling (conversation with author).

8. Wright (1942:1272) also mentions the possible influence of the "average dominance of a political party in democratic countries" of 40 to 60 years. This seems less plausible, however, since it would apply only to recent times and would be internationally synchronized only if connected with economic long waves and/or wars.

Among psychological factors, Wright suggests the *alternation of generations* as an explanation for the recurrence of major war about every fifty years: "The warrior does not wish to fight again himself and prejudices his son against war, but the grandsons are taught to think of war as romantic" (p. 230). This generation cycle theme is picked up by Toynbee (see below).

Among economic factors, Wright argues that the *costs of war* create a "tendency to postpone a new war until there has been time to recover economically from the last" (p. 1272). Wars cost money, so countries fight until they run out of money and then save up to fight again. The cost of war theme is picked up by Farrar (see below).

The economic factor for Wright operates in the context of a balance-of-power system with an inherent *tendency towards war*. Countries consistently try to build up their war-making capabilities, which rest on national economic strength. After a major war, nations rebuild their capabilities, and shifts begin to occur in the balance of power. Then, "after the activity of building up from the losses of a great war, heavy industries find it possible to induce armament-building at an increasing rate and for this purpose mobilize demands first for imperialistic expeditions, then for defense from reported aggressions" (p. 1319). Gradually the great powers tend to polarize into two hostile alliances, and the side that calculates time running against it in the new dynamic provokes "a war which is now considered inevitable" (p. 230).

Wright sums up the possible causes of war cycles as: (1) "fading social memory with the passage of a generation"; (2) economic factors; (3) "the lag of national policies and constitutions behind changing international conditions"; and (4) "the tendency of unsettled disputes to accumulate, aggravating the relations of states" (p. 1318).

Wright is not explicit about any longer-term cycles and does not elaborate on the alternation of more severe and less severe war recurrences (which, as Toynbee argues, form a one-hundred-year cycle). Wright does, however, delineate four long-term periods (about 150 years) that define the stages of development of military technology in Europe:[9]

1450–1648:	Experimental adaptation of firearms and religious wars
1648–1789:	Professional armies and dynastic wars
1789–1914:	Industrialization and nationalist wars
1914– :	The airplane and totalitarian war

I will refer to these long-term periods later, in chapter 13, since they line up fairly closely with the divisions I will use to date the hegemony cycle.

Fifty-Year Cycles in War and Politics

The first main branch from Wright's work consists of studies of fifty-year cycles (synchronous with long waves) in war, foreign policy, social values, and public opinion. I will review each area in turn.

9. Wright (1942:294–303) cited in Klingberg (1970:505).

War

William Thompson and L. Gary Zuk (1982:624–25) revive the central question of the war school of the long wave debate—the role of war in the long wave. They consider three hypotheses: (1) the initiation of a major war inaugurates the upswing of the Kondratieff long wave; (2) the termination of major war inaugurates the downswing of the Kondratieff long wave; and (3) major wars significantly reinforce the upswing of the Kondratieff long wave.[10]

Thompson and Zuk find that, contrary to hypothesis 1, "upswings tend to precede major wars" (p. 632). As for hypothesis 2, they find that "the termination of major wars . . . may initiate downswings, but downswings may occur in their absence. Thus, a major war termination is not a *necessary* cause of the Kondratieff downswing, but . . . may have been a *sufficient* cause" (p. 632). Hypothesis 3 receives the strongest support—although economic upswings have preceded major wars, those wars have in turn caused "an impressive proportion of the [eventual] price upswings" (p. 639). "Overall, one gets the impression that, were it not for wars . . . , Kondratieff's long waves might well have more closely resembled ripples" (p. 634).

Thompson and Zuk then statistically analyze the impact of war on prices, focusing on British and U.S. wholesale prices from 1750 and 1816, respectively, to the present. They use Box-Tiao intervention analysis, a statistical technique designed to ascertain the immediate and subsequent effects of an event on a time series. Thompson and Zuk find "significant percentage increases [in prices] during the war followed by a drawn-out period of readjustment that may last as long as twenty years" (p. 637). Only the biggest wars,[11] however, had a statistically significant impact.

W. W. Rostow (1975a:753)[12] likewise concludes that wars play a role in "reinforc[ing] the inflationary tendency at work in the Kondratieff upswings." In the first Kondratieff upswing (about 1790 to 1815), war "reinforced, if, indeed, it did not largely create" the price upswing. But in the next three upswings, "the price increases of the early 1850's, 1890's, and late 1930's, preceded the relevant wars." Thus wars do not seem to be the only factor in price upswings, Rostow notes.

Paul Craig and Kenneth Watt (1985)[13] show a strong correlation of war with economic long waves, using L. F. Richardson's data on war fatalities.[14] They date long waves since World War II in an unusual way—with the trough in 1936, the peak in 1955, and the next trough due around 1987.[15]

---

10. The third hypothesis is considered a contradiction of the first, but not necessarily of the second.
11. Global wars as defined by Modelski (see chap. 6).
12. See chap. 3 on Rostow's approach to long waves.
13. Craig and Watt—an engineer and a zoologist—illustrate the variety of disciplines represented in the long cycle debate (creating problems of disciplinary cohesion within the field).
14. These results converge with my results based on Levy's war data, reported in Goldstein (1984b, c; 1985; 1986).
15. They note that World War II was "premature," coming early in an upswing, "for reasons probably relating to the extremely harsh terms of the Versailles treaty" (p. 26).

Foreign Policy

In addition to studies directly relating war and long waves, there have been several studies of long waves in American foreign policy, beginning with the work of Frank Klingberg (1952), who traces his roots from Quincy Wright (Klingberg 1970:505).

Klingberg argues (1952) that American foreign policy since 1776 follows alternating phases of "extroversion" and "introversion."[16] These alternating twenty-to-thirty-year-long phases are dated as follows (p. 250):

Introvert	Extrovert
1776–1798	1798–1824
1824–1844	1844–1871
1871–1891	1891–1919
1919–1940	1940–?

Klingberg supports this theory with empirical indices based on such events as treaties, wars, armed expeditions, annexations, and diplomatic warnings (p. 241). He also judges the "popular mood" by means of political platforms, election results, and contemporary writers and speakers. Klingberg observes that "all but two of America's wars were fought during the extrovert phases, and these two wars were begun near the close of extrovert phases" (1979:40).[17] During the extrovert phase, he argues, presidential leadership is widely supported, while during the introvert phase Congress reasserts its constitutional prerogatives.[18]

Klingberg's phases correspond very closely with the base dating scheme for long waves—the introvert phases corresponding to the economic downswings and the extrovert phases to the upswings. Klingberg himself, however, does not (in 1952) connect his cycles with long waves. Rather, he suggests internal (self-generating) explanations for the cycles of foreign policy moods, such as "a need for a period of rest and relaxation following a period of intense activity" (p. 262).[19] Klingberg

16. For instance, the mood of the 1930s was introvert, because "America was unwilling to exert much positive pressure upon other nations." The mood from 1941 through the time of writing in 1952 was extrovert, as seen by the country's "willingness to bring its influence to bear upon other nations, to exert positive pressure (economic, diplomatic, or military) outside its borders" (pp. 239–40).

17. The Revolutionary War of 1775 and the Vietnam War of 1966/67. The latter is just past the end of Klingberg's extrovert phase in 1966 but before the period 1968–74, in which most long wave scholars date the end of the upswing.

18. Klingberg (1979:39) describes the alternation of foreign policy moods as "spiral in character, with the U.S. becoming more deeply involved abroad during each extrovert phase, followed by a relative plateau or modest withdrawal." Klingberg states that each complete cycle has been devoted to a particular problem: (1) 1776–1824, building independence; (2) 1824–71, responding to the challenges of slavery and manifest destiny; (3) 1871–1918, becoming an industrial world power; (4) 1918–66, meeting the special crisis for world democracy; and (5) 1966–, "apparently being challenged to lead in establishing a stable world order." The argument is reminiscent of Trotsky's stages, Rostow's phases, and Schumpeter-Kuznets's "Industrial, Bourgeois, and Neo-Mercantilist Kondratieffs."

19. He notes a correspondence of his periods with a possible "world political cycle" (p. 263) as reflected in periods of intense diplomatic pressures and wars among the European powers—but doubts this causes the American foreign policy cycle, noting that "it is more likely that some larger factor or inherent tendency affected both" (p. 266).

(1979:39) speculates that the length of the cycle derives from the length of a " 'political generation' . . . of about 25 years."[20] Neither economic causes nor the effects of recurring war play a role in Klingberg's theory.

Klingberg (1979) predicts that a current introvert phase[21] will last through about 1986 or 1987 and warns that "another Great Power might be able to move aggressively, in some significant region of the world, with impunity" (p. 45). Nonetheless, challenges from abroad would be likely to stimulate the United States toward extroversion sooner than would otherwise be the case (p. 40).

Jack Holmes and Robert Elder follow up on the work of Klingberg (see also Alexander 1985). Elder and Holmes (1985a,b) present a variety of empirical data—based mainly on content analysis of political documents—in support of Klingberg's conclusions. Holmes (1985), and Holmes and Elder (1985), focus particularly on the relationship of Congress and the president as correlated with the foreign policy cycle (and hence with long waves). Holmes and Elder tabulate (by phase period) such phenomena as presidential vetoes, struggles over executive privilege, war powers actions, Congressional action on treaties and supreme court nominations, and the results of content analysis of inauguration speeches. Holmes and Elder (1985) conclude that "institutional interactions between the Presidency and Congress are roughly congruent with Klingberg/Holmes mood phases."[22]

Social Values

Possibly related to foreign policy "moods" are more general phases of "social values," studied by J. Zvi Namenwirth and (his student) Robert Philip Weber. They use content analysis of political documents to connect "value changes" in society to economic long waves.[23]

Namenwirth (1973) develops a theory of cyclical value shifts (as measured by U.S. party platform analyses) closely synchronized with the long wave.[24] He finds cycles of various lengths, the most important being a 152-year cycle and (in its simplified description) a 48-year cycle with four alternating sets of concerns that he calls the conservative, parochial, progressive, and cosmopolitan phases of value concerns (see fig. 5.2).

In the *parochial* phase, economic concerns and "wealth" values reach a peak; "there is little concern with the world, and long-range planning or the concern with wealth is associated with a 'Fortress America' stance" (p. 678). The *progressive* stage sees a "preponderant concern with political strifes" (p. 676), as economic

20. He also (1983) suggests connecting the foreign policy cycle with a longer cultural-political-spiritual cycle.
21. He calls the 1980s a "presumed neo-isolationist period" (1979:37).
22. My reading of Holmes and Elder's evidence finds it generally convincing.
23. This work builds on Namenwirth and Lasswell's (1970) use of content analysis to measure the frequency of key words in (American) Democratic and Republican party platforms. Namenwirth and Lasswell distinguish such value categories as "power," "affection," "respect," and so on. They argue that party platforms are "especially suitable for the study of values of the whole society" (p. 8), representing the party's best guess about policies that will win popular support.
24. "The history of value change is neither progressive nor regressive, but basically cyclical" (p. 649).

Figure 5.2. Namenwirth's 48-year Value Change Cycle

The Internal Structure of Short-Term Value Changes (Cycle lengths set at 48 years, Variable Origins)

Source: Namenwirth (1973: 674). Reprinted from *The Journal of Interdisciplinary History*, III (1973), 674, with permission of the editors of *The Journal of Interdisciplinary History* and The MIT Press, Cambridge, Mass.

growth accelerates and concern with economic matters diminishes. Then, "with increasing surplus, attention turns again to the world scene, [and] value articulations become more cosmopolitan" (p. 681). The *cosmopolitan* phase stresses long-range planning; an increasing concern with technology, industry, and training; and "a maximum concern with the world at large" (p. 677). Finally, there follows a *conservative* "preoccupation with authoritative restoration of former structures and values" (p. 677) as the economy begins to decline again.

Namenwirth notes "a rather striking fit" between these value cycles and the long wave (p. 680) and suggests the long economic wave as "the most plausible explanation" (p. 682) for the sequential articulation of value categories: "During long-wave economic deterioration, the nation turns inward, gradually relinquishing international ventures and then obligations, becoming more and more parochial in its orientations" (p. 681).

Namenwirth's analysis suffers from certain methodological problems,[25] particularly in fitting data to sine waves and then averaging the resulting wavelengths.

25. Including the inadequate length of the time series relative to the cycle lengths postulated—most notably using a 120-year data set to identify a 152-year cycle.

For instance, cycles varying from 104 years to 232 years are "assumed" to have a "true wave length" of 152 years, with "deviations due either to measurement error or to estimation procedures" (p. 659). But cycles of widely varying wavelengths cannot be at all synchronous, which goes against the idea of long waves as synchronous movements of different variables.

Namenwirth's resulting cycle of value change corresponds closely to the economic long wave. His methodology, although problematical, does not appear biased to give those results. This suggests that Namenwirth's results do reflect an underlying relationship of long waves with social values.

Namenwirth's theory receives further support when Weber (1981) finds corresponding results in a similar analysis of British "speeches from the throne."[26] Weber tests Namenwirth's theory against the British data (1795 to 1972, or 178 years), again using content analysis. He finds, after removing a secular trend and a longer sine curve (the latter being equivalent to Namenwirth's 152-year cycle), that a short sine curve emerges in many content categories. The wavelengths vary from 27 to 89 years, and Weber (like Namenwirth) "assumed that change in concern with these categories proceeds at one rate or wavelength . . . . Therefore the estimated wavelengths . . . were standardized to the median wavelength" of 52 years (p. 1134). As with Namenwirth, this is a dubious methodology, but the resulting curve again correlates well with Namenwirth's cycle and the long wave (see table 5.1). Weber concludes that "as in America, the British . . . cycle is correlated with the Kondratieff economic cycle. In addition, the British and American thematic and Kondratieff cycles are all in phase" (p. 1132).

John Langrish (1982), like Namenwirth and Weber (but independently), studies long cycles in social values. Langrish finds that periods of technological optimism and confidence in science and technology have corresponded with the upswings of the long wave. Conversely an "anti-science" mood since 1965 may be connected with the downswing. Langrish analyzes changes in social "optimism," using a content analysis of advertisements in the *Journal of Decorative Art*—each of which he classifies as forward-looking, backward-looking, or time-neutral (p. 156).[27] He constructs an "optimism index" based on these categories and tabulates the average index value in each long wave period to show that optimism increases on the upswing and decreases on the downswing (p. 156). However, the analysis covers only selected years in the period 1924–81 (one long wave).

Michael Barkun (1984) considers another aspect of social values—the formation of utopian communities in America. Of 270 such communities founded between 1787 and 1919, fully one-third began during two seven-year-long concentrations—

26. Delivered at the opening of each parliamentary session and similar to the American "state of the union" address. Weber "assume[s] that these speeches reflect . . . the dominant concerns of at least the upper classes of British society" (p. 1132).

27. Forward-looking advertisements contain such words as "modern" and "scientific" and futuristic symbols, while backward-looking ones refer to established traditions and such symbols of the past as coats of arms.

Table 5.1. Weber's Economic and Value Cycles Compared

	Minima Economic Cycle*	Parochial Value Phase**	Maxima Economic Cycle*	Cosmopolitan Value Phase**
Britain	1789	1790	1819	1816
	1849	1842	1873	1868
	1896	1894	1920	1920
	1932	1946		
America	1790	1788	1814	1812
	1849	1836	1866	1860
	1896	1884	1920	1908
	1932	1932		

	Minima Economic Cycle***	Parochial Value Phase**	Maxima Economic Cycle***	Cosmopolitan Value Phase**
Britain	1783	1790	1815	1816
	1837	1842	1866	1868
	1884	1894	1921	1920
	1938	1946	1967	1972
America	1783	1788	1815	1812
	1837	1836	1866	1860
	1884	1884	1921	1908
	1938	1932	1967	1956

*From Table 1 in Kondratieff (b, 110). Kondratieff did not estimate the minima corresponding to the Great Depression; 1932 is used as an approximate date.

**The estimates for the American short cycle are from Namenwirth (674).

***Estimates from van Duijn (b, 563).

Reprinted from Social Forces 59 (June 1981). "Society and Economy in the Western World System" by Robert Phillip Weber. Copyright c The University of North Carolina Press.

1842–48 and 1894–1900. He identifies a third concentration in the 1930s. Each of these three concentrations corresponded with an upsurge of "millenarian movements" in America. Barkun notes (p. 43) that each period comes near the trough of a long wave. A fourth concentration in the late 1960s, however, does not fit the pattern. "While the first three waves indisputably took place in times of severe deprivation, the most recent did not" (p. 47).[28]

A different approach to social values is found in Arthur M. Schlesinger, Sr.'s (1939), suggestion that American politics since 1765 have swung between alternating periods of (roughly speaking) liberalism and conservatism. These cycles (like so

28. The fourth wave of millenialism might fit the long wave better if one used Rostow's unusual dating scheme, in which the 1950s and 1960s are considered a downswing.

much else in the long cycle field) have recently been resurrected (Arthur Schlesinger, Jr., 1986). These Schlesinger cycles, however, average 16.6 years in length and do not correspond with the cycles being discussed here. As Schlesinger (1939:226) notes, "a scrutiny of the [liberal/conservative] oscillations reveals no clear relationship to any rhythms which students of the business cycle have yet discovered in our economic life."

Public Opinion

A final line of work relevant to fifty-year political cycles concerns data from public opinion polling. Do these data reflect changes in public attitudes toward extroversion and introversion? The available data extend back only through one long wave,[29] but within that period the evidence is supportive.

Lloyd A. Free and Hadley Cantril (1967:62–65) study shifts in American public opinion on foreign policy questions. They distinguish between generally "internationalist" and "isolationist" outlooks. Public opinion polls show strongly isolationist tendencies in the 1930s (a long wave downswing) but strongly internationalist tendencies in the 1960s (an upswing phase):

Results from 1936–37:
If another war like World War I developed in Europe, should America take part again?
                        Yes   5%   No 95%
If one foreign nation insists upon attacking another, should the U.S. join with other nations to compel it to stop?
                        Yes 29%   No 71%
Would you like to see the United States join the League of Nations?
                        Yes 33%   No 67%

Results from 1964:
The United States should mind its own business internationally and let other countries get along as best they can on their own. Do you agree or disagree?
                Disagree 70%, Agree 18%, Don't Know 12%
The United States should cooperate fully with the United Nations. Do you agree or disagree?
                Agree 72%, Disagree 16%, Don't Know 12%

These results, although limited in time, are consistent with the hypothesis that "internationalist" public opinion correlates with the expansion phase along with extrovert foreign policy, "cosmopolitan" values, and increased war.

Furthermore, recent public opinion data show a return movement toward isolationism, coinciding with the current long wave downswing phase. Free and William Watts (1980:47) present data that show a sharp shift toward isolationism in the 1970s (which has partially eroded in the 1980s):[30]

29. And I have evidence only for the United States.
30. There were no meaningful differences between Republicans, Democrats, and Independents on the internationalist-isolationist spectrum.

	U.S. should mind its own business: Agree (%)	U.S. should cooperate with the U.N.: Agree (%)
1964	18	72
1974/76	41	46
1980	30	59

Free and Watts interpret the partial decline in isolationism since 1975 as a sign that "defense-oriented internationalism has come of age"—that there is "a new desire to put an end to what is seen as a weakening U.S. role in the world, and to resume the position of being 'number one' " (p. 47).

However, such a conclusion seems exaggerated and is contradicted by William Schneider's (1983:7–8) poll results, which indicate that "in areas not related to America's own defense and security, the trend in public opinion since the late 1960's has been away from internationalism." The response to the question, "Do you think it will be best for the future of the country if we take an active part in world affairs or if we stay out of world affairs?" showed a steady trend away from internationalism from the 1950s through the present:[31]

1950s	about 70%
Mid-1970s	66%
1978	59%
Nov. 1982	54%

Although the United States is not currently as isolationist as in the 1930s (neither is the economy as depressed), the mood has shifted in that direction since the 1960s.[32]

In conclusion, results from a number of scattered research projects that search for fifty-year cycles in war, foreign policy, and social values consistently support the presence of long waves at this level of society, and not just in economics.

The Search for Periodicity

The second line flowing from Wright's work is the search for periodicity in war data.[33] This research was part of the larger enterprise of creating quantitative "behavioral" data on war for statistical analysis as exemplified in the research program of J. David Singer's Correlates of War (COW) project begun in the 1960s at the University of Michigan.

31. Elites ("a leadership sample of Americans in senior positions") followed a similar pattern over time but were more internationalist across the board than the general public.

32. The most recent polling data available to me (Gallup-*Newsweek* poll, *Boston Globe*, Apr. 8, 1985, p. 4) seems to show continuing sentiment against at least the military side of internationalism. As of April 1985, 63% of those polled felt the United States made a mistake in sending troops to Vietnam (27% disagreed), and 75% felt the United States should be more cautious in using military force (17% favored more military force).

33. See also Goldstein (1984a) and Thompson (1985a) for further reviews of this literature.

Singer is not primarily concerned with war cycles, but he looked into the periodicity of war along with other aspects of the "correlates of war" (see Small and Singer 1982:143–57). Singer and Thomas Cusack (1981:411) use the cow project data (1816–1965, or 150 years) to test for constancy in the elapsed time between one war and the next. "The passage of time since the prior war experience seems to have little effect" on the probability of a country finding itself at war again. After considering other possible ways to measure war periodicity, Singer and Cusack find little supporting evidence and take a "dim view" of war periodicity (p. 419).

Aside from the work of Singer and his associates, there have been a few other studies of war "periodicity." The first of these, J. E. Moyal (1949), followed closely after Quincy Wright and used Wright's data, which covered 450 years. Moyal claims to show a 200-year cycle in the outbreak of war, using statistical means, including 50-year moving averages. But Moyal's methodology is problematical, and his 200-year cycle has not been pursued.

Frank Denton and Warren Phillips (1968:185) find "a definite tendency for a periodic increase in the level of violence about every 25 years," as well as a longer cycle of 80–120 years, in Quincy Wright's data (for 420 years up through 1900). They use 20-year averages to bring out this longer cycle graphically. Denton and Phillips interpret these data to support a long cycle theory, but their long cycle matches up neither with the 100-year cycle of Wright (and of Toynbee and Farrar, see below) nor with economic long waves, and their data are unconvincing.

Singer (1981:1) sums up the war-periodicity line of research thus: "Much research on periodicity in the occurrence of war has yielded little result." The efforts to identify war cycles based on fixed periodicities are a self-proclaimed dead-end and may be seen as a "degenerate research program" in Imre Lakatos's terms (see chapter 7).

Longer Cycles of War and Hegemony

The third strand of research coming out of Quincy Wright's work leads into the current debate on cycles of war and hegemony. The influences of Ludwig Dehio, Arnold Toynbee, and A. F. K. Organski come to bear, as shown on the right-hand side of figure 5.1.

This strand focuses not on fifty-year cycles (long waves) but on longer cycles defined by the very biggest wars, which I will call "hegemonic wars."[34] This conception of war cycles flows out of Wright's observation that every other fifty-year war concentration was "more severe." Toynbee formulated this into a one-hundred-year war cycle scheme, and his contemporary Dehio formulated a similar scheme based on the recurrent efforts of Continental powers to gain hegemony in Europe.

34. I follow Farrar (and Gilpin) in this usage. Other terms referring to the same concept but with different emphases are general war (Toynbee, Levy), global war (Modelski), world war (Wallerstein), and systemic war (Midlarsky). Levy (1985) reviews these interpretations (see chap. 6). My choice of "hegemonic war" is explained early in chap. 13.

This concept of a cycle of hegemonic challenges eventually drew Organski's "power transition" theory into the debate, since that theory deals with the outbreak of war when a rising challenger surpasses the dominant power in capabilities.

Different conceptions of what constitutes hegemony, hegemonic war, or a hegemonic challenge lead to different interpretations and datings of these phenomena. By hegemony I mean the position of the leading country in the world, which is able, by virtue of superior economic and military capabilities, to largely shape the rules by which international relations (both economic and security relations) are conducted.[35] I will return to the definition of hegemony in chapters 6 and 13.

Ludwig Dehio

German historian Ludwig Dehio ([1948] 1962), writing in the shadow of World War II, argues that European history over five centuries has been structured by the recurrent drives of Continental powers (Spain, then France twice, then Germany) for world domination. Each drive was eventually defeated by island nations that controlled the seas (Insular nations).[36] Unlike Wright, Dehio relies on interpretive history rather than quantitative data and does not explicitly refer to the recurrence of hegemonic challenges as "cyclical." But Dehio's instances match Wright's "more severe" war concentrations closely:

Wright's "more severe" war concentrations	Dehio's drives for world domination
—	Spain (Charles, Philip)
Spanish Succession (1701–14)	France (Louis XIV)
Napoleonic wars (1795–1815)	France (Napoleon)
World War (1914–18; 1939–45?)	Germany (WWI and WWII)

Venice for Dehio ([1948] 1962:37) was the prototype of an insular power. He dates the rise of the modern system of states from the beginning of the struggle among the great powers over Italy in 1494. Only Venice "preserved its freedom," and that success derived from its insular position as an "island empire."

Portugal, Dehio argues (pp. 51–52), was the first nation in the European state system to develop long-distance trade to Asia by sailing ship and hence capture Venice's role as "the intermediary . . . between two worlds"—Europe and Asia. But Portugal lacked the "insular" security of Venice, especially against Spain's armies, and so "Portugal's legendary glory was as fleeting as a meteor." In 1494 Portugal had to concede half the globe to its Spanish rival, and "in 1580 she lost her

35. This usage contrasts with those referring to "hegemony" as the (unsuccessful) drives for military conquest of Europe.
36. Continental powers, militarily strong on land but weak at sea, tend to be "totalitarian," while Insular (naval) powers are militarily invincible at sea but weak on land, and are associated with the "free spirit of humanity" protected by the "shield of insularity" over the centuries ([1948] 1962:272).

independence, together with all her overseas possessions, to Spain, not to regain it for two generations.''

Under Charles V and Philip II Spain mounted the first big push for domination of the European state system, according to Dehio. Charles V came of age in 1515, inheriting both the Spanish and Hapsburg empires, including the Netherlands, and battled France throughout the middle sixteenth century with considerable success before abdicating in favor of his son, Philip II. After conquering Portugal (which had in turn taken much of the Asian trade from Venice) in 1580, ''Philip held both the Spanish and the Portuguese colonial empires in his mighty hand. Did not this colonial monopoly appear to be the harbinger of Spanish supremacy in Europe? Was not the end of the European system of states in sight? . . . To understand how it was saved, we must take stock of England'' (p. 53). Since France was unable to contain the Hapsburgs, England emerged as Spain's adversary: ''Thus, the supreme Continental power, seemingly at the peak of its strength, [faced] the small and untested island power . . . . Now, for the first time in the European setting, two ways of life confronted each other. Their derivatives have remained face to face right down to our own times'' (p. 55). The decisive showdown came in 1588, when the Spanish armada, ''like a tract of continent on the high seas'' (p. 56), was decimated by the longer-range artillery and experienced seamanship of the British under Sir Francis Drake.[37] The decades after 1588 saw Spain's gradual downfall, which culminated in Spain's big land defeat in 1643 at Rocroi.[38]

The defeat of Spain, according to Dehio, laid the foundations for the second great drive for world domination, under Louis XIV of France.

The defeat of the Armada dried out the veins of the Spanish lands while it swelled those of the opposing countries. However, the political and economic decline was so gentle that . . . not until the Peace of the Pyrenees in 1659 and Louis XIV's assumption of power in 1661 did the wave of France gather majestically, to attain its proud crest a century after the defeat of the Armada.

The broad trough between these two waves is packed with incident in many forms and ramifications. But they lack paramount significance (p. 66).

Louis XIV, like Philip II, found England in his way, and the English defeat of the French fleet in 1692 repeated the experience of the Spanish armada 104 years earlier. After this defeat, according to Dehio, France had ''passed her zenith,'' but her decline, ''like that of Spain before, ensued by degrees.'' Eight years after the defeat of the French fleet, the dying king of Spain left all of Spain's dominions to Louis's grandson, and France fought to claim them in the War of the Spanish Succession,

37. ''The Armada shared the fate of the Persian fleet at Salamis [in Ancient Greece] and foreshadowed that of the Russian fleet at Tsushima [in the 1905 Russo–Japanese War]: in each case, the squadrons of a giant continental power with long voyages behind them were sent to the bottom in the home waters of the small opposing naval power'' (p. 56).

38. Sweden having defeated the Hapsburgs the previous year, the Treaty of Westphalia in 1648 saw Sweden and France the big winners, Spain and the Hapsburgs the losers.

1701–13. France was defeated by a coalition again led by England, and France signed peace treaties in 1713 and 1714.[39]

The next drive, at the end of the century, again came from France under Napoleon and again ran up against Britain. The British declared war in 1803, and the French attempt to invade England resulted in yet another French naval defeat, in 1805. The French fleet regrouped in the Mediterranean and was decisively beaten by Adm. Horatio Nelson at Cape Trafalgar, near Gibraltar.[40] It had been just over a century since the French fleet was decimated under Louis XIV.

Shortly after Trafalgar, "Napoleon was destroyed on land, and this defeat, in turn, was an effect of his inability to master Britain at sea, for otherwise he never would have had to march on Moscow" (p. 164). The invasion of Russia in 1812 was a disaster for Napoleon, and his defeat was ratified at the Congress of Vienna in 1815, which shifted borders westward to France's disadvantage.

The next drive for domination came from Germany. With the defeat of France, Germany moved into the vacuum and began to grow and evolve in new ways:

The economic strength which the early stages of industrialization had brought to this agricultural country made it vulnerable as industrialization advanced; self-sufficiency was transformed into dependence on foreign raw materials and markets . . . . This sense of constriction also became increasingly tangible in foreign affairs (p. 225–26).

Dehio argues that as Germany industrialized and expanded into the world scene, it found itself competing with Britain everywhere (p. 231).

[T]he building of the German battle fleet, designed for decisive operations in British coastal waters . . . constituted a direct threat to Britain's insular strength. The prosperity of Germany enabled her to embark on a breathtaking armaments race. Moreover, Germany's lunge into the Near East pressed the more disturbingly on the [British] Empire's major artery since the Reich had no need, as France had had under Napoleon I, to make claims on the sea route (p. 236).

The German challenge was, however, like those of Spain and France, defeated in World War I by a coalition led by Britain (with the addition of the United States and Japan, which in Dehio's terms increased the insular strength of the coalition). But Britain's costly "victory" in World War I "sucked at the vitals of her world position" (p. 240). The power of America thus emerged as the crucial new insular factor in the world.

Tragically, "America, unprepared in spirit for the global role suddenly proferred her, rejected it, and withdrew into the 'splendid isolation' of her giant island"

---

39. Austria emerged the big winner. Twenty years later, however, in 1733, France, Spain, and Savoy declared war on a growing Austria and won; the Turks also defeated Austria in 1737–39. By 1755 France again faced England at sea and lost, and by 1763 the end of the Seven Years' War left Austria whittled back down to size. These 1733–63 wars centering on France, Austria, and England correspond with Quincy Wright's "less severe" cluster of wars.

40. According to Dehio, though, the critical moment had come seven years earlier, when a British fleet under Nelson destroyed a French fleet of equal size in the Mediterranean (at Aboukir in 1798), ruining Napoleon's Egyptian expedition. "At the cost of only 900 dead, Britain was able to thwart the grand-scale sortie of a dominant Continental power into the world outside" (p. 153).

(p. 244). The "withdrawal of Russia and the United States from the world scene" destabilized the shaky peace of Versailles, allowing some in Germany to "misread the situation" (p. 256). Thus Germany mounted another full-blown attempt at world domination in World War II—but Dehio argues that, although "still vigorous and vital, [Germany] was in fact engaged in a death struggle" (p. 259).

Dehio notes that the world wars transformed the European balance-of-power system into a bipolar world order, raising the possibility "that the great game of the modern era . . . has been played to a finish" (p. 263). But in fact the new "global order," which is "going through its birth pangs," has recreated the pattern of an insular power (the United States) trying to contain a Continental power (the Soviet Union) (p. 266). "Once again, the continental and insular principles are face to face, stripped down to their essence and at the same time magnified to global proportions" (p. 267).

Dehio closes hopefully, in 1948, since the new world order faces different dangers than the "peculiar mechanism of European history" (p. 268). But in a 1960 epilogue, Dehio argues that Soviet technological development after World War II aims ultimately at supporting a drive for "communist world domination" (p. 275). Furthermore, the insular principle is "gravely menaced" by new technology, since naval power can no longer protect an island from rockets and aircraft (p. 281). Dehio suggests that "a broad and deep current in world politics has begun to favor the continental principle" and threatens to bring about the "decline of the West" (p. 286). But, although the Western powers have lost their trump cards, "they have by no means lost the game" (p. 287). What is required is renewed strength and vigilance:

Is not the nightmare that weighs upon us—a third world war—the product of experience in an earlier epoch unthinkingly applied to the present? To answer this question in the affirmative, and to ignore the need to prepare for the worst, would be a dangerous error. God grant that the world of Western culture may not suffer the fate of the ancient world when the cry of "panem et circenses" could still be heard even as the barbarians, thirsting for plunder, burst into the limes (p. 287–88).

This quote, which ends Dehio's book, conveys the deeply conservative flavor of his approach.

Arnold Toynbee

Toynbee (1954 9:322) structures the past five centuries around the same timing that Wright and Dehio followed. He builds from Wright's "more severe" war concentrations (every other long wave)[41] a roughly 115-year cycle of war and peace (table 5.2). The three regular modern cycles are dated 1568–1672, 1672–1792, and 1792–

41. Toynbee describes long waves in war as having an average span of 57.66 years. (He really does state their periodicity to two decimal points, which is to say within four days!) By comparison, Toynbee finds war-and-peace intervals in combined Hellenic, Western, and Chinese history averaging 44.76 years in length (p. 287).

Table 5.2. Toynbee's War-and-Peace Cycle

Phase		Overture (1494-1568)	First Regular Cycle (1568-1672)	Second Regular Cycle (1672-1792)	Third Regular Cycle (1792-1914)	Fourth Cycle (1914 -)
(i)	Premonitory Wars (the Prelude)	--	--	$1667\text{-}8^1$	--	$1911\text{-}12^2$
(ii)	The General War	$1494\text{-}1525^3$	$1568\text{-}1609^4$	$1672\text{-}1713^5$	$1792\text{-}1815^6$	1914-18
(iii)	The Breathing-space	1525-36	1609-18	1713-33	1815-48	1918-39
(iv)	Supplementary Wars (the Epilogue)	$1536\text{-}59^7$	1618-48	$1733\text{-}63^8$	$1848\text{-}71^9$	$1939\text{-}45^{10}$
(v)	The General Peace	1559-68	1648-72	1763-92	1871-1914	--

1 Louis XIV's attack on the Spanish Netherlands.
2 The Turco-Italian War of 1911-12; The Turco-Balkan Wars of 1912-13.
3 1494-1503, 1510-16, and 1521-25.
4 1568-1609 in the Spanish Hapsburg Monarchy; 1562-98 in France.
5 1672-78, 1688-97, and 1702-13.
6 1792-1802, 1803-14, and 1815.
7 1536-38, 1542-44, [1544-46 and 1549-50, England v. France], [1546-52, Schmalkald League of Protestant Princes in the Holy Roman Empire v. Charles V], 1552-59.
8 1733-35, 1740-48, and 1756-63.
9 1848-49, 1853-56, 1859 [1861-65, civil war in the United States; 1862-67, French occupation of Mexico], 1864, 1866, and 1870-71.
10 This recrudescent general war of 1939-45 was heralded by a splutter of premonitory wars: the Japanese attack on China, launched in Manchuria in 1931; the Italo-Abyssinian War of 1935-36; the War of 1936-39 in Spain; and the fateful one-day campaign in the Rhineland on March 7, 1936, which was to pay for its bloodlessness at compound interest in the holocausts of the years 1939-45.
Source: Toynbee (1954: 255). Copyright Oxford University Press.

1914 (p. 255). Each cycle begins with a general war and is followed by a "breathing space", "supplementary wars," and, finally, a general peace.

Toynbee's (p. 255) dating of "general war" periods corresponds with Dehio's "drives for world domination": the first of these, in 1568–1609, corresponds with Philip II's wars and the defeat of the Spanish armada by Britain.[42] Toynbee's second cycle begins with general war in 1672–1713, corresponding with Louis XIV's drive for supremacy.[43] His third general war period, 1792–1815, corresponds with the Napoleonic challenge.[44] And the fourth cycle begins with general war in 1914–18.[45]

Toynbee sees similar patterns in each of the four cycles. In each, a centrally located Continental power, "with sally-ports opening into the back-yards of the countries that were . . . the stakes of contention," strives aggressively to break out of encirclement. This role, corresponding with Dehio's Continental powers, was played successively by the Spanish Hapsburg monarchy, by France (twice), and by Germany. Like Dehio, Toynbee suggests that by 1952 the Soviet Union had inherited the role (p. 258).

42. After a breathing space (1609–18), Toynbee's "supplementary war" period consisted of the Thirty Years' War (1618–48), followed by a general peace from 1648 to 1672.

43. The supplementary war period (1733–63) contained the Seven Years' War, followed by general peace (1763–92).

44. With a supplementary war period in 1848–71 (German, Italian, Crimean wars).

45. The supplementary war period, 1939–45, is considered anomalous by Toynbee.

Toynbee notes the correspondence of his war-and-peace cycle with the long wave (pp. 254, 287). Whereas Kondratieff claimed that long waves cause the cyclical recurrence of war, Toynbee takes the opposite position:

The apparitions of economic 'long waves' might not be hallucinations but might be economic reflections of political realities that had already been 'a going concern' in the Modern Western World for some three hundred years before the outbreak of the Industrial Revolution in Great Britain (p. 235).

This argument resembles that of the war school of the long wave debate.[46]

Toynbee explains the war-and-peace cycle as a result of a "Generation Cycle in the transmission of a social heritage":

The survivors of a generation that has been of military age during a bout of war will be shy, for the rest of their lives, of bringing a repetition of this tragic experience either upon themselves or upon their children, and . . . therefore the psychological resistance of any move towards the breaking of a peace . . . is likely to be prohibitively strong until a new generation . . . has had time to grow up and to come into power. On the same showing, a bout of war, once precipitated, is likely to persist until the peace-bred generation that has light-heartedly run into war has been replaced, in its turn, by a war-worn generation.

Thus Toynbee explains the alternation of war and peace periods along the long wave "as effects of the periodic breach that is made in the continuity of a social tradition every time that an experience has to be transmitted by the generation that has experienced it in its own life to a generation that has merely learnt of it at second hand" (p. 322).

This generation cycle theory[47] derives from that of Wright (see above), but whereas it explains Wright's 50-year war cycle plausibly, it does not account for the 115-year cycle that Toynbee builds out of the "more severe" war periods. The longer cycle, Toynbee argues, could arise from a "concatenation of four generations" needed to erase the memory of general war sufficiently for a new generation to "have the heart to re-perform the tragedy on a grand scale"—even though two generations would suffice to "give the next generation the nerve to embark on supplementary wars of limited scope" (p. 326).

If this explanation is accepted, however, the case of World War II, which Toynbee includes with "supplementary wars," becomes particularly problematical. "The structural novelty of the fourth cycle was . . . the portentous one of capping one general war with another one of still greater severity, atrocity, and inconclusiveness, instead of following it up with a burst of milder, but nevertheless more conclusive, supplementary wars" (p. 254). This irregularity undermines the generation cycle theory of war fluctuations: "If it normally requires two or three inter-generational caesuras to nerve a society to plunge into a general war again, the reduplication of a

46. But Toynbee does not cite the war school proponents.
47. On generation cycles, see also Beck (1974) and Huntington (1977).

general war after a single caesura is manifestly something contrary to Human Nature'' (p. 326). At least it is contrary to Toynbee's theory.[48]

Two other ''peace researchers'' following in Wright's tradition in this period are relevant to Toynbee's generation cycle theory. The first is Pitirim Sorokin. The theme that grandchildren reflect values of their grandparents runs ''like a red thread'' through Sorokin's writings, Mensch (1979:5) observes. Sorokin (1957:561), however, does not find the evidence of war cycles convincing. ''No regular periodicity is noticeable'' in war and peace periods. ''Instead, we find an enormous variety of rhythms. After prolonged wars several times there occur long periods of peace, but not always.'' Sorokin dismisses Quincy Wright's 50-year war cycles as unproven and unprovable and likewise refutes the possibility of war cycles in a study of 2150 years of Chinese history (pp. 561–63).[49] The generation cycle, according to Sorokin, would not give rise to a war cycle because, in fact, ''periods of peace as long as one quarter of a century have been exceedingly rare,'' so that ''almost every generation (25 to 30 years) in the past, with very few exceptions, has been a witness of, or an actor in, war phenomena'' (p. 559).[50]

The work of Lewis F. Richardson (1960b) would seem to be more supportive of Toynbee's approach. Richardson finds that the frequency of retaliatory wars drops off in the years following a war (as ''forgiving and forgetting'' takes place) but picks up again after thirty years. Richardson speculates that ''the generation who had not fought in the earlier war, but who were brought up on tales about its romance, heroism, and about the wickedness of the enemy, became influential from 30 to 60 years after the war ended and so delayed the process of forgetting and forgiving'' (p. 200). Richardson himself does not, however, subscribe to a cyclical (or a secular trend) theory of war, finding war distributions to be more of a ''random scatter'' (p. 136).

A. F. K. Organski's Power Transition

While Toynbee's generation cycle embodies the psychological elements in Quincy Wright's approach, other scholars have been more interested in the material or economic elements that might lead to a regular recurrence of war. These approaches have drawn on the ''power transition'' theory of A. F. K. Organski in which the relative growth of national economic capabilities is seen to affect the conditions for war. While Organski's theory is not explicitly cyclical, it becomes integral to later cyclical theories.[51]

The power transition theory is an offshoot from the general approach of ''realism'' in the study of international politics, of which Hans Morgenthau became the preemi-

48. Colby wrote in 1926: ''As wounded men may limp through life, so our war minds may not regain the balance of their thoughts for decades'' (p. 15). Nonetheless, little more than a decade later those ''war minds'' were again returning to war.
49. See also Lee (1931) on periodic Chinese wars.
50. Sorokin (1957:564) also rejects ''linear theories of war evolution.''
51. Beginning with Farrar's synthesis of the power transition approach with Wright's ''cost of wars'' approach and Toynbee's 100-year cycle (see below).

nent spokesperson after World War II. Realism "maintains the autonomy of the political sphere" from economics (Morgenthau [1948] 1967:14). The purpose of realism is to contribute to the development of the study of politics in terms of its own standards, based on interests and power and not on either economic or moral standards (p. 14). Power, according to Morgenthau, derives from three psychological influences of one actor over another: expectation of benefits, fear of disadvantages, and respect or love for people or institutions (p. 27). Elements of national power include such economic factors as resources, industrial capacity, and population ([1948] 1967:chap. 9). Thus, as in classical mercantilism, national wealth and economic strength serve politics.[52] A nation's wealth directly affects its ability to wage war as well as to give or respond to other incentives and threats short of war.

Organski (1958)[53] follows on Morgenthau and the realist tradition in emphasizing *power:* "Shifts in the international distribution of power . . . create the conditions likely to lead to at least the most important wars, and power is the most important determinant of whether a war will be won or lost. And power, again, is the resource that leaders hope to preserve or to increase by resorting to armed conflict (Organski and Kugler 1980:4). And like other realists, Organski sees economic factors as crucial in building national power.[54]

But Organski parts company with the traditional realist balance of power theory. Balance of power theory assumes a set of roughly equal nations that form alliances based on power considerations and that maintain peace by maintaining the "balance" and preventing predominance by one nation. Organski, however, finds this to be historically inaccurate. "Balance" is unusual; it is more common for one country to dominate the international system.[55] Thus Organski assumes a *hierarchical* world order in which there is a "most powerful nation" at the "very apex of the pyramid" (Organski and Kugler 1980:19). Just below are other great powers that have less ability to influence other nations and that receive fewer benefits from the international order.

Organski argues that differentials in national economic growth affect the rise or fall of different countries' *relative capabilities* in this international hierarchy and that these changes underlie major wars:

The manner and speed of national growth and development change the pools of resources available to nations . . . . If one nation gains significantly in power, its improved position relative to that of other nations frightens them and induces them to try to reverse this gain by war. Or, vice versa, a nation gaining on an adversary will try to make its advantage permanent by reducing its opponent by force of arms. Either way, changes in power are considered causae belli (Organski and Kugler 1980:8, 13).

52. Current neorealists such as Gilpin (see below) and Krasner are thus sometimes called neomercantilists.
53. The core ideas put forth by Organski (1958) are elaborated in Organski and Kugler (1980).
54. Organski (and Organski and Kugler) in fact use national income as an index of national power or capabilities.
55. Britain did not act as a "balancer" in European politics but acted to maintain her own dominant position, according to Organski.

According to Organski, *challenges* to the world order arise from changes in relative national power:

The powerful and dissatisfied nations are usually those that have grown to full power after the existing international order was fully established and the benefits already allocated . . . . The challengers, for their part, are seeking to establish a new place for themselves in international society . . . . They have reason to believe that they can rival or surpass in power the dominant nation, and they are unwilling to accept a subordinate position in international affairs when dominance would give them much greater benefits and privileges.[56]

Thus, Organski argues, the greatest danger of war lies not in the preponderance of one nation but in a balance of power, since equally distributed power encourages challenges to the status quo. War is most likely when challengers catch up to or surpass the dominant power, and peace is most likely when one nation or coalition predominates so clearly as to make a challenge to the status quo impractical.

It is not hard to put together Organski's theoretical "challengers" with Dehio's historical "challenges," which, as discussed above, correspond roughly with Toynbee's war cycles. Organski and Dehio represent conservative approaches in terms of the prescriptions flowing out of their theories. Protection of the status quo is the best guarantee of peace; erosion of American predominance should be resisted.

L. L. Farrar, Jr.

Farrar (1977) combines Organski's power transition with Toynbee's one-hundred-year war cycle. Farrar adopts Toynbee's dating of hegemonic wars every hundred years with smaller war periods in between.

Farrar finds a repeating sequence in historical data of "hegemonic wars" alternating with "adjusting wars," with "probing wars" scattered in between. These categorizations are shown in figure 5.3 superimposed on Quincy Wright's graph of battle frequencies. Farrar's war phases coincide with those of Wright and Toynbee but have a different terminology:

Wright	Toynbee	Farrar
Major wars	General war	Hegemonic wars
(peace)	Breathing-space	Probing wars
Minor wars	Supplementary wars	Adjusting wars
(peace)	General peace	Probing wars

Farrar lists several possible causes of the existence of this cyclical pattern and of its length (94 to 130 years in all). Among these causes are such psychological explanations as Toynbee's generation cycle, which he finds unsatisfying. Farrar prefers two explanations based on economic factors—Wright's cost of war argument and Organski's power transition argument.

---

56. Organski ([1958] 1968:364–67) quoted in Organski and Kugler (1980:19–20).

Figure 5.3. Farrar's Modern Battles by Type of War

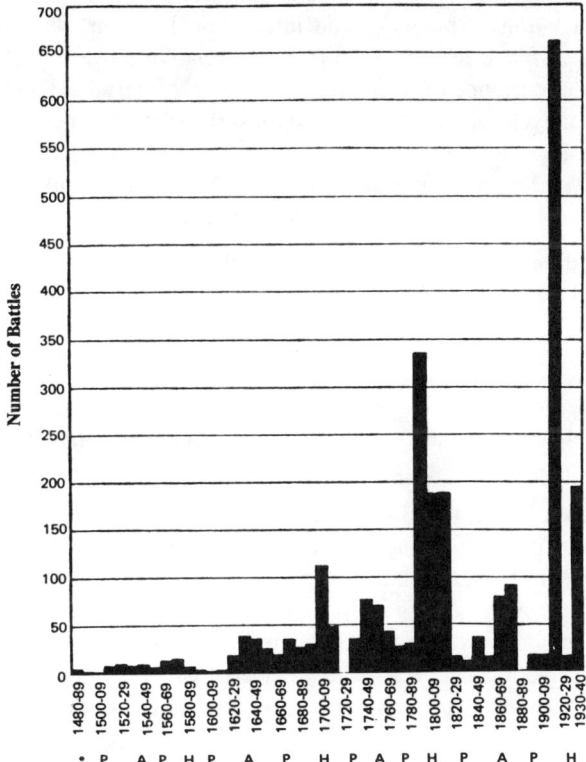

Abbreviations refer to types of wars: P = *probing war;* A = *adjusting war;*
H = *hegemonic war.*

Note: Graph represents number of important battles per decade in modern
civilization, 1480-1940. Data from Wright (1942: 627).

Source: Farrar (1977: 164) by permission of *International Interactions,*
Gordon and Breach, Science Publishers, Inc.

The cost of war argument holds that countries tend to store up a surplus for war purposes, then fight a major war until it is concluded or money runs out, then begin saving up again. "War can be seen to require a surplus of material-human resources," argues Farrar, and hence "can continue only as long as the surplus exists and must be discontinued when the surplus is either actually exhausted or seen to be exhausted" (p. 171). The rapid augmentation of Europe's economic surplus-generating capability over the past five centuries did not shorten the war cycle's length, according to Farrar, because war itself incorporated the new technology. "The time required to expend surplus [on war] consequently remained relatively constant" (p. 171). This cost of war argument, however, applies to fifty-year rather than one-hundred-year war cycles. In the latter area, Farrar draws on the power transition theory.

Farrar follows Organski in focusing on the dynamic nature of power-seeking in the European state system (pp. 166–67). Like Organski, he argues that economic factors help determine a nation's "power" in the international system. National capabilities change at different rates, leading to shifts in the relative power of different nations that underlie the recurrence of hegemonic war. Farrar interprets the duration of the one-hundred-year cycle as the time required for shifts in relative power to occur in the international system. Periods of probing wars (low violence) alternate first with adjusting wars (middle violence) and then with hegemonic wars (high violence), taking about 94 to 130 years for a complete sequence.

Probing wars test the existing status quo and indicate that it is sound in the sense of reflecting the distribution of power . . . . But internal change meanwhile continues and makes that status quo less realistic. These pressures for change of the status quo eventually precipitate new adjusting wars which alter the status quo to conform more closely with the new distribution of power. This new status quo is then tested again in probing wars . . . . Hegemonic wars follow . . . when new adjustments in the status quo coincide with the attempt of a great power . . . to dominate the system . . . . [They are] the most extreme form of an adjusting war (p. 167).

Farrar thus casts the power transition theory in a cyclical model, explaining the cycle of hegemonic war in terms of long-term changes in international power distribution.

Farrar's approach, then, sees the hegemony cycle as a roughly one-hundred-year process in which a country emerges from a period of hegemonic war as the dominant nation but is eventually overtaken in economic strength by a rising "challenger." The century-long period between bouts of hegemonic war represents the time required for major changes to occur in the relative capabilities of the leading nation and the "catch up" nation or nations.

Farrar's synthesis pulls together the main elements around which the current debate on long cycles of war and hegemony has coalesced. That debate is the subject of the next chapter.

CHAPTER SIX

The War/Hegemony Debate 2: The Current Debate

As I noted in the last chapter, the current debate grows out of the confluence of Toynbee's long war cycle and Organski's theory of military challenges to the hierarchical world order. In the current debate, as in the long wave debate (chapter 3), three theoretical groupings, or research schools, have developed (see fig. 6.1). One school is descended from Toynbee and Wright, with the incorporation of Organski's and Farrar's influence. This is the current *leadership cycle* school, led by Modelski. A second school, led by Wallerstein, is the *world-system* school, which has engaged the Toynbee/Organski problem of war and hegemony from a Marxist perspective. This school has interacted, but not agreed, with the leadership cycle school. The third school, shown at the right, is the *power transition* school, growing out of Organski's approach.

Each current research tradition grows out of a more general approach to international relations—peace research, neo-Marxism, and realism, respectively. And these three approaches in turn correspond roughly with the three world views (liberal, revolutionary, and conservative) discussed in chapter 1. In general, the peace research approach is oriented toward the quantitative and qualitative study of war to understand its causes and bring about its reduction. The neo-Marxist approach emphasizes the importance of the world-system structured by the inequality (and unequal dependency) between core and periphery and seeks to change the underlying socioeconomic context that leads to war. The realist approach focuses on national power and balance-of-power politics and seeks "timeless" laws of national behavior.

These differences in approach are reflected in different foci for the three current schools in the war/hegemony debate. The leadership cycle school focuses on the role of global war in establishing a new international order under a world leader roughly every century. The neo-Marxist world-system school focuses on hegemony and rivalry in the core of the world economy, linking hegemonic cycles to pairs of long waves. The power transition school focuses on changes in national power and their effects on war and hegemony.

Hegemony

The hegemony cycle is based on the idea that one country rises, during hegemonic war, to a preeminent position in a hierarchical international

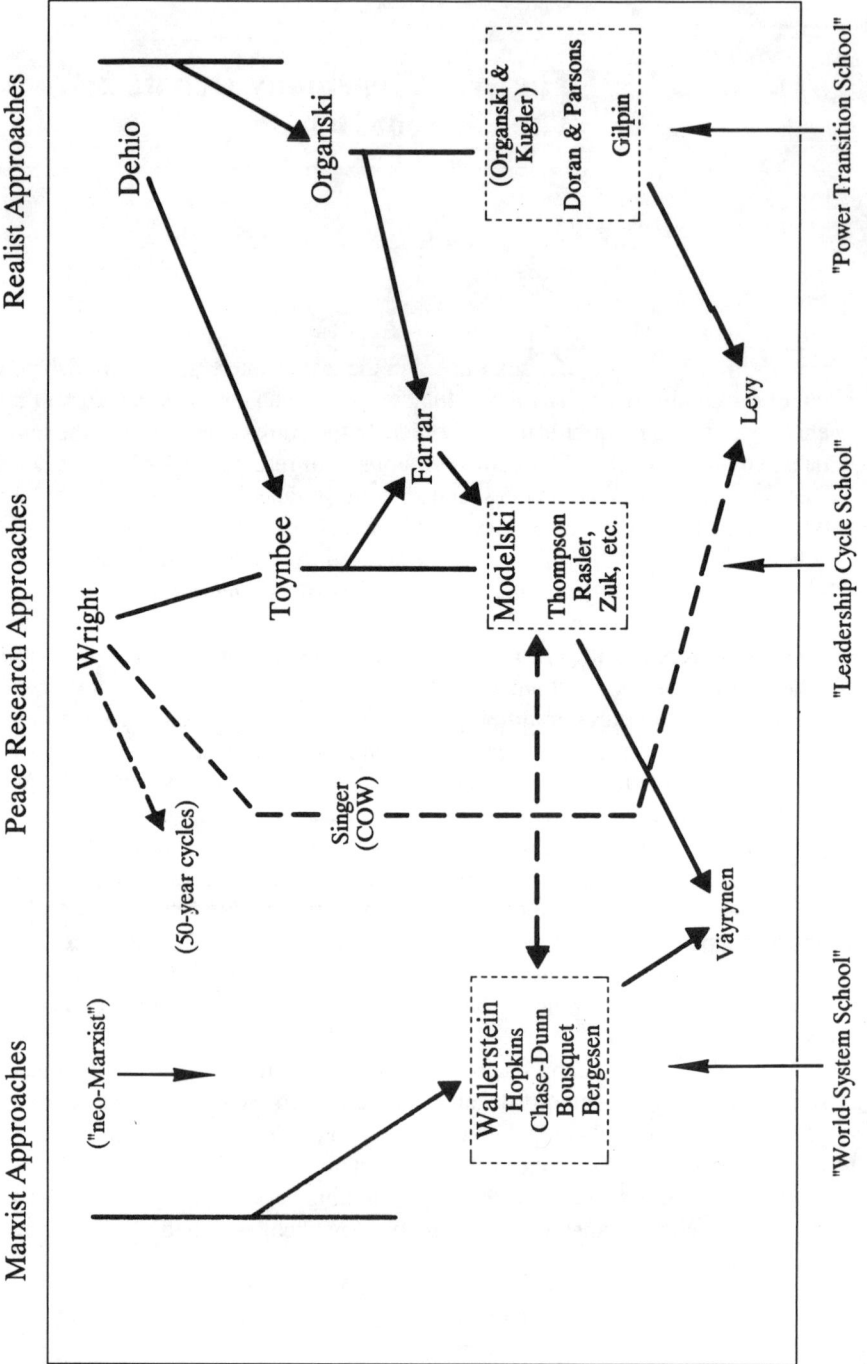

Figure 6.1. The Current War/Hegemony Debate

Realist Approaches

Peace Research Approaches

Marxist Approaches

Dehio

Organski

(Organski & Kugler)

Doran & Parsons

Gilpin

"Power Transition School"

Farrar

Levy

"Leadership Cycle School"

Wright

Toynbee

Modelski

Thompson Rasler, Zuk, etc.

(50-year cycles)

Singer (COW)

Väyrynen

"neo-Marxist"

Wallerstein Hopkins Chase-Dunn Bousquet Bergesen

"World-System School"

order, a position from which it eventually falls and to which another country succeeds. This preeminent position is called *hegemony*.

Hegemony has different meanings: some scholars refer mainly to military and political predominance, while others refer to economic predominance. I use the term in a broad sense including both. Also, some scholars (for example, Doran 1971) use hegemony to refer to the failed attempts at military supremacy within the great power system (for example, Napoleonic France), while others use it to refer to the leading country emerging victorious after such a challenge is suppressed (for example, post-Napoleonic Britain). The latter usage is more common, and I will follow it.[1]

In referring to a preeminent nation as "hegemonic" I do not mean to imply a necessarily oppressive or inequitable arrangement (as the flavor of the term sometimes implies) but only the "dictionary" sense: "leadership; preponderant ascendancy or authority, as among states."[2] Modelski prefers the term *world leadership,* with its cooperative rather than exploitive overtones, while Organski refers to "one country at the apex of the pyramid" of world politics.

Hegemony seems to have acquired two connotations, positive and negative. In the positive image, "benign hegemony," the leading country takes on the burden of maintaining international order and pays a disproportionate price for doing so. In this approach, international order is seen as a "public good" benefiting all countries, supported by the hegemonic power. Kindleberger (1973:28) argues that "the international economic and monetary system needs leadership, a country which is prepared, consciously or unconsciously, under some system of rules that it has internalized, to set standards of conduct for other countries; and to seek to get others to follow them, to take on an undue share of the burdens of the system." Britain had this role from 1815 to 1913, and the United States after 1945, according to Kindleberger, but in the interwar years Britain was unable, and the United States was unwilling, to accept this leadership role; Kindleberger sees in this lack of leadership the main causes for the severity of the depression of the 1930s. "Hegemonic stability theory" (see Keohane 1980), to quote McKeown's (1983:73) summary, argues that "it is the power of hegemonic states that leads to the emergence of open international economic systems" with free trade, benefiting all.[3]

In the negative image of hegemony, the preeminence of one country is seen as an exploitative dominance of the world system gained by one country over other competitors. Kurth (1971:20) uses the term *hegemony* to refer to great power domination of small states.[4] Kurth notes that since World War II, "while the practice

1. This usage includes the shared understanding that the period after World War II was one of American hegemony.

2. Webster's Collegiate Dictionary, S. V. "hegemony."

3. McKeown (1983:89–90) himself is doubtful about this, however. While such a theory has "obvious attractions," consensus on it is "at best premature. The theory has been plagued by numerous conceptual ambiguities and omissions . . . Its predictive accuracy is poor." McKeown suggests instead (for the 19th and 20th c.) that open trading systems occur at times of general world prosperity and that closure of the system occurs at times of general depression.

4. A great power controlling a network of these states in a region has a "hegemonial system." Kurth lists ten such systems since 1648.

of hegemony increased, especially by Americans, the mention of hegemony declined, especially by Americans.''[5] In current usage by the world-system school (see below), *hegemony* implies that one core country dominates exploitive core-periphery relations.

These are some of the different implications the term *hegemony* can evoke. Different views of hegemony will be elaborated under each school.

The Leadership Cycle School

George Modelski (1978), like Farrar (1977), builds on Toynbee's roughly one-hundred-year cycle of general war. Modelski argues (1978) that a "global political system . . . defined as the institutions and arrangements for the management of global problems or relations" has existed since about the year 1500. In contrast to Wallerstein's (1974) contention that the world system arose from capitalism, Modelski's (1981:63) approach is "distinguished by the emphasis it lays on the autonomy of global political [versus economic] processes."

Modelski (1978) defines "world powers" as those units that monopolize the function of order-keeping in the global system. Since 1500 this role has been played by four states in turn: Portugal, the Netherlands, Britain, and the United States. Each power remained dominant for about a century (except Britain, which repeated for another century), and each of these centuries constitutes one "world leadership cycle."[6]

Each cycle begins with a period of weak organization that gives way to "global war" (roughly corresponding in dating to Toynbee's periods of general war). One world power emerges from the global war as the dominant power and maintains order in the world system. However, "the time comes when the energy that built this order begins to run down" (p. 217) and competitors come forward. The system becomes multipolar, order gradually dissolves, and the cycle returns to its starting point with the coming of the next global war.

Modelski dates the five "global war" periods and the world powers that arose from them as follows:

1494–1517	Portugal
1579–1609	Netherlands
1688–1713	Britain (1)
1792–1815	Britain (2)
1914–1945	United States

Modelski's account of the five cycles since 1500 parallels Dehio's history but emphasizes the winners rather than the losers. Whereas Dehio stresses the role of the

---

5. He credits Charles de Gaulle with keeping the term *hegemony* alive after World War II, in referring to the "two hegemonies" (the Soviet Union and United States in Eastern and Western Europe).

6. Modelski thus argues that "a succession of world powers shaped the global system" (1978:216). The world leadership cycle has "produced . . . the emergence of the nation-state as the dominant organization in world politics" (1978:230–31). Nation-states defined the identity of successive global systems, and global power in its turn strengthened those states that attained it.

unsuccessful aspirants to world hegemony (Spain, France, Germany), Modelski emphasizes the successful powers that built world orders based on control of shipping and trade (Portugal, Netherlands,[7] Britain, United States). The two schemes can thus be combined as follows:

hegemonic powers:	Portugal	Netherlands	Britain	Britain	United States
failed aspirants:	Spain		France	France	Germany	(USSR)

Modelski (1984b:19) argues that a coalition formed in each global war to contain the challenger. In the century after each global war (except after 1710), the winning coalition fractured and one of its members became the new challenger (p. 23).

In his historical interpretation of the past five centuries, Modelski (1978:218) writes that around 1500 "the global system was a dispersed one" lacking "provision for self-maintenance and defence against interlopers" despite the system of long-distance trade linking Europe with Asia (controled at the western end by Venice). Venice, which monopolized trade with Alexandria, was the Mediterranean's "leading power and has since served as the model for later world powers."

"The kings of Portugal determined to break into that system," according to Modelski (p. 218). In 1498 Vasco da Gama reached India by sea, and, "in the series of swift naval campaigns that followed, a string of bases was established and rival fleets were wiped off the oceans." A series of major wars in Italy drastically curtailed the power of Venice, and by 1515 "a new order had been established. . . . Portugal rose to global status in circumstances of severe conflict of global dimensions." Portugal monopolized the Asian trade and explored Africa and Brazil.[8]

By the second half of the sixteenth century, "Portugal . . . was feeling the strain of maintaining this far-flung system on a rather slender home base" (p. 219). Pressure from Spain mounted, and when Spain in 1580 seized Portugal, "the Portuguese global system was merged with the domains of the Spanish Hapsburgs. For a short time (but in truth only for a fleeting moment) the union seemed to be raising an intercontinental structure of towering proportions, but the defeat of the Great Armada (1588) soon punctured this illusion" (p. 219).

With the fall of Portugal and the failure of Spain's drive for dominance, Spain's rebellious subjects in the Netherlands came out on top:

These wealthy provinces derived much of their income from trade with Lisbon, and Antwerp had until a short time before served as the banking and distribution center of the Portuguese system. But when the King of Spain, some years after his success in Portugal, banned all rebel

---

7. Dehio does not see Portugal or the Netherlands as what Modelski would call a world power but instead stresses the superiority of England from as early as 1588.

8. While Wallerstein (1974) sees Spain as dominant in the 16th c. (see below), Modelski argues that "it was Portugal that first seized the heart of the preexisting world system and thus drastically altered its structure" (p. 219). Although "there is something to be said for describing the system as bipolar," since the two powers divided the periphery in the Treaty of Tordesillas, nonetheless "Spain operated on the fringes and never developed a truly global outlook."

trade, the Dutch took matters into their own hands, sailed to the East and proceeded to capture the spice trade from the Portuguese (p. 220).

By 1609, when the United Provinces signed a truce with Spain, "the essentials of the Dutch global system were in place." Drawing support from England and France (who opposed Spain), the Dutch "maintained a pattern of global activity as intricate and possibly even more daring than that of their predecessors." The Dutch navy established its clear superiority over the Spanish, and by around 1660 three-quarters of the seagoing merchant ships of Europe sailed under the Dutch flag. "Control of the Baltic trade and a near monopoly of the carrying trade in Europe was combined with influence in Venice, a firm hold over the spice trade of the Indies and substantial interests in Africa and the Americas" (p. 220).

In the latter part of the seventeenth century, however, the Dutch encountered French pressure and had to ally with England to hold back France. The great wars against Louis XIV continued until his defeat in 1713.

The Dutch had held their own against the French, but the price was the effective transfer of global power to what had just become Great Britain. As the English navy took over the chief burden of fighting the French on the high seas and the Dutch concentrated on the land campaigns, the Dutch navy lost the impetus of its expansion and began to suffer neglect (p. 221).

The British global system was born in the struggle against the French and was, like the Dutch system before it, "firmly anchored in the control of world trade" (p. 221). Amsterdam, tied in with the British system, retained its position as the center of investment finance but fell behind in maritime strength and trade. Portugal granted important privileges to English merchants in 1703, and the Lisbon-London trade siphoned off gold and diamonds from overseas Portuguese possessions. Even Spanish Latin America was opened slightly to English trade. "Thus without assuming direct control over the colonial territories of earlier world powers England put in place the superstructure whereby the cream might be skimmed off the top and the whole fitted into a global economic pattern" (p. 222). By 1763 England had gained strength in Asia and the Americas (against France), the English East India Company "had become a great Asian power," and England was playing the role of "power balancer" on the European continent, preventing the rise of any power that aspired to continental supremacy.

After the American War of Independence, the French Revolution, and the Napoleonic wars, "another generation of global warfare was required before a global order was reestablished and reaffirmed by the settlements of 1814–15" (p. 222). The resulting second cycle of British dominance, according to Modelski, "repeated some of the essential properties of the first: the European balance . . . ; the command of the sea, and a controlling position in extra-European and world trade." But novel elements also appeared—"the development of London into the center of world banking and shipping; newly emerging industrial and technological superiority" (p. 223).

In the second half of the nineteenth century, the world order again "began to lose vigor'' (p. 223). European and American challengers broke Britain's industrial monopoly; railways cut into the importance of Britain's dominance in shipping. In the world depression that followed the year 1873, ''commercial competition grew fierce and put British traders on the defensive for the first time in two centuries. Britain's industrial mainstays, coal and cotton, ceased to be world growth leaders.'' By 1900 ''it had become clear to many that Pax Britannica was well past its prime and that the world system was swiftly losing its ordering capacities'' (p. 223).

The ensuing global war period, in Modelski's framework, includes both world wars. The transition to U.S. leadership was not smooth. The outcome of World War I

seemed to assure the United States of a leading role in the . . . laying of the foundations of the new international order. But President Wilson was repudiated at home, and the United States neither took up the position that was its own for the taking nor proffered an alternative scheme for world order. The resulting vacuum of authority attracted another challenge and another cataclysmic clash (p. 223).

Modelski treats World Wars I and II ''as one generation-long period of global conflict forming the world order that emerged in 1945'' (pp. 223–24). The final step in the succession of power ''occurred in 1947 when in the Truman Doctrine and the Marshall Plan American leaders declared their willingness to step into Britain's place'' (p. 224).

This sketch summarizes Modelski's (1978) historical description of the leadership cycle. He then discusses (1981) the theoretical underpinnings of that cycle. Modelski's theory connects the leadership cycle with pairs of long waves and stresses innovation as the driving force. He argues that economic and political innovations alternate on successive phases of the long wave. Modelski distinguishes four phases of the world leadership cycle (p. 73):[9]

Long wave upswing 1:	Global war
Long wave downswing 1:	World power
Long wave upswing 2:	Delegitimization
Long wave downswing 2:	Deconcentration

The dominant world power has also historically been the leading economy of the world, Modelski argues, and has shaped the international economic order.[10] In addition, Modelski sees an evolution, in successive cycles, of political structure[11] and military techniques—which he calls ''waves of political innovations'' (p. 66). Each world power played the key role in both economic and political innovation (p. 68).[12]

---

9. Only two phases were distinguished in 1978 (p. 232).

10. The role of leading economy requires the political stability that only a world power can provide. And the high cost of operating as a world power cannot be maintained without a strong and growing economy (Modelski 1981:70).

11. Residential diplomacy from 1500 onward; international law consolidated after 1600; balance of power theory and practice around 1700; the Concert of Europe after 1815; and the emergence of international organizations in the 20th c.

12. Including the growth of new leading sectors of the world economy and new techniques of global communications.

Modelski argues that there is a trade-off between political development and economic growth in that both consume limited social resources (pp. 75–76). Periods of high political innovation, in Modelski's view, alternate with periods of economic innovation. The political innovation periods match the expansion phases of the long wave, while the economic innovation periods match the stagnation phases (p. 77).[13]

Modelski's empirical evidence for this idea is weakened by its reliance on a self-selected list of political innovations (p. 78), and his periodization of long waves is out of phase with that of Kondratieff and most other scholars after 1890:

Kondratieff/Mandel:[14]	Modelski:
1870/75–1890/96 down	1874–1913 down
1890/96–1914/20 up	
1914/20–1940/48 down	1913–1946 up
1940/48–1968 up	1946–1973 down
1968–? down	1973–? up

Modelski considers 1913–46 a single "up" period of global war in which the depression of the 1930s was an interlude. The 1946–73 period was a "down" phase with relatively low price inflation, while the period since 1973 is an "up" phase with high inflation.[15]

The major problem with Modelski's "alternating innovations" model is that it does not explain the pairing of long waves to make up a longer "leadership cycle." Modelski (1981:79) says only that "the global wars form the major pulse of the world system, while the in-between 'up' periods serve the function of mid-course correction." But why two long waves per leadership cycle rather than three or one? And how does the innovation dynamic lead to the one-hundred-year period necessary for the erosion and restructuring of global order?

Modelski does not answer these questions, and by 1984 he changes direction, moving away from long waves. The alternating innovations model (1982:108) rests on an assumption of a "single logic for the politico-economic process" at the world system level—an assumption that "these two structures of the world system [are] related." However, in 1984 Modelski (1984a:5) argues that, although the leadership cycle may be linked or partially synchronous with the long wave, they should not be described as one cycle; the cycle periods and patterns of recurrence differ. "[W]e need . . . to keep distinct the two processes, one political and the other economic."

Modelski's view of the future considers two processes: the decline of U.S. leadership, and the possible transformation of the global war process into a more

---

13. Modelski states that the idea of alternating innovations is "simpler, thus more plausible" than a model of simultaneous political and economic growth and innovation (p. 75). This is not elaborated, however.

14. Kondratieff until 1914/20, then Mandel.

15. Modelski (1982:108) claims to follow Rostow in this dating.

peaceful transition process. On the first point, Modelski (1981:80–81) argues that the period since 1973 "cannot be defined as that of a loss of position as leading economy for the United States or . . . a decline of American economic power . . . . The United States remains the single most important economic unit in the world." Modelski's timing of phases puts declining U.S. power ("deconcentration") still decades in the future. The most important condition for the United States to retain its role is the successful management of political and economic innovation (p. 80).[16]

As for the future, Modelski (1979:16) argues that those who take the leadership cycle with its component of global war seriously will be "impelled to devise drastic measures of political innovation for the modern world system."[17] He (1984b:3) stresses that the long leadership cycle is not a "war cycle" but a "political cycle." Even though world political leadership has been decided by global war in the past, other leadership selection processes—parallel to the role of elections in domestic politics—could be used in the future.

Modelski's approach reflects a liberal world view in its emphasis on innovation and on the role of the individual nation-state in the evolution of the nation-state system. Modelski's political innovations reflect Schumpeter's economic innovations on the level of world politics. Modelski (1982:98) prefers the term *world leadership* to *hegemony*."[18] Leadership is "the ability to innovate and move ahead in the common interest" (p. 104). Modelski and Thompson (1981:2) "conceive the global political system . . . as cooperative action . . . for the attainment of common interests, or the production of public goods." These are liberal conceptions of international order.

By the mid-1980s, Modelski's approach had spawned what I call the leadership cycle school.[19] Modelski (1983) provides a bibliography of works in this school by twenty authors, including Modelski himself, William Thompson, and Thompson's coauthors Karen Rasler and L. Gary Zuk. The leadership cycle school has gained attention in the political science discipline[20] but seems to be supported by only a minority.

William Thompson and his coauthors have conducted a series of empirical tests on particular aspects of the world leadership cycle theory. Some of these will be

16. The present phase is a "crisis of world order . . . of legitimacy . . . a political and moral crisis." The United States retains the chief responsibility for solving such global problems as the international monetary order and the problems of world oil. "The absence of resolute leadership and failure to deal with these problems . . . has produced a period of disarray that gravely contributes to further undermining the legitimacy of the international economic order" (p. 81).

17. "This is the period in which strategic emphasis needs to be placed on political innovation" (Modelski 1981:81).

18. "When a leading state acts in the public interest and its actions are thought legitimate, then its behavior cannot be described as hegemonial" (p. 98).

19. Its members generally refer to this cycle simply as "the long cycle," a term that Modelski himself (1984a) admits should be reserved for a general class of which the leadership cycle and the long wave are two members.

20. For instance, Modelski's panel on Alternatives to the Next Global War at the 1984 American Political Science Association conference attracted an audience of over 100.

discussed in chapter 12, below, but the following summary indicates the type of work going on in this research school.

Thompson (1984:12a) analyzes data on naval capabilities as measured by capital warships[21] in the five centuries since 1495. Thompson lists the years in which one nation holds more than 50 percent of the indexed world naval capabilities as follows:

1502–44
1608–19, 1624, 1632–33, 1635–36, 1640–42
1719–23 [mean concentration of .472 for 1714–50]
1809–12, 1814–34, 1843, 1854–57, 1861, 1880–81, 1889–90
1944–

The years in which the future leader passed the declining leader's naval power score are listed as:

Netherlands   1602
England   1676
United States 1941

Thompson calculates average naval power concentration scores (percentage of world capabilities held by leader) by *long wave* phase periods (not quite synchronous with those I have been using, however) and finds that the changes in naval concentration do *not* correlate with the long wave (p. 14a).

Rasler and Thompson (1983) study the impact of global wars on long-term public debt, especially for the leading power. They argue that war has strongly affected national debts, which in return have affected the ability to wage war:

[The] winners in the struggle for world leadership owed a significant proportion of their success to the ability to obtain credit inexpensively, to sustain relatively large debts, and in general to leverage the initially limited base of their wealth in order to meet their staggering military expenses. . . . [But] winning leads to successively higher levels of permanent debt burdens (p. 490).

Thus, through access to credit, the winners defeat nations with larger populations and economic capabilities, but at the price of a permanent high debt burden that eventually undermines their position. Rasler and Thompson illustrate this dynamic with narrative and data for each world power in the "leadership cycle."[22] The lingering debts resulting from war contribute to the "high overhead costs of the world-power role" (p. 515)—costs that erode the position won through military victory.

Several other works in this school may be mentioned. Thompson and Zuk (1982) examine the correlation of major wars with economic long wave phases and the effects of major wars on prices in Britain and the United States. Rasler and Thomp-

21. The definition actually changes several times, measuring different naval assets in different time periods.

22. For example, "both Spain and France [losers] experienced critical difficulties in obtaining further credit when it was most needed during periods of global warfare" (p. 497). Spain declared bankruptcy six times between 1557 and 1647. The Dutch and British, by contrast, "were able to develop and exploit their innovational and institutionalized access to short- and long-term credit" (p. 499).

son (1985b) examine the effects of war on economic growth. Modelski and Thompson (1981) test a "cobweb" model (borrowed from econometric modeling of market fluctuations) based on the world leadership cycle. Strickland (1982) attempts to integrate leadership-cycle theory with "lateral pressure" theory. Raymond and Kegley (1985) investigate the connection of internationalized civil wars wtih phases of the leadership cycle. Several of these studies will be discussed further in chapter 12, below.

Recently Thompson appears to have moved, along with Modelski, away from the idea of a close linkage of the leadership cycle with long waves. He argues (1984) that the two kinds of cycle show "fundamental traces of dissynchronization" and concludes that the leadership cycle and long wave should be treated as "separate, albeit interdependent, processes." Thus, although the leadership cycle originated through Wright and Toynbee as a concept rooted in the long wave, it has now taken on a separate existence in the theoretical debate.

The World-System School

A second major school to emerge in the current debate is rooted in a neo-Marxist framework. I call this school the world-system school (see fig. 6.1).

Neo-Marxist approaches differ from more traditional Marxism in emphasizing core-periphery relations in the world system rather than just the most advanced (core) capitalist countries. Chase-Dunn and Rubinson (1979:295) write:

In Marxist terminology the institutional constants of the modern world system are capitalist commodity production with expanded reproduction in the core, and primitive accumulation in the periphery in the context of the core-periphery division of labor and the state system. This is a departure from Marx's own understanding of the fully developed capitalist mode of production which, focusing on the core of the system, defined capitalism as synonymous with the wage system of labor exploitation.

Bergesen (1980) refers to "class struggle on a world scale":

The core-periphery division of labor and the process of unequal exchange are direct consequences of the class struggle between core and periphery . . . Since the sixteenth century the vast majority of the world's territory has been brought under colonial control. What we now call the periphery represents social formations and local modes of production that were either destroyed or significantly modified such that their productive activity came to be directed toward generating surplus value that was transferred . . . to the core (p. 124).

The world-system school approaches the war/hegemony question in the context of the capitalist world-economy and at first connected it with economic long waves. This school in fact forms the main link between the long wave debate and the hegemony cycle debate.[23] Later (as with the leadership cycle school), the two kinds of cycles were separated.

---

23. The journal *Review*, edited by Wallerstein, has printed a number of long wave articles. Wallerstein also puts out an occasional *Newsletter on Long Waves* internationally. Wallerstein himself (1984a) has also written about long waves, discussing whether long waves existed before industrial times and arguing that too few long wave studies use profit rate as the key variable.

Hopkins and Wallerstein (1979) and their "research working group on cyclical rhythms and secular trends" argue that "the growth of the capitalist world-economy exhibits a 'cyclical' character and [that] this cyclical pattern is *constitutive* of the world-economy." The capitalist world-economy contains "such contradictions that its growth cannot be unremittingly linear and still be capitalist" (p. 485).[24] This approach is consistent with other Marxist theories of the long wave. However, Hopkins and Wallerstein criticize explanations that focus too much on "an abstract model of the accumulation process" without including "the social structures through which capitalism operates," which "permit a wide variety of modes of accumulation" (p. 493). Also, theories focusing solely on the European component of capitalism rather than the world-system as a whole are seen as limiting. Hopkins and Wallerstein "therefore presume the interrelationship of 'politico-cultural' and 'economic' processes, and will always specifically take account of the axial division of labor in the world-economy between core and periphery" (p. 493).

This connection of economics and politics is embodied, for Hopkins and Wallerstein, in a long political-economic cycle made up of paired long waves (parallel to the pairing suggested by Toynbee, Modelski, and others). The long wave is seen as arising from the self-limitations of capital reproduction ("stagnation theoretically *must* follow expansion" [p. 493]). These limits derive from the lack of coordination of production decisions.[25]

Hopkins and Wallerstein suggest that long waves come in pairs that affect the core and periphery differently (p. 495). They name the successive phase A1–B1–A2–B2, where A1 and A2 are upswings and B1 and B2 are downswings. The core is a high-wage zone and the periphery a low-wage zone. During the A1 upswing, production of low-wage goods expands faster than high-wage goods as the economy expands into new regions, and terms of trade favor low-wage goods and raw materials. Terms of trade then even out as the supply of low-wage goods exceeds demand, and eventually the expansion turns to stagnation. This brings class struggle and a consequent redistribution of income, which increases demand and leads to a new expansion.[26] This time the expansion favors high-wage goods because of the higher income elasticity of the demand for high-wage goods. But this expansion also peters out, and there is a "crash" leading back to the beginning of the cycle (p. 496). During the downswings, world specialization reduces (that is, production of high-wage goods shifts toward the periphery and low-wage goods toward the core), and during upswings specialization increases.

24. A major consequence of this cyclical character of growth is that "spatial shift in the locus of the zones of the world-economy [core, semiperiphery, periphery] is continuous and inevitable" (p. 485). These geographical shifts do not change the system's basic structure, however; "they are primarily a game of 'musical chairs' in which the *relative* roles of core and periphery remain the same" (p. 485).

25. See "rationality" discussion in chap. 7.

26. Note that the hypothesis of increased class struggle during the stagnation phase opposes that of Mandel and Cronin (chap. 3). For Mandel, class struggle reduces profits, contributing to the end of an upswing; for Hopkins and Wallerstein, class struggle increases demand (by redistributing income), contributing to the beginning of an upswing.

This is the economic side of Hopkins and Wallerstein's theory. The political side addresses "hegemony":[27]

Interstate relations center around the relation among core powers, and their ability to control peripheral areas. If we assume a number of core states, we can assume 'rivalry' as a normal state of affairs, with exceptional periods in which one core power exceeds all others in the efficiency of its productive, commercial and financial activities, and in military strength. We can call this latter 'hegemony'.

If hegemonic powers always 'decline', because the technological edge of efficiency is inherently subject to disappearance through emulation, while the wage-levels of technologically-advanced production are subject to endemic real rise (in order to maintain, via politico-economic concession, a high rate of production), then there are always potential successors among the rivals.

There would then be periods, in terms of the world-economy, of ascending hegemony, hegemony, and declining hegemony (p. 497).

Hopkins and Wallerstein relate these periods of hegemonic succession to the paired long waves just discussed:

A1 (up): Ascending Hegemony—acute conflict between rivals to succession

B1 (down): Hegemonic Victory—"new" power bypasses "old" declining power

A2 (up): Hegemonic Maturity—true hegemony

B2 (down): Declining Hegemony—acute conflict of hegemonic power versus successors

Figure 6.2 illustrates these relationships along with dates for the last four cycles (the hegemonic cycles of the Hapsburgs, Netherlands, Britain, and the United States).[28] Hopkins and Wallerstein's dating of the A1 phases, that is, ascending hegemony, corresponds roughly to Toynbee's periods of "general war." The A2 phases (hegemonic maturity) correspond with Toynbee's "supplementary wars"—except in the most recent cycle.[29] Hopkins and Wallerstein theorize that A2 periods are "moments of 'free trade' because the hegemonic power imposes a general 'openness' on the

27. McKeown (1983) gives a non-Marxist response to the Wallerstein–Chase-Dunn approach to hegemony.

28. As noted earlier, Wallerstein, in contrast to Modelski, considers Hapsburg Spain (not Portugal) the first hegemon.

29. Toynbee considered World War I a general war, the 1920s and 1930s as the breathing space, and World War II as an anomalous supplementary war, with the general peace from 1945 on. Hopkins and Wallerstein, like Modelski, put both world wars into one phase. They consider it a downswing, however, while Modelski considered it an upswing, putting them out of phase after 1914:

Hopkins and Wallerstein	Modelski
D (Hegemonic victory) 1913/20–1945	U 1913–1946
U (Hegemonic maturity) 1945–1967	D 1946–1973
D (Declining hegemony) 1967–	U 1973–

In previous cycles, hegemonic victory corresponded with Toynbee's "breathing space" and maturity with Toynbee's "supplementary wars."

Figure 6.2. Hopkins and Wallerstein's Paired Long Waves

Rivalry among core powers

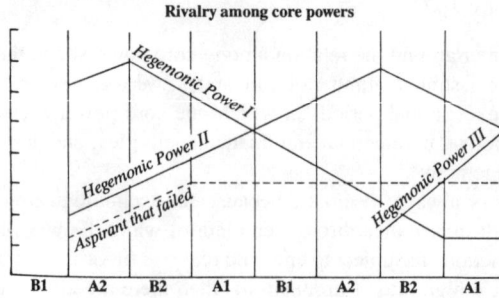

| | B1 | A2 | B2 | A1 | B1 | A2 | B2 | A1 |

Paired Kondratieffs and Hegemony/Rivalry.

Hegemonic power	I: Dorsal spine (Hapsburgs)	II: Netherlands (United Provinces)	III: Great Britain	IV: U.S.A.
A_1 (ascending hegemony) (shortage of LW)	1450-	1575-1590	1798-1815	1897-1913/20
B_1 (hegemonic victory) (balance)		1590-1620	1815-1850	1913/20-1945
A_2 (hegemonic maturity) (increasing *relative* HW production)	-1559	1620-1650	1850-1873	1945-1967
B_2 (declining hegemony) (shortage of markets for HW)	1559-1575	1650-1672	1873-1897	1967-?

IIa:

A^3	1672-1700
B^3	1700-1733/50
A^4	1733/50-1770
B^4	1770-1798

Source: Hopkins and Wallerstein (1979: 497,499).   From Review.

system. It can be said that the system is enjoying at such moments the temporary effects of the Ricardian model'' (p. 498). B2 periods, by contrast, ''would be moments of colonization, as rival core powers move to 'pre-empt' potential peripheral zones'' (p. 498).

This scheme thus encompasses various economic and political dynamics within one framework. However, it fails to show why these processes should follow so regular and mechanistic a rhythm. In this sense it resembles Modelski's (1981, 1982) attempt to tie hegemony cycles to long waves (see above). And as in that case, recent emphasis (see below) has shifted toward describing a war/hegemony dynamic less tightly connected with long waves.

Chase-Dunn and Rubinson (1979) study both long waves defined in terms of ''the relative rate of capital accumulation and overall economic activity'' and cycles of ''core competition'' marked by unicentricity or multicentricity among core states (p. 279). Chase-Dunn and Rubinson state (p. 295) that ''we do not yet understand the causal structure which produces these cycles," and they do not link long waves and hegemonic cycles as Hopkins and Wallerstein do. Instead they define three historical cases of hegemony in the world-system: the United Provinces (Netherlands), the United Kingdom, and the United States (p. 279).[30] Wallerstein (1983) later also adopts this framework (a switch from Hopkins and Wallerstein 1979). This dating of hegemony cycles not built from paired long waves contrasts with that of the leadership cycle school.[31]

Wallerstein (1983) defines hegemony in these three instances as "that situation in which the ongoing rivalry between the so-called 'great powers' is so unbalanced that . . . one power can largely impose its rules and its wishes (at the very least by effective veto power) in the economic, political, military, diplomatic, and even cultural arenas" (p. 101).[32] Wallerstein refers to hegemony as "one end of a fluid continuum" of competitive relations between core powers in which both ends— hegemony and multipolar equality—are rare and unstable (p. 102). Wallerstein (p. 102) lists the three periods of hegemony as maximally defined by roughly these dates:

United Provinces	1625–72
United Kingdom	1815–73
United States	1945–67

Each hegemon achieved its preeminent position based on its ability to operate more efficiently in three economic areas—agroindustrial production, commerce, and finance (p. 103). The hegemon's edge in efficiency is so great that enterprises based in the hegemonic power can outbid those based elsewhere in the world, even within the latter's home countries. Wallerstein argues that each hegemonic power first gains and then loses its edge in production, commerce, and finance, in that order. Hegemony exists during the short period in which all three overlap.

Wallerstein points to broad similarities between each hegemonic power. Each advocated global liberalism, including free trade (antimercantilism), anticolonialism, parliamentary institutions, civil liberties, and a relatively high standard of living for their own national working classes. Each was primarily a sea (then sea and air) power.

In the long ascent to hegemony, they seemed very reluctant to develop their armies, discussing openly the potentially weakening drain on state revenues and manpower of becoming tied down in land wars. Yet each found finally that it had to develop a strong land army as well to face up to a major land-based rival which seemed to be trying to transform the world-economy into a world-empire (p. 103).

---

30. Chase-Dunn and Rubinson (1979:287) argue that "the Pax Americana was quite short. The fall of the Bretton Woods agreement signaled the end of the use of the US dollar as *the* world currency."

31. It contains three cycles in the space of Modelski's four (he has two British cycles). Also, while Modelski calls Portugal the first hegemonic power (preceding the Netherlands), Chase-Dunn and Wallerstein suggest a less hegemonic situation dominated not by Portugal but by Spain.

32. Hegemony is distinguished from empire, since "omnipotence does not exist within the interstate system" (p. 102).

Each instance of hegemony, Wallerstein notes, "was secured by a thirty-year-long world war." His definition of world war is "a land-based war that involves (not necessarily continuously) almost all the major military powers of the epoch in warfare that is very destructive of land and population" (p. 103).[33] The world wars corresponding with each instance of hegemony were in 1618–48 (triumph of Dutch over Hapsburgs), 1792–1815 (triumph of British over French), and 1914–45 (triumph of America over Germany). World wars, in contrast to other more limited wars, have (like hegemony itself) been "a rarity" in the world-system, according to Wallerstein.

In the aftermath of each world war, according to Wallerstein, came

a major restructuring of the interstate system (Westphalia; the Concert of Europe; the U.N. and Bretton Woods) in a form consonant with the need for relative stability of the now hegemonic power. Furthermore, once the hegemonic position was eroded economically . . . and therefore hegemonic decline set in, one consequence seemed to be the erosion of the alliance network which the hegemonic power had created . . . .

In the long period following the era of hegemony, two powers seemed eventually to emerge as the "contenders for the succession"—England and France after Dutch hegemony; the U.S. and Germany after British; and now Japan and western Europe after U.S. Furthermore, the eventual winner [turned] the old hegemonic power into its "junior partner" (p. 104).[34]

All of this parallels Modelski's leadership cycle, except that the dating of world wars and their hegemonic winners differs:[35]

Wallerstein		Modelski	
		1494–1517	Portugal
1618–1648	Netherlands	1579–1609	Netherlands
		1688–1713	Britain (1)
1792–1815	Britain	1792–1815	Britain (2)
1914–1945	United States	1914–1945	United States

This difference in dating hinges on the question of the Thirty Years' War (1618–48), which falls in the middle (that is, not the global war period) of the world leadership cycle (and of Hopkins and Wallerstein's earlier paired long wave scheme). If the Thirty Years' War is considered a hegemonic war (cf. Midlarsky 1984a) the timing of the hegemony cycle follows Wallerstein (stressing land warfare). Otherwise the timing follows Modelski (stressing naval warfare).

These two major approaches to dating hegemony cycles correspond with two datings already mentioned in chapter 5. Toynbee's dating of war cycles based on pairs of long waves corresponds with Modelski's dating of global wars. Quincy

33. Note the difference from the leadership cycle school's emphasis on naval war.

34. Note the difference from Toynbee, Dehio, and Modelski, who suggest the Soviet Union as the probable next challenger.

35. Wallerstein (1983, 1984a) places world wars near the peak of each "logistic" cycle (see chaps. 3 and 13), whose troughs are in 1450, 1730, and 1897.

Wright's division of military history into successive eras corresponds with Waller-stein's dating of world wars and implies a somewhat longer hegemony cycle less closely linked to the long wave.

Bousquet (1979:516), another member of Wallerstein's Research Working Group, paralleled Chase-Dunn (and preceded Wallerstein) in deemphasizing the link of hegemony to long waves. She finds the "argument of the Research Group that there exists a 'hegemonic cycle' linked to two pairs of Kondratieffs . . . open to empirical skepticism. . . . Political cycles are in fact longer than two pairs of Kondratieffs." Bousquet suggests a revision that incorporates a longer and more variable ascending phase and (like Wallerstein and Chase-Dunn) condenses the five cycles of the paired long wave scheme into four (p. 509).[36]

Bousquet's (1980:49) theoretical explanation of these long cycles of hegemony centers on the role of innovation in promoting productive superiority in one core country. Hegemony for Bousquet is defined as "supremacy in the realms of produc-tion, commerce, and finance, and . . . a position of political leadership."[37] This supremacy is based on the creation of a new leading sector concentrated in one country. "It is precisely the uneven distribution of innovation at the core that causes temporary gaps between different countries" (p. 52). National economies, Bousquet argues, are "different environments within which the process of diversification of products and processes unfolds" (p. 53). The differences from one national economy to another[38] affect the production techniques favored in each country, and the hegemonic nation achieves superiority by "finding radically new methods of produc-tion in one or more sectors" (p. 53).[39]

Bousquet lists these nationally based historical leading sectors as follows:

Holland: Shipbuilding and sea transport, providing a more general model of low profit-margin operations.

England: Textiles (spinning devices) and mining (steam engine), spilling over into widespread mechanization.

America: Electronics and computers, revolutionizing the management of enter-prises across the board.

She writes:

Thanks to these major innovations, the entity wherein they occur finds itself in a position of production supremacy within the world-economy, and eventually obtains other dimensions

36. According to her scheme, the U.S. period of hegemonic maturity covers from 1960 through the present, and "declining hegemony" has not yet begun.

37. Economic hegemony means that "the products of one core power predominate in the world-market over those of other nonhegemonic powers; . . . its merchants or equivalent economic institutions carve for themselves a large part of the world network of exchange; . . . it controls and owns the largest part in relative terms of the world production apparatus. Thanks to the lion's share in world trade and invest-ments, the currency of the predominant power becomes the universal medium of exchange and its metropolis becomes the financial center of the world" (p. 49).

38. These include scarcity or abundance of labor and of capital and the structure of demand.

39. Weber (1983:44) shares with Bousquet "the view that each crisis is resolved through a structural reorganization of political economy" but rejects her views on the role of innovation in hegemony.

characteristic of authentic hegemony, namely, commercial and financial supremacy, and political leadership coupled with military supremacy (p. 79).[40]

Bousquet (1980:68) argues that hegemonic decline is rooted in overspecialization by the hegemonic power, which reduces innovation while competing powers "catch up."

It is as though the hegemony carries the seeds of its own destruction. In our view the very success of the hegemonic power's advanced sectors within the world-economy contributes, at some half-way stage in its hegemonic life, to shifting the innovation process away from major changes in the methods of production, and toward merely repeating and improving what had been so successful . . . . So, the growth of key advanced sectors is simultaneous with a technological lull in terms of major innovations. As we know, technological lulls are dangerous: they allow others to buy time (p. 68).

"Catching up," Bousquet argues, "is a complex process" that involves emulation of innovations[41] and is linked with protectionism (p. 68). "Protectionism does not happen at any given phase of some kind of national development process" (p. 77) but at certain conjunctures in the world system.[42]

Bergesen (1980) focuses on relations between the core and periphery. He sees two waves of colonization:

1500–1815   First wave of colonial expansion
1820–1870   First trough of colonialism
1870–1945   Second colonial expansion
1945–1973   Second trough

Bergesen ties these movements to hegemony: "Colonialism expands when there is instability within the core and contracts when there is stability" (p. 119). He argues (1980:121; 1983:74) that hegemony correlates with colonial contraction and with "free trade," while lack of hegemony correlates with colonial expansion and mercantilism.[43]

---

40. I might add that the country creating a major cluster of innovations often finds immediate military applications and propels itself to hegemonic status by that mechanism as well.

41. Raymond Vernon's product cycle theory (see also Kurth 1979) could help explain Bousquet's "emulation process." In the product cycle, an innovative product is first produced in one core country, where it saturates the domestic market, then is exported to foreign markets. Eventually direct foreign investment replaces exports, and foreign production takes off. Finally home production levels out and declines, while foreign production increases, and the product is imported to the home market from foreign countries.

42. Under hegemony, protectionism is defensive and limits itself to protecting production in the home economy, abandoning the periphery to the hegemonic country. Under nonhegemony, by contrast, protectionism is more aggressive, including "political expansion at the periphery" (Bousquet 1980:77).

43. Bergesen (1982; 1985) relates the economic long wave to hegemonic succession. Bergesen (1982) speculates that long downswings bring mergers, but mostly in nonhegemonic countries, and that nonadaptation by hegemonic countries leads to hegemonic decline and succession. However, his dating of upswings and downswings (as with Bergesen and Schoenberg 1980) does not match that of other long wave scholars.

The world-system school as a whole, then, contains differences regarding the historical timing and characteristics of hegemony cycles, but Chase-Dunn, Bousquet, Wallerstein (after 1984), and Bergesen all argue that these cycles are longer than a pair of long waves. Chase-Dunn and Wallerstein agree on the rough timing of the cycle (starting with the Netherlands), and I consider this the main line of the school. The world-system school is fairly consensual in seeing hegemony as correlated with free trade, multilateral trade, and looser core-periphery relations; whereas lack of hegemony is correlated with protectionism, bilateral trade, and tighter core-periphery relations.

The parallel work of the world leadership school and the world-system school has led to various exchanges between them. This interschool debate is taken up in a volume edited by Thompson (1983) and in an exchange by Chase-Dunn and Sokolovsky (1981; 1983) with Thompson (1983a, b).[44] The debate culminates in what Thompson calls the Cool Hand Luke Syndrome, which refers to a failure of communication. As with the long wave debate, communication across schools is difficult.[45]

The Power Transition School

The third major school of the current war/hegemony debate, which I call the power transition school, is descended from Organski's (1958) approach.

Charles Doran and *Wes Parsons* (1980; Doran 1983) remain essentially within Organski's framework but add a cyclical component. They assume a regularity in the rise and fall of a nation's relative capabilities in the international system, which they call a "power cycle." Like Organski, they assume that a state's relative power position[46] affects the likelihood of war.[47]

As shown in figure 6.3, Doran and Parsons (1980:949–53) fit regularized curves to data for each of nine great powers, indicating each country's relative power (that is, share of total capability) for 1815–1975 (or however long the country was a "great power"). Countries seem to (more or less) follow logistic curves, gradually gaining

---

44. These differences include vocabulary differences, such as the question of hyphenating *world-system* (Marxists do, others do not).

45. Rapkin (1984:28–29) attempts to "cobble together" arguments from the leadership cycle and world-system schools, along with hegemonic stability theory and structural Marxism. Rapkin generally endorses Modelski's approach but tries to merge the two schools' vocabularies, adopting the term *hegemony/leadership*.

46. Doran and Parsons measure the capability of countries not by GNP (as did Organski and Kugler) but by a combined measure on two dimensions: size (iron and steel production, population, and size of armed forces) and development (energy use, coal production, urbanization). War data come mainly from the Correlates of War project (Singer and Small).

47. Doran and Parsons (1980:947) study "the impact of long-term nonlinear changes in a state's relative power on its propensity for extensive war."

Figure 6.3. Doran and Parsons' Relative Power Curves

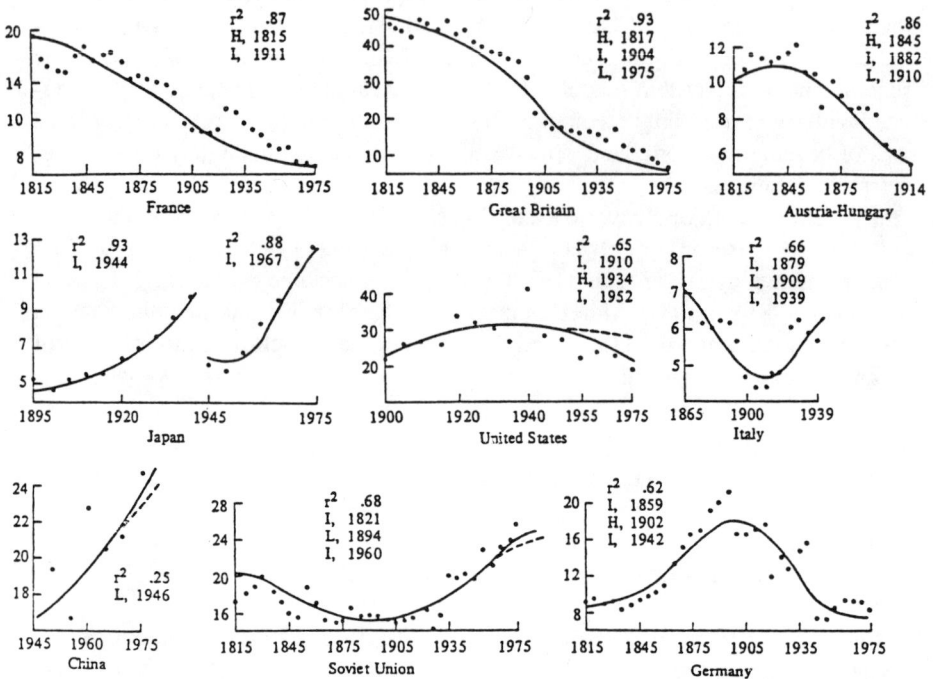

Notes: Data points and fitted curves are graphed. L = year of low point; H = year of high point; I = year of inflection point. Doran and Parsons note that their data on five indicators of capability drawn from over forty sources are available from the authors upon request.

Source: Doran and Parsons (1980: 956).   Reprinted from the <u>American Political Science Review</u>.

or losing their share of world power.[48] Doran and Parsons conclude that "major powers pass through a cycle indexed by relative capability" (p. 952).

They hypothesize that "at critical points during this cycle where change is most rapid and disruptive of past trends, namely, at the inflection and turning points, the probability is highest of major power initiation of extensive war" (p. 953), because "it is at these points that the government is most vulnerable to overreaction, misperception, or aggravated use of force which may generate massive war" (p. 949).[49]

Doran and Parsons analyze seventy-seven cases of war initiation by major powers. Using simple statistical groupings of wars by "critical periods" versus "remaining

48. The curve-fitting exercise has some of the familiar problems of fitting long cycles to short data sets.
49. These inflection and turning points, Doran and Parsons argue, "may engender feelings of power-lessness, determinism, and subsequent helplessness in a governing elite anxious about security" (p. 952).

intervals,'' they conclude that indeed ''a major power is more prone to initiate a war that becomes extensive (i.e. escalates) during one of the critical periods on the cycle of relative power than at other times'' (p. 960). Further, they find that the inflection points (where the rate of growth or decline shifts rather suddenly) rather than the turning points (where the level of relative capability is maximum or minimum) were most conducive to war.[50] I am somewhat skeptical of these results because of ad hoc elements in the methodology.

Robert Gilpin (1981) also follows the main thrust of the power transition school, though not in a cyclical framework. He argues that war is a resolution of systemic disequilibrium resulting from a differential growth of power among the actors in the international system. Gilpin integrates this theory with that of another neorealist, Waltz (1979), who makes an analogy between international politics and micro-economics. According to this approach, states act like firms and the international system like a market, so the ''rational actor'' model of economists can be applied to world politics. The nation-state, according to Gilpin, behaves ''rationally'' and seeks to change the international system only when the perceived benefits of doing so exceed the costs (p. 11). Hence the system is stable only when no actor thinks the benefits of change exceed the costs. The principle method of systemic change through history has been hegemonic war—war to reorder the international system (p. 15).[51] Gilpin's theory suggests a ''power transition'' explanation of the hege-mony cycles—periodic hegemonic wars arising from (and correcting) systemic disequilibrium. But Gilpin's theory is not explicitly cyclical.

The distinctions between the three schools discussed in this chapter are captured by Modelski (1983:2), who distinguishes his approach from realist and neo-Marxist approaches as follows:

In contrast to *realism*, [it] strives not for universal generalizations about the behavior of states but only for propositions about time and space-bound systems. It represents politics not as something eternal or unchanging but subject to innovation and learning. . . . It also rejects the characterization of world politics as anarchical but is particularly sensitive to the role global wars have played in its organization.

On the other hand, in contrast to the *world-systems* approach, [it] eschews economic determinism and has a fuller conception of the role of the political process, and in particular global war, in the shaping of the modern world. It does, however, share with it a systemic and evolutionary perspective, a concern for space and time, and attention to global economic processes.

---

50. ''Our findings show that most extensive wars involving major powers are not initiated at the top of their relative capability curves as is popularly supposed'' (p. 963).

51. Just as the central ordering mechanism of the nation-state internally is property rights (here the argument draws on North and Thomas 1973) and the nation-state represents an efficient innovation relative to feudal states in this respect (see Organski and Kugler 1980:116), so the central ordering mechanism of the international system is territory, which plays a similar role internationally to the domestic role of property (Gilpin 1981:37).

Hybrid Theories

In addition to the three main schools of the current war/hegemony debate, several syntheses—hybrid theories—draw on more than one school.[52]

Raimo Väyrynen

Väyrynen (1983a, b) synthesizes ideas from the world system, power transition, and leadership cycle schools.[53] Väyrynen (1983b:392) argues that "the role of power transitions and political management in the outbreak of warfare between major powers is affected by the socio-political context associated with various phases of the long economic cycle [long wave]." He thus (pp. 393–402) links long waves with hegemony, using the following datings:

Hegemonic phase	Accelerated growth (Up)	Decelerated growth (Down)
Hegemonic victory		1825–1845
Hegemonic maturity	1845–1872	
Declining hegemony		1872–1892
Ascending hegemony	1892–1913/29	
Hegemonic victory		1929–1948
Hegemonic maturity	1948–1973	
Declining hegemony		1973–

Väyrynen's long wave phases match the base dating scheme, and the phases of hegemony match the dates of Hopkins and Wallerstein (1979:499),[54] at least roughly.[55] Väyrynen's analysis extends back only to 1825, however.

Väyrynen then considers the "war-proneness" of the international system. He argues (1983b:409) that the periods of hegemonic decline (1872–92 and 1973–) have been marked by little major-power war, while phases of ascending hegemony (1892–1929) were marked by much major-power war.[56] The two other phases, hegemonic victory and maturity (a long wave downswing and upswing, respectively) had a mix of "some" or "little" major-power war.

52. In addition to the hybrid theories, there are occasional works that do not engage the current debate and are not referred to by others in the field. An example is Zambell (1984), who links Kondratieff waves, war, and a 150-year "world supremacy cycle." His dating of the latter is unusual: the world leaders are listed as Spain (1580s–1730s), France (1680s–1830s), England (1780s–1930s), and the U.S. (1880s–2030s). The 150 years of each leader contains three long waves, the first of which coincides with the last long wave of the previous leader's reign. Zambell's scheme seems rigidly mechanistic and does not engage the existing debate.

53. From his relatively neutral base in Finland, Väyrynen is aware of the distinctions between these schools and open-minded toward possibilities for synthesis among them.

54. But not of the later Wallerstein or of Chase-Dunn.

55. There is a one-to-one correspondence, but dates of turning points differ somewhat.

56. This accounts for the increased amount of war on the long wave upswing, which Kondratieff had noted.

Väyrynen (1983b:411) tabulates war data by phase period as follows:

Phase	Wars	Dates	Magnitude[a]	Severity[b]
Ascending hegemony	Russia-Japan	1904–1905	38	130
(U)	World War I	1914–1919	608	9000
	Russian civil	1917–1921	39	50
Hegemonic victory	USSR-Japan	1939	13	28
(D)	World War II	1939–1945	888	15000
Hegemonic maturity	Crimean	1853–1856	116	246
(U)	Austro-Prussian	1866	14	36
	Franco-Prussian	1870–1871	27	188
	Korean	1951–1953	514	2000
Declining hegemony (D)	none			

[a]Number of nation-months of war
[b]Number of battle deaths in 1,000s

He notes that, in line with Kondratieff's theory, seven of the nine wars among major powers since 1825 took place on long wave upswings and the other two in the recovery stage at the end of the downswing. Most interestingly, "no wars among major powers have been waged during periods of hegemonic decline" (p. 414).[57]

Väyrynen's work thus draws upon several traditions in the war/hegemony and long wave debates and dates hegemony cycles as paired long waves. His empirical study provides some clues to the connections of the long wave with hegemony but is weakened by the short period of time he studies (since 1825).

Jack Levy

Levy draws upon both the Singer tradition of behavioral research (see chapter 5)[58] and the "realist" tradition. He develops (1983a) a data set similar to the basic components of the cow data but covering all wars that involve "great powers" from 1495 to 1975 rather than from 1815 to 1975.[59] Levy then analyzes those data statistically to test various hypotheses about great power war.[60]

Levy (1984) focuses on the idea, derived from Organski, of a "preventive war by the dominant power to weaken or destroy a rising challenger while that opportunity is

---

57. Elsewhere, Väyrynen (1983a) pursues the cost-of-wars argument (see Wright and Farrar discussions, chap. 5), connecting war with long economic upswings. He argues that during the upswing phase the cost of a growing military is easier to carry than during the downswing.

58. Levy (1981:609) calls his work "part of an ongoing tradition of research, initiated by Singer and Small."

59. Levy (1983b) contrasts his "Great Power framework" with "world system" approaches.

60. For example, Levy (1981:610) finds that evidence from five centuries contradicts the hypothesis that alliance formation correlates with or precedes high levels of war. Levy and Morgan (1984) show empirical support for the hypothesis that the frequency of war in a given period is inversely related to its seriousness.

Table 6.1. Comparison of Definitions of General War

War	Dates	Levy	Toynbee	Modelski/ Thompson	Wallerstein	Gilpin	Doran[a]	Mowat
Italian wars	1494-1525[b]		X	X				X
Wars of Charles V								
War of Dutch Independence/ Spanish Armada	1585-1609[c]	X	X	X			X	
Thirty Years' War	1618-1648	X			X	X	X	X
Dutch War of Louis XIV	1672-1678	X	X			X	X	X
War of the League of Augsburg	1688-1697	X	X	X		X	X	X
War of the Spanish Succession	1701-1713	X	X	X		X	X	X
War of Jenkins' Ear/ Austrian Succession	1739-1748	X						X
Seven Years' War	1755-1763	X						X
French Revolutionary & Napoleonic wars	1792-1815	X	X	X	X	X	X	X
World War I	1914-1918	X	X	X	X	X	X	X
World War II[d]	1939-1945	X		X	X	X	X	X

Levy's notes:
a It is not clear which wars Doran (1983a: 179) includes in the "Hapsburg attempt to dominate Europe" or which of Louis XIV's wars he includes.
b Regarding ending dates: Toynbee uses 1525, while Modelski and Thompson use 1517. Mowat includes the wars of Charles V by identifying 1559 as the end of the war.
c Toynbee opens the war in 1568, Modelski in 1579; Thompson and I [Levy] wait until the internationalization of the civil war in 1585.
d Toynbee classifies World War II as a "supplemental war" but in a footnote refers to it as a "recrudescent general war" (p. 255). Modelski, Thompson, Wallerstein, and Gilpin all treat the two world wars of this century as a single global war.

Source: Jack S. Levy, "Theories of General War", World Politics 37, no. 3 (April 1985). Copyright (c) 1985 by Princeton University Press.
Table reprinted with permission of Princeton University Press.

still available." He reviews the theories and definitions relating to preventive war, drawing on and distinguishing the approaches of Morgenthau, Organski, Doran, Gilpin, Modelski, and Thompson.

Levy and Morgan (1985) study "war-weariness"—the hypothesis that a war between the great powers affects the likelihood of another war in a subsequent period. Such a hypothesis could help to explain the cyclical character of major wars. But, in agreement with previous behavioral studies of this question, Levy and Morgan find no evidence for the war-weariness hypothesis (p. 17).

Levy (1985) reviews different approaches to the question of "general war," drawing on major works from all three schools in the war/hegemony debate.[61] He shows that different assumptions on the part of different scholars lead to differing definitions of general war and hence to varied lists of wars included in this category. Levy puts forward his own three criteria for general war and a resulting list of ten wars (see table 6.1). Levy himself (1985) adopts a "realist" approach to general war, and particularly to the role of coalitions in those wars[62]—in explicit contrast to the approaches of Modelski and Wallerstein. He argues that "a traditional realpolitik

61. He reviews Toynbee, Modelski, Thompson, Organski, Doran, Gilpin, Wallerstein, Chase-Dunn, and Väyrynen. See also Midlarsky (1984b).
62. Levy finds that coalition formation in general wars fits the idea—central to balance-of-power theory—that a threat by any single power to gain a dominant position will generate an opposing coalition to restore equilibrium.

perspective provides a better explanation . . . than do other perspectives based on economic or global assumptions.''[63]

However, Levy's rejection of Modelski's approach seems to stem partly from incommensurable vocabularies. In Levy's terminology, the ''leading power'' is the power that threatens to gain a dominant position—such as France or Germany—while in Modelski's framework the ''world leader'' is the leader of the peripheral coalition that contains these challengers.

This misunderstanding reflects a different area of attention in Levy's work from that of Modelski. For Levy, the key arena is continental Europe, where the wars between the great powers are fought. For Modelski, it is the oceanic arena, where naval powers struggle for dominance of extra-European avenues.[64]

63. The ''economic'' assumptions clearly are those of the world system school, and ''global'' assumptions are those of the leadership cycle school.

64. While Levy argues that the great powers have always feared their Continental neighbors more than the more distant oceanic powers, Modelski argues that the oceanic powers order the international system through their ''world-reach'' capabilities.

CHAPTER SEVEN

Knowledge Cumulation in
the Long Cycle Field

Having now reviewed both the long wave and war/ hegemony debates, I will conclude Part One by considering the cumulation of knowledge in the long cycle field as a whole. Why has it proved difficult to reach agreement concerning what we know about long cycles?[1]

World Views and Research Schools

The *long wave* debate is currently structured by the interplay of three research schools, each based on a different theory of the central causes of long waves (chapter 3). Each of these three theories reflects a different world view in its conception of social change. The capitalist crisis theory of Mandel and Trotsky is most revolutionary (transformation of order) in seeing long waves as recurrent restructurings of capitalism in the face of universal crises. The capital investment theory of Forrester and Kondratieff is most conservative (preservation of order) in seeing long waves as endogenously generated fluctuations in a system whose underlying rules do not change. The innovation theory of Mensch and Schumpeter is most liberal (evolution of order) in seeing long waves as innovational spurts in the development of society.

The central scholars in each of the three research schools reflect their respective underlying world views in their conceptual frameworks, their models of the long wave, and their prescriptions for society:

Trotsky/Mandel:
    Framework   Marxist dialectics; stages of development in mode of production
    Model   Crisis tendency / class struggle
    Prescription   International socialist revolution

---

1. In this section I explore the ways in which the field has or has not fit a model of "scientific" inquiry. I will conclude that the long cycle debate resembles a scientific research effort in some ways but that many of the requirements of a working scientific community (Kuhn's "disciplinary matrix") are lacking. This has been a major obstacle to the cumulation of knowledge about long cycles.

148

Schumpeterians:

Framework	Liberal economics; the role of the individual in economic evolution
Model	Technological innovation / leading sector
Prescription	Increased innovation to spur upswing

Forrester:

Framework	Conservative management; effective policy decisions in a complex environment
Model	Capital investment / system dynamics
Prescription	Correct investment policies to dampen cycle

The differences among world views are illustrated by the views of different scholars regarding *rationality* in the long wave. Why do capitalist firms overinvest in fixed capital or fail to apply innovations at the right time?

For Marxist approaches, actions that are individually rational for capitalists are collectively self-destructive because of the fundamental contradiction of capitalism—*private* ownership of the *social* means of production. The individual capitalist, although acting rationally, makes decisions that for all capitalists together are self-destructive.[2] Mandel says of over- and under-investment by capitalists: "What is rational from the standpoint of the system as a whole is not rational from the standpoint of each great firm taken separately."[3] Kleinknecht likewise finds the timing of innovations to be individually rational (for the single firm), although undesirable from the point of view of the society as a whole.

For liberals like Mensch, by contrast, the investment and innovation decisions that lead to long downswings are "mistakes" on the part of managers, that is, irrational (not in the best interest of those making them). And from Forrester's more conservative angle, incorrect investment decisions result from the complex dynamics of capitalism that cannot be grasped by the human brain unassisted by the computer.[4] In Mandel's (revolutionary) view, by contrast, Forrester's computer would be irrelevant since the capitalist firm is in fact already acting in its own (individual) best interest; only socializing the ownership of production could bring about socially rational decisions.[5]

As in the long wave debate, the *war/hegemony* debate contains three current schools that reflect different approaches to the study of international relations. These

2. On this theme, see also non-Marxists Mancur Olson (1965), and Garrett Hardin (1968:1244): "Ruin is the destination toward which all men rush, each pursuing his own best interest in a society that believes in the freedom of the commons." These issues of collective and individual rationality are also explored in the extensive literature on "rational choice."

3. Quoted in Wallerstein (1979:666).

4. Sterman (1984:6) and Morecroft (1983) show how the system dynamics model is consistent with Herbert Simon's theory of "bounded rationality," which states that individuals do not reach optimal decisions, but instead settle for satisfactory outcomes ("satisficing" rather than "optimizing"). Since bounded rationality arises from the idea that "human beings have a limited ability to process information" (Sterman 1984:7), it fits in with the use of computer simulation to arrive at more fully rational outcomes.

5. I will not explore the issue of rationality beyond pointing out these differences among schools.

schools are the neo-Marxist world system school led by Wallerstein, the leadership cycle school of Modelski, which grows out of Toynbee's historical peace-research approach, and the neorealist power transition school, in which Organski is central. Each school sees the question of hegemony cycles, and their connection to economics, differently.

The world-system school embraces the Marxist assumption that political change flows from the dynamics of capitalism as a mode of production (and defined broadly as a world-system). It differs from traditional Marxist approaches, however, in its orientation to the international level. Hegemony and competition refer to relationships among core states struggling to control the periphery and the world-economy as a whole. The hegemonic power plays the leading role (but not the role of an empire) in a worldwide system of exploitation, and long cycles of world politics are intrinsic to the development of that system. For the world-system school, world war and hegemony are outgrowths of a world capitalist system structured by the division between core and periphery. Some scholars have linked the rise and fall of hegemonic states in the core with the rhythm of paired long waves in the world economy. However, recent opinion in this school has moved away from seeing hegemony cycles as paired long waves.

The leadership cycle school is liberal in its emphasis on the evolution of the system of nation-states. Modelski's model of alternating economic and political innovations transposes innovation theory to the level of international politics. The school portrays leadership as a public good benefiting all and expresses hope that nonviolent alternatives can replace global war as a leadership selection mechanism. For the leadership cycle school, global war and world leadership are central elements in a world political dynamic that is assumed to be largely autonomous of economics. The leadership cycle and the long wave were once considered to be linked (two long waves per leadership cycle), but, as with the world-system school, recent work suggests greater independence between these two cycles.[6]

The power transition school[7] reflects the conservative world view underlying realist approaches to international politics. These approaches tend to see the recurrence of war as deeply rooted in the power-seeking behavior of nation-states.[8] Nations attempt to increase their share of power in the international system, using economic capabilities as a means toward that end. The power transition school sees the rise and fall of hegemonic orders, and the major wars that attend these, as resulting from differentials in the dynamics of national capabilities. Although the

6. They are moving further apart in dating hegemonic orders and world wars (especially before 1815). When both were tied to the idea of synchrony with the long wave (Modelski 1981; Hopkins and Wallerstein 1979), their datings of "global war" and "ascending hegemony" generally corresponded. But as each moved away from that linkage (Modelski 1984a; Wallerstein 1983), their datings diverged. Modelski has five hegemonic cycles since 1495, while Wallerstein now has three, starting in 1625.

7. Especially Gilpin's synthesis of Organski's theory with Waltz's microeconomic model of international relations.

8. Dehio's focus on the lust for world domination or Organski's focus on challenges to the international order.

Figure 7.1. Six Current Schools of Long Cycle Research

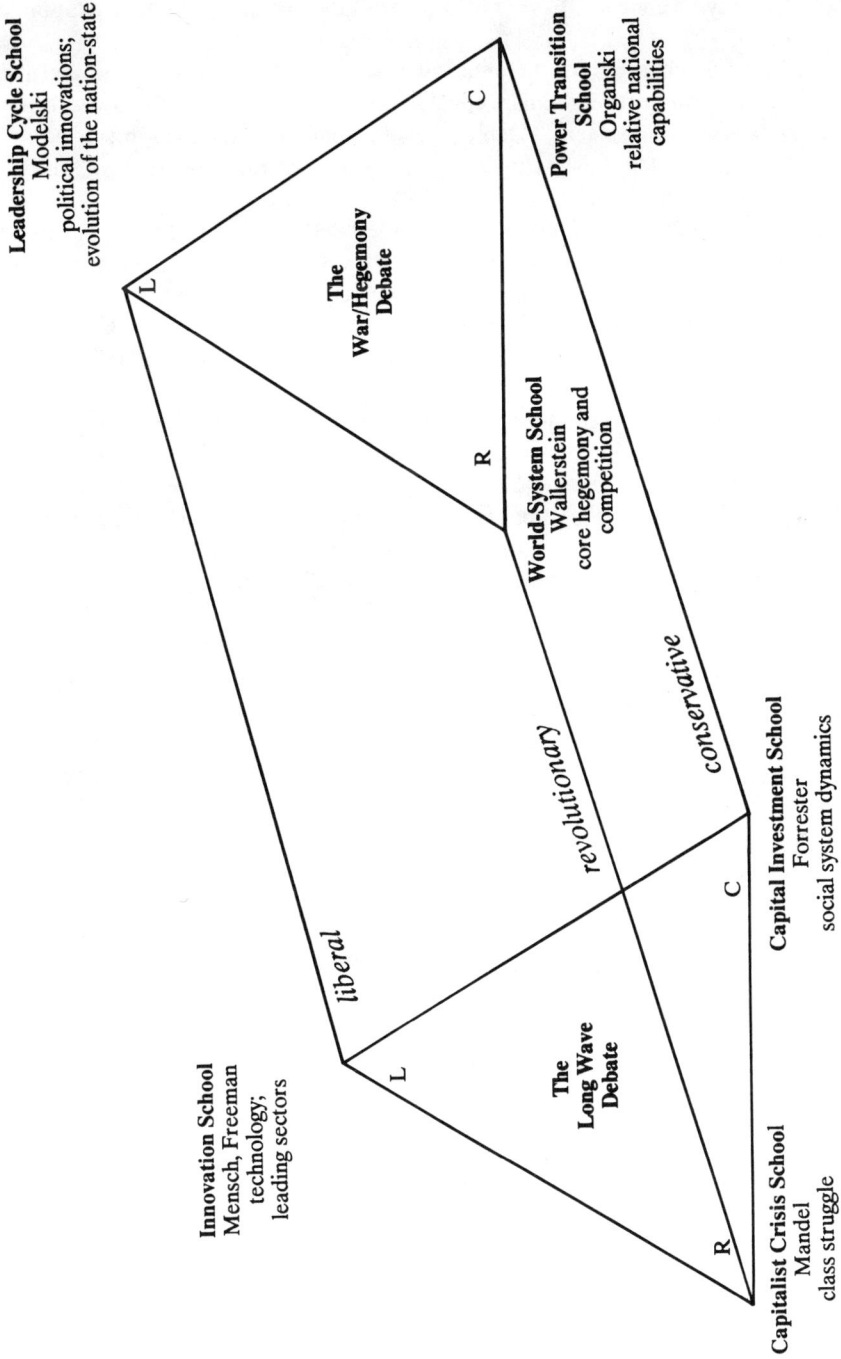

Leadership Cycle School
Modelski
political innovations;
evolution of the nation-state

Power Transition School
Organski
relative national
capabilities

The
War/Hegemony
Debate

World-System School
Wallerstein
core hegemony and
competition

conservative

revolutionary

liberal

Capital Investment School
Forrester
social system dynamics

Innovation School
Mensch, Freeman
technology;
leading sectors

The
Long Wave
Debate

Capitalist Crisis School
Mandel
class struggle

process may be conceived as cyclical (as does Doran), it is not tied to economic long waves.

The three schools have different approaches to the current period and the near future. Power transition scholars consider the likelihood of war as power shifts occur in the international system.[9] Dehio, Toynbee, and Modelski are interested in U.S.-Soviet rivalry.[10] Marxist scholars consider the declining position of the U.S. as hegemonic power.[11]

Figure 7.1 illustrates the structural parallels between the long wave debate and the war/hegemony debate.[12] On the revolutionary axis, the world-system school (Wallerstein) and the capitalist crisis school (Mandel) tie long cycles to the contradictions of capitalism—Mandel at the domestic level and Wallerstein at the international level. Both Mandel and Wallerstein explicitly link the economic and political levels.[13]

On the liberal axis, the world leadership school (Modelski) is clearly working in the same paradigmatic framework as the innovation school (Schumpeter)—rewriting Schumpeter (economic evolution through technical innovation) at the political level (political evolution through political innovation). Schumpeter's starting point is the individual (entrepreneur) in the competitive economic setting; Modelski's is the individual nation-state in the competitive international setting.

On the conservative axis, the power transition school (Organski) and capital investment school (Forrester) stress systemic rules generating nonevolving behavior that persists over time. In both approaches, individually rational decisions lead to problematical systemic outcomes.

In figure 7.1 there are two kinds of barriers—those among schools on each triangle (reflecting differences in world views) and those between the two triangles themselves (reflecting disciplinary barriers between economics and politics).[14]

Philosophy of Science Issues

Why has the long cycle field failed to coalesce around agreed-upon theories and empirical results? Can knowledge cumulation take place where research is fragmented into schools that do not fully communicate? These issues will now be explored in a "philosophy of science" framework.[15]

9. Farrar specifically predicts a period of adjusting wars from 1973 until about 2000.

10. Toynbee and Dehio specifically see the USSR as the new rising continental power in the tradition of Spain, France, and Germany; while Modelski sees a crisis (but not an insuperable one) for the United States in maintaining world leadership.

11. Both Hopkins and Wallerstein and Bergesen see a declining hegemony from 1967 onward, and Bousquet sees a period of hegemonic maturity from 1960 on (with decline to follow later).

12. In view of Kuhn's discussion of paradigm shifts (see below), I cannot resist making the figure itself an optical illusion that shifts in or out of the page—leaving either politics or economics on top.

13. And both try to afford more autonomy to political "superstructure" than does traditional Marxism.

14. The area of 50-year war cycles, with the most promise of connecting these two debates, has been largely neglected in recent decades (chap. 6).

15. Here I use the term *science* broadly to refer to knowledge cumulation.

Karl Popper, Thomas Kuhn, and Imre Lakatos

Philosophy of science discussions in recent years have centered on the work of Thomas Kuhn (1970), who focuses on the social and community aspects of science. Scientific communities share certain values, standards, agendas, and models that shape their work. "Normal science" on a day-to-day basis takes place within a research framework, or paradigm, that guides a scientific community. Most scientific work aims to solve puzzles within the paradigm framework, extending and articulating it over time. Only when anomalies within the paradigm become increasingly severe—forcing more and more ad hoc adjustments to theory in order to account for new empirical findings—does a scientific crisis develop. At such times a new paradigm can be put forward, and, after debate between the two competing frameworks, the new paradigm can gain converts in the scientific community and become the dominant framework for research. Kuhn calls this a scientific revolution.

Kuhn's focus on "normal science"—seeing scientific revolutions as relatively rare—differs from that of Karl Popper, who dominated the philosophy of science debate in the generation before Kuhn's (see Alker 1982). Popper argued that science advances by bold conjectures and empirical refutations—putting forward theories and then trying to falsify them.[16] Theories are systems from which hypotheses can be logically deduced and empirically tested. The "corroboration" of a theory is a matter of degree, based on how well it solves problems, its degree of testability, the severity of tests it has withstood, and how well it stood up to them.

Kuhn, however, argues that Popper's "bold conjectures" are relatively rare. Most science consists of "normal science" within a framework that sets out a general view and a set of puzzles to be solved. It is the ingenious attempts to solve outstanding puzzles *within* a theoretical framework that generate the incremental growth of knowledge. In this paradigm-governed research, the failure to solve a puzzle is taken not as a challenge to the paradigm itself but as a reflection on the quality of the particular scientist. Thus negative empirical results do not falsify a theory but are seen only as anomalies (which no theory is completely free of). Only after repeated failures throughout a field does a "crisis" occur, allowing a new paradigm to be put forward and to gain adherents in the scientific community.[17]

In the course of a scientific revolution (a paradigm shift), different subcommunities may work simultaneously within different paradigm-governed frameworks, each partially incommensurable with the others in terms of theories, vocabularies, methods, instruments, and so forth. A somewhat similar situation occurs in an immature field, where no paradigm framework for research has yet emerged. Many of the social sciences apparently fall in this "immature," or "preparadigm," category. The long cycle field certainly does.

The choices between competing scientific theories, according to Kuhn (here

16. In Popper's view, theories cannot be proven but only falsified. Scientific progress is defined as the increasing truth content of nonfalsified theories.
17. Such a community may be as small as 25 to 50 specialists, according to Kuhn.

differing from Popper) cannot be made on the basis of any neutral or objective algorithm (bringing theory closer to an objective truth) but only through group discussion and debate in the scientific community, a sociopsychological and historical process. A theory is never "falsified" unless there is a better one to replace it, and the process whereby one paradigm replaces another as the dominant framework for research in a field is one of winning converts within the community.[18]

Kuhn later (1970 postscript) notes that he used the word *paradigm* to refer both to "shared examples of successful practice" (which operate as rules to guide research) and to all the group commitments in a scientific community. These group commitments, he suggests, might better be called a "disciplinary matrix." A disciplinary matrix includes metaphysical paradigms (cosmological models and beliefs), scientific values, symbolic generalizations (formal laws, definitions, and theories), and exemplars (shared examples of applications—that is, the narrow meaning of paradigm).

Imre Lakatos (1970) disagrees with Kuhn's idea of paradigm shifts as irrational leaps[19] but agrees that Popper's idea of falsification is inadequate. In Lakatos's view, theories are embodied in competing "research programs" that progress or degenerate depending on the relative strength of their theories. Lakatos's research programs have many of the elements of Kuhn's disciplinary matrices. A research program, Lakatos argues, has a "core" of nonfalsifiable assumptions, including metaphysical beliefs, negative heuristics (directions of research that are *not* to be pursued; assumptions that the program must *not* try to falsify), and positive heuristics (promising areas for research where falsification *may* be applied). Around this core, a sequence of testable theories develops.

Lakatos disagrees with Kuhn's view that mature scientific communities give a monopoly to one paradigm (except during revolutions) and suspend all others. Rather, Lakatos argues that research programs are *never* definitively falsified; they either progress or degenerate. A progressive research program is one that generates sequences of theoretical respecifications that fit reality better and better; a degenerate program requires more and more ad hoc adjustments to make theory conform to new evidence.

Long Cycle Schools as Research Paradigm Complexes

Alker (1982) combines the ideas of paradigm exemplar, disciplinary matrix, and research program into what he calls a "research paradigm complex."[20] The six

18. Since paradigms themselves govern the conceptualization of problems, methodologies, and agendas in the research effort—and are partially incommensurable—the winning of adherents takes place through a conversion experience, in which a member of the community rather suddenly switches his or her entire view of the problem, seeing it in the new framework. After the new paradigm has succeeded in supplanting the old one and establishing a dominant position, scientific history is rewritten in scientific textbooks to fit with the new paradigm and downplay the old, so that the new generation entering the field is trained within the new framework. This in retrospect makes scientific progress appear rational and linear, while understating the actual debates and incommensurabilities between paradigms.

19. Lakatos (1970:178) calls Kuhn's mechanism "mob psychology."

20. This approach, unlike that of Kuhn and Lakatos, is specifically addressed to social science.

elements composing Alker's research paradigm complex are embodied in the research schools of the long cycle debates.

1. "Metascientific beliefs and values":[21] These correspond with what I have called world views—the revolutionary, liberal, and conservative orientations that shape the major approaches. Examples include different views of capitalism and of the relationship of economics and politics, differing concerns with preserving or destroying capitalism, and differing approaches to methodology in defining and identifying social cycles.

2. "Originating exemplars and positive heuristics": Kondratieff's work is an exemplar for all long wave schools, and the major figures within each school have also provided exemplars for that school (notably Mandel, Mensch, and Forrester).[22]

3. "Symbolic generalizations which facilitate the application of exemplars, including empirically-revisable theories":[23] Such generalizations are central to the broad differences among long cycle research schools that propose different causal theories.

4. "A cumulative literature, containing some increase in corroborated content":[24] In the long cycle field, each school has its own literature that is largely cumulative in its limited domain.

5. "A scholarly community sharing items 1–4 above, and internally tending toward theoretical monopoly (but possibly substructured)": Here the long cycle schools reflect internal theoretical monopoly in general but in several cases are seriously fragmented on specific causal theories.

6. "The external research situation as it impinges on the complex":[25] Subsumed in this category are the "knowledge interests" served by research,[26] which affect the motives and practices of the members of the research paradigm complex. In the long cycle debates, different knowledge interests and application contexts apply to different schools.

21. Metascientific beliefs include ontologies, cosmologies, and analogies, nonfalsifiable core beliefs protected by negative research heuristics, problem definitions, and research-related policy concerns, value commitments, and critical epistemological standards (Alker 1982).

22. Included in this category are technical exemplars (e.g., Mandel's methodology, followed by four other studies in his school, of averaging growth rates by phase period), and research priorities (e.g., different economic variables studied by the innovation school than by the capitalist crisis school).

23. This category includes representational languages and formalisms, ideal types, and theoretical specifications.

24. This literature may include new evidence of successes, new data discoveries, updated lists of anomalies, revised standards of validity, or reference to a changed social context confirming the worth of the research.

25. This includes forgotten or unknown research experience, the effects of other research paradigms subsuming, overlapping, or competing with the complex (e.g., the other long cycle schools), and sponsorship and application contexts. The sponsorship context must be at least tolerant of the metascientific beliefs of the school, willing to not interfere in day-to-day science, and supportive of research and literature cumulation (Alker 1982).

26. As discussed by Ashley (1981), these include prediction-and-control (technical) interests, interpretation interests, and emancipation interests (using knowledge to overcome oppressive social structures).

The Structure of the Long Cycle Community

Kuhn's (1970:109–10) description of the "incommensurability" between paradigms applies well to the competing research schools of the long cycle debates:

To the extent . . . that two scientific schools disagree about what is a problem and what a solution, they will inevitably talk through each other when debating the relative merits of their respective paradigms. In the partially circular arguments that regularly result, each paradigm will be shown to satisfy more or less the criteria that it dictates for itself and to fall short of a few of those dictated by its opponent.

Kuhn's (p. 148) reasons for paradigm incommensurability also apply to the long cycle schools. First, "the proponents of competing paradigms will often disagree about the list of problems" to be solved. In the long cycle debates, this has been reflected in the different foci of different schools. Second, different paradigms use similar vocabulary and conceptual apparatus, but with different meanings. This has been seen in the confused debates between long cycle schools about the meanings of words.[27] Third, and most fundamentally, according to Kuhn (p. 150) different paradigms reflect and are defined in terms of different world views. Proponents of different approaches, ordering their perceptions and theories around different paradigms, actually see different "worlds." "Practicing in different worlds, the two groups of scientists see different things when they look from the same point in the same direction" and see those things in different relations to each other.

The structure of the long cycle community is fractured and divided on several levels. The ideological and metatheoretical differences have been discussed: each school has its own theories couched in its own vocabulary and shaped by fundamentally different concerns for the policy implications of its work. In addition to these divisions between schools, the field is fragmented by other, more random divisions—linguistic, national, and disciplinary borders. Figure 7.2 shows the nationalities of the participants in the long wave debate. The major contributions are written in five languages: English, French, German, Russian, and Dutch.[28] Some of the most interesting material has been largely ignored in the English literature (the predominant language of the debate) because it was unavailable in English—for example, the Trotsky-Kondratieff debate (Russian), the war theory of Åkerman (Swedish), and the war-innovation synthesis of Imbert (French).

The division between disciplines seems to be another important source of the lack of cohesion in the long cycle field. The scholars of the debate come from a variety of disciplines—economics, sociology, political science, history, and others. Each discipline has its own terminology, its own methodological leanings, its own disci-

27. For instance, the world-system school talks about "world war" and "hegemony," the leadership cycle school talks about "global war" and "world leadership," and the power-transition school talks about "hegemonic war" (Gilpin) and a "dominant nation" (Organski). While these are parallel vocabularies, they are rooted in different theoretical contexts.
28. While much of the theoretical debate is now available in English or French, this was not true until recent years.

Figure 7.2. Long Wave Scholars' Nationalities/Languages

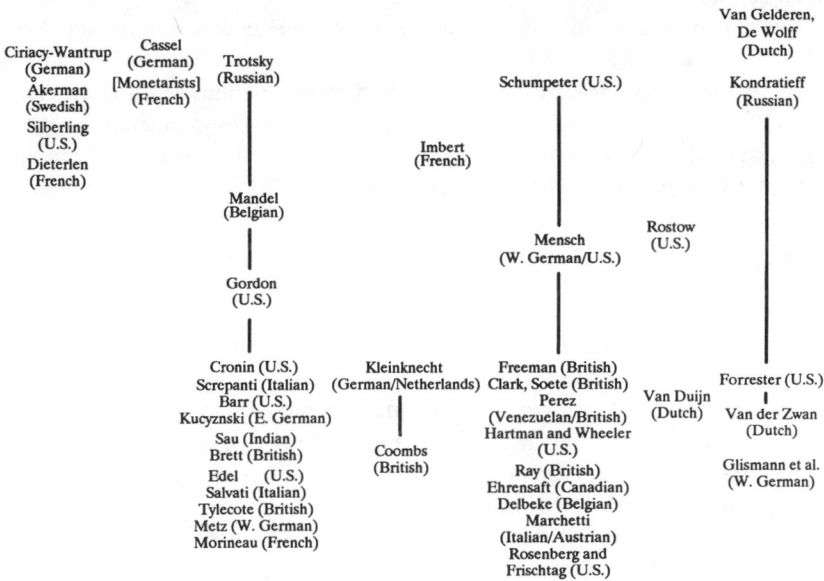

```
                                              Van Gelderen,
                                              De Wolff
Ciriacy-Wantrup  Cassel                       (Dutch)
(German)        (German)   Trotsky
Akerman         [Monetarists] (Russian)       Schumpeter (U.S.)   Kondratieff
(Swedish)       (French)                                          (Russian)
Silberling
(U.S.)                                Imbert
Dieterlen                             (French)
(French)
                   Mandel
                   (Belgian)
                                                          Rostow
                                          Mensch          (U.S.)
                                          (W. German/U.S.)
                   Gordon
                   (U.S.)


Cronin (U.S.)      Kleinknecht        Freeman (British)
Screpanti (Italian) (German/Netherlands) Clark, Soete (British)   Forrester (U.S.)
Barr (U.S.)                            Perez             Van Duijn   |
Kucyznski (E. German)                  (Venezuelan/British) (Dutch)  Van der Zwan
Sau (Indian)                           Hartman and Wheeler          (Dutch)
Brett (British)    Coombs              (U.S.)
Edel    (U.S.)     (British)           Ray (British)               Glismann et al.
Salvati (Italian)                      Ehrensaft (Canadian)        (W. German)
Tylecote (British)                     Delbeke (Belgian)
Metz (W. German)                       Marchetti
Morineau (French)                      (Italian/Austrian)
                                       Rosenberg and
                                       Frischtag (U.S.)
```

plinary associations, conferences, and journals. In each discipline, the long cycle scholars are a tiny minority surrounded by a majority unsupportive of long cycles either as a useful theory or as an important agenda for research. Long wave scholars from different disciplines, unlike scholars working within a discipline, have the opportunity for contact only at special conferences on long waves or through other special channels of communication specific to the long wave debate. By contrast, one advantage for communication among schools in the war/hegemony debate as opposed to the long wave debate is that the principals are overwhelmingly American, are concentrated in two disciplines—political science and sociology—and write in English.

Given the divisions inherent in the structure of the long cycle community, it is hardly surprising that communication between schools has been less than adequate. Numerous examples of poor communication can be found in the materials presented in earlier chapters. I will elaborate seven elements of the miscommunication among schools, using further examples drawn from the long wave debate.[29]

1. Theoretical schools make reference primarily to work in their own school and may actually be unaware of entire research traditions in one or more of the other schools. For example, the introduction to the 1984 translation of Kondratieff's 1928 book refers to the second wave of interest in long waves almost entirely in terms of

29. The examples referred to are not meant as criticisms of the individual authors but as illustrations of the difficulties in cross-paradigm communication.

Forrester's work (parallel to Kondratieff's capital investment theory) while ignoring all other schools.

2. Two schools discussing similar aspects of the same phenomenon often do so in apparent ignorance of each other's work (they do not cite the other school). For example, Perez (1983:358), from the innovation school, defines a "structural crisis" in terms of "the visible syndrome of a breakdown in the complementarity between the dynamics of the economic subsystem and the related dynamics of the socio-institutional framework." This parallels Gordon's (1980:20) concept of economic crises that threaten the stability of the "social structure of accumulation" (this social structure represents socioinstitutional conditions for the continued operation of capitalism). Yet Perez does not cite Gordon. Likewise, in her criticism of Schumpeter's exclusion of socioinstitutional factors from the economy and her conceptualization of long waves as "successive phases in the evolution of the total system" (p. 360), she cites neither Trotsky nor Mandel.

3. Theoretical schools tend to talk to themselves rather than address other groups conducting parallel research under the framework of a different paradigm. For example, Perez's (1983:1) paper at the 1983 Florence conference on long waves begins with the statement: "I believe we all agree here that an appropriate theory of long waves should provide an explanation *endogenous* to the system."[30] That conference included the leaders of the innovation and capital investment schools but not the capitalist crisis school or war theorists—and hence was limited to precisely those who agree on the conceptualization of long waves as endogenous (see fig. 7.3).

4. Even when two schools present parallel theories or empirical evidence, these are embedded in different systems of reference and couched in different vocabularies. Different terms are used to refer to the same phenomenon—for example, "long waves" and "Kondratieff cycles." Similarly, a term such as *long cycle* can refer to several very different phenomena. Gordon (1978) uses the term *long swing* to refer to long waves, while Hoffmann (1955) uses the term *long waves* when actually referring to long swings (Kuznets cycles).[31]

5. Differences among long wave schools often reflect parallel differences among the underlying world views and/or the individuals themselves in other arenas. I referred in chapter 2 to the parallels between the Trotsky-Kondratieff long wave debate and the earlier and more general split between Lenin and Kautsky (communism and socialism). More recently, the debate between the capital investment school, led by Forrester, and the innovation school, centered around Freeman, reflects similar conservative-liberal dynamics found in the Forrester-Freeman debate over "limits to growth."[32]

30. She goes on to argue that the "system" should include both social/institutional and economic components.
31. An extreme example of the lack of standardized vocabulary is Kuczynski's (1982:28) reference to "a" and "b" phases (upswings and downswings). His usage is directly reversed from the usage of other long wave scholars (this does not reflect an interschool difference but does indicate the severe lack of consistency in vocabulary in the field, which is in turn partly due to interschool differences).
32. Freeman edited a major book, *Models of Doom,* criticizing Forrester's "limits to growth" models.

Figure 7.3. Long Wave Conferences in 1983

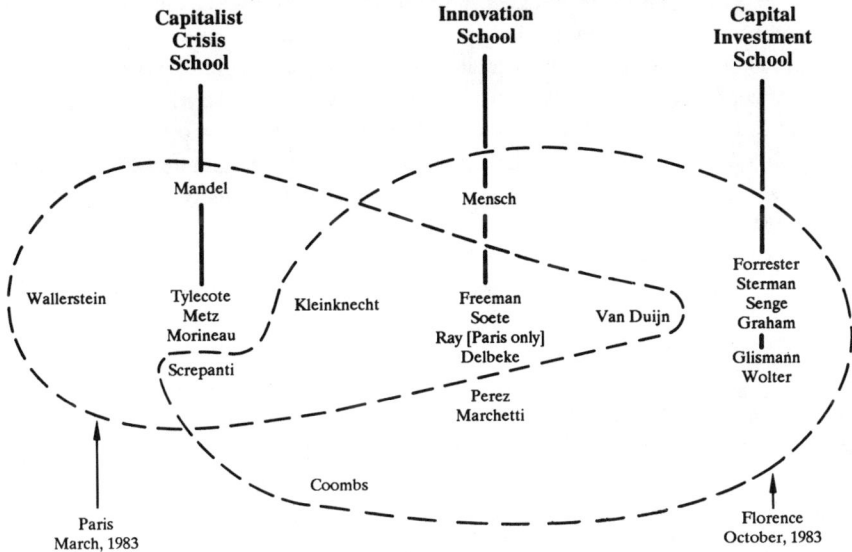

6. Those outside a theoretical school tend to apply their own standards, rather than those of the school itself, in evaluating the work of the school. They tend to see the school as monolithic and are not aware of divisions either within it or between it and other schools to which the outsider does not belong. For instance, Hussain's (1980: 355–56) review of Mandel (1978) is a broadside attack on Marxism,[33] which he sees as a monolithic bloc: "If Marxists claim that capitalism goes through various stages . . . then they have to reconcile those stages with the recurrence of long term cycles . . . [which] straddle different stages of capitalism. . . . This question does not bother Mandel, for he is not interested in analysis but in crystal ball gazing." Mandel, of course, was very interested in such questions as he grappled with the debate *within* Marxism, between Kondratieff and Trotsky, on cycles versus stages of development.[34]

7. The failure of knowledge cumulation across schools is self-reinforcing, since it

33. Hussain begins by dismissing the entire Marxist approach for arguing that capitalism inherently produces crises that can only be permanently resolved by socialism.

34. Baqir (1981:117) also reflects the common assumption among non-Marxists that there is one Marxist theory of long waves, failing to recognize the divisions between Kondratieff and Trotsky. Baqir says that Kondratieff "followed Karl Marx in regarding the long-wave cycles as the result of the nature of the capitalist system. For the Marxists these causes, and in particular, wars, are integral parts of capitalism" (p. 119). Actually, Kondratieff saw long waves as integral to capitalism and as causing wars, but Trotsky held the opposite. Baqir similarly misreads Forrester's approach (pp. 120–21) as attributing long waves to technological changes and "Schumpeterian causes." Forrester's central causal argument is actually based on capital investment, not innovation. These examples illustrate the way theoretical distinctions become blurred and tangled when viewed from outside a school.

obstructs support for long wave research by larger disciplinary communities, which in turn obstructs the kind of research that could contribute to the cumulation of knowledge. Onuf (1984:50) stresses the need for the long wave debate to acquire a unity within the context of the larger directions of social science and finds this undermined by the debates within the long wave community. He argues that in order to gain acceptance, "long waves must be endowed with the same paradigmatic significance that the report *Limits to Growth* granted to the idea of limits to growth. The writers who come closest to doing this are Mensch, the Schumpeterian liberal, and the great Trotskyite economist, Ernest Mandel. Neither succeeds because of the other's effort" (p. 51).

Gordon (1980:10–11) and Ehrensaft (1980:78) argue that long waves should be on the research agenda for the sake of prudence: "If such waves exist in some form, our reasoning about the economy will be quite flawed if the phenomenon is ignored. . . . [If they do not exist,] the most that scholars have to lose is a certain amount of time spent on negative findings, which is less risky than ignoring a major force in the world economy" (Ehrensaft 1980:78). This view, however, ignores the fact that disciplinary communities do not reward negative findings and hence are not inclined to support research on long waves unless they believe such waves exist (which they presently do not). Thus, for an individual scholar, the pursuit of long waves is more risky than other lines of work, and the perceived likelihood of negative findings deters the expenditure of effort in this direction.[35] These considerations help explain why many scholars from various disciplines "toy" with long waves without committing their full resources in that area.

Contact and Cumulation between Schools

Kuhn (1970:201–2) does, however, suggest that those who experience communication breakdowns due to paradigm differences "have some recourse."

Briefly put, what the participants in a communication breakdown can do is recognize each other as members of different language communities and then become translators. Taking the differences . . . as itself a subject for study, they can first attempt to discover the terms and locutions that, used unproblematically within each community, are nevertheless foci of trouble for inter-group discussions. . . . Each may . . . try to discover what the other would see and say when presented with a stimulus. . . . [T]hey may in time become very good predictors of each other's behavior. Each will have learned to translate the other's theory and its consequences into his own language and simultaneously to describe in his language the world to which that theory applies.

Furthermore, says Kuhn, there is an incentive for this kind of work, because translation "is a potent tool both for persuasion and for conversion."

The kind of "translation" described by Kuhn has been rare in the long cycle

---

35. Wallerstein (1984a) argues that "the investment of scholarly energy is a decision and a risk, and will only be pursued if it seems likely to be rewarded by additional interpretive insight. Most scholars have not been willing to invest at all in the construction of Kondratieffs."

debate, but not entirely absent. In a number of ways schools have come in contact and have partially synthesized perspectives drawn from each other.

A first type of contact is the universal reference of long wave schools to the work of Kondratieff, which provides a shared exemplar.[36] Kondratieff provided exemplary analyses and outlined the puzzles to be pursued in a way that has shaped the debate for sixty years.[37]

A second type of communication has been the emergence of "hybrid" theories—particularly those of Van Duijn and Kleinknecht in the long wave debate and of Väyrynen, Farrar, and Levy in the war/hegemony debate. These theories integrate two schools, providing bridges for communication between them and for reconciling differences in vocabularies, interpretations, and theories. In a somewhat analogous role in bridging the two debates as a whole are Wallerstein and (potentially) the scholars of fifty-year political cycles.[38]

A third avenue of communication for long wave schools has been the journal *Futures,* which has made a point of publishing articles from the innovation school (its primary focus), the capital investment school, and (to a lesser extent) the capitalist crisis school. In 1981 *Futures* published a special issue (later published as a book) with articles from all three long wave schools and the two hybrid theories connecting them.[39] Another journal important in long wave research is *Review,* edited by Immanuel Wallerstein. However, it has published mainly studies from the capitalist crisis school. In the war/hegemony debate, an example of this kind of cross-school forum is found in Thompson, ed. (1983) and in Johnson and Thompson, eds. (1985).

A fourth type of contact between schools has occurred in conferences devoted specifically to long waves.[40] Two conferences in Europe in 1983 each brought together two schools, with the innovation school overlapping both (see fig. 7.3).[41] These conferences increased contact between different schools, even though no conference brought all three long wave schools together (and contact between those three and the war/hegemony schools remained even more limited).

Fifth, in recent years a few articles from members of one school have dealt substantively with the central issues of another school. This has occurred several times between the innovation and capital-investment long wave schools—for example, in recent articles on innovation written by Jay Forrester (1978; 1981b) and members of his group (Graham and Senge 1980) or on capital investment by Mensch, Coutinho, and Kaasch (1981).

Finally, of course, this book itself aims to translate among research schools and to bring together past work from different schools in one framework.

---

36. The war/hegemony debate has no comparable exemplary work.

37. As Marchetti (1983:337) perhaps too enthusiastically puts it, "not much has been said after [Kondratieff] that he himself did not say."

38. The latter are, however, a disparate group at present, largely unaware of each other's existence.

39. Mandel, Mensch, Freeman, Forrester, Kleinknecht, and Van Duijn.

40. I know of no parallel conferences on war/hegemony.

41. The first (Paris) included the main proponents of the innovation and capitalist crisis schools, while the second (Florence) included the innovation and capital investment schools.

In conclusion, then, the long cycle debates reflect many of the elements of Kuhn's "immature" scientific community or Lakatos's competing research programs. The internal fragmentation of the long cycle research community goes a long way toward explaining the difficulties of knowledge cumulation in the field.

Alternative Hypotheses

In the remainder of this chapter I will list and sort out alternative hypotheses from the long cycle debates. From the array of long cycle hypotheses that have been touched on in Part One, I seek to structure a set of hypotheses that cover the main points of the debates. I translate each hypothesis into my own terminology (in order to bring them into one internally consistent vocabulary), while providing references to the scholars whose theories support the hypothesis.[42]

Opinions frequently converge across the major research schools. These consensual hypotheses point to common historical realities cutting through the diversity of definitions and methodologies that should be preserved in building theory consistent with empirical reality. There are also many direct contradictions between mutually exclusive hypotheses,[43] and these salient points of disagreement must be resolved (however tentatively) by empirical testing in order to render a long wave theory internally consistent. Beginning with the next chapter, I will present the results of my own empirical testing and theory-building efforts on the question of long waves. My empirical tests seek to favor one hypothesis over a mutually exclusive alternative (rather than to test a hypothesis in isolation against the "null hypothesis"), so that theory may be built in a manner consistent with favored hypotheses.

I have pulled from the preceding chapters ninety-eight hypotheses, which are marked henceforward with asterisks (*). One or more principal scholars are listed for each hypothesis.[44] Mutually exclusive, contradictory sets of hypotheses are separated from each other with a dotted line.

In going through these hypotheses, I have made two kinds of judgment: (1) What is the standing of this hypothesis within the existing long cycle debate? Is it advocated by a majority of any school or by a minority of more than one school? Is it compatible or irreconcilable with existing frameworks of research? (2) What is my judgment of the evidence for this hypothesis? Were reported results consistent among different scholars? Were methodologies appropriate? Did results using different approaches converge? Through this process, I will make a first pass at provisionally accepting

42. The hypotheses are not identical to those of the scholars cited but rather the "mapping" of those scholars' theories onto my vocabulary and framework.
43. And between clusters of hypotheses having slightly different interpretations of the same basic relationship.
44. The persons cited would generally agree with the hypotheses as stated, but the hypotheses are not technically theirs, since I have translated them into my own framework and language in order to integrate them.

Table 7.1. Hypothesized Causal Relations -- Long Wave

Economics and politics:

Long waves are generated endogenously in the economy. [A] (Kondratieff, Gordon)

Long waves are generated exogenously to the economy. [A] (Trotsky, Mandel)

Capital investment:

Capital investment causes long waves. [A] (Forrester, Van der Zwan)

 Increased investment causes upswing. [A] (Van Duijn)

The long wave causes changes in capital investment. [A] (Mandel)

Innovation:

Innovation causes long waves. [A] (Schumpeter)

The long wave causes changes in innovation. [A] (Forrester)

 Long wave downswing causes innovation to increase. [A] (Kleinknecht)

Class struggle:

Class struggle causes the long wave. [A] (Screpanti)

 Class struggle causes the long wave upswing. [A] (Gordon, Mandel)

The long wave causes class struggle. [A] (Cronin)

War:

Long waves in the economy cause concentrations of war. [A] (Kondratieff)

 Long wave upswings cause increases in war. [A] (Imbert)

War causes the long wave. [A] (Akerman, Silberling, Dickinson, Toynbee)

 War causes the long wave downswing. [A] (Imbert)

 War causes the price upswing. [A] (Kuznets)

 War does not create but reinforces the price upswing. **[A] (Thompson and Zuk)**

 War causes changes in innovation. [A] (Rose)

 War causes changes in capital investment. [A] (Dickinson)

 The cost of war causes long waves in war. [A] (Wright, Farrar)

Gold production:

Fluctuations in gold production cause long waves in prices. [A] (Cassel)

Long waves cause fluctuations in gold production. [A] (Åkerman)

and rejecting hypotheses. Those that are internally inconsistent, are incompatible with the major theoretical frameworks, or are contradicted by convincing empirical evidence will be provisionally rejected (marked [R]).[45] The others will be provisionally accepted (marked [A]), even though many in this group directly contradict each other. The criteria for acceptance at this stage are thus broad, allowing the inclusion of mutually exclusive hypotheses from alternative research traditions.

I have grouped the hypotheses into three categories. First are twenty-two causal hypotheses concerning the dynamics of long waves. These are listed in table 7.1 and show the opposed theories of different groups of scholars on almost every important question of causality. The causal hypotheses are not empirically testable, however, and will not be pursued further here.[46]

The second group of hypotheses concern the scope and correlations of long waves. These hypotheses are discussed immediately below. They are empirically testable and will be the focus of Part Two. The third group of hypotheses, concerning the scope and correlations of hegemony cycles, will be discussed after the long wave hypotheses and will set the stage for further elaboration in Part Three.

Long Wave Hypotheses

This section summarizes the hypotheses regarding the scope and correlations of long waves. There is consensus among scholars of long waves that long economic cycles (whether called waves, stages, phases, or cycles) of about fifty years' length do exist as a historical fact at the world level (despite disputes about why they exist). On this point the long wave schools all agree and all differ from the dominant view in the social sciences that long waves do *not* exist:[47]

Existence of long waves

Long waves exist. [A]
(Most long wave researchers)

Long waves do not exist. [R]
(Most social scientists; see Rosenberg and Frischtak)

There is no consensus on the *scope* of the long wave—the variables, time periods, and countries in which it is found:

Scope: Variables
Long waves exist in prices, production and investment. [A]
(Kondratieff, Mandel, Kuczynski, Gordon, Kleinknecht, Delbeke, Van Duijn, Forrester)

Long waves exist in prices only, not production and investment. [A]
(Kuznets, Silberling, Cleary and Hobbs, Van Ewijk, Van der Zwan)

---

45. The idea here is to sort out stray theories that use the language of long cycles but are not really talking about the same phenomena as the rest of the community is. Provisionally accepted long wave hypotheses should be compatible with the consensual base dating scheme (see chap. 4).

46. I have not drawn up a comparable list of causal hypotheses for the hegemony cycle hypotheses. I find that debate to be less well defined and less focused on questions of causality.

47. I reject the hypothesis that no long waves exist, given significant (if scattered) evidence of their existence reviewed in chaps. 2–4.

Long waves exist in world trade. [A]
(Kondratieff, Mandel, Mauro, Kuczynski)

Long waves do not exist in trade. [A]
(Oparin, Van der Zwan, Van Ewijk)

Long waves exist in wages. [A]
(Kondratieff)

Long waves do not exist in wages. [A]
(Oparin)

Innovations cluster at one point on the long wave. [A]
(Kondratieff, Mensch, Freeman, Forrester, Mandel, Gordon)

Innovations do not occur in clusters. [A]
(Kuznets)

Long waves exist in war and related political phenomena. [A]
(Kondratieff, Wright, Väyrynen, Craig and Watt).

Long waves of war do not exist. [A]
(Sorokin)

These form five pairs of contradictory hypotheses. I provisionally accept all ten, noting these as fertile areas for empirical research.[48] The duration of the long wave over historical eras is also nonconsensual.

Scope: Temporal

Long waves exist only after about 1790. [A]
(Kondratieff, Ischboldin)

Long waves, at least in prices, exist before 1790. [A]
(Imbert, Braudel, Wallerstein)

Long waves in prices and harvests exist before 1790. [A]
(Morineau, Baehrel)

The first two hypotheses are contradictory and should be tested. The third hypothesis is an elaboration of the second. Most long wave studies are restricted to the period after about 1790, many explicitly arguing that this is the appropriate time frame. But a minority, cutting across schools, argue for long waves in preindustrial times.[49] I include the longer time period within the scope of my empirical study where possible and try to compare the earlier and later epochs.

48. As regards the scope of long waves in terms of countries, I have defined long waves at the level of the core of the world system and find no benefit from defining long waves in terms of "capitalist countries." To the extent the core of the world system has been capitalist the long wave is a capitalist phenomenon; to the extent that socialist economies are nonetheless tied into a world capitalist economy the distinction becomes meaningless. In any case available data relate only to capitalist countries.

49. That group seems to agree roughly on Imbert's datings (through 1650), as his seems to be the most complete study. These are roughly compatible with the base dating scheme.

The next area is the historical dating of long wave phases. There is a strong consensus that phase dates roughly follow those given by Kondratieff for the 1790–1920 period. Datings by a wide variety of scholars fall within a few years of each other for each turning point up until World War II.[50] As discussed in chapter 4 (p. 67), I created a base dating scheme using dates given by Kondratieff, Mandel, Braudel, and Frank. I then showed that such a base dating scheme comes close to a consensus among thirty-three scholars from a variety of schools, interests, and methodologies. Therefore my base dating scheme is provisionally accepted. Acceptance of the base dating scheme means provisionally accepting Mandel's side in the Mandel-Rostow dating debate (for reasons discussed in chapter 3) and provisionally rejecting two alternative datings:

Historical dating of phases
The dating of phases is captured in my base dating scheme. [A]
(Goldstein, based on 33 scholars reviewed in chapter 4)

1940/45–1968/74 was an upswing; 1968/74– is a downswing. [A]
(Mandel, Dupriez)

The 1951–72 period was a downswing; since 1972 an upswing. [R]
(Rostow)

The 1913–46 period was an upswing; 1946–73 a downswing. [R]
(Modelski)

I also reject Metz's irregular long waves, which do not match the base dating on which other scholars converge:

Irregular "long waves" exist in grain prices before 1790. [R]
(Metz)

The next set of hypotheses concern the correlations and timing among the different variables that may play a role in long waves. As noted above, there is no consensus about whether long waves in *production* do exist, but if so, most scholars put production phases in synchrony with price phases. Only Imbert offers a slightly different sequence:

Correlations: Production
Production phases are synchronous with price phases. [A]
(Most long wave researchers)

---

50. For example, the beginning of the upswing that Kondratieff dates at 1890–96, is dated at 1896 by De Wolff, 1895 by Ciriacy-Wantrup, 1897 by Schumpeter, 1898 by Kuznets, 1895–96 (depending on country) by Burns and Mitchell, 1895–96 by Dupriez, 1894 by Mandel, 1896 by Rostow, and 1892 by Van Duijn (see Van Duijn 1983:163).

Production increases precede price increases. [A]
(Imbert)

Next come correlations concerning long-term *capital investment*. Most research-ers link investments in long-lived fixed assets with emerging technologies in new leading sectors, though they disagree on the cause-effect relationship. Most scholars put the timing of a surge of capital investment early in the expansion phase, and the rare instance of the opposite hypothesis is provisionally rejected:

Correlations: Capital investment
Capital investment increases early in the upswing. [A]
(Kondratieff, Mandel, Gordon, Forrester)

Capital investment is low during the downswing. [A]
(Van Duijn)

Capital investment increases on the downswing. [R]
(Hartman and Wheeler)

Innovation is the next area of concern. All three schools work innovation into the long wave in one way or another. Most researchers hold that innovations increase late in the stagnation phase or early in the upswing phase (when stored innovations may be put to use):[51]

Correlations: Innovation
Innovations cluster late in the downswing. [A]
(Gordon, Schumpeter)

Innovations cluster on the downswing. [A]
(Mensch)

Innovations are fewer late in the upswing. [A]
(Forrester)

Innovations cluster early in the upswing. [A]
(Kondratieff, Mandel, Freeman et al.)

"Product" innovations cluster early in the upswing. [A]
(Van Duijn)

Innovations are fewer late in the downswing. [A]
(Freeman et al.)

51. The innovation school (and those who have borrowed from it, Gordon and Kleinknecht) sees innovation as a necessary precondition for the expansion phase and hence hypothesizes that innovation peaks late in the downswing. Most people in the capitalist crisis and capital investment schools see innovation as a result rather than a cause of the long wave and hence place the peak of innovation early in the upswing. But the divisions do not always follow school boundaries.

Note also that some researchers distinguish both invention and the diffusion of innovations from innovation itself:

Inventions cluster on the downswing.* [A]
(Hartman and Wheeler.)

*Innovations *diffuse* faster during upswings.* [A]
(Mensch et al.)

The next area of interest is the role of *class struggle:* the most common view is that workers' movements intensify late in the upswing, reducing profits and pushing capitalism toward crisis. But every other timing correlation has also been hypothesized, and none can yet be rejected:

Correlations: Class struggle
Class struggle peaks during the upswing. [A]
(Kondratieff, Cronin)

Class struggle peaks during the downswing. [A]
(Imbert)

Class struggle peaks late in the upswing. [A]
(Mandel, Screpanti)

Class struggle peaks late in the downswing. [A]
(Gordon)

Finally, there is the question of long waves in *war.* I accept the cluster of compatible hypotheses with the most theoretical and empirical support, correlating war with the upswing phase (and reject the opposite correlation):

Correlations: War
War concentrations occur on long wave upswings. [A]
(Kondratieff, Åkerman, Rose, Wright, Craig and Watt, Väyrynen)

   Foreign policy "extrovert" moods occur on upswings. [A]
   (Klingberg, Holmes and Elder)

   Cosmopolitan/parochial social values on up/downswings. [A]
   (Namenwirth, Weber)

   "Internationalist" public opinion increases on upswings. [A]
   (Goldstein; see chapter 5)

   Price upswings precede major wars.[52] [A]
   (Rostow, Thompson and Zuk)

War clusters early in the downswing. [R]
(Mensch)

---

52. This is a more specific timing and not consensual.

These are the hypotheses that can be tested in the following chapters. I note, however, several other less central hypotheses concerning the correlations of *other long wave variables:*

Correlations: Other variables

Downswings in agriculture correspond with general upswings. [A]
(Ehrensaft)

  Harvest downswings correspond with price upswings, pre-1790. [A]
  (Baehrel)

Labor cost upswings correspond with general downswings. [A]
(Gordon et al.)

High employment corresponds with the upswing. [A]
(Freeman et al.)

Mergers cluster on the upswing. [A]
(Mensch)

Millenarian movements cluster late in the downswing. [A]
(Barkun)

Social "optimism" in design is high during upswings. [A]
(Langrish)

Currency issue follows long wave phases. [A]
(Dupriez)

War/Hegemony Hypotheses

The war/hegemony hypotheses are less well defined than the long wave hypotheses (less agreement about what compose phenomena of interest and how to define and measure them). The cycle is longer, and empirical testing of it is consequently harder. There has been little empirical work; rather, the flavor of the debate is more theoretical, interpretive, and historical.

The convergent hypotheses that are consensual among the schools include the general dynamic of war and hegemony:

Hegemonic war follows hegemonic decline (rising challenges). [A]
(Wallerstein, Modelski, Organski)

Hegemony follows hegemonic war. [A]
(Wallerstein, Modelski)

Few wars occur in periods of declining hegemony. [A]
(Väyrynen)

There is agreement that each hegemonic war episode represented a major struggle for control of the European-centered state system. But there are two definitions of which wars were hegemonic:

Hegemonic war/challenges: Spain, France (2), Germany. [A]
(Dehio, Toynbee, Modelski)

Hegemonic war/challenges: Thirty-Years', Napoleonic, WWI/WWII. [A]
(Chase-Dunn, Wallerstein)

These two approaches constitute two dating schemes for historical hegemony cycles. Whereas for long waves I identified a consensual dating scheme (and then rejected outliers from it), here there are two competing dating schemes, the first based on pairs of long waves (Toynbee's dating), and the second on longer cycles (Chase-Dunn's dating):

"Hegemonic war" occurs on every other long wave. [A]
(Wright, Toynbee, Farrar, Modelski)

  Hegemony cycles consist of pairs of long waves. [A]
  (Hopkins and Wallerstein, Väyrynen)

  Hegemony recurs: Portugal, Netherlands, Britain (2), U.S. [A]
  (Modelski)

  Portugal was the first hegemonic power (world power). [A]
  (Modelski)

  Venice was the prototype insular power/world power. [A]
  (Dehio, Modelski)

  The USSR is the next likely "challenger." [A]
  (Dehio, Toynbee)

Hegemony cycles are longer than pairs of long waves. [A]
(Chase-Dunn, Bousquet, Wallerstein)

  Hegemony recurs: (Hapsburgs), Netherlands, Britain, U.S. [A]
  (Hopkins and Wallerstein, Wallerstein, Chase-Dunn, Bousquet)

  Spain was the first hegemonic power. [A]
  (Wallerstein)

  Military technology enters new stages: 1648, 1789, 1914. [A]
  (Wright)

For now, I provisionally accept both possible dating schemes for hegemony cycles.[53] But I reject other dating schemes that find little corroboration:

53. In chap. 13, however, I will eventually adopt the second of these dating schemes.

There is a 200-year cycle in war. [R]
(Moyal)

There are 25-year and 100-year war cycles (irregular). [R]
(Denton and Phillips)

Relative national capabilities in world are cyclical. [R]
(Doran and Parsons)

The idea that wars are not cyclical at all is rejected in light of the evidence that war at the least correlates with long waves.

Wars are not cyclical. [R]
(Singer, Sorokin, Richardson)

Several subsidiary hypotheses fit into one or the other hegemony dating scheme that I have accepted. I accept these as possibilities within the hegemony dynamic (two also relate to long waves):

Naval capabilities are most concentrated after global wars. [A]
(Thompson)

Naval capabilities are not correlated with long waves. [A]
(Thompson)

"Free trade" is high in times of strong hegemony. [A]
(Hopkins and Wallerstein, Bergesen)

Colonization diminishes in times of strong hegemony. [A]
(Hopkins and Wallerstein, Bergesen, Bousquet)

"Logistic cycles" (150–200 years) exist before 1790. [A]
(Wallerstein, Bousquet)

Stagflation on long wave downswing in "logistical" upswing. [A]
(Wallerstein)

This last group of hypotheses is a scattered set, not split into opposed clusters. In general, the war/hegemony hypotheses are fewer, less well defined, and more difficult to judge than the long wave hypotheses. When the hegemony cycle is taken up again, in Part Three, it will be in a historical, interpretive vein rather than a quantitative, empirical one.

In conclusion, I have taken as ideal types three generative "world views"— revolutionary, liberal and conservative—and have shown how these world views structure the debates over long cycles at both the economic and the political level. The six current schools of the long cycle debates—three in the long wave debate and three in the war/hegemony debate—represent the present mainline traditions flowing out of the three world views, respectively, in each debate. I have treated them as paradigm-governed research programs, in the sense of Kuhn and Lakatos, in which the different metaphysical core-beliefs (world views), vocabularies, theories, methodologies, and knowledge interests all contribute to the partial incommensurability of schools.

The fragmented structure of the long cycle research community has contributed to a disappointing lack of knowledge cumulation over the decades of debate on long cycles. Although in the preceding chapters I have sorted out the competing approaches and hypotheses of the debates and encompassed them within one framework, I have yet to resolve the substantive differences.

In Part Two of this book I present my own empirical analysis on long waves, which is informed and shaped by the theoretical arguments of the long wave debate and is oriented toward making some progress in resolving those arguments. The coming chapters do not, of course, resolve all issues between the competing schools, nor do they arrive at a full and final understanding of long waves. They aim, rather, for limited but tangible progress in sorting out relevant empirical questions, in judging between contradictory hypotheses, and in moving toward greater consensus regarding the state of knowledge in the field.

Part Two: ANALYSIS

CHAPTER EIGHT

Defining Long Cycles:
Epistemology and Methodology

The following questions are of central importance in the long wave debate: (1) Can long waves be identified in a variety of economic time series? (2) In which time periods, countries, and types of economic variables can long waves be found? (3) Is there a connection between the ups and downs of wars and the phases of the long wave? (4) From the above, what relationships among various economic and political elements can be adduced and what causal theories of the long wave do these relationships suggest?[1] Through these questions, I have tried to address the gap between theory and empirical investigation that has plagued past work on long waves.[2]

The long wave field is weak in data, and this sharply limits what is possible. In this study I try to push out the frontiers where little research has been done and data are very limited. In a sense everything is provisional. I believe the analysis presented below shows that the long wave theory proposed can account for empirical data in a coherent manner. But I do not believe it is the last word on long waves, and I expect parts of the theory to be revised in the future as further evidence emerges. I am seeking new possibilities, not final conclusions.

The Definition of Social Cycles

The first subject of this chapter is the conceptualization of social cycles in general and long waves in particular. There has been much confusion about definitions of "cycles" or "waves." I will start with a dictionary definition: "Cycle: an interval of time during which one sequence of a regularly recurring

---

1. Van der Zwan (1980:185) calls the long wave "a pre-eminent methodological problem," while Ehrensaft (1980:78) calls long wave research "an intimidating process because of the very scope of the questions that must be raised."

2. Wallerstein (1984a) notes that the results of empirical research to date "have been meager." And he agrees with Gordon (1980:10), who writes that long wave scholars have failed "to elaborate a coherent (much less a unified) theoretical foundation for their interpretation of long cycles." My overall approach is: (1) Define research schools and their hypotheses; (2) Test alternative hypotheses against others' and my own evidence; (3) Synthesize surviving hypotheses into an adduced theoretical framework; (4) Identify anomalies, unanswered questions, and potentially fruitful avenues of future research; and (5) Use the adduced theoretical framework to develop new interpretive insights into history (in Part Three).

succession of events or phenomena is completed."[3] This definition contains two elements: an interval of time and a repeating sequence. If the time interval is fixed in length, the definition corresponds to *periodicity,* but if the time interval varies, then the *repeating sequences* define the cycle.

Periodicity versus "Cycle Time"

I distinguish two general approaches to social cycles. The first defines cycles in terms of "periodicity" relative to a fixed external time frame. The second approach defines cycles as repeating sequences best measure in "cycle time."[4]

Time itself is always relative to some referent, not absolute. Time is always measured by a *repeating* change of state in some phenomenon and is thus inherently cyclic. Physical time is measured by physical cycles—the rotations and orbits of atoms and planets. "Social time" may likewise be measured by such social cycles as long waves. Allan (1984; 1987) suggests the desirability of building "social clocks" in which the succession of social phenomena is timed against its own internal dynamic rather than against a fixed external time line.[5]

The regular periodicities of the physical world make possible a variety of measurement and statistical analysis techniques that are appropriate only to cycles defined by fixed periodicities.[6] These techniques include spectral analysis, Fourier analysis, and related approaches that use sine waves as the underlying model of cyclicity.[7]

But periodicity is not appropriate to the social world. While physical phenomena underlie social phenomena, the latter constitute a higher level of analysis, exhibit greater complexity, and contain the added elements of intention and choice. Complex social phenomena are not well described by physical laws of mechanical motion (see Alker 1981).

Kondratieff ([1928] 1984:81–82) argues that "in social and economic phenomena, there is nothing like strict periodicity." Kondratieff holds that the "regularity" of long waves should refer not to periodicity but to "the regularity of their repetition in time" and to the international synchrony of different economic series. Trotsky[8] suggests that the long cycle does not resemble the fluctuations of a wire under tension

3. *Webster's 3d New International Dictionary,* S. V. "cycle."
4. As I will argue, the periodicity approach is conducive to the use of inferential statistics, while for the cycle time approach descriptive statistics are more appropriate.
5. Allan criticizes the social sciences for using a time referential "directly borrowed from physics" (1984:2). He proposes looking at the interrelationships of social processes in time in terms of the "sequence and covariations at different phase lags, where the phases are defined as relevant theoretical parts of the dynamic process under consideration" (p. 3). See also Ruggie (1985).
6. In the biological sciences, periodicities tend to be less regular. Although cycles still exist on many levels (biochemistry to population), the cycles can be irregular in duration and timing (e.g., menstrual cycles, life cycles).
7. Spectral analysis produces a curve showing how well the sine wave fits the data as a function of the wavelength of the sine wave (see chap. 4). Fourier analysis finds a set of sine waves (of varying wavelengths), the sum of which at a given point in time approximates the value of a time series.
8. Trotsky (1921), quoted in Day (1976:70).

(periodicity) but might better be compared with a heartbeat.[9] As Sorokin (1957:563) puts it: "History seems to be neither as monotonous and uninventive as the partisans of the strict periodicities . . . think; nor so dull and mechanical as an engine, making the same number of revolutions in a unit of time. It repeats its 'themes' but almost always with new variations." Wallerstein (1984a) suggests an analogy between social cycles and the process of breathing in animal life:

> Physiologists do not argue about whether breathing occurs. Nor do they assume that this regular, repetitive phenomenon is always absolutely identical in form or length. Neither do they assume that it is easy to account for the causes and consequences of a particular instance. . . . [Nonetheless,] all animals breathe, repetitively and reasonably regularly, or they do not survive.

Critics will say that what I call a cycle is not a cycle but just a series of ups and downs, a "random walk." Only periodicity would satisfy them that a cycle exists. But periodicity is only the superficial aspect of a cycle—the essence of the cycle is a (sometimes unknown) inner dynamic that gives rise to repetition. In a single time series variable, there is no way (other than periodicity) to distinguish superficial ups and downs from a deeper cyclic dynamic. But when ups and downs correlate throughout a worldwide political-economic system, it is safe to conclude that there is a deeper systemic dynamic at work, not just a scatter of random ups and downs.

Past studies of social cycles have had little success when using a mechanistic definition of cycles as fixed periodicities and the statistical techniques appropriate to such a definition. In the long wave field, Bieshaar and Kleinknecht (1984:281) note that "research experience has shown that spectral analysis is not a very promising method for the analysis of long waves."[10] And as I noted in chapter 5, the search for war cycles based on periodicity was a self-proclaimed dead end.

An example of the problems inherent in periodicity approaches is the work of E. R. Dewey and his Foundation for the Study of Cycles[11] (Dewey and Mandino 1971). This foundation subjects all manner of time series—on social, economic and natural processes—to Fourier analysis. Each series is broken down as the sum of, say, 4.8-year, 11.2-year, 51.9-year, and 211.4-year cycles, and these numbers vary for every series.[12] Dewey's journal lists so many alleged cycles that they are indexed in the

---

9. For once Kondratieff and Trotsky agree (that periodicity is the wrong definition). Rose (1941:107) agrees that "we may speak of long waves . . . without being concerned with . . . the periodicity of those two-phase wave movements." Morineau (1984) likewise prefers sequences to "rigid cycles" as a basis of defining long waves. By contrast, some long wave studies rely heavily on the concept of periodicity. Kuczynski (1978:81), for example, argues that "generally, Kondratieff's hypothesis can be described as a set of trigonometric functions."

10. Both because time series are too short compared with the wave length and because the results are too sensitive to the method used to eliminate long-term trends (to make the series "stationary," which is necessary for spectral analysis).

11. Which puts out the journal *Cycles*.

12. Dewey (1970), for example, claims to find a cycle of close to 50 years in an index of international battles over the past 2,500 years. However, he also claims to find cycles of several other lengths in the same series (it is the sum of these cycles that approximates the series).

back of each volume according to the length of the cycle. Mechanistic work of this kind may be largely responsible for the skepticism many social scientists express toward cycles.

In contrast to the periodicity approaches, my analysis defines long waves in terms of a simple repeating sequence, that of two alternating phases. Each long wave phase is one unit of cycle time, although the lengths of the phases vary in terms of calendar time. The unit of analysis is thus the phase period rather than the year, and the methodology I develop seeks to identify patterns of regular alternation between successive phase periods. Eventually the analysis moves beyond a simple two-phase analysis, as I look for lagged correlations among variables *within* cycle time. This opens up a fuller theory of timing and causality among variables (see chapter 12).

Several other methodologies relevant to the reconceptualization of social cycles in terms of sequences deserve mention here, although I do not pursue them. Kruskal (1983) summarizes recent research on "sequence comparison" in fields as diverse as macromolecular genetics, speech recognition, and bird-song analysis. These approaches embody techniques for identifying isomorphic sequences even when particular elements have been inserted or deleted from one sequence or when the time axis has been compressed or expanded. Such techniques could someday form the starting point for the statistical analysis of *repeating* sequences of political, economic, and social processes. Mefford (1984) uses "artificial intelligence" techniques to develop a sequence-matching algorithm for political events, finding common patterns in similar (but not identical) case histories.[13] Similar techniques could prove useful in identifying political cycles defined by repeating sequences in political events.

World History: The N=1 Problem

The move away from periodicity to cycle time means defining the long wave as a unique, historically defined set of alternating phases. The level of analysis is thus world history. History is a unique process, and the past five centuries of the core of the world system present only one such history to be studied. It is not a sample of a larger population but the "universe" of cases, and the number of cases in a real sense is one.[14]

This raises methodological problems because the statistical tools useful in testing hypotheses in randomly drawn samples are not appropriate to testing hypotheses in a single historical sequence.[15] Because there is only one history, the underlying thrust

13. His application is the analysis of historical precedents in decision-making—specifically the response of the Soviet leadership to the Czech situation in 1968, based on outcomes of previous Soviet actions in Eastern Europe.

14. And at best, in comparing the repeating pattern over time we can find only ten cases of a long wave in the past five centuries.

15. As Freeman and Job (1979:125, 134) point out, problems with inference increase as one moves to higher levels of analysis and as the number of cases decreases: "our ability to understand contextual novelty decreases rapidly because we have less and less information about the contingencies and effects of structural transformations."

of this study will be toward the statistical *description* of that history rather than toward the inferential statistics appropriate to the analysis of statistical samples within "confidence intervals." I will draw on such simple inferential techniques as bivariate regressions and t-tests, but mainly as tools toward building the most consistent and compelling *description* of long waves. The emphasis, furthermore, is on testing alternative contradictory hypotheses against each other rather than testing a general long cycle hypothesis against the null hypothesis.

Adduction

The logic of inquiry in this approach is adductive. Fischer (1970:xv) calls adduction the most appropriate "logic of historical thought."[16] The study of history

consists neither in inductive reasoning from the particular to the general, nor in deductive reasoning from the general to the particular. Instead, it is a process of *adductive* reasoning in the simple sense of adducing answers to specific questions, so that a satisfactory explanatory "fit" is obtained. The answers may be general or particular, as the questions may require. History is, in short, a problem-solving discipline. A historian is someone (anyone) who asks an open-ended question about past events and answers it with selected facts which are arranged in the form of an explanatory paradigm.

These questions and answers, according to Fischer, affect each other in "a complex process of mutual adjustment." The resultant explanatory paradigm—expressed as some combination of statistical generalization, narrative, causal model, or analogy—is "articulated in the form of a reasoned argument." This is the spirit of my analysis, and I repeat that those who expect "behavioral science" will not find it here.

Alker (1984:167) notes that this kind of explanation is incomplete, offering neither "sufficient causes" nor "counter-arguments as to alternative determinants." Adductive accounts thus "belong in the realm of probabilistic or contingent reasoning; they are not necessarily valid inferences. Nor are they conventional inductive statistical inferences." Yet these "practical inferences" can give a "how possible" rather than "why necessary" account of behavior, and these accounts are in fact useful in a world of imperfect information.[17]

The cumulation of knowledge, as discussed in chapter 7, relies on adduction in important ways. Since theories, according even to Popper, are never "proven" but only imperfectly corroborated, all of science is in a sense adductive. But this is more evident in such a field as long wave research than in, say, physics.

The above considerations, then, shape my overall methodological approach—an approach that stresses adduction, historical datings, descriptive statistics, and cycle time.

16. See also Alker (1984), Braudel ([1958] 1972; [1969] 1980), and Le Roy Ladurie ([1978] 1981).
17. Wallerstein (1984a) argues that cycles, like all concepts, are "a construct of the analyst." A construct "must have an empirical base" to distinguish it from fantasy, but "a construct is not a 'fact,' somehow there, irremediably objective, unmediated by collective representations and social decisions. A construct is an interpretive argument. . . . Its justification is in its defensibility and its heuristic value."

Data Considerations

The search for historical empirical evidence of long waves is greatly constrained by data limitations. Quantitative data regarding economic history are spotty (especially for preindustrial times). Most quantitative data are estimates of particular quantities at particular (occasional) years (or for such longer periods as decades). These are of little use in identifying trends over specific phase periods that do not generally correspond with the years or decades given. Long waves can be identified only by finding trends in the data over phase periods as short as ten to twenty years, and only *annual time series* data will adequately capture such relationships.[18]

Furthermore, in looking for long waves of roughly five decades' length, few meaningful conclusions can be drawn from time series of less than about one hundred years. The series should, at the minimum, pass through several adjacent phase periods—so that differences in the trend behavior within different phase periods may be identified.

Data considerations bear on the issue of what variables to include in the analysis. As I showed in Part One, past work on long waves in different theoretical schools has focused on different variables. I have included in some manner each of the seven categories of variables outlined at the beginning of chapter 4.[19] But I have been constrained by using "available data" in each category (since I did not have the resources to create new time series from primary sources). For some variables data are woefully inadequate, and for some variables the only "available" data are those developed by long wave scholars working within a paradigmatic framework that stresses both the particular variable *and* a theoretical role for that variable (particularly for innovation). Thus my empirical analysis is not free of the "debates" of Part One, since data are themselves influenced by research frameworks.[20]

Another data consideration is what time period to examine. Most past studies of long waves have restricted their analysis to industrial times. Barr (1979:677) refers to "a gap in the literature—*viz.*, the empirical study of long waves before the so-called Industrial Revolution." I have sought to include data from both before and since the beginning of industrial times, going back to 1495 (the beginning of Levy's "great power system" and approximate start of Wallerstein's world-system). But again this has been only partially possible. Data for *price* series both before and since about 1790[21] are adequate for a fairly detailed analysis. However, *production* series are available only since around 1790—and this limits the analysis. Still more spotty are time series for innovation, trade, wages, and capital investment. I have included at

---

18. On long time series, see Granger and Hughes (1971).

19. Prices, production, innovation, capital investment, wages/working-class behavior, trade, and war.

20. I often find that my own analysis of another long wave researcher's data confirms his or her own conclusions.

21. Again, I use the year 1790 to distinguish the preindustrial from the industrial period, since the 1790 long wave trough begins Kondratieff's part of the base dating scheme.

least two time series in each of these categories, but two series are insufficient to draw far-reaching conclusions. The capital investment area is particularly under-represented. In these parts of the theoretical debate, then, the analysis will be able to do no more than tentatively look for consistency between alternative hypotheses and the limited data.

My data set consists of fifty-five economic time series (see table 8.1) as well as Levy's war data to be discussed below. The general type of data is annual time series for different economic variables. The time period of interest is 1495 to 1975. However, only one economic time series comes close to covering the entire 481-year period (South English consumer price index). Most of the time series are about 100–200 years long. Thus the five-century period is covered through an overlap of different series in different periods.

The fifty-five time series comprise six *classes* of variables:

1. Prices   28 series
2. Production   10 series
3. Innovation and invention   9 series
4. Capital investment   2 series
5. Trade   4 series
6. Real wages[22]   2 series

To my knowledge, no comparable compilation of economic time series for Europe and the United States covering the past five centuries exists. The series have been rescaled and converted to a standard format,[23] as described in Appendix A, and are listed in Appendix B.[24]

The sources of historical economic time series data are varied and fragmentary. The fifty-five economic time series used in this study have been drawn from twenty-seven sources. Only a few of these sources compile series from different countries (Mitchell 1980; Maddison 1982). More often, an economic historian has reconstructed a time series for a particular commodity and in some cases has compiled a set of such series for a particular country (for example, Beveridge 1939; Jörberg 1972; Maddalena 1974). Some economic historians have gone on to construct indexes of

22. I had no time series data on class struggle.

23. The original data series are given in a wide variety of units, ranging from arbitrarily scaled indexes to units of national currency or of physical volume. The particular units in the original source are of no interest in analyzing the dynamic patterns of ups and downs in the series—provided one remains consistent about measurement concepts. Specifically, all the price series are expressed in current terms in the national currency (unless already converted to price indexes in the original form). All production, trade, innovation, investment, and wage series are expressed in "real" terms, i.e., in "constant prices," so changes in those series do not reflect changes in prices (with one exception, "English exports in current prices"). In most such cases the data have been converted from current prices to constant prices by the original author using some sort of deflator (an index of inflation). In no cases have I converted data to constant prices myself.

24. Appendix A describes the source of each time series, my judgment of its accuracy and consistency, and any special considerations relevant to its interpretation. It also explains what was done to transform each series from its original form to the standardized format as printed in Appendix B.

Table 8.1. List of Economic Time Series

Period	Length (years)	Variable	Source
Price indexes (14 series)			
1495-1954	460	S. English consumer price index	Phelps-Brown [a]
1495-1640	146	S. English industrial price index	Doughty (1975)
1495-1640	146	S. English agricultural price index	Doughty (1975)
1651-1800	150	New Castile textile price index	Hamilton (1947)
1651-1800	150	New Castile animal product prices	Hamilton (1947)
1661-1801	141	English producers' price index	Schumpeter (1938)
1780-1922	143	British commodity prices	Kondratieff [b]
1791-1922	132	U.S. commodity prices	Kondratieff [b]
1750-1975	226	British wholesale price index	Mitchell (1980)
1798-1975	178	French wholesale price index	Mitchell (1980)
1792-1918	127	German wholesale price index	Mitchell (1980)
1801-1975	175	U.S. wholesale price index	Fellner, Census [c]
1822-1913	92	Belgian industrial price index	Loots (1936)
1835-1913	92	Belgian agricultural price index	Loots (1936)
Commodity Prices (14 series)			
1495-1788	294	French wheat prices (Paris)	Baulant (1968)
1531-1786	256	German wheat prices (Cologne)	Ebeling and Irsig. (1976)
1658-1772	115	German bread prices (Cologne)	Ebeling and Irsig. (1976)
1597-1783	187	Amsterdam prices for Prussian rye	Posthumus (1964)
1595-1831	237	English malt prices (Eton College)	Beveridge (1939)
1622-1829	208	English hops prices (Eton College)	Beveridge (1939)
1630-1817	188	English wheat prices (Winchester)	Beveridge (1939)
1653-1830	178	English coal prices (Eton College)	Beveridge (1939)
1694-1800	107	English bread prices (Charterhouse)	Beveridge (1939)
1701-1860	160	Italian wheat prices (Milan)	Maddalena (1974)
1701-1860	160	Italian hard coal prices (Milan)	Maddalena (1974)
1732-1914	183	Swedish wheat prices	Jorberg (1972)
1735-1914	183	Swedish pine wood prices	Jorberg (1972)
1732-1914	183	Swedish iron ore prices	Jorberg (1972)
Production indexes (10 series)			
1740-1850	111	World industrial production (1)	Haustein and Neuwirth [d]
1850-1975	126	World industrial production (2)	Kuczynski (1980)
1850-1975	126	World agricultural production	Kuczynski (1980)
1850-1975	126	World total production	Kuczynski (1980)
1820-1975	156	French real gross national product	Maddison (1982)
1830-1975	146	British real gross national product	Mitchell (1980)
1889-1970	82	U.S. real gross national product	U.S. Census (1975)
1801-1938	138	British industrial production	Mitchell (1980)
1815-1913	99	French industrial production	Crouzet (1970)
1840-1975	135	Belgian industrial production	Vandermotten (1980)
Trade indicators (4 series)			
1506-1650	145	Volume of Seville-Atlantic shipping	Chaunu (1956)
1700-1775	76	British net volume of wheat exports	Minchinton [e]
1700-1775	76	English exports in current prices	Minchinton [f]
1850-1975	126	Total world exports	Kuczynski (1980)
Innovation indicators (5 series)			
1764-1975	212	List of innovations [g]	Haustein/Neuwirth (1982)
1856-1971	116	List of innovations [g]	Van Duijn (1981/83)
1904-1968	65	List of innovations [g]	Clark et al. (1981)
1879-1965	87	List of "product" innovations [g]	Kleinknecht (1981b)
1859-1969	111	List of "improvement" innovations [g]	Kleinknecht (1981b)
Invention indicators (4 series)			
1738-1935	198	Number of British patents	Haustein/Neuwirth (1982)
1790-1975	186	Number of U.S. patents (1)	Haustein/Neuwirth (1982)
1837-1950	114	Number of U.S. patents (2)	Schmookler (1966)
1837-1950	114	U.S. patents in buildings and railroads	Schmookler (1966)
Capital investment (2 series)			
1830-1957	127	U.S. private building volume	Schmookler (1966)
1870-1950	81	U.S. railroad gross capital expenditure	Schmookler (1966)
Real wages (2 series)			
1700-1787	88	Real wages for London	Gilboy (1936)
1736-1954	219	South English real wages	Phelps-Brown [a]

Notes:
a. Phelps-Brown and Hopkins (1956).
b. Kondratieff's index as listed in Van Duijn (1983). Data in Kondratieff ([1928]/1984.)
c. Fellner (1956) until 1889, then U.S. Census (1975; 1983).
d. Haustein and Neuwirth (1982), who cite Hoffmann.
e. Minchinton (1969), who attributes the source as Marshall.
f. Minchinton (1969), who attributes the source as Schumpeter.
g. Time series constructed from a list of innovations (the value for a year is zero or a small integer).

prices or other economic variables for a national economy as a whole (for example, Doughty 1975; Crouzet 1970). I drew two time series on average from each source, and no more than five from any one source.

For prices, twenty-eight series are included—fourteen price indexes and fourteen commodity price series.[25] In the case of commodities, some of the series were drawn from compilations of many commodities for a given national economy, and in such cases (Beveridge, Jörberg, Maddalena, Posthumus) only a few commodities were selected. The few commodities were selected on the basis of their central role in the economy, the quality of data for those particular series, and the availability of the same variable (for example, wheat prices) for different countries. Thus many more price series than are analyzed here are available if one wishes to analyze various commodity series for the same country and time period and from the same source. This was not my intent; rather, I wanted to analyze a variety of series from different sources, time periods, and countries in order to investigate common patterns in them. With regard to nonprice data, my intentions were the same, but in practice the choices were much more limited, and I generally "took what I could get."

In addition to the economic series, my data set includes several war series (severity, intensity, and incidence) as well as non-time-series war indicators (numbers and types of wars aggregated by long wave phases). The best compilation of war data that is consistent across the five centuries under study is Levy's (1983a) study of war in the "modern great power system." Levy's work traces its roots to the approach of Singer and the Correlates of War project mentioned in chapter 5. He takes the conceptual and methodological framework of the project and extends its most central indicators (participants and battle fatalities) back to 1495, instead of just 1815 as in the COW project. All my war series[26] derive from Levy's data, although I have transformed them quantitatively.

A Methodology for Long Waves

In designing an appropriate methodology for a quantitative analysis of long waves, many choices must be made. As I showed in chapter 4, there have been six major methodologies in past empirical research. The first task of this section is to sort through these methodologies and explain why I find phase period analysis to be the best approach. I will then explore the methodological issues in phase period analysis itself.

The methodological problems with each of the methodologies used in the past may be summarized as follows. First, the inappropriateness of *spectral analysis,* and related techniques based on fixed periodicities, has just been discussed. In addition to the problems mentioned, these techniques generally require transforming a time

25. The national indexes are of most interest, and prices of individual commodities of less interest, in the overall assessment of long waves. However, the commodity series are included as supplementary data covering different countries and time periods than are available in price index form.
26. With the exception of one very tangential analysis of Sorokin's war data for the period before 1495.

series to achieve stationarity (no long-term trend), raising the problems of trend deviation discussed below.

Trend deviation has been particularly problematical, due to disagreements over the correct specification of a long-term secular trend in a time series (see Reijnders 1984). Past studies that have claimed to find long waves in this manner have used unduly complicated equations for the trend and have specified the trend differently for each series. This introduces an ad hoc element and weakens the idea of long waves as simple and unified movements of the world economy.

Moving averages, as was noted in chapter 4, can introduce distortions in the cyclical character of the time series, possibly exaggerating and lengthening intermediate-range cycles.

Analysis in terms of *business cycles* also presents problems in terms of how the business cycle is measured or compared with adjacent cycles. To measure from one peak to the next (as in Van Duijn 1980) means using only one data point in each business cycle (throwing away most of the information in the data) and a data point that is probably an "outlier" at that (since it is a peak).

Visual inspection relies on qualitative interpretation to describe phase periods and turning points in a time series. By itself, visual inspection is not convincing since it is subjective and may tend towards ad hoc interpretations of historical data.[27]

I find *phase period analysis* the methodology most appropriate to the definition of cycles developed above. Unlike spectral analysis, trend deviation, or moving averages—all of which relate to calendar time—phase period analysis relates to cycle time. The unit of analysis is the historical phase period. This approach identifies long waves by the differences in averages, growth rates, or other attributes of a series in successive phase periods.[28]

Phase period analysis has been used most often by Marxist researchers—perhaps because it corresponds well with Trotsky's conception of long waves, which, as Day (1976:71) says, "implied a trend broken into discontinuous periods each represented by a distinct line with a different slope." But Rostow's (1979) view of long waves as a "sequence of erratic but quite clear alternating trend periods" is a parallel statement of the same basic idea from a different theoretical camp.

Past phase period analyses have suffered from two problems. First, the dating of phases has been inadequate; many past studies have dated phases differently in each series (each according to its own unique turning points) rather than with a global dating scheme,[29] and this introduces an ad hoc element. Second, the methods of calculating trends or averages within each phase period have also been problemat-

---

27. The reader cannot be expected to wade through the source materials used by the analyst in making judgments through visual inspection; thus statistics should be used in order to convey to the reader overall characteristics of the data under study.

28. Statistical techniques may be used to find whether a certain set of series consistently tend toward a higher trend or average on upswing phases than on downswing phases.

29. I have criticized this in chap. 4. Note it is inconsistent with the concept of a system-wide "cycle time."

ical, differing from one study to another and often remaining unspecified in published articles. I will now try to resolve both problems.

My approach for dating turning points between phases begins with a single set of dates that applies to the core of the world system—to different countries and different variables. For these dates I use the base dating scheme developed in chapter 4, which comes reasonably close to a consensus of datings drawn from thirty-three long wave scholars.[30] The base dating scheme thus defines cycle time for my long wave analysis.[31]

Estimating Growth Rates

The method of measuring trends within a given phase period is not straightforward. What distinguishes the alternating phases of the long wave? What characteristic of the expansion and stagnation phases should be measured, and how should it be measured to compare the two phases? These are not trivial questions, since different scholars have used different methodologies to measure long wave expansion and stagnation phases and have arrived at different results (see chapter 4). Like most phase period analyses, I stress *growth rates* as the characteristic that distinguishes expansion from stagnation phase periods. The growth rate of prices (inflation rate) and other economic variables is higher in expansion phases and lower or negative in stagnation phases. But how, given the dates of a historical phase period, should the growth rate of the series in that period be estimated?

This turns out to be difficult. As indicated in chapter 4, five Marxist studies using phase period analysis claimed to find long waves in production variables (Mandel 1975; Gordon 1978; Kleinknecht 1981a; Kuczynski 1982; Screpanti 1984).[32] These authors typically report a figure for the "average growth rate" of some variable during a particular set of years but do not fully explain their methodology for measuring the average growth rate during that period.[33]

I will first discuss four methods I chose *not* to use and why each one is problematical. Then I will explain the method I use to estimate growth rates in a phase period.

1. Probably the most common method of measuring an "average growth rate" for

30. For reasons explained in chap. 10, I eventually changed the last turning point in the base dating scheme from 1968 to 1980 to reflect new insights (production peak around 1968, price peak around 1980). The results reported here use the 1980 date for consistency, except where otherwise noted. An earlier set of results using the 1968 date differed little (only one or two phase periods in a few series are affected by the change). In a rare few instances, as noted, I failed to rerun a 1968 result using 1980, and I report the 1968 result instead—but never with any substantive effect.

31. The dates of turning points are explicitly drawn from sources other than the particular data series under analysis. Certainly I could have developed a statistical routine to find the "best" dates to fit a given set of time series. This is much better than dating the ups and downs of *each* series separately. But drawing that dating scheme from the particular set of economic time series analyzed would still introduce an ad hoc element in the analysis. The base dating scheme, on the other hand, is largely independent of the time series I analyze except in the (unresolvable) sense that there is only one history from which both my data and other scholars' datings derive.

32. One other study using a similar methodology found no long waves (Van der Zwan 1980).

33. Although studies of prices generally have not used phase period analysis, similar concerns arise in making a phase period analysis for prices (as I will do below) as for production.

a phase period is to convert the time series to annual growth rates[34] and then average these annual growth rates for all the years in the phase period. The problem here is that the average of the annual growth rates is not necessarily a good indicator of the overall growth of the series during the phase. This is because a percentage growth rate when the series rises is not the same as the percentage (negative) growth rate when it falls again by the same amount. To illustrate this problem, consider a hypothetical series that alternates between 100 and 125 each year, without any trend up or down, over a phase period of twenty years. The series is in fact stationary, but the "average annual growth rate" would be 2.5 percent[35] and would hence be indistinguishable from a series showing steady growth.

2. This problem with annual percentage growth rates can be solved by converting the series to annual *changes* on a fixed scale (not percentages), thus giving equal weight to upward and downward changes. However, in such a methodology the net change during a given historical phase period is by definition equal to the difference between the starting and ending points. This is identical to the following methodology.

3. The growth rate of a phase could be defined by the turning point years alone, as the change (or the percentage change) from the trough to the peak, or vice versa. However, this approach relies on just one data point for each phase, throwing away the rest of the data in the series—data that could provide much richer information about the structure of trends in the data. It is also unduly sensitive to the exact specification of turning points, which have been defined as inexact within a few years in either direction.

4. A methodology that resolves all the problems with the above three approaches uses statistical regression to estimate the slope of the data curve within a phase period. Several past studies have estimated growth rates by logging the data series and then fitting a straight line to the series within a phase period.[36] Van der Zwan (1980:191) argues for this method. Bieshaar and Kleinknecht (1984:282) also use a methodology along these lines. They estimate (through linear regression) the slopes of the log-linear trend curves of national production series within each phase period.[37] They also constrain the trend lines so that they intersect at the turning points, forming a zigzag pattern for the sequence of trend lines.[38]

34. Each year's data point being expressed as a percentage change from the previous year's data point.

35. The growth rate on the up years is 25/100, or 25%, while that on the down years is −25/125, or −20%. The average is 2.5%. Fluctuations of this magnitude are common in many price series, especially in preindustrial commodity prices.

36. Logging the data means that a growth curve is transformed to a linear increase and that the slope of the line should in theory represent the growth rate of the series.

37. The phase periods are "assumed to be known a priori from the literature" (p. 284) are hence predefined in terms of the study. They use Mandel's dates of turning points (p. 286), except that the turning point in 1968 is changed to 1974 (p. 288).

38. The estimation is done through an iterative process to find the best-fitting linear slopes (with logged data) subject to the restraint that values of slope lines in adjacent periods must be equal at the turning point. This constraint I find undesirable because it complicates the estimation and puts too much importance on the particular years chosen as turning points.

While this approach of estimating log-linear slopes comes close to the ideal, I do not find the log transformation necessary or useful, because it assumes an underlying form to the series (exponential growth).[39] This may not be the best model of underlying change, particularly in stagnation phases and particularly for price series. I prefer to avoid making such assumptions about the underlying trend or form of the series, if possible.

My solution, then, is to estimate the linear slope of the (unlogged) data within each phase period and then standardize that slope to the mean of the series in that phase period, giving a number equivalent to a growth rate.

The growth estimation procedure is as follows: Starting with the historically defined phase periods given by the base dating scheme, each phase period is treated as a separate segment ten to forty years long.[40] For each of these segments the best-fitting slope is estimated by linear regression.[41] No attention is paid to inferential indicators of how well the slope line fits the data (R squared) but only to the descriptive indicator (the slope itself). I converted these slopes (expressed in term of whatever units the series is in) to growth rates by dividing each slope by the mean of the series during that period.[42] A series whose slope line increases two units per year at a mean level of one hundred units has an estimated growth rate of 2 percent during the period.

This method for estimating growth rates allows trends during phase periods to be compared from one phase period to another and from one variable to another. It is not overly sensitive to the particular dating of turning points, since the moving of the turning point by a year weights the regression by the addition or deletion of only one data point. The trend line is not forced to intersect the data point for any particular year. The methodology makes fullest use of all the data points in the time series and does not require any rigid assumptions about the structure of the underlying long-term secular trend.

This methodology is compatible with a variety of theoretical models of the underlying form of long waves, since all have in common a difference in slope between adjacent phase periods. Figure 8.1 illustrates five different conceptions of the underlying model of long waves: (1) a stationary series of up and down phases (of unequal length), (2) a rising secular trend with alternate rising and stagnating phases,

39. As chapter 4 showed, such assumptions can be controversial.

40. If the beginning or end of the time series falls within a particular phase period, then that segment will consist of a shorter series covering only part of the phase period. I ran a set of analyses in which phase periods containing data for less than half the years were first included and then excluded, and the results showed no substantial differences. The results I report are those in which all periods are included for which the time series is at least five years long. Note also that in those few series extending to 1980 the year 1980 was included erroneously in the last phase period (as though 1981 were the peak). The effect was negligible.

41. The ordinary-least-squares regression procedure was used. The slope of the best-fitting line (i.e., the coefficient estimated by the regression, with no restraint on the intercept) represents the best estimate of the series trend during the phase period, expressed in terms of the units in which the series is measured.

42. A slope of 2 when the mean of a series is 100 will be equivalent to a slope of 20 when the mean is 1000.

Figure 8.1. Phase Periods in Five Long Wave Models

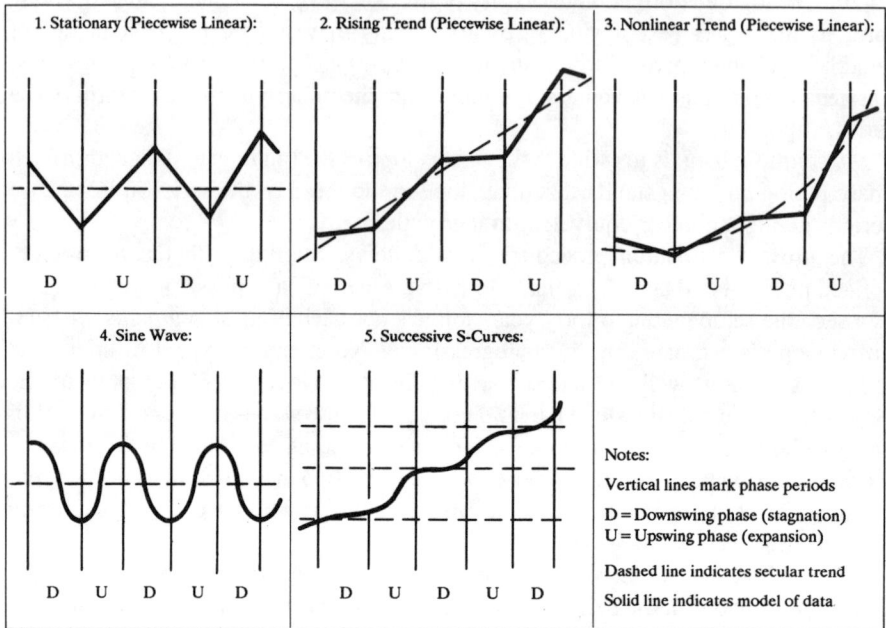

1. Stationary (Piecewise Linear):	2. Rising Trend (Piecewise Linear):	3. Nonlinear Trend (Piecewise Linear):

(chart)

D	U	D	U

(chart)

D	U	D	U

(chart)

D	U	D	U

4. Sine Wave:	5. Successive S-Curves:	

(chart)

D	U	D	U	D

(chart)

D	U	D	U	D

Notes:

Vertical lines mark phase periods

D = Downswing phase (stagnation)
U = Upswing phase (expansion)

Dashed line indicates secular trend

Solid line indicates model of data

(3) a long wave defined around a more complicated secular trend (exponential, S curve,[43] and so forth, (4) a long wave defined as a sine wave (with time-invariant periodicity), and (5) a long wave defined as successive S curves of growth. These models all have in common that the growth rates between turning points (defined by mean-standardized slopes) are higher during upswing than downswing phases. Thus my methodology works under a variety of theoretical specfications, not just for one model.

Testing for Differences in Alternate Phases

These methods allow us to compare, for a single series, the growth rates in successive phase periods (in order to look for an alternating pattern). However, since the data set includes hundreds of phase periods, it is also useful to summarize the growth rates on upswing and downswing phases for an entire class of series at once. This requires a statistical method to summarize both the overall difference in slopes between the upswing and downswing periods and the likelihood that such a difference would result from random differences in growth rates in different phases.

The appropriate statistical tool for this purpose is the *paired t-test*. A t-test looks

---

43. Van Duijn (1980:224) suggests that long waves be conceived as fluctuations around long-term S curves.

Figure 8.2. Paired T-tests

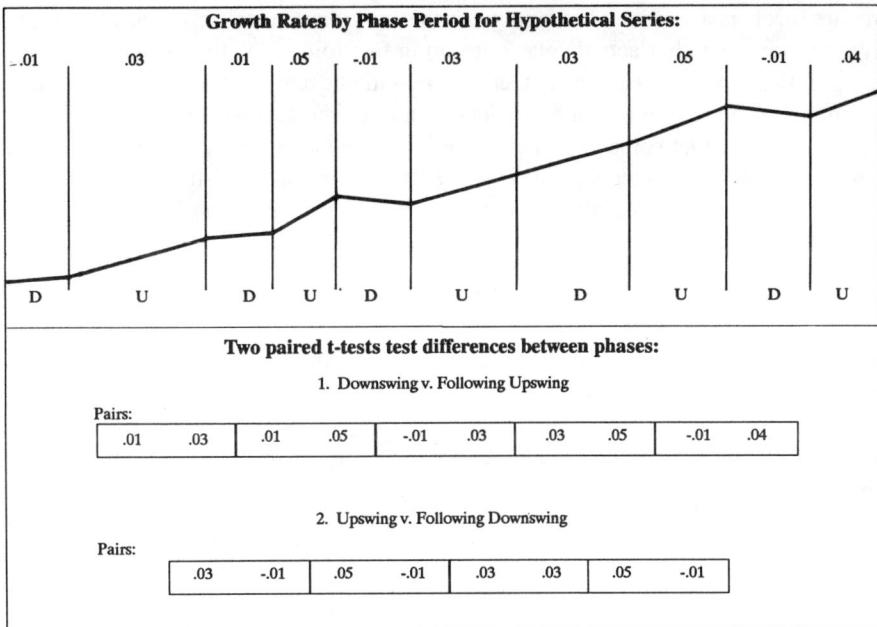

Growth Rates by Phase Period for Hypothetical Series:

| -.01 | .03 | .01 | .05 | -.01 | .03 | .03 | .05 | -.01 | .04 |

| D | U | D | U | D | U | D | U | D | U |

Two paired t-tests test differences between phases:

1. Downswing v. Following Upswing

Pairs:

| .01 | .03 | .01 | .05 | -.01 | .03 | .03 | .05 | -.01 | .04 |

2. Upswing v. Following Downswing

Pairs:

| .03 | -.01 | .05 | -.01 | .03 | .03 | .05 | -.01 |

for a statistically significant difference in the means of two groups of numbers. The groups in this case are the growth rates on upswing and downswing phases for a class of series. Since successive phases of a system cannot be assumed to be independent of each other (a requirement of the ordinary t-test), I use a paired t-test in which data points from the two groups are paired with each other.[44]

As shown in figure 8.2, this requires two paired t-tests—one pairing each downswing against the following upswing, and one pairing each upswing against the following downswing.[45] I use these tests for each class of variables and (for prices where data permit) for different time periods within the five centuries under study.[46]

44. This is the appropriate methodology for a before-and-after analysis—in this case the growth rate before and after a turning point is passed.

45. Sometimes there are more pairs in the down/up test (the first one in figure 8.2) than in the up/down test, or vice versa, and generally the test with more pairs (more degrees of freedom) shows stronger results (chaps. 9 and 10).

46. When the direction of the difference in means is hypothesized ahead of time, a one-tailed t-test is appropriate rather than the more common two-tailed test, which simply indicates a significant difference in means in either direction. This applies to prices, production, and capital investment (all presumed to increase on the upswing) but not to innovation, wages, or trade, where both directions of correlation were hypothesized by different scholars (chap. 7). For these latter variables I have used two-tailed probabilities (the two-tailed probability of error is twice that of the one-tailed distribution). In actual practice I was able to perform t-tests only on prices, production, innovation, and wages. The first two of these were one-tailed and the last two were two-tailed.

Identifying Lagged Correlations

The approach just outlined disaggregates the long wave into only two phases per cycle and tests whether actual data series do in fact follow the trends defined by the dating of those phases. However, there are two major reasons for trying to examine the timing of the long wave in more detail than just the two phases.

First is simply that some hypotheses specify more exact timing than can be tested using a two-phase framework alone. For example, to distinguish between the following two hypotheses requires resolution down to a period of one-fourth of a cycle:

Innovations cluster late in the downswing. [A]
(Gordon, Schumpeter)

Innovations cluster early in the upswing. [A]
(Kondratieff, Mandel, Freeman et al.)

And the following hypothesis could require even greater resolution:

Production increases precede price increases. [A]
(Imbert)

The second reason for looking more closely at the timing within long waves is that variables defined differently may appear to lead or to lag each other, obscuring their correlation with the long wave. Figure 8.3 illustrates two definitions, which have not been closely distinguished in past long wave research. The first, which I generally follow, defines a long wave upswing phase as a period of increased *growth* in the series, lasting from a trough until a subsequent peak. The second model defines an upswing phase as a period of higher *levels* in the series, or a *cluster* of discrete events.[47]

As figure 8.3 indicates, this difference in definition has the effect that for a single series the phases defined in terms of growth rates *lead* the phases defined in terms of levels by about one-fourth of a cycle (half a phase).[48] This principle can be understood intuitively since there is a lag after a rate change before levels ''catch up.''

The effect of this lag on the phase period analysis is potentially serious, since using the ''wrong'' definition[49] will shift the correlation by about one-fourth of a cycle. This shift could ''wash out'' any correlation with the long wave phases (since each

---

47. The first definition has often been used for continuous variables like prices and production, while the second has been used for correlating discrete events, such as innovations and wars, with the long wave. A statement such as ''more innovations (wars) occur during the downswing (or upswing) phase'' is based on the second model of levels rather than growth rates. But the distinctions can be unclear even for price or production series when, for example, the series has been ''detrended.'' The hypothesis that the curve is above the trend line during upswings reflects the second model (levels, not rates).

48. This is a deductive conclusion and not drawn from actual data, although it can be found in the data as well.

49. That is, using levels when rates are actually correlated with the historical phases, or vice versa.

Figure 8.3. Phases Defined by Rates v. Levels

Two ways to date schematic curve are shown:
First based on phases defined by growth rates, then on phases defined by levels.

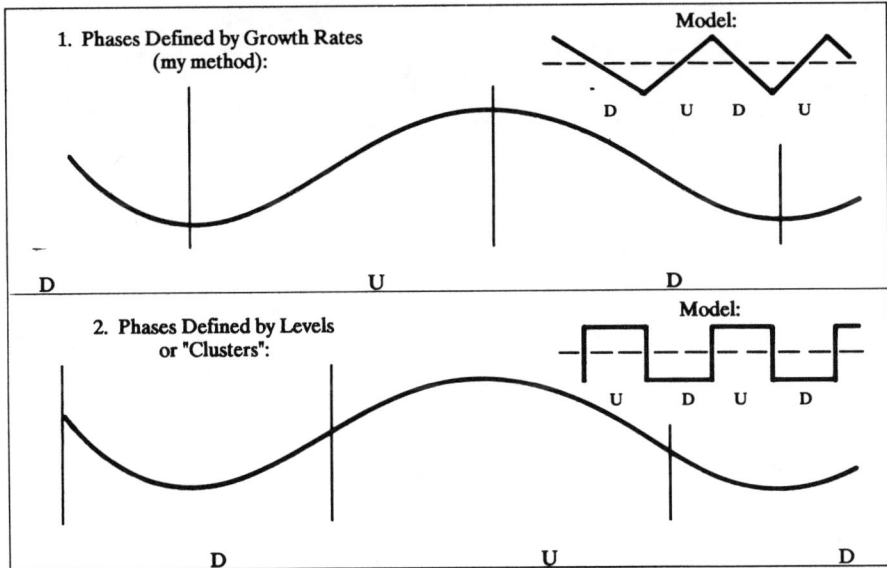

1. Phases Defined by Growth Rates
   (my method):

Model:

D   U   D   U

D   U   D

2. Phases Defined by Levels
   or "Clusters":

Model:

U   D   U   D

D   U   D

Note that the phase periods in #1 lead those in #2 by 1/4 cycle.

phase will have data drawn half from an upswing, half from a downswing). Only by looking at more detailed timing relationships, not just two phases, can such correlations be recovered. This was a second reason to disaggregate the timing beyond just two phases.

To this end, I developed a methodology to identify *lagged correlations* of a series with the base dating scheme. To identify lagged correlations within cycle time, I developed a descriptive statistic that I call the "lag structure" of a time series. Figure 8.4 is a schematic diagram of a lag structure. The lag structure is a curve showing how well the data series fits the upswing and downswing phases as a function of shifting the base dating scheme backward and forward a year at a time.[50] The goodness of fit indicator derives from the difference between growth rates on the upswing phases and those on the downswing phases for the series.[51] This approach

50. The horizontal axis goes from −20 to +20 years of shift in the dating scheme; the vertical axis represents the goodness of fit (of the data to the shifted dating).

51. In calculating the fit to the dating scheme, I used a method similar to that of the t-tests described above (with only one series there are not enough cases to do the t-test for the growth rates for each lag). For each lagged dating scheme, the average change in growth rate at peaks and the change at troughs are calculated, as is the difference between these. If indeed growth rates are higher on upswings than on downswings, then the mean change at peaks will be negative and at troughs positive. The difference will be positive, and that difference is the indicator of the fit of a series to a particular dating scheme. As the dating scheme is shifted through time, this indicator should be maximum at the time lag that "best fits" the data.

Figure 8.4. Schematic Lag Structure

(Example shown is for a series unlagged, directly correlated to base dating.)

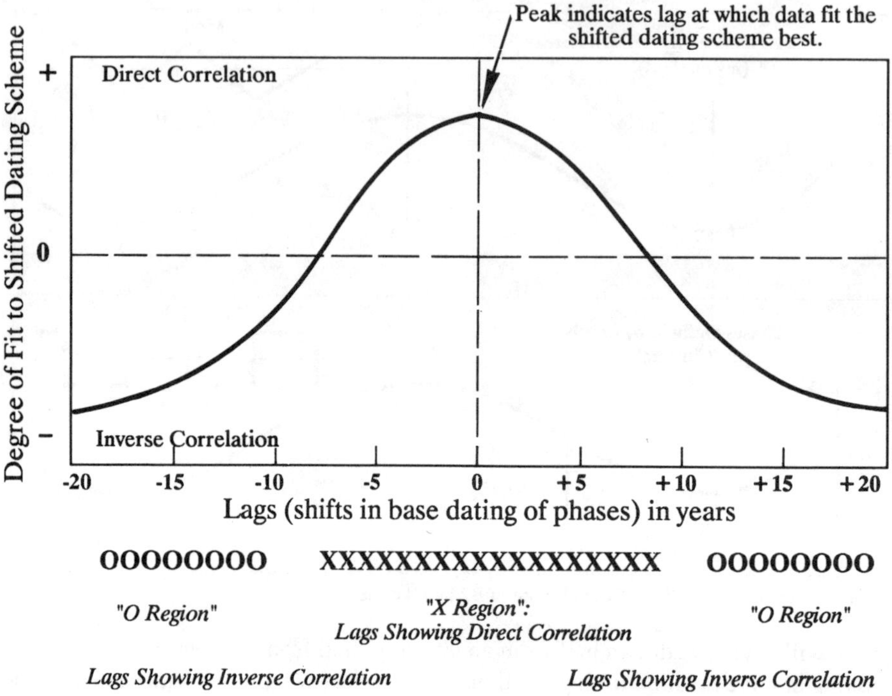

Peak indicates lag at which data fit the shifted dating scheme best.

[Vertical axis: Degree of Fit to Shifted Dating Scheme; + Direct Correlation; 0; − Inverse Correlation]

Lags (shifts in base dating of phases) in years: -20, -15, -10, -5, 0, +5, +10, +15, +20

OOOOOOOO   XXXXXXXXXXXXXXXXXX   OOOOOOOO

"O Region"   "X Region":   "O Region"
          Lags Showing Direct Correlation

Lags Showing Inverse Correlation   *Lags Showing Inverse Correlation*

thus examines small shifts in calendar time (years) within each phase, while remaining in cycle time (base dating scheme phases) overall.[52]

For each variable's lag structure (see fig. 8.4) several points or regions on the horizontal axis are labeled. First is the maximum point, the lag for which data fit dating scheme best. Second, I identify with an "X" the lags for which a minimal fit to the dating scheme is found.[53] A set of such minimally fitting lags I call the "X region" of the lag structure. Conversely, the lags for which a minimal inverse correlation is found are called the "O region," and the minimum point of the lag structure indicates the best fit for an inverse correlation.[54]

52. This is an adequate but not ideal solution, since shifts of up to 20 years in either direction may or may not bring one into the next phase. But since the data are annual I cannot break down each phase into cycle-time subunits such as $\frac{1}{10}$-phase (about 2.5 years, but variable). Therefore I live with calendar time as the secondary units within cycle time, and I find this works reasonably well within 10–15 years of each turning point.

53. The difference between growth rates on downswings and those on subsequent upswings is positive; between rates on upswings and subsequent downswings, negative.

54. Because of the nonsynchrony of cycle time and calendar time, as noted above, the maximum/minimum points and the "X" and "O" regions are more reliable close to zero lags and less so near the left or right edge (−20 lags or +20 lags).

These time shifts also indicate the sensitivity of the long wave to turning points. If small shifts in the dating scheme (along the horizontal axis) cause sudden changes in how well the data fit the periods (along the vertical axis), then the fit is too sensitive to the particular turning points chosen and not *robust* (the word I will use for this particular kind of time stability).[55]

The purpose of the lag structures is to identify possible lagged correlations with the base dating scheme in different series. As a final step, in cases where a class of variables seems to follow a certain lagged correlation, I then return to the paired t-test to find out whether the class as a whole does in fact correlate well with a lagged dating scheme. I calculate the growth rates by phases for all the series in the class, using an appropriately lagged dating scheme,[56] then use t-tests as above (and compare these results to the earlier t-tests). The interpretation of probability levels in these lagged t-tests is problematical, since I choose the "best" lags for the test;[57] therefore these t-tests are weak. They are included both to facilitate comparison between unlagged and lagged results for a class of variable and to support the adduction of the most plausible theory based on lagged correlations.[58]

Methodologies for War Data Analysis

In the analysis of war data in chapter 11, all of the above methodologies will be brought into play. However, because of the different nature of these data (originally given as discrete events in time, converted to time series by me), I have also drawn on a variety of other methodologies. I will reserve explanation of these methodologies for chapter 11, but in summary there are four additional approaches used. The third and fourth methodologies listed pertain to short-term relationships among variables, not to long cycles per se.

First, since wars may be seen as discrete events rather than a continuous flux in a system, I supplement the analysis of growth rates in phase periods by looking at *levels* (counting events) in each phase period.[59] A variety of war indicators are

55. In the base dating scheme, the dates of turning points were said to be approximate within a few years in either direction. Thus it is important that the statistical analysis not be too sensitive to the particular dating of turning points. In addition to the use of lag structures, the basic method using best-fitting slopes within each period (unconstrained by data in adjacent periods) minimizes sensitivity to turning points.

56. As suggested by the "best" lags in individual series in the class. Only lags at 5-year intervals (5, 10, 15, etc.) were experimented with—I felt that the data would not support a more exact specifications of lags than this and wanted to minimize the ad hoc nature of looking around for particular lags that might happen to fit better than others.

57. This increases the probability that a random difference in upswing and downswing growth rates will be interpreted as a lagged long wave correlation. In practice, the problem is not as serious as it might appear, since in most cases the lag structure is fairly "robust" and the "X" region of adequate fit to a long wave pattern covers ⅓ to ½ of the 41 lags. Also, I do not select the best lag for each series but a 5-year-interval lag for an entire class of series together.

58. They are not, to repeat, a test against the null hypothesis in the usual sense. The lag structure is intended as a descriptive statistic; it "uses up degrees of freedom" and thus weakens statistical confidence.

59. The same, incidentally, is done for innovations, which are also given as discrete units (see chapter 10).

tabulated for each phase period, allowing a comparison of war levels in upswing versus downswing phases. This allows such hypotheses as "more wars occur on upswings" to be tested.

Second, in the course of reinterpreting the findings of Levy (1983a), who followed the COW approach methodologically, I use a technique based on periodicity (Auto-Correlation Functions) to look at war cycles defined in calendar time. The results provide new insights into the research on war periodicity.

Third, in order to identify connections between war and price data over rather short periods (a few years), I use visual inspection of graphs showing annual fluctuations in war and price series over long time periods. Some of these graphs are reproduced in chapter 11.

Fourth, for the same purpose of identifying war-price connections, I use a methodology called Granger Causality, which aims to identify the effect of one time series on another. Although somewhat flawed for this purpose,[60] it nonetheless provides corroborating evidence for the relationships identified through visual inspection.

In the next three chapters, I will take up long waves in prices, in real economic variables,[61] and in war, respectively.[62]

---

60. The long-term autocorrelation in the war series as I have constructed it goes against assumptions of the model.

61. A "real" variable is one defined in terms of physical volumes, not monetary values, and hence does not reflect price movements.

62. Statistical packages used in this study include the following: (1) on the MIT IBM VM/SP mainframe, TROLL ARIMA (for ACFs) and TROLL graphing routines (for war graphs); (2) on the Sloan School of Management PRIME computer, NAG Fortran library (for growth rates by phase period), SPSSX (for paired t-tests), and SHAZAM (for Granger causality analysis).

CHAPTER NINE

Data Analysis 1: Prices

Ⅰn this chapter and the next I will analyze the fifty-five economic time series with respect to the historically defined phase periods of the base dating scheme (cycle time). In this chapter I consider the price series, which include fourteen price indexes and fourteen series for individual commodity prices. I examine the "fit" of different types of price series (from different time periods, countries, and commodities) to the base dating scheme and then look for possible leads and lags in different price series relative to cycle time. I will reflect these results back on the hypotheses presented at the end of chapter 7 to test among alternative hypotheses advanced by different theoretical schools.[1] Chapter 10 will then take up the other five classes of economic variables in a similar manner.

Phase Period Correlations

Growth rates for the price series generally follow the alternating pattern hypothesized (see table 9.1).

Price Indexes

The South English consumer price index fits the phase periods (base dating scheme) very well over the entire period 1495–1967 (see table 9.1; each line in the table represents one unit of cycle time,[2] and the growth rates alternate in every successive phase period). The growth rates for both the industrial and the agricultural price indexes for South England also fit the phase periods perfectly. Along with the above, this strongly corroborates the hypothesis of long price waves in preindustrial times in England. Unfortunately, no price indexes for countries other than England are available for this period.

In the period around 1650–1800, two Spanish and one English price indexes are available. The Spanish series show some degree of fit to the long wave pattern, but not as closely as in the earlier English series. Textile prices follow the phase periods

1. Central among these are the hypotheses concerning the existence of long waves in prices in preindustrial times.
2. Over time, changes in the mean show the secular trend of the series and might also be useful in examining levels rather than growth rates in certain series (chap. 8).

Table 9.1. Prices -- Growth Rates by Phase Period

Spanish Textile Price Index

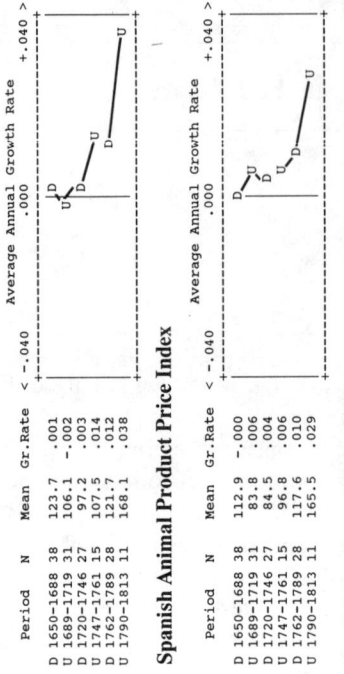

Average Annual Growth Rate   < -.040   .000   +.040 >

	Period	N	Mean	Gr.Rate
D	1650-1688	38	123.7	.001
U	1689-1719	31	106.1	-.002
D	1720-1746	27	97.2	.003
U	1747-1761	15	107.5	.014
U	1762-1789	28	121.7	.012
U	1790-1813	11	168.1	.038

Spanish Animal Product Price Index

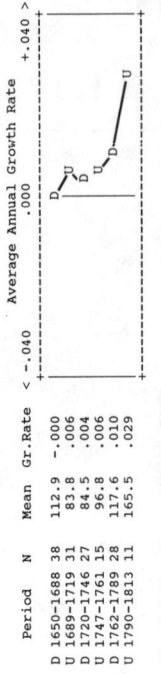

Average Annual Growth Rate   < -.040   .000   +.040 >

	Period	N	Mean	Gr.Rate
D	1650-1688	38	112.9	-.000
U	1689-1719	31	83.8	.006
D	1720-1746	27	84.5	.004
U	1747-1761	15	96.8	.006
U	1762-1789	28	117.6	.010
U	1790-1813	11	165.5	.029

English Producers' Price Index

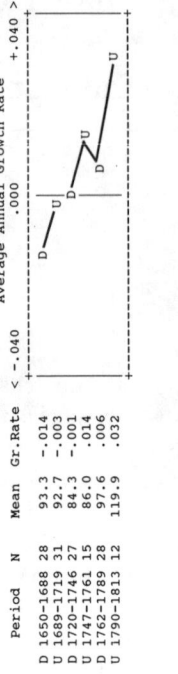

Average Annual Growth Rate   < -.040   .000   +.040 >

	Period	N	Mean	Gr.Rate
D	1650-1688	28	93.3	-.014
U	1689-1719	31	92.7	-.003
D	1720-1746	27	84.3	-.001
U	1747-1761	15	86.0	.014
U	1762-1789	28	97.6	.006
U	1790-1813	12	119.9	.032

British Commodity Price (Kondratieff)

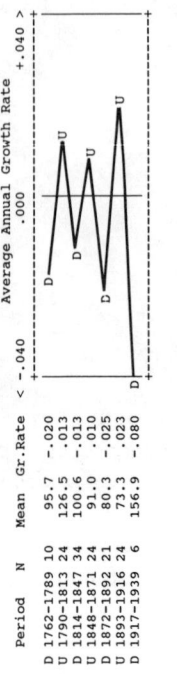

Average Annual Growth Rate   < -.040   .000   +.040 >

	Period	N	Mean	Gr.Rate
D	1762-1789	10	95.7	-.020
D	1790-1813	24	126.5	.013
D	1814-1847	34	100.6	-.013
D	1848-1871	24	91.0	-.010
D	1872-1892	21	80.3	-.025
D	1893-1916	24	73.3	-.023
D	1917-1939	6	156.9	-.080

South English Consumer Price Index

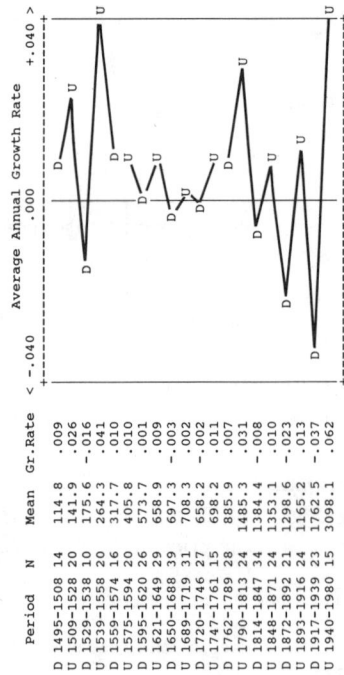

Average Annual Growth Rate   < -.040   .000   +.040 >

	Period	N	Mean	Gr.Rate
D	1495-1508	14	114.8	.009
U	1509-1528	20	141.9	.026
D	1529-1538	10	175.6	-.016
D	1539-1558	20	264.3	.041
D	1559-1574	16	317.7	.010
D	1575-1594	20	405.8	.010
D	1595-1620	26	573.7	.001
U	1621-1649	29	658.9	.009
D	1650-1688	39	697.3	-.003
U	1689-1719	31	708.3	-.002
D	1720-1746	27	658.2	-.002
U	1747-1761	15	698.2	.011
D	1762-1789	28	885.9	.007
U	1790-1813	24	1485.3	.031
D	1814-1847	34	1384.4	-.008
U	1848-1871	24	1353.1	-.010
D	1872-1892	21	1298.6	-.023
U	1893-1916	24	1165.2	-.013
U	1917-1939	23	1762.5	-.037
U	1940-1980	15	3098.1	.062

South English Industrial Price Index

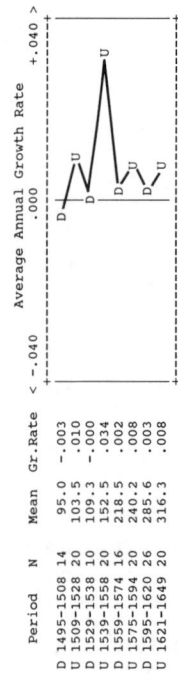

Average Annual Growth Rate   < -.040   .000   +.040 >

	Period	N	Mean	Gr.Rate
D	1495-1508	14	95.0	-.003
U	1509-1528	20	103.5	.010
D	1529-1538	10	109.3	-.000
D	1539-1558	20	152.5	.034
D	1559-1574	16	218.5	.002
U	1575-1594	20	240.2	.008
U	1595-1620	26	285.6	.003
U	1621-1649	20	316.3	.008

South English Agricultural Price Index

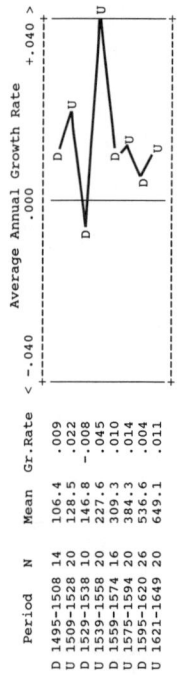

Average Annual Growth Rate   < -.040   .000   +.040 >

	Period	N	Mean	Gr.Rate
D	1495-1508	14	106.4	.009
U	1509-1528	20	128.5	.022
D	1529-1538	10	146.8	-.008
D	1539-1558	20	227.6	.045
D	1559-1574	16	309.3	.010
U	1575-1594	20	384.3	.014
U	1595-1620	26	536.6	.004
U	1621-1649	20	649.1	.011

U.S. Commodity Prices (Kondratieff)

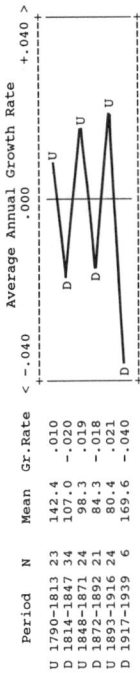

Period	N	Mean	Gr.Rate
U 1790-1813	23	142.4	.010
D 1814-1847	34	107.0	.020
U 1848-1871	24	84.3	.019
D 1872-1892	21	80.4	.018
U 1893-1916	24	169.6	.021
D 1917-1939			.040

British Wholesale Price Index

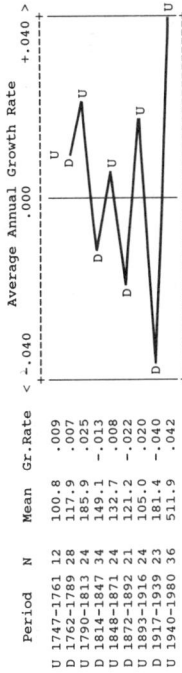

Period	N	Mean	Gr.Rate
U 1747-1761	12	100.8	.009
D 1762-1789	28	117.9	.007
U 1790-1813	24	185.9	.025
D 1814-1847	34	149.1	.013
D 1848-1871	24	132.7	.008
U 1872-1892	21	121.2	.022
D 1893-1916	24	105.0	.020
D 1917-1939	23	181.4	.040
U 1940-1980	36	511.9	.042

French Wholesale Price Index

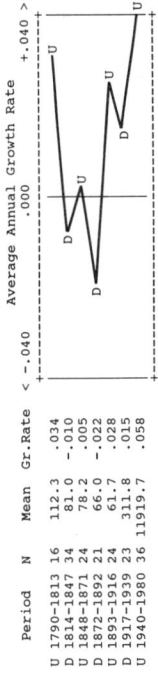

Period	N	Mean	Gr.Rate
U 1790-1813	16	112.3	.034
D 1814-1847	34	81.0	.010
D 1848-1871	24	78.2	.005
D 1872-1892	21	66.0	.022
U 1893-1916	24	61.7	.028
D 1917-1939	23	311.8	.015
U 1940-1980	36	11919.7	.058

German Wholesale Price Index

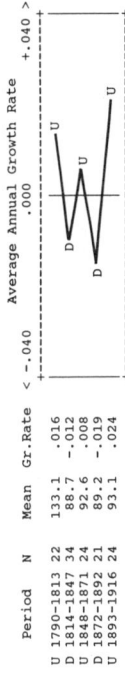

Period	N	Mean	Gr.Rate
U 1790-1813	22	133.1	.016
D 1814-1847	34	88.7	.012
U 1848-1871	24	92.6	.008
D 1872-1892	21	89.2	.019
U 1893-1916	24	93.1	.024

U.S. Wholesale Price Index

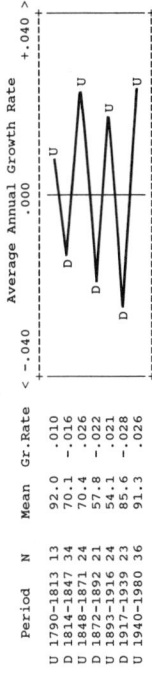

Period	N	Mean	Gr.Rate
U 1790-1813	13	92.0	.010
D 1814-1847	34	70.1	.016
D 1848-1871	24	70.4	.026
D 1872-1892	21	57.8	.022
U 1893-1916	24	54.1	.021
D 1917-1939	23	85.6	.028
U 1940-1980	36	91.3	.026

Belgian Industrial Price Index

Period	N	Mean	Gr.Rate
D 1814-1847	26	91.3	-.004
U 1848-1871	24	94.6	.006
D 1872-1892	21	98.4	-.009
U 1893-1916	21	98.4	.015

Belgian Agricultural Price Index

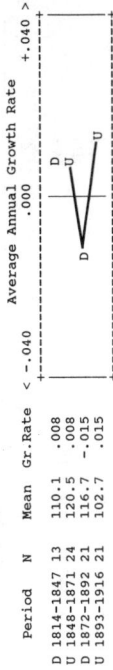

Period	N	Mean	Gr.Rate
D 1814-1847	13	110.1	.008
U 1848-1871	24	120.5	.008
D 1872-1892	21	116.7	-.015
U 1893-1916	21	102.7	.015

Commodity Prices:

French Wheat Prices (Paris)

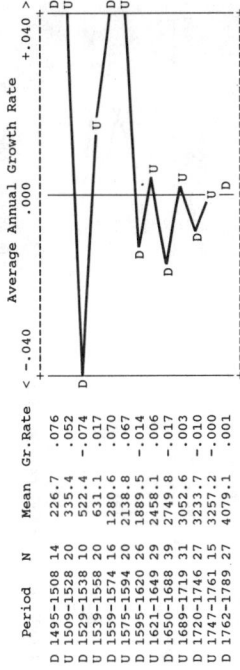

Period	N	Mean	Gr.Rate
D 1495-1508	14	226.7	.076
U 1509-1528	20	335.4	.052
D 1529-1538	10	522.4	-.074
D 1539-1558	20	631.1	.017
D 1559-1574	16	1280.6	.070
U 1575-1594	20	2138.8	.067
D 1595-1620	26	1889.5	.014
U 1621-1649	29	2458.1	.006
D 1650-1688	39	2749.8	.017
U 1689-1719	31	3052.6	.003
D 1720-1746	27	3233.7	.010
U 1747-1761	15	3257.2	-.000
D 1762-1789	27	4079.1	.001

German Wheat Prices (Cologne)

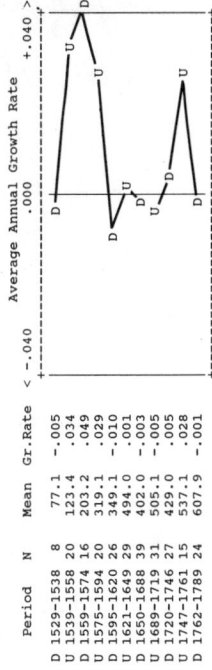

Period	N	Mean	Gr.Rate
D 1529-1538	8	77.1	-.005
U 1539-1558	20	123.4	.034
D 1559-1574	16	203.2	.049
U 1575-1594	20	319.1	.029
D 1595-1620	26	349.1	-.010
U 1621-1649	29	494.0	.001
D 1650-1688	39	402.0	-.003
U 1689-1719	31	505.1	-.005
D 1720-1746	27	429.0	.005
U 1747-1761	15	537.1	.028
D 1762-1789	24	607.9	-.001

German Bread Prices (Cologne)

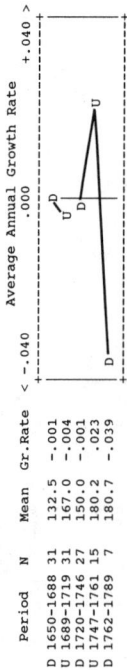

	Period	N	Mean	Gr.Rate
D	1650-1688	31	132.5	-.001
U	1689-1719	31	167.0	-.004
D	1720-1746	27	150.0	-.001
D	1747-1761	15	180.2	-.023
D	1762-1789	7	180.7	-.039

Netherlands Prussian-Rye Prices (Amsterdam)

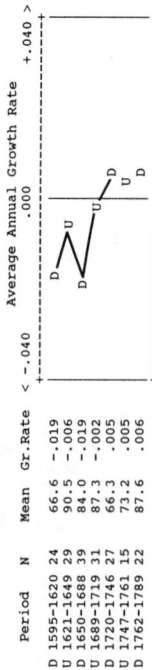

	Period	N	Mean	Gr.Rate
D	1595-1620	24	66.6	-.019
U	1621-1649	29	90.5	-.006
U	1650-1688	39	84.0	-.019
U	1689-1719	31	87.3	-.002
D	1720-1746	27	66.3	-.005
U	1747-1761	15	73.2	.005
D	1762-1789	22	87.6	.006

English Malt Prices (Eton College)

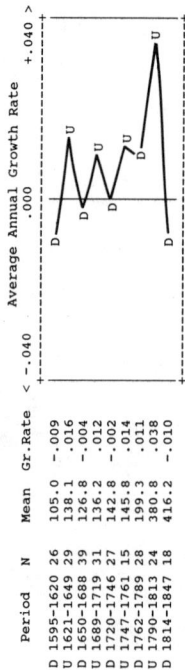

	Period	N	Mean	Gr.Rate
D	1595-1620	26	105.0	-.009
U	1621-1649	29	138.1	-.016
D	1650-1688	39	126.8	-.004
D	1689-1719	31	136.2	-.012
D	1720-1746	27	142.8	-.002
U	1747-1761	15	145.8	-.014
U	1762-1789	28	199.3	-.011
D	1790-1813	24	380.2	-.038
D	1814-1847	18	416.2	-.010

English Hops Prices (Eton College)

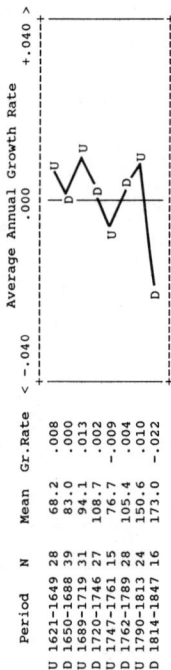

	Period	N	Mean	Gr.Rate
U	1621-1649	28	68.2	.008
D	1650-1688	39	83.0	.000
D	1689-1719	31	94.1	.013
D	1720-1746	27	108.7	.002
U	1747-1761	15	76.7	-.009
U	1762-1789	28	105.4	.004
U	1790-1813	24	150.6	.010
D	1814-1847	16	173.0	-.022

English Wheat Prices (Winchester College)

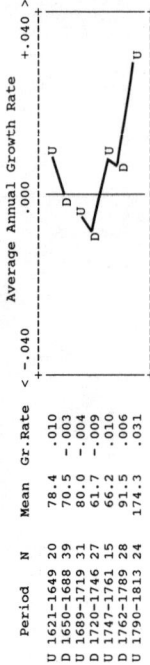

	Period	N	Mean	Gr.Rate
U	1621-1649	20	78.4	.010
D	1650-1688	39	70.5	-.003
D	1689-1719	31	80.0	-.004
D	1720-1746	27	61.7	-.009
D	1747-1761	15	66.2	-.010
U	1762-1789	28	91.5	.006
U	1790-1813	24	174.3	.031

English Coal Prices (Eton College)

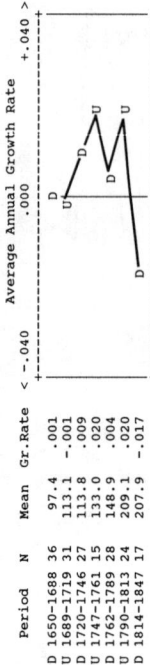

	Period	N	Mean	Gr.Rate
D	1650-1688	36	97.4	.001
D	1689-1719	31	113.1	-.001
D	1720-1746	27	113.8	.009
D	1747-1761	15	133.0	.020
D	1762-1789	28	148.9	.004
D	1790-1813	24	209.1	.020
D	1814-1847	17	207.9	-.017

English Bread Prices (Charterhouse)

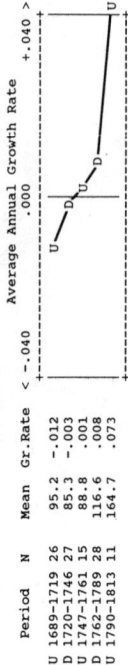

	Period	N	Mean	Gr.Rate
U	1689-1719	26	95.2	-.012
D	1720-1746	27	85.3	-.003
U	1747-1761	15	88.8	.001
D	1762-1789	28	116.6	.008
U	1790-1813	11	164.7	.073

Italian Wheat Prices (Milan)

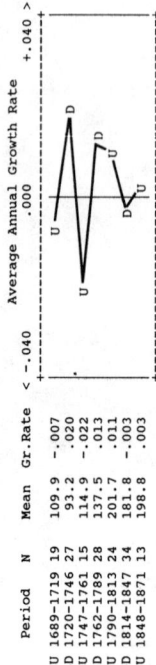

	Period	N	Mean	Gr.Rate
U	1689-1719	19	109.9	-.007
D	1720-1746	27	93.2	.020
D	1747-1761	15	114.9	-.022
D	1762-1789	28	137.5	.013
D	1790-1813	24	201.7	.011
U	1814-1847	34	181.8	-.003
U	1848-1871	13	198.8	.003

Italian Hard Coal Prices (Milan)

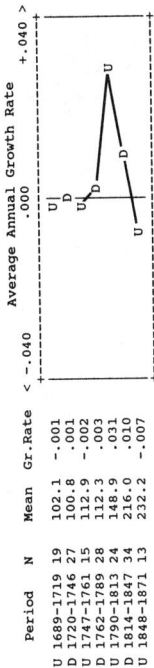

Period	N	Mean	Gr.Rate
U 1689-1719	19	102.1	-.001
D 1720-1746	27	100.8	.001
U 1747-1761	15	112.9	-.002
D 1762-1789	28	112.3	-.003
U 1790-1813	24	148.9	.031
D 1814-1847	34	216.0	.010
U 1848-1871	13	232.2	-.007

Swedish Wheat Prices

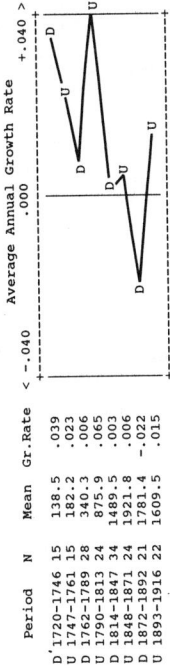

Period	N	Mean	Gr.Rate
D 1720-1746	15	138.5	.039
U 1747-1761	15	182.2	.023
D 1762-1789	28	340.3	.006
U 1790-1813	24	875.9	.065
D 1814-1847	34	1489.5	.003
U 1848-1871	24	1921.8	.006
D 1872-1892	21	1781.4	-.022
U 1893-1916	22	1609.5	.015

Swedish Pine Wood Prices

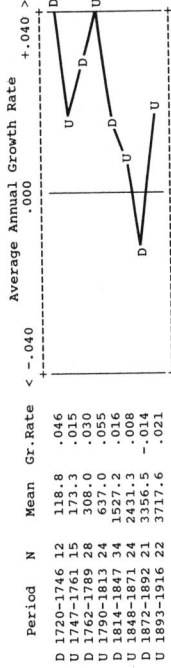

Period	N	Mean	Gr.Rate
D 1720-1746	12	118.8	.046
U 1747-1761	15	173.3	.015
D 1762-1789	28	308.0	.030
U 1790-1813	24	637.0	.055
D 1814-1847	34	1527.2	.016
U 1848-1871	24	2431.3	-.008
D 1872-1892	21	3356.5	-.014
U 1893-1916	22	3717.6	.021

Swedish Iron Ore Prices

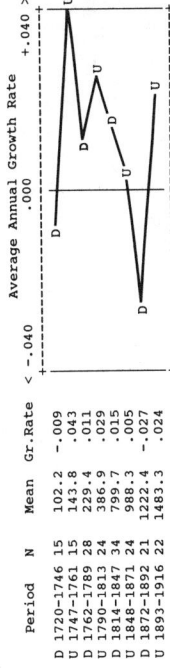

Period	N	Mean	Gr.Rate
D 1720-1746	15	102.2	-.009
U 1747-1761	15	143.8	.043
D 1762-1789	28	229.4	.011
U 1790-1813	24	386.9	.029
D 1814-1847	34	799.7	.015
U 1848-1871	24	988.3	.005
D 1872-1892	21	1222.4	-.027
U 1893-1916	22	1483.3	.024

Notes: N = number of years of data in each phase period. Average growth rates are graphed on standardized scale. Growth rates above 4% or below -4% are shown just outside the graphed range. "D" is plotted in a nominal downswing period, and "U" in a nominal upswing period.

199

only after 1720 (the 1689–1719 nominal upswing in fact saw a drop in prices). Prices of animal products follow the long wave phases except in 1762–89 (when the growth rate increases in a nominal downswing period). The English producers' price index in this period follows the phase datings fairly well.[3] These results suggest that long waves in prices around 1650–1800 are not limited to Britain, although they seem stronger in the British series.[4]

The remaining eight price indexes refer to industrial times (since about 1790). All show very strong correlations with the long wave phase periods. The commodity price indexes for Britain and the United States were put together by Kondratieff, and since I have adopted his dating of phase periods, the close fit is not surprising.[5] In the wholesale price indexes for Britain, France, Germany, and the United States, respectively, the growth rates in prices clearly alternate in successive phase periods. The two Belgian (industrial and agricultural) price indexes also fit the long wave phases well.[6]

These results for prices indexes may be summarized thus:

1. British prices fit the phase periods closely during all historical periods.
2. Since at least the late eighteenth century prices in all five countries closely follow the long wave phases, indicating a synchrony in these core economies.
3. In the period before 1650, the only available price indexes are British, and in the period 1650–1800 the only non-British indexes are for classes of Spanish commodities which fit the long wave, but not as closely as the British indexes.

Commodity Prices

The fourteen individual commodity price series are by their nature more sensitive to particular conditions and disturbances than the economy-wide price indexes. They cannot be expected to follow the long wave phase periods as closely as the price indexes, and indeed they do not. Nonetheless, they provide useful information, particularly since they cover a variety of countries.

The Paris wheat price series covers the entire period through 1788. Of the thirteen phase periods included, three are problematical, while the rest fit the long wave datings.[7] The two German (Cologne) price series, for wheat and bread, cover the

3. Only one downswing has higher growth than the previous upswing, and that by only a small amount; upswing growth rates, by contrast, are much higher than the previous downswings.

4. This could be because: (1) long waves were stronger in Britain than Spain in this period; (2) long waves were stronger in the overall price indexes (Britain) than in indexes for just one class of commodity (Spain); (3) long waves were more synchronous with the base dating in Britain than Spain; or (4) the British data are of higher quality.

5. These are the only two series for which the dating of turning points derives from the data series themselves (since Kondratieff's dates, which I use in the base dating scheme, came from these series, among others).

6. The industrial price index fits better in the first phase period but possibly only because the series starts earlier in the phase period, 1822 rather than 1835.

7. The three problem periods are the first, the last, and the period 1559–74—all nominal downswings marked by strong inflation. The first and last periods cannot be explained by the lack of data, since almost all years in the phase period are included.

period from 1531 and 1658, respectively, through the end of preindustrial times (1785, 1769). Neither series fits the long wave datings very well, although both series weakly correlate with the long wave.[8] Prices for Prussian rye on the Amsterdam produce exchange cover roughly the same period.[9] Through 1719, Amsterdam rye prices follow long wave datings, but later growth rates are relatively constant (and higher) across all phase periods.

English prices for malt, hops, wheat, coal, and bread, respectively, in the same seventeenth-to-eighteenth-century period, each come from just one original source (the records of one institution's purchases), so they are particularly subject to local disturbances. The price trends in the first four series fit the long wave periods fairly well, notwithstanding some anomalous phase periods for particular variables.[10] Only the bread price series does not match the long wave. Thus the English, Dutch, German, and French commodity price series in the seventeenth and eighteenth centuries generally support the existence of long waves in that era, most strongly in the case of Britain. These results supplement the indexes above (for which data are almost entirely British in the early centuries) and suggest that long waves exist in non-British countries in this era but appear stronger for Britain.[11]

The last five series cover late preindustrial and early industrial times for Italy and Sweden (1701–1860 and 1732–1914, respectively). Like Germany, Italy was not a core country in this period. The price trends for Milan wheat and coal do not follow the long wave pattern, and, in the first two, long waves even appear to be reversed with respect to the upswing and downswing phases. The Swedish series show mixed results.[12] Wheat prices follow the long wave after the first period,[13] iron ore prices show a weaker correlation, with some unusual behavior around 1848–71, and wood prices do not correlate with the long wave phase periods. These results suggest that long waves were absent or very weak in this era in Sweden and Italy.

The results for the individual commodity prices may be summarized as follows:

1. Commodity prices correlate with the long wave, but less consistently than price indexes.
2. The fit of price series to the long wave phase periods in preindustrial times decreases as one moves from British series to French, German, Prussian at

---

8. The wheat price series shows a tendency for growth rates on upswings to be higher than on adjacent downswings, but with several cases of the opposite tendency. The trends in bread prices parallel those of wheat. Both show low inflation in the nominal upswing of 1689–1719. Chapter 11 mentions other problems with dating the 1689–1719 phase period and suggests 1712 as possibly a better ending date.

9. In this period Amsterdam, unlike Germany, was at the center of the European world economy. Unfortunately the only series of suitable quality that I found for the Netherlands was for Prussian rye—a primary commodity imported from a noncore area.

10. Deflation during the nominal upswing of 1747–61 for hops and of 1689–1719 for wheat and coal.

11. Again, it is unclear whether the British prices actually followed long waves more closely or whether the British data are of higher quality.

12. The three Swedish series each derive from an average of a number of regional prices, which should make them more reliable than those drawn from a single location.

13. For which only half the years' data were available.

Amsterdam, Swedish, and Italian series in that order—corresponding roughly with outward movement from the core of the European world economy.

3. Wheat prices seem to follow the long wave pattern more closely than prices of bread and of nonfood commodities (coal, iron, wood); this may reflect either the centrality of grain in preindustrial economies or perhaps higher quality data for wheat prices.

T-tests

The above analyses for each of twenty-eight price series showed that many correlated well with the long wave phases hypothesized. But how strong is the correlation for the entire class of price series as a whole? And how strong is it in different subperiods of the total five-hundred-year period? I use the paired t-test (see chapter 8) to measure the overall fit to long wave phases.[14] I also make separate analyses of three shorter eras within the five-hundred-year period under study—1495–1650 (early preindustrial), 1650–1813 (late preindustrial), and 1790–1939 (the industrial period considered by Kondratieff).[15]

The t-test results for the twenty-eight price series as a class are shown in table 9.2. The "mean growth rate" columns give the average slope rates for the first phase periods of all pairs, then the average slope for the second periods, then the difference between them. The difference is hypothesized to be positive in comparing downswings to upswings, and negative in the upswing/downswing pairs, and this turns out to be the case in all the time periods analyzed. The "t" column gives the t statistic, which is then shown as a probability that the difference in slopes would occur randomly.

For the 1495–1975 period as a whole, the first line in the table indicates there were ninety-seven matched pairs consisting of a downswing and the following upswing among the twenty-eight price series (see table 9.2). The average growth rate was −.001 on the downswings and .018 on the upswings for a difference of .019. The value of t was 7.96, which is very high, indicating an extremely small probability of such a difference arising from random chance. In the next line, which shows upswings paired with following downswings, the sign of the difference is negative as hypothesized and t is still very high.[16]

The subperiod of 1790–1939 roughly matches the industrial era studied by Kon-

---

14. To recap, the input to the t-test consists of all the growth rates for all series available in a given era (different eras encompass different series). The growth rates are paired, and the t-test tests the difference across each pair. First downswing phase periods are paired with the following upswing periods (D/U), and then in a separate t-test the upswings are paired with the following downswings (U/D). Since the sign of the difference is as hypothesized (higher inflation on upswings), a one-tail probability is used here.

15. The period 1790–1939 is the one in which long price waves are most commonly assumed to exist. The earlier divisions follow roughly the divisions between series themselves, as well as the divisions between "eras" discussed in Part Three.

16. This and all other t-tests below used the 1968 turning point rather than 1980, but the effect was negligible. The t-statistic for the 28 price series, 1495–1975, using the 1980 date, comes out to 7.94 for the U/D pairs and −6.87 for the D/U pairs.

Table 9.2. T-test Results for 28 Price Series

Variable	Period	Pairs[a]	Mean Growth Rate[b]			DF[c]	t	Probability[d]
			1st	2d	Diff.			
Prices	1495-1975	Down/Up	-.001	.018	.019	96	7.96	< .0005**
		Up/Down	.016	-.002	-.017	90	-5.47	< .0005**
Prices	1790-1939	Down/Up	-.011	.014	.025	25	6.34	< .0005**
		Up/Down	.020	-.017	-.036	32	-11.59	< .0005**
Prices	1495-1813	Down/Up	.004	.018	.014	65	5.24	< .0005**
		Up/Down	.012	.001	-.011	57	-3.23	.001**
Prices	1495-1649	Down/Up	.004	.022	.018	20	3.08	.003**
		Up/Down	.029	.002	-.027	13	-2.44	.015*
Prices	1650-1813	Down/Up	.004	.016	.012	44	4.26	< .0005**
		Up/Down	.008	.002	-.006	34	-1.94	.030*

a. Paired phases: D/U = Downswing with following upswing; U/D = upswing with following downswing. Note that for all subperiods under study except 1790-1939, the U/D runs always lop off the first phase period (a downswing) and the last one (an upswing), resulting in fewer degrees of freedom. For 1790-1939 (which begins with an up phase and ends with a down), the D/U run lops off the first and last phase period.

b. 1st = average growth rate for 1st phase in pair; 2d = average growth rate for 2d phase in pair; Diff. = difference in growth rates (2d phase minus 1st). (Differences may show discrepancy due to rounding.)

c. DF = Degrees of freedom = number of phase period pairs minus 1.

d. 1-tailed probability (D/U positive; U/D negative as hypothesized).

** indicates statistical significance level below .01;
* indicates statistical significance level below .05.

dratieff and most other long wave scholars (excluding both the controversial pre-1790 period and the controversial post-1940 period). Here the significance of t is even higher, indicating a very strong long wave pattern in prices.

For preindustrial times as a whole, 1495–1813, t remains very high and is significant at the .01 level (indeed, at the .001 level). Breaking this subperiod into two eras, both have slightly lower, but still significant, t statistics. The lower statistical significance may in part reflect the smaller number of cases in these earlier eras (fewer degrees of freedom). The era 1495–1649 (fourteen to twenty-one pairs) continues to show a significant difference between the paired downswing and upswing phases, though only at the .05 confidence level for the up-down pairs. The same result holds for the second era, 1650–1813, in which there are thirty-five to forty-five pairs.

Thus these t-tests corroborate the correlation of the twenty-eight price series as a whole with the long wave in both preindustrial and industrial times.[17] The results thus far, then, corroborate these hypotheses:

17. This conclusion is tempered only by the fact that most of the best correlations in the preindustrial period occurred in British series.

> *Long waves exist.* [A]
> (Most long wave researchers)
>
> *Long waves at least in prices exist before 1790.* [A]
> (Imbert, Braudel, Wallerstein)
>
> *The dating of phases is captured in my base dating scheme.* [A]
> (Goldstein, based on thirty-three scholars reviewed in chapter 4)

The following hypothesis is now *rejected:*

> *Long waves exist only after about 1790.* [R]
> (Kondratieff, Ischboldin)

Lagged Correlations

As discussed in chapter 8, leads and lags in the correlations of different variables can be important in finding the "fine structure" of sequences in the long wave (within cycle time) as well as in clarifying confusion between methods of dating phases (by growth rates or by levels) that could lead to apparent time shifts.

In looking at these finer divisions of time (calendar time within phase-time, rather than just phase-time itself) there is an inescapable loss of precision, however. These methods are "weaker" statistically—the answers more tentative and more open to challenge—than the above correlations with the unlagged base dating scheme. Yet, despite these reservations, I will use the available information to the fullest in adducing the most plausible relationships in the long wave.[18]

Lag Structures: An Example

The lag structure of each time series in relation to the base dating scheme, as explained in chapter 8, graphs the relative fit of the time series to the nominal phase periods as those phase periods are shifted forward or backward through time.[19]

Consider the lag structure for the first price series, South English consumer price index, 1495–1954 (fig. 9.1). The figure represents the difference between two numbers: (1) the mean difference in the growth rates of downswings compared with following upswings, and (2) the mean difference when pairing upswings with following downswings.[20] The difference between these two is graphed, and

18. The data are, after all, given at the annual level.

19. A computer program shifts the entire base dating scheme back 20 years (keeping each phase the same length) and calculates the growth rates within each phase period and the differences between adjacent periods. The indicator of "fit" is the value of the "lag structure" for −20 years. The entire dating scheme is then shifted forward one year at a time, to +20, and the same procedure is repeated, yielding an indicator of the fit for each lag.

20. In this particular example the series is unusually long, so a mean growth rate is an average of about

Figure 9.1. Lag Structure, South England Consumer Prices, 1495-1954

1495-1954

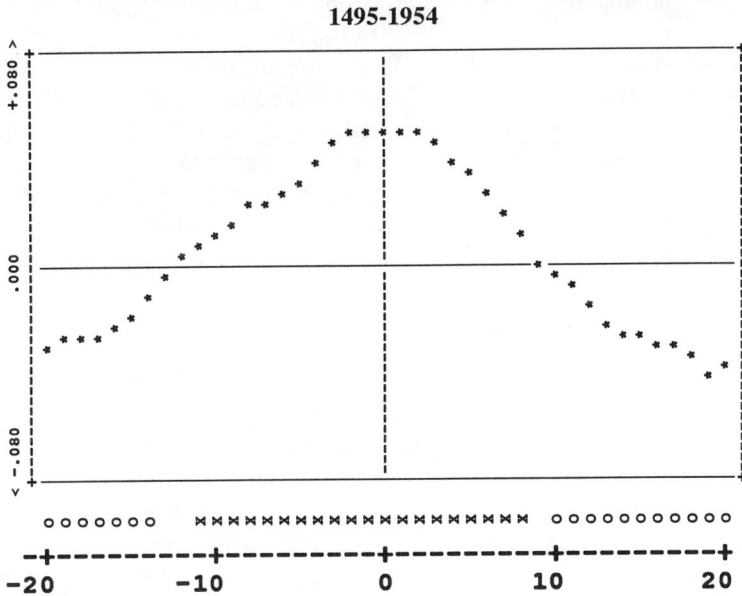

this function will be at its maximum when the shifted dating scheme best fits the data.[21]

A direct correlation with the long wave is indicated when growth rates change in a positive direction when moving from downswing to upswing phase and in a negative direction when moving from upswing to downswing. The lags for which both these conditions are true are marked with an "X" at the bottom of the graph (the "X region" of the lag structure). Those lags for which the reverse is true, indicating an inverse (phase-reversed) correlation of the time series to the long wave phases, are marked with an "O."[22]

The lag structure of a variable provides three types of information about the variable. First, the location of the peak (if there is a clear peak) indicates whether the variable leads or lags the base dating scheme. A class of variables all tending to have peaks around the same lag indicates a lagged correlation of that class of variables. Second, the amplitude of the peak indicates how strongly the data fit a long wave pattern at that peak. Third, the lag structure indicates the sensitivity of the correlation to the particular dates of turning points by shifting all the turning points together

ten phase changes. For shorter series the mean may be the average of as few as two to three phase changes. Also, in a given series the number of phase changes included in this average may vary slightly in different lags (since turning points can shift past the beginning or end of the time series).

21. Or in the case of inverse correlations, minimum.

22. The remaining unmarked lags are those for which the mean change in the D/U and U/D columns have the same sign as each other.

backward and forward a year at a time (see chapter 8). The behavior of the curve in the few years around the peak shows how robust that peak is against minor dating shifts.

The lag structure of South English consumer prices (fig. 9.1) is a good example of robustness against minor time shifts. The peak is around zero lags, indicating a fit to the unlagged base dating scheme. The peak amplitude of 5.3 percent reflects an average change in growth rates of +2.8 percent at troughs and −2.5 percent at peaks. On either side of the peak, a time shift of two years does not affect the fit at all, and then for several more years the fit drops off. With fifteen to twenty years of shift in either direction, the lag structure becomes negative, or inversely correlated with the phases.

Price Indexes

The lag structure for the South English consumer price index (1495–1954) (fig. 9.1), is time-stable (robust) and shows no time shift from the base dating scheme. A similar pattern is found in the English industrial and agricultural price indexes (1495–1640). The respective peaks are around −3 to +9 lags and −2 to +2 lags. The agricultural price index is less robust than the industrial price index, which about equals the robustness of the English consumer price index.

The two Spanish price indexes (1651–1800) are less robust, but both seem to show at least a weak peak leading the base dating scheme by about five years. For the English producers' price index (1661–1801), the lag structure is less robust, with two peaks at around −12 and +1 lags. The highest peak of the curve is at 0 to +2 lags. This series thus correlates basically with the unshifted dating scheme but has some anomalous behavior.

In the four national wholesale price indexes—for Britain, France, Germany, and the United States—the peaks are high and very close to 0 lags (around +1 for Britain and the United States, +2 for France), and the lag structures are robust in all but Germany (fig. 9.2). This strong correlation of wholesale prices in the core industrial countries corroborates that the long wave in prices is internationally synchronous.

Both Kondratieff's British and American price indexes (1780–1922 and 1791–1922) have fairly robust lag structures (the British more so), peaking at +1 lags. The Belgian industrial and agricultural price indexes (1822–1913) also have a robust lag structure. They peak around 0, lagging just slightly (+2 to +3 lags).

The fourteen price indexes, then, consistently show price waves to be synchronous with the nominal phase dating with no important lags in either direction.

Commodity Prices

For the individual commodity prices, the lag structures are less robust—curves are more jumpy and the location of peaks varies more. This is to be expected, since individual commodities are subject to more fluctuations from unrelated causes and local conditions.

The lag structure for French wheat prices (1495–1788) peaks at around 0. For

Figure 9.2. Lag Structures, Four National Price Indexes

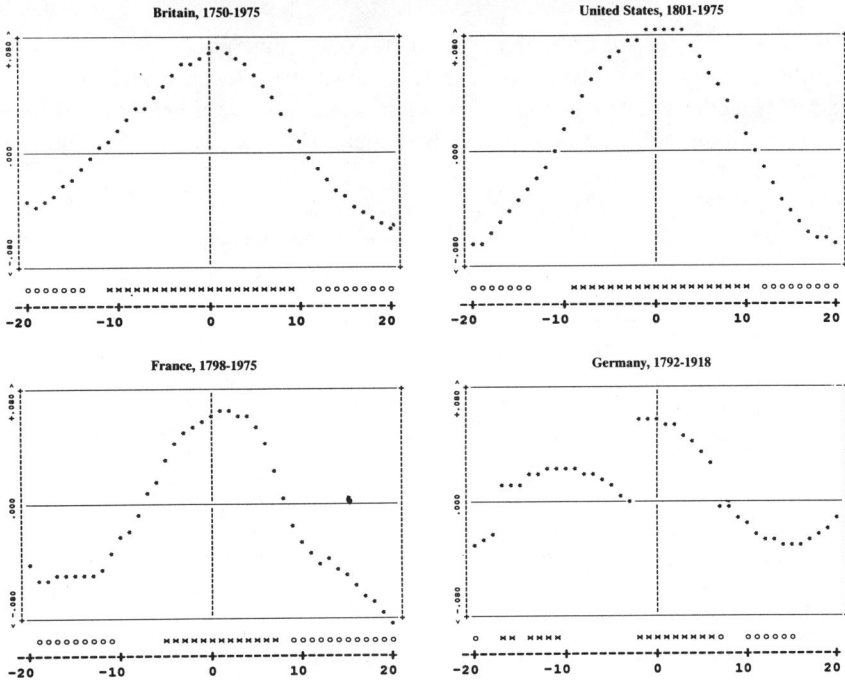

Britain, 1750-1975

United States, 1801-1975

France, 1798-1975

Germany, 1792-1918

German wheat and bread prices (1531–1786 and 1658–1772, respectively), the peaks fall somewhere between 0 and −15 lags (seemingly leading the nominal phase dating), though they are hard to identify.[23] The bread price lag structure is not very robust (especially around +13 lags). For the price of Prussian rye at Amsterdam (1597–1783), the lag structure is also rather jumpy but seems to peak at −14 to −11 lags.

For the five British commodity price series (malt, 1595–1831; hops, 1622–1829; wheat, 1630–1817; coal, 1653–1830; and bread, 1694–1800), the lag structures are not very robust but peak around zero—there is no clear shift for the whole set of variables. Malt, wheat, and coal, which have the more robust lag structures, seem to peak a few years before zero, while hops and bread peak a few years after zero but have extremely nonrobust lag structures.

The two Italian price series (wheat and coal, 1701–1860) lead the base dating scheme by about ten to twelve years and three to thirteen years, respectively. The lag structures are relatively robust, although in the case of coal prices the amplitude is small. The Swedish price series (1732–1914) are fairly robust (wood less so than

23. For wheat prices, the "X" region extends from at least −20 lags to +2, and within that region the peak period stretches from −15 to −2 lags (single highest peak at −3 lags). For bread prices, the "X" region similarly extends from at least −20 lags to +2, and there seem to be two peaks, one at −20 lags or less, and one around −3 to 0 lags.

wheat or iron), and all peak at around three years' lag (that is, reasonably close to zero).

To summarize for the fourteen individual commodity price series, some lag structures are more robust than others, and as a rule they are less robust than the price indexes. Nonetheless, the patterns of lag structures indicate a general correspondence to the base dating scheme, with sometimes a shift one way or the other for a particular country's prices.

While the data are really too fragmentary to draw any but the most tentative conclusions about the behavior of individual countries, the lag structures are suggestive of a possible lagged relationship among prices in different countries as follows:

17th c.	Prussian/Amsterdam:	about −11 to −14
18th c.	Italian:	about −3 to −13 lags
18th c.	Spanish	about −5
17th–19th c.	German	about 0 to −5
16th–20th c.	British	about 0
19th–20th c.	U.S.	about +1
16th–20th c.	French	about 0 to +2
19th c.	Belgian	about +2 to +3
18th–19th c.	Swedish	about +3

Could this indicate that price waves actually rolled across Europe from south to north, or from the semiperiphery to the core?[24]

To check on this possibility of a geographic pattern in price lags, I examined different researchers' datings of long waves in various countries (see chapter 4) and asked whether their datings were consistently shifted from the base dating (see table 9.3).[25] These lags do not correspond with those shown above, however. In fact, if anything the opposite is seen (the more central countries leading the more peripheral ones).

A better interpretation of my results is simply that both the price indexes and the commodity prices in core countries cluster around 0 lags, while commodity prices, especially in semiperipheral countries,[26] show more shifts in peaks and are less robust (see table 9.4). The first group of series, which shows leads, and the last group, which shows lags, are almost entirely commodity prices. The middle group of series, with 0 to +3 lags, are almost all national indexes. The data for national

24. The latter would be consistent if Sweden's positive lags were ignored and Prussian/Amsterdam was treated as Prussian. I examined phase correlations in the German, Spanish, Italian, and Prussian series with the dating scheme shifted up 10 years (−10 year lag). I also ran phase correlations with a shift of 5 rather than 10 years. The results were largely the same for the 5- as for the 10-year shift. The fit of the German and Italian series is considerably better than with no lags, but the improvements in the Prussian and Spanish series are not dramatic.

25. If a similar pattern emerged to that shown above, this could corroborate the idea of geographical lags in long waves. This attempt is difficult, since almost all the countries included are core countries.

26. Where data are worse and long waves seemed to be weak (see earlier in this chapter).

Table 9.3. Possible Lags in Other Authors' Datings

For industrial times:

Britain	– 0.9 years	Imbert (1959)
Britain	– 0.1	Burns and Mitchell (1946)
United States	– 1.3	Imbert (1959)
United States	– 2.3	Burns and Mitchell (1946)
United States	+ 0.1	Ischboldin (1967
United States	– 1.4	Cole (1938)
France	+ 1.4	Imbert (1959)
France	+ 2.0	Burns and Mitchell (1946)
France	+ 5.0	Simiand (1932b)
Germany	– 0.2	Imbert (1959)
Germany	0.0	Burns and Mitchell (1946)
Belgium	+ 2.6	Imbert (1959)
Italy	+ 2.3	Imbert (1959)
"Europe"	+ 1.0	Ischboldin (1967)

For preindustrial times:

England	– 2.7	Imbert (1959)
France	– 5.3	Imbert (1959)
S. France	+ 5.1	Baehrel (1961)
Spain	– 5.3	Imbert (1959)
Germany	– 18.7	Imbert (1959)

Note: Numbers indicate average lag of a turning point from the comparable turning point in my base dating scheme.

indexes are simply of higher quality. On the whole, in twenty of the twenty-eight price series (including thirteen of the fourteen national indexes) the lag structures peak within three years of zero, corroborating that price waves in the core of the world system are internationally synchronized and synchronized with the base dating scheme.[27]

In sum, the empirical analysis strongly corroborates long waves in price data— both before and after the onset of industrialization in the late eighteenth century.[28] Price waves go back as early as the sixteenth century, although in the earliest centuries they seem strongest in the most central core countries (especially Britain) and weakest in outlying areas of Europe. Since the late eighteenth century, price waves appear in, and are synchronous among, various European countries, reflecting the expansion of the core of the world system and its increasing integration in the industrial era.

27. Outside the core, price waves seem to be weaker and less synchronous. Again, this may be partly due to lower quality data.

28. This also corroborates the idea of the world system itself as a useful unit of analysis with its own internal coherence. As Braudel (1984:75) notes, "prices that rise and fall in unison provide us with the most convincing evidence of the coherence of a world-economy penetrated by monetary exchange and developing under the already directive hand of capitalism."

Table 9.4. Summary of Lags in Price Series

Series	"X Region"			Best
Amsterdam prices for Prussian rye (1597-1783)	-20	to	+4	-13
Italian wheat prices (Milan) (1701-1860)	-20	to	-5	-10
Italian hard coal prices (Milan) (1701-1860)	-14	to	+9	-6
Spanish animal product price index (1651-1800)	-8	to	-1	-4
English wheat prices (Manchester) (1630-1817)	-10	to	+7	-4
Spanish textile price index (1651-1800)	-9	to	-1	-3
German wheat prices (Cologne) (1531-1786)	-20	to	+2	-3
English malt prices (Eton College) (1595-1831)	-20	to	+4	-2
English coal prices (Eton College) (1653-1830)	-20	to	+4	-2
German bread prices (Cologne) (1658-1772)	-20	to	+2	-1
French wheat prices (Paris) (1495-1788)	-11	to	+11	0
South English consumer price index (1495-1954)	-11	to	+8	0
South English agricultural price index (1495-1640)	-12	to	+6	0
German wholesale price index (1792-1918)	-17	to	+6	0
English producers' price index (1661-1801)	-16	to	+5	+1
British commodity prices [Kondratieff](1780-1922)	-7	to	+9	+1
U.S. commodity prices [Kondratieff] (1791-1922)	-9	to	+5	+1
British wholesale price index (1750-1975)	-11	to	+9	+1
U.S. wholesale price index (1801-1975)	-9	to	+10	+1
Belgian agricultural price index (1822-1913)	-7	to	+12	+1
Swedish iron ore prices (1732-1914)	-6	to	+10	+1
French wholesale price index (1798-1975)	-5	to	+7	+2
S. English industrial price index (1495-1640)	-8	to	+8	+3
Belgian industrial price index (1822-1913)	-5	to	+13	+3
Swedish wheat prices (1732-1914)	-13	to	+10	+3
Swedish pine wood prices (1732-1914)	-5	to	+20	+4
English hops prices (Eton College) (1622-1829)	-1	to	+14	+6
English bread prices (Charterhouse) (1694-1800)	-11	to	-4	+6

CHAPTER TEN

Data Analysis 2:
Real Economic Variables

A s has been mentioned, the change from examining prices to examining production, innovation, and other economic variables is not a straightforward one. The nature of the data used in the analysis changes in two ways. First, very few data are available for preindustrial times; and second, the quality of data even in industrial times is lower than for price data. For production data most of the period since the late eighteenth century is covered by time series of reasonable quality for the major core countries. But for the other economic variables only scattered series of mixed quality are available. These series are eclectic, consisting of a scattering of particular variables, countries, and time periods that in no way "cover" any class of variable. A correlation with long waves can provide only fragmentary evidence; and a lack of correlation may merely reflect the low quality of the data.

Thus the conclusions throughout this chapter must be more tentative than those in the previous chapter, and the conclusions regarding economic variables other than production and prices must be considered preliminary at best. Nonetheless, these tentative results offer little bits of evidence—clues if you will—regarding some of the other economic variables thought by various schools to play a role in long waves.

Production

Phase Period Growth Rates

To analyze the ten production series I first estimated the growth rates for each phase period of the base dating scheme (table 10.1).[1]

The ten production series begin with four series at the "world" level of analysis. Two series cover world industrial production: the first (1740–1850) is from Haustein and Neuwirth (who cite Hoffman); the second and later series (1850–1975) is from Kuczynski. In addition to his world industrial production series, Kuczynski gives series for world agricultural production and world total production (the third and fourth series). World industrial production before 1850 does not follow the long

1. Note that the few data points after 1968 are not included on this table, since I had not yet changed the last turning point from 1968 to 1980. The 1940–80 phase ends in 1967.

Table 10.1. Production -- Growth Rates by Phase

World Industrial Production [Series 1]

Average Annual Growth Rate < -.040   .000   +.040 >

Period	N	Mean	Gr.Rate
D 1720-1746	7	105.4	.027
U 1747-1761	15	124.8	-.001
D 1762-1789	28	163.3	.021
D 1790-1813	24	340.5	.026
D 1814-1847	34	837.5	.034

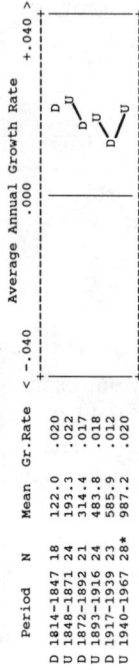

World Industrial Production [Series 2]

Average Annual Growth Rate < -.040   .000   +.040 >

Period	N	Mean	Gr.Rate
U 1848-1871	22	166.7	.034
D 1872-1892	21	340.4	.035
U 1893-1916	24	800.0	.037
D 1917-1939	23	1350.6	.024
U 1940-1967	28*	3615.3	.040

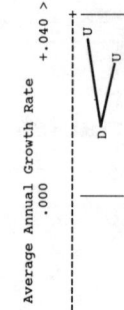

World Agricultural Production

Average Annual Growth Rate < -.040   .000   +.040 >

Period	N	Mean	Gr.Rate
U 1848-1871	22	116.5	.016
D 1872-1892	21	184.6	.021
U 1893-1916	24	290.2	.017
D 1917-1939	23	429.5	.022
U 1940-1980	36	648.9	.021

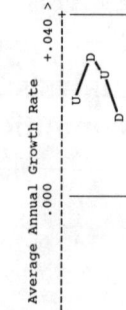

World Total Production

Average Annual Growth Rate < -.040   .000   +.040 >

Period	N	Mean	Gr.Rate
U 1848-1871	22	128.3	.021
D 1872-1892	21	222.3	.026
U 1893-1916	24	414.5	.027
D 1917-1939	23	655.7	.022
U 1940-1980	36	1563.1	.036

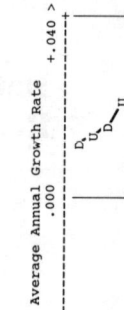

French Real Gross National Product

Average Annual Growth Rate < -.040   .000   +.040 >

Period	N	Mean	Gr.Rate
D 1814-1847	28	127.1	.016
U 1848-1871	24	190.7	.015
D 1872-1892	21	252.9	.009
D 1893-1916	24	340.7	.014
U 1917-1939	23	439.3	.020
U 1940-1967	28*	724.0	.054

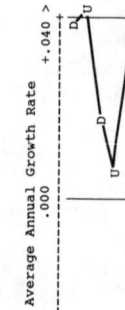

British Real Gross National Product

Average Annual Growth Rate < -.040   .000   +.040 >

Period	N	Mean	Gr.Rate
D 1814-1847	18	122.0	.020
U 1848-1871	24	193.3	.022
D 1872-1892	21	314.4	.017
D 1893-1916	24	483.8	.018
U 1917-1939	23	585.9	.012
U 1940-1967	28*	987.2	.020

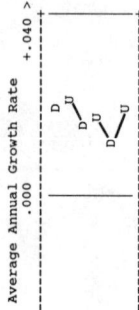

U.S. Real Gross National Product

Average Annual Growth Rate < -.040   .000   +.040 >

Period	N	Mean	Gr.Rate
U 1893-1916	24	194.9	.038
D 1917-1939	23	344.9	.013
U 1940-1980	28	867.3	.032

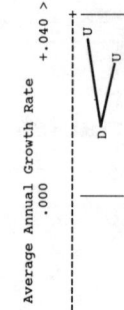

British Industrial Production

Average Annual Growth Rate < -.040   .000   +.040 >

Period	N	Mean	Gr.Rate
U 1790-1813	13	117.0	.021
D 1814-1847	34	237.3	.032
D 1848-1871	24	582.7	.029
U 1872-1892	21	1003.9	.018
U 1893-1916	24	1568.6	.016
D 1917-1939	22	2228.4	.030

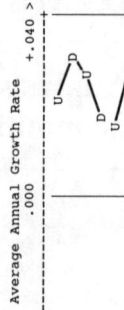

French Industrial Production

Average Annual Growth Rate < -.040   .000   +.040 >

Period	N	Mean	Gr.Rate
D 1814-1847	33	119.6	.013
U 1848-1871	24	194.9	.014
D 1872-1892	21	270.4	.016
D 1893-1916	21	386.3	.023

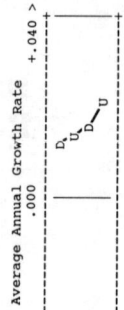

Belgian Industrial Production

Average Annual Growth Rate < -.040   .000   +.040 >

Period	N	Mean	Gr.Rate
D 1814-1847	8	102.8	.040
D 1848-1871	24	219.3	.043
D 1872-1892	21	434.3	.019
D 1893-1916	24	704.2	.006
U 1917-1939	23	955.2	.035
U 1940-1967	28*	1556.7	.047

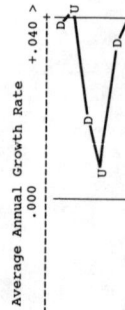

See notes to Table 9.1.

wave pattern of upswings and downswings. Since 1850, or at least from 1893 on, the pattern matches, but this is only a short period and does not justify any broad conclusions. World agricultural production seems to follow a pattern of inverse correlation with the nominal phase periods. This supports the hypothesis:

Downswings in agriculture correspond with general upswings. [A]
(Ehrensaft)[2]

However, this corroboration is weak, since the differences in growth rates are slight (growth rates always remain between .016 and .022) and since only one series is analyzed. The series for world total production (industrial plus agricultural) does not match the long wave phases.[3]

The next three series measure real gross national product (GNP) for France, Britain, and the United States, respectively. The French GNP follows the long wave phase datings only weakly (due to strong growth in the 1917–39 nominal downswing).[4] British GNP follows the long wave pattern. The differences between the upswing and downswing phases, however, are slight (growth rates ranging from .012 to .020). The U.S. GNP series fits the long wave phases; but only one-and-a-half cycles (seventy-five years) of data are available.

The last three production series measure the volume of British, French, and Belgian industrial production, respectively. In none of these series do the growth rates correlate with the long wave phases.

To summarize, the estimated growth rates by phase period match the long wave phases rather weakly[5] for national GNP series and not at all for world production series and national indexes of industrial production. For production variables taken as a class (ten series), a correlation with long wave dating cannot be corroborated. In the results of t-tests on the growth rates of the production series (twenty-two to twenty-five pairs of phase periods), the sign of t in each of the two tests was as expected, but in neither case was t statistically significant (table 10.2).[6]

Lagged Correlations: Production

In the lag structures for production series, a striking pattern appears repeatedly (though not in every case). For the majority of series (and those with greatest

2. "Agriculture entered a B-phase as the economy as a whole entered an A . . . phase" (Ehrensaft 1980:77). Note that Ehrensaft considered only the most recent upswing.

3. This is not surprising, given the weak correlation in world industrial production and the inverse correlation in world agricultural production.

4. Problems could arise from the particular datings of the 1917 and 1940 turning points during wars that caused substantial fluctuations in French GNP.

5. Less consistently and with smaller variations in growth rates across phase periods than the price series.

6. As with the price t-tests, the 1968 turning point is used here rather than 1980. Since 1968 is presumed to be closer to the actual production turning point, using the 1980 date would only make this insignificant t-test slightly less significant.

Table 10.2. T-test Results for Ten Production Series

Variable	Period	Pairs[a]	Mean Growth Rate[b] 1st	2d	Diff.	DF[c]	t	Probability[d]
Production	1740-1975	Down/Up	.022	.025	.003	21	1.35	.096 −
		Up/Down	.025	.025	.000	24	-0.08	.468 −

a. Paired phases: D/U = Downswing with following upswing; U/D = upswing with following downswing.

b. 1st = average growth rate for 1st phase in pair; 2d = average growth rate for 2d phase in pair; Diff. = difference in growth rates (2d phase minus 1st). (Differences may show discrepancy due to rounding.)

c. DF = Degrees of freedom = number of phase period pairs minus 1.

d. 1-tailed probability (D/U positive; U/D negative as hypothesized).

− indicates not statistically significant.

robustness in their lag structures), the lag structure peaks *lead* the base dating scheme (and hence prices) by about ten to fifteen years (or one-fourth of a cycle) on average.

In the case of the two world industrial production series, both lag structures are fairly robust and peak around ten to fifteen years before the zero (fig. 10.1).[7] The fact that the patterns in these two series are so similar is a powerful corroboration of a lagged correlation in production, because the series cover two different periods of time (1740–1850 and 1850–1975, respectively) and come from two different sources affiliated with different long wave schools.[8] It is also noteworthy that the correlation emerges most clearly in these ''world'' (rather than national) series.

Other production series showing a similar pattern include World total production (1850–1975), British real GNP (1830–1975), U.S. real GNP (1889–1970), British industrial production (1801–1938), French industrial production (1815–1913) and Belgian industrial production (1840–1975):[9]

Series	Approximate Peak	"X" Region
World industrial production 1	−15	−20 to −6
World industrial production 2	−16	−20 to +2
World total production	−18	−20 to −1 except −9 to −7
British real GNP	−5	−19 to +2
U.S. real GNP	−4	−18 to +4
British industrial production	−9	−20 to −5
French industrial production	−19	−7 to −3
Belgian industrial production	−17	−10 to +15? (interspersed)

7. For the two series the peaks are at −17 to −13 lags, and −17 to −15 lags, respectively.

8. The 1740–1850 series is from non-Marxists—Hoffman, reprinted by Haustein and Neuwirth (1982:76). The 1850–1975 series is from a Marxist, Kuczynski (1980:309).

9. The last two series are less robust than the others.

Figure 10.1. Lag Structures, World Industrial Production

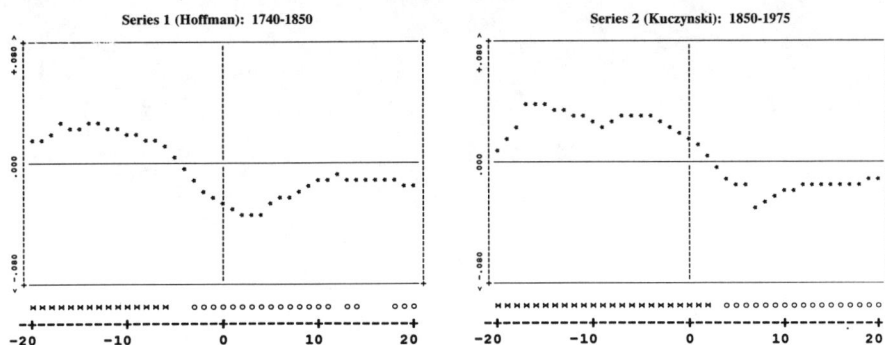

By contrast, two production series showed both less robustness and a different lag structure. First, French real GNP peaks at about +7 lags.[10] Second, world agricultural production seems to be out of phase with world industrial production, with a trough at about −8 lags and a peak around +15 ("O" region, −13 to +2). This inverse correlation, mentioned above, appears to be robust, although the difference between the peak and trough of the lag structure is small.

For the production variables as a class, then, lag structures for eight of the ten series show production leading the base dating scheme and hence leading prices by about ten to fifteen years on average.[11] Agricultural production, by contrast, follows an inverse correlation with the long wave.[12] I therefore reconceptualized production as leading prices by ten to fifteen years and adopted a dating scheme for production that is shifted from the base dating. How does this affect the overall strength of long waves in this class of variable as reflected in the pattern of alternating growth rates and in the t-test?

I reestimated the growth rates for the ten production series first with −10 years and then with −15 years shift in the base dating scheme.[13] In production growth rates with the −15-year time shift, the alternating pattern in successive phases is now visible in the world industrial production indexes, world total production, United States GNP, and (less strongly) in British and French industrial production—but not in the other four production series (table 10.3). The pattern was similar in the estimates using a −10-year dating shift (not shown here).

10. The lag structure stays at a high positive level, however, for an extended "X" region from −20 to +13 lags (except 0). Thus it is not entirely inconsistent with the behavior of the first six production series, which lead the base dating scheme.

11. Six of these eight are fairly robust against time shifts, while the other two are less robust. A ninth series is also less robust but not entirely inconsistent.

12. The hypothesis that agricultural production downswings correspond with general upswings, if accepted, would imply that agricultural production does not really belong in this class of variables. But it would be too "ad hoc" to draw such a conclusion on the basis of one time series. Thus for purposes of testing the class of production variables as a whole, I have retained the agricultural production series.

13. In lagging a class of variables, I have used only five-year increments (e.g., −5 lags, −10 lags, etc.) in the time shifts (see chap. 8).

Table 10.3. Production -- Growth with Phases Shifted

World Industrial Production [Series 1]   Time Shift -15

Average Annual Growth Rate
< -.040   .000   +.040 >

Period	N	Mean	Gr.Rate
U 1732-1746	7	105.4	.027
D 1747-1774	28	132.7	.009
U 1775-1798	24	213.5	.032
D 1799-1832	34	513.0	.028
U 1833-1856	18	1179.9	.031

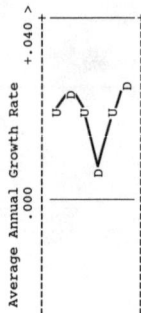

World Industrial Production [Series 2]   Time Shift -15

Average Annual Growth Rate
< -.040   .000   +.040 >

Period	N	Mean	Gr.Rate
U 1833-1856	7	127.2	.069
D 1857-1877	21	207.2	.033
U 1878-1901	24	448.0	.038
D 1902-1924	23	987.4	.018
U 1925-1965	41	2701.7	.036
D 1966-1975	10	7724.8	.040

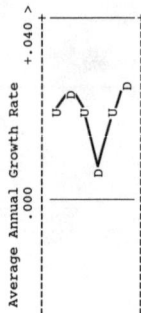

World Agricultural Production   Time Shift -15

Average Annual Growth Rate
< -.040   0   +.040 >

Period	N	Mean	Gr.Rate
U 1833-1856	7	103.9	.015
D 1857-1877	21	131.4	.021
U 1878-1901	24	216.8	.020
D 1902-1924	23	325.8	.011
U 1925-1965	41	536.7	.012
D 1966-1975	10	845.9	.022

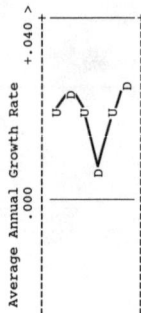

World Total Production   Time Shift -15

Average Annual Growth Rate
< -.040   0   +.040 >

Period	N	Mean	Gr.Rate
U 1833-1856	7	109.4	.029
D 1857-1877	21	149.3	.025
U 1878-1901	24	272.9	.027
D 1902-1924	23	488.2	.015
U 1925-1965	41	1045.9	.026
D 1966-1975	10	2423.4	.036

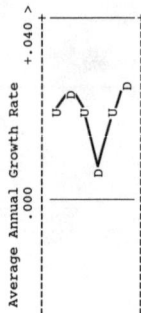

French Real Gross National Product   Time Shift -15

Average Annual Growth Rate
< -.040   .000   +.040 >

Period	N	Mean	Gr.Rate
U 1799-1832	13	112.1	.012
D 1833-1856	24	150.1	.015
U 1857-1877	21	214.4	.013
D 1878-1901	24	276.3	.013
U 1902-1924	23	360.9	.004
U 1925-1965	41	606.0	.027
D 1966-1975	10	1647.2	.049

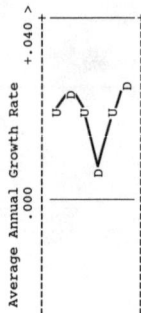

British Real Gross National Product   Time Shift -15

Average Annual Growth Rate
< -.040   .000   +.040 >

Period	N	Mean	Gr.Rate
U 1833-1856	24	139.3	.021
D 1857-1877	21	230.8	.025
U 1878-1901	24	363.8	.021
D 1902-1924	23	526.3	.006
U 1925-1965	41	832.5	.020
D 1966-1975	10	1507.9	.026

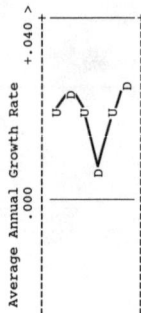

U.S. Real Gross National Product   Time Shift -15

Average Annual Growth Rate
< -.040   .000   +.040 >

Period	N	Mean	Gr.Rate
U 1878-1901	13	129.7	.040
D 1902-1924	23	253.9	.026
U 1925-1965	41	660.9	.034
D 1966-1975	5	1420.8	.026

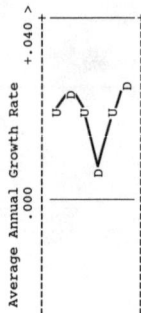

British Industrial Production   Time Shift -15

Average Annual Growth Rate
< -.040   .000   +.040 >

Period	N	Mean	Gr.Rate
D 1799-1832	32	154.2	.028
U 1833-1856	24	365.1	.032
U 1857-1877	21	722.0	.027
U 1878-1901	24	1174.9	.023
U 1902-1924	23	1710.8	.007
U 1925-1965	14	2494.1	.029

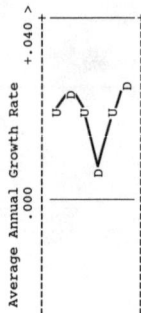

French Industrial Production   Time Shift -15

Average Annual Growth Rate
< -.040   .000   +.040 >

Period	N	Mean	Gr.Rate
D 1799-1832	18	107.7	.004
D 1833-1856	24	149.7	.024
D 1857-1877	21	216.1	.013
U 1878-1901	24	304.5	.016
D 1902-1924	12	419.7	.037

Belgian Industrial Production   Time Shift -15

Average Annual Growth Rate
< -.040   .000   +.040 >

Period	N	Mean	Gr.Rate
U 1833-1856	17	129.2	.049
D 1857-1877	21	293.8	.037
D 1878-1901	24	525.3	.027
D 1902-1924	23	705.9	-.007
U 1925-1965	41	1349.0	.023
D 1966-1975	10	3091.2	.037

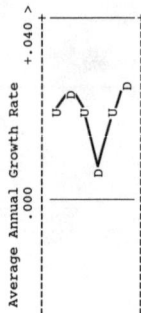

See notes to Table 9.1.

Table 10.4. T-test Results for Production with Phases Shifted

Variable	Lag	Pairs[a]	Mean Growth Rate[b]			DF[c]	t	Probability[d]
			1st	2d	Diff.			
Production	-10	Down/Up	.021	.028	.007	21	3.03	.003 **
		Up/Down	.028	.023	-.005	24	2.12	.022 *
Production	-15	Down/Up	.017	.025	.008	20	3.43	.002 **
		Up/Down	.027	.022	-.005	25	-1.70	.050 —

Note: All production series, 1740-1975, are included.
a. Paired phases: D/U = Downswing with following upswing; U/D = upswing with following downswing.
b. 1st = average growth rate for 1st phase in pair; 2d = average growth rate for 2d phase in pair; Diff. = difference in growth rates (2d phase minus 1st). (Differences may show discrepancy due to rounding.)
c. DF = Degrees of freedom = number of phase period pairs minus 1.
d. 1-tailed probability (D/U positive; U/D negative as hypothesized).
** indicates statistical significance level below .01;
* indicates statistical significance level below .05;
— indicates not statistically significant.

In the t-tests for the production series growth rates using dating schemes shifted −10 and −15 years, the signs of the growth rate differences are as expected (table 10.4). For the −10 year shift, the difference is statistically significant at the .001 level for D/U pairs and at .05 for U/D pairs. For the −15 year shift, the difference is significant at .01 for the D/U pairs and not quite significant for the U/D pairs. Overall, I conclude that the production series fit rather well to a shifted long wave pattern that leads prices by ten to fifteen years.

Thus I accept the hypotheses that long waves exist in production as well as prices and that production leads prices:

Long waves exist in prices, production, and investment. [A]
(Kondratieff, Mandel, Kuczynski, Gordon, Kleinknecht, Delbeke, Van Duijn, Forrester)

Long waves exist in prices only, not in production and investment. [R]
(Kuznets, Silberling, Cleary and Hobbs, Van Ewijk, Van der Zwan)

Production increases precede price increases. [A]
(Imbert)

Production phases are synchronous with price phases. [R]
(Most long wave researchers)

Stagflation: A New Interpretation

The lag between long waves in production and those in prices opens the way to resolving a central anomaly and dispute in the long wave literature—the stagflation of the 1970s. Mandel argues that production began a downswing around 1968; Rostow argues that prices rose rapdily through the 1970s. Both are correct if production leads prices—a production peak around 1968 would go with a price peak around 1980.

Furthermore, if production leads prices, then the dates in the base dating scheme must be reconsidered. Braudel's dates seem to derive from prices (see chapter 4). Frank's dates claim to describe rapid and slower development, but since they are from preindustrial times it must be assumed that price data also played a large role there (since few data other than prices are available in that era). Kondratieff's dates, too, fit best for his price data and less well for production data. Only Mandel's turning points seem to be truly based on production.

I therefore changed the last date in the dating scheme to reflect a new understanding of the production-price lag, making the base dating consistent and resolving the stagflation problem. The peak of 1968 was changed to 1980, representing a price peak ending an unusually long upswing from 1940. The base dating scheme is then explicitly a dating of prices.

I chose 1980 as the best date for this peak for several reasons. First, if 1968 is the production peak (following Mandel), then the price peak should be about ten to fifteen years later. Second, inflation did in fact subside in the United States in the 1980s. Third, the change in U.S. inflation seems to come just after 1980:

	Annual percentage change		
Producer prices[14]		Consumer prices[15]	
1978–79	12.6%	1980	12.4%
1979–80	14.1%	1981	8.9%
1980–81	9.2%	1982	3.9%
1981–82	2.0%	1983	3.8%
		1984	4.0%
		1985	3.8%

The stagflation of the 1970s, then, becomes not an anomaly but only a particularly strong instance of a phenomenon that may often mark the late upswing phase.[16] The previous historical instance was the hyperinflation following World War I, in the early 1920s. In the instance before that, Dupriez (1978:203) sees a similar pattern around 1872. And the instance before that, around 1815, is discussed by Mokyr and Savin (1976) explicitly as a case of "stagflation."

---

14. Annual percentage change in the producer price index for major commodity groups from U.S. Census (1983:486).

15. Bureau of Labor Statistics, reprinted in *Boston Globe,* Jan. 23, 1986, p. 19.

16. Often associated with war; see chap. 11.

Table 10.5. Innovation -- Growth Rates by Phase

List of Innovations [Haustein & Neuwirth]

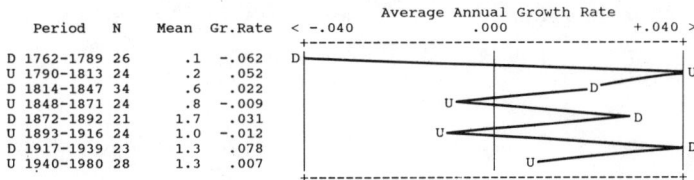

Period	N	Mean	Gr.Rate
D 1762-1789	26	.1	-.062
U 1790-1813	24	.2	.052
D 1814-1847	34	.6	.022
U 1848-1871	24	.8	-.009
D 1872-1892	21	1.7	.031
U 1893-1916	24	1.0	-.012
D 1917-1939	23	1.3	.078
U 1940-1980	28	1.3	.007

```
                        Average Annual Growth Rate
                   < -.040              .000              +.040 >
                   +------------------------------------------+
D 1762-1789     D |
U 1790-1813                                                   | U
D 1814-1847                                          D
U 1848-1871           U
D 1872-1892                                       D
U 1893-1916       U
D 1917-1939                                                   | D
U 1940-1980                           U
                   +------------------------------------------+
```

List of Innovations [Van Duijn]

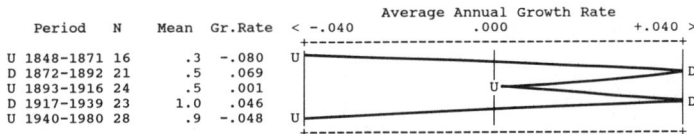

Period	N	Mean	Gr.Rate
U 1848-1871	16	.3	-.080
D 1872-1892	21	.5	.069
U 1893-1916	24	.5	.001
D 1917-1939	23	1.0	.046
U 1940-1980	28	.9	-.048

```
                        Average Annual Growth Rate
                   < -.040              .000              +.040 >
                   +------------------------------------------+
U 1848-1871     U |
D 1872-1892                                                   | D
U 1893-1916                           U
D 1917-1939                                                   | D
U 1940-1980     U |
                   +------------------------------------------+
```

List of Innovations [Clark et al]

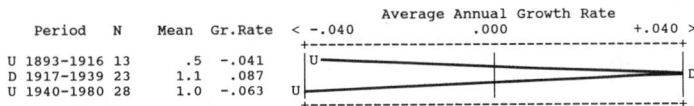

Period	N	Mean	Gr.Rate
U 1893-1916	13	.5	-.041
D 1917-1939	23	1.1	.087
U 1940-1980	28	1.0	-.063

```
                        Average Annual Growth Rate
                   < -.040              .000              +.040 >
                   +------------------------------------------+
U 1893-1916    |U
D 1917-1939                                                   | D
U 1940-1980    U|
                   +------------------------------------------+
```

List of "Product" Innovations [Kleinknecht]

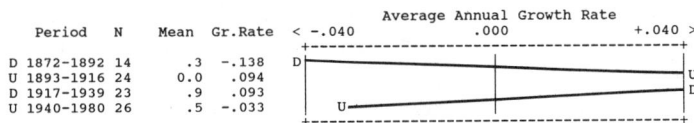

Period	N	Mean	Gr.Rate
D 1872-1892	14	.3	-.138
U 1893-1916	24	0.0	.094
D 1917-1939	23	.9	.093
U 1940-1980	26	.5	-.033

```
                        Average Annual Growth Rate
                   < -.040              .000              +.040 >
                   +------------------------------------------+
D 1872-1892     D |
U 1893-1916                                                   | U
D 1917-1939                                                   | D
U 1940-1980          U
                   +------------------------------------------+
```

List of "Improvement" Innovations [Kleinknecht]

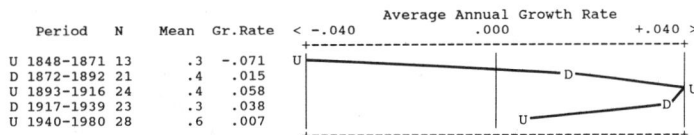

Period	N	Mean	Gr.Rate
U 1848-1871	13	.3	-.071
D 1872-1892	21	.4	.015
U 1893-1916	24	.4	.058
D 1917-1939	23	.3	.038
U 1940-1980	28	.6	.007

```
                        Average Annual Growth Rate
                   < -.040              .000              +.040 >
                   +------------------------------------------+
U 1848-1871     U |
D 1872-1892                                          D
U 1893-1916                                               | U
D 1917-1939                                            D
U 1940-1980                           U
                   +------------------------------------------+
```

See notes to Table 9.1.

Innovation and Invention

The next five series derive from lists of innovations.[17] The first four are counts of basic innovations, while the fifth is of "improvement" innovations in contrast to basic innovations.[18]

In the estimated growth rates for the innovation series, the first (Haustein and Neuwirth) matches the long wave base dating scheme phases (inversely) only after

17. Four of these I transformed into time series (one was already a time series).
18. Kleinknecht claims that only product innovations, not improvement innovations, cluster on the downswing phases.

Table 10.6. Innovation -- Changes in Mean Levels

Haustein and Neuwirth's data:				Kleinknecht's data — "product" innovations:		
Mean change U/D:[a]	.4	.9	.3	Mean change U/D:	.9	
Mean change D/U:[b]	.1	.2 -.7	0	Mean change D/U:	-.3	-.4

Van Duijn's data:			Kleinknecht's data — "improvement" innovations:		
Mean change U/D:	.2	.5	Mean change U/D:	.1	-.1
Mean change D/U:	0	-.1	Mean change D/U:	0	.3

Clark, Freeman and Soete's data:

Mean change U/D:	.6
Mean change D/U :	-.1

a. Change in mean level from upswing to downswing, calculated from table 10.5.
b. Change in mean level from downswing to upswing.

1815 (table 10.5).[19] The next two series (Van Duijn; Clark, Freeman, and Soete) consistently fit the phase periods (again inversely). The final two innovation series— Kleinknecht's lists of ''product'' (basic) and ''improvement'' (non-basic) innovations—show no long wave pattern.

As discussed in chapter 8, some confusion exists about whether the correlation hypothesized for innovation is for levels (clusters) or for growth rates.[20] Therefore, for these series I tabulated changes in mean *levels* (for each phase period) from one phase period to the next (table 10.6), in addition to analyzing the estimated growth rates.[21] For Haustein and Neuwirth's data, the levels correlate (inversely) with phases more closely than did the growth rates for the same series.[22] For Van Duijn's and Clark, Freeman, and Soete's data, the levels match the long wave phases (inversely), as had the growth rates. And Kleinknecht's data for ''product'' (but not ''improvement'') innovations also matched long wave phases more strongly in the analysis of levels than of growth rates.

To summarize, the growth rate estimates within phase periods fit the long wave pattern, inversely, in only two of the four basic innovation series. The innovation levels, however, fit the base dating inversely for the same two basic innovations

19. The last eight years of data for this series, 1968–75, are omitted as in table 10.1 (see note 1, above). A 1968–75 phase is included in the t-test results below, but including it in the 1940–80 phase would actually strengthen the significance of t slightly.

20. The innovation series are counts of discrete events, and for some hypotheses it is the rate of *occurrence* (not of growth) that differs on upswing and downswing phases.

21. The numbers shown are the changes in mean levels for each phase period (calculated directly from table 10.5).

22. The changes in mean levels indicate that while the average annual number of innovations grew over time, the annual number during *downswings* registered the biggest increases compared with the previous upswings.

Figure 10.2. Lag Structures, Four Innovation Series

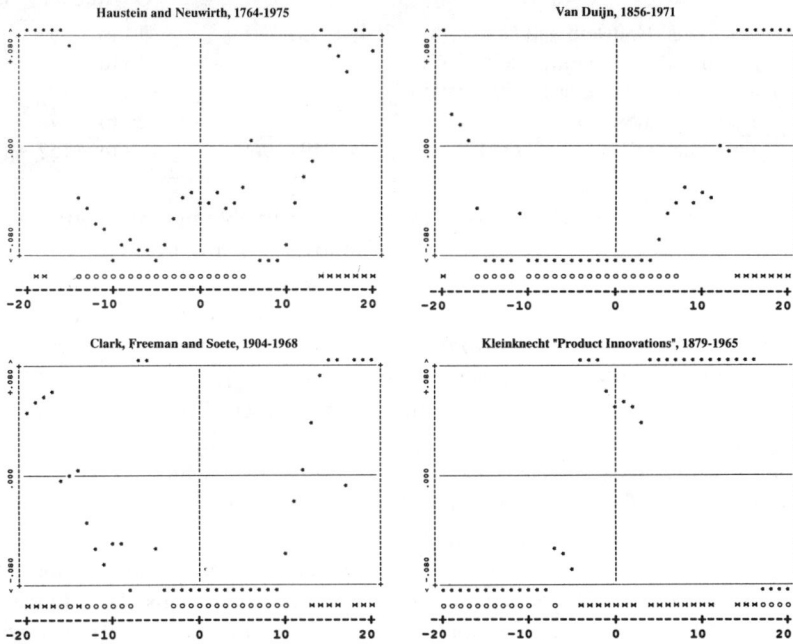

Haustein and Neuwirth, 1764-1975

Van Duijn, 1856-1971

Clark, Freeman and Soete, 1904-1968

Kleinknecht "Product Innovations", 1879-1965

series and (more weakly) for the other two basic innovation series.[23] For the "improvement" innovation series, no fit to the long wave was found. These results, although limited and tentative, are consistent with the hypothesis that basic innovations cluster on the downswing phase of the long wave.

As shown in chapter 8, to say that levels correlate with long wave phases is equivalent to saying that growth rates lead the nominal phases by about one-fourth of a cycle (ten to fifteen years). These leads should be evident in the lag structures for innovation growth rates. Since the correlation is inverse, we should look for a trough in the lag structure leading the base dating.

The lag structures for the four basic innovation series (fig. 10.2) do in fact indicate such a pattern, but with less than one-fourth of a cycle of lead. The pattern is rather weak, and the lag structures are not very robust against time shifts.[24] But the "O" regions and troughs are shifted to the left of zero for all four series (this similarity is important since the series come from four different data sources).

23. Secular growth in these two series made the correlation weaker, but the means on downswings were *higher* above the mean of the previous upswing than vice versa.

24. Part of the problem with these series may be their lack of fine structure—each year is either a zero or a very small integer according to whether any innovations on a limited list are dated in that year. It is difficult to estimate growth rates in such a series, and one must be very cautious in interpreting the results.

Series	"O" Region	Best
List of innovations [Haustein and Neuwirth] (1764–1975)	−14 to +5	−5
List of innovations [Van Duijn] (1856–1971)	−16 to +7	−4
List of innovations [Clark et al] (1904–1968)	−16 to +10	0
List of "product" innovations [Kleinknecht] (1879–1965)	−20 to −7	−19?
List of "improvement" innovations [Kleinknecht] (1859–1969)	+8 to +15?	+15?

For Haustein and Neuwirth's series, there is a discernable inverted pattern with a trough at −5 lags.[25] For Van Duijn's list of innovations, the inverted wave is the most strongly defined of all the innovation series, while the lag structure for Clark et al.'s innovation list is more jumpy. Kleinknecht's list of "product" innovations is not robust against time shifts, but from the "O" and "X" regions it appears to show a trough at about −19 lags and a peak around +14.[26]

The last innovation series, Kleinknecht's "improvement" innovations, has "X" and "O" regions interspersed, with very low robustness (fig. 10.3). But there is a discernible peak around −10 lags and a trough around +15, which is consistent with Kleinknecht's hypothesis that "improvement" innovations cluster at a point opposite on the long wave to "basic" innovations.

I grouped the four innovation series together as a class of variables[27] and tested time shifts of −5 and −10 years in the base dating scheme for this class. In the −5-year shift (table 10.7), the alternation of upswing and downswing periods matches

Figure 10.3. Lag Structure, "Improvement" Innovations

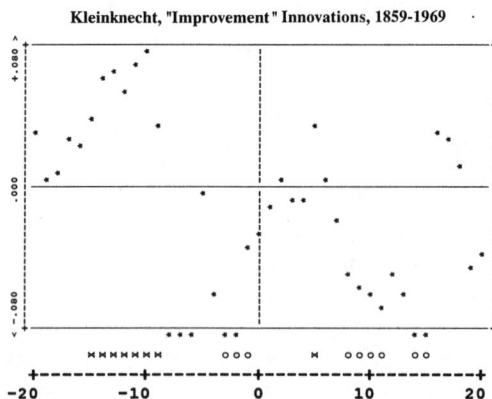

Kleinknecht, "Improvement" Innovations, 1859-1969

25. There is a (deeper) trough at +7 lags, but it is not stable with respect to minor time shifts (+6 lags gives an opposite correlation).

26. This is somewhat phase-shifted as compared with the previous three series, perhaps reflecting Kleinknecht's different criteria in distinguishing types of innovations. The long lead in this series would explain why it correlated only in terms of levels, and not at all when measured by growth rates, in the analysis above.

27. Excluding the "improvement innovations" series hypothesized to *not* correlate with the other innovations.

Table 10.7. Innovation -- Growth with Phases Shifted

List of Innovations [Haustein & Neuwirth]   Time Shift -5

Average Annual Growth Rate

Period	N	Mean	Gr.Rate	< -.040	.000	+.040 >
D 1757-1784	21	.1	-.027			
U 1785-1808	24	.1	-.031			
D 1809-1842	34	.5	-.013			
U 1843-1866	24	.9	-.015			
D 1867-1887	21	1.5	.086			
U 1888-1911	24	1.0	-.032			
D 1912-1934	23	.9	.016			
U 1935-1975	41	1.4	-.021			

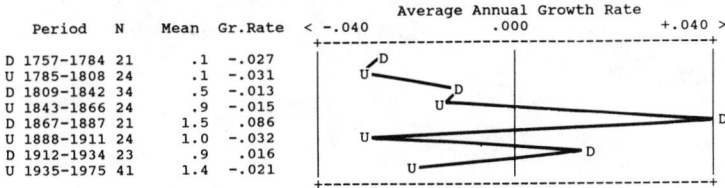

List of Innovations [Van Duijn]   Time Shift -5

Average Annual Growth Rate

Period	N	Mean	Gr.Rate	< -.040	.000	+.040 >
U 1843-1866	11	.4	-.125			
D 1867-1887	21	.3	.027			
U 1888-1911	24	.6	-.074			
D 1912-1934	23	.8	-.010			
U 1935-1975	37	1.0	-.051			

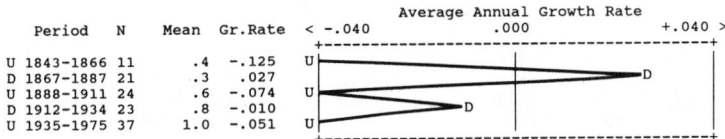

List of Innovations [Clark et al]   Time Shift -5

Average Annual Growth Rate

Period	N	Mean	Gr.Rate	< -.040	.000	+.040 >
U 1888-1911	8	.6	.133			
D 1912-1934	23	.7	.067			
U 1935-1975	34	1.2	-.056			

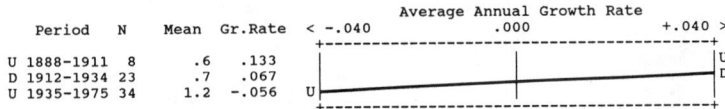

List of "Product" Innovations [Kleinknecht]   Time Shift -5

Average Annual Growth Rate

Period	N	Mean	Gr.Rate	< -.040	.000	+.040 >
D 1867-1887	9	.3	-.200			
U 1888-1911	24	.1	-.021			
D 1912-1934	23	.4	.071			
U 1935-1975	31	.8	-.067			

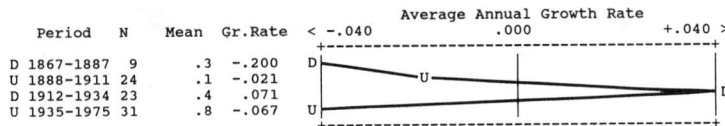

See notes to Table 9.1.

changes in the growth rates in all but two phase periods.[28] For the −10-year shift, the results were not as consistent.

In the t-tests for this class of series, with lags of 0, −5, and −10 years, the number of cases (pairs of phase periods) is only eight or nine for each test (table 10.8). In all cases the sign of t indicates an inverse correlation to the base dating but is not statistically significant. The lags of both −5 and −10 years are better than the unlagged case, and the lag of −5 years is closer to being significant than is the lag of −10 years. The lack of significance is not of great concern given the few degrees of freedom and the jumpy character of the original time series.[29] What I find more important is the consistency of results across four different data sources and the fact that the lag of −5 years gives the strongest correlation.

28. Both of them "end" phases of the series with less than ten years' data.
29. The series consisted of zeroes and small integers. I constructed three of the four series from simple lists of innovations and their dates.

Table 10.8. T-test Results for Four Innovation Series

Time Shifts of 0, -5, and -10 Years

Variable	Lag	Pairs[a]	Mean Growth Rate[b]			DF[c]	t	Probability[d]
			1st	2d	Diff.			
Innovation	0	Down/Up	.025	-.001	-.026	8	-0.64	.536 —
		Up/Down	.002	.026	.025	7	0.61	.564 —
Innovation	-5	Down/Up	.002	-.041	-.043	8	-1.31	.227 —
		Up/Down	-.024	.035	.058	6	2.23	.068 —
Innovation	-10	Down/Up	.021	-.028	-.049	7	-2.18	.066 —
		Up/Down	-.048	-.019	.030	6	0.42	.692 —

Note: Four innovation series, 1764-1975, are included.

a. Paired phases: D/U = Downswing with following upswing; U/D = upswing with following downswing.

b. 1st = average growth rate for 1st phase in pair; 2d = average growth rate for 2d phase in pair; Diff. = difference in growth rates (2d phase minus 1st). (Differences may show discrepancy due to rounding.)

c. DF = Degrees of freedom = number of phase period pairs minus 1.

d. 2-tailed probability (Either direction of correlation hypothesized).
 — indicates not statistically significant.

Overall, I find the evidence most consistent with the hypothesis that long waves in innovation are inversely correlated with prices and production and lead prices by about five years.[30] Innovations hence follow production by five to ten years, which is consistent with the hypothesis that an upturn in production tends to dampen innovation, while a downturn in production stimulates innovation. Thus I sort out the innovation hypotheses as follows:

Innovations cluster at one point on the long wave. [A]
(Kondratieff, Mensch, Freeman, Forrester, Mandel, Gordon)

Innovations do not occur in clusters. [R]
(Kuznets)

Innovations cluster late in the downswing. [A]
(Gordon, Schumpeter)

   Innovations cluster on the downswing. [A]
   (Mensch)

   Innovations are fewer late in the upswing. [A]
   (Forrester)

----

30. The inverted five-year lead in growth rates means that innovations *cluster* at the end of the nominal downswing phase.

Innovations cluster early in the upswing. [R]
(Kondratieff, Mandel, Freeman et al.)

  "Product" innovations cluster early in the upswing. [R]
  (Van Duijn)

  Innovations are fewer late in the downswing. [R]
  (Freeman et al.)

Invention

Invention is hypothesized by some researchers to correlate with the long wave, but perhaps with a different timing from innovation. One British and three U.S. annual patent series were examined (table 10.9). The results are anomalous in that *British* patents appear inversely correlated with the long wave (patents increasing more

Table 10.9: Invention -- Growth Rates by Phase

Number of British Patents

```
                                    Average Annual Growth Rate
   Period    N    Mean  Gr.Rate  < -.040            .000             +.040 >
                                 +----------------------------------------+
D 1720-1746   9     4.8   -.042  D
U 1747-1761  15     9.8    .012                           U
D 1762-1789  28    34.0    .039                                         D
U 1790-1813  24    85.1    .032                                    U
D 1814-1847  34   242.5    .054                                       D
U 1848-1871  24   480.7    .005                    U
D 1872-1892  21   831.8    .023                       D
U 1893-1916  24  1289.0    .006                   U
D 1917-1939  19  1537.3    .025                       D
                                 +----------------------------------------+
```

Number of U.S. Patents [Series 1]

```
                                    Average Annual Growth Rate
   Period    N    Mean  Gr.Rate  < -.040            .000             +.040 >
                                 +----------------------------------------+
U 1790-1813  24    84.8    .111                                          U
D 1814-1847  34   394.1    .034                              D
U 1848-1871  24  4870.6    .114                                        U
D 1872-1892  21 17446.9    .040                                  D
U 1893-1916  24 30238.3    .034                              U
D 1917-1939  23 42343.3    .005                 D
U 1940-1980  36 48372.4    .029                       U
                                 +----------------------------------------+
```

Number of U.S. Patents [Series 2]

```
                                    Average Annual Growth Rate
   Period    N    Mean  Gr.Rate  < -.040            .000             +.040 >
                                 +----------------------------------------+
D 1814-1847  11   480.5    .015                        D
U 1848-1871  24  4859.9    .114                                          U
D 1872-1892  21 17212.1    .038                                 D
U 1893-1916  24 32066.3    .031                              U
D 1917-1939  23 44865.6   -.009                 D
U 1940-1980  11 37860.6    .037                                         U
                                 +----------------------------------------+
```

U.S. Patents in Building and Railroads

```
                                    Average Annual Growth Rate
   Period    N    Mean  Gr.Rate  < -.040            .000             +.040 >
                                 +----------------------------------------+
D 1814-1847  11    16.8   -.001                      D
U 1848-1871  24   174.8    .114                                          U
D 1872-1892  21  1071.7    .071                                        D
U 1893-1916  24  2069.7    .029                            U
D 1917-1939  23  1656.3   -.024            D
U 1940-1980  11   792.3   -.013                U
                                 +----------------------------------------+
```

See notes to Table 9.1.

Figure 10.4. Lag Structures, Four Invention Series

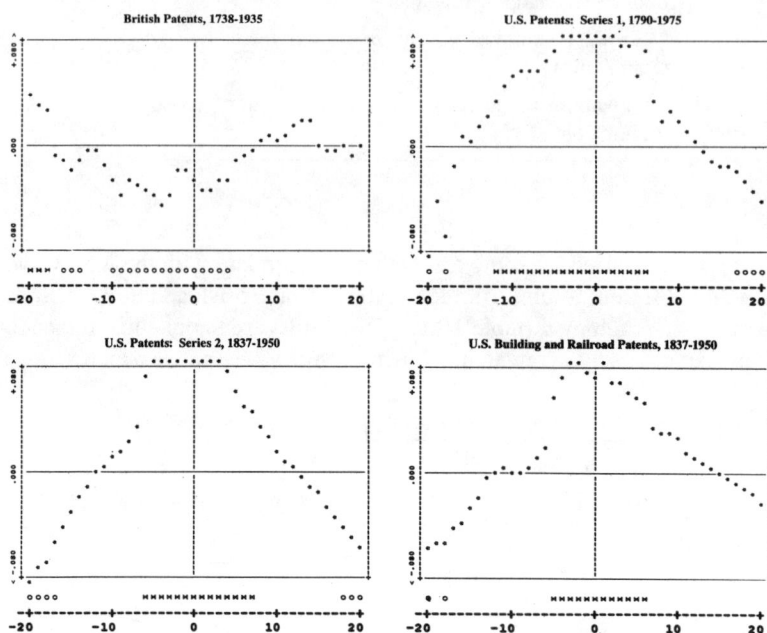

rapidly during downswings), while *U.S.* patents are directly correlated, though less consistently.[31]

The lag structures do not solve this anomaly (fig. 10.4). For the British series, there is a clear inverted pattern (of moderate robustness), with a trough around −4. But for all three U.S. patent series there is a clearer and quite robust lag structure peaking around 0 (and thus inverted as compared with British patents):

Series	"X"/"O" Region	Best
Number of British patents (1738–1935)	O −16 to +4	−4
U.S. patents in building and railroads (1837–1950)	X −5 to +6	−3
Number of U.S. patents (1790–1975)	X −12 to +6	−2
Number of U.S. patents (1837–1950)	X −6 to +7	0

The contrary behavior of British and U.S. patent series remains an anomaly; further investigation (perhaps encompassing more countries) would be useful.

I did not run any t-tests on invention as a class, since the U.S. and British results would clearly just cancel each other out and since there is no theoretical basis for postulating an inverse timing in Britain from the United States.

31. The exception to the British pattern is the first period, which, however, contains only nine years of data. The growth rates are parallel in the three U.S. series (which cover the same time frame), and all three contain a deviant period, 1893–1916, of slackened growth on an upswing.

Table 10.10. Capital Investment -- Growth Rates by Phase

U.S. Private Building Volume

```
                                        Average Annual Growth Rate
     Period    N    Mean   Gr.Rate   < -.040        .000         +.040 >
                                     +------------------------------------+
 D 1814-1847  18    213.5    .001    |                   D               |
 U 1848-1871  24    537.2    .007    |                    U-----         |
 D 1872-1892  21    897.2    .062    |                          -----    | D
 U 1893-1916  24   1428.0    .017    |                      -U---        |
 D 1917-1939  23   1072.4   -.025    |   D-----                          |
 U 1940-1980  18   1536.4    .082    |                                   | U
                                     +------------------------------------+
```

U.S. Railroad Gross Capital Investment

```
                                        Average Annual Growth Rate
     Period    N    Mean   Gr.Rate   < -.040        .000         +.040 >
                                     +------------------------------------+
 D 1872-1892  21     69.6    .029    |                              D-    |
 U 1893-1916  24     88.4    .043    |                                   | U
 D 1917-1939  23     73.9   -.031    |       D-----                      |
 U 1940-1980  11     75.7    .040    |                              -U   |
                                     +------------------------------------+
```

See notes to Table 9.1.

Capital Investment

For capital investment, only two series were available, both of them for the U.S. and neither very central (see growth rates in table 10.10). United States private building volume does not fit the phase periods well. United States gross capital investment in the railroad industry, however, correlates strongly (and directly) with the long wave (although the series spans only two long waves). The data are too limited to draw any firm conclusions, and there are not enough data for a t-test.

The two capital investment series show somewhat similar lag structures, both with three somewhat ill-defined peaks around −17, −5, and +7 lags, respectively, and dropping off to a trough somewhere beyond +20 lags. The lag structures are not very robust but suggest that capital investment may lead the base dating by perhaps ten years (hence closely following production trends).[32] Shifting the two capital investment series by −5 years (leading prices) only slightly improved the resulting growth rates over the unlagged ones.

There are not nearly enough data to draw any firm conclusions about capital investment. But to the extent that the evidence supports any position, it is the hypothesis that long waves in capital investment lag production but lead prices:

Capital investment increases early in the upswing. [A]
(Kondratieff, Mandel, Gordon, Forrester)

   Capital investment is low during the downswing. [A]
   (Van Duijn)

Capital investment increases on the downswing. [R]
(Hartman and Wheeler)

---

32. For U.S. private building volume, the "X" regions are from −20 (at least) to −14 lags, −9 to −3, and +5 to +8 lags, with the strongest peak coming in the first of these, around −18 lags. The subsequent

The analysis of capital investment on the long wave could be a fruitful area for future research.

Trade

The four trade series were an eclectic lot, consisting of: (1) the volume of Atlantic shipping at Seville in the earliest era, 1506–1650; (2) the net volume of British wheat exports, 1700–1775;[33] (3) English exports in current prices, 1700–1775;[34] and (4) Kuczynski's series for total world exports, 1850–1975. The four trade series do not correlate well with the long wave (table 10.11).[35] There are not enough data, and the four series are not comparable enough, to support a t-test for trade indicators.

The results of the lagged correlation analysis do not help much. The lag structure for Spanish trade (1506–1650) is quite nonrobust, with "X" and "O" regions interspersed. For British wheat trade (1700–1775), the lag structure is extremely time-sensitive around 0 and +14 lags.[36] For British exports (1700–1775), the lag structure is more robust and indicates a peak at around −8 lags. But since this series is in current prices, the degree of correlation is probably attributable to prices and not volume of trade. The lag structure for total world exports (1850–1975) shows a very long "X" region roughly in phase with the base dating scheme (−18 to +16, with peak around +6).[37]

To summarize, no consistent correlation is found in the trade series either for lagged or unlagged datings. I conclude that long waves cannot be identified in this group of series—either because long waves do not affect volumes of trade or because these very limited data are inadequate. Provisionally, I reject the trade hypothesis:

Long waves do not exist in trade. [A]
(Oparin, Van der Zwan, Van Ewijk)

Long waves exist in world trade. [R]
(Kondratieff, Mandel, Mauro, Kuczynski)

---

two peaks drop off toward the eventual trough at +20 lags or more. For U.S. railroad gross capital investment, the "X" regions correspond to the second and third peaks, −11 to +2 lags and +10 to +11 lags. The second peak, around −4 lags, is the strongest, while the third is much weaker, dropping off toward the trough beyond +20 lags.

33. The value is negative if imports exceed exports.

34. This is the only non-price series expressed in current rather than constant prices; hence any long waves found in this series might be just a by-product of price waves.

35. British wheat exports seem to show an inverse correlation, but the high volatility of this series makes me skeptical of any conclusion.

36. There is a possible inverse correlation, with the "O" region extending from 0 to +11 lags, and the trough around +7. This would mean that wheat exports begin declining (imports pick up) just after inflation picks up. But the results are only weakly suggestive of such a conclusion.

37. Mauro's (1964:313) datings of long waves in world trade lead the base dating scheme by only about one year.

Table 10.11. Trade -- Growth Rates by Phase

Volume of Seville-Atlantic Shipping

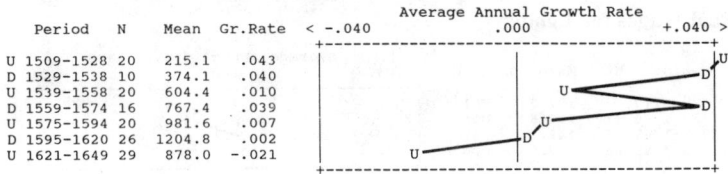

Period	N	Mean	Gr.Rate
U 1509-1528	20	215.1	.043
D 1529-1538	10	374.1	.040
U 1539-1558	20	604.4	.010
D 1559-1574	16	767.4	.039
U 1575-1594	20	981.6	.007
D 1595-1620	26	1204.8	.002
U 1621-1649	29	878.0	-.021

Average Annual Growth Rate: < -.040 … .000 … +.040 >

British Net Volume of Wheat Exports

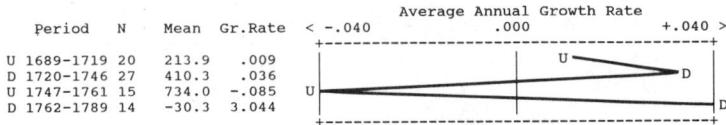

Period	N	Mean	Gr.Rate
U 1689-1719	20	213.9	.009
D 1720-1746	27	410.3	.036
U 1747-1761	15	734.0	-.085
D 1762-1789	14	-30.3	3.044

Average Annual Growth Rate: < -.040 … .000 … +.040 >

English Exports in Current Prices

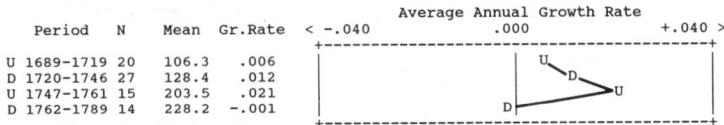

Period	N	Mean	Gr.Rate
U 1689-1719	20	106.3	.006
D 1720-1746	27	128.4	.012
U 1747-1761	15	203.5	.021
D 1762-1789	14	228.2	-.001

Average Annual Growth Rate: < -.040 … .000 … +.040 >

Total World Exports

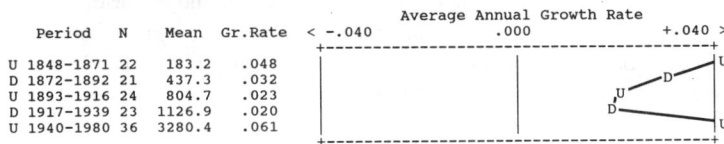

Period	N	Mean	Gr.Rate
U 1848-1871	22	183.2	.048
D 1872-1892	21	437.3	.032
U 1893-1916	24	804.7	.023
D 1917-1939	23	1126.9	.020
U 1940-1980	36	3280.4	.061

Average Annual Growth Rate: < -.040 … .000 … +.040 >

See notes to Table 9.1.

Real Wages

The final two time series measure real wages in England; the first for London alone (1700–1787), the second for South England (1736–1954). Growth rate estimates for both series, (table 10.12) match the long wave phase periods perfectly and inversely. This indicates that wages fail to keep pace with inflation during price upswing phases (hence real wages fall) but do not drop as fast as prices during downswings.[38]

The lag structures show the inverse correlation to be fairly robust, especially for the second, longer series. For the first wage index (London), the "O" region is from −6 to +15 lags, with the trough around −4 lags. For the second index (South England), the "O" region is from −15 to +8 lags, with the trough around −2.

These results suggest that wage changes may *lead* price changes by a few years.

38. This inverse relationship is consistent with Braudel's observations for preindustrial times (see chap. 3).

Table 10.12. Real Wages -- Growth Rates by Phase

Real Wages for London

```
                                      Average Annual Growth Rate
    Period     N   Mean  Gr.Rate  < -.040        .000         +.040 >
                                +---------------------------------------+
U 1689-1719 20  107.3   .001    |                   U                   |
D 1720-1746 27  119.8   .005    |                    >D                 |
U 1747-1761 15  118.1  -.007    |                  U                    |
D 1762-1789 26   97.9  -.006    |                  D                    |
                                +---------------------------------------+
```

South English Real Wage Index

```
                                      Average Annual Growth Rate
    Period     N   Mean  Gr.Rate  < -.040        .000         +.040 >
                                +---------------------------------------+
D 1720-1746 11   93.0   .001    |                    >D                 |
U 1747-1761 15   87.6  -.011    |            U<                         |
D 1762-1789 28   76.7   .003    |             <D                        |
U 1790-1813 24   66.3  -.009    |          U<                           |
D 1814-1847 34   89.2   .008    |             >D                        |
U 1848-1871 24  105.1   .003    |              U<                       |
D 1872-1892 21  143.2   .024    |                     >D                |
U 1893-1916 24  175.2  -.005    |        U<                             |
D 1917-1939 23  269.1   .038    |                      >D               |
U 1940-1980 15  256.7  -.008    |        U<                             |
                                +---------------------------------------+
```

See notes to Table 9.1.

However, the troughs are close enough to 0 lags that synchrony is equally plausible.[39] In growth estimates with the dating scheme lagged by −5 years, the alternating pattern of ups and downs is as strong as in the unlagged case.[40]

By combining the two wage series, and thanks to the length of the 1736–1954 series, there are six pairs, barely enough for a t-test (table 10.13). But in the unlagged case, t is significant at the .05 level. With the lag of −5 years, the t-test results are not quite as good.[41] Therefore I tentatively accept that real wages move synchronously (and inversely) with prices and do not lead prices.

These results corroborate long waves in real wages:

Long waves exist in wages. [A]
(Kondratieff)

Long waves do not exist in wages. [R]
(Oparin)

If a decrease in real wages sparks an increase in "class struggle" (strikes, labor insurgencies, etc.), these findings would be consistent with the hypothesis that class struggle peaks late in the upswing:[42]

39. And theoretically preferable, given the effect of prices on real wages.
40. Perfect except one truncated six-year "end" period.
41. The t-test for −5 years is significant at the .05 level for only the U/D pairs, not the D/U pairs.
42. This would be the point in the long wave when real wages were reaching their lowest point, yet production is still high and just beginning to stagnate.

Class struggle peaks during the upswing. [A]
(Kondratieff, Cronin)

Class struggle peaks late in the upswing. [A]
(Mandel, Screpanti)

Class struggle peaks during the downswing. [R]
(Imbert)

Class struggle peaks late in the downswing. [R]
(Gordon)

Summary of Economic Results

In the case of *prices,* there was a strong alternation of estimated growth rates in successive phase periods, unlagged from the base dating scheme. This was strongest in England and in recent centuries (but perhaps just because of better data quality) and weakest in the individual commodity prices in non-core countries. For *production,* long waves were found to lead prices by ten to fifteen years but were weaker than in prices. For *innovation,* long waves were inversely correlated and seemed to lead prices by about five years (lagging production by five to ten years). For *invention,* the results were anomalous—Britain and the United States both seemed to follow the long wave but were out of phase with each other. For *capital investment,* data were inadequate but weakly followed long waves, lagging slightly behind production. For *trade,* no long waves were found. Finally, *real wages* correlated strongly and inversely with the long wave.

The analysis in chapters 9 and 10 has helped sort out the hypotheses concerning

Table 10.13. T-test Results for Two Real Wage Series

Variable	Lag	Pairs[a]	Mean Growth Rate[b] 1st	2d	Diff.	DF[c]	t	Probability[d]
Real Wages	0	Down/Up	.013	-.006	-.019	5	-3.09	.027 *
		Up/Down	-.005	.012	.017	5	2.72	.042 *
Real Wages	-5	Down/Up	.006	-.007	-.013	5	-0.96	.379 —
		Up/Down	-.005	.012	.018	5	3.01	.030 *

Note: Real wage series from 1700 to 1954.

a. Paired phases: D/U = Downswing with following upswing; U/D = upswing with following downswing.

b. 1st = average growth rate for 1st phase in pair; 2d = average growth rate for 2d phase in pair; Diff. = difference in growth rates (2d phase minus 1st). (Differences may show discrepancy due to rounding.)

c. DF = Degrees of freedom = number of phase period pairs minus 1.

d. 2-tailed probability (Either direction of correlation hypothesized).

* indicates statistical significance level below .05.

Table 10.14. Provisionally Accepted Economic Hypotheses

Existence of long waves:
 Long waves exist. [A]
 (Most long wave researchers)

Scope — variables:
 Long waves exist in prices, production and investment. [A]
 (Kondratieff, Mandel, Kuczynski, Gordon, Kleinknecht,
  Delbeke, Van Duijn, Forrester)

 Innovations cluster at one point on the long wave. [A]
 (Kondratieff, Mensch, Freeman, Forrester, Mandel, Gordon)

 Long waves do not exist in trade. [A]
 (Oparin, Van der Zwan, Van Ewijk)

 Long waves exist in wages. [A]
 (Kondratieff)

Scope — temporal:
 Long waves at least in prices exist before 1790. [A]
 (Imbert, Braudel, Wallerstein)

Historical dating of phases:
 The dating of phases is captured in base dating scheme. [A]
 Base dating is for prices and 1980 is most recent peak.
 (Goldstein, modified)

  1940-1980 was a price upswing; 1980- a downswing.
  1933-1968 was a production upswing; 1968- a downswing.
  (Modified hypotheses resulting from analysis) [A]

Correlations — production:
 Production increases precede price increases. [A]
 (Imbert)

Correlations — capital investment:
 Capital investment increases early in the upswing. [A]
 (Kondratieff, Mandel, Gordon, Forrester)

  Capital investment is low during the downswing. [A]
  (Van Duijn)

Correlations — innovation:
 Innovations cluster late in the downswing. [A]
 (Gordon, Schumpeter)

  Innovations are fewer late in the upswing. [A]
  (Forrester)

Correlations — class struggle:
 Class struggle peaks late in the upswing. [A]
 (Mandel, Screpanti)

232

economic variables in the long wave. Which hypotheses have been provisionally accepted, and which provisionally rejected, as a result of the economic analysis?

The surviving, provisionally accepted hypotheses concerning the scope and timing of the long wave are listed in table 10.14. The empirical analysis was not able to address the hypotheses concerning "other economic variables" (such as employment, mergers, and currency). But regarding the existence and timing of long waves in the main economic variables, the analysis succeeded in sorting out the contradictory hypotheses into a single consistent scheme. Long waves are tentatively corroborated in prices, production, investment, innovation, and wages (the last two are inversely correlated) but not in trade. They extend from 1495 (at least for prices) through the present. The variables are lagged within cycle time in the following sequence: production, investment, innovation, prices, and wages.

These results corroborate the central hypotheses of each theoretical school. The results support Kondratieff and Forrester on capital investment, Schumpeter on innovation, and Mandel on class struggle and production.

To a large extent the directions of the research presented here have been driven by data. Where few data were available, I pursued what was available. Where only one school of the debate cared to collect data for a certain variable, that school's data were used. As a final comment on the economic time series, I note the relationship between data sources and the results emerging from those data.

The strongest results are found in the class of variables with the highest quality data—prices—and the results become progressively weaker as the data do, moving through production, innovation, and investment. Data sets developed by researchers in one theoretical school tend to support the theory of that school, even though I apply my own methods to the analysis of the data. Kondratieff's price series corroborated his long wave datings. Kuczynski's world production data corroborate his theory of long waves in production. Kleinknecht's innovation data corroborate his distinction between "product" and "improvement" innovations. Thus each school's data tend to support its own theory. While I have sorted out many conflicting hypotheses, the central hypotheses of all three long wave schools remain and are potentially compatible within a single framework. Before that framework can be built, however, the last major long wave variable—war—must be analyzed.

CHAPTER ELEVEN

Data Analysis 3: War

Measuring War

As I mentioned in chapter 8, high quality data on war covering the past five centuries have been lacking until a few years ago, when Levy (1983a) extended the approach of the Correlates of War project from 1815–1975 to cover the period 1495–1975.[1] With one minor exception,[2] this chapter relies entirely on Levy's data.[3] Levy's list of great powers is shown in table 11.1. Membership in the great power system changes over time, with old powers like Spain and Turkey dropping out and new ones like the United States and Japan joining. Table 11.2 lists the wars in Levy's data set.

While there is only one data set, there are several ways to cut into the data. I looked at the war data from a variety of angles generated by the combination of three dimensions: (1) different classes of wars, (2) different indicators of war, and (3) different methods for analyzing those indicators and correlating them with phase periods. While the same methodological tools are used as in the past two chapters, they are supplemented by other methods oriented to the distinct qualities of war and of the war data, which are not shared by the economic time series.

Classes of Wars

What is a war, and what wars are of interest? Many arguments have taken place concerning the proper definition and measurement of war. As a practical matter I have accepted Levy's definitions deriving from the cow approach (see chapter 6). Levy's data include only wars involving the "great powers," so I am limited to investigating these wars at the core of the world system. But from the list of such wars, six overlapping classes of wars may be distinguished:

1. All wars on Levy's list: 119 wars in which "great powers" fought, either against each other or against less powerful, more peripheral countries.
2. Great power wars:[4] 64 wars *between* great powers—that is, with one or more

---

1. The cow data are a standard data set on war. For the period since 1815, Levy's data set is essentially the same as the cow data.

2. A tangential investigation into Sorokin's data for the pre-1495 period.

3. Levy's work is reviewed in chap. 6. His data are shaped by his realist approach to international relations (see Levy 1985a), emphasizing "Great Power" politics.

4. The categorization of wars as great power wars is Levy's, not my own.

Table 11.1. Membership in Levy's "Great Power System"

Country	Years
France	1495-1975
England/Great Britain	1495-1975
Austrian Hapsburgs/Austria/ Austria-Hungary	1495-1519; 1556-1918
Spain	1495-1519; 1556-1808
Ottoman Empire	1495-1699
United Hapsburgs	1519-1556
The Netherlands	1609-1713
Sweden	1617-1721
Russia/Soviet Union	1721-1975
Prussia/Germany/West Germany	1740-1975
Italy	1861-1943
United States	1898-1975
Japan	1905-1945
China	1949-1975

Source: Levy (1983a).

great powers participating on each side. This class is, along with the first, the most relevant to the *core* of the world system.

3. Core-periphery wars: the 55 wars not in class 2—that is, those with a great power on one side only, fighting against a non-great-power country.
4. Great power wars *except* wars of European powers against Turkey. This class is largely similar to class 2 but in the earliest centuries conceives of Turkey as external to the European system. This class thus includes only wars within the emergent *European* core.
5. All wars involving Britain. This represents the total war effort of Britain whether directed against other great powers or less powerful countries.
6. All wars involving France. France and Britain were examined because they were the longest-standing central actors in the great power system.

War Indicators

A variety of indicators of war may be used to examine each class of war. My primary measure is battle fatalities, which Levy (after Singer and Co.) refers to as the *severity* of war. It is an indicator of the scale of violence, getting at the dimension of "how big" a war is. Several secondary indicators are also used. One of these is what the cow project, and Levy, call *intensity*—the ratio of battle fatalities to the European population. This might be more appropriate than total fatalities in measuring war's impact on society or on society's ability to make war. In practice, the results turned out largely similar to severity and I have reported the severity results since it is a simpler and more straightforward indicator. Another indicator is the *incidence* of war—the presence or absence of wars of a certain type in the system in a given year. I

Table 11.2. Levy's List of Wars

#	GP?	Name	Years	#GPs	Sev.	Country	Int.
1	*	War of the League of Venice	1495-1497	3	8	F SA	119
2		Polish-Turkish War	1497-1498	1	3	T	45
3		Venetian-Turkish War	1499-1503	1	4	T	60
4		First Milanese War	1499-1500	1	2	F	29
5	*	Neapolitan War	1501-1504	2	18	F S	269
6		War of the Cambrian League	1508-1509	3	10	F SA	145
7	*	War of the Holy League	1511-1514	4	18	FESA	261
8	*	Austro-Turkish War	1512-1519	2	24	AT	343
9		Scottish War	1513-1515	1	4	E	57
10	*	Second Milanese War	1515-1515	3	3	F SA	43
11	*	First War of Charles V	1521-1526	3	30	FE H	420
12	*	Ottoman War	1521-1531	2	68	TH	958
13		Scottish War	1522-1523	1	3	E	41
14	*	Second War of Charles V	1526-1529	3	18	FE H	249
15	*	Ottoman War	1532-1535	2	28	TH	384
16		Scottish War	1532-1534	1	4	E	55
17	*	Third War of Charles V	1536-1538	2	32	F H	438
18	*	Ottoman War	1537-1547	2	97	TH	1329
19		Scottish War	1542-1550	1	13	E	176
20	*	Fourth War of Charles V	1542-1544	2	47	F H	629
21	*	Siege of Boulogne	1544-1546	2	8	FE	107
22	*	Arundel's Rebellion	1549-1550	2	6	FE	79
23	*	Ottoman War	1551-1556	2	44	TH	578
24	*	Fifth War of Charles V	1552-1556	2	51	F H	668
25	*	Austro-Turkish War	1556-1562	2	52	AT	676
26	*	Franco-Spanish War	1556-1559	3	24	FES	316
27	*	Scottish War	1559-1560	2	6	FE	78
28	*	Spanish-Turkish War	1559-1564	2	24	S T	310
29	*	First Huguenot War	1562-1564	2	6	FE	77
30	*	Austro-Turkish War	1565-1568	2	24	AT	306
31	*	Spanish-Turkish War	1569-1580	2	48	S T	608
32	*	Austro-Turkish War	1576-1583	2	48	AT	600
33		Spanish-Portuguese War	1579-1581	1	4	S	50
34		Polish-Turkish War	1583-1590	1	17	T	210
35	*	War of the Armada	1585-1604	2	48	ES	588
36		Austro-Polish War	1587-1588	1	4	A	49
37	*	War of the Three Henries	1589-1598	2	16	F S	195
38	*	Austro-Turkish War	1593-1606	2	90	AT	1086
39		Franco-Savoian War	1600-1601	1	2	F	24
40	*	Spanish-Turkish War	1610-1614	2	15	S T	175
41		Austro-Venitian War	1615-1618	1	6	A	70
42		Spanish-Savoian War	1615-1617	1	2	S	23
43		Spanish-Venetian War	1617-1621	1	5	S	58
44	*	Spanish-Turkish War	1618-1619	2	6	S T	69
45		Polish-Turkish War	1618-1621	1	15	T	173
46	*	Thirty Years' War-Bohemian	1618-1625	4	304	ESA N	3535
47	*	Thirty Years' War-Danish	1625-1630	6	302	FESA NW	3432
48	*	Thirty Years' War-Swedish	1630-1635	4	314	SA NW	3568
49	*	Thirty Years' War-Swedish/French	1635-1648	5	1151	F SA NW	12933
50		Spanish-Portuguese War	1642-1668	1	80	S	882
51		Turkish-Venetian War	1645-1664	1	72	T	791
52	*	Franco-Spanish War	1648-1659	2	108	F S	1187
53		Scottish War	1650-1651	1	2	E	22
54	*	Anglo-Dutch Naval War	1652-1655	2	26	E N	282
55	*	Great Northern War	1654-1660	3	22	A NW	238
56	*	English-Spanish War	1656-1659	2	15	ES	161
57		Dutch-Portuguese War	1657-1661	1	4	N	43
58	*	Ottoman War	1657-1664	3	109	F AT	1170
59		Sweden-Bremen War	1665-1666	1	2	W	11
60	*	Anglo-Dutch Naval War	1665-1667	3	37	FE N	392
61	*	Devolutionary War	1667-1668	2	4	F S	42
62	*	Dutch War of Louis XIV	1672-1678	6	342	FESA NW	3580
63		Turkish-Polish War	1672-1676	1	5	T	52
64		Russo-Turkish War	1677-1681	1	12	T	125
65	*	Ottoman War	1682-1699	2	384	AT	3954
66	*	Franco-Spanish War	1683-1684	2	5	F S	51
67	*	War of the League of Augsburg	1688-1697	5	680	FESA N	6939

#	GP?	Name	Years	#GPs	Sev.	Country	Int.
68	*	Second Northern War	1700-1721	2	64	E W	640
69	*	War of the Spanish Succession	1701-1713	5	1251	FESA N	12490
70		Ottoman War	1716-1718	1	10	A	98
71	*	War of the Quadruple Alliance	1718-1720	4	25	FESA	245
72	*	British-Spanish War	1726-1729	2	15	ES	144
73	*	War of the Polish Succession	1733-1738	4	88	F SA R	836
74		Ottoman War	1736-1739	2	38	A R	359
75	*	War of the Austrian Succession	1739-1748	6	359	FESA RG	3379
76		Russo-Swedish War	1741-1743	1	10	R	94
77	*	Seven Years' War	1755-1763	6	992	FESA RG	9118
78		Russo-Turkish War	1768-1774	1	14	R	127
79		Confederation of Bar	1768-1772	1	14	R	149
80	*	War of the Bavarian Succession	1778-1779	2	0.3	A G	3
81	*	War of the American Revolution	1778-1784	3	34	FES	304
82		Ottoman War	1787-1792	2	192	A R	1685
83		Russo-Swedish War	1788-1790	1	3	R	26
84	*	French Revolutionary Wars	1792-1802	6	663	FESA RG	5816
85	*	Napoleonic Wars	1803-1815	6	1869	FESA RG	16112
86		Russo-Turkish War	1806-1812	2	45	E R	388
87		Russo-Swedish War	1808-1809	1	6	R	51
88		War of 1812	1812-1814	1	4	E	34
89		Neapolitan War	1815-1815	1	2	A	17
90		Franco-Spanish War	1823-1823	1	.4	F	3
91		Navarino Bay	1827-1827	3	.2	FE R	2
92		Russo-Turkish War	1828-1829	1	50	R	415
93		Austro-Sardinian War	1848-1849	1	5.6	A	45
94		First Schleswig-Holstein War	1849-1849	1	2.5	G	20
95		Roman Republic War	1849-1849	2	.6	F A	4
96	*	Crimean War	1853-1856	3	217	FE R	1743
97		Anglo-Persian War	1856-1857	1	.5	E	4
98	*	War of Italian Unification	1859-1859	2	20	F A	159
99		Franco-Mexican War	1862-1867	1	8	F	64
100		Second Schleswig-Holstein War	1864-1864	2	1.5	A G	12
101	*	Austro-Prussian War	1866-1866	3	34	A GI	270
102	*	Franco-Prussian War	1870-1871	2	180	F G	1415
103		Russo-Turkish War	1877-1878	1	120	R	935
104		Sino-French War	1884-1885	1	2.1	F	16
105		Russo-Japanese War	1904-1905	1	45	R	339
106		Italo-Turkish War	1911-1912	1	6	I	45
107	*	World War I	1914-1918	8	7734	FE A RGIUJ	57616
108	*	Russian Civil War	1918-1921	5	5	FE R UJ	37
109		Manchurian War	1931-1933	1	10	J	73
110		Italo-Ethiopian War	1935-1936	1	4	I	29
111		Sino-Japanese War	1937-1941	1	250	J	1813
112	*	Russo-Japanese War	1939-1939	2	16	R J	116
113	*	World War II	1939-1945	7	12948	FE RGIUJ	93665
114		Russo-Finnish War	1939-1940	1	50	R	362
115	*	Korean War	1950-1953	4	955	FE U C	6821
116		Russo-Hungarian War	1956-1956	1	7	R	50
117		Sinai War	1956-1956	2	0	FE	0
118		Sino-Indian War	1962-1962	1	.5	C	1
119		Vietnam War	1965-1973	1	56	U	90

Legend:

GP?   * indicates a "great power war" (between greatpowers).
#GPs Number of great powers participating in war.
Sev   Severity of war -- total battle fatalities sufferedby great powers, in thousands.
Int   Intensity of war -- Battle fatalities suffered by great powers, per million European population.

Countries (letter indicates participation in war):

F = France	W = Sweden	
E = England	R = Russia	Source: Levy (1983a)
S = Spain	G = Germany	
A = Austria-Hungary	I = Italy	Copyright University Press of Kentucky.
T = Turkey	U = United States	
H = United Hapsburgs	J = Japan	Reprinted by permission.
N = Netherlands	C = China	

measure war incidence at three levels by determining whether average annual battle
fatalities per million European population (intensity) from great power wars exceed
zero, one hundred, or five hundred in a given year.[5] The final indicator is the number
of wars occurring in a given period—that is, the *frequency* of wars in a given class.
Each of these war indicators provides different information about the pattern of war
at the core of the world system—how often wars occur, how big they are (absolutely
and relative to population), and how long they last.

Methods

Several methods are used to analyze these indicators of war. Some use *time series* of
annual battle fatalities (severity), which I calculate from Levy's data. Since the
fatality data are given only by war, not by year within a war, I distribute each war's
fatalities among the years spanned by the war—giving the first and last years half the
fatalities of the intermediate years since on average wars begin and end in the middle
of a year.[6]

This severity time series has extreme variation and nonstationarity in later centuries with the abrupt high-fatality wars between great powers. To control the
nonstationarity somewhat (and thus avoid having the twentieth century overwhelm
the earlier centuries), I generally use the *logged* time series. The logged series used
the following scale:[7]

Annual fatalities:	0	1,000	10,000	100,000	1,000,000	10,000,000
Logged scale:	0.0	0.5	1.5	2.5	3.5	4.5

The main war time series are listed in Appendix B.

To get at the correlation of war with long wave phase periods, two methods of
counting or averaging wars by phase period are used. The first is to treat the war time
series like the economic time series, segmenting the series at each turning point and
calculating averages within phases.[8] I refer to this as fatalities "strictly" within a
phase period.[9] The second method is to place each war in the phase period that it

5. The first level, 0, indicates whether any war involving a great power is in progress, 100 excludes the
very minor wars, and 500 includes only the most major wars.
6. If the beginning and ending years were allocated a full year's share of the fatalities, then the time
series would seem to jump to twice the fatality rate whenever one war gave way to another in the same
year, even though they never actually overlapped (this happens, e.g., when Levy distinguishes phases of a
conflict as separate wars).
7. Since the years with no fatalities cannot be logged (the log of 0 is negative infinity), such years were
set to an arbitrary low number: -0.5 on the log scale in which 0 equals 1,000 annual fatalities, 1 equals
10,000, and so on. The -0.5 value translates to 316 fatalities a year, which is close enough to 0 to
represent a "peace" year adequately. However, having negative numbers in the series is problematical in
certain applications, so 0.5 was added to the above series, creating a new series defined as shown: original
series in 1,000s, logged, $+0.5$, and 0 in original set to 0.
8. Averages rather than growth rates are taken as the most appropriate measure to test hypotheses of
higher *levels* of war on upswing phases.
9. Of course, without data on the annual distribution of fatalities within a war, I cannot actually say
how many fatalities really occurred in one phase period or the other when a war overlaps a turning point.

"mainly" fell into.[10] A few wars that fall on the turning points do not qualify for inclusion in either period. By including wars in the period they mainly fall in, this method is less sensitive to the particular dating of turning points than the first method (counting overlapping war years in the phase they overlap into). The comparison of both methods is useful in finding out how sensitive the war results are to the particular turning points used.[11]

Finally, I examine time series graphs showing the continuous behavior of war and economic variables over the entire five centuries, which help to identify both dynamic patterns in the data and relationships between different variables. Log scales are used to bring out the ups and downs of the series in spite of long-term upward secular trends.

War Cycles

The great power war[12] severity times series (fig. 11.1) strongly suggests fifty-year cycles.[13] In the middle years of the graph, around 1600–1800, are four regularly recurring war peaks (marked "WP"). Each is a sustained, high-fatality war that ends a series of wars of escalating severity. These peaks are spaced about fifty years apart and are followed by two more peaks (around 1870 and around 1915), also spaced about fifty years apart, though of shorter duration and not preceded by a series of escalating wars. Only the final peak, World War II, does not fit the pattern, following too closely after the World War I peak. Going back to the years before 1600, three more peaks are visible, although much more weakly in the first two cases, which have similar though slightly shorter spacing.

Furthermore, there is a dramatic one-to-one correspondence between the recurring war peaks shown on the graph and the long wave peaks (from the base dating scheme), which are indicated on the figure by small arrows at the top. For nine successive long waves, until 1918, each war peak occurs near the end of an upswing phase period.[14] From this, I date ten war cycles since 1495 (table 11.3).

10. This is defined as at least 60% of the war years falling within the period and no more than three war years falling in a different period.

11. In both cases, results are expressed in terms of average annual levels within a phase period to equalize for the varying lengths of historical phases.

12. Great power wars, excluding wars against Turkey. A log scale is used to condense the upward trend in fatalities.

13. Again, this is only an average annual rate within each war, not a truly annual series. In reading this and later graphs of war data, remember that the first and last years of a war have half the annual fatalities as the middle years, creating a pattern in the graph like this (see, e.g., pattern at World Wars I and II in the figure):

.   .

The lower points for the first and last years should not be mistaken for separate wars.

14. Note that the economic peak in 1720 (from Frank's dating for England) could be moved to about 1713—the end of the war peak—and would then fit international prices as well as war better. Prices appear to fall in 1713–20. This might resolve the problem with prices in the downswing of 1720–46, noted earlier for several series (chap. 9).

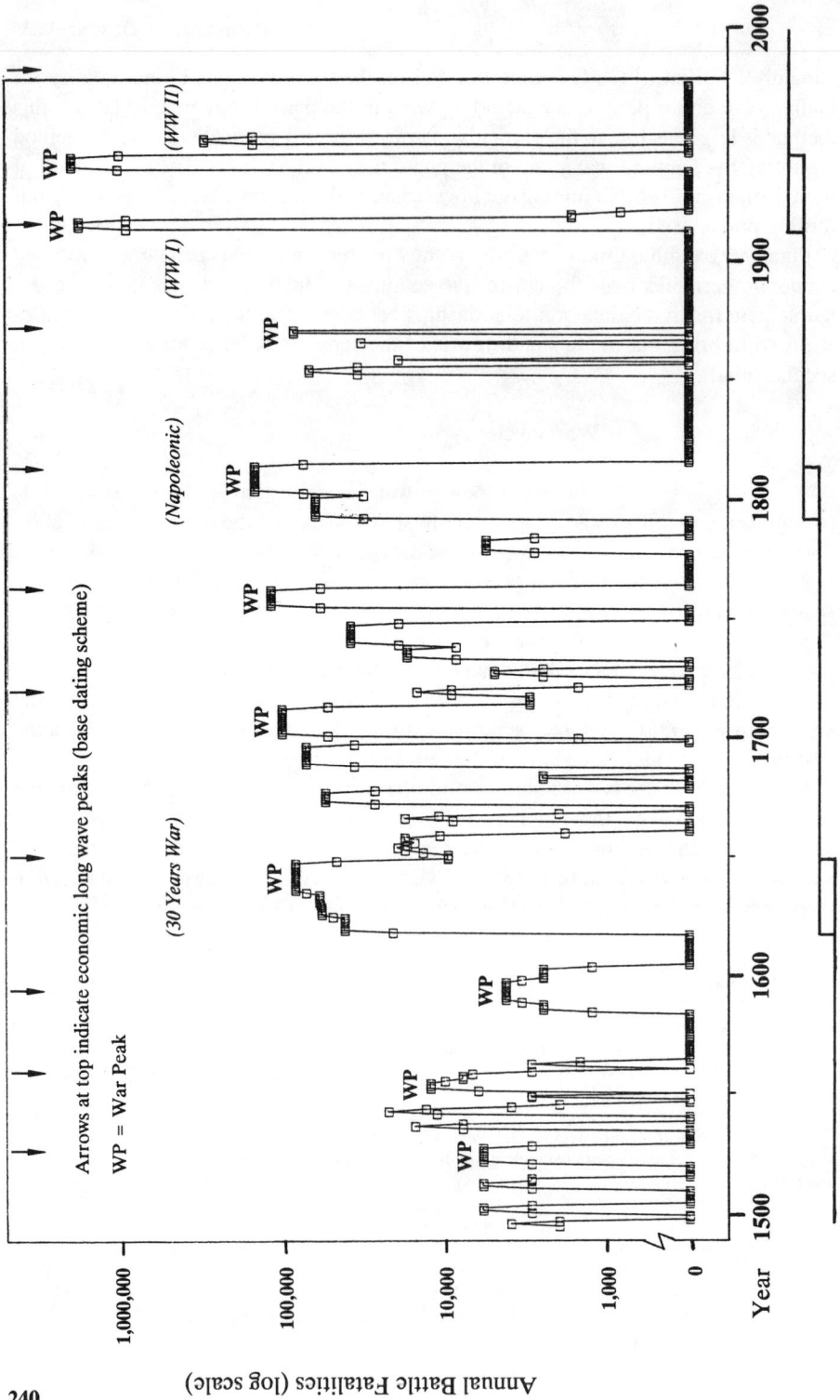

Figure 11.1. Great Power War Severity, 1495-1975

Arrows at top indicate economic long wave peaks (base dating scheme)

WP = War Peak

(WW II)

WP

WP

(WW I)

WP

(Napoleonic)

WP

WP

WP

(30 Years War)

WP

WP

WP

WP

Year

1,000,000

100,000

10,000

1,000

0

Annual Battle Fatalities (log scale)

1500   1600   1700   1800   1900   2000

Wallerstein's 3 "world war" periods (see text)

Table 11.3. Dating of Long War Cycles, 1495-1975

Cycle	Starting date of war cycle	Peak war years	Length (years)	Ending date of corresponding long wave phase period
1	(1495)	1521-1529	(35)	1528
2	1530	1552-1556	28	1558
3	1558	1593-1604	47	1594
4	1605	1635-1648	44	1649
5	1649	1701-1713	65	1719
6	1714	1755-1763	50	1761
7	1764	1803-1815	52	1813
8	1816	1870-1871	56	1871
9	1872	1914-1918	47	1917
10	1919	1939-1945?	(27)	(1968/80?)

Cycle	Peak wars	Annual fatality rate at peak (thousands)
1	First and Second Wars of Charles V; (Ottoman War v. Hapsburgs) [a]	13
2	Fifth War of Charles V; (Ottoman War v. Hapsburgs) [a]	22
3	War of the Armada; (Austro-Turkish War) [a]	11
4	Thirty Years' War: Swedish/French Phase	88
5	War of the Spanish Succession	107
6	Seven Years' War	124
7	Napoleonic Wars	156
8	Franco-Prussian War	90
9	World War I	1,934
10	World War II	2,158

[a] Dating of war peaks in cycles 1-3 based primarily on intra-European wars rather than those against Turkey. Wars against Turkey are included in the statistics, however, and are shown above in parentheses.

Three Eras

In describing the war cycles in fig. 11.1, I find it helpful to look at the war pattern as evolving and passing through successive stages of development, which I call "eras." In each successive era, the recurring pattern of war severity resembles the previous era in some ways but differs in others:

1. From 1495 until about 1618/1648, great power wars fluctuate up and down around a level of about ten thousand fatalities per year (from 1511 to 1606 there are only three "peace" years out of ninety-four). Three war peaks, albeit weak ones, can be picked out on the basis of sustained, high-fatality wars: 1521–29, 1552–56, and 1593–1604.[15]

2. From about 1618/1648 to 1793/1815, there is a repeating pattern, or "signature," of great power war, in which a series of wars of escalating severity culminates in a high-fatality war and a relatively peaceful period follows. This pattern repeats four times, the war peaks ending respectively in 1648, 1713, 1763, and 1815. The fatality levels of these war peaks are an order of magnitude higher than in the previous era—about one hundred thousand annually—and rise steadily during the two centuries. In these centuries a trend toward more peace years breaking up the years of great power war is observable.

3. From about 1793/1815 to 1914/1945, the peace years become predominant and the pattern of escalating wars within a long wave is replaced by one or more peaks of short duration. In this era the wars are shorter and, in the case of World Wars I and II, more severe by an order of magnitude (about two million battle fatalities per year).

I hypothesize that a fourth era may have begun around 1945 in which even fewer great power wars will occur, but any that do will be of even greater severity and shorter duration.

Note that Wallerstein's (1983) three "world war" periods (fig. 11.1, bottom), each followed by the start of a new hegemony (see chapter 6), seem to correlate with the eras just described. These issues will be taken up further in the discussion of hegemony cycles in chapter 13.

World War II: An Anomaly

World War II is anomalous, coming at the beginning rather than the end of a long wave upswing.[16] World War I marks the end of one upswing, and World War II the beginning of the next, with a downswing of economic stagnation and reduced war in between. The timing of World War II at the start of an upswing might be explained in

15. The peak at 1552–56 is higher but shorter than 1521–29, while 1593–1604 is again lower but longer; 1576–80 (not considered a peak) is both lower and shorter than the neighboring peaks. George Modelski has suggested to me that the Dutch-Spanish war of around 1585–1609 be added to Levy's data set (Levy did not consider it a great power war). Doing so does not change the war curve in fig. 11.1 in any important way, although it does change the first "peace" years in that period to 1615–17 rather than 1607–9, and it increases fatalities on the downswing of 1595–1620 (fig. 11.3).

16. It is not bad to have one anomalous case out of ten; but when it is the most recent case there is no way to know whether it is a single deviant case or the start of a new pattern. These issues are taken up in chap. 15.

part by the unusual irresolution that resulted from World War I. The costs of that war were far above any previous experience, constituting a severe shock to the world economic and political system.[17] World War I ended in mutual exhaustion without resolving the issue of hegemony (particularly since the rising powers, Russia and America, withdrew into revolution and isolationism after that war). Only at the outset of the next long wave upswing (production having turned upward sometime around 1933), could hegemonic war resume. The upswing thus began at a high level of war severity instead of war building up to a peak late in the upswing as in previous long waves.

But once World War II occurred, how could the world economy sustain a continued upswing phase instead of being driven into a long downswing as in previous war peaks? Here the answer may be the expansion of the core of the world economy. By the time of World War II, the United States had become the world's largest industrial power, Soviet industrialization had proceeded at a rapid pace, and Japan had also industrialized rapidly and benefited from sitting out World War I. This expanded core could support another hegemonic war before Europe alone could have. The increased severity of World War I, coupled with the extension of the European system to a global one (Barraclough 1964:268), thus created the conditions for World War II to occur early rather than late in the upswing phase.[18]

The rest of the 1940–80 upswing phase saw continuing war, but not directly between great powers. Three "Pacific" wars—World War II, Korea, and Vietnam—go together on this upswing (see chapter 14). The upswing ended with an unusually small war, Vietnam (although it did take its toll on the world economy), as it had begun with an unusually large one.

Singer, Levy, and War Cycles

Given the evidence of cycles in Levy's war data, I became curious why Levy, who was aware of the debate on fifty-year cycles in war, had concluded that no cycles could be found in his data.[19] The answer seems to be a combination of two factors. First, Levy used visual inspection to look for cycles in the data and did not find them evident. Second, Levy (1983a:137) did not search for cycles statistically, since he did not spot them in visual inspection of his own data and since past research had not shown evidence of cycles. On the latter point he specifically cites (in addition to Sorokin) Singer and Small's (1972:206) negative findings using spectral analysis. Levy concludes that "it is very unlikely that sophisticated statistical techniques could uncover any patterns that are sufficiently strong to have any substantive significance. For this reason these tests are not applied here."[20]

17. See Carnegie 1940; Kindleberger 1973; Bogart 1920, 1921; Dickinson 1934, 1940; Jeze 1926; Kohn and Meyendorff 1932; Seligman 1919; and Berger 1928.
18. While this "explains" the anomaly, I recognize it is an ad hoc explanation.
19. Levy (1983a:137) writes that "there are no hints of any cyclical pattern in either the occurrence of war or in any of its other dimensions." Periods of war and peace "appear to be scattered at random."
20. This is a good illustration of the power of a research paradigm to shape what one looks for—and hence what one finds or does not find.

Ironically, Levy's data *would* have allowed even the methodology of Singer and company to identify long waves in great power war. To illustrate this, I use the type of methodology applied by the Correlates of War—a methodology based on fixed periodicities—even though I think it is inappropriate for social cycles. The Auto-Correlation Function (ACF) is a function expressed in terms of lags in a time series. For a given lag n, the value of the ACF is the correlation of all the data points in the series with the corresponding set of data points n years earlier.[21] The set of such correlations for sequential lags makes up the ACF.[22] In an autoregressive time series,[23] the ACF starts out high but generally falls rapidly in the first few lags to a statistically insignificant level. If there are cycles in the data (periodic in calendar time), the ACF will then rise again in a bump centered somewhere around the cycle length.

The top part of figure 11.2 shows something like what David Singer and the COW project must have looked at—the ACF for war severity for the period after *1815* (the data available to the COW project before Levy extended them). In this ACF no fifty-year cycle is visible. A weak twenty-six year cycle is visible, but this derives entirely from the single case of World War I followed by World War II. And indeed these are exactly the conclusions that Singer and Cusack (1981:413) reported, which in turn discouraged Levy from searching statistically for cycles in his data.

But the bottom part of the figure—the ACF for great power war severity from *1495* on—reveals a different pattern. There is a clear bulge in the ACF peaking around fifty to sixty years. Depending on the exact formulation,[24] the peak is either just barely, or not quite, significant at the .05 level. Thus even methods based on fixed periodicity are able to pick up the long wave in Levy's five centuries of war data.

For no economic variable—even the best price series—can I find a peak at around fifty years on its ACF.[25] The peak in the ACF for war severity thus indicates that the war cycle is more periodic in calendar time than are economic movements. This is consistent with the hypothesis that sociopolitical dynamics, such as a generation cycle in war, help to stabilize the temporal recurrence of economic long waves.

War and Long Wave Phases

The connection between economic phase periods and wars is investigated in several ways. Levy's "great power wars" (class 2, above) are

21. As the number of lags increases, the degrees of freedom decreases (terminal years are lopped off), so it takes a larger value of the ACF at high lags to make the ACF statistically significant at a given confidence level. The confidence limits in a graph of an ACF therefore curve outward as they move to the right.
22. My "lag structures"—relative to a scheme of alternating phases of uneven length—get at somewhat the same thing as an ACF but in cycle time rather than calendar time.
23. The value of one year's data point is correlated with the value in the previous year.
24. Whether the series is logged or not, and so on.
25. I tried a variety of different data treatments, such as logging the series and transforming them to differences and to growth rates—all with little effect.

Figure 11.2. ACFs for War Severity, 1815 on and 1495 on

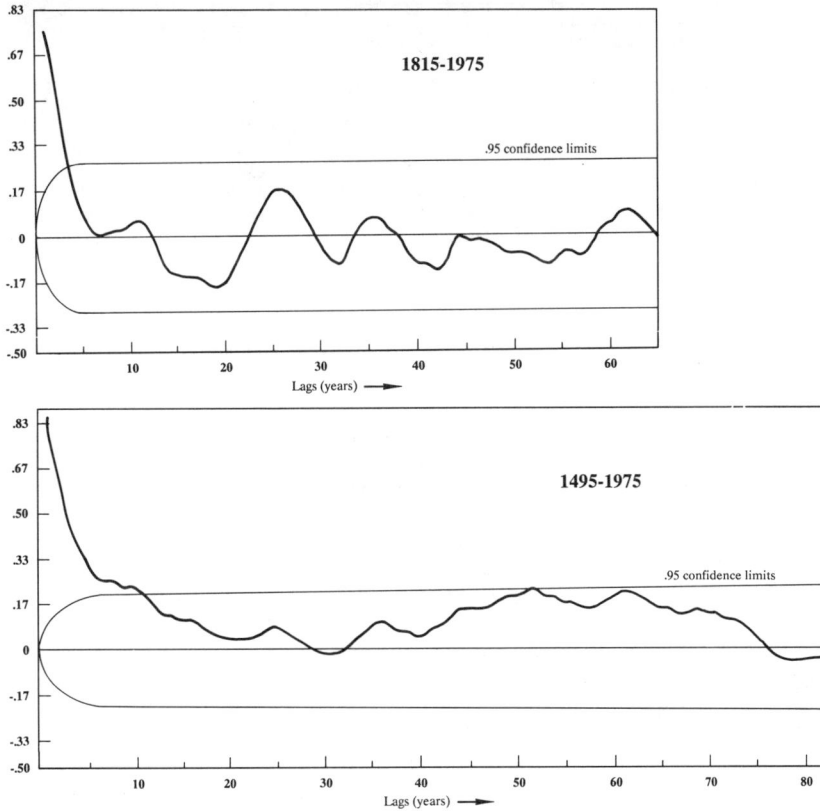

1815-1975

.95 confidence limits

Lags (years) ⟶

1495-1975

.95 confidence limits

Lags (years) ⟶

categorized (table 11.4) according to the economic phase period in which the war
"mainly" fell (see definitions above, p. 239). Thirty-one wars occurred during
upswings, twenty-seven during downswings, and six seriously overlapped phase
periods (see also table 11.5, column 7). Thus hardly any *more* wars occurred on the
upswing phases than the downswings. But in total battle fatalities (severity), except
for the 1575–94 upswing, there is a clear alternation between upswing and downswing phases. More severe wars occurred during upswing phases.

I have tabulated six war indicators by phase period (table 11.5).[26] The first
indicator (col. 3) derives from the list of fatalities (table 11.4), here expressed as an
average annual fatality rate in each phase.[27] This indicator is also displayed as a bar
chart in figure 11.3. With the exception of the (low-fatality) upswing of 1575–94,
fatalities follow the pattern of upswings and downswings throughout the 481-year

26. Note that 1968, not 1980, is used here as the date of the last turning point, because these analyses
were done while using the unmodified dating from Mandel. The categorization of those twelve years
makes no substantial difference in any reported results, so I have not recalculated them with 1980.
27. To compensate for the different lengths of phases.

Table 11.4. Great Power Wars by Phase Period

Period	Fatalities ('000)		Great power wars mainly in period
	Upswings	Downswings	
(1495)–1508		26	League of Venice; Neapolitan War
1509–1528	161		Holy League; Austro-Turkish; Second Milanese; Ottoman War; 1st and 2nd Wars of Charles V
1529–1538		60	Ottoman War; 3rd War of Charles V
1539–1558	227		Ottoman; 4th of Charles V; Siege of Boulogne; Arundel's Rebellion; Ottoman; 5th of Charles V; Franco-Spanish
1559–1574		60	Scottish; Spanish-Turkish; 1st Huguenot; Austro-Turkish
1575–1594	48		Austro-Turkish
1595–1620		111	Austro-Turkish; (2) Spanish-Turkish
1621–1649	1 767		Thirty Years' War: Danish; Swedish; Swedish-French
1650–1688		668	Franco-Spanish; Anglo-Dutch Naval; Great Northern; English-Spanish; Ottoman; Anglo-Dutch Naval; Devolutionary War; Dutch War of Louis XIV; Franco-Spanish
1689–1719	2 020		League of Augsburg; 2nd Northern War; Spanish Succession; Quadruple Alliance
1720–1746		462	British-Spanish; Polish Succession; Austrian Succession
1747–1761	992		Seven Years' War
1762–1789		34	Bavarian Succession; American Revolution
1790–1813	2 532		French Revolutionary; Napoleonic Wars
1814–1847		0	—
1848–1871	451		Crimean; Italian Unification; Austro-Prussian; Franco-Prussian
1872–1892		0	—
1893–1916	7 734		World War I
1917–1939		21	Russian Civil War; Russo-Japanese War
1940–1967	13 903		World War II; Korean War
1968–(1975)		(0)	—

Note: Wars not categorizable by phase period: Austro-Turkish (1556–1562); Spanish-Turkish (1569–1580); War of Armada (1585–1604); War of the Three Henries (1589–1598); Thirty Years' War/Bohemian (1618–1625); Ottoman War (1682–1699). Total fatalities in these wars: 852,000.
Source: Goldstein (1985: 438).

span of the data. Up through 1892, the average annual fatality rate was six times higher on upswings than on downswings; if the twentieth century is included, it is twenty-one times higher on upswings than downswings.

Categorizing the same fatality data "strictly" by phase period (col. 4),[28] in conjunction with the method just discussed, points to sensitivities to the exact dating of turning points. Not surprisingly, the main effect is on the twentieth century's two world wars, each overlapping one to two years into an adjacent phase. The results also show the weakest correlation to be in the period 1495–1620. Nonetheless, the fatality rate on upswings is still more than four times higher than on downswings for

28. As explained above, a war that overlaps slightly into another phase period then has a proportion of its fatalities allocated to the other period (relative to the percentage of years in each period).

Table 11.5. Selected War Indicators by Phase Period

Phase period (1)	(2)	Great power wars					Other wars
		Avg. ann. fatal.		Percent war years		No. of wars mainly in period	Avg. ann. fatalities mainly in period
		Mainly in period (3)	Strictly in period (4)	All GP wars (5)	Above 500 ann. fatalities per 10^6 Euro. pop. (6)	(7)	(8)
1495–1508 D		1.9	1.9	50	0	2	0.6
1509–1528 U		8.0	7.0	85	0	6	0.4
1529–1538 D		6.0	9.5	100	0	2	0.4
1539–1558 U		13.8	14.0	95	0	7	0.6
1559–1574 D		3.8	7.4	100	0	4	0
1575–1594 U		2.3	5.8	95	0	1	1.2
1595–1620 D		4.3	9.2	77	8	3	1.2
1621–1649 U		60.9	68.2	100	97	3	0
1650–1688 D		17.1	21.5	85	13	9	0.6
1689–1719 U		63.1	71.2	100	71	4	0.3
1720–1746 D		17.1	15.3	74	0	3	1.8
1747–1761 U		66.1	57.7	60	47	1	0
1762–1789 D		1.2	7.9	32	7	2	1.0
1790–1813 U		105.5	95.8	92	83	2	10.4
1814–1847 D		0	6.9	6	6	0	1.6
1848–1871 U		18.8	18.8	33	17	4	0.8
1872–1892 D		0	0	0	0	0	5.8
1893–1916 U		322.2	201.4	12	12	1	2.1
1917–1939 D		0.9	173.9	26	13	2	11.5
1940–1967 U		496.5	458.0	36	36	2	0.3
1968–1975 D		0	0	0	0	0	7.0
1495 to 1975:							
All downs		5.9	26.0	50	6	27	2.6
All ups		126.6	110.6	71	40	31	1.6
Between		—	0	0	0	6	—
Total[a]		65.1	66.9	60	22	64	2.1
1495 to 1892 only:[b]							
All downs		7.3	9.6	60	6	25	1.5
All ups		44.8	45.6	84	44	28	1.8
Between		—	0	0	0	6	0
Total[a]		25.6	27.8	72	24	59	1.6

Explanation of columns:

1. Dates of economic phase period (from literature).
2. Nominal type of period (D=downswing; U=upswing).
3. Average annual fatalities over period, from great power wars falling primarily during the phase period [see bar chart]; excludes six wars not definable as mainly in either phase period.
4. Average annual fatalities from great power wars during phase period based on time series and including overlap from wars falling primarily in an adjacent period.
5. Percent of years in phase period in which any great power wars were in progress.
6. Percent of years in phase period in which time series of annual average fatalities per million European population exceeded 500.
7. Number of great power wars (GP on both sides) falling primarily during the phase period.
8. Average annual fatalities over period, from non-great power wars (GP on one side only) falling primarily during the phase period.

Note: 'Fatalities' refers to battle fatalities only.

[a]Totals exclude wars falling between periods for variables categorized as 'mainly in period' (Variables 3 and 8).

b Twentieth century omitted because 2 turning points fall during extremely severe wars, making results sensitive to dating.

Source: Goldstein (1985: 423).

Figure 11.3. Battle Fatalities by Long Wave Phases

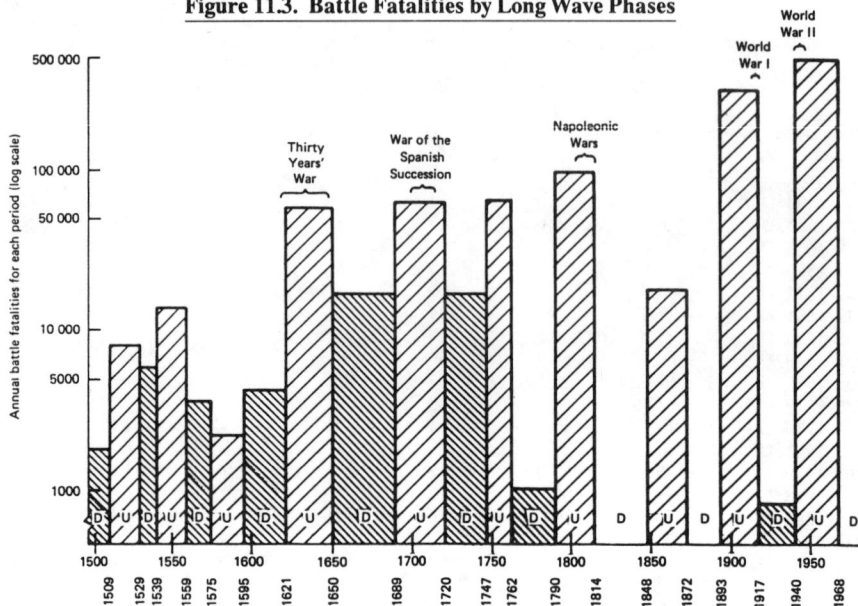

Battle fatalities from great power war in each economic phase period, 1495–1975. U = economic upswing; D = economic downswing. (Wars with over one million total fatalities are noted.)

Source: Reprinted from Goldstein (1985: 422).

both 1495–1892 and 1495–1975. The greater severity of war on long wave upswings, then, is a very strong and consistent correlation.[29]

The years in which any great power war was in progress (col. 5) match the upswing/downswing pattern from 1595 on except for two periods (1747–61 and 1917–39). Overall, 71 percent of the upswing years saw great power wars in progress, as compared with 50 percent of the downswing years. This reflects only a weak correlation with phase periods. Counting only years in which very major wars were in progress produces a stronger correlation (col. 6). There were no wars this severe before 1595, but after 1595 the upswing/downswing pattern matches the ups and downs of war incidence with only one exception (1917–39 slightly above 1893–1916). Of the upswing years, 40 percent saw a very major great power war in progress, as compared with only 6 percent of the downswing years.

The frequency of wars (col. 7) does not correlate with the phase periods; roughly equal numbers of wars took place on downswings as on upswings.

These results for great power wars indicate that the long wave upswing periods are characterized neither by *more* wars than on the downswings nor by wars that last much *longer*, but by much *bigger* wars—roughly one order of magnitude bigger.[30]

29. The severity data also show a strong secular increase over the past five centuries. Particularly strong jumps in the fatality rate occurred with the Thirty Years' war (1618–48) and World War I (1914–18).

30. Orders of magnitude refer to numbers ten times as large, as 10, 100, 1,000, and so on.

These bigger wars are more costly, more destructive, and have greater political and economic impact.

In wars involving great powers on *one side only,* fighting lesser powers (col. 8), there is weak evidence of an inverse correlation to long wave phases from 1600 on (with the exception of 1790–1813).[31] Such a pattern would suggest a displacement of war from core-core conflicts during the upswing to core-periphery wars during the downswing. While this possibility remains intriguing, the evidence thus far is weak.[32] For the other classes of war listed in chapter 8, any cyclical patterns seem to result only from their overlap with the great power war class.

War and Inflation

From the seventeenth century on, most of the major inflationary periods appear to be connected to wars. This pattern is evident in fig. 11.4, a graph of the fluctuations of war severity and of the most central price indexes along with long wave phase periods (shown by vertical lines). Beginning in 1621 each upswing phase in the price series is dominated by a period (or two periods in the case of 1848–71) of major inflation lasting from three to twenty years. These periods of major inflation (identified by visual inspection) are labeled on figure 11.4 ("MI") and listed in table 11.6. Each major inflation period is associated with the later, high-fatality stages of the escalatory war upswing (though not always the final war peak). In all but two cases, 1755 and 1914, the increase in great power war precedes the price increase (see table 11.6).[33] But these relationships are somewhat irregular. Not every war escalation is inflationary; price deflation does not always follow the end of great power wars; and prices sometimes drift downward after an inflationary period while war continues.

Granger Causality: War and Prices

As a supplementary test of the relationship between war and prices, I used Granger causality analysis (J. Freeman 1983). This methodology can help to identify lagged correlations between two time series, indicating temporal precedence of one variable relative to another and hence possible causality. Given two times series x and y,[34] Granger causality asks whether, once the past behavior of series x itself is taken into account, the past behavior of series y still has a significant effect on x. The same

31. The high-fatality upswing of 1790–1813 results from the spillover of the great power Napoleonic wars into Turkey, which was no longer considered a great power.

32. Overall the rate is only slightly higher on downswings than upswings, and even this disappears if 20th-c. data are excluded. Visual inspection of a time graph of these wars showed no clear pattern in relation to the phase periods.

33. In 1755, the price increase precedes the war onset by one year, but most of the price rise in the 1754–60 inflation period follows the onset of war. In 1914, mild inflation had been underway since 1898, but sharper inflation was triggered by the onset of war. A similar pattern occurs in 1939 (mild inflation underway since 1933/36).

34. The raw data are logged and then differenced to ensure stationary and to control variance; Granger causality is preserved across these transformations (J. Freeman 1983).

Figure 11.4. Great Power War, Prices, and Phase Periods

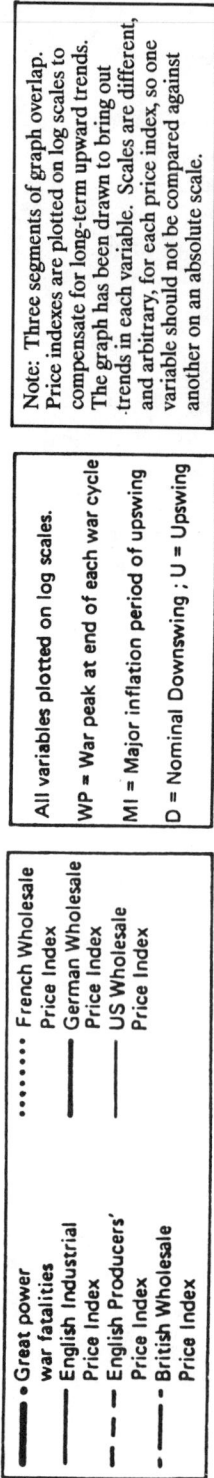

• Great power war fatalities	French Wholesale Price Index
English Industrial Price Index	German Wholesale Price Index
English Producers' Price Index	US Wholesale Price Index
British Wholesale Price Index	

All variables plotted on log scales.

WP = War peak at end of each war cycle

MI = Major inflation period of upswing

D = Nominal Downswing ; U = Upswing

Note: Three segments of graph overlap. Price indexes are plotted on log scales to compensate for long-term upward trends. The graph has been drawn to bring out trends in each variable. Scales are different, and arbitrary, for each price index, so one variable should not be compared against another on an absolute scale.

Source: Goldstein (1985: 424-9).

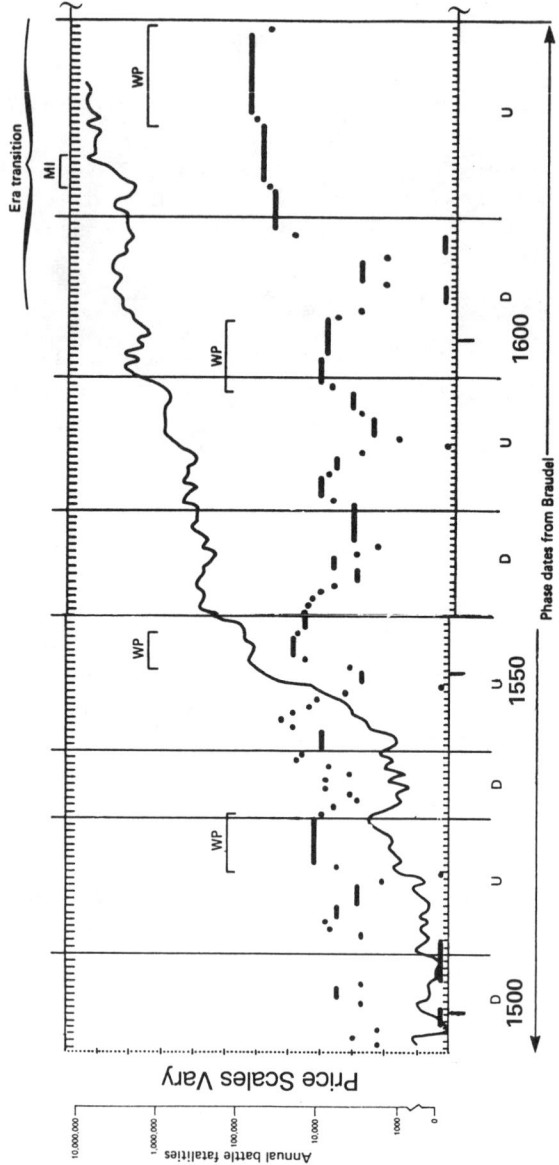

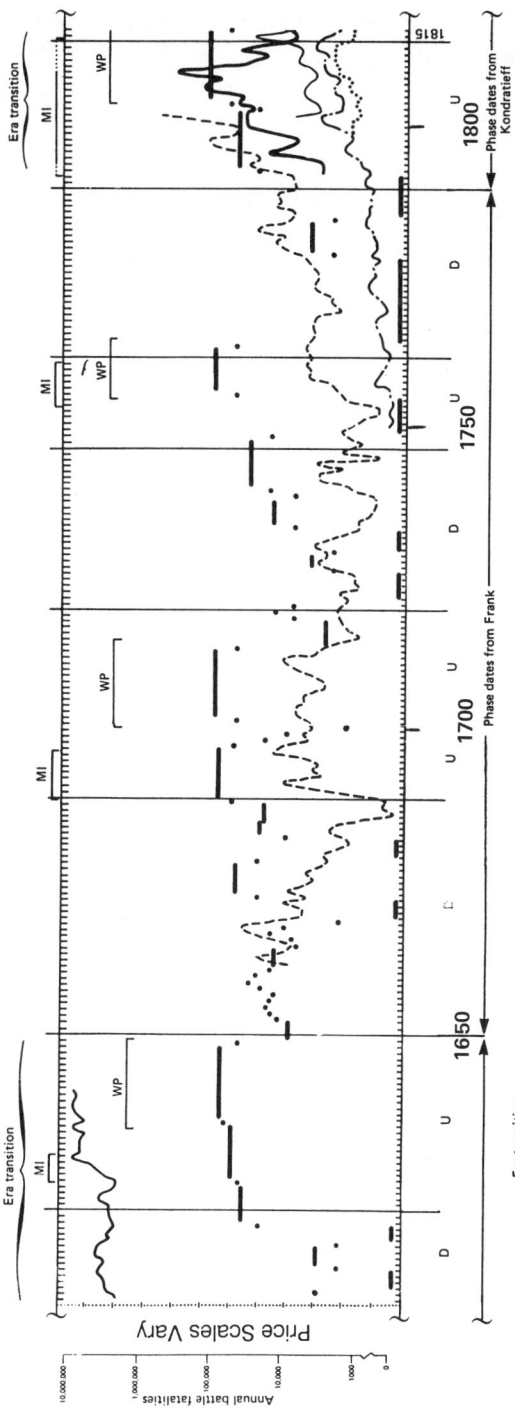

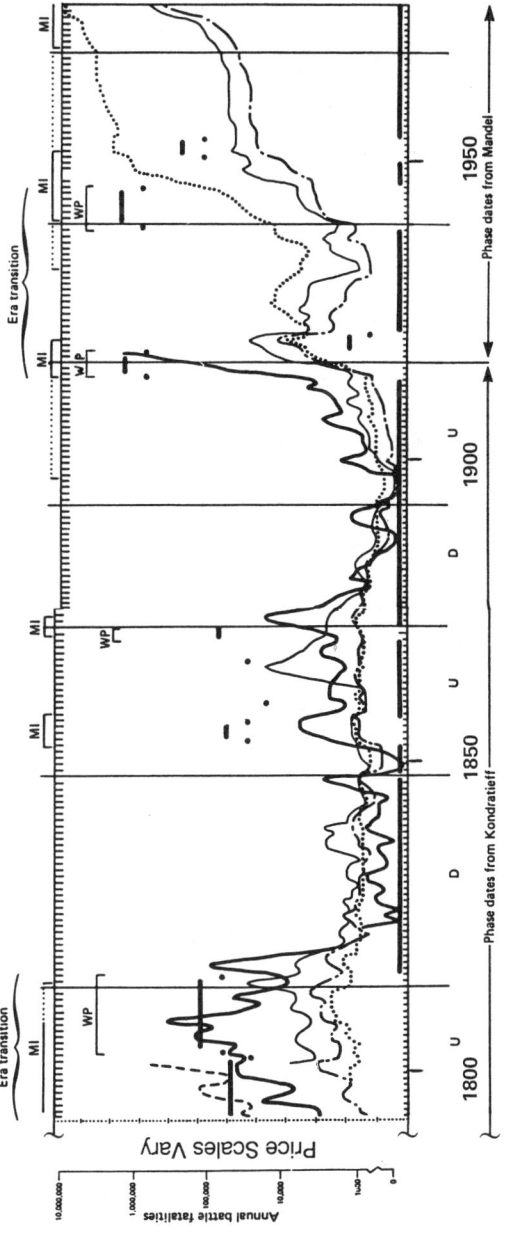

Table 11.6. Major Inflation Periods and Associated Wars

Inflationary period	Great power war occurrence
1626-29	Escalation of Thirty Years' War, 1625
1689-96	Onset of War of League of Augsburg, 1688
1754-60	Onset of Seven Years' War, 1755
1792/94-1808/14	Onset of French Revolutionary wars, 1792
1851-55 Germany only	—
1853-57 Britain, France	Onset of Crimean War, 1853
1862-65 U.S. only	(U.S. Civil War)
1871-73	Onset of Franco-Prussian War, 1870
1898-1914 (mild)	—
1915-1920 (steep)	Onset of World War I, 1914
1933/36-1939 (mild)	—
1940-51 (steep)	Onset of World War II, 1939
1952-68 (mild)	—
1969-80 (steep)	(Vietnam?)

question is asked of the effect of x on y. This is done by regressing each variable on its own past values and the past values of the other variable in a two-equation system and testing for the joint significance of the other variable's coefficients.[35]

There are methodological problems with Granger causality in this application—chiefly the extreme autocorrelation of the war time series. In long periods of "peace," and during certain prolonged wars, the series remains constant for long time periods (longer than the eight lags included in the equation). When changes do occur, they are very abrupt. The economic time series, by contrast, fluctuate from year to year. Nonetheless, a statistically significant result in this application would very likely reflect actual temporal precedence of war and prices, since the autocorrelation problem would not account for such a result.

The results of this analysis, shown in table 11.7, demonstrate consistently significant Granger causality from war to prices, but not vice versa, in the era *since 1790*. The three series in which this relationship is statistically significant at a level of less than .01 are the British commodity price index, French wholesale price index, and German wholesale price index. In all the post-1790 series, the evidence is strong that wars play a major role in the price wave.

The period *1648–1815* shows evidence of Granger causality from war to prices, but the relationship is weaker than in the nineteenth and twentieth centuries. For the period *before 1648,* the Granger-causal relationships are not statistically significant.

35. These are estimated with ordinary-least-squares as "seemingly unrelated regressions." Only a limited number of past lags can be included when estimating the equation. I estimated each equation twice, once with eight lags of the first variable and four lags of the second variable, then with eight and ten lags included respectively. Results reported are for the latter.

Table 11.7. Granger Causality Results for War and Prices

1495-1648:

Period	Variable 1	Dir./ sign	Variable 2	Sig. Lags	Significance
1496-1788	GP War		French Wheat Prices		—
1496-1788	French Wars	< −	French Wheat Prices	5*	—
	French Wars	− >	French Wheat Prices	8*	—
1496-1640	GP War		English Ag. Prices		—
1496-1640	British Wars	< +	English Ag. Prices	7*	—
1496-1640	GP War		English Ind. Prices		—
1496-1640	British Wars	< −	English Ind. Prices	2,9*	—

1618-1815:

Period	Variable 1	Dir./ sign	Variable 2	Sig. Lags	Significance
1631-1817	GP War	+ >	English Wheat Prices	1*	—
1631-1817	British Wars	+ >	English Wheat Prices	8*	*

1790-1945:

Period	Variable 1	Dir./ sign	Variable 2	Sig. Lags	Significance
1781-1922	GP War	+ >	British Kondratieff Prices	1-4**	**
1802-1922	GP War	+ >	U.S. Kondratieff Prices	2,3**	*
	GP War	< m	U.S. Kondratieff Prices	2,3*	*
1802-1975	GP War	+ >	U.S. Wholesale Prices	2**	*
1751-1975	GP War	+ >	British Wholesale Prices	1-3,6*	*
1799-1975	GP War	+ >	French Wholesale Prices	2,6**;8,9*	**
	GP War	< m	French Wholesale Price	2,8*	*
1793-1918	GP War	+ >	German Wholesale Prices	1-4**;5-7*	**

Notes: Variable 1 = 1st variable of Granger analysis; Variable 2 = 2d variable of Granger analysis. Dir./sign = direction of Granger causality and sign of coefficients (m = mixed signs on different lags);
Sig. Lags = Particular lags found significant in the equation. Significance = Overall significance level: * < .05 ; ** < .01. Results shown are for 8 lags by 10 lags.

In that period, either wars had less impact on prices (wars were less sharply defined in that period), or data are simply of lower quality.

Lag Structure for War

If wars do lead prices, this should be evident in the lag structure for the war severity time series.[36] In the lag structure of war severity relative to the nominal (price) long wave phases (fig. 11.5), note that the "fit" is much stronger than in the economic series and that I have therefore extended the scale threefold at both the top and bottom. The structure is robust, although the shift from "X" to "O" regions is quite abrupt. The "X" region is from at least −20 lags to +2, and the "O" region from

---

36. The scale of the series was described earlier. The logged series was used to control the extreme variance of the series, particularly in the 20th c. (sudden jumps to extreme severity levels would overwhelm data from the previous four centuries).

Figure 11.5. Lag Structure, War Severity

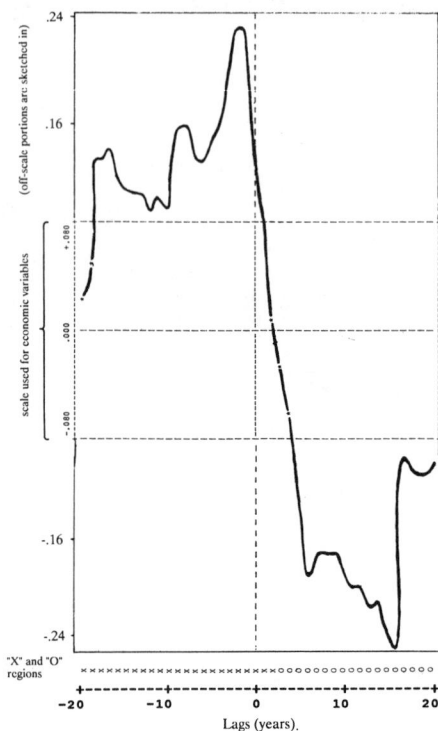

+3 to at least +20. The peak comes near the end of the "X" region, −1 to −2 lags, and the trough at +16 lags. This structure indicates that war *leads* prices, by about one to five years (for the strongest correlation). This of course implies that war *lags* production by about ten years.

War Cycles before 1495?

It is really outside the scope of this project to consider war cycles before 1495 in any serious way. Nonetheless, Sorokin (1957) provides some fatality data going back well before 1495, and Imbert (1959) gives datings of claimed long wave phase periods back to 1286,[37] so I checked whether the two match up. But I can find no strong correlation between Imbert's economic phases and Sorokin's war data. For instance, for Imbert's French phases for all wars involving France, the upswing phases contain 550 battle fatalities annually on average, while the downswing phases contain 440 annually (610 annually during transition years between phases as given by Imbert). In English-French wars, categorized by English phase periods (a dif-

---

37. Unfortunately, Imbert's datings are quite different for different countries (England and France).

Figure 11.6. English-French Battle Deaths, 1300-1500

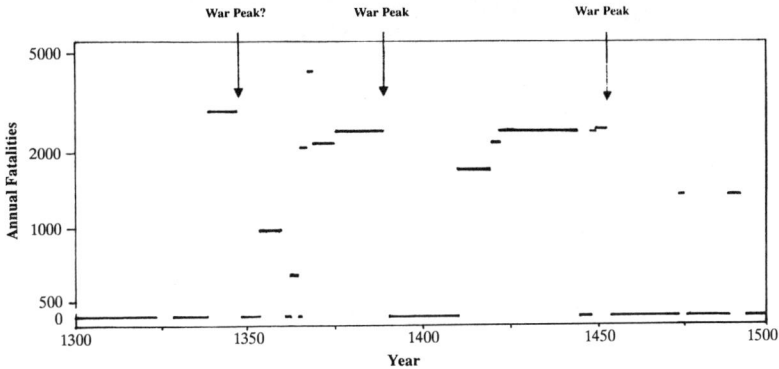

Note: Data, converted to time series and graphed on log scale, are from Sorokin (1957: appendix).

ferent dating scheme), the average annual fatalities are 600 on the upswings and 1180 on the downswings (950 in transition years).

The only intriguing results came not from Imbert's data but from graphing the Sorokin fatalities alone. One series—English-French wars, essentially battle fatalities from the Hundred Years' War (1339–1453)[38]—seemed to show fifty-year cycles at least weakly (fig. 11.6). A series of three war peaks seem to exist in 1347, 1389, and 1444 (the peaks are separated by forty-two and fifty-five years, respectively). The data for other countries—Austria-Hungary, Russia, and Poland—did not follow these patterns, however, nor did fatalities for Europe as a whole.

A long wave in the Hundred Years' War might point to the centrality of Britain and France at a very early point in the development of the "core" in Europe, but the evidence here is much too weak to support that conclusion. Future research into long waves before 1495, however, might pay particular attention to England and France.

Hypotheses of War and the Long Wave

The results reported in this chapter bear directly on the long wave hypotheses dealing with war. The existence of long waves of war is corroborated and provisionally accepted, while the contrary hypothesis may now be rejected:

Long waves exist in war and related political phenomena. [A]
(Kondratieff, Wright, Väyrynen, Craig and Watt)

Long waves of war do not exist. [R]
(Sorokin)

38. This class was perhaps the closest thing to great power wars that existed before 1495.

The hypothesis connecting higher levels of war with the long wave upswing has been strongly corroborated, and the opposite timing rejected:

War concentrations occur on long wave upswings. [A]
(Kondratieff, Åkerman, Rose, Wright, Craig and Watt, Väyrynen)

War clusters early in the downswing.[39] [R]
(Mensch)

And more exact statements can now be made about the timing of war relative to the long wave phases. This hypothesis:

Price upswings precede major wars. [R]
(Rostow, Thompson and Zuk)

---

is true only if interpreted as referring to changes in the *rate* of price increases and the *level* of war.[40] Major wars tend to occur late in the price upswing, before the price peak. But, overall, changes in war precede changes in prices.

Summary of Empirical Analysis

Chapters 9–11 have presented the results of my empirical analysis on long waves in economic variables and in war. This analysis began from a conception of long waves as alternating historical phase periods in which cycle time rather than calendar time is the appropriate statistical framework. I defined these phase periods, a priori, by a single base dating scheme that applies across the board to all the time series studied.

Fifty-five economic time series and several war series were assembled into a coherent data base, which was analyzed to find whether the behavior of the series in fact alternates in successive phase periods. The analysis consistently identified synchronous long waves in a variety of price series from different core countries as well as in the two (English) real wage series. The analysis of time-shifted correlations further identified long waves in production, innovation, and capital investment— although the paucity of data, especially for capital investment, makes this conclusion quite tentative. The production variables lead prices by about ten to fifteen years, allowing a new interpretation of the "stagflation" of the 1970s as the start of a production downswing and the end of a price upswing. Innovation seems to lead

---

39. This timing is off by only ¼ cycle, not ½, since it refers to levels of war, not rates. Clusters occur late in the upswing phase.

40. The difference between rates and levels can appear as a roughly ¼-cycle shift in timing (see chap. 8).

prices, inversely, by about five years, and capital investment seems to lead prices by about ten years. Long waves in trade are not evident. The severity of great power war correlates strongly with the long wave, leading prices by about one to five years. The pattern of recurring war, while remaining fairly synchronous with the long wave, passes through several different eras over the course of five centuries.

The lagged correlations of the different classes of variables suggests the following *sequence* of the long wave, which I adduce as most plausible given all empirical evidence:

−15 lags	
	Upturn in production
−10	Upturn in capital investment
−5	Downturn in innovation
	Upturn in war severity
0	Upturn in prices; downturn in wages

These results form the starting point for the next chapter, in which I develop a theory of the long wave, building on both the empirical analysis of chapters 9–11 and the theoretical debates of Part One.

While the results arrived at in chapters 9–11 are in many places tentative, and the data supporting them often fragmentary, I have nonetheless tried to piece together the most coherent picture possible—admittedly, only a "rough sketch"—from the available information. This effort does not "prove" anything about long waves but helps to build theory consistent with available evidence. Further research into one or another class of variable may well turn up contradictory evidence at some later point, forcing a revision of theory (or resolving an unsolved puzzle, such as the British-U.S. patent mystery). But for now, the picture described in chapters 9–11 is the most consistent and supportable interpretation that can be made of the available evidence.

In closing, I note that the competing long wave hypotheses tested in the preceding chapters may be seen as the bottom level of a hierarchy of hypotheses. At the upper levels, the results corroborate three metahypotheses:

1. The existence of a world system—corroborated by the international synchrony of political-economic movements.
2. The unity of economics and politics in that system—corroborated by the strong correlations among political and economic variables.
3. The existence of long waves of political economy within the world system—corroborated by the alternating growth rates in the data series.

CHAPTER TWELVE

Toward a Theory of Long Waves

The theoretical model of the long wave developed in this chapter is both consistent with the findings of chapters 9–11 and resonant with the most promising theories of chapters 2–7.[1] It includes those aspects of war relevant to the long wave but puts off discussion of other aspects of war (war and hegemony) for Part Three.[2]

The long wave theory proposed is a best guess—an approximation, given presently available information both from my own analysis and from the work of other scholars. It is put forward as a working model that is both internally consistent and generally consistent with the evidence. But (like any scientific model) it is incomplete, contains anomalies, and will be subject to modifications as it faces the challenges of new evidence.

I will present this theory in stages, beginning with the most central and most empirically consistent elements—war, prices, and production—and working outward to less well defined elements that may play a role in long waves.[3]

The Long Wave Sequence

The *sequence* of an idealized long wave within cycle time, based on the lagged correlations emerging from chapters 9–11, is depicted in figure 12.1. Starting on the left-hand side, there is a peak[4] in production at about −10 to −15 years in cycle time—the growth of production turns downward. Within a few years capital investment also turns downward, and within ten years the growth of innovation is stimulated, turning upward. Soon after this, about ten years into the

---

1. The theory attempts to integrate both the *consensual* hypotheses found in Part One and the hypotheses *selected* from mutually contradictory pairs in Part Two.

2. The long waves in systemic severity of war are relevant here, while I leave the longer-term recurrence of hegemonic war for the next chapter. The dynamics of relative national capabilities are mainly left for the hegemony discussion, but are touched on in this chapter as a possible factor in the long wave dynamic.

3. The variables for which weakly supportive evidence was found—innovation and capital investment—are discussed as possible elements in the long wave dynamic. The dynamics of generational change and of relative national capabilities are also taken up as possible contributing elements.

4. *Peak* refers to the end of the upswing phase.

Figure 12.1. Sequence and Timing of Idealized Long Wave

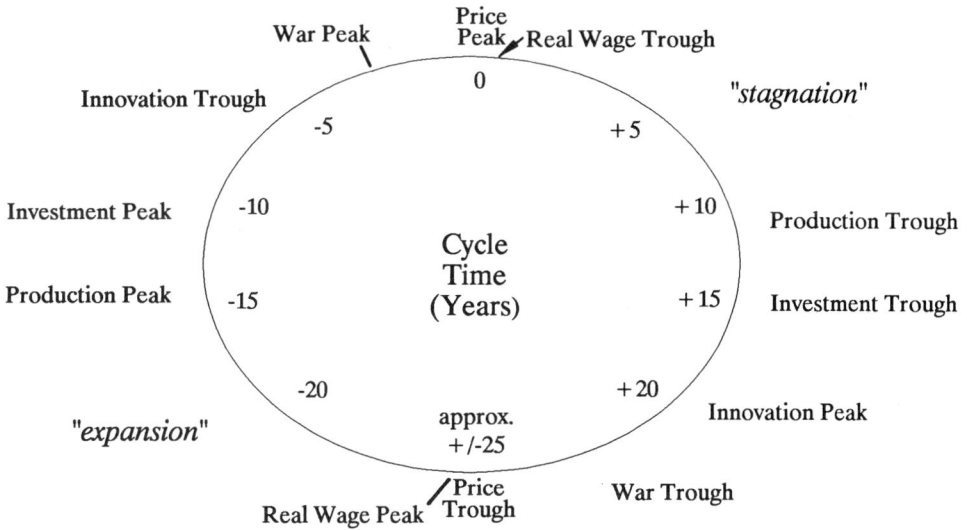

production downswing, the severity of great power war peaks and turns downward. A few years later prices follow and turn downward, and this triggers an upturn in real wages.[5] A decade follows in which the growth of production, war, and prices are all stagnant but innovation grows briskly. Then production growth turns upward, investment follows, innovation is dampened, and, about ten years into the production upswing, war severity turns upward. Prices turn upward following war, and as prices rise, real wages stagnate. This brings on a decade in which production, war, and prices are all growing steadily while innovation stagnates and real wages are held down (money going into war and investment instead).

The *causal* theory of long waves that I adduce comes essentially straight out of this sequence, giving production, war, and prices key roles. I will step through the sequence, elaborating each link in the theory using both theoretical and empirical materials from my own and others' work. My long wave theory is built on lagged structural relationships among variables. Each relationship, marked by an arrow in schematic diagrams in this chapter, will be discussed in turn.

Figure 12.2 shows the connections between production, war, prices, and wages in

5. This timing for wages seems to me anomalous for recent instances. The correlation of wages with long waves was clear in chap. 10, but only British wages were examined.

Figure 12.2. Adduced Causality, Production/War/Prices/Wages

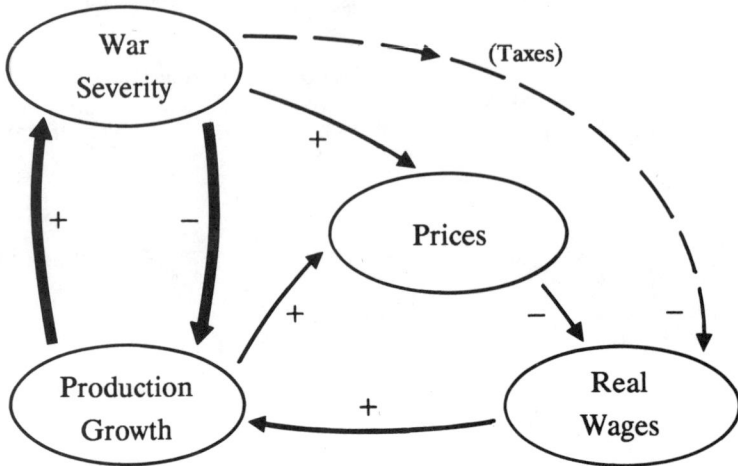

my long wave theory. This sketch will be elaborated toward the end of the chapter with the addition of other elements. I have borrowed the language of system dynamics modelers in sketching out theoretical relationships—arrows indicate causal relationships, and plus or minus signs indicate positive or negative effects on the target variable. The generative dynamics of the long wave may be seen as a set of "negative feedback loops" with time delays.[6]

Production, War, Prices, and Wages

The heart of the theory, as seen in figure 12.2, is the two-way causality between war and production—a dialectical movement in which economic growth generates war and is disrupted by it. Great power war is an expensive activity: it depends on but undermines prosperity.[7]

The cyclical sequence of production and war is illustrated in figure 12.3. A sustained rise in production supports an upturn in great power war. Increased war contributes to a downturn in production growth. Economic stagnation curtails war severity. And low war severity contributes to the resumption of sustained growth. This sequence takes roughly fifty years to complete—forming one long wave. While war and economic growth are the main "driving" variables, prices react primarily to growth and war.

6. The time lags are not indicated on the sketch, but are those shown in fig. 12.1, above.
7. The drive to increase capabilities for purposes of war stimulates long-term secular economic growth (not part of the long wave dynamic), yet that growth is disrupted by recurring wars and lurches forward in 50-year waves.

Figure 12.3. Primary Causal Sequence of Long Wave

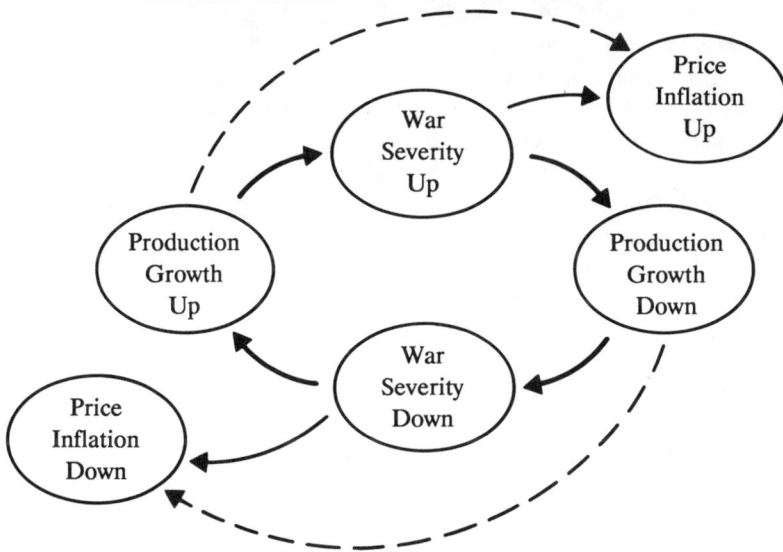

The Effect of Production on War

Why should an upturn in economic growth lead, about a decade later, to an upturn in great power war severity?[8] Several theoretical arguments may be adduced in support of this idea.

The first theoretical argument, which I call the "cost of wars" argument, was mentioned in chapter 6 (Farrar 1977). The biggest wars occur only when the core countries can afford them, which is after a sustained period of stable economic growth. When treasuries are full, countries are willing and able to wage big wars; when they are empty, countries are not able to undertake such wars.[9] Thus when the growth of production in the core of the world system accelerates, the war-supporting capacity of the system increases as well, and bigger wars ensue.[10] Hansen ([1932] 1971:97) wrote more than fifty years ago: "Nations do not fight wars after prolonged periods of depression. Following long periods of predominantly good times, in periods of the long-wave up swing, war chests are accumulated, navies are built, and armies are equipped and trained."[11]

One constant over the span of history has been that wars cost money. More than

---

8. Or a downturn in growth lead to a downturn in war severity.

9. The step between economic growth and full treasuries is taxation (see discussion below).

10. As noted in chap. 11, it is not more frequent nor longer wars that correlate with long waves, but bigger ones.

11. As noted elsewhere, since World War II the contrary view—that depressions (the 1930s) lead to war (the 1940s)—has become popular. But, as I have shown in chap. 11, this was the exception to the historical rule, and Hansen's argument better fits the past five centuries.

two thousand years ago, Sun Tzu wrote in the Chinese classic *The Art of War* that the cost of a military campaign, which generally involved 1,000 four-horse chariots, 1,000 four-horse wagons, and 100,000 troops, would come to 1,000 pieces of gold per day. "After this money is in hand, one hundred thousand troops may be raised" (p. 72). In 1423, the Venetian doge Francesco Foscari warned that in the event of war, "the man who has 10,000 ducats now will be left with a thousand," and so forth across the entire economy (Braudel 1984:120). And in the sixteenth century, the king of Spain was told by his adviser that three things were required to wage war—money, money, and more money!

The cost of wars argument is especially applicable to preindustrial times. In the first few centuries after 1500, wars were fought primarily with money, that is, with mercenaries hired by a monarch. If the mercenaries were not paid, they would not fight—or worse, they might turn on their master. Thus the link between prosperity and war was fairly direct.

Braudel (1972:897–99) identifies two types of wars in Europe around the sixteenth century. "Internal" wars took place within Christendom or Islam, and "external" wars were between these two hostile civilizations. Braudel notes that the second type (jihad or crusade), as well as the outbreaks of anti-Semitic violence in the Christian world, coincide with times of economic depression. But wars of the first type—corresponding more closely to what are here called great power wars—are "usually preceded by a 'boom'; they come speedily to a halt when the economy takes a downward turn" (p. 898).

Braudel (1972) describes fifteenth-to-seventeenth-century European wars as moving in surges—the economy recovered from one war and was in turn drained by the next, bringing war temporarily to a halt. Braudel describes the constraining effect of finances on the Spanish-French war in 1557 (p. 943), the European conquest of Tunis in 1574 (p. 1134), and the Spanish-French war in 1596–97 (p. 1218). In the latter case, the "state bankruptcy of 1596 had once more brought the mighty Spanish war machine to a halt" (p. 1221). Braudel cites a number of cases in which spectacular state bankruptcies, especially by Spain, brought a sharp reduction in war.

In industrial times the costs of war, no longer restricted to purchased mercenaries, continued to place a strain on the total resources of society. Although by industrial times European society was able to sustain a much higher level of economic production and surplus, the costs of war kept pace with this growth (Farrar 1977).[12]

The second argument for why production affects war I call the "lateral pressure" argument. Production upswings bring increased national growth by a number of great powers at once, leading to heightened competition for world resources and markets. This competition increases the propensity toward major conflicts and wars among core countries (even though the things over which they conflict may lie outside the core).

Lateral pressure theory (North and Lagerstrom 1971; Choucri and North 1975;

12. On war costs, see also Bogart (1921) and Warren (1940).

Ashely 1980) seeks to explain linkages between national economic growth and international conflict. It focuses on the importance of a country's population size, level of technology, and domestic resource availability—and changes in these—in shaping that country's international behavior. According to this theory, each member of a population creates demands for (at a minimum) food, water, shelter, clothing, and other basic needs. At higher levels of technology, these demands multiply, since machines and infrastructure must also be supported. These demands create a need for resources, and if the country does not have the needed resources domestically it will tend to seek them internationally.

The propensity to extend activity beyond a country's own borders to help meet demands is called lateral pressure. It can take various forms, including trade, colonial expansion, and military activity. Different countries develop different national capabilities—such as armed forces, merchant marines, financial institutions, and communications networks—that go with different forms of expansion. The intersections of lateral pressure from two or more countries, often in other parts of the world, create competition—for resources, for markets, for trade routes, for military position, and so forth—that can intensify into conflicts.[13]

The lateral pressure literature has not addressed cycles in the past. Since it concerns the effects of economic expansion, the past work has focused on expansionary periods.[14] But the implications for long wave theory are clear. During the upswing of the world economy, demands will rise, countries will expand and intersect, and competition and war will increase.

Kondratieff himself ([1928] 1984:95) attributes the correlation of major wars with economic upswings to a process much like lateral pressure:

The upward movement in business conditions, and the growth of productive forces, cause a sharpening of the struggle for new markets—in particular, raw materials markets. . . . [This] makes for an aggravation of international political relations, an increase in the occasions for military conflicts, and military conflicts themselves.

Earlier authors have suggested similar effects of economic expansion. Sorokin (1957:565–66) tentatively advances the hypothesis that

in the life history of nations, the magnitude of war, absolute and relative, tends to grow in the periods of expansion—political, social, cultural, and territorial. . . . In such periods of blossoming the war activities tend to reach the highest points, probably more frequently than in the periods of decay.

The expansion of any empire . . . [except in a sparsely settled area] can be made only at the cost of the territory of other nations. . . . These other nations must be conquered, because

---

13. Choucri and North (1975) use lateral pressure theory to illuminate the dynamics of six European powers from 1870 to 1914. The study combines econometric analysis with historical narrative to explain the processes that led to the outbreak of World War I. The model is considered a "first-order approximation" of the linkage between domestic growth and international violence. Ashley (1980) uses a lateral pressure approach to examine the dynamics of the United States, Soviet Union, and China, 1950–72.

14. The periods 1870–1914, which began with the long downswing and led into the upswing, ending with World War I, and 1950–72, an upswing.

none is willing to present itself, its population, its territory, and its resources as a free gift to any other nations. Since the victim of the expansion must be subjugated and conquered, this means war, the only real instrument of subjugation. Hence war's increase in the period of expansion.[15]

John Maynard Keynes (1936:381) likewise argues that "war has several causes. . . . [Above all] are the economic causes of war, namely, the pressure of population and the competitive struggle for markets."[16] And Lasswell (1935:121) argues that "in a world divided into states whose ultimate differences are to be settled by violence, prosperity expands markets, intensifies contact, sharpens conflict and war."

The lateral pressure argument, in which sustained economic growth increases the *propensity* for major wars in the system, complements the cost of wars argument, in which sustained growth increases the *ability* to wage bigger wars.

In addition to the cost of wars and lateral pressure arguments, there may be a psychological link from increased economic growth to a kind of "gung-ho" social mood to bigger wars. Lasswell (1935:116–19) considers the political effects of prosperity and depression as articulated through Freudian psychology. Prosperity allows for human impulses to be dealt with indulgently, bringing "a steadily expanding myriad of individual demands." This increases the likelihood of war because "it is the threat of war which counteracts the individualizing tendencies unleashed in prosperity."

Depression, on the other hand, brings "blows to the self-esteem of those affected." The first effect "is to turn aggressive impulses back against the primary self." During times of depression, however, the individuals notice many others similarly affected and hence turn frustration outward onto secondary (political) symbols. The psychology of a depressed economy thus increases "the probability that the ruling order itself may be the target of an attack." The ruling order may, however, avoid such revolutions by "meeting the psychological exigencies of the population".

Lasswell's theory is consistent with the idea that wars occur on upswings and revolutions on downswings. This fits with Braudel's comment (see above) that times of prosperity brought increased war between neighboring great powers, while times of depression brought increased scapegoating—the deflection of internal tensions in Christian Europe against Moslems and Jews.

The Effect of War on Production

While a sustained increase in production tends, with some delay, to increase war severity, increasing war severity in turn dampens the long-term growth of produc-

15. By itself, however, Sorokin does not find a theory of economic causes of war adequate. "None of these factors [economic, psychological, climatic, and so forth] can account for a greater part of the fluctuation of war magnitude" (p. 569).

16. Pigou (1940:21), however, cautions that the economic causes of war are limited. To "seek an exclusively economic interpretation of war would be to neglect evident truths." The economic gains from war, Pigou reasons, could theoretically be greater than the cost of the war but this actually is "improbable." Particular factions, such as financiers with large overseas investments or arms merchants, however, can benefit from war and have some influence in lobbying for war (pp. 24–26).

tion. As Hansen ([1932] 1971:97) argues, "the long-wave up swing . . . produces favorable conditions for the waging of war. But wars and their aftermath tend to produce a reversal of the long-wave movements." Why, theoretically, should more severe wars lead to diminished economic growth?

Despite the popular American belief that "war is good for the economy,"[17] common sense as well as historical experience indicate that war is not, on balance, good for the economy. Resources allocated to war are not available for productive economic purposes (including both consumption and investment), and economic assets destroyed by war (houses, factories, farms, and so forth) no longer contribute to production.

For the twentieth century, in which data are fairly good, war has clearly acted to set back economic growth. In the case of World War I, Burns and Mitchell (1946:90–91) write: "In Great Britain and Germany, production of basic commodities dropped, as did employment. At the same time, the price level soared . . . [and] the output of consumer goods, especially of the durable type, slumped."

Data on total economic output for Britain, France, Germany, and the United States (from Maddison 1977:130) confirm that during World War I the outputs of Germany and France dropped by over 10 percent and 25 percent, respectively, while those of Britain and the United States continued to grow.[18] In World War II the outputs of Germany and France dropped by over 50 percent each, while Britain grew and the United States grew sharply.

National production curves for Britain, France, and the United States (data from sources listed in chapter 8) are graphed in figure 12.4. The clear major disruptions to sustained growth came in the 1914–45 period and were triggered not by the financial crash of 1929 but the outbreak of war in 1914.

It is noteworthy that each of the three countries shown in figure 12.4 resumed a different growth curve after 1945 from the curve it followed before 1914. The curves are shown on a log scale so that a constant growth rate appears as a straight line. For Britain, a fairly steady growth rate prevails from 1800 until 1914. The curve falls below this trend in 1914–45, then resumes roughly the same growth rate but lags about thirty years behind the original curve (this shows on the figure as a parallel but lower trend line). The disruption to France's pre-1914 growth rate was severe in the 1914–45 period. But after 1945 France resumes a higher growth rate and by the 1960s is above where it would have been on the original growth curve.

For the United States the pre-1914 growth also slows down in the 1914–45 period (and again, not just after 1929). In the World War II years, U.S. production surges but by 1947 has dropped back to where it would have been without the war. Since 1947, U.S. production follows roughly the same growth curve as held from 1933 to 1940, a lower curve than prevailed before 1914. So even in World War II, which

17. This belief is clearly rooted in the American experience of World War II, which seemed to pull the country out of the Great Depression and propel it into the prosperity of the 1950s and 1960s. The same historical case underlies the popular idea that depression causes war (Russett 1983).

18. But not rapidly enough to keep the pace of world production from being diminished by the substantial reductions in other countries.

Figure 12.4. Great Power Wars and National Production

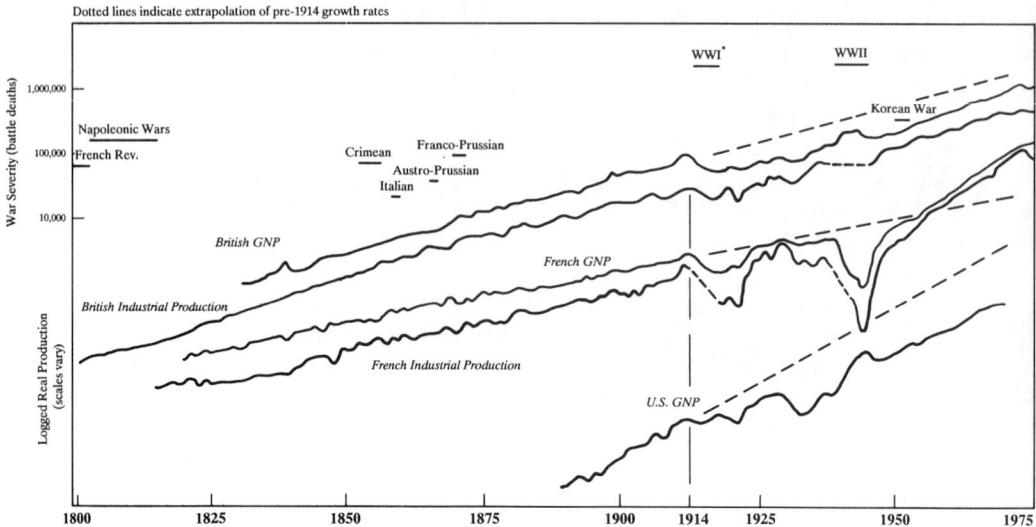

Dotted lines indicate extrapolation of pre-1914 growth rates

*Followed by Russian Civil War at very low severity (not graphed).

shaped the American belief in the economic "benefits" of war, war appears to have played a significant role not in sustained economic growth but only in the short boom of 1939–44.[19]

In the recent past, there is evidence that the costs of war and of war preparations continue to exert a "drag" on economic growth in the major core countries. The proportion of a country's GNP devoted to the military is inversely correlated with the increase in that country's productivity in 1973–83 (fig. 12.5).

Melman (1986:64) argues that while the U.S. military budget currently is only 6.5 percent of the GNP, "it siphons off a much larger share of the country's production resources." He calculates the ratio of military to civilian capital formation as follows:

USSR	.66
United States	.33
West Germany	.20
Japan	.04

"Those numbers show why Japan has been so successful in international [economic] competition." Melman estimates that the planned buildup of U.S. military forces

---

19. Nonetheless, the American *victory*, which allowed a restructuring of a stable Western international order led by the United States, may have been a major factor in sustained economic growth in the 1950s and 1960s. This aspect will be considered under "hegemony" in Part Three. But this is different from the idea that war itself increased growth by stimulating demand.

Figure 12.5. Military Spending and Productivity

| Proportion of Gross Domestic Product Devoted to the Military, 1983 | Improvement in National Economic Productivity, 1973-1983* |

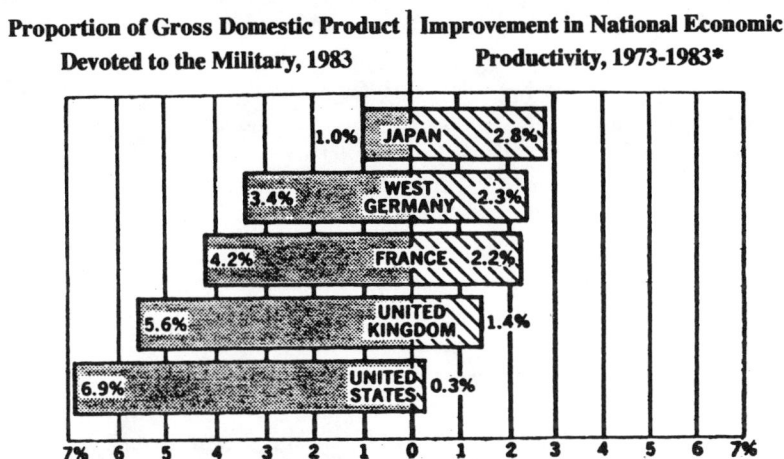

1.0%	JAPAN	2.8%
3.4%	WEST GERMANY	2.3%
4.2%	FRANCE	2.2%
5.6%	UNITED KINGDOM	1.4%
6.9%	UNITED STATES	0.3%

7% 6   5   4   3   2   1   0   1   2   3   4   5   6   7%

* Average annual increases in productivity, measured
as Gross Domestic Product per employed person.

Note: Data from Stockholm International Peace Research Institute
and President's Commission on Industrial Competitiveness.

Source: *The Washington Post*, Dec. 1, 1985: A20.

and budgets would push the U.S. ratio to .87 by 1988. Currently, according to Melman, the United States allocates 70 percent of federally funded research and development to the military. He quotes the American Electronics Association (hardly a peacenik organization!): "We cannot siphon off a disproportionate share of our skills and technical resources to military application and still stay ahead of Japan in commercial markets."[20]

All of the above notwithstanding, war *may* be economically profitable for one country under special circumstances—if the war is fought on foreign territory, knocks out some sizable economic competitors, and one's own side wins the war. World War II met all three conditions for the United States. Japan in World War I experienced similar benefits while sitting out the war. The U.S. war in Vietnam, which met only the first condition, was clearly *not* good for the U.S. economy and seems to have played a major role in the production stagnation that began in the late 1960s.

The impact of wars on long-term economic growth has been statistically analyzed by Wheeler (1980) and by Rasler and Thompson (1985b). Wheeler (1980) uses the data and methods of the Correlates of War project to analyze postwar industrial growth (measured by iron production to 1870, then energy consumption) in major

20. Hiatt and Atkinson (1985) also present evidence of the draining effect of arms spending on the U.S. economy.

nations since 1815. Using multivariate regression analysis for forty-four national cases, Wheeler finds that except for World War II, the effects of war on industrial growth were "overwhelmingly" negative (p. 275).[21] This conclusion converges with the conclusions of five earlier studies by other authors (Wheeler 1980:261–62).

Rasler and Thompson (1985b) use a Box-Tiao statistical analysis in which wars are regarded as an "intervention" in the process of economic growth. The scope of the study was defined by the availability of GNP data—Britain since 1700, the United States and France since about 1800, and Germany and Japan since about 1875. "Global wars" as defined by Modelski's leadership cycle theory (see chapter 6) are distinguished from other interstate wars. Rasler and Thompson find that interstate wars "in general . . . have no statistically significant impact on economic growth." But for global wars, each of which they test separately, eight of the thirteen country-war combinations are statistically significant at the .05 level.

Rasler and Thompson's conclusions are tentative (the statistical significance is borderline and the methodology somewhat ad hoc), and they point out that their results largely contradict those of Wheeler (1980) in terms of the effects of World Wars I and II on economic growth in specific countries. Nonetheless, they conclude that at a minimum, "the evidence indicates that global war does not seem to pay" and does "cost . . . in terms of permanently increasing the costs of maintaining and operating competitive states" (p. 534).

The empirical evidence thus corroborates war's negative impact or production. Theoretical arguments support this conclusion as well. Wars cost money to fight and use up limited resources. And in the war zone itself existing capital plant is damaged and economic output reduced. War conditions, with centralized governmental control and sacrifices on the part of the population, may manage to "squeeze" the maximum production out of the economy in the short-term (using full capacity). But those very conditions disrupt the long-term growth of the economy (growth of capacity).

These arguments have already been mentioned, in the discussion of the war school of the long wave debate, in chapter 2. Silberling (1943:61), for example, argues that the "dislocating effects" of war on the economy "appear to follow long after the event."[22] He concludes that "great wars generate . . . disturbance of such magnitude that the broad course of industrial progress may be appreciably modified for several decades" (p. 63).[23]

---

21. If World War I is included, the results are "mixed."

22. The disturbing effects of war are particularly felt in the sectors of primary production—agriculture and mineral production—and transportation. In these areas the war triggers emergency demands that stimulate capital-intensive expansion under difficult conditions. Heavy government borrowing for these purposes depletes capital markets (p. 62), forcing banks to "come to the rescue" with loans to producers at favorable rates. Under war conditions, the "temptation to borrow and expand" multiplies indebtedness, and fixed charges on these debts "remain long after the war is over and the prices . . . have probably collapsed" (p. 62).

23. After the war ends, according to Silberling (1943:64), prices deflate faster than wages of industrial wage-earners, creating postwar demand for goods and housing and redistributing income from farmers to

Bernstein (1940:529), another war school writer, argues that even for a neutral country, the effects of war are negative. The *initial* effects of a war can stimulate economic growth for a neutral, due to the increased demand for war goods from belligerents and for raw materials to be used in war industries.[24] But, after two to three years of war, the neutral countries themselves will experience economic depression when "foreign exchange reserves [of belligerents] have been depleted, when shipping has been destroyed, and when blockades have become most effective."

Writers from outside the long wave debate agree with these theoretical arguments of the war school. Pigou (1940:11) writes that there is "a strong presumption that any interference with the free play of economic forces . . . will . . . divert resources from more to less productive channels, and so will make the country somewhat less well-off than it would have been if the claims of defence had been silent." Although a national government can use various techniques to "squeeze out" higher production during wartime (p. 30), these increases are unlikely to match the very high costs involved in fighting war (p. 47). Thus the overall long-term effect on the economy can hardly be positive.

Quincy Wright (1942:1180) agrees that war disrupts long-term growth. The extreme increases in commodity prices and the burdens of war debts combine to reduce purchasing power and dampen long-term growth.

Rostow (1962:145) shares this negative view of war's economic effects.[25] He writes that "the direct contribution of war to economic change has been, on balance, negative."[26]

War is a process of mobilizing and applying resources for destructive purposes. That is its essence. . . . Over the long period soldiers kill each other. They destroy capital equipment, houses, and ships. They drain resources away from the normal maintenance and enlargement of society's capital stock (p. 148).

Rostow particularly notes the negative effects of war in raising taxes and in indirectly raising taxes through inflation (p. 161). He calls war a form of "communal capital investment" (p. 161) but one that has not by and large paid off: "It must be concluded that war constituted a great net waste of British resources" (p. 164). Rostow finds that some long-term benefits of war, however, may be found in the

---

industrial workers (this is consistent with the evidence on real wages presented in chap. 10). But imbalance in the entire economy eventually limits the postwar revival and brings on a secondary postwar depression.

24. In addition, the lagging nonwar production in the belligerent countries may open up new export markets for the neutrals.

25. Rostow (pp. 156–58) examines the British experience in particular, making many of the points that have been stressed earlier in this section—that war diverts economic resources from productive uses, that it destroys capital, that it increases taxes, and that these negative effects are only partially offset by short-term positive effects of war in raising employment and capacity utilization. Rostow details the effects of historical British wars as early as the 16th c. in disrupting the development of trade, production, and domestic investment.

26. This conclusion Rostow also attributes to Nef (1950).

social and political changes it engenders. Precisely because it places society under strain, war may speed up beneficial changes in the organization of society that ultimately allow sustained growth to continue (p. 165).

Tinbergen and Polak (1950:131) also share the negative assessment of "the consequences of wars on the long-run process of development." They stress (p. 137) the scarcity of all three factors of production—labor, capital, and land—in wartime conditions and the disruptive effects of the ensuing inflation.

One particular way that severe wars may disrupt long-term economic growth is through sudden increases in national debt. Rasler and Thompson (1983:500) find that increases in real national debt for the countries they consider winners of global wars[27] are relatively permanent following those wars. Using Box-Tiao statistical procedures (to test the effects of an "intervention" on a time series), global wars are shown as statistically significant, "abrupt, permanent interventions" on U.S. and British debt levels (p. 507). Such debt increases might contribute to the disruption of stable, long-term economic growth following severe wars.

At least three countereffects can be postulated, nonetheless, in which war exerts a *positive* effect on production. While these are weaker than the negative effects, they deserve mention.

First, in the short term, war can effectively "squeeze" maximum production out of a national economy.[28] Pigou (1940:32) reasons that productive power can increase in wartime "by the direct action of patriotic sentiment. Volunteers flow into the army and munition-makers readily accept long hours, just as a family would do which suddenly discovered its house burning and in crying need of salvage." These effects are augmented by direct and indirect coercion (conscription and taxation).

Second, war seems sometimes to "shock" a national economy into a reorganized mode based on a new "technological style."[29] After a sharp drop in production during the war, production may resume growth at a more rapid rate than before the war—as was the case for French national production discussed above (fig. 12.4). Organski and Kugler (1980) refer to the "phoenix factor" in which a country that has been decimated by losing a major war recovers economically and within fifteen to twenty years restores its capabilities to levels competitive with the other leading powers (the distribution of power that would have ensued had the war not taken place).[30] West Germany and Japan are the two most recent and most striking such cases. But John Stuart Mill refers to the same kind of phenomenon centuries earlier:

---

27. The leadership cycle school's definition.

28. Economists distinguish actual GNP from potential GNP, which would be achieved at 100% capacity utilization. War, while reducing potential GNP, may in the short-term increase actual GNP by increasing capacity utilization.

29. To use the language of the innovation school.

30. Government reorganizations brought about by losing a war may play a role in this renewal process. Beer (1981:174) notes that war played a major role at least in recent centuries in causing domestic regime changes in the losing countries. He categorizes 10 countries as winners and 9 as losers in the Franco-Prussian War, Russo-Japanese War, and World Wars I and II (countries are listed once for each war they participated in). All 9 losers had changes of domestic regime as a result of losing the war, while none of the 10 winners had such changes.

The great rapidity with which countries recover from a state of devastation . . . has so often excited wonder. . . . An enemy lays waste a country by fire and sword, and destroys or carries away nearly all the moveable wealth existing in it: all the inhabitants are ruined, and yet in a few years after, everything is much as it was before.[31]

A third possible positive effect of war on production, although beyond the scope of this book to explore, is war's role in shaping the formation of the nation-state itself and hence the overall context of production. As Tilly (1975:42) puts it, "war made the state, and the state made war."

These three positive effects of war on growth operate on different time scales. The squeezing of higher production can be sustained only over the short-term (a few years); the "phoenix effect" is relevant to a period of decades following a major war;[32] and the role of war in state-making operates on an even longer time-scale more relevant to hegemony cycles than long waves.

The Effect of War on Prices

In my theory, prices are not crucial but are mainly a reflection of the more crucial elements production and war. They are a good indicator by which to date long wave phases, because of the availability of high-quality data. The link from war to inflation has been strongly corroborated in my empirical work (chapter 11) and that of other scholars (chapters 2 and 5). As the war school argued, major wars increase demand, interrupt supply, and hence lead to strong inflation.

Thompson and Zuk (1982:622) write: "Most observers are prepared to accept the idea that wars tend to be inflationary. . . . It is much less commonly accepted that the relationship between war and war-induced inflation may have functioned as a continuous historical process with some regularity over the past two centuries." In light of the evidence discussed in previous chapters, the past two centuries would seem to be the "tip of the iceberg" in a much longer historical continuity. Indeed, the Chinese military strategist Sun Tzu wrote some 2,400 years ago: "Where the army is, prices are high; when prices rise the wealth of the people is exhausted" (p. 74).[33]

The Effect of Production on Prices

While prices certainly are affected by war, they may also respond to production, with a ten-to-fifteen-year lag. The relationship of production and prices is not easy to unravel historically. Long wave scholars have widely presumed that the long-term fluctuations of prices and production are synchronous.[34] But my analysis (see chapter

---

31. Quoted in Rasler and Thompson (1985b). While this has been historically true, we may assume it has changed in the case of nuclear war at least potentially.

32. And may thus play a role in the production upswing that follows the downturn in war by about 15 years.

33. In fig. 12.2, above, this statement maps directly onto a positive arrow from war to prices and a negative arrow from prices to real wages.

34. This theory may owe its popularity in part to the fact that what can be empirically measured most readily is prices, while what is of greatest interest to long wave scholars theoretically is production. So one measures prices and makes claims about production.

Figure 12.6. Timing of Production Growth and Price Levels

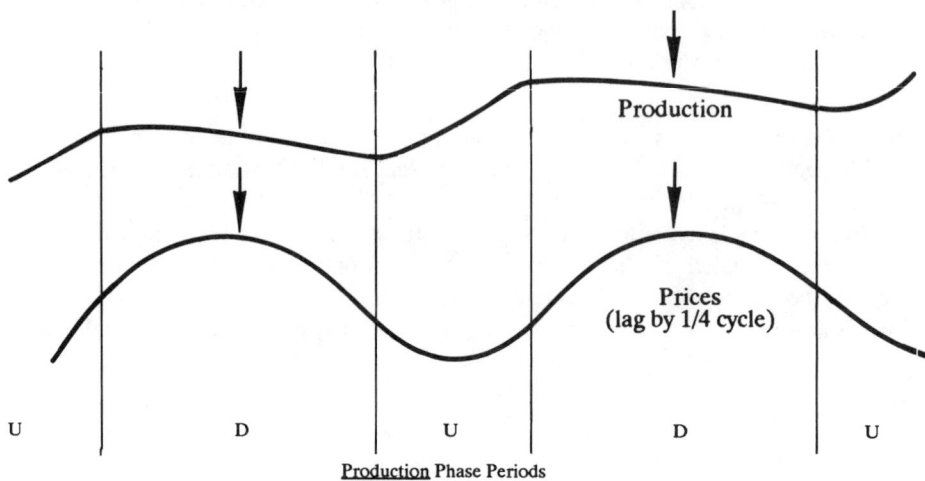

Lowest growth rate of production corresponds with highest price level (arrows).

10) suggests that prices lag production. Since the difference between measuring trends and measuring levels corresponds to a shift of about one-fourth of a cycle in the timing of the long wave (see chapter 8), it follows that the *level* of prices (rather than the rate of inflation) is *inversely* correlated with the *rate* of production. Figure 12.6 illustrates this relationship. The period of lowest production growth coincides with the highest level of prices, and the highest production growth coincides with the lowest price levels.[35] These relationships, however, seem only to supplement the primary relationship that connects production to prices through war.[36]

Production, War, and Real Wages

The empirical analysis in chapter 10 showed strong evidence that real wages correlated inversely with the long wave (although the data covered only Britain). When prices rise, money wages do not keep pace, and so real wages fall. In price downswings, the reverse occurs and real wages rise.

This timing of real wages in the long wave makes sense theoretically for two reasons: First, real wages appear to be inversely correlated with capital investment (capital investment leads by about ten years). This suggests that, on the long wave upswing, as more resources are funneled into capital investment (a necessary aspect of increasing production growth), fewer resources go into real wages. There is a trade

35. It is in that period of most rapid growth that prices begin to rise again.
36. It should also be noted that prices seem to respond to money supply as well, at least since World War II. Fusfeld (1979:8), for instance, shows data linking the increase in inflation after 1967 with the fact that money supply (M1 and M2) began increasing faster than the potential GNP growth rate. I have no theory that ties in money supply, however, except as it is used to finance wars.

off, in real terms, between capital and labor. Thus sustained growth late in the production upswing may be subsidized in part by workers' standards of living.[37]

Second, and more important, real wages are affected by taxes, which are affected by war. Inflation and taxes combine to redistribute income away from real wages and toward the government in time of war.[38] Tilly (1975:23) notes that "taxation was the chief means by which the builders of states in the sixteenth century and later supported their expanding armies. . . . Conversely, military needs were in those first centuries the main incentive for the imposition of new taxes and the regularization of old ones." Taxation and the military fed on each other, since military forces were required to overcome resistance to taxation and taxation was required to support military forces. In 1787, Thomas Paine wrote: "War involves in its progress such a train of unforeseen and unsupposed circumstances that no human wisdom can calculate the end. It has but one thing certain, and that is to increase taxes."

But direct taxation is not the only way to redistribute income away from real wages to finance wars. Hamilton (1977:17–18) sees inflation itself as a tax to pay for war and a way to avoid paying from current taxation. "Of all forms of de facto taxation, inflation is the easiest to levy, the quickest to materialize, and the hardest to evade."[39] Hamilton argues that "wars . . . without taxation to cover the cost have been the principal causes of hyperinflation in industrial countries in the last two centuries."[40] He blames the high inflation of the 1970s on the Vietnam war and "the unwillingness of our political leaders in both parties to attempt to pay the cost of the war through taxation. For this method of payment would have revealed the true cost, and thus ended the war."

The main causal links involving prices have been drawn *from* war and production *to* prices. But there may also be a "feedback loop" (though perhaps of lesser importance) from prices to production, perhaps through the intermediate variables of real wages and "class struggle."[41] This dynamic, consistent with the mainstream of the capitalist crisis school, would entail higher production growth leading (through inflation and with a decade's delay) to lower real wages, which in turn would lead to

37. This is not to deny, of course, that over the long term the secular growth of production contributes to higher standards of living for workers in the core of the world system.

38. On this subject, see also Rasler and Thompson (1985b).

39. In the unlikely event that governments did try to pay for wars from current taxation, Hamilton predicts that the people would see that "the cost of the war was too great and the probable benefits entirely too small . . . and would clamor for peace." Consequently, "if only one side resolved to pay as it went, it would be one of the surest possible ways to lose the war."

40. He cites inflation figures from World War I (1913–20) of 120% in the United States, 145% in Canada, 200% in Britain, and 400% in France. The "hyperinflation which reduced the value of money in Germany to zero from 1919 to 1923 would have been inconceivable without World War I and its aftermath." U.S. inflation following the War of 1812 and the Civil War ran at similar levels to that following World War I. And World War II, according to Hamilton, "again forced commodity prices sharply upward in virtually all countries throughout the civilized world, whether industrial or agricultural, belligerent or neutral."

41. Regarding the direct effects of prices on production, Kaldor (1978:257) argues that "*any* large change in commodity prices . . . retards industrial growth." But these effects seem relatively minor in the overall long wave dynamic.

an upsurge of "worker militancy" late in the price upswing phase (see chapters 2 and 3), which would dampen the growth of production. Heightened worker demands resulting from low real wages might help explain the downturn of capital investment in the last ten years of the price upswing phase.[42] And the increases in real wages in the first decade of the price downswing phase could contribute, with a delay, to a reduced worker militancy (and a buildup of demand) that helps spark the production upturn ten to fifteen years into that phase.

Other Elements in the Theory

In this long wave theory I try to synthesize the most consistent and plausible long wave hypotheses in a way that makes them compatible both with each other and with the empirical evidence uncovered by myself and others. Figure 12.7 is a schematic diagram of an expanded model incorporating the dynamics of innovation, capital investment, the memory of war, and the distribution of national capabilities among nations.[43]

The model as a whole is consistent internally, consistent with my empirical findings, and consistent with the main conclusions of the schools of long wave research discussed in Part One. Note that the three negative feedback loops connecting with production in the "economic" half of the diagram correspond with the respective theories of the three long wave research schools. The two negative feedback loops connecting with war on the "political" half of the diagram contain the main causal elements of the three war/hegemony schools in their reading of long waves.[44] Some elements of this "full" model may turn out to be unnecessary at a later time, but for now all add something and none are ruled out.

Innovation

First consider the innovation cycle (fig. 12.7, lower left). My tentative conclusion (chapter 10), resonant with the main line of thinking in the innovation school, was that innovation is inversely correlated with production, lagging production by about ten years. Secondary relationships may also exist between innovation and war and between innovation and national capabilities.

The relationship of innovation and production somewhat parallels that between war and production in that the lagged negative feedback between the two variables gives rise to a long cyclical pattern. Increased growth of production leads to decreased innovation, but decreased innovation leads to decreased growth of production. Conversely, decreased production growth stimulates renewed innovation,

42. This would be consistent with the argument of Screpanti (1984) that higher worker militancy discourages investment (see chap. 3).
43. Social memory of war refers to Toynbee's generation cycle (see chap. 5). National capabilities distribution refers to the international distribution of capabilities, their differential growths, and the conditions of hegemony or competition in the core (linking to the longer hegemony cycle), which are central to Modelski and Organski (chap. 6).
44. The national capabilities distribution loop resonates with Organski, but he does not address long waves. It also resonates with Modelski, but he would apply that dynamic only to longer hegemony cycles. The social memory of war loop embodies Toynbee's explanation for 50-year war cycles.

Figure 12.7. Theoretical Model of Long Wave Dynamics

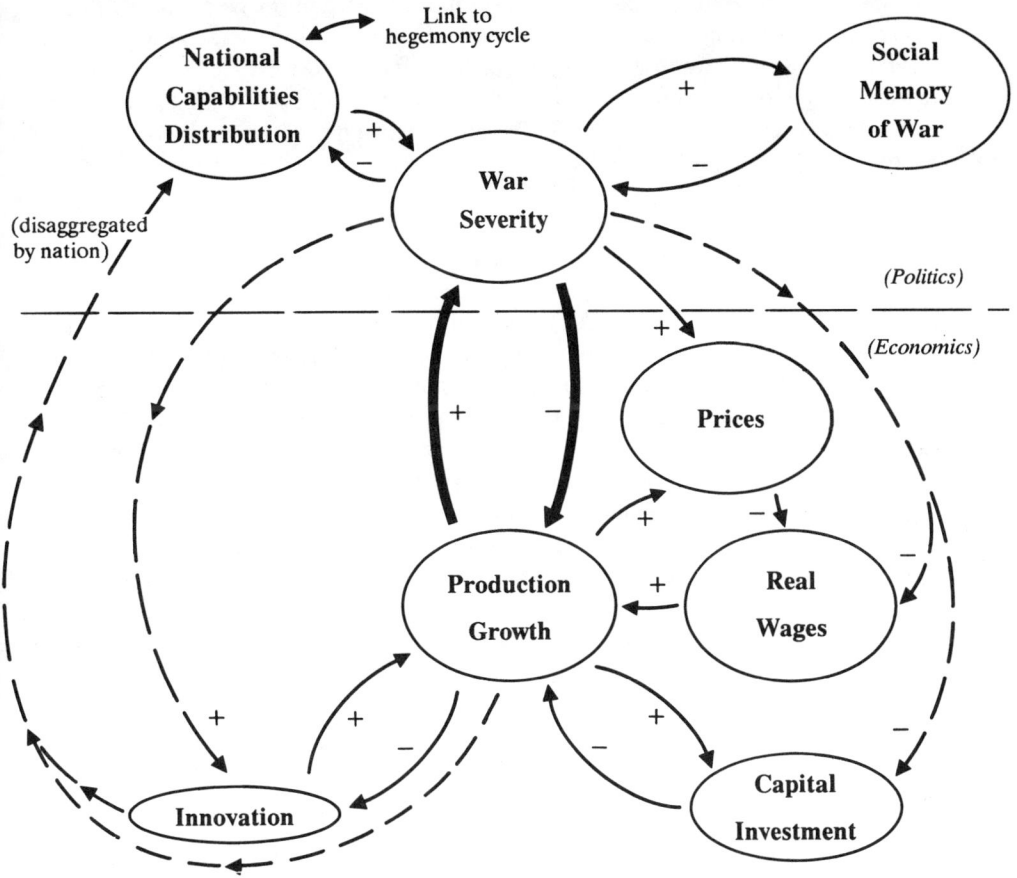

which triggers faster growth. This innovation cycle theory was discussed in detail in chapters 2 and 3.

War's effect on innovation is indicated by a dashed line on the figure. Does war stimulate or depress innovations? Many basic innovations have come about under the exigencies of war conditions. World War II, for example, spurred innovations that helped develop the electronics sector in the United States. Van Duijn ([1981] 1983:25) states that "war conditions . . . have historically been a major force in bringing about innovations." He argues that in the "innovation-rich decades" of the 1930s and 1940s, the innovations did not cluster around the Great Depression but around the war.[45] Kleinknecht (1981b:297) indicates that 37 of his list of 120 innovations were connected with a "war armament strategy."

45. "If a specific cause of basic innovations in the 1930s and 1940s has to be singled out, it would have to be rearmament and war-related demand" ([1981] 1983:29).

But is the experience of World War II generally applicable or (as in some other respects) unique? I cannot answer this question, but if war does stimulate innovation, this does not fit the timing of lagged relationships adduced at the beginning of this chapter. In that timing sequence, the upturn of war severity comes nearly synchronously with the downturn of innovation. If innovation is stimulated by war, this is a weak countervailing force relative to the stronger production-war and production-innovation cycles.[46] But this area remains something of a puzzle for future research.

Capital Investment

The relationship between capital investment and production—like that between innovation and production or between war and production—may be seen as a negative feedback loop with time lags. The upturn in production is closely followed by an upturn in capital investment. But this surge of investment overshoots the equilibrium level and eventually causes a downturn in production and investment. This is the theory of the capital investment school discussed in chapters 2 and 3.

As with innovation, we must also assume a connection between war and capital investment. The net effect of war (although varying from country to country) is to disrupt capital investment—indeed, war devastation constitutes negative capital investment. In the long wave sequence adduced above, the downturn in investment comes just as wars are approaching their peak and production is turning downward. Like the war-innovation link, the war-investment connection seems to be secondary, largely following the war-production dynamic.[47]

War and Social Memory

Toynbee's theory (chapter 5) that the social memory of war causes cycles in war may also be integrated into this framework. The memory of recent severe war works against its recurrence. But as that memory fades over the decades, the chances of war recurrence increase. While I am not sure that social memory can be shown to play a role in the long wave,[48] and while I have not done empirical research in this area, a role for social memory in the long wave has a certain theoretical appeal and should not be ruled out.

Such a theory is consistent with the finding, in chapter 11, that war severity is more "periodic" than other elements in the long wave with respect to calendar time.[49] Thus the social memory element of the long wave theory could serve to stabilize and give greater regularity to the recurrence of major wars, which in turn would stabilize the entire long wave.

---

46. Note the production-war-innovation cycle is a positive feedback loop, in contrast to the other negative loops.

47. As with innovation, I cannot elaborate in any detail the connections of war and capital investment but consider this an area of potentially fruitful future research.

48. And recent empirical analyses do not support hypotheses of "war-weariness" (Levy and Morgan 1985).

49. The relatively fixed length of a generation becomes a clock that links long waves to calendar time.

War and National Capabilities Distribution

Finally, the element of national capability dynamics, including the differentials in the growth of capabilities in different countries, may also be integrated into this theoretical model. This element of the theory links long waves to hegemony cycles.

The most important connection here, in my view, is a negative loop between war severity and the distribution of national capabilities. If the "power transition" approach (see chapter 5) were applied to long waves, severe wars might be seen as resulting from a shift toward more equal distribution of national capabilities ("challengers" try to "catch up" with the leading economic and military power). But a severe war in turn unequalizes the distribution of capabilities again.

Thus, after a war peak, the winners emerge with a predominant position in terms of national capabilities (this almost has to be the case since they have just defeated the other side). This advantage in relative economic and military capabilities then erodes over the following decades, as new (and renewed) challengers come forward. Capabilities again begin to equalize, and a new escalation of war follows.

In addition to this war-capabilities loop, I adduce two other possible elements affecting the distribution of national capabilities—the relative national changes in production and innovation (disaggregated at the national level). These are indicated on the figure by the dashed line at the left connecting innovation and production with capabilities.

The growth rate of each country's production affects its prospects for increasing or decreasing its share of world capabilities. To incorporate this element in the model, production should be broken out into its national components, each of which affects a corresponding national capability component (which together determine the systemic distribution of capabilities).[50]

Likewise, the theoretical model could incorporate the effects of relative rates of innovation on relative national capabilities (again, ultimately affecting the systemic-level distribution of capabilities) by disaggregating innovations by country. A country in which an innovative new leading sector develops gains an advantage in war (by translating the new "technological style" into military innovations). Military innovations allow a nation's overall economic potential to be leveraged into greater effective military capabilities.[51] In addition, innovations in one country will also increase that country's relative capabilities indirectly by stimulating production.

The Theoretical Model as a Whole

To summarize, the theoretical model as illustrated in figure 12.7 contains eight variables. There are six basic two-way causality relationships, which I have portrayed as negative feedback loops with time delays. The primary relationship is between production and war. Of secondary importance are three

---

50. This level of detail is not shown in fig. 12.7 but would be necessary in a formalization of the model.
51. But military technology diffuses to competing powers, so the technological edge tends to erode.

feedback relationships involving production (innovation, investment, and real wages) and two involving war (social memory and national capabilities). As noted earlier, these encompass most major causal theories of the long wave, which are seen not as competing explanations but as pieces of a larger dynamic.

A further set of possible relationships, less well articulated and of lesser importance, were sketched into the long wave model. These include the effects of war on innovation and on investment and the effects of production and innovation on the distribution of capabilities.[52]

This long wave theory integrates elements normally considered political with those considered economic. A horizontal line through figure 12.7 separates the disciplinary spheres of politics and economics. Many of the relationships in the theoretical model—including the primary war-production relationship—cross this disciplinary divide. Indeed, if this model at all closely approximates the dynamics of the long wave, those dynamics could not be understood while remaining on just one side of this disciplinary border.

Conclusion to Part Two

Part Two has addressed some of the outstanding issues of the long wave debate (from Part One) through empirical analysis and theoretical reformulation. I have by no means answered all questions, and I have explicitly noted a number of anomalies or puzzles for future research. Nonetheless, in Part Two I have largely succeeded in building an integrative theoretical framework within which the alternative hypotheses of different theoretical schools have been sorted, translated into common terms, and partially tested.

The implications of the results for other research efforts in the long wave field are clear. More attention should be paid to the role of war than most long wave theories have given it. Those approaches that have emphasized war (for example, Imbert 1959) should be reexamined and built on. Studies that have developed theoretical accounts of the economic aspects of the long wave *without* giving adequate attention to the role of war (for example, Forrester, Mass, and Ryan 1976; Mensch 1979; Van Duijn 1983) should be extended to include war. Schumpeterian innovation theorists should look more closely at the effects of war on innovation (Rose 1941). Theorists of capital investment, likewise, should consider the role of war in the destruction of existing capital plant and its subsequent rebuilding. The ''capitalist crisis'' theorists should consider the effects of war on production, distribution, and class struggle. At the same time, those who have studied war only in the context of longer (hegemony) cycles should not ignore the fifty-year cycle.

In Parts One and Two I have moved from theoretical debate to empirical analysis to theoretical synthesis in the long wave debate. In Part Three I will take up the longer hegemony cycle. In this context the long wave is an intermediate unit of time within a larger unfolding of world history.

52. My empirical data analysis, and the timing sequence it suggested, formed the starting point for the model, but the theory far exceeds the bounds of what can be induced directly from data.

Part Three: HISTORY

CHAPTER THIRTEEN

Continuity and Change: 1495 to 1648

The methodology of Part Three differs from either the hermeneutical analysis of Part One or the quantitative analysis of Part Two. This part relies on historical interpretation and is more overtly adductive. It turns from abstract, statistical, and theoretical understandings of long cycles to their historical instantiation in the European-centered world system over the past five centuries. Hegemony cycles, unlike long waves, seem to be completely inaccessible to quantitative statistical analysis.

In this chapter I lay out the framework for, and begin to elaborate, a new synthesis of historical material. I adduce a dating scheme for hegemony cycles based on three hegemonic wars and the corresponding rise and decline of three hegemonic powers—the Netherlands, Great Britain, and the United States. I discuss the idea of "structural history" and give the background of European political economy around 1500 (the starting point for the study). I then present a historical reconstruction of the first era (the first hegemony cycle), lasting through the Peace of Westphalia in 1648. The historical period since 1648 is left for chapter 14.

Hegemony and Hegemonic War

Hegemony essentially consists of being able to dictate, or at least dominate, the rules and arrangements by which international relations, political and economic, are conducted (see chapters 5 and 6). Economic hegemony implies the ability of one country to center the world economy around itself. Political hegemony means being able to dominate the world militarily.

Marxist analyses tend to emphasize the economic side of hegemony. Wallerstein (1974, 1980) and Braudel (1977, 1984) give predominant emphasis to the economic sphere, with less emphasis on war. In Wallerstein's framework, the "core" dominates the "semi-periphery" and "periphery," imposing unequal terms of exchange and thus extracting surplus value (wealth) toward the core, where capital accumulation is concentrated (see chapter 1). A hegemonic power is a core country that temporarily dominates all other core powers economically (Wallerstein 1983).

Braudel's (1984:27–39) definitions are similar but narrower. He stresses the single city at the center of every world-economy around which is a narrow "core" (the country containing the central city), a broad "middle zone," and a large periphery. Dominant cities do not remain dominant forever; they replace one another in sequence. But there is room for only one center at one time; the rise of one means the downfall of another, according to Braudel.

More traditional Marxists also see hegemony in economic terms but concentrate on the core itself rather than core-periphery relations. Mandel (1980:31) sees hegemony within the core as necessary for capitalist stability: "Only a high degree of international concentration of economic and political-military power makes it possible to impose on the capitalist world currently pragmatic solutions in times of crisis."

Realist and peace-research approaches focus more on military than economic hegemony. Organski (1958) stresses the pyramidlike structure of international power—one country at the apex and others trying to maintain or improve their position in the political hierarchy. Modelski (1978) emphasizes military capabilities and sees hegemony in terms of preponderant "global reach" capabilities.

In my approach, consistent with my theory of the reciprocal influence of war and economics (chapter 12), the military and economic aspects of hegemony receive equal billing. I am particularly interested in the connections between the two aspects.

In my conception of the hegemony cycle, countries rise and decline in relative position within the hierarchical international structure in the core.[1] The hegemony cycle is defined by the succession of countries that occupy the very top position in the international hierarchy. At the end of each hegemony cycle, and the beginning of the next, is a period of very intense great power war, out of which emerges a new hegemonic power with a predominant share of world capabilities (economic and military). This war period ends with a restructuring of the world order around the new hegemonic power. I refer to this war period as "hegemonic war."[2]

The overwhelming predominance that emerges at the end of, and as a result of, a hegemonic war is temporary. Gradually other powers rebuild from the war, and the gap begins to narrow.[3] New technologies underlying the hegemonic power's economic advantage are imitated in other countries. Countries rebuilding from war incorporate a new generation of technology, eventually allowing competition with the hegemonic country. For these reasons, each period of hegemony gradually erodes. Recurring wars, on several long wave upswings, eventually culminate in a new hegemonic war,[4] bringing another restructuring of the core and a new period of hegemony.

Each new hegemonic power emerges from the leading position in the winning

1. Position indicates how much power a country has to "get its way" in international affairs and to benefit from international arrangements.

2. Other terms that have been used are reviewed in chap. 6. In my opinion, "hegemonic war" (Farrar) best gets at the special nature of these wars in revamping the world order. "World war" (Wallerstein) or "global war" (Modelski) could imply only a war of global scope (in which case other wars like the Seven Years' War should be included). "General war" (Toynbee, Levy) implies the participation of all great powers, again suggesting the inclusion of other wars. "Systemic war" (Midlarsky) may connote a change in system structure but can also be taken to mean a war of systemwide scope.

3. See Organski and Kugler (1980) on the "phoenix factor."

4. The connection between declining hegemony and hegemonic war (where and how a hegemonic war occurs) would seem to be the most unpredictable part of the cycle.

coalition in hegemonic war. Among the winners are countries heavily damaged by war and others relatively insulated from war damage. The new hegemonic power comes from the latter group.[5] After each hegemonic war, the winning coalition has fragmented. The next challenger has come from within the ranks of the winning coalition in the last hegemonic war.

This outline of the hegemony cycle has been cast in general terms and is largely consistent with both Wallerstein's (1983) and Modelski's (1978) approaches. However, when it comes to describing the historical instances of hegemonic war and hegemony—dates and countries—the two approaches diverge (see chapter 6).

The Historical Dating of Hegemony Cycles

Wallerstein's dating concentrates on war periods about 150 years apart, which have recurred three times since 1618. Modelski stresses war periods about 100 years apart, recurring five times since 1500. I have chosen Wallerstein's datings as the basis of hegemonic wars and periods of hegemony in the scheme adduced below. There are a number of reasons for this choice.

First, of course, this dating of hegemony cycles fits with the shifts in economic hegemony described by both Braudel and Wallerstein. Maddison (1982:29) comes to parallel conclusions in terms of economic leadership in the world: "Since 1700 there have been only three lead countries"—the Netherlands until the 1780s, then Britain until around 1890, then the United States. He documents these changes in terms of productivity (gross domestic product [GDP] per worker-hour)[6] and elaborates them with interpretive historical narrative for each case.[7]

It seems to me that three is indeed the correct number of identifiable shifts in world leadership since the sixteenth century and that even Modelski acknowledges this (but reconciles it with his dating by having two British cycles in a row). While different scholars date the shifts at somewhat different points, they line up more or less with Wallerstein's dates.

These three shifts also line up with the most cataclysmic wars. Looking back over the past five centuries, three great war peaks stand out above all the others:

The Thirty Years' War, 1618–48
The French Revolutionary and Napoleonic wars, 1793–1815
World Wars I and II, 1914–45

These are empirically (see chapter 11) the most severe wars,[8] corresponding with the highest peaks of inflation and hence presumably the most "costly" wars. They also

---

5. The effect of a war front passing through territory (from mercenary days on) is devastating. A central realist principal of war is to try to keep war off one's own territory (Machiavelli).

6. GDP per worker-hour expressed in 1970 $U.S.: Netherlands falling from 0.35 in 1700 to 0.33 in 1785; Britain rising from 0.32 in 1785 to 0.38 in 1820, to 1.00 in 1890; U.S. rising from 1.06 in 1890 to 8.28 in 1979 (Maddison 1982:30).

7. Maddison suggests (pp. 40–42) that the continuing erosion of U.S. productivity relative to Europe and Japan will likely cause technical leadership to "pass from the U.S. to a collective grouping."

8. Respective battle fatalities are 2.1 million, 2.5 million, and 21 million. Only the War of the Spanish Succession at 1.2 million and the Seven Years' War at 1 million come close to these levels.

seem to divide the war data into eras marked by shifts in the nature of war recurrence (chapter 11). From my perspective, the crucial issues are how costly a war period was, how disruptive it was of the world economy, and what effect it had in restructuring relations among the core countries. From this perspective, the three wars included are the most important landmarks on the historical map.

Each of these three wars marks a transition, a transformation of world politics and its reconstitution on a new level of development. While slow, underlying change takes place all the time and transitions from one era to another are long and drawn out in many ways, one can still identify the most visible, most intense phases of these transitions as residing in the three hegemonic war periods, 1618–48, 1793–1815, and 1914–45.

At the end of each of these three war periods, a new configuration of international politics at the core of the world system emerged. The Treaty of Westphalia, the Congress of Vienna, and the arrangements of 1945 each revamped the hierarchical system of great powers, coronating a new hegemonic power at the head of a fresh world order. Each war period thus brought a political restructuring of the core and a realignment of economic relations among core countries (winners and losers, new trading spheres, differential costs of the war to participants, bankruptcies, reparations, and so forth).

This dating of hegemony cycles also resonates well with the work of several other scholars. In chapter 5 I mentioned Quincy Wright's dating of eras in military evolution: 1450–1648; 1648–1789; 1789–1914; and 1914–. Again, while the specific dates vary, the overall scheme corresponds with the dating of Wallerstein rather than Modelski.

Tilly (1975:46), in discussing the role of wars among established states in creating new states, lists the most "dramatic demonstrations" of this as the Treaty of Westphalia, the Congress of Vienna, and the Treaty of Versailles.[9] These major reorderings of the international system again correspond more closely with Wallerstein's than Modelski's dating of hegemony cycles.

The division of time into these eras also resonates with Doran's (1971) study of the "assimilation" of losing countries after drives for European supremacy. His list of such drives is: the Thirty Years' War, the War of the Spanish Succession, the Napoleonic wars, and World Wars I and II. However, he finds the Treaty of Utrecht (1713), which ended the War of the Spanish Succession, to have been a "failure" of assimilation (p. 110), allowing France's drive for supremacy to resume later. Leaving this case aside, then, the remaining wars are the same "big three."

The importance of these three wars is reflected in evidence from prices as well. A graph of wheat prices for most of the past five centuries (Valley Camp Coal Co. 1942) shows that the greatest inflationary peaks accompany the same three hege-

---

9. In general, however, states went out of rather than came into existence: from 1500 to 1900 the number of independent political units in Europe dropped from 500 to about 25 (Tilly 1975:15). I would add that the world order born around 1945 (especially the United Nations and the decolonization process) led to dramatic additions to the membership of the state system.

Table 13.1. Summary of Historical Hegemony Cycles

Era Dates	Initial hege-mon	Eventual challenger	Culminating hegemonic war	Restruc-turing treaty	Evolution of world system	Military evolution
1 1350(?) –1648	Venice[a]	Hapsburgs	Thirty Years'War 1618-1648	Westphalia 1648	Expansion of periphery; increased surplus finances wars to consolidate core nation-states.	Mercenary wars
2 1648– 1815	The Nether-lands	France	Fr. Rev. & Napoleonic Wars 1793-1815	Congress of Vienna 1815	Balance-of-power system in core; consolidation of periphery.	Professional wars
3 1815– 1945	Great Britain	Germany	World Wars I and II 1914-1945	Yalta[b] 1945	Industrialization; railroads & steamships; dividing up the remaining periphery.	National wars
4 1945–	United States				Shift from Europe to Pacific center; nuclear war; space; information age.	Technological wars

a. Hegemony in 1st era is unclear but seems to predate 1495.
b. Formal and de facto arrangements following World War II (Yalta, United Nations, Bretton Woods, etc.).

monic wars. Warsh (1984:77) notes that the price data of Phelps-Brown and Hopkins (1956) resembles "a cross section of a set of steps." Major price "explosions" have taken place three times: once in the late sixteenth century, once in the late eighteenth century, and once in the mid- to late twentieth century. These correspond with Braudel's (1984:77) "logistics," described in chapter 3, and again divide the five centuries since 1500 at roughly (though not exactly) the same places.

The adduced historical dating and characteristics of hegemony cycles are summarized in table 13.1. The *first cycle* is dated from sometime before the start of this study in 1495 and may go back to a period of Venetian hegemony in the fourteenth century, already in decline before 1495 (see below).[10] The date of 1350 as a possible start for the first cycle is taken from Braudel's dating of "logistic" price movements, in which the corresponding dates are 1650, 1817, and 1974.[11] In the part of this cycle after 1495 hegemony is unclear and there are disagreements between Modelski, Wallerstein, and Braudel about which power was dominant (see chapter 6). Eventually, the first cycle culminated in a challenge for hegemonic position by the Hapsburgs that ended in the Thirty Years' War, in which the Hapsburgs were defeated and the Netherlands succeeded to hegemony.[12] The *second cycle* began

10. The possibility of Venetian hegemony is outside the scope of this study. If it existed, it seems to have been more a commercial than a military hegemony.
11. Braudel marks 1974 with a question mark.
12. Dutch military hegemony was quite short-lived, apparently resting on a temporary advantage gained from the weakening of competitors by war (see chap. 14).

with the ascendancy of the Netherlands in the Thirty Years' War and continued through the decline of the Netherlands and the rivalry of France and Britain for succession. The era ended with the French drive for hegemony in 1793–1815, its failure, and the resulting restructuring of world order around British hegemony in the Congress of Vienna in 1815. Britain dominated the early decades of the *third cycle* and declined more slowly than the Netherlands had. The third era culminated in the German hegemonic challenge in World Wars I and II and the succession of the United States to hegemony after German failure. The *fourth cycle* began with U.S. hegemony and has continued, to date, through the initial stages of partial U.S. decline.

The Secular Evolution of the World System

I refer to each hegemonic cycle as an era in recognition of the secular evolutionary change from one to the next. The very long-term evolution of the world system encompasses the decline of the Mediterranean "world" (Braudel 1972) and the rise of Europe as the most advanced economic and political region, the development of capitalism and of the nation-state, and the eventual "take-off" of industrial growth in Europe. Europe comes to embrace the entire world in its economic and political reach, dividing up the rest of the world's territory into colonies and spheres of influence. And eventually, Europe itself declines with the rise of the superpowers outside Europe and the loss of European control over the periphery (Barraclough 1964).

Wallerstein sees the rise of capitalism as starting around 1500 and as rooted in expanded world trade through which Europe extracted the world's wealth toward the center. This is not a consensual approach among Marxists. Brenner, for instance, likens Wallerstein's approach to that of Adam Smith, not Karl Marx (see Thomas and Denemark 1985). Whereas Wallerstein sees international trade as crucial in the development of capitalism, Brenner sees the impetus coming from domestic sources within the advanced countries.[13]

The issue of when and why capitalism began lies outside the scope of this book. I assume merely that at my starting point of 1495, capitalism and nation-states were beginning to emerge, and the European system was taking shape with the decline of Venice and the rise of Portugal, Spain, Austria, France, and England.

During the first hegemony cycle, before 1648, the evolution of the world system was characterized by a long steady process of expanding the reach of the Eurocentric system, extracting economic surplus from the periphery, and using that wealth as

---

13. Wallerstein, generally following Sweezy's line, sees the transition from feudalism to capitalism arising from trade: "the provision of luxury goods (and weapons) via trade engendered in feudal lords a need to increase their incomes. This need manifested itself in the search for more efficient forms of accumulation" (Thomas and Denemark 1985:2). Brenner, following Dobb's general approach, stresses internal changes in productivity, innovation, and worker alienation as driving the transition from feudalism to capitalism. Wallerstein defines capitalism in terms of "production for exchange in a market," while Brenner argues that the commodification of labor power, not just the trade-based division of labor, must be central to the definition (Thomas and Denemark 1985:3). Thomas and Denemark (1985) review this debate in the context of Polish history in this era and come out generally on Wallerstein's side.

well as Europe's own surplus production to finance wars between emerging nation-states (see table 13.1, right columns). The culmination of this stage came in the formalization of the nation-state system in the Peace of Westphalia, in 1648. The stage of military evolution in this first cycle was one of wars fought by paid mercenaries on behalf of monarchs.

The second era was characterized by a multipolar balance-of-power system in the core, which led to the most regular recurrence of great power wars on long wave upswings in any era (see chapter 11). Europe's hold on the periphery was further extended, and its control was consolidated, in this era (at least until Britain's loss of America near the end). The military technology in this era was characterized by large, trained, professional armies.[14]

The third era was initially dominated by Britain and was characterized by the industrialization of the core at a rapid pace. Railroads and steamships opened up the world to European penetration on a new scale, and as British hegemony slowly declined, the great powers competed to colonize the remaining peripheral areas of the globe. Industrialization also changed the nature of war, ushering in national wars that mobilized an entire national economy toward sustaining mechanized warfare.

The fourth era marks a very different stage of development for the world system. Europe's conquest of the world ultimately drew the center of power away from Europe—leaving Europe itself split in half. This is an era of technological wars fought by small groups operating expensive weapons at large stand-off distances. New developments in world politics include the presence of nuclear weapons, the extension of global reach into space, and the effects of an information revolution still in progress.

Hegemony Cycles and Long Waves

Given the above dating and overall outline of hegemony cycles, then, how do those cycles relate to long waves? I find the connection between the causal dynamics of these two cycles—long waves and hegemony cycles—to be weak. They are not synchronized, and there is no exact number of long waves that "makes up" a hegemony cycle. Rather, I see the two cycles as playing out over time, each according to its own inner dynamic but each conditioned by, and interacting with, the other. The world system can thus occupy, in rough terms, any position in a two-dimensional space at a given time, depending on the phases of the two cycles (see chapter 15):

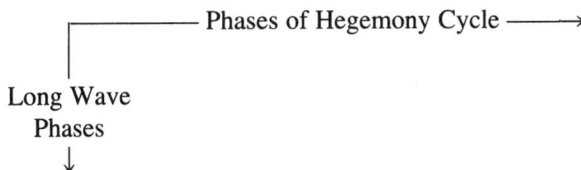

```
        ┌────────── Phases of Hegemony Cycle ────────→
        │
        │
  Long Wave
   Phases
        ↓
```

14. In each era, the hegemonic war initiating the era seems to be the instance where the new stage of military practice emerges in force. Professional armies emerged in the Thirty Years' War, national armies in the Napoleonic wars, and technological armies in World Wars I and II (submarine, air, nuclear).

The path of the world system may be seen as moving repeatedly from top to bottom in this space, while more slowly drifting toward the right (weak hegemony) and then suddenly pulling back to the left (hegemonic war and renewed hegemony).

Each hegemony cycle contains several long waves, but not a fixed number. Each of the long waves *within* the hegemony cycle ends in a war peak[15] that readjusts the international power structure *without* bringing in a new hegemony.[16] The treaties marking the end of each long wave are as follows (war peaks ending a hegemony cycle are marked with arrows):[17]

	1529	Paix des Dames
	1559	Cateau-Cambresis
	1598	Vervins
→	1648	Westphalia
	1713	Utrecht
	1762	Paris [end of Seven Years' War]
→	1815	Congress of Vienna
	1871	Frankfurt [end of Franco-Prussian War]
	1920	Versailles
→	(1945)	(Yalta, etc.) [before long wave peak]
	1970s	Helsinki, SALT I/II(?)

In the first era, to 1648, the war peaks coinciding with long waves all concerned north-south competition for succession to hegemony, culminating in the Thirty Years' War. In the second era, to 1815, the war peaks all concerned French-British competition, culminating in the Napoleonic Wars. In the third era, to 1945, the war peaks concerned Germany's drive for hegemony, culminating in World Wars I and II.

Overlaid on the long wave is the longer-term sequence from hegemony to hegemonic decline to hegemonic challenge to hegemonic war. The two are loosely synchronized in that hegemonic war tends to occur on the ''war upswing'' of the long wave. But the synchrony is imperfect, as World War II shows.

Toward a Historical Synthesis

The above pages have laid out the general concept of the hegemony cycle, its historical dating, and its interaction with the long wave. I will now move toward using the hegemony cycle as a framework for looking at history.

15. To recap, economic growth creates surplus, providing the revenue base for great powers to wage war (a costly activity). War, however, drains this surplus (away from reinvestment, which means growth) and disrupts the stable growth of production, undermining the economic base on which war depends. Thus the world system lurches forward in long waves with this sequence: prosperity-war-stagnation-peace.

16. All great power wars affect relative positions in the international ''pecking order.'' Hegemonic wars determine the top position in that order.

17. Braudel (1972:897–98) gives these dates up through 1648. It would be interesting to do a comparative study of all nine treaties.

Structural History

The development of world political economy may be seen as an intersection of processes operating on four time scales:

1. Very long-term evolution—the development of the world system and its changing geographical size and composition.
2. Hegemony cycles—the rise and fall of successive international orders.
3. Long waves in economics and war at the core of the world system.
4. Day-to-day and year-to-year change, including short cycles, events, and random or local influences.

My historical interpretation emphasizes the first three levels of change: secular evolution, hegemonic cycles, and long waves. The fourth level of change—people, events, locations, and dates—will be largely ignored.

This "structural history," pioneered by Braudel,[18] emphasizes the systemic level of analysis, especially the level of the world as a whole, and examines the traces of long-term forces of change in society.[19] Those who study history, Braudel argues, help society to develop and refine its collective self-temporalization—how we see our society in time. "World time" is Braudel's (1984:17) term for time "experienced on a world scale," which governs certain realities and excludes others.[20]

For Braudel, structural history means not only a new time scale but a change in focus, from the political to the economic/social/cultural aspects of history. His interpretations tend toward "geohistory" in which politics is "secondary to other historical ensembles of action" and the emphasis is on "a space ecologically articulated rather than on a nation politically expressed" (Kinser 1981:103). While shifting the focus away from the state and "politics," Braudel (1984:19) also steers clear of the approach in which economics drives all other aspects of society (economism):

It would be a mistake to imagine that the order of the world-economy governed the whole of society. . . . An economy never exists in isolation. Its territory and expanse are also occupied by other spheres of activity—culture, society, politics—which are constantly reacting with the economy.

Reality is a totality, the "set of sets," in which each set (economics, politics, culture, society) "extends beyond its own area" (Braudel 1984:45).[21]

18. Kinser (1981) discusses Braudel's structural history.

19. *Structure* refers to the deeper forces of social change and *conjuncture* to the actual course of history. One can look at long-term change (structure), medium-term change (conjuncture), or very rapid change, "the shortest being the easiest to detect" (Braudel 1984:17).

20. Ruggie (1985:8) quotes Jacques Le Goff to the effect that history of *"la longue durée"* means not only lasting a long time but "having the structure of a system."

21. Wallerstein's (1979:673) view of long cycles resonates with "structural history." He sees cyclical patterns as a "central part" of "long-term, large-scale social reality." "To seize this reality, we need data over wider space and longer time, and we have to search first of all for the continuities."

The Geopolitical Economy of Europe

The political economy of Europe is rooted in the physical geography of Europe, a huge peninsula surrounded by water on three sides. The rivers—the central inland arteries for trade—run from the center of the peninsula outward toward the water on every side (see fig. 13.1). Trade took place between the major cities up and down the long coastline of Europe and up and down the rivers that connected the inland areas to that coastline. There was also trade with North Africa and with the Middle East, the latter connecting with the land routes to Asia.

The areas of Europe that would become great power nation-states are located circularly around the continent, each with its river basins and ports (fig. 13.2). Some twelve countries played a central role during the evolution of the core of the system. Each went through various political embodiments, ranging from disunified groups of political entities to nation-states to empires and so on. Some played a significant role in great power politics for only a limited period. But each of the twelve has played a major role during the past five centuries. They are, clockwise from the corner facing Turkey:[22]

Austria
Italy
Spain
Portugal
France
Great Britain
The Netherlands
Germany
Sweden
Russia

United States ⎫   (non-European countries
Japan   ⎬   joining core in third era)

By 1500, according to Tilly (1975:18), Europe had a ''cultural homogeneity'' that grew out of earlier Roman unification, which had ''produced some convergence of language, law, religion, administrative practice,'' and so forth. Most of Europe by 1500

shared a common culture and maintained extensive contacts via an active network of trade, a constant movement of persons, and a tremendous interlocking of ruling families. A single relatively centralized church dominated the continent's religious life, an enfeebled empire sprawled over the continent's central sections, clutching fragments of a common political tradition.[23]

22. I exclude Turkey from the list, considering it external to Europe, although important to Europe's development.
23. Wight (1977) argues that Europe went from a more unified to a less unified political system (from empire to bipolar order to multipolar order) in the early modern period.

Figure 13.1. Europe -- Physical Geography

Figure 13.2. The Major Nations

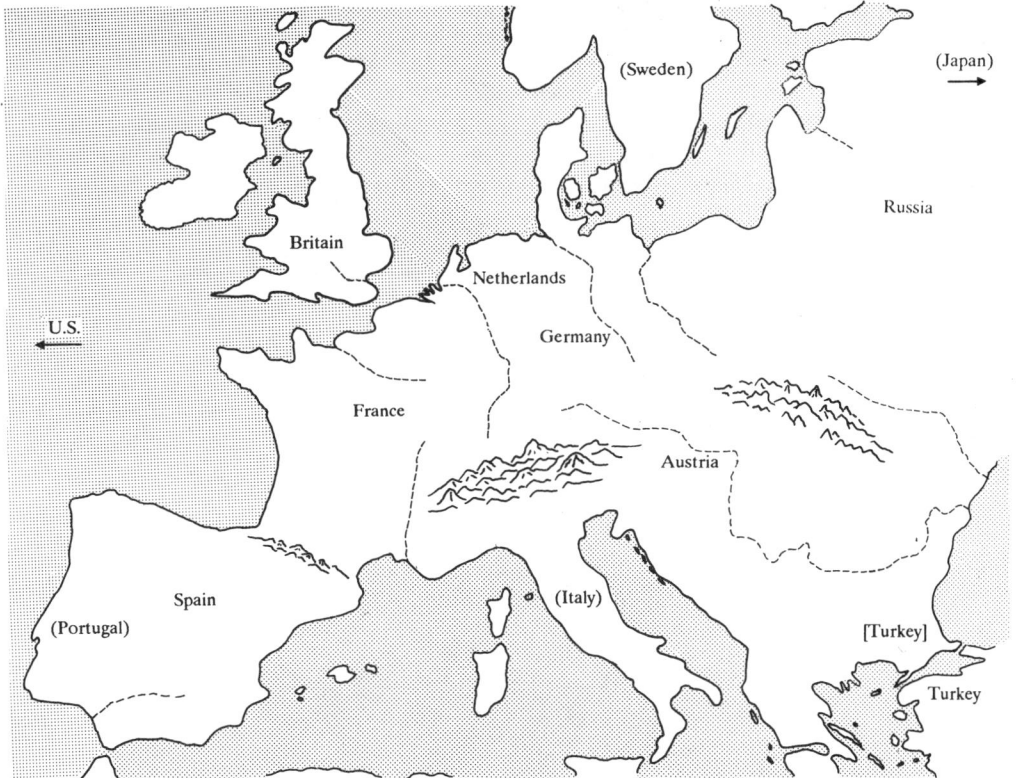

Figure 13.3. Towns in Contact with the Champagne Fairs

Note: Map represents twelfth and thirteenth centuries.

Source: Hektor Ammann, *Hessisches Jahrbuch fur Landesgeschichte*, 8, 1958. Reprinted in
    Braudel (1984: 113).

Braudel (1984) describes Europe before 1500 as already a ''world-economy.'' By this he does not mean that the extended system centered in Europe had yet embraced the entire world but rather that it was ''an economically autonomous section of the planet able to provide for most of its own needs, a section to which its internal links and exchanges give a certain organic unity'' (p. 22). Boundaries between such world economies are zones that are rarely economical to cross, according to Braudel (p. 26).

Venetian Hegemony?

By the end of the fourteenth century, according to Braudel (1984:119), Venice had become the central city in this European ''world-economy.'' Europe itself contained two ''complexes'' of advanced growth, one in the Northwest, centered around the Netherlands, and one in the South, centered around Italy (p. 97). Each had its own trading basin based on water routes—the Baltic/North Sea trade in the north, and the Mediterranean trade in the south.

The Champagne fairs in the thirteenth century epitomized the land trade between these two complexes (pp. 98, 111). The northern and southern clusters of towns in contact with the Champagne fairs are distinguishable already in the thirteenth century (fig. 13.3). The trading community represented on the map follows in many respects what were to become the borders of the French nation-state. For France, however, the Champagne fairs were "the first and last time that France saw the economic centre of the West located on her soil" (p. 116). The sea trade routes linking the North Sea with the Mediterranean, as well as the overland routes linking Germany with Italy, had already (by the thirteenth century) foreshadowed the bypassing and encirclement of France that was to prevail hundreds of years later.

Braudel refers to a "Venice-Bruges-London axis," along which the most advanced development was taking place and away from which lay more peripheral areas. At the southern end of this axis, where it intersected the Mediterranean trading area, lay the dominant city of the whole system, Venice. Venice linked this north-south trade with the east-west trade to distant countries in Asia, via the Middle East. Venice was "a sort of universal warehouse of the world" (p. 125). From the northwestern complex came textiles, and from Germany and Austria came copper and other metals. Venice's "merchants firmly controlled all the major commodity trades in the Mediterranean—pepper, spices, Syrian cotton, grain, wine and salt" (p. 123). Most importantly, Venice had a string of outposts that formed a secure trading route to the Middle East, where goods from Europe were exchanged for goods from Asia.[24]

The Decline of Venice

At about the time that my study begins, the end of the fifteenth century, Venice lost its position as the dominant economic power.[25] In just over fifty years Venetian trade routes were drastically reduced (fig. 13.4). Several factors at this time both undermined Venice and laid the basis for a new stage of competitive great power relations.

First was the development by the Portuguese of efficient sailing ships, allowing a relatively small crew to move a ship over long distances. These ships could carry cargo or cannons (or both) and thus laid open new areas of the world for conquest and economic exploitation. The Portuguese "voyages of discovery" started in 1416 and worked their way down the west coast of Africa throughout the fifteenth century, reaching the Cape of Good Hope in 1487. In 1497, Vasco da Gama sailed around the cape and reached India. Using their guns freely on ships and ports in the Indian Ocean, "the newcomers made themselves masters and before long reigned unchallenged" (Braudel 1984:139). The Portuguese expansion "culminated spectacularly in the direct shipment of pepper and spices to Lisbon." The Asian trade was pulled out from under Venice.[26]

24. Venice captured Candia (Crete) in 1204, Corfu in 1383, and Cyprus in 1489. It lost Cyprus in 1572 and Candia in 1669 (Braudel 1984:89, 34).

25. It is not clear that Venice was ever hegemonic in the sense used for later cases. But the situation in 1500, in any case, resembled weak or declining hegemony.

26. China had launched its first maritime expeditions from Nanjing early in the 15th c., but in 1421 the Ming rulers moved the capital from Nanjing to Beijing to face dangers coming from the north. This created a "new landlocked metropolis . . . deep in the interior [that] began to draw everything towards it" (Braudel 1984:32), and China lost out in maritime competition.

Figure 13.4. Decline of Venetian Trade Routes

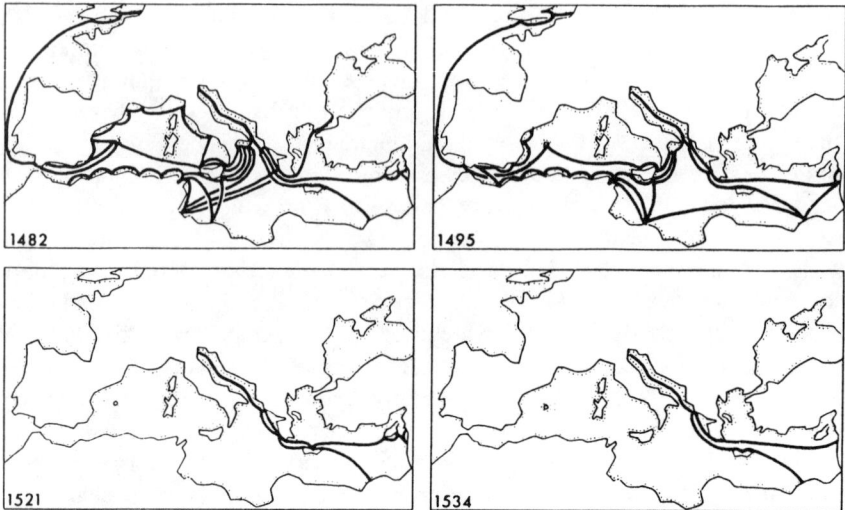

Note: Sketch maps summarize the decline of the system of convoys of *galere da mercato* linking Venice with Flanders, Aigues-Mortes, Barbary, the "Trafego," Alexandria, Beirut, and Constantinople.

Source: Alberto Tenenti and Carrado Vivanti, *Annales E.S.C.* (1961). Reprinted in Braudel (1984: 127).

Spain, England, and France soon followed in Portugal's path, expanding the European trading system to reach most of the coastlines and ports of the world (fig. 13.5). Spain, not surprisingly given its location, was first to follow Portugal's successes and concentrated on Latin America. The Treaty of Tordesillas in 1494 divided the world, giving Portugal all rights in Asia and in the Atlantic up to Brazil and Spain all rights in lands west of Brazil.[27] Britain and France, however, made sure that their exclusion did not last long, and all four countries developed colonies outside Europe.

A second element of change in Europe around 1500 was the overrunning of Italian city-states by larger, territorial states—Austria, France, and Spain. These nation-states, because of their size, could concentrate more economic surplus (more revenue) in one central authority (the monarchy, the central government) than could the smaller nation-states, even the wealthy ones. They thus had bigger armies that no city-state could stand up to. To play in this league, one had to become a nation-state or risk being overrun by one.

A new style of warfare came with the new nation-states. Taylor ([1921] 1973:2) writes:

The fruit of this period of intensive cultivation of the art of war was the military science of the modern world. . . . When, in 1529, the treaty of Cambrai brought the Italian wars to a close

27. It was Portugal's bad luck that Spain, with a much smaller overseas domain, was eventually able to extract from it large amounts of gold and silver—Europe's monetary standards—and use this wealth to purchase large land-based military forces against which Portugal was helpless.

Figure 13.5. Voyages of Discovery, circa 1500

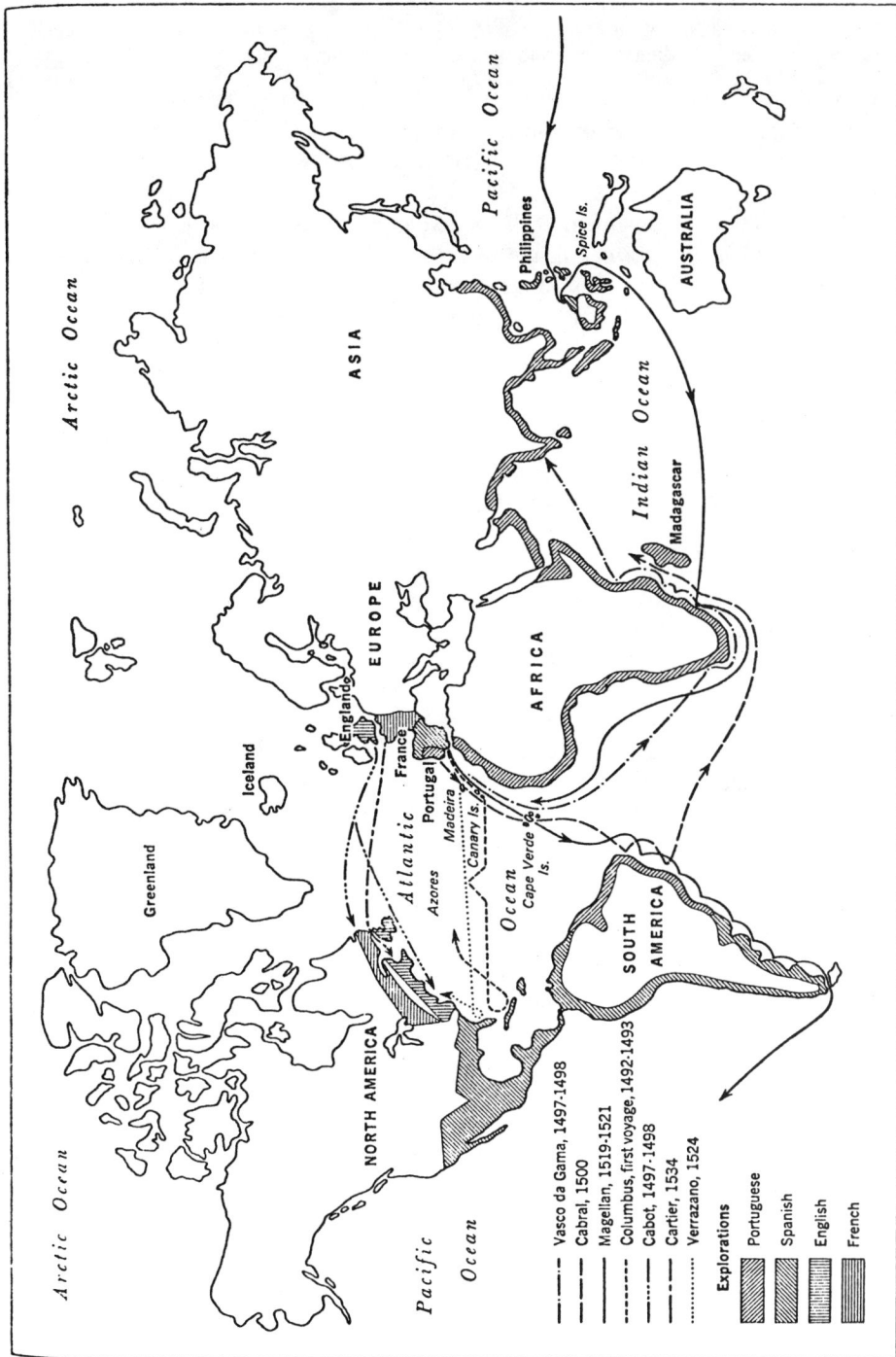

Legend:
- Vasco da Gama, 1497-1498
- Cabral, 1500
- Magellan, 1519-1521
- Columbus, first voyage, 1492-1493
- Cabot, 1497-1498
- Cartier, 1534
- Verrazano, 1524

Explorations
- Portuguese
- Spanish
- English
- French

Source: Clough (1968: 133) by permission of the McGraw-Hill Book Company.

there had already appeared in Europe such modern phenomena as the principle of the balance of power, trained standing armies, and competitive armaments.

Howard (1976:20) describes the army of Charles VIII of France as "the first 'modern' army," made up of soldiers paid from a central treasury and organized in three "arms"—cavalry, infantry, and artillery—deployed for mutual tactical support.[28]

A third noteworthy element of the period around 1500 was the crystallization of the theory of *power politics* in the writings of Machiavelli. The practice of Machiavellian power politics has been at the heart of the great power system from that time until the present. I will touch on this again in chapter 15.

The First Era (1495)–1648

The first hegemonic era begins before 1495 and lasts through the end of the Thirty Years' War in 1648. It is characterized by protracted competition between northern and southern European countries.

Hegemonic Decline

I pick up the first era in 1495 at a time of weak hegemony. The economic decline of Venice was in full swing. It is perhaps a good indication of weak hegemony that scholars disagree about what country was dominant after 1495. Modelski claims that Portugal, by virtue of its dominance of long-distance sea trade and naval capabilities, was the "world leader" until around 1579–1609. Braudel, however, argues against Portugal and states that the economic center of the European world economy shifted to Antwerp and then to Genoa in this period. Wallerstein (1980:64) argues against considering any power hegemonic at this early point but calls Spain the "dominant naval power"—directly contradicting Modelski.[29] Despite these disagreements, it is clear that the early part of this era saw the displacement of Venice and the rise of a Portugal/Antwerp combination (but not to the exclusion of Spain, Austria, France, the Netherlands, and England, which also were rising).

As the era progressed, a grand competition emerged for predominance between the southern and northern European countries. Several deep factors worked against the south and in favor of the north, in this rivalry. These included industry, trade, and war.

North-South Industrial Competition

Three industries predominated in Europe in this era: shipbuilding, textiles, and mineral extraction (Wallerstein 1980:16).

---

28. Howard (1976:21) notes, however, that the transition was gradual. In the early 16th c. "warfare still consisted of personal quarrels between individual princes over rights of inheritance, and not in any sense conflicts between states, let alone nations."

29. By 1600 (nearing the end of the era) Wallerstein (p. 37) locates the "core of the European world-economy" in "northwest Europe"—the United Provinces, England, and France.

Figure 13.6. Textile Industry in the Northern "Pole"

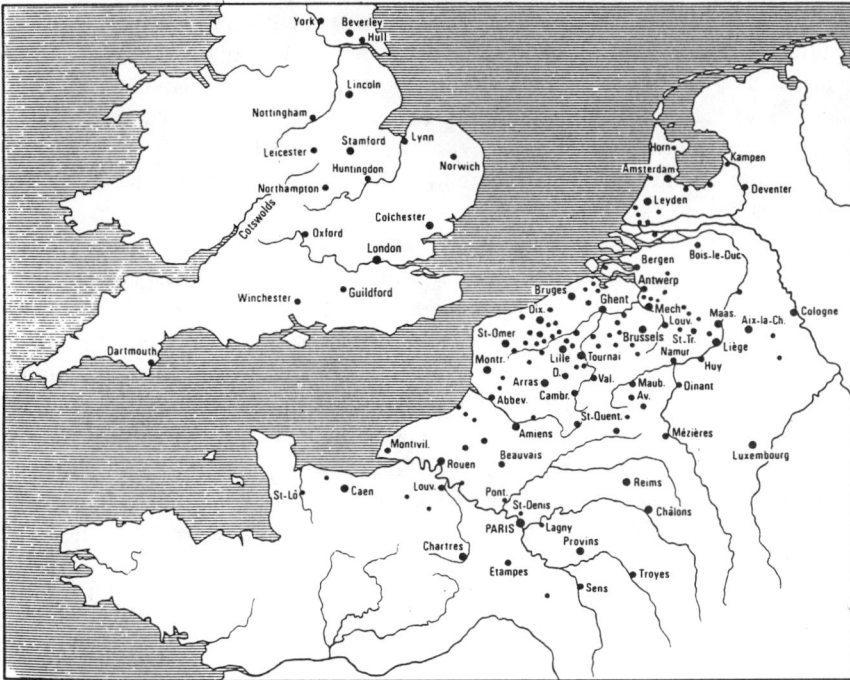

Note: Map indicates the cluster of textile workshops, from the Zuyder Zee to the Seine valley, before 1500.

Source: Hektor Ammann in *Hessisches Jahrbuch fur Landesgeschichte*, 8, 1958. Reprinted in Braudel (1984: 97).

Shipbuilding flourished all along the Atlantic coast (Portugal, Spain, France, the Netherlands, England), but increasingly through the period the advantage in this industry shifted to the Dutch (Wallerstein 1980). By 1570, the Dutch had developed a new merchant ship, the flute, which could operate with a 20 percent smaller crew on long journeys—a significant innovation in an industry where labor costs were the single greatest expense (Braudel 1984:190).

The textile industry had also been concentrated in the north (the Low Countries and southern England) since before the fifteenth century (see fig. 13.6). The "largest single industrial agglomeration in Europe" by the seventeenth century was the textile industry at Leiden in the Netherlands. The Netherlands textile industry in turn depended on English wool.[30]

Thus productive advantage in both shipbuilding and textiles was shifting to the Netherlands and England in this era. In addition, industrial production in England was beginning to expand rapidly. Braudel (1984:552), after Nef, calls 1560–1640 the "first British industrial revolution." Braudel attributes this British advance in

30. England made efforts throughout this era to divert wool from raw export to domestic textile production in order to export cloth instead of wool (Glamann 1974:501).

industry to a fuel switch from scarce wood to abundant coal and to the enlargement of British home markets in the sixteenth century due to population growth and growing agricultural income. The switch to coal meant that "one way or another, coal was introduced to glassmaking, to breweries, brick-works, alum manufacture, sugar refineries and the industrial evaporation of sea-salt. In every case, this meant a concentration of the workforce and inevitably of capital" (p. 553). Thus large-scale manufacturing emerged earlier in Britain than in other countries that had larger timber resources.

The third major industry of Europe, mineral extraction, was centered in the northeast—in Germany and, to a growing extent, Sweden—where copper, silver, and other metals were mined. The German silver mines were overwhelmed in the course of this era with silver and gold from the Americas, imported to Europe by Spain and then by Portugal. Copper, however, was used by the Hapsburgs in the sixteenth century and by Sweden in the seventeenth as an export product by which to finance war. Glamann (1974:490) calls copper "a key to much of the great-power politics of Europe." Copper had "high strategic value" because it was used to make bronze cannons. Virtually all the copper in international trade in the sixteenth century came from three producing districts in Central and Eastern Europe (Glamann 1974: 491).

Copper remained important throughout this era, but iron cannons gradually replaced bronze ones (Wallerstein 1980:101). Cipolla (1965) dates the innovations in cannon production as follows:

1530–60   Wrought iron
1560–80   Cast bronze
1580–   Cast iron

By the end of the era, the switch to cast iron gave great advantage to Sweden with its advanced iron production (when combined with imported Dutch entrepreneurship and technology).[31]

The Baltic Trade

Also strengthening the north was access to the Baltic trade, which became crucial in this era as a source of food and wood. Grain was grown for export in Eastern Europe and shipped via the Baltic to areas that were not self-sufficient in grain, including the Mediterranean.

Economics in this period centered around agricultural production, especially the production of grain. As Braudel (1984:84) put it, "wealth in the sixteenth century meant the accumulation of sacks of grain." Bulky and heavy, grain was particularly suitable for long-distance transport by water (Glamann 1974:455). The Baltic taps four rivers—the Oder, the Vistula, the Memel, and the Duna—that "reach deep into

---

31. Exports of cast-iron cannon from Sweden increased from 20 to 1,000 metric tons between the 1620s and 1640s, during the Thirty Years' War (Sella 1974:388).

Figure 13.7. Baltic Trade Around 1400

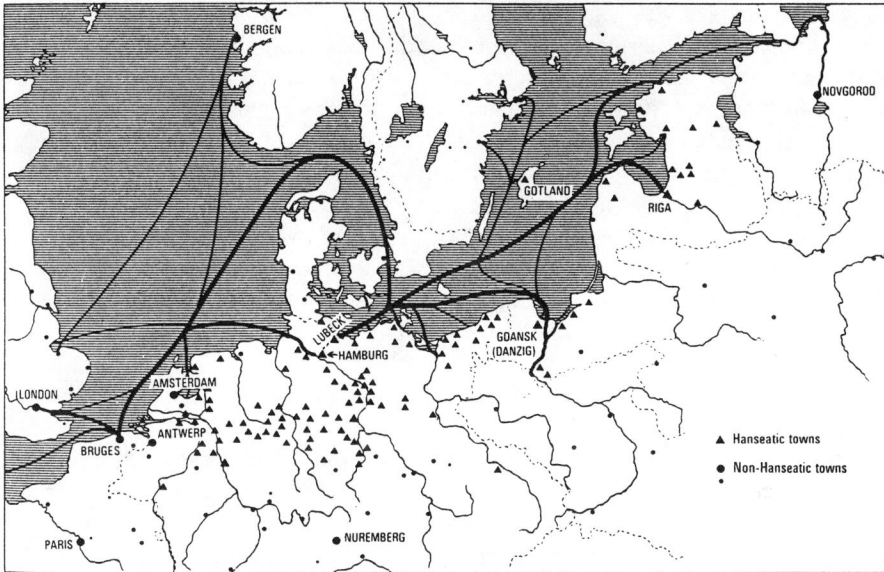

Note: Map indicates trade of the Hanseatic League in about 1400.
Source: F.W. Putzger, *Historischer Weltatlas* (1963): 57. Reprinted in Braudel (1984: 105).
Reprinted by permission of Cornelsen-Velhagen & Klasing, Berlin.

the heartlands of central Europe,'' where climate and geography favor grain production, and that hence ''can tap the agricultural surpluses of a very extensive area'' and
''provide inexpensive water transport'' to move these to the Baltic (Miskimin
1977:58). Thus the Baltic was ''the granary of northern Europe'' (Glamann 1974:
441). Poland had gained secure access to the Baltic by conquering Danzig in the war
of 1454–66, and thereafter grain exports through Danzig increased sharply.[32]

The Netherlands developed agricultural productivity but had little land for a large
population and hence depended on grain imports in order to feed its population.[33] For
the Low Countries, the Baltic trade was the ''mother trade,'' carrying imported
grain. The Dutch called the grain trade ''the source and root of all trade in this
country'' (Glamann 1974:457). Already in the 1490s, Dutch ships formed a majority
of those passing through the Baltic Sound, the Dutch having pioneered this route to
bypass the sea–land route via Lubeck and Hamburg (Glamann 1974:442) (see fig.
13.7). The main terminal for Dutch ships in the Baltic was in Danzig (Gdansk), at the
head of the Vistula River (Glamann 1974:457–58). The Baltic region was also a

32. From about 150,000 bushels annually to about 500,000 by 1500, 3 million by 1560, and a peak of
about 6 million by 1618–48 (Thomas and Denemark 1985:13).

33. Verlinden, Craeybeckx, and Scholliers ([1955] 1972:60) argue that the dependence of the Low
Countries on imported grain in the 1560s was as low as 13% of the total, which was tolerable except in bad
harvest years. But even in moderate harvest years ''the least threat of a bad harvest or a ban on shipping in
the Sound would result in hoarding and speculation on the part of wholesalers.''

source of salt herring and of cattle, which were raised in the Eastern European countries and moved westward overland.[34]

In addition to grain, Eastern Europe produced wood for export. Wood played a key role as both a fuel and a building material, the latter particularly as seaborne shipping took off in this era. The fuel problem affected different countries differently. In England, as mentioned above, by the mid-sixteenth century wood had already become scarce and costly, forcing a fuel shift away from wood and toward coal. In the Netherlands, peat was a major fuel, being shipped downriver from the inland areas to the coastal cities (see Zeeuw 1978). In France, wood was more plentiful.

Perhaps more important than the use of Baltic wood for fuel was its use in construction, particularly shipbuilding. England was a major importer of Baltic timber for this purpose. Spain also came to rely on Eastern Europe for timber and other naval supplies.

The Asia and America Trade

Most trade in this era was between adjacent regions; the volume of trade dropped off as the distance increased. The most profitable trade, however, and hence a trade that played a disproportionate role in the development of the core despite its small volume, was the long-distance trade—particularly the Asia trade.

The Asia trade centered on the exchange of precious metals, primarily from Germany (and later Latin America), for pepper and spices primarily from India and the East Indies. Pepper was one of the first goods imported from outside Europe to reach the poorest classes in Europe (it was used to make old meat palatable) and hence had "the character of an article of mass consumption" (Glamann 1974:475). The East Indies also produced gold and tin for Europe.

As mentioned above, Portugal captured the Asia trade from Venice early in the era, using the sea route around the Cape of Good Hope. But the pepper and spice trade by sea from Asia was an uncertain proposition throughout the sixteenth century, triumphing decisively over the land route only in the seventeenth century (Glamann 1974:477). The Portuguese depended on a string of bases that controlled access to the Persian Gulf and other routes in order to block trade across the Middle East and to protect its own trade around Africa (Glamann 1974:480). The Turks contested these bases in the 1530s to 1550s. In 1586–91, only about two-thirds of the shipments from Goa reached Lisbon (Glamann 1974:477). Again in the 1630s supplies of pepper to Europe dropped, especially with the Dutch blockade of Goa around 1636–45 and their capture of Malacca in 1641.[35]

The second important long-distance trade in this era was the shipment of silver and gold from South and Central America to Spain and Portugal, which was supported by

34. On Eastern European production, see Wallerstein (1980:133).
35. All three instances—the 1540s to 1550s, the 1580s, and the 1630s to 1640s—were on long wave upswing periods. The disruption of imports from Asia may have contributed to price inflation in Europe in these periods. Extreme pepper prices in 1639–40 (during the Thirty Years' War) caused an upsurge of imports, and by 1652 (after the war) "Europe was glutted with pepper" and prices dropped (Glamann 1974:485).

the slave trade from Africa to America, largely controlled by the Portuguese at the outset.

Where did these patterns of industry and trade leave Spain and Portugal? They were not mining centers, and they fell behind on cannon production by the late sixteenth century, becoming dependent on imported weaponry (Cipolla 1965). They were not competitive with the northwest European countries in textiles. And although they had advanced shipbuilding industries, they became increasingly dependent on imports of timber and other naval supplies from northeastern Europe. Against these disadvantages, Spain and Portugal had the profits from the long-distance trade, including the inflow of bullion from the New World, to pay for the supplies and weapons they needed. But over the course of the sixteenth century, as the inflow of bullion accelerated, its value declined (the prices of things bought with bullion rose) and the southwest corner of Europe became more and more squeezed. Austria, in the southeast, was not competitive in advanced sectors of production and was not favorably located to benefit from either the long-distance or Baltic trades. All these factors may have contributed to the decline of the southern countries and the rise of the northern countries at the end of the era.

Antwerp

Also favoring the north was the difficulty of operating the long-distance trade from Portugal or Spain as a center (much less Austria in its awkward inland location). Both Portugal and Spain were forced to use Antwerp as a center for world trade. The reason is probably the same as that mentioned by Glamann (1974:446) for the later rise of Amsterdam: the timing of the arrival of grain in Danzig simultaneously with Asian spices in Lisbon meant that only in the Low Countries could the two meet before the onset of winter. Furthermore, as Braudel (1984:143) notes, about nine out of ten consumers of pepper lived in the north.

The first Portuguese ship carrying pepper arrived in Antwerp in 1501, and Antwerp soon became the distribution center for northern Europe. Copper and silver now flowed from Germany to Antwerp, rather than south to Venice. In just six years— 1502–3 to 1508–9, the proportion of Hungarian copper going to Antwerp increased from 24 percent to 49 percent, while only 13 percent ended up going to Venice by 1509 (Braudel 1984:149). In the early sixteenth century, then, Antwerp brought together Baltic and German products—metal, food, and wood—with spices from Asia.[36]

Long Waves in Antwerp and Genoa

After 1523, according to Braudel (1984:150), Antwerp experienced "lean years."[37] Venice fought to regain its share of the pepper trade with some success (transport by

36. Braudel (1984:56) writes that Antwerp "gained control of the whole of Europe and of those areas of the world dependent on the old continent."
37. During the trade slump of 1521–35, capital in Antwerp shifted toward loans, and an Antwerp money market came into being (Braudel 1984:151).

sea lowered the quality of Portugal's pepper). Meanwhile Portugal and Spain began to get silver from America rather than Germany, making Lisbon itself the logical meeting place of silver and pepper (but still not of food or wood).

After about 1535, though, so much silver was flowing into Spain from the Americas that Spanish expansion became dependent on products from northern Europe—shipbuilding materials, food, and products that could be sold in America. Thus the "Portuguese Antwerp" was replaced by a "Spanish Antwerp" (Braudel 1984:151). This second period of Antwerp prosperity "came to an abrupt end with the Spanish state bankruptcy of 1557" (Braudel 1984:153), which resulted from war with France.

These two waves of prosperity in Antwerp correspond fairly closely with the first two long waves in the base dating scheme.[38] This correspondence further corroborates long waves in this era, which had previously (chapter 9) been found primarily in English prices.

With the decline of Antwerp, the financial center (though not the trade center), according to Braudel, passed to Genoa, where it remained until the ascendancy of Amsterdam. The Genoese rose to ascendancy by bailing out the Spanish in 1557, used control of gold to exert influence, particularly on the Spanish, and declined by around 1627 (Braudel 1984:173),[39] when the Spanish again went bankrupt. The height of Genoese prosperity thus seems to correspond generally with the third long wave upswing (1575–95).

Long Waves in Prices and Wages

The "price revolution" of the sixteenth century also follows long waves—sharply inflationary periods are followed by leveling-out periods. The causes of sixteenth-century inflation are disputed. Earl Hamilton's (1947) "quantity theory" of money attributes the inflation to the influx of silver and gold from America. The more precious metal poured in, the less it was worth and the more was needed to pay for a given good. Others contest this theory. Cipolla ([1955] 1972:46) argues that the connection of the influx of American metals with the price curve is not "mechanical" or "obvious." Chabert ([1957] 1972) responds to Cipolla, and so forth.[40]

According to the data of Clough (1968:150), shown in table 13.2, Spanish imports of gold from America were highest from about 1530 to 1620, peaking in the 1550s. Spanish silver imports were high from about 1560 to 1650, peaking in the 1590s. These two peaks correspond roughly with successive long wave upswing periods and may help to account for inflation on those upswings as due to the surplus of precious metals.[41]

My reading of Cipolla's ([1955] 1972:44) data on price movements in this period

---

38. Upswing from 1509 to 1529, then down to 1539, then up to 1559 (see chap. 4).

39. Elsewhere, however, Braudel (1977) dates the shift to Amsterdam earlier, in 1590–1610.

40. See Braudel and Spooner (1967) and Hoszowski ([1961] 1972).

41. But, as discussed elsewhere, I think wars are even more important in explaining these inflationary periods (and perhaps in explaining the higher influx of precious metals).

Table 13.2. Spanish Imports of American Gold and Silver

Period	Silver	Gold	Long Wave Phase Periods[a]
1503-1510		4,965,180	1509
1511-1520		9,153,220	U
1521-1530	148,739	4,889,050	1529
1531-1540	86,193,876	14,466,360	D 1539
1541-1550	177,573,164	24,957,130	U
1551-1560	303,121,174	42,620,080	1559
1561-1570	942,858,792	11,530,940	D
1571-1580	1,118,591,954	9,429,140	1575
1581-1590	2,103,027,689	12,101,650	U
1591-1600	2,707,626,528	19,451,420	1595
1601-1610	2,213,631,245	11,764,090	D
1611-1620	2,192,255,993	8,855,940	1621
1621-1630	2,145,339,043	3,889,760	
1631-1640	1,396,759,594	1,240,400	U
1641-1650	1,056,430,966	1,549,390	1650
1651-1660	443,256,546	469,430	
Total	16,886,815,303	181,333,180	

Source: Earl J. Hamilton, American Treasure and the Price Revolution in Spain (Cambridge, Mass.: Harvard University Press, 1934), cited in Clough (1968:150). Reprinted by permission of Harvard University Press.

a. Base dating scheme (not shown in original table).

supports an interpretation in which the effects of wars (whose correlation with inflationary upswings has been shown) are supplemented by the effects of precious metals. Cipolla notes an inflationary period (5.2 percent annually) from 1552 to 1560 that is "hard to explain . . . in terms of the influx of American gold and silver." The war peak of the second long wave, in 1552–56, might help to explain it. The next inflationary period, 1565–73 (3.3 percent inflation after an interlude of −1.2 percent) might be best explained by the influx of Spanish silver, which more than tripled in the decade from the 1550s to the 1560s (Clough 1968:150). Cipolla's final inflationary period, 1590–1600,[42] like the 1552–60 period, corresponds with a long wave upswing and is probably best explained by the war peak of 1593–1604.

The data analysis in chapter 10 suggests an inverse movement of real wages, and hence possibly of "class struggle," with prices. This relationship seems to "fit" in this era. Verlinden, Craeybeckx, and Scholliers ([1955] 1972) discuss the effects of the sixteenth-century inflation on workers in Belgium, who were dependent on imported grain. Revolts followed price increases and tended to be aimed primarily at grain merchants (p. 67).

In the eyes of contemporaries, including the government, monopolies were . . . the main if not the only cause of high prices. It was not until 1568, when high prices had long been a

42. This period has 3.1% inflation and comes between two deflationary periods, 1573–90 (−0.4%) and 1600–1617 (−0.8%).

universal fact of life, that Jean Bodin suggested that increased stocks of money were the chief and almost the sole explanation (p. 69).

Verlinden et al. also note periods of crisis in which wages remained far below prices in Belgium: 1531–32, 1565–66, and 1586–87 (p. 77). The first two roughly match up with the long wave price peaks (real wage troughs) and hence also with the end of each of Braudel's periods of prosperity in Antwerp. The third such crisis, however, does not match the long wave.

These observations on long waves in the prosperity of Antwerp and Genoa, and in prices and class struggle, are consistent with my long wave theory but tangential to the main issue at hand—the evolution of European society and the north-south struggle. The economic factors at work in this struggle have been discussed. I will now consider the military struggle, beginning with some general considerations concerning the state of military practice as it evolved in this era.

Military Evolution

As noted earlier in this chapter, the nature of great power war changed at the outset of this era with the advent of large national armies that city-states could not match.[43] Advances in military technology in this era, as in all subsequent eras, had the effect of making war more deadly and more costly. Braudel (1984:57) writes that by the sixteenth century, "advanced warfare was furiously engaging money, intelligence, the ingenuity of technicians, so that it was said that it changed its nature from year to year." In this era a "rising and unprecedented amount of resources was channelled into military use" (Sella 1974:384). The "favorite Latin tag of the period," according to Howard (1976:27), was *"pecunia nervus belli"* (money is the nerves of war). Only the core powers could afford to engage in the new style of war,[44] and small political units could not muster the wealth required. War was "an ever-open abyss into which money poured. States of small dimensions went under" (Braudel 1984: 61).[45]

Strategically, a central rule in this era was to "always take the battle on to the enemy's territory, taking advantage of the weaker or the less strong" (Braudel 1984:61). This avoided the cost of damage from the new weapons and tactics in the home country, if not the cost of waging war itself at a distance. But even those latter costs could often be reduced by living off the enemy's countryside.

At the outset of this era, cavalry (the heart of war-making in the Middle Ages) was still regarded as "the most important instrument of battle" (Taylor [1921] 1973:8) but began to be displaced by infantry, guns, and artillery (Sella 1974:385). Artillery had made its appearance in this era, but its initial "effectiveness was slight compared with [its] heavy cost" (Howard 1976:30). By the end of the sixteenth century a single

43. Denis (1979:155) argues that the political-military structures of the Italian cities were inadequate in the context of the "new European reality."
44. Indeed, Braudel (1984:58) states that such a style of warfare was not even effective outside the core.
45. See also Braudel (1972:840ff.) on the ruinous costs of war in this era.

artillery gun required sixty horses to draw it and its ammunition carts. "The effect of these lumbering convoys on the movement of armies over the unsurfaced roads of Europe may be well imagined" (Howard 1976:31). Artillery played a lesser role, though a necessary one in the case of seige warfare, up until the Thirty Years' War (1618–48).

Artillery had looked promising at the beginning of the era when it proved effective against fortifications (feudal society had been structured around fixed fortifications). Previously, only a long, slow siege could guarantee the defeat of a castle. In 1494 Charles VIII of France used artillery to bring Italian fortresses to terms in short order (Howard 1976:35). But defenses also adopted artillery and were able to keep the offense at bay with the help of redesigned fortifications ("the arrangement of mutually supporting bastions projecting from the walls").[46] These fortifications "began to develop into that system of continuous frontiers" that emerged in the seventeenth century. The new defenses blunted the offense, because the fortifications could neither be taken by assault nor bypassed (leaving supply lines vulnerable) but had to be masked by leaving a force behind (weakening the main force) or besieged (losing much time).[47]

Thus, after the changes in warfare that had occurred around the beginning of this era (about 1500), there followed a "prolonged" and "indecisive" period of warfare in Europe that lasted through the rest of the era, until the Thirty Years' War (Howard 1976:37). Howard (1976:34, 26) writes of "the virtual disappearance of major battles from European warfare" from 1534 to 1631. Big battles were replaced with "a long succession of sieges."[48]

Cautious professional competence took the place of the quest for glory in the planning and conduct of campaigns . . . ; and not the least effective way of terminating a campaign successfully was to prolong it, avoiding battle and living off the enemy's country until his money ran out, his own mercenaries deserted and he had to patch up the best peace he could (p. 27).

Long Waves and North-South Wars

The war peaks corresponding with long wave upswings in this era all consist of north-south wars. These north-south wars recur on each long wave until the ultimate resolution of the north-south struggle. The first war peak was the First and Second Wars of Charles V, the Hapsburg ruler, against France and England in 1521–29. Charles V became king of Spain in 1516 and emperor of the Holy Roman Empire in 1519. His Hapsburg forces made war against France with initial success. Francis I of

46. "Fortifications of this kind, at first improvised ad hoc by the Italian cities in the last decade of the fifteenth century, spread all over Europe during the next fifty years" (Howard 1976:35).

47. And "for sixteenth-century armies time was money, and money meant, or failed to mean, troops" (Howard 1976:36).

48. "By the end of the Italian wars in 1529 the broad outlines of siegecraft had been established" (Howard 1976:36). Siege warfare, relying heavily on tunnels, mines, and above all trench warfare, was a "tedious, dangerous, murderously unhealthy" business, not unlike the later conditions in World War I (p. 36).

France was taken prisoner in battle in 1525, and the peace agreement of 1529 went against France.[49]

A lull coincided with the long wave downswing, and the fighting between the Hapsburgs and France began again in 1542, near the start of the next long wave upswing. This next upswing (1539–59) culminated in the second war peak—the Fifth War of Charles V against France (1552–56) and its continuation in the Franco-Spanish war (1556–59). In these wars, France and Spain battled to a standoff by 1557, when both declared bankruptcy due to the costs of war (Wallerstein 1974:183, 185; Braudel 1972:943). The treaty of Cateau-Cambresis in 1559 followed from this exhaustion and marks the end of the long wave upswing. The negative impact of Spain's bankruptcy in particular was felt throughout Europe, weakening the extended Hapsburg empire, especially Germany (Wallerstein 1974:185–86). Cateau-Cambresis "led directly to the beginning of Spain's decline," according to Wallerstein (p. 185).[50]

The long wave downswing after 1559 saw a decrease in great power wars, but at the outset of the following upswing, in 1572, the Dutch rebelled against Spain. The third war peak was the War of the Armada,[51] pitting (Hapsburg) Spain against England and the rebellious Dutch, in 1585–1604. A truce in the Dutch-Spanish fighting prevailed during the next long wave downswing, from 1609 to 1621, but the war resumed in 1621 (along with the Thirty Years' War) at the start of the next upswing. The fourth war peak was the Thirty Years' War, 1618–48, which saw the northern countries finally break the power of the Hapsburg countries. Each war peak in this era, then, pitted the southern Hapsburg countries against the northern powers.[52]

North-South Military Competition

Militarily, Europe was divided on a north-south basis. This division became more polarized as the era went on and culminated in the great war at the end of the era, the Thirty Years' War.

Initially, naval predominance was held by the south, first by Portugal and then by Spain. Wallerstein (1980:64) stresses the naval predominance of Spain during most of the era, arguing that even after the "invincibility" of Spain was disproved in the War of the Armada (1588), Spain's navy was still, in 1600, larger than the English

49. The draining effect of the war peak is illustrated by the sack of Rome for plunder in 1527 (after the treaty of Madrid in 1526), by the unpaid imperial army.

50. Wallerstein (1974:184) argues that 1557 marks the defeat of the attempt of the Hapsburgs to "recreate political empires that would match the [expanded] economic arena." He says that "a whole world had come tumbling down." But it seems to me that the treaty of 1559 was indecisive in the sense that bankruptcy on both sides halted the fighting without resolving the central issues—a situation somewhat analogous to that of World War I some centuries later. Thus not long afterwards the same battle lines began to be drawn.

51. See Howarth (1981) and Mattingly (1962).

52. Each of the final three successive long wave peaks in this era is emphasized by one or another scholar as important turning points in the European power balance: 1557 for Wallerstein (1980); 1579–1609 for Modelski (1978); and 1618–48 for Wight (1977), Wallerstein (1983), and others.

Figure 13.8. Europe Around 1610

Source: Steinberg (1966: 1).
Reproduced from THE THIRTY YEARS' WAR and the Conflict for European Hegemony, 1600-1660, by S. H. Steinberg, by permisssion of W. W. Norton & Company, Inc. Copyright (c) 1966 by S. H. Steinberg.

and Dutch navies combined. It was not until 1645, when the Dutch gained control of the Baltic Sound (through which passed their ''mother trade'') that Dutch naval power triumphed (Wallerstein 1980:64).

On land Spain was also a formidable power and was closely allied with Austria throughout the era. The Hapsburgs—centered on the Spain-Austria alliance—thus had one of the two great land armies on the Continent. The second great land army belonged to France, the central power on the northern side of the European division. Wight (1977:137) calls the Hapsburgs and the French the ''superpowers'' in a bipolar order. The strongest naval power in the north, emerging as a formidable force in this era, was England.[53] England eventually aligned with France as the polarization of Europe proceeded in this era.

The Hapsburgs unified Austria, Spain, and the Netherlands in the early sixteenth century (redivided but still allied after 1556) and also gained effective control of Italy. This threatened to encircle France, but France also stood between Spain and its prized possession, the Netherlands (see fig. 13.8). Spanish troops had to follow a circuitous route from Italy to the Netherlands, inside what is today France (see fig. 13.9).

53. Dehio ([1948] 1962) particularly stresses England's role.

Figure 13.9. Spanish Military Corridors, circa 1600

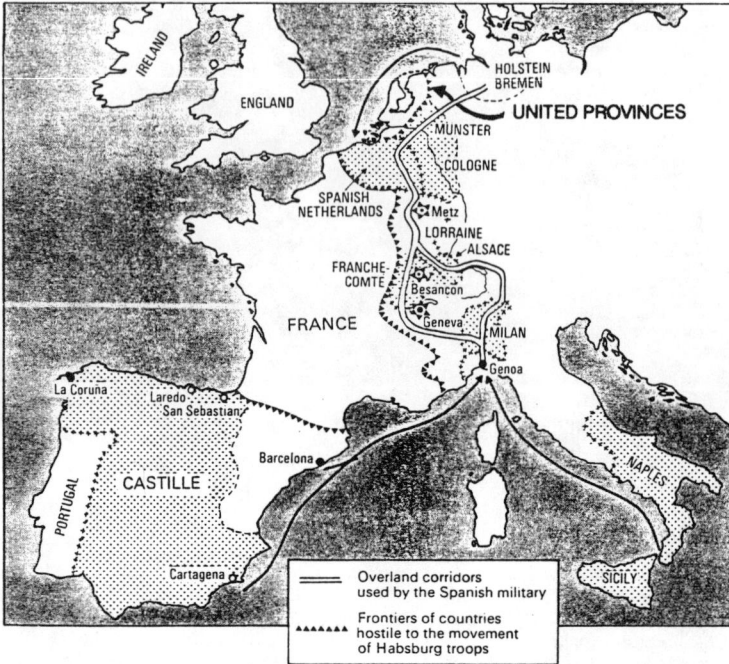

Note: Map indicates logistical system for Spanish war effort, with routes over Alps and up to North Sea. Holstein was an area of recruitment of soldiers for the Flanders army.

Source: Geoffrey Parker, *The Army of Flanders and the The Spanish Road, 1567-1659*; 1971, p. 51. Reprinted in Braudel (1984: 203). Copyright Cambridge University Press. Reprinted by permission.

When Spain under Philip II took over Portugal in 1580—thereby consolidating in one family alliance the two great overseas trading empires along with the bulk of European land power—the Hapsburgs reached their pinnacle and were well on their way to taking full control of the European "world."[54]

The reaction to the Hapsburg expansion came from the north of Europe and largely overlapped the division between northern Reformation and southern Catholicism. Two northern revolts played an important role in the period leading up to the decisive showdown of 1618–48. First, the Netherlands rebelled against Spain, and although the southern (Spanish) Netherlands[55] reunified with Spain fairly quickly, the northern United Provinces won independence after an eighty-year struggle. The second revolt came from the mostly northern Protestant princes in Germany, who rebelled

54. Braudel (1984:55) downplays this "spectacular" but "anachronistic" achievement of the Hapsburgs; Wallerstein (1974:165) calls it a "valiant attempt to absorb all of Europe" that "failed."
55. Roughly corresponding to modern Belgium.

against Hapsburg rule as embodied in the fragmented Holy Roman Empire to which they still nominally belonged.[56]

Thus in the last part of this era both the Spanish and Austrian Hapsburgs faced revolts in northern territories. This increased the north-south polarization of Europe: France, England, the Netherlands, and Sweden on one side and Austria, Spain, and Portugal on the other. The decisive showdown between these blocs came with the hegemonic war of 1618–48, the Thirty Years' War.

Hegemonic War

As Rabb (1981a:ix) notes, the designation of the Thirty Years' War is only shorthand for a set of overlapping wars among the European powers: the Dutch war of independence against Spain of 1568–1648, the Franco-Spanish war of 1635–59, and others. The majority of the fighting took place in Germany, and the dates of that fighting, 1618–48, have come to stand for all the wars of the first half of the seventeenth century. But in fact the fighting raged throughout the European "world" and is sometimes referred to broadly as "the crisis of the seventeenth century" (see fig. 13.10).

"Above all," writes Rabb (1981a:x), "the wars of the early seventeenth century have been regarded, ever since their own day, as one of the worst catastrophes in history." There has been much debate in recent years about the true extent of the war and its effect on society and economy[57] as well as on the causes of the war.[58] Despite these continuing debates, the main points concerning the war for present purposes are clear—that the war took place on a scale previously unknown (Levy's data confirm this); that it caused tremendous economic losses, particularly in Germany; and that it ended with the defeat of the Hapsburgs by the northern coalition.

The scale of the Thirty Years' War is important in classifying it, along with the Napoleonic wars and World Wars I and II, as one of the three "great wars" of the five-century period. Rabb (1975:119) refers to the "frightful specter of total anarchy raised by the new military tactics, the unprecedented slaughter." He stresses the perception of the war by its contemporaries as an unprecedented human disaster, as reflected in paintings and writings from that period. Langer (1978) captures this spirit in a book filled with pictures of the war as seen by contemporaries. The images of wholesale destruction of civilian society are familiar to us inhabitants of the twentieth century. Figure 13.11, an etching from 1633, conveys this gruesome atmosphere.[59] Howard (1976:37) writes that "warfare seemed to escape from rational control . . . and to degenerate instead into universal, anarchic, and self-perpetuating violence." Mercenary forces could survive only by plundering the civilian population, and

---

56. Wallerstein (1974:186) suggests that this German revolt, nationalist in character, was a reaction to the decline of the Hapsburgs beginning with the Spanish bankruptcy of 1557.

57. Rabb (1962; 1975; 1981b); Steinberg (1966:2–3).

58. Polišenský (1981); Wedgwood (1981); Mehring (1981).

59. The "looters" being hanged are no doubt civilians deprived of their livelihood by the war and essentially competing with soldiers for subsistence.

Figure 13.10. The General Crisis of the 17th Century

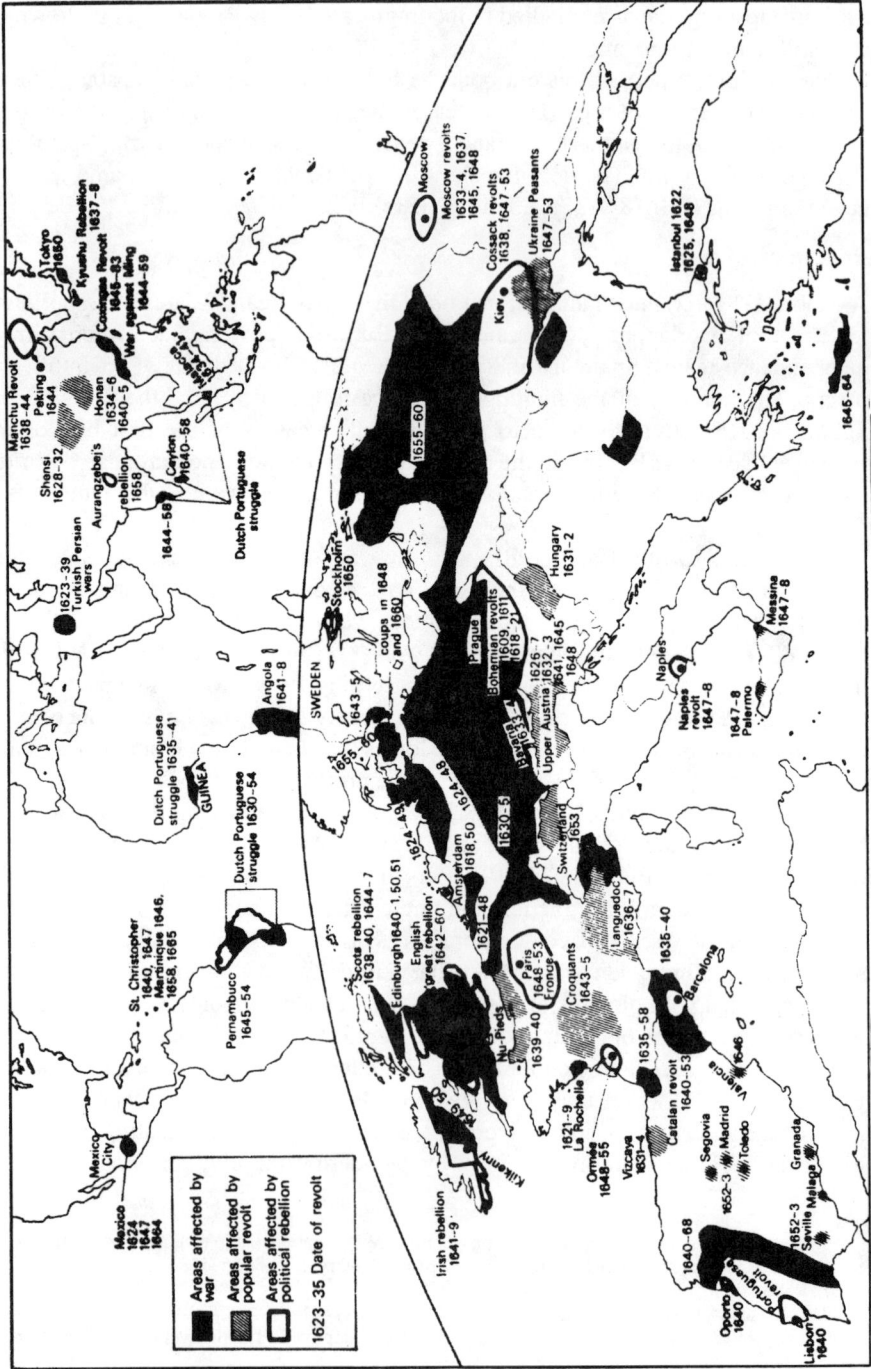

Source: (Parker & Smith, 1978: 5)   The General Crisis of the 17th Century   (London: Routledge & Kegan Paul).

Figure 13.11. "The Hanging", Jacques Callot, 1633

Note (from Mehring, 1981: 14): Jacques Callot (1592-1635), a seventeenth century master of etching, received a number of commissions from princes who wanted representations of heroic moments in battle. Near the end of his life, however, he became deeply unhappy about the effects of warfare, and in 1633 he produced two magnificent series of etchings entitled *The Miseries of War*. *The Hanging*, his most famous, depicts a mass execution of looters, surrounded by the panoply of war and religion, a scene almost certainly inspired by a real incident.

Reprinted courtesy of The Art Museum, Princeton University. Bequest of Junius S. Morgan.

311

civilians in turn could survive only by turning mercenary. "A soldier, in this period, was well described as a man who had to die so as to have something to live on" (Howard 1976:37).

The war and its accompanying hardships, including famine and plague, reduced the German population by as much as one-third and put a severe strain on the entire European economy. It ended the period of economic prosperity of the sixteenth century and inaugurated the "unusually prolonged depression"[60] (or at least long-term secular stagnation) of 1650–1750.

The Thirty Years' War brought, predictably, huge increases in tax burdens. Tilly (1981:119) estimates that the amount of time a taxpaying French household worked for the government may have tripled in the seventeenth century.[61] Tax resistance also rose. "Warmaking and statemaking" took place at the expense of ordinary people and "placed demands on land, labor, capital, and commodities" already committed for other uses (Tilly 1981:121).

The political effect of the war was primarily to break the power of the Hapsburgs and shift the center of European military and economic power northward. Wedgwood ([1938] 1981:31) claims that "the war solved no problem . . . it is the outstanding example in European history of meaningless conflict." But in fact major changes in the structure of European international relations emerged from the war. As Steinberg (1966:1–2) notes, the war brought to a close the "struggle for European hegemony between Bourbon and Habsburg" that lasted from 1609 to 1659 and succeeded, from France's point of view, in breaking France's encirclement by the Hapsburgs.

At the outset of the war, the anti-Hapsburg camp was "a free grouping of 'maritime' powers under the leadership of the United Netherlands," the latter having broken away from Spain (Polišenský 1978:12). From 1621 on, the Netherlands used financial subsidies to enlarge the coalition, which culminated in the Hague Coalition of 1625 (Netherlands, England, Denmark, and Norway, among others). Denmark collapsed in 1629, and Sweden entered the coalition in its place. France supported the coalition unofficially beginning in 1631. After 1635 the anti-Hapsburg German princes played an increasing role, and France took over leadership of the coalition from the Dutch, who eventually withdrew along with England (whose civil war began in 1642). In 1648 the Peace of Westphalia was concluded, giving major concessions to France and Sweden at the expense of the Hapsburgs.[62]

Westphalia was a restructuring of international relations based on the principle of

60. Slicher van Bath's phrase, from Wallerstein (1980:3).
61. The Thirty Years' War brought "a spectacular rise in the per capita tax burden" in France. The French government "raised money for its military purchases in a variety of ways"—through forced loans, sale of offices, confiscations, "and a number of other devices to which officials increasingly applied their ingenuity as the seventeenth century wore on. But . . . one form of taxation or another provided the great majority of the essential funds" (Tilly 1981:119).
62. The Treaty of the Pyrenees (1659) completed this settlement.

balance of power and giving predominance to the northern coalition that had defeated the Hapsburgs. Albrecht-Carrié (1965:40) writes that Westphalia

registered the final failure of the unitary tendency in Europe. For, if Westphalia registered a French success and a corresponding Habsburg setback, it did not substitute one hegemony for another, but established instead an equilibrium of forces. What is more, this condition of equilibrium came to be recognized and accepted until it was enshrined as the desirable principle which was the strongest guarantee of . . . the equal right of all to separate existence.

Thus "Westphalia is usually spoken of as the event that marks the birth of the European state system."

But Wight (1977:152) seems closer to the mark in calling Westphalia not the birth but the "coming of age" of the states system, culminating more than a century of previous political development. By 1648 a "system of states acknowledging, and to some extent guaranteeing, each other's existence" had crystallized (Tilly 1975:45). "Over the next three hundred years," Tilly adds, "the Europeans and their descendants managed to impose that state system on the entire world."

CHAPTER FOURTEEN

Continuity and Change: Since 1648

The Second Era, 1648–1815

The second era began with the victory of the northern bloc, dominated by the Netherlands, England, and France, over the southern Hapsburg bloc, dominated by Austria and Spain. The Netherlands had won independence from Spain after an eighty-year struggle.[1]

Dutch Hegemony

Wallerstein (1980) dates Dutch economic hegemony from about 1625 to 1675.[2] At the peak of Dutch hegemony, in the second half of the seventeenth century, "the volume of Dutch-owned shipping considerably exceeded Spanish, Portuguese, French, English, Scottish and German combined" (Glamann 1974:452). The Dutch fleet—as large as all the other European fleets put together—consisted of six thousand ships and about fifty thousand crewmen, "fantastic figures for the time" (Braudel 1984:190). Amsterdam was the undisputed commercial center of the world.

Seaborne trade, including both the Baltic and Asian trade, was firmly in Dutch hands at the outset of this era. The Baltic trade continued to be the "mother trade" and was Amsterdam's lifeline to such needed supplies as grain, wood, metals, and fish—both for the Dutch's own use and for reexport to other areas. Of particular importance was imported grain for home consumption; grain was also shipped on to the Mediterranean. Already in the sixteenth century, 60 percent of the Baltic trade had been in Dutch hands, and this dominance continued through most of the seventeenth century despite British attempts to break in (Wallerstein 1980:52). In exchange for grain, the Dutch shipped textiles and pepper, among other items, to the Baltic. The Baltic trade linked Amsterdam and Danzig, the latter well-suited as a grain-exporting terminus (Glamann 1974:458). In the seventeenth and eighteenth centuries, according to Glamann (p. 457), the Amsterdam exchange determined the grain prices for Europe.[3]

1. The southern Netherlands (roughly what is now Belgium) remained Spanish.
2. As discussed earlier, Wallerstein considers hegemony a "momentary summit" in which "a given core power can manifest *simultaneously* productive, commercial, and financial superiority *over all other core powers*" (Wallerstein 1980:39). Dutch productive advantage preceded 1625, and financial advantage extended beyond 1675, according to Wallerstein.
3. However, in this era Baltic grain trade did not keep expanding as it had in the era before 1650. "Southern and western Europe seem [after 1650] to have become more self-sufficient in grain" (Glamann

In the Asian trade, the Dutch faced competition from the British. The English East India Company had been founded in 1600, and the Dutch East India Company in 1602 (Glamann 1974:516). Trade with Asia in this era concentrated on imports (Glamann 1974:447). Bullion was sent to Asia in exchange for silk, pepper, and spices. Then Indian textiles began to replace spices and pepper on Europe's import list, accounting for over 40 percent of the Dutch East India Company's imports by 1700. In the 1720s to 1740s, imports of coffee and tea became important, reaching about 25 percent of the company's imports (Glamann 1974:447).

Dutch control of shipping concentrated world trade at Amsterdam, turning the city into a "warehouse" for the world. Braudel (1984:236) writes that "the warehouses of Amsterdam could absorb and then disgorge any amount of goods." The Bank of Amsterdam, created in 1609, was the central institution of a large financial sector connected with the "warehouse" trade.

The Dutch also pioneered the global "triangular trade," a trade innovation that reduced warehousing and increased efficiency. Silver could be shipped directly from America to Asia to be traded for spices and tea, which could be shipped back to Amsterdam. An earlier version of this seems to have occurred in the Baltic trade, with ships sailing from Amsterdam to Brouage to buy salt, then to the Baltic to sell salt and buy grain and timber, which went back to Amsterdam (Glamann 1974:458). The triangular trade was widely used by France, Britain, and the American colonies later in the era.[4]

Dutch hegemony, according to Wallerstein, rested on productive superiority, particularly in shipbuilding. The shipyards at Saardam could turn out a warship every week at peak production (Braudel 1984:191). Wallerstein (1980:40, 55) stresses the importance of controlling the Baltic trade, which provided Amsterdam with shipbuilding materials. The advantage in shipbuilding in turn helped the Dutch control the Baltic trade, creating a "circular reinforcement of advantage."[5]

As mentioned in the last chapter, during the previous era the Dutch had built up a lead in the design of ships that were cheaper to *operate* (requiring smaller crews). This advantage seems to have persisted in the second era. A French report from 1696 stated that Dutch ships of 250–400 tons needed only twelve to eighteen crewmen, compared to eighteen to twenty-five men on a French ship of similar size (Braudel 1984:191). Between the lower production costs and the lower operating costs, Dutch shipping outcompeted that of all other countries. Warships as well as commercial ships could be built cheaply (and the revenues from commerce could support a navy

---

1974:464). Agriculture also picked up in England, supporting increased English grain exports. Wallerstein (1980:280) says a shift of agricultural production from the periphery to the core took place. It is not clear to me why this occurred.

4. Wallerstein (1980:51). In the British version, British manufactures were sent to the North American colonies, which sent lumber and provisions to the West Indies, which sent sugar and tobacco to England (Wallerstein 1980:237). In the American colonies' version, slaves were shipped from Africa to the Caribbean, which sent molasses to the northern colonies, which sent rum to Africa.

5. Braudel (1984:191) stresses access to easy credit, in addition to access to naval stores from the Baltic and technological superiority in shipbuilding, as a Dutch advantage.

disproportionate to the small size of the Dutch population), so the Dutch were able to take over the Asian trade routes from Portugal by military force. This gave the Netherlands control of both the intra-European and long-distance trades.

Dutch agricultural technology was quite advanced, concentrating on industrial crops rather than food crops (Wallerstein 1980:41). Among these were dyes, which were produced more cheaply there than anywhere else and which allowed the Netherlands to build up a substantial industry of importing British cloth, dying it, and reexporting it at twice the value.

The Dutch also excelled in their own textile production. Dutch industrial production, primarily textiles, expanded fivefold between 1584 and 1664 (Wallerstein 1980:42). The import of grain from the Baltic allowed the Netherlands to concentrate on industrial crops, and in turn the production of such export goods as textiles gave the Dutch something to trade for the grain. In sum, Wallerstein (1980:44) says that "no other country showed such a coherent, cohesive, and integrated agro-industrial complex."

The role of the Dutch state in Dutch hegemony is controversial. Tilly (1975:45) argues that Holland was economically central but "did not mount a particularly strong state" and that this makes the Netherlands an exception to Wallerstein's assertion that state-making is more likely to succeed in the core (where the flow of resources from the periphery supports it) than in the periphery. Wallerstein, however, argues that the Netherlands did indeed have a strong state, and Braudel (1984:203) agrees that "the United Provinces had . . . a strong state" as demonstrated by their very often playing the "leading role" in the Thirty Years' War.

Hegemonic Decline

Militarily as well as economically, the second era after 1648 began with Dutch predominance. But as Europe recovered from the Thirty Years' War, the Dutch immediately faced military and economic competition from two of its winning coalition partners in that war, England (Davis 1975) and France. Wallerstein (1980: 80) attributes Dutch military decline to the rising costs of warfare, which had made a quantum jump in the Thirty Years' War (chapter 13). The Netherlands was too small, in total population and total economic strength, to support the costs of great power war, even with the wealth derived from trade.

Directly after the end of the Thirty Years' War, the English began moving against Dutch trade, restricting imports from the Netherlands in the Navigation Act of 1651[6]—a move designed to cripple the Amsterdam "warehouse" trade, according to Wallerstein (1980:78).

War broke out between the Dutch and English in the following year, 1652, and twice more in the next two decades. An English general, when asked the reason for

6. This was the period of strong mercantilist sentiment, as captured by an English Writer around 1651: "What nation soever can attaine to and continue the greatest trade and number of shipping will get and keepe the Sovereignty of the Seas, and consequently the greatest Dominion of the World" (Howard 1976:46).

declaring war on the Dutch, said: "What matters this or that reason? What we want is more of the trade the Dutch now have" (Howard 1976:47). Thus, as the late seventeenth century wore on, there emerged what Howard (p. 38) calls the Wars of the Merchants—naval battles in the North Sea between England and the Netherlands in which both sides began to learn "organized naval tactics and strategy" (p. 47). The British navy generally got the better of these encounters.[7]

Meanwhile, in 1667 the French invaded the Spanish (southern) Netherlands and by 1672 nearly conquered the Dutch republic as well. Thus the Dutch were not militarily strong enough to stand up to the British on the sea and could barely hold off the French on land, despite their trade-derived wealth. And the failure to secure superiority at sea undercut the basis of that wealth.

The Dutch military decline occurred rapidly in the decades following the Thirty Years' War. I find this no mystery. In 1648, Dutch hegemony rested in part on Dutch superiority but also largely on the weakness of other powers. The Netherlands had sat out the last years of the Thirty Years' War, which had drained much of Europe, and had taken advantage of the war to take over other countries' trade. Meanwhile the Hapsburgs were defeated. England had been engaged in civil war for six years. France had borne heavy costs toward the end of the Thirty Years' War and was still at war with Spain. But none of this would last, and as other great powers rebuilt their strength, the Dutch lead evaporated. Wallerstein (1980:80) argues that until 1672, England and France both saw the Dutch as their primary threat, while after that date "the Dutch suddenly became a secondary factor" and the English and French turned on each other.

Economic decline seems to have set in more gradually than military decline for the Netherlands. But by the late seventeenth century, Dutch textile industry was "running into trouble" (Wallerstein 1980:91). The industry was located in the towns, where taxes and labor costs were high, while the textile industries in other countries had moved to the countryside to avoid these costs. "The town, with its restrictive guild system, its higher taxation, and its greater hazards of plague, fire, and enemy action, was not a place where the enterprising organiser of industry could thrive" (Pennington 1970:55).[8] Dutch shipbuilding also declined in the last decades of the seventeenth century, just as English shipbuilding was rapidly expanding.[9]

Dutch decline in *trade* proceeded more slowly. As late as 1786, almost all of the fifteen hundred ships arriving in Amsterdam (from Prussia, Russia, France, America, and elsewhere) were Dutch-registered (Braudel 1984:238).[10] The market value

---

7. The reasons for British advantage are not obvious.

8. Other than this shift to the countryside, European industry did not register striking changes in the 17th c., except in mining and metalworking, where the demands of war stimulated rapid growth in copper and then iron mining (Pennington 1970:59).

9. North American shipbuilding also became quite competitive in the late 17th to mid-18th c. since low lumber costs more than compensated for high wages. By 1775, nearly a third of all ships registered in Britain as British-owned had been built in the northern colonies (Wallerstein 1980:240).

10. Glamann (1974:443) writes that Dutch trade "was finished" after 1730; this seems overstated since Amsterdam seems to have remained a strong trade center for at least several decades more.

of goods shipped from the East Indies to Amsterdam nearly quadrupled from the mid-seventeenth to the mid-eighteenth century (Van Dillen 1974:203). As Pennington (1970:60) puts it, after Amsterdam's preeminence had been established in the early sixteenth century, "not even the incessant rivalry of England and then of France could do more than slowly erode it."

In the Asian trade, the Dutch "had to fight a constant and in the end losing battle" (Pennington 1970:60). But most of the trade of the European world economy was still concentrated within Europe itself, and it was in this intra-European seaborne trade, rather than the long-distance trade, that the Dutch proved strongest and most enduring.

Dutch economic strength, ironically, may have been prolonged by military decline, which diverted the attentions of Britain and France to each other and spared the Netherlands the costs of war. In the Seven Years' War (1755–63), Dutch neutrality paid off in "unparalleled commercial prosperity" (Braudel 1984:269), as the Dutch moved in to capture French trade routes in America.[11]

But as the era progressed, through the eighteenth century, Britain gained greater and greater trade predominance, while the Netherlands declined. By the late eighteenth century, European trade networks encompassed the coastal areas throughout the world, and the British network predominated (Braudel 1984:28).[12]

Finally, financial decline followed, perhaps a century behind military decline. Dutch finance was shaken by three major credit crises between 1763 and 1783 (Braudel 1984:267)[13] Dutch capital had gradually shifted from industry to commerce to finance, and much of it ended up invested in England—280 million florins by 1782, compared to 425 million invested in the Netherlands themselves (Braudel 1984:267).

British-French Rivalry

As Dutch hegemony declined, Britain and France competed to fill the gap.[14] Competition to achieve greater economic strength (through production and trade) was an important component of British-French rivalry. The country that became strongest economically would likely come out on top in the next hegemonic war. The English seem to have won the economic contest for three main reasons, despite the considerable strengths of France—in particular France's larger population and resource base and its self-sufficiency in both wood and iron.

First, England's forests began to run out before those of France—a blessing in disguise, because while France was still comfortable using wood for fuel, England switched to coal. As mentioned in chapter 13, this favored the development of large-

11. The English had done the same to the Dutch during the long continental wars of the early 17th c. (Wallerstein 1980:77).
12. Braudel (1984:273) calls the treaty of 1784 with England "the knell of Dutch greatness."
13. On the long wave downswing of 1762–90.
14. See Kindleberger (1964). The military aspects of this competition will be discussed later in this chapter.

scale manufacturing. The shortage of wood also encouraged England to take over aggressively the Baltic trade from the Dutch in order to secure high-quality masts for shipbuilding (as well as Swedish iron).

Second, England, a compact, island nation, was pushed toward seaborne trade at a time when sea transport was becoming cheaper than land transport (Wallerstein 1980:104). The "tyranny of distance" in France (Braudel 1984:316) is conveyed by the fact that in 1765 it took three weeks to cross France by land. Braudel (1984:315) calls France "a victim of her size."

A third factor, stressed by Wallerstein, is the structure of the state. Wallerstein (1980:101) argues that both England and France expanded their industrial production in the eighteenth century at roughly comparable rates. Thus, it was the

steady increase in the relative strength of the English state—rather than significant differences [which were minor (p. 90)] in how French and English production was organized in the period from 1600 to 1750 or in their value systems—that accounted for the ability of England to outdistance France decisively in the period from 1750 to 1815 (p. 288).

By the late eighteenth century, France's national product (GNP) was still more than double that of England (due to France's larger size), but England's budget was almost equal to France's. The English, by using indirect taxation of consumer goods and by benefiting from a high *per capita* GNP, were able to concentrate in their national government (whence it could be used for military purposes) a greater proportion of the national wealth than did the French.

Much of the British-French competition in this era centered on access to wealth from the extra-European periphery. By 1700 European colonies extended around the globe, but the largest and most extensively colonized areas were the Americas (see fig. 14.1). There was intense competition between the Netherlands, England, France, Spain and Portugal in this era for trade in America, particularly in the Caribbean, which had become a production center for tropical agriculture using slave labor. The Caribbean became in the late seventeenth century "the haven of pirates and buccaneers" (Wallerstein 1980:157). Ships from one country were not safe from seizure by other countries (a strategy dating back to Sir Francis Drake's seizures of Spanish ships in the Caribbean a century earlier). Contraband smuggled to the English through Jamaica broke the Spanish monopoly on trade with the Caribbean region (Wallerstein 1980:159). These British successes in America strengthened its position relative to France.

Despite the high visibility of the American trade, three-fourths of England's shipping around 1700 was with the nearby areas of Europe—and the highest profit ratios (though only a small portion of total volume) were for Asian trade (Wallerstein 1980:97; Davis 1973a). Pennington (1970:63) estimates that in 1700 England and the Netherlands "were sending perhaps a tenth of their tonnage across the Atlantic, and a little more to the east." Of the total shipping tonnage used for English imports around 1700, half was for timber; on the export side, coal accounted for 60 percent of the shipping tonnage (Glamann 1974:454).

Figure 14.1. European Overseas Empires, circa 1700

Source: Clough (1968: 141) by permission of the McGraw-Hill Book Company.

The era under consideration was one of great trade competition generally because of the decline of Dutch predominance. It is known as the "age of mercantilism." Mercantilism was used by economically weaker countries at all levels of the international hierarchy against stronger ones. Braudel (1984:53) writes that "mercantilism was above all a means of self-defence." A hegemonic power generally promotes "free trade," since its products, being superior and less expensive, can penetrate all markets under such conditions. When, in the eighteenth century, Britain moved away from its earlier mercantilist stance (epitomized by the Navigation Acts), Braudel (1984:53) takes it as a sign that "Britain's power and greatness on a world scale had dawned," and by 1846 Britain "could embrace free trade without running any risk at all."

Rising Powers of the Future

While the center of great power rivalry in this era was in Britain and France—the Netherlands being in decline and the southern countries having been defeated in a hegemonic war—new powers were rising at the edges of the European world that would become important only in the next era. The United States became an important economic center in its own right, winning independence in the 1770s and consolidating it in 1812. Japan had asserted its independence from the European "world economy" in 1638 and was following its own path to development—a path that would eventually bring it into the world system as a great power.

Meanwhile, the Russian empire at the outset of this era was completing a major expansion into huge new territories stretching to the Pacific, as illustrated in figure 14.2. In this era, Russia still "tended to manage her affairs on the margins of the rest of Europe, as an autonomous world-economy" (Braudel 1984:442). But Russia's territorial growth would lay the basis for its eventual rise to great power and then superpower status. Russia adopted an unusually strong and dominant state structure in the sixteenth century under Ivan the Terrible (1547–84). Braudel (1984:446) attributes this to the effects of three centuries of war against the Tatars. After defeating the Tatars decisively in 1552, Ivan expanded his empire eastward, and Siberia was opened to conquest beginning with the expedition of 1583 (Braudel 1984:455).

Long Waves in Prices and Wages

The second era, like the first, is divided into several long waves, each with its war peaks (discussed below) and its movements of prices and real wages. Prices showed little secular trend throughout the second era (in contrast to the secular inflation of the first era), until the last upswing of hegemonic war.[15]

Strangely, although the inverse correlation of prices and real wages in the long wave continued in this era, the longer-term trends of both variables declined in this

---

15. This may be due in part to decreasing Spanish imports of silver from America, which peaked in the 1590s and declined throughout the 17th c. (Wilson and Parker 1977:46, 48).

Figure 14.2. Russian Expansion in Siberia, 1550-1660

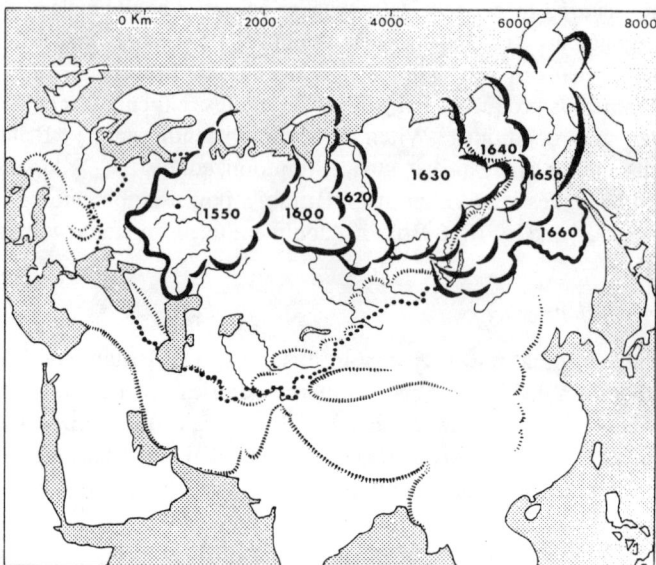

Note: The dotted line indicates the present-day frontier of the USSR.

Source: Braudel (1984: 24).
Map of Russian expansion in Siberia from THE PERSPECTIVE OF THE WORLD, Civilization and
Capitalism 15th-18th Century, Vol. III by Fernand Braudel. Copyright (c) 1984 by William Collins
Sons & Co., Ltd.,and Harper & Row, Publishers, Inc.

era as compared with the previous era. Prices changed from inflation to stationarity,
and real wages went from stationarity to decline.[16] This suggests that the inverse
correlation of prices and wages in the long wave time frame does not hold up over a
longer term.

The secular decline in real wages in this era probably resulted from two influences:
the working people were paying the costs of the new style of larger great power wars
fought by professional armies, and economic surplus was being invested in the early
stages of industrialization to the detriment of immediate consumption. Economic
surplus used for investment in industrial expansion, and for making war, was not
available for improving the lot of the working class. Thus over the course of the
eighteenth century real wages declined. Only in the next era, as great power war
diminished under British hegemony and industrialization reached full swing, did
working-class conditions improve.[17]

16. The estimates of Phelps-Brown and Hopkins ([1956] 1962) for English real wages show that they
declined from a peak of 104 (1736 = 100) in 1744—at the start of the long wave upswing—to a low of 64
in 1772 (ten years past the end of the same long wave upswing), then climbed during the long wave
downswing back to 78 by 1786. On the next upswing, wages again lost ground, to 58 in 1813.
17. I advance these explanations as tentative and partial answers.

Military Evolution

As discussed in the last chapter, the Thirty Year's War, which started this era, ended a long period of stalemate in European war. That stalemated period, which had lasted from the Italian wars at the outset of the first era, was characterized by much siege warfare but few major battles.

In the Thirty Years' War, it will be recalled, mercenary war reached its "nadir of brutality," and war seemed to "escape from rational control" (Howard 1976:37). But, adds Howard, there was "one great exception" from this condition, "the armies of the United Provinces; and they were exceptional for the very simple reason that they were regularly supplied and paid." This allowed the Netherlands to maintain a regular force of *trained* professionals: "The wealth which the Dutch derived from their overseas trade enabled them, almost alone among the states of the early seventeenth century, to keep their force under arms throughout the year" (p. 55). The first thing such an army could be trained to do, which mercenary armies could not, was to dig and maintain high-quality fortifications (Howard 1976). Braudel (1984:203) writes: "Like any self-respecting economic centre, the United Provinces kept war at arm's length: a string of forts along the frontiers reinforced the obstacles created by the many waterways." Well-paid and well-trained troops "had the task of seeing that the Provinces remained an island sheltered from conflict" (Braudel 1984:204).

The second thing the professional army could do was *drill* soldiers, which enabled them to make use of firepower in new and devastating ways (as well as to maintain order in the face of firepower). Maurice of Orange, at the end of the sixteenth century, developed formations of musketeers ten deep "countermarching in their files, reloading as they did so, so that their front rank was always giving continuous fire" (Howard 1976:56). The effect of this war machine on the ragtag mercenary armies of the seventeenth century can be imagined.

Sweden picked up these techniques during the Thirty Year's War and refined them,[18] developing faster reloading so that infantry formations could be only six deep and combining this with a new, lighter, and more mobile artillery developed by the Swedish iron industry. The superiority of the new military system developed by the Netherlands and refined by Sweden was proven in 1631 at Breitenfeld when "the Habsburg forces suffered a cataclysmic defeat which transformed the pattern of power in Europe" (Howard 1976:58). This new military style required discipline and control in order to work, and that required a professional army, which cost money. A quantum leap in the social burden of war had again taken place, as had happened around 1495. An Englishman wrote at the end of the seventeenth century: "Nowadays the whole art of war is reduced to money" (Howard 1976:48).

Where could a state in the seventeenth century find the "ample and continuous supplies of money" needed for warfare in the new style? "Money in the necessary

18. Military service in Sweden lasted 20 years, for one in ten citizens, supporting the existence of a professional army as in the Netherlands.

quantities could come only from trade'' (Howard 1976:37). Howard argues that ''the capacity to sustain war and so maintain political power in Europe became, during the seventeenth century, increasingly dependent on access to wealth either extracted from the extra-European world or created by the commerce ultimately derived from that wealth'' (p. 38). World trade supported Dutch hegemony, and world trade would support British hegemony next. Between the British and their future, however, lay the French.

Long Waves and British-French Wars

This era saw recurring war peaks, on each long wave, in which Britain opposed France. Dutch military decline was already evident by the end of the long wave downswing of 1650 to 1689.[19] Beginning with the next war peak, the rivalry of France and England shaped each major round of great power war. In each long wave, England pulled further ahead of France in controlling world trade and dominating the seas militarily. France repeatedly fought to gain dominance on the Continent but was repeatedly put down—as were the Hapsburgs in the last era—by a succession of coalitions led by England.

The first long wave upswing phase in the era began around 1689. Ralph Davis (1975:5) writes that 1689 opened a new phase in British maritime expansion, ''with French wars that were marked by fierce privateering operations against English merchant shipping.'' These wars first catalyzed Anglo-Dutch cooperation against the French threat.[20] The war peak of the upswing was the War of the Spanish Succession (1701–13), in which France under Louis XIV united with Spain but was defeated by a coalition led by England and including the Netherlands. Wallerstein (1980:188) sees that war as an unsuccessful attempt by Spain to resist English domination. The war also continued British and French efforts to ''destroy each other's trade networks, especially by privateering'' (Wallerstein 1980:188).[21] After the War of the Spanish Succession, the European economy entered another long wave downswing (1720–47), and France and Britain's ''mutual destruction of each other's property'' in the Caribbean ''died down'' (Wallerstein 1980:164).

Figure 14.3 shows the political map of Europe during this period. Spain and Portugal were past their prime and under English domination; Austria-Hungary was a shrunken remnant of past Hapsburg grandeur, although the Ottoman Empire had receded somewhat; Germany and Italy were fragmented; and the Dutch republic was in decline. France had failed in the War of the Spanish Succession but was not knocked out, and only France had the potential to challenge Britain's ascent.

The following upswing from 1747 to 1762 saw the same issues build to a new war

---

19. A particularly long phase, no doubt because of the high toll of the Thirty Years' War on the European economy.

20. Throughout the 18th c., Dutch investments in England helped the English fight wars against the French with minimal economic disruption, a ''symbiotic arrangement between a formerly hegemonic power and the new rising star'' (Wallerstein 1980:281).

21. As had the Anglo-French wars in the Caribbean in 1666–67, 1689–97, and since 1702.

Figure 14.3. Europe in 1740

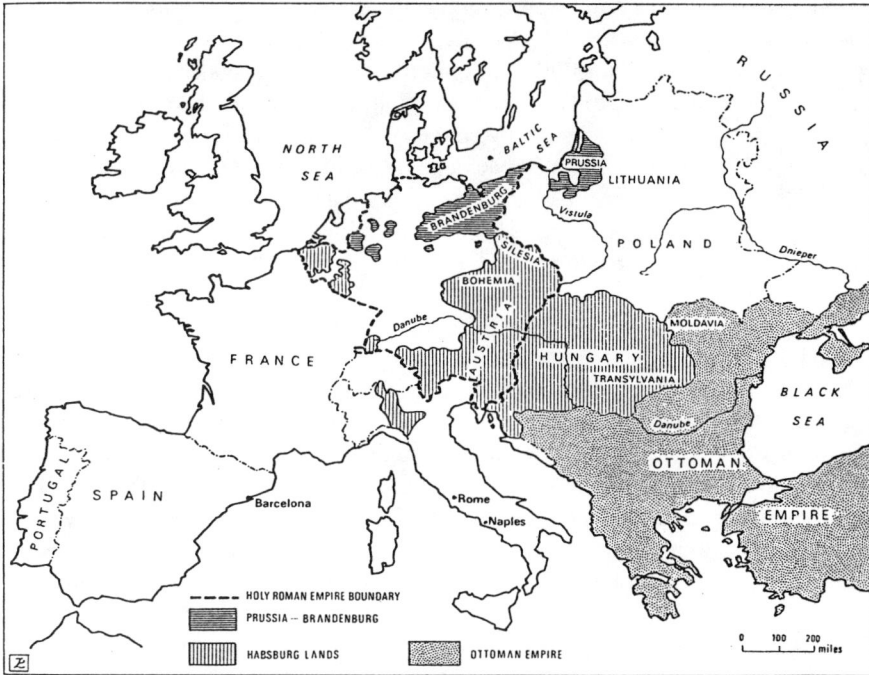

Source: Seaton (1973: 13) by permission of Osprey Publishing LTD.

peak in the Seven Years' War (1756–63). In the Seven Years' War, fought at various locations throughout the world, the British essentially defeated France in the periphery and deprived France of its right to compete outside Europe (Wallerstein 1980: 191; see also Furneaux 1973; Gradish 1980; Kaplan 1968).

The long downswing that followed the Seven Years' War, from 1762 to 1790, was punctuated by one relatively small British-French war, which the French got the better of by 1783.[22] Britain also lost her North American colonies during this downswing, so it was a time of slowdown in the British move toward hegemony. But by the end of the downswing, in 1787, the French were forced to open their ports to English shipping (under the Eden Treaty of 1786), letting in an "avalanche of British goods" (Braudel 1984:380). This coincided, Braudel suggests, with a crisis in French industry, which was "still suffering from antiquated structures." These pressures may have contributed to France's path during the next upswing, 1790 to 1814—a period of hegemonic war that finally resolved the English-French rivalry.

22. In 1772 a French writer said: "We open our campaigns with armies that are neither adequately recruited nor properly paid. Whether they win or lose, both sides are equally exhausted. The National Debt increases, credit sinks, money runs out" (Howard 1976:74). This statement well reflects conditions on a long wave downswing.

Hegemonic War

The French revolutionary and Napoleonic wars represent the last effort of France to avoid British hegemony and, if possible, to dominate Europe itself. At first, the French Revolution seemed to offer an opportunity for France's rivals to do her in. "As the French state sank to its knees the vultures gathered. In 1792 an Austro-Prussian army marched on Paris" (McEvedy 1972:70). The French, however, not only repulsed this attack but struck back and "surged forward all along their eastern frontier," overrunning several neighbors. "This onslaught by forces that had been thought incapable of defence amazed and alarmed Europe. . . . 1793 saw the formation of an anti-French coalition that included just about everyone" (McEvedy 1972:70).

The French fleet proved unable to withstand the British on the seas in 1798 (Aboukir) and 1805 (Trafalgar), but on land France was stronger due to a new military innovation. The professional armies of the other great powers (professional armies that had replaced the mercenary armies of the first era) were countered with French superiority in numbers, gained through a reordering of the state under a revolutionary ideology. The upkeep of regular military forces drained the budgets of other European states, but for revolutionary France a new relationship between the national economy and the war machine was possible. In 1793 all Frenchmen were put "on permanent requisition for military service," and within eighteen months Carnot had put over a million men under arms and obtained "a crushing numerical superiority on every battlefield" (Howard 1976:80). "If men could be conscripted, so also could the resources of the nation to arm, equip, clothe, and feed them; and in order to do so Carnot and his associates attempted to create a planned war economy, based on the fear of the guillotine" (Howard 1976:81).

Furthermore, it became impossible either to demobilize this huge army or to support it on French soil.

The Directory did not much care where the French armies went so long as they and their generals stayed abroad. The young Bonaparte led his starving and ragged forces into Italy in 1796 with a simple promise of plunder. . . . The spirit of romantic heroism . . . thus coexisted happily in the Grande Armée with a more straightforward zest for loot (Howard 1976:82–83).

This style of fighting meant that the army had to stay constantly on the move and had to win all its battles in order to resupply itself from the defeated country. The French army ate its way across Europe like a swarm of locusts:

Carnot, 'the organizer of war', supplied [the French army] with conscripts and munitions at a truly revolutionary rate. As he sent nothing else but men and guns the French had to attack to keep alive. . . . [T]he new state could function only on a war footing and its armies only in an offensive role" (McEvedy 1972:70).

This new kind of war produced battle casualties and civilian suffering on a greater scale than any previous war. Average annual battle fatalities exceeded 150,000— compared with about 88,000 in the Thirty Years' War (see chapter 11).

Ultimately, even France with its large population, area, and resources could not sustain its offensive against a coalition, again led by England, that had grown to include Russia. Within ten years, the "quality of conscripts deteriorated" and "supply became a nagging and insoluble problem," particularly as Napoleon began penetrating less fertile areas of Europe after 1807. Russia had remained outside the European world economy until the eighteenth century, Braudel (1984:27) writes, because "distance was forever taking its revenge." Now that distance took its revenge on Napoleon.

France was decisively and finally beaten on land, and its fleet was decimated by Britain. The Congress of Vienna in 1815 marked another restructuring of the great power system, with Britain assuming a predominant position. France was whittled back, and a "pentarchy" of great powers emerged with Britain in the most powerful role. The congress brought about the restoration of conservative rule after revolutionary challenge: "[t]he Congress asserted one theory of government—the rulers' right to rule—and denied another—the peoples' right to rule themselves" (Albrecht-Carrié 1965:85).[23]

The Third Era, 1815–1945

The third era extends from the end of the Napoleonic wars in 1815 to the end of World War II in 1945. British hegemony seems to have been stronger at the outset and to have lasted longer than Dutch hegemony in the previous era.

British Hegemony

The following sections on British hegemony will rely heavily on Thomson (1950) as a convenient historical summary. I chose Thomson because his periodization of phases of British social development fits my long wave phases (see below).[24]

After 1815, Britain was the strongest country in Western Europe and the Mediterranean and "supreme in the colonial world of North America, the West Indies, and India. The markets of the world lay wide open to her manufactured goods, and the undeveloped areas of the globe to her capital investment" (Thomson 1950:26).

Britain had benefited greatly by having the war fought elsewhere.[25] At the height of the British land expedition to the Continent, the Peninsular War against Napoleon, only forty thousand British lives were lost, of a British population of about thirteen million. High prices hurt the British working class, but "the war had scarcely upset the delightful routine" of the landed gentry (pp. 1, 15).[26]

During this era industrialization proceeded in earnest, and Britain led the way. At the outset of the era, "agriculture was still Britain's largest national industry"

---

23. See also Kissinger (1973).
24. Unlike Wallerstein's and Braudel's accounts, which I relied on heavily in describing Dutch hegemony, Thomson's is not a Marxist account.
25. Thanks to what Dehio would call Britain's "insular" position.
26. On the effects of the war on the British economy, see Mauro (1971:7–10).

Table 14.1. Estimated Real Per Capita National Product

	1700	1760	1800	1820	1830	1840	1850	1860	1870	1880	1890	1900	1910
Great Britain*	333	399	427		498	567	660	804	904	979	1130	1269	1302
Belgium							534	637	738	832	932	1013	1110
Denmark				358	382	402	489	497	563	617	708	850	1050
Germany							418	481	579	602	729	868	958
France					343	392	432	474	567	602	668	784	883
Sweden								292	351	419	469	597	763
Norway								420	441	486	548	605	706
Finland								300	390	407	458	529	561
Italy								451	467	466	466	502	548
Russia								236	252	253	276	342	398

Estimates apply to the boundaries as at the dates shown.
* England and Wales prior to 1800.
    Note that national income levels in 1970 were derived from Kravis
et al., 1978, pp. 236–237, column (5).

Note: Values shown are in 1970 U.S. dollars.
Source: Crafts (1983: 389).   From <u>Explorations in Economic History</u>.

(p. 137), but textiles were a close second, and industry was just beginning to take off. Coal was the main fuel, and the era saw the rapid growth of railroads and steamships.[27] Railroad expansion created demand for coal and iron and stimulated heavy industry, metallurgy, and mining (p. 42). Britain's per capita GNP remained higher than all others during the nineteenth century (see table 14.1).[28]

Throughout the nineteenth century, Britain dominated world trade by any standard. By 1851, more than half the world's tonnage of seaborne shipping was British (Thomson 1950:142). The long wave upswing around 1848 to 1872 saw a particularly rapid increase in this trade, which tripled in volume in just two decades (p. 138). During this upswing period "Britain enjoyed to the full the economic benefits of having become the 'workshop of the world' "—an advantage over other countries that Thomson (p. 101) attributes to successful industrialization, inventiveness, and political stability. By the end of that upswing, British foreign trade was greater than that of France, Germany, and Italy combined (p. 101).

At the beginning of this era, trade with America was crucial to Britain. As noted earlier, exports to America amounted to only about 10 percent of Britain's total around 1700, but this had risen to 37 percent by 1772 (Crouzet 1980:69). But the importance of the American trade seems to have peaked by 1815 (Crouzet 1980:77).

27. Thomson (1950:41) calls the period 1830–50 the "era of railways and steamships in Britain." Railroads became "one of the chief sources of national wealth" (p. 13). Boom years of railway construction occurred in 1836–37 and 1844–47—perhaps a sign of the upturn in capital investment that would be expected about ten years before the long wave price upturn in 1848 (see chap. 12).

28. Unfortunately, data for the Netherlands are of lower quality, and Crafts (1983:394) lists them separately, only from 1870 on. These data show per capita GNP (in 1970 $U.S.) in the Netherlands at 591 in 1870, 707 in 1880, 768 in 1890, 840 in 1900, and 952 in 1910—lagging well behind Britain in this late part of the era.

The slave trade was officially abolished in 1815, though smuggling continued (Braudel 1984:440). In the downswing years after 1815 (the beginning part of this era), British exports to the United States "fluctuate[d] wildly" (Crouzet 1980:73), and the "state of the American market was—at least in the 1830s—the most important single factor in bringing prosperity or depression to British export industries" (Crouzet 1980:75). During the upswing of 1848–72, exports to North America grew more slowly than those to northern Europe. The final years of the price upswing ending in 1872 saw "a big boom in trade."[29] The Suez Canal was opened in 1869. But after 1872, trade stagnated.[30]

Along with its productive advantage and commercial predominance, Britain in this era was also the financial center of the world economy. "Sterling . . . became the money of international finance" (Thomson 1950:140). E. H. Carr writes that the "corollary of an international commodity market was an international discount market, an international market for shipping freights, an international insurance market, and, finally, an international capital market."[31] Thomson (1950:141) argues that "the world economic order, which was regarded by *laissez-faire* economists as part of the natural order, was in fact controlled by a highly centralized authority situated in London." British financial hegemony seems to lag somewhat behind commercial hegemony, as Wallerstein's theory of hegemony suggests. Paris was considered a rival financial center until about 1870.

Long Waves and Phases of British Hegemony

Thomson (1950) divides British history in the extended Victorian age into three phases, each marked by a distinct character.[32] The dividing lines between these phases correspond with turning points of the long wave.[33] First is the postwar generation of 1815–50 (corresponding with the long wave downswing), marked by international peace and the consolidation of government in Britain. Second is the golden age of Victorian Britain, 1851–74 (a long wave upswing), in which a spate of minor great-power wars occurred, free trade reached its peak, and a liberal hegemony prevailed in the British government.[34] The third phase, 1875–1914, combines a long wave downswing and the following upswing and could be broken into subphases on that basis. It was marked by the scramble for colonies as British

29. 1868–74, according to Thomson (1950:139).

30. British exports came to £256 million at their peak in 1872 and did not reach that level again until around 1900. By 1913 the export value had grown again (on the upswing) to £525 million (Thomson 1950:194).

31. Cited in Thomson (1950:141).

32. In this extended period, within Britain three political groupings competed for power—the Tories, Whigs, and Radicals—although the distinctions between them were not "over-sharp" (Thomson 1950: 25). These groupings correspond with the triangle of world views discussed in Part One.

33. Thomson does not note this.

34. This period was marked by "growing material prosperity" and a rising standard of living. The Crystal Palace of 1851 in London, a "Great Exhibition of the Works of Industry of all Nations," symbolized British optimism, internationalism, and prosperity (Thomson 1950:97–100).

hegemony declined (on the long wave downswing) and then the escalation of great power tensions in the prewar generation before 1914 (on the long wave upswing).

The rival philosophies of mercantilism and free trade also seem to follow the long wave in this era.[35] Free trade gained sway on the upswing, and mercantilism on the downswing. The first downswing of this era began with the passage of the Corn Law in Britain (1815), which restricted imports of corn. The first upswing was initiated by the repeal of the mercantilist Navigation Acts (dating from mid-seventeenth century) in 1849. And the next downswing "revived the old policy of protectionism within the Conservative ranks, under the slogan of 'fair trade' " (Thomson 1950:182).[36]

These same long wave periods also seem to reflect an alternation in "social values" (to use Namenwirth's term; see chapter 5). Thomson (1950:119) calls the period from 1846 to 1874 (the long wave upswing) a period of "Liberal hegemony" in British government. The period from 1874 to 1891 (the downswing) Thomson (p. 182) refers to as "Conservative hegemony."[37]

Hegemonic Decline

British hegemony did not decline as quickly as had Dutch hegemony. It was not until the second half of the nineteenth century that Britain began to lose its lead; even then it remained the strongest military and economic power until around the turn of the twentieth century.

British economic decline seems to have accompanied a shift toward production for export. Crouzet (1980:79) cites data showing that British exports grew from about 14 percent of the national product in 1811 to 25 percent by 1871. The greatest acceleration of exports was after 1848, on the long wave upswing—"it was only after 1850 that Britain really became 'an export economy' " (Crouzet 1980:81). By the end of the upswing, around 1872, Britain was exporting something like 40 percent of its wool production, 70 percent of its cotton, and 40 percent of its iron (Crouzet 1980:86). Britain paid the "penalty of industrial leadership" as it became increasingly dependent on food imports—by 1875 nearly half the wheat consumed was imported, and this rose to nearly 70 percent with bad harvests in the late 1870s (on the downswing). The acreage under cultivation in Britain fell by 30 percent from 1871 to 1901 (Thomson 1950:195).

Meanwhile, in the 1850s and 1860s Britain had a great technological lead but, unlike France and the United States, "did not originate any of the great naval

35. Over the longer term, free trade was favored by the hegemonic country at times of greatest productive and commercial hegemony. "The open door . . . was the creed natural to any people which has great natural advantages and a long lead in methods of production. Free competition is of most value to those who need not fear any competition" (Thomson 1950:27).

36. But I wonder if this relationship is specific to the 19th c. with its low great power war severity. Mercantilist measures were used as a source of revenue (and a way to control shipping for security reasons), more than to protect domestic industries. In Britain in the late 1820s, customs and excise contributed £36 million annually, and all other sources of taxation only £13 million (Thomson 1950:78).

37. The five years of Liberal government in this period, in 1880–85, coincided with the temporary upsurge of prosperity between the depressions of the 1870s and 1890s.

developments'' (Thomson 1950:98). In fact, ''naval shipbuilding passed through a baroque phase'' (p. 98).[38] British industrial growth slowed down, from perhaps 3 percent annually to 2 percent in the downswing of the 1870s to mid-1890s (p. 163). Not only Britain but the world experienced a Great Depression from about 1873 to the early 1890s (see Gordon 1978:23).

During the long wave upswing starting around 1893, British exports shot up to record levels, but this increase came primarily in coal exports and ''masked the stagnation in the textile industries and the positive decline in the iron and steel industries'' and did not reverse the agricultural decline (Thomson 1950:194; see also McCloskey 1973).

British overseas financial expansion, based on the export of capital as foreign investments, peaked in the 1848–72 (upswing) period. Britain exported surplus capital amounting to roughly 15 million pounds sterling annually, in addition to reinvesting abroad the earnings from existing foreign investments (about 50 million pounds sterling annually by the 1870s). The situation was reversed after 1872, however. Income from foreign investments was diverted to home consumption in Britain, and surplus capital was directed toward bridging an adverse trade balance rather than toward new foreign investments (Thomson 1950:165). ''No change marks more decisively than this the end of [Britain's] great era of economic expansion'' (p. 166).

By the late 1870s Britain's position was one of

diminished prestige, loss of initiative in foreign diplomacy, and increasing economic dependence . . . , though all these changes were at first masked by the continuing aura of prestige . . . [and] the continued pre-eminence of Britain financially and commercially in the world (p. 163).

Long Waves in Prices and Wages

This era, like the previous one, saw level and even slowly declining prices up until World War I, then very sharp inflation. Prices returned to their pre–World-War-I level only momentarily, if at all, at the height of the depression in the 1930s and then inflated rapidly again in World War II.

Thomson (1950:139, 192) writes that real wages experienced a sudden increase in 1870–73 (around the time of the price downturn) and notes a ''sharp check in the rise of real wages'' between 1900 and 1913 (the price upswing). These fluctuations are consistent with the inverse connection of prices and wages discussed in chapter 12. Around 1910 (late in the long wave upswing), ''class struggle'' seems to have reached a peak throughout the core. This period, Screpanti (1984:512) argues, was ''announced'' by the Russian revolution of 1905, which was followed by a wave of strikes and occasional street fighting in the West—especially France, Italy, and the United States. The peak of industrial unrest and violence came in 1911–15, accord-

38. This might reflect a dampening of innovation on the production upswing, as suggested by long wave theory.

ing to Screpanti (see also Phelps Brown 1975:5). This fits with the theory adduced in chapter 12, in which the late upswing period brings decreasing real wages, rising prices, and stagnating production.

Encouraged by this corroboration, I categorized the points of most visible class struggle, as described in Thomson's (1950) account, according to long wave phases. The results were not convincing, however:

→ Downswing of 1815–48:

1825–35: Remarkable growth in trade union movement (p. 52).
1830: Starving field laborers riot for wage demands (p. 16).
1832: Reform Bill, major Whig Parliamentary reform (p. 73).
1833: Owen's Factory Act passed, regulating child labor, under pressure for more radical reforms (p. 47).
1838–48: Chartist movement; put down in 1848 (p. 83).
1847: Ten-Hour Bill limits working hours of adults (p. 47).

→ Upswing of 1848–72:

1850–70: 10 percent increase in prosperity of working class (p. 144).
1867: Second (Conservative) Parliamentary Reform Bill (p. 126).
1871: Start of new wave of strikes (p. 148).

→ Downswing of 1872–93:

1879: Depression; high unemployment weakens labor (p. 148).
1890s: Big strikes (p. 198).

→ Upswing of 1893–1917:

1910–14: Great strike movement (p. 188).

Thus working-class agitation seems to have peaked toward the end of the first downswing (1838–48), again at the beginning and end of the next downswing (early 1870s and 1890s), and again at the end of the following upswing—not correlating with long waves.

Military Evolution

The decades after 1815 "witnessed the transformation of land and sea transport by the development of the steam engine," and this affected military affairs greatly. The railway eliminated prolonged marches and allowed huge armies to be moved quickly and without exhausting them (Howard 1976:97). The professionalism of the armed forces of the eighteenth century could be combined with the massive armies that had emerged after the French Revolution. In the eighteenth century problems of supply limited the size of armies that could be fielded. While Napoleon transcended those bounds, the disaster in Russia showed that "even this ruthless improvization had its limits. With the introduction of railways these limits disappeared" (Howard 1976: 99).

The new military techniques made possible by steam power were perfected by Germany in its ascent to great power status during the 1860s and 1870s, when Prussia unified Germany. A key ingredient of Prussian success was its General Staff, which coordinated the administrative details of moving large numbers of troops and supplies by railway.[39] In 1870–71 Prussia deployed 1.2 million soldiers against France—not the ragtag million of Napoleon's army but an organized force brought to bear in a coordinated manner. The Prussians also developed breech-loading guns (first used against Austria in 1866 and soon adopted by other European armies) that could be fired both three times as fast as muzzle-loaded guns and from a lying position (Howard 1976:102). And after a poor showing by Prussian artillery in 1866 against Austria, the Prussians also created a new breech-loading steel cannon (developed by Friedrich Krupp), which dominated the battlefield in 1870 against France. France and Austria continued to use brass guns, and Britain used wrought iron, until after 1870–71, but the Prussian steel cannons proved superior (Craig 1964:174).

After the German unification, then, "it was accepted by all the states of Europe that the military effectiveness on which they relied to preserve their relative power and status depended . . . on a combination of the manpower of the population and a strategically appropriate railway network" (Howard 1976:106).

Finally, Germany used nationalism itself as a sort of military innovation, borrowed from France. A group of young officers in the Prussian army became convinced that the Grande Armée had been "something new in warfare" based on "the release of national energies evident in the French revolution" (Howard 1976:86). Nationalist ideology could facilitate raising a large army of "serious, intelligent, reliable patriots" (p. 87). Conscription was introduced throughout Germany in 1813 (during a "burst of patriotic enthusiasm" following Napoleon's defeat in Russia).

By the end of the nineteenth century European society was militarized to a very remarkable degree. War was no longer considered a matter for a feudal ruling class or a small group of professionals, but one for the people as a whole. The armed forces were regarded . . . as the embodiment of the Nation. (Howard 1976:110).

Long Waves and German Ascent

The close correlation of the long wave with great power wars is quite apparent in the nineteenth century. The first downswing, 1815–48, following the Congress of Vienna, was marked by an absence of great power wars and has been called "the Thirty Years' Peace."[40]

The long wave upswing, 1848–72, contained a spate of major wars in Europe, although only one of these involved the British (the Crimean War). This period may be seen as a time of jockeying for position among the European powers without challenging British hegemony itself.

During this upswing, Prussia waged three wars in the decade from 1862 to 1872 to unify Germany as an empire and great power. In 1863–64 Prussia and Austria

39. "This General Staff was perhaps the great military innovation of the nineteenth century" (Howard 1976:100). The Prussian General Staff studied closely the first war that had used railways extensively, that between France and Austria in northern Italy in 1859. A French force of 120,000 troops reached the front in eleven days by rail, as opposed to two months on foot (Howard 1976:97).
40. Harriet Martineau, quoted in Thomson (1950:95).

conquered Schleswig-Holstein, a strategic region at the base of Denmark that controlled the land bridge between the Baltic and North seas. Prussia then defeated Austria in 1866, resolving a long-standing "struggle for supremacy in Germany" (Craig 1964:2).[41] And in 1872, Prussia defeated France largely by virtue of superior organization, supply, and economic base and established the German Empire. The result of this upswing period, then, although it did not upset British hegemony, was a "complete revolution in the balance of power in Europe" with the appearance of a powerful united Germany (Thomson 1950:160).[42] Quigley (1966:211) goes so far as to say that "the unification of Germany . . . ended a balance of power in Europe which had existed for 250 or even 300 years." Nonetheless, up until the 1890s Britain "tended to welcome the rise of Germany" as a counterbalance to France (Quigley 1966:211).

Britain started off this upswing phase of 1848–72 in a more "self-assertive" mood than it ended on.[43] Britain's one major war of the phase, the Crimean War (1853–56), was not successful. The war arose from British and French fears of Russian expansion toward the Mediterranean (which could be blocked by maintaining the Ottoman Empire as a barrier). The war cost Britain seventy million pounds and 25,000 lives and "gave her no clear advantage beyond postponement of the break-up of Turkey" (Thomson 1950:157–58).

Thus the rise of Germany on the long wave upswing of 1848–72 coincided with a weakening of British position—although no power could yet challenge British hegemony outright. The downturn in British overseas economic expansion, discussed above, coincided with shifts in the European balance of power, resulting in an erosion of British hegemony (Thomson 1950:166).

The downswing of 1872–93 saw a halt in great power wars in Europe and a simultaneous "race for colonies," particularly in Africa. Britain and France led this race because of their existing overseas possessions and advanced industrialization. But Germany and even Portugal also participated in the European conquest and partition of virtually all of Africa after 1880 (Fieldhouse 1973:map 3). Figure 14.4 shows the colonial empires of the great powers as they stood at the end of the subsequent upswing, on the eve of World War I in 1914. European control of the world had reached its peak, extending to all the earth's inhabited landmass except for a stretch from Japan to Turkey that was never conquered and most of America, which had become (at least formally) independent following European colonial rule.

41. General von Moltke, chief of the Prussian General Staff, wrote that "the war of 1866 was entered on . . . for an ideal end—the establishment of power. Not a foot of land was exacted from conquered Austria, but she had to renounce all part in the hegemony of Germany" (quoted in Craig 1964:1). A Viennese newspaper wrote of the outcome that Austria's "Great Power status" had been destroyed; "German Power" would henceforth overwhelm Austria and "Prussia's word would be the decisive one in all central European questions" (quoted in Craig 1964:170).

42. As well as the concurrent rise of a united Italy.

43. Especially in the optimistic age of Palmerston, 1855–65 (Thomson 1950:153). In 1848–72, the navy began to improve, after a long period of neglect since 1815 (Thomson 1950:97).

Figure 14.4. The Colonial Empires, 1914

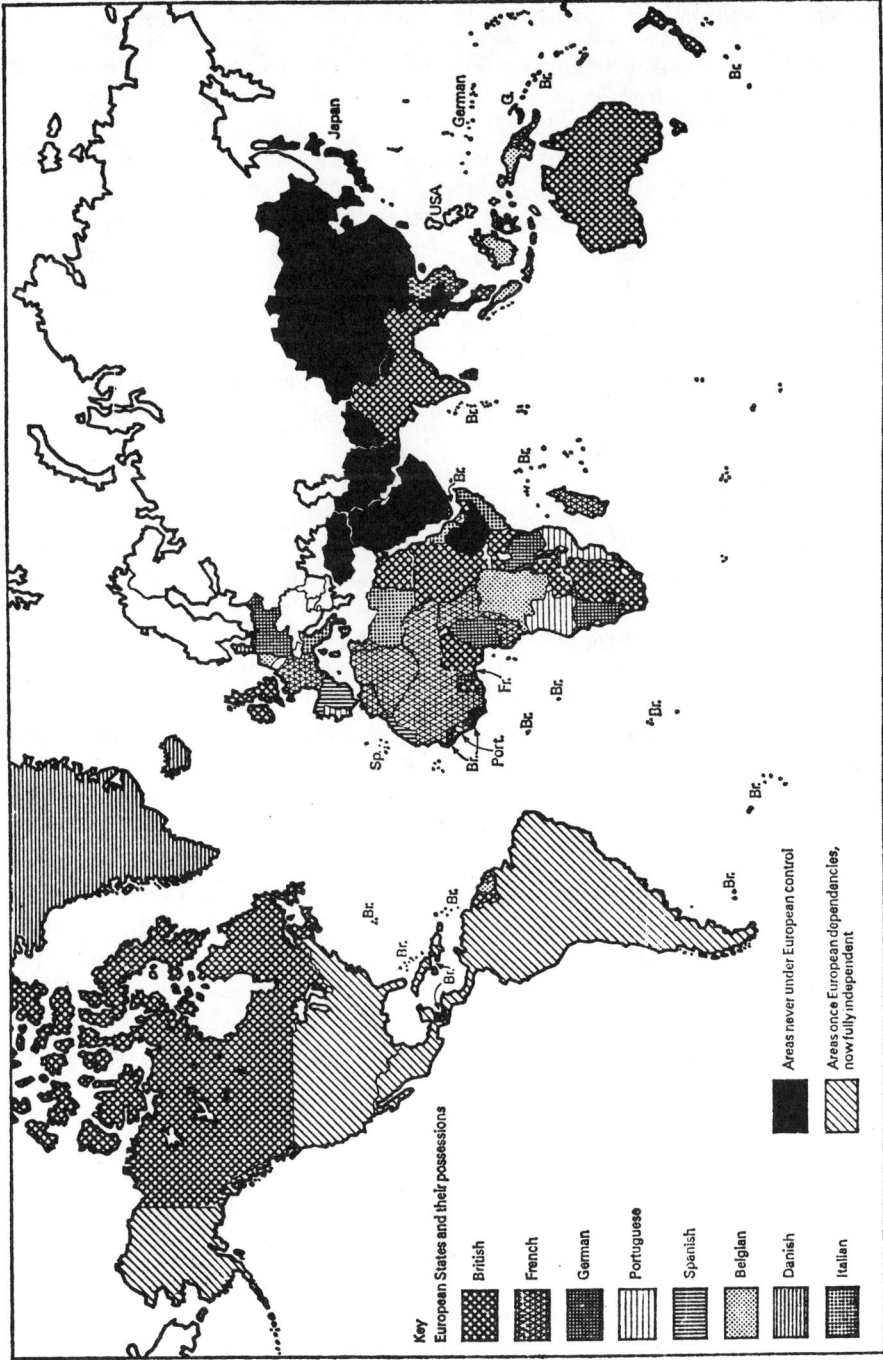

Key
European States and their possessions

British
French
German
Portuguese
Spanish
Belgian
Danish
Italian

Areas never under European control

Areas once European dependencies, now fully independent

Source: Fieldhouse (1973: Map 9) by permission of George Weidenfeld and Nicolson LTD.

Russian, American, and Japanese Ascent

Russia's eastward expansion, meanwhile, had reached the Pacific, and Russia turned southward in this period, consolidating its hold over a huge landmass outside of Europe (Fieldhouse 1973:map 1).

The United States for its part emerged as a major military power in the era of 1815–1945, particularly in the upswing phase of 1893–1917. This phase began with a dispute with Britain over Venezuela (1895) and the Cuban revolt against Spain (1895), which precipitated the U.S. war against Spain in 1898 (see Vanderlip, 1898). The United States emerged from this war as an established naval power and gained possession of Puerto Rico, Guam, and the Philippines. The expansionary drive continued with the annexation of Hawaii (1898), intervention in the Boxer Rebellion in China (1900), conquest of Panama (1903), occupation of Nicaragua (1912), and intervention in Mexico (1916) (Quigley 1966:75). The Panama Canal was opened in 1914.

The upswing phase of 1893–1917 also saw Japanese expansion through war parallel that of the United States (both being attempts to enlarge regional spheres of influence at the expense of European powers). Most important were Japan's defeat of China in 1894–95 and of Russia in 1905. Japanese expansion continued in World War I as Japan took advantage of the European war to capture German colonial possessions in Asia and to gain extensive commercial advantages in China (Quigley 1966:244). From 1918 to 1922 Japan tried to take advantage of the Russian revolution by seizing Vladivostok and the eastern end of the trans-Siberian railroad but ultimately gave these up when the anti-Bolshevik factions supported by Japan were defeated in the Russian civil war (Quigley 1966:245).

Rivalry for Hegemonic Succession

The century from 1815 to 1914 was marked by a prolonged low level of great power wars. By the early twentieth century the ''age of general European wars . . . seemed to be at an end. Only after 1900 did even the notion of another general European war loom above the horizon'' (Thomson 1950:111).[44] During the long wave upswing of the mid-nineteenth century, Britain was still too strong to be challenged. By the time of the next upswing (after 1893), however, British hegemony had weakened, Germany had emerged as a leading industrial economy, and tensions between the great powers had increased.

In the Anglo-German naval race, beginning in the 1890s, Germany challenged British naval superiority. Rapid technological change in the last half of the nineteenth century had important military implications, especially in naval war. The ships that Britain had used to defeat Napoleon at the beginning of the century (less than two thousand tons displacement) had been made obsolete by the 1840s first by steamships

---

44. Thomson (1950:221, 220) writes almost in the same breath that the 19th c. in Britain was above all ''a period of extraordinary peace'' and yet that World War I was ''historically the culmination of the nineteenth century.''

and then by iron (rather than wooden) ships,[45] reaching nine thousand tons displacement by the 1860s and twenty thousand tons by 1900 (Howard 1976:123).

The last half of the nineteenth century saw a frantic competition between the British on the one hand and their chief imperial rivals, the French and the Russians on the other—a competition in size of guns, thickness of armour, and speed. At the very end of the century the Germans joined in the race with all the power of the most highly developed industry in Europe behind them. The real competition was now, not at sea, but in the dockyards; and Germans and British set to outbuild one another in the new all big-gun ships, *Dreadnoughts* and *Super-Dreadnoughts,* on which command of the sea and with it, so it was thought, command of the world now appeared to depend (Howard 1976:123–24).

The "Bible of European navies at the turn of the century" (Howard 1976) was *The Influence of Sea Power on History* by American naval theorist Alfred Mahan (1890). Mahan advocated the use of large capital fleets to run the enemy fleets out of the seas so that the ocean could serve as a highway for one's own trade and an obstacle to the enemy's trade. This would undermine the enemy's war-making capabilities, especially if the enemy was a country with a large population dependent on imported food, such as Germany.

Thomson (1950:218) describes the decades leading up to World War I as a period "of rivalry in power . . . ; of periodic war-scares and crises; of feverish competition in armaments; of nervous tensions and anxieties." Quigley (1966:218) lists nine crises that "brought Europe periodically to the brink of war" in the upswing phase before World War I:

The First Moroccan Crisis, 1905–6
The Bosnian Crisis, 1908
Agadir and the Second Moroccan Crisis, 1911
The Tripolitan War, 1911
The First Balkan War, 1912
The Second Balkan War, 1913
The Albanian Crisis, 1913
The Liman von Sanders Affair, 1913
Sarajevo, 1914

By 1914, in the description of J. A. Spender, "the equilibrium was so delicate that a puff of wind might destroy it, and the immense forces on either side were so evenly balanced that a struggle between them was bound to be stupendous."[46]

Hegemonic War

The year 1914 (in some ways as much as 1945) seems to mark a sudden change in the nature of world politics. After a century of only occasionally broken peace between

45. The superiority of ironclad ships over wooden ships was demonstrated by Russia at the beginning of the Crimean War. Ironically, the Russian fleet did not keep up with technological change and was decimated by Japan in 1904–5.
46. Quoted in Thomson (1950:216).

the great powers, war erupted on a scale utterly unprecedented.[47] The annual costs and destruction of hegemonic war increased more than tenfold in World War I over the previous high (Napoleonic wars).

I agree with both Wallerstein and Modelski that World Wars I and II are, in effect, two stages of a single hegemonic war period. In the seventeenth century the costs of hegemonic war might be sustained for three decades, but in the twentieth century this was reduced to about five years, and the war had to proceed in pieces, with a long readjustment and recovery period in between.[48]

In World War I, each side's war plans called for rapid mobilization and quick, decisive attacks carried out along preplanned lines—the lessons drawn from the German successes against Austria in 1866 and against France in 1871.[49] Van Evera (1985) refers to the "cult of the offensive" that had grown out of these recent precedents.

As it turned out, the strategists were "fighting the last war," and the offensive strategy had already become obsolete. Since 1871, defense had caught up with offense, so that by 1914, prevailing methods of offense (infantry assaults) were prohibitively costly against prevailing methods of defense (entrenched positions with machine guns). In late 1916, on a single front about twenty-five miles wide (the Somme), a maximum gain of seven miles was achieved in four months at a cost of over one million casualties on both sides (Quigley 1966:231). In 1917, in three months, the British used over four million artillery shells against an eleven-mile front (at Passchendaele, Belgium), almost five tons for every yard of the front, and then lost four hundred thousand men in the ensuing attack, which failed (Quigley 1966: 231).

The magnitude of World War I was not expected by political and military leaders but first impressed itself in "the problem of how to pay for [war] supplies."[50] It had been thought that although a great war might be very expensive, it was unlikely to last more than six months:

In July 1914, the military men were confident that a decision would be reached in six months because their military plans and the examples of 1866 and 1870 indicated an immediate decision. This belief was supported by the finanacial experts who, while greatly underestimating the cost of fighting, were confident that the financial resources of all states would be exhausted in six months (Quigley 1966:256).

In fact, the countries at war all broke from the gold standard and issued currency unbacked by gold, in effect taxing their national economies through inflation (see

47. Though not unforeseen by the more thoughtful observers in the pre-1914 years, such as Bloch ([1899] 1903)—see chap. 15.
48. The time it took to exhaust the world economy had been reduced from several decades, to about 15 years, to about 5 years, in the three hegemonic wars, respectively—as annual fatalities climbed from 88,000 to 160,000 to 2 million.
49. The perceived need to stick to these tightly scheduled plans in order to achieve success was one reason that in 1914, once one country mobilized its forces, it was unlikely that the outbreak of total war could be avoided.
50. Quigley (1966:256); see also Hirst (1915:297–303).

Hamilton 1977). And by draining their national economies in this way, the European powers were able to sustain the war for four years.

Everything had changed, to anticipate the famous words of Einstein in 1945, except the way people were thinking. Militarily, the old rules of strategy held sway—there was to be a continuous front in which the attacker would "break through" the strong points of the enemy line by frontal infantry assault with bayonets. Great importance continued to be placed on cavalry, including great demands on supply lines for horse feed (more feed was transported than ammunition), even though cavalry was "obsolete for assult" (Quigley 1966:227). The development of new military innovations was spurred by the war, but they were not employed for decisive advantage by either side because of the initial drain of the war, the long, rigid, front line, and the old-fashioned strategy still prevailing.[51] The nature of war had changed in many ways, but the theory and practice of warfare—from both the immediate military and the long-term political-economic points of view—had lagged behind.

In naval warfare, however, significant innovations did occur and eventually played a major role in World War I. Britain still had the strongest capital fleet, which Germany could not overcome, and Britain was able to impose a crippling economic blockade on Germany.[52] But Germany developed the submarine into a potent counterweapon with which it also crippled the British economy (Howard 1976:126).

The overall costs of World War I were estimated by the Carnegie Endowment for International Peace at over four hundred billion dollars, a figure five times greater than the value of everything in France and Belgium at that time (Carnegie Endowment 1940; Quigley 1966:256).[53] Caron (1979:247) estimates the direct destruction of French industrial capital by the war as only 7.5 percent. But industrial production in France was reduced to 57 percent of its 1913 level by 1919. In Germany, both agricultural acreage and agricultural productivity fell, and food imports ceased. The blockade of Germany caused an estimated eight hundred thousand civilian deaths (Quigley 1966:261). The German submarine warfare against British shipping destroyed almost a million tons of shipping in the month of April 1917 alone and brought Britain within three weeks of exhausting its food supply (Quigley 1966:235).

At the outset, this war of military and economic attrition, pitting the entire economy and social structure of countries against each other, was evenly balanced. According to Thomson (1950:194), the ratio of the industrial potentials of Germany, Britain, and France was three to two to one by 1914. Maddison (1977:126) lists aggregate GNP in 1913 (in 1970 U.S. dollars) for Germany at $70 billion, Britain at $67 billion, and France at $48 billion.[54] The combined national products of the Triple

---

51. The first German gas attack, in 1915, opened a gap in Allied lines for five weeks, but German military leaders who opposed the new weapon did not take advantage of the opening to advance (Quigley 1966:231). Similarly, the use of tanks by the British to break through fortified positions was "resisted by the generals" and their effective use delayed for two years (Quigley 1966:232).

52. A lesson taken from Admiral Mahan's book.

53. See also Day (1927) and Keynes (1920).

54. Figures are actually for Gross Domestic Product (GDP), little different from GNP.

Entente side were greater than those of Germany, Austria-Hungary, and Italy by something like $171 billion to $104 billion,[55] but the economic clout of the central powers could be brought to bear on the fighting more easily than the more distant resources of Britain or Russia, so the balance was indecisive. Germany was able generally to carry the war beyond its borders but was vulnerable to economic blockade over the long term.

By January 1918, Germany had defeated Russia and was losing men at half the rate of the Triple Entente powers in the West (Quigley 1966:235). But the entry of the United States into the war, particularly at this late stage when the European powers were exhausted and the United States was fresh, decisively swung the balance to the Entente side. By 1914 the United States had already become the world's leading industrial economy, with a national product in 1913 of $176 billion[56] (Maddison 1977:126), a large and growing population, and vast natural resources. The relative position of the United States only improved during the war. Germany was forced to make an expensive and humiliating peace.

The Delayed Transition

The long wave downswing of the 1920s and 1930s seems to follow rather directly from the enormous costs of World War I.[57] Kindleberger (1973:21) argues that the timing of economic phenomena in the 1920s and 1930s paralleled that which followed the Napoleonic wars after 1815.

But while the economic downswing after World War I resembled previous instances, the political situation did not. The United States was instrumental in winning the war in Europe, but the United States was not a European power.[58] The situation in Europe itself was unsettled. Although the devastation of the European economies, coupled with the rise of the American economy, propelled the United States into a leading position in the world, Woodrow Wilson's attempt to translate this into a new world order failed. Instead of a new hegemony, a shaky armistice prevailed for two decades as the world economy recovered from the shock of World War I.

Two factors seem to have contributed to making the transition around 1914–45 unlike previous hegemonic transitions. These factors played a role in the indecisive outcome of World War I, the unstable hegemonic situation that followed it, and hence the quick renewal of hegemonic war at the outset of the next upswing phase.

First, the unprecedented jump in the cost and destructiveness of great power war allowed the European powers to exhaust themselves without a decisive victory by any European power. In the 1920s and 1930s, the core economies were too shaky from the shock of the war to renew the struggle. The withdrawal of the United States

55. Calculated from Maddison's data. I estimated Russian GNP based on per capita GNP figures from Crafts (1983:389) and population figures from Quigley (1966:393, 398).

56. That is, greater at the outset of the war than either of the two coalitions fighting the war.

57. See Kindleberger (1973:20) on the connection of World War I to the Great Depression. Dickinson (1940:332) argues that World War I "cast a long economic shadow over two and possibly three postwar decades."

58. The United States had a long history of dislike for European great power politics, a desire just to be "left alone" by Europe.

into isolationism and the Soviet Union into revolution, along with the further weakening of British hegemony, left an unstable political power balance.

Second (and accelerated by World War I), the rise of the United States as the leading world economy shifted the ''center'' of the world system for the first time away from Europe. Britain's decline was unmistakable, but Germany, France, and Russia had all been even more devastated by the war. The Soviet Union did not regain its 1913 level of national production until the end of the 1920s (Quigley 1966:393). Japan had gained during the war, capturing German territories in Asia. Thus, not only had the core of the world system expanded beyond Europe, but its ''center of gravity'' was shifting away from Europe. Barraclough (1964:75) writes: ''In every decade after 1900 it became more clear to more people that future centres of population and power were building up outside Europe, that the days of European predominance were numbered, and that a great turning-point had been reached and passed.'' The rise of the United States was the most visible aspect of that transition, according to Barraclough, but deeper factors were at work. Population trends were shifting—European population growth was slackening, while growth in the rest of the world was increasing due to the importation of techniques from Europe in medicine, agriculture, and transportation (Barraclough 1964:77).[59]

With the decline of Europe—and the rise of America, Russia, and Japan—the center of attention shifted from Europe and the Atlantic to the Pacific (Barraclough 1964).[60] At the outset of the twentieth century, Teddy Roosevelt proclaimed: ''The Mediterranean era died . . . , the Atlantic era is now at the height of its development, and must soon exhaust the resources at its command; the Pacific era, destined to be the greatest of all, is just at its dawn.''[61]

The expansion of the European system, then, may have combined with the indecisive outcome of World War I to produce the unique (by historical standards) timing and character of World War II at the beginning of the 1940–80 upswing phase.

World War II will receive only scant discussion here, because it is within living memory and because I wish to emphasize long-term patterns of social change, which tend to become lost when one focuses on important recent events in detail. World War II did, however, see major developments in military evolution that deserve mention because of their role in the transition to the post-1945 era.

World War II was a continuation of the European war begun in 1914 and halted in mutual exhaustion in 1918,[62] combined with the Pacific War—a continuation of

59. This dialectic, in which European conquest of the world led to Europe's loss of centrality in the world, was noted by Morgenthau (1948:370): ''Europe has given to the world its political, technological, and moral achievements, and the world has used them to put an end to the pre-eminence of Europe.''

60. Braudel (1984:627) also mentions the possibility of a shift to the Pacific.

61. Barraclough (1964:76). Roosevelt's enthusiasm should be tempered by Barraclough's (1964:23) warning that, despite the appeal of the ''Pacific age'' concept, ''the new period which we call . . . 'post-modern' is at its beginning and we cannot yet tell where its axis will ultimately lie.''

62. The continuity of the two wars is underscored by the fact that the armies at the outset of World War II ''had no new weapons which had not been possessed by the armies of 1918,'' despite changes in tactics (Quigley 1966:661).

Japan's military strategy for enlarging its economic sphere in East Asia, dating from at least 1894. In World War II, offensive strategy had adjusted to the new realities, and, in place of a continuous front, armored assaults were used to break through the front at selected points and penetrate behind it. In turn, defense adjusted, adopting defense-in-depth to blunt these breakthroughs behind the lines and, if possible, isolate the enemy's advanced units before their armies could catch up with them. The front thus became much more fluid.

Air warfare was a further influence against the fixed front and was an important innovation in World War II. Air forces both on land and at sea evolved from a reconnaissance mission to a primary method for delivering destructive force. After 1941, the aircraft carrier supplanted the battleship as the "primary instrument of naval domination" (Howard 1976:128). Furthermore, air power developed from a tactical to a strategic weapon—a weapon used against the industrial heartland of the enemy country. "Total war" depended on the civilian populations and economies of entire nations, and with the entire population mobilized for war, the entire population became an explicit and not just incidental target of war. The killing of one hundred thousand civilian city dwellers in a great firestorm was not a military art invented at Hiroshima, as the experiences of Dresden and Tokyo attest. The difference at Hiroshima was not the outcome but the *cost*—one plane, one bomb, no losses, assured destruction of target. Offense, which had been prohibitively expensive twenty-five years earlier, had just become prohibitively cheap.

The Fourth Era, 1945–

As with the war that initiated it, I will say less about the current era than the three preceding it, for two reasons. First, it is within the direct experience of the current generation and hence less in need of historical reconstruction. Second, we have reached only an indeterminate middle point in the current hegemonic cycle, and historical perspective is lacking.

The year 1945 marks one of those restructurings of the international system following a great war that has initiated each era. The United States assumed the hegemonic role but the Soviet Union, which had borne much of the cost of defeating Germany in Europe, won an expanded sphere of control and the status of a separate (but not equal) superpower in a bipolar order.

Continuity or Discontinuity?

The era starting in 1945 seems to differ in some important ways from the previous three. The European system was transformed into one no longer centered in Europe; simultaneously, the nature of war changed with the introduction of atomic weapons. While American hegemony in many ways resembles earlier cases, the current era also represents in several ways a break from the past five centuries and a discontinuity in the development of the world system.

The continuity of the present era with the past is stressed by writers from various world views. Chase-Dunn and Rubinson (1979:280) write:

We contend that, at the level of the basic processes of development, not much is really new in the contemporary period. This flies in the face of most interpretations of the changes which have occurred in the twentieth century. . . . We contend that many of the patterns of change in the contemporary period can be seen in the earlier epochs of world-system development, and that there has not yet been a fundamental reorganization at the systemic level.[63]

And Gilpin (1981:211ff.) argues that despite nuclear war, economic interdependence, and the beginnings of global society, the nation-state is still not dead and the practice of international relations has not changed much.

But other scholars have made the discontinuity argument. Barraclough (1964:268) argues that "the European age—the age which extended from 1498 to 1947—is over." Quigley (1966:831) writes that "the age which began in 1945 was a new age from almost every point of view." Howard (1976:135) says of the atomic bombs dropped on Japan:

Used by one extra-European power against another, in termination of a conflict between them in which Europeans had figured only as auxiliaries, they marked the end of that era of European world dominance which the voyages of Columbus and Vasco da Gama had opened nearly five hundred years earlier.

Morgenthau ([1948] 1967:21) argues that the transition period around 1945 brought a three-fold revolution in the political structure of the world.[64] And as early as 1941 Rose (p. 106) argued that the long wave "has come to an end. . . . The destructive war of 1914–1918 dealt it a mortal blow," and World War II "destroyed it completely."

The anomalous relation of World War II to the long wave (coming at the beginning of an upswing) is an indication of possible discontinuity in this era. It was unprecedented for the world economy in 1939–45 to absorb the costs of a hegemonic war at the beginning of an upswing and then to continue sustained growth for another two decades after the war.[65]

Not only was economic growth sustained after 1945 but so was permanent mobilization for war.[66] "Military Keynesianism" assumed an important role in national economic planning. National economies had become thoroughly restructured around the exigencies of the war system. The permanent war economy marks another way in

---

63. Braudel (1984:20) also stresses the hold of the past on the present: "Is not the present after all in large measure the prisoner of a past that obstinately survives, and the past with its rules, its differences and its similarities, the indispensable key to any serious understanding of the present?" And he quotes Marx: "Tradition and previous generations weigh like a nightmare on the minds of the living" (p. 628).

64. First, the multiple-state system gave way to a bipolar world with centers outside Europe. Second, the "moral unity of the political world" (in the 19th c. especially) was split into "two incompatible systems of thought and action." Third, modern technology created the possibility of total war resulting in universal destruction.

65. As mentioned above, this may have been made possible by the economic strength of the United States and its ability to insulate itself from the effects of the war. The ability of the United States to generate sustained economic growth at the heart of the world system facilitated the restoration of growth in war-damaged countries—Britain, France, Germany, Japan, and elsewhere.

66. The high rate of military innovation, created by the industrialization of the core countries, means that weapons and equipment must be continually replaced.

which the era after 1945 is dissimilar to those preceding it. The permanent war economy has also apparently brought permanent inflation. After previous wars, wartime inflation had given way to postwar deflation. But since World War II, prices have not declined.[67]

American Hegemony

Despite these differences in the world system after 1945, American hegemony resembles previous instances of hegemony in many ways. The United States emerged from World War II with a monopoly on nuclear weapons and military predominance throughout the world except in the Soviet Union and Eastern Europe (a de facto outcome recognized at Yalta). Like previous hegemons, the United States had survived the war with a healthy economy, while those of the other major powers were in ruins.

According to the data of Rupert and Rapkin (1984), the United States around 1950 accounted for over 70 percent of the total GNP and the total capital formation in the seven leading core countries and held over 50 percent of the world's financial reserves. The United States completely dominated both the Pacific trade and the Atlantic trade. The world's financial center was in New York, the central international financial institutions (including the World Bank and the International Monetary Fund) were located in the United States, and the dollar was the international currency standard. Thus the United States enjoyed superiority in production, trade, and finance (Wallerstein's three categories) as well as in military affairs.

The philosophical debates on protectionism and free trade under American hegemony resemble those under Britain. The long wave upswing period of 1940–80 saw "free trade" predominate, particularly in the years of strongest U.S. hegemony. In this respect the period resembled the upswing of 1848–72, the height of British hegemony.[68] In the current downswing (since 1968 for production and 1980 for prices), the protectionist position seems to be making a comeback in the United States, resembling the downswings of 1872–93 and 1917–40.[69]

As for American wars in the current era, the "Pacific era" concept just discussed gives a unifying character to the 1940–80 upswing. The U.S.-Japanese war, Korean War, and Vietnam War were all Pacific wars (Bushkoff 1985).[70] They all concerned

67. Under such conditions prices would rise rapidly on long wave upswings and level off during downswings, as happened in the 16th-c. secular inflation. Keynesian economics in general may also have promoted permanent inflation as the government used monetary policies, including deficit spending and control of money supply, to control the economy.
68. The period 1848–72 combined a long wave upswing with continuing British preeminence.
69. Even the same phrase, "fair trade," used to justify British protectionism in 1872–93, is now heard in the U.S. Congress.
70. Barraclough (1964:28) stresses the Pacific aspect of World War II, dating its start in 1937 with Japan's invasion of China rather than the traditional (European) date of 1939. The Korean and Vietnam wars were not of course, great power wars in the same sense as World War II, but they involved one superpower directly and the other by way of close material and political support. Levy (1983a) counts the Korean War as a great power war because of the participation of Chinese troops, but I find this questionable. In certain logistical ways, the Vietnam War resembled a great power war—for example

American hegemony in the Pacific basin. The Vietnam War in some ways resembles the Crimean War, Britain's unsuccessful interventionary attempt at containment to prop up hegemony. And, just possibly, in the potential coming U.S.-Soviet race for military advantage in space can be seen shadows of the Anglo-German naval race of the late nineteenth century.

Soviet Ascent?

The Soviet Union continued to industrialize in this era. The doctrine of "socialism in one country," dating from the 1920s, had required industrialization at "breakneck speed" (Quigley 1966:396) to support a military buildup against foreign threats to the Soviet Union. This program had succeeded, though at staggering cost, in the 1930s.[71] "There can be little doubt that this tremendous achievement in industrialization made it possible for the Soviet system to withstand the German assault in 1941" (Quigley 1966:400). After World War II, and helped by the integration of Eastern Europe into its economic sphere, the Soviet Union continued to industrialize. While the USSR has been unable to keep up with the advanced U.S. sectors in technology, it has been able (drawing on a larger population) to roughly equal the United States in overall military strength by the 1980s.

The Soviet Union, incidentally, seems not to have been immune from the production downswing beginning around 1968. Mikhail Gorbachev said in June 1985 that "one cannot fail to see that since the early 1970s certain difficulties began to be felt in economic development."[72]

Five Centuries of War and Hegemony

Chapters 13 and 14 have focused on three major transitions in the world system, shifts from one "era" to another, in which the international political-economic system was restructured under a new hegemonic power after a period of extremely severe war.

The succession of countries playing the central roles in each of the three hegemonic wars can be summarized thus (see table 14.2):

1. The losing "hegemonic challenger" is the country or empire decisively defeated in the hegemonic war. These countries become "has-beens"—relegated to a lesser role in the future international order.

2. The new hegemonic power emerging from the war is a leader of the winning coalition in the war that survives the war with its economy intact (while that of most great powers is severely drained). These countries reign as hegemon after the war,

---

more bombs were used than in World War II—and this may help account for the negative impact of the Vietnam War on the world economy.

71. Quigley (1966:398) says that 12 million peasants died in the agricultural reorganization that supported this rapid industrialization.

72. Major speech quoted in Brown (1985:19).

Table 14.2. Succession of Hegemonic Wars

Role in war	*Hegemonic Wars*			
	Thirty Years' War	**Napoleonic Wars**	**World Wars I/II**	**Eventual Status**
Losing hegemonic challenger; defeated in war	Hapsburgs	France	Germany	"Has been"
New hegemon; emerges from war economically intact at head of winning coalition	Netherlands	Britain	U.S.	Comfortable Retirement
(Future challenger); an economically decimated member of winning coaltion	France (Germany?)	Germany (Russia?)	USSR?	Future Challenger

then decline, and eventually take up a comfortable "retirement" under the shield of the next hegemon.

3. Other members of the winning coalition are economically drained by the war, despite being on the winning side, and from these ranks arise future challengers.

Challenges, it seems, are rooted in the previous hegemonic war. They start very early in each era. France's direction very soon after the Thirty Years' War, under Louis XIV,[73] put France on the road to hegemonic challenge. The first war peak in the era (War of the Spanish Succession) already revolved around this challenge. Likewise, Germany's response to the Napoleonic wars was a nationalist upsurge and military reorganization that played a central role in the next war peak (Franco-Prussian War). And looking back to the Hapsburgs, their drive toward world empire certainly goes back more than a century before the Thirty Years' War.[74] Thus each hegemonic challenge has taken a century to mature. It is not a sudden lunge for power, an attempted coup. It is no surprise which country becomes the eventual challenger but is clear from early in the era.

The same cannot be said of the future hegemon. A century ahead of time, it is anything but clear who will emerge on top after the next hegemonic war. The Netherlands in the early sixteenth century was firmly in the Hapsburgs' grasp. Britain after 1648 was embroiled in civil war, and although it soon emerged to challenge the

73. Who came of age in 1659.
74. Charles V was crowned emperor in 1519.

Dutch on the seas, Britain was not obviously stronger than France, the Netherlands, or Sweden. Likewise, the United States after the Napoleonic wars was just emerging as an independent nation, had yet to face its own civil war, and hardly looked like the next world leader.

These patterns suggest new perspectives on the contemporary world situation. Currently, the United States seems to be in an early stage of hegemonic decline. The next hegemon is indeed unclear—China? Japan? A Western European consortium?[75] But, if history is a guide, the "challenger" would be the Soviet Union. This suggests that, for at least the next few decades, the issues of U.S.-Soviet balance, cold war, detente, and related matters will remain central to world politics and to the now-imperative effort to avoid the recurrence of great power wars. But these are issues for the next chapter, in which I take up the relevance of long cycles—and of history—to the rapidly changing world of the present and future.

75. China, in my view, best fits the profile of a possible successor to hegemony. It "got on its feet" after the last hegemonic war, and its population and resource base are large and young. I can imagine possible paths of rapid Chinese industrialization in a new "technological style" (bypassing oil-steel industrialization in favor of silicon and plastics) that could eventually make China economically preeminent. To actually succeed to hegemony in the traditional manner, however, would require China to remain insulated from a U.S.–USSR hegemonic war, which is highly problematical. Thus, as I argue in chap. 15, hegemony itself will more likely give way to a new kind of world order.

CHAPTER FIFTEEN

The Past and the Future

I n looking back over the past five centuries, I am reminded
of a comment made by an octogenarian friend. "Old age," she said, "is like
climbing a mountain. When you get to the top you're out of breath and your legs are
shaky—but the view is terrific!" This seems to me an apt analogy for the modern
world. Over five centuries of development, the world system has been shaken by
recurrent great power wars and stands, fragile, at the brink of a possible catastrophe—but from the late twentieth century we have a terrific view of the modern age.

That view is called history. For all the sudden developments of the twentieth
century, the world today is still a product of its history.[1] In this chapter I will address
the relevance of the historical development of the world system—including long
waves and hegemony cycles—to the future of that system. I will look at the present
from a "long cycle perspective"—a perspective grounded in an awareness of long-
term cyclical dynamics as they have historically unfolded. This perspective offers
new interpretive insights into contemporary issues, seeing present-day issues in their
historical context, political issues in their economic context (and vice versa), and
national issues in their global context.

PROJECTION AND PRECEDENT

In this chapter I look toward both the past and the future of
the world system, to both future projection and historical precedent. Like the Roman
god Janus, we need two faces looking in opposite directions, forward and backward.
The two-faced Janus was the god of gates and doors and hence of *beginnings*. The
development of the world system may be seen as a series of gateways stretched
through the past, each representing a crisis, a transformation, and a new beginning.
The past gateways are fixed, but there are many possible future gateways to choose
among. The present is another beginning.

---

1. Fischer (1970:307) criticizes a contemporary "powerful current of popular thought which is not
merely unhistorical but actively antihistorical as well. . . . Many of our contemporaries are extraor-
dinarily reluctant to acknowledge the reality of past time and prior events, and stubbornly resistant to all
arguments for the possibility or utility of historical knowledge."

348

Future Projection

Some people think it is inherently deterministic to project long cycles into the future. I do not agree. This is more of the baggage carried by the long cycle field under the title of astrology, mysticism, and so on.

In my view, the past is determined but the future is uncertain. Nobody has unrestricted "free will" because all are partially constrained by physical forces as well as the choices of other human beings. But everyone has latitude for *choice*. In a world system containing many millions of people, the macro level of aggregate social patterns may be beyond any individual's power to change. Nonetheless whole societies do make choices and change social patterns (that is what politics is all about), so even the macro-level social rules are only conventions, and not physically binding. Social rules can be manipulated, bent, and even rewritten.

All science seeks to understand the rules of the world we live in, not to show that those rules bind us but to open up new possibilities for liberating ourselves from them.[2] Long cycles are no different, in my view (except that our knowledge of them is cloudier, and our basis of action hence less reliable, than in the case of the natural sciences). Long cycles are a manifestation of certain deep-seated dynamics in world society. Our understanding of those dynamics will increase, not diminish, our freedom to choose a future we want.

If long cycles were mechanistic—if long cycle dynamics did not change and if the world system did not evolve—then my projection could be a prediction. But long cycles are not mechanistic or deterministic. They have evolved through several transitions over five hundred years, and that evolution has only recently reached a new and ill-defined era in which some of the regularities of the past have changed.[3] Thus I am emphatically *not* making a prediction, much less engaging in prophecy!

The truth is that we all make projections of the future, consciously or unconsciously, all the time. My cyclical projection, however tentative and rough, challenges the assumptions of the more conventional projections. Most projections of world politics are based on either of two questionable assumptions. First is the assumption that the world will continue just as it is now—resulting in a *static* projection into the future. Second is the slightly more sophisticated assumption that the types and directions of change characteristic of the recent past will continue in the future. This second assumption results in a *linear* projection into the future.[4] If in fact

2. As even Mao Tsetung ([1940] 1972:204) has said: "For the purpose of attaining freedom in society, man must use social science to understand and change society and carry out social revolution. For the purpose of attaining freedom in the world of nature, man must use natural science to understand, conquer and change nature and thus attain freedom from nature."

3. Long cycles are particularly ill-suited to prediction, especially the prediction of hegemonic war. As Freeman and Job (1979:126) point out, "those analysts who persist in trying to forecast (predict) the 'big event,' e.g. the outbreak of total war . . . , proceed on very shaky ground" because only a few instances exist on which to base the projection. Second, the level of analysis is the world system, of which only one case exists, and this makes generalizations difficult (Freeman and Job 1979:132). Third, the length and scope of long cycles mean that significant evolutionary change can occur from one instance to the next.

4. A good example of the shortcomings of linear projection was provided by the expectation in the 1960s that sustained economic growth would continue unabated indefinitely.

there is a cyclical dynamic at work in the world system, then both of these types of projection will be seriously flawed. My *dynamic* projection, by contrast, is based on the assumption that long cycles will continue.

This provides a *baseline* projection from which to start a discussion, not a final statement about the future. It is an educated guess about the likely sequence and timing *if* past dynamics continue into the future. I offer it as a viable alternative perspective with which to temper the conventional wisdom rather than as an ultimate truth. My projection offers a way to think about our choices as a world society from a new baseline, a new context.

The basis of my projection will be to locate the present phase of the world system and find its rough directions and rates of change within the two-dimensional space defined by the long wave on one dimension and the hegemony cycle on the other. I will project first the long wave, then the hegemony cycle, and finally consider the two together. Here, more than ever, I must rely on adduction, striving for a plausible and consistent range of possibilities, not a definitive answer.

Projecting the Long Wave

The first task in projecting the long wave sequence is to locate the present in that sequence. The most recent upswing phase seems to have had roughly the following sequence:

1933   Upturn in production
1937   Upturn in great power war
1940   Upturn in prices
1968   Downturn in production
1975   Downturn in great power war
1980   Downturn in prices

The economic turning points have been discussed in chapter 11. To recap, around the late 1960s the world economy moved into a production downswing phase[5] of slower and less stable growth, which had not ended by 1986. Inflation continued upward after 1968 until the price peak of 1980, since which point inflation has remained quite low.

The "war upswing" phase from about 1937 to 1975 requires some discussion now. The year 1937 marked the opening shots of World War II—Japan's invasion of China (Barraclough 1964)—while 1975 marked the end of the Vietnam War. The major war (World War II) came at the beginning of the phase and was followed by smaller wars (which, as noted above, is an anomalous pattern historically). Nonetheless the entire phase was a period both of continuous mobilization for great power war and of frequent great-power involvement in war, often directed consciously but obliquely at another great power. The major national economies remained on a "war

5. For which the Vietnam War bears some responsibility.

footing'' throughout most of this period (see Melman 1974 on the ''permanent war economy'' in the United States).[6]

The use of military force by the great powers, especially the United States, declined sharply after 1975, with the coming of ''detente'' and U.S.-Chinese rapprochement in the mid-1970s. A few years, from the fall of Saigon in 1975 until the Soviet intervention in Afghanistan in 1979, were particularly free of great power involvement in international wars.[7]

Some people would be surprised at my description of the present as a war downswing. True, in the early 1980s, great power war activity and military spending increased somewhat, and within a four year period (1979–83) every member of the United Nations Security Council became involved in military combat beyond its borders—the USSR in Afghanistan, the United States in Grenada, China in Vietnam, Britain in the Falklands-Malvinas, and France in Chad. But these interventions were limited to the country's immediate neighbor or to a ''sphere of influence'' not strongly contested by another superpower. So I see the present superpower maneuvering as essentially different, and less prone to actual great power war, than that of the cold war years in the 1950s and 1960s.[8]

But can present U.S. behavior really be seen as part of a war downswing phase in light of the Reagan administration's military buildup in the United States? I believe so. While U.S. military spending is being pushed to new peacetime highs in absolute terms, it is still well below the levels of the 1950s and 1960s in terms of percentage of GNP, as shown in figure 15.1. And while President Reagan clearly would *like* to keep building up the military, it now (1987) looks as though the U.S. economy simply cannot support such a buildup and that the buildup of the early 1980s was a one-time feat accomplished at the price of a huge jump in the federal deficit. By 1986, Melman (p. 65) could argue that

there is a growing awareness in Congress and among the public that the United States cannot have both guns and butter. The huge federal deficit, much of it stemming from the recent increase in the military budget, is creating serious problems for U.S.-based production in both domestic and foreign markets.

By 1986, Congress was mandating at least slight cuts, rather than continued rapid buildups, in real military spending—not because they opposed the buildup but because they did not want to pay for it.

6. The exception, Japan, was also the most successful in economic growth, probably because of its ability to keep military spending around 1% of GNP (compared to 5–10% of GNP in many core powers). The difference of a few percent of GNP being reinvested productively instead of wasted on the military could account for much of Japan's higher growth rate.

7. The peace-making trip of President Anwar Sadat of Egypt to Jerusalem in 1977 seems to symbolize these years.

8. As this manuscript was being revised, in 1986, several new signs of the potentially peaceful character of the current period emerged. These include the Soviet peace initiatives and nuclear testing moratorium, the U.S. Congress's near-passage of test-ban legislation, and the sweeping ''almost'' agreement of Gorbachev and Reagan in Reykjavík.

Figure 15.1. U.S. Defense Outlays as a Percent of GNP

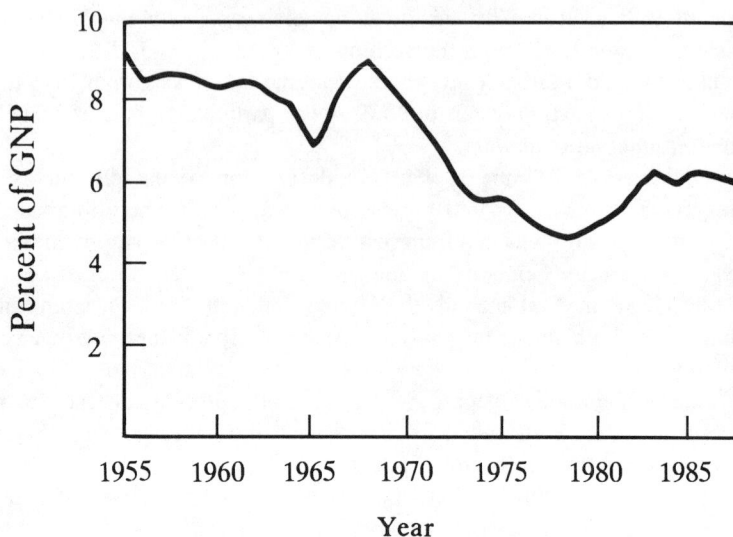

Source: U.S. Department of Defense. Your Defense Budget, Fiscal Year 1987
(Washington, DC, 1986), p. 30.

Meanwhile, the growth of military spending in the Soviet Union also seems to have slowed down after about 1974. Recent reports from the Central Intelligence Agency and the Defense Intelligence Agency[9] estimate that Soviet military spending, which grew by nearly 50 percent between 1965 and 1974,[10] slowed to virtually no real growth from 1975 through at least 1981.[11]

To summarize our present position with respect to the long wave, then, we are in a period of low and unstable production growth, reduced great power war activity, and low inflation. Looking to the future, the long wave sequence suggests an upturn in production growth,[12] followed by an upturn in great power war activity (war likelihood, propensity towards war?), followed by an upturn in prices.

The next point in the usual sequence would be an upturn in production growth. I do not see this turning point yet, especially in the U.S. economy, which is still the world's leading economy. The "recovery" of the U.S. economy in 1984 did not last. The United States has recently joined much of the third world in a massive debt

9. See *Boston Globe*, Mar. 31, 1986, p. 3.
10. That is, about 3% real annual growth, above the inflation rate of about 1%.
11. For 1982–1984, the "more comprehensive" CIA report estimates that this spending freeze continued, while the DIA estimates growth of 2–3% above inflation. See also *Christian Science Monitor*, July 30, 1987, p. 9, on "massive cuts" in China's military in the 1980s.
12. The production upturn will be distinguishable only after it has been sustained for some years, since only then can growth be called stable.

crisis. And I do not yet see a new leading economic sector emerging into strong growth—rather, the relevant sectors seem to be going through shake-downs and consolidations.[13]

The next leading sector might most plausibly be an information sector incorporating telecommunications,[14] computers (electronic information processing) and perhaps biogenetics (control of biological information). This new leading sector does not yet seem to be in place.[15] By the early 1990s, however, these new technologies may begin to settle into place. For what it is worth, a production upturn around the mid-1990s would mean a phase length of about twenty-five years since 1968. However, an upturn in the late 1990s or even the late 1980s would be about equally plausible.

Given a production upturn around the 1990s, the long wave sequence would suggest a war upswing phase beginning around the first decade after 2000 and lasting through sometime around the decade of the 2020s.[16] The most plausible projection would then be something like this (rough dates):

1995–2020	Production upswing phase
2000/05–2025/30	War upswing phase
2010–2035	Price upswing phase

As a first approximation, I suggest the period around 2000 to 2030 as a "danger zone" for great power war. The greatest danger of war, in my opinion, will come later rather than earlier in this period. Unlike the upswing that *began* with World War II, there is no great unresolved issue of hegemony left over from the last upswing period. Instead, like the upswing that *ended* with World War I, there is a more gradual erosion of an existing hegemonic system and the rise of potential challengers to that hegemony (see below on declining hegemony). Given the exceptional costs of great power war in this era (see below), it seems that war would come only at the end of a long buildup with persistent pressure toward war. I consider most plausible a return to the pattern before the 1930s (to which World War II was an exception), in which great power wars peak toward the end of the upswing phase. This would put the highest danger of great power war sometime around the decade of the 2020s, or almost forty years in the future as of this writing.

---

13. The latest data as of 1987 show adjusted U.S. GNP growth of 3.0% in 1985 and 2.9% in 1986, following low growth in every year since 1980, except 1984 (election year?). Although the U.S. economy might just limp along until the next production upturn, I would not discount the possibility of a sharp deflationary jolt and reorganization before that time. If, as argued below, the most relevant precedent for the 1980s is the 1870s, then the equivalent of the great depression of the 1890s (deeper than that of the 1870s) would lie just ahead, before the production upturn.

14. "An obvious candidate for the next great leap forward is the telecommunications industry" (Kurth 1979:33).

15. Computers have become important in the core economies, but the most pervasive applications appear to be still some years in the future, and costs are still dropping sharply. Biogenetics for its part has just begun making products of significance and is mostly a promise of things to come.

16. Again, these dates could easily be shifted somewhat in either direction.

Figure 15.2. Indicators of Declining U.S. Hegemony

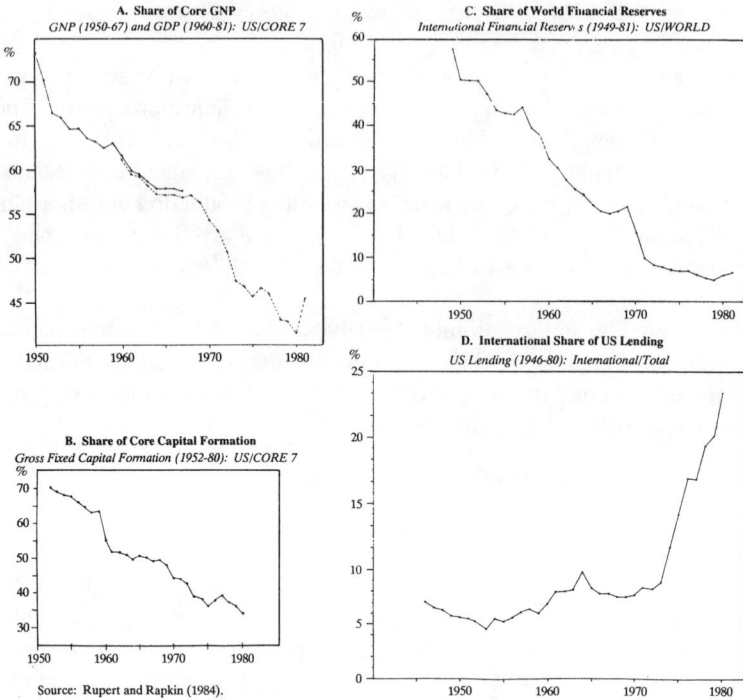

A. Share of Core GNP
GNP (1950-67) and GDP (1960-81): US/CORE 7

B. Share of Core Capital Formation
Gross Fixed Capital Formation (1952-80): US/CORE 7

C. Share of World Financial Reserves
International Financial Reserves (1949-81): US/WORLD

D. International Share of US Lending
US Lending (1946-80): International/Total

Source: Rupert and Rapkin (1984).

Projecting Hegemonic Decline

Moving from the long wave to the hegemony cycle, again the first task is to locate the present along the sequence of hegemonic decline. How far and how fast has American hegemony eroded in terms of both military and economic predominance?

The economic erosion is illustrated in figure 15.2. The U.S. share of core GNP fell from 70 percent to 40 percent, at an accelerating rate after 1970. Share of capital formation also fell from about 70 percent to 40 percent. The U.S. share of core production of motor vehicles, radio, and television, its share of world manufactured exports, and its share of world financial reserves all decreased substantially, while the ratio of U.S. imports to exports increased. Dawson and Rupert (1985:10) have graphed U.S. manufacturing exports and motor vehicle production (fig. 15.3). They express exports of manufactures relative to imports, creating "a measure capable of reflecting the production and exchange relations which inhere in hegemony" (Dawson and Rupert 1985:11). The decline of such an indicator, they argue, would show that "world markets for core production are being recaptured by competing core powers and . . . the domestic market of the hegemonic society is increasingly penetrated by its competitors" (p. 11). Such a decline occurs in the U.S. in the period 1945–80; a similar decline also occurs in the U.S. share of core motor vehicle

Figure 15.3. The Rise and Decline of U.S. Production Hegemony

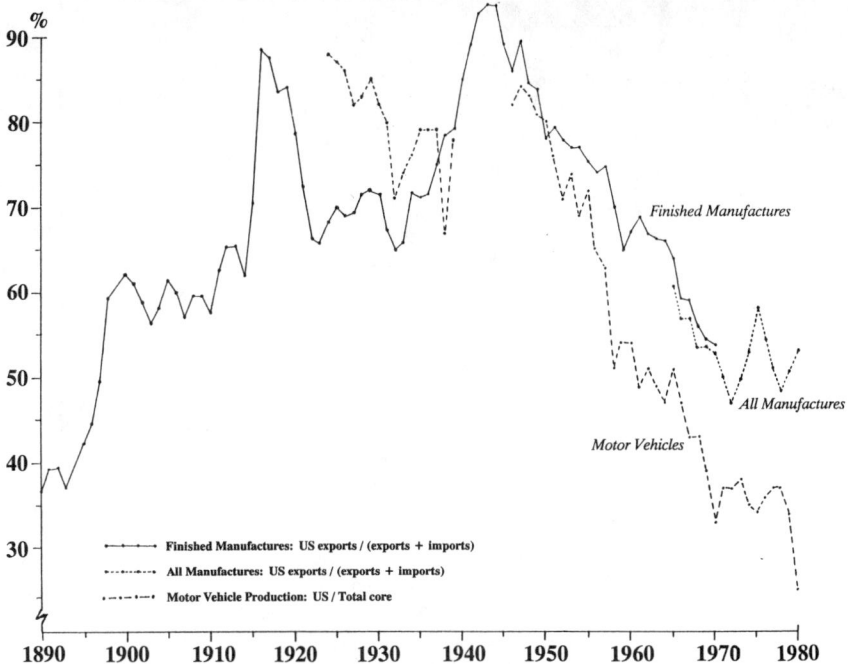

Source: S. Dawson and M. Rupert, *Hegemony and the Dynamics of Core Periphery Relations,* paper presented to the International Studies Association, March, 1985.

production ("an indicator of the more purely productive aspect of hegemony," according to Dawson and Rupert).

W. D. Burnham has graphed the decline of corporate profits relative to net interest rates in the United States from 1948 to 1983 (see figure 15.4). The decline in profits and rise in interest rates are particularly sharp from 1965 to 1970, and since 1980 net interest rates have been higher than profit rates.

Bergesen, Fernandez, and Sahoo (1986) evaluate U.S. hegemony in terms of the nationality of the fifty largest manufacturing corporations in the world (which they define as constituting "hegemonic production") from 1956 to 1981.[17] They categorize each company by industry and ask how many industries each leading country was active in at this top level. The United States declined from thirteen to seven such industries, while Europe remained constant at about six to seven, Japan rose from zero to three, and the "semi-periphery" rose from zero to one.

The U.S. military position has seen somewhat parallel decline. From total superiority in 1945, the United States went on to lose the war in Vietnam and accept a position equal with, not superior to, the Soviet Union in the nuclear standoff (SALT

17. See also Bergesen (1986).

Figure 15.4. U.S. Corporate Profits and Net Interest

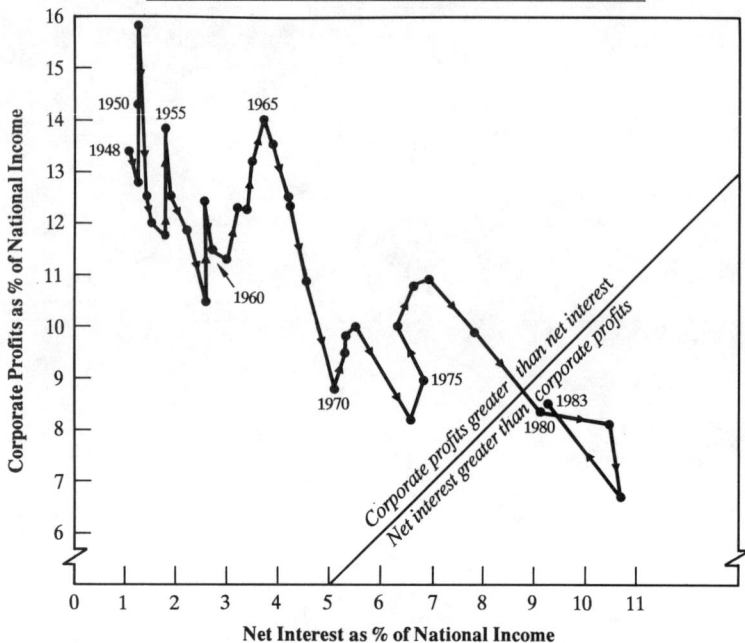

Note: Graph represents both corporate profits and net interest as a percent of national income, for 1948-83. Data from National Income and Product Accounts.
Source: Courtesy of Walter Dean Burnham, M.I.T.

agreements). The United States, however, continues to be the strongest great power in terms of global-reach capabilities.

There are differing interpretations of how significant the decline in U.S. position has been. In sharp contrast with the scholars just discussed, President Reagan said in a recent interview that "I firmly believe that the United States is still in the upswing of the cycle" of rise and decline of empires. Furthermore, according to Reagan, "America . . . , which is unique in the world, could be the first exception to the historical rule" of decline.[18]

A more moderate position is that of Russett (1985), who argues that U.S. hegemony has declined, but not as far as is commonly believed. Between 1950 and 1983, according to Russett's data, the United States has maintained parity with the Soviet Union on military expenditures and has remained far ahead on GNP and manufacturing production.[19] The U.S. share of the world economy has declined, but the United States remains the most powerful single country.

In these discussions of U.S. economic and military decline the different view-

18. Interview with Brazilian news magazine *Veja,* Oct. 5, 1986, quoted in *Los Angeles Times,* Oct. 6, 1986, p. 13.
19. He puts the Soviet Union in 1950 at 29% of the U.S. GNP and 24% of its manufacturing production. By 1983 the figures had risen, but only to 41% and 47%.

points seem to converge on some basic points even though interpretive conclusions vary. The U.S. position has declined from its post-World War II high (President Reagan's view notwithstanding), but the United States is still the single most powerful nation in the world. Some people focus on the decline, others on the continuing strength.

As American hegemony (slowly or rapidly) declines, is the Soviet Union ascending? The position of the Soviet Union has, since 1945, become much stronger. It recovered economically from utter devastation in World War II and has attained a position of rough parity with the United States in the strategic arms race.[20] Perhaps, with its larger size and greater remaining natural resources, the Soviet Union will overtake the United States in overall economic and military strength in the coming decades, but this is debatable. To some observers, the USSR seems far more concerned about securing its own borders than controlling the world.

Alker, Biersteker, and Inoguchi (1985:32–39) argue that the Soviet Union was never more than a regional hegemon and that as such it "reached its period of maximal extension between 1955 and 1965" and is now in decline. In their view, the U.S. policy of containment raised the costs of Soviet expansion (though possibly "the Soviet Union never intended to extend itself very far beyond its borders"). The USSR, they argue, has been able to end U.S. hegemony in the world system without being able to assert its own hegemony. Thus, "it appears we have entered a period of a global devolution of power, a period in which no single actor can dominate."

Does declining U.S. hegemony imply that hegemonic war is imminent? I believe not. In the past, hegemonic decline has been a long, drawn-out process. The speed with which hegemony declines and the point in that process when hegemonic war might be triggered are indeterminate. What *can* be said is that we are moving toward the "weak hegemony" end of the spectrum and that this seems to increase the danger of hegemonic war.

Two-Dimensional Cycle Time

I have now estimated the location and direction of change for both long waves and hegemony cycles. These may be combined using the two-dimensional space described in chapter 13. Figure 15.5 is a sketch of the path followed by the world system since 1815 in the space defined by the long wave on the vertical axis and the hegemony cycle on the horizontal axis.

Beginning in the lower left of the figure, 1815 ended a hegemonic war period and a price upswing and marked the emergence of strong hegemony. Hegemony eroded gradually through the following long wave (price trough in 1848, price peak in 1872) and then eroded somewhat more rapidly in the following long wave, ending in World War I. Hegemonic war was resumed near the outset of the next upswing (1939),

20. Lester Thurow (1986:15) finds American plans to "bankrupt" the Soviet Union through high defense spending absurd: "The Soviet economy may look cumbersome and inefficient from our vantage point, but if it did not collapse in the face of Hitler's armies it is not going to collapse in the face of American military spending."

Figure 15.5. Historical Path and Future Projection

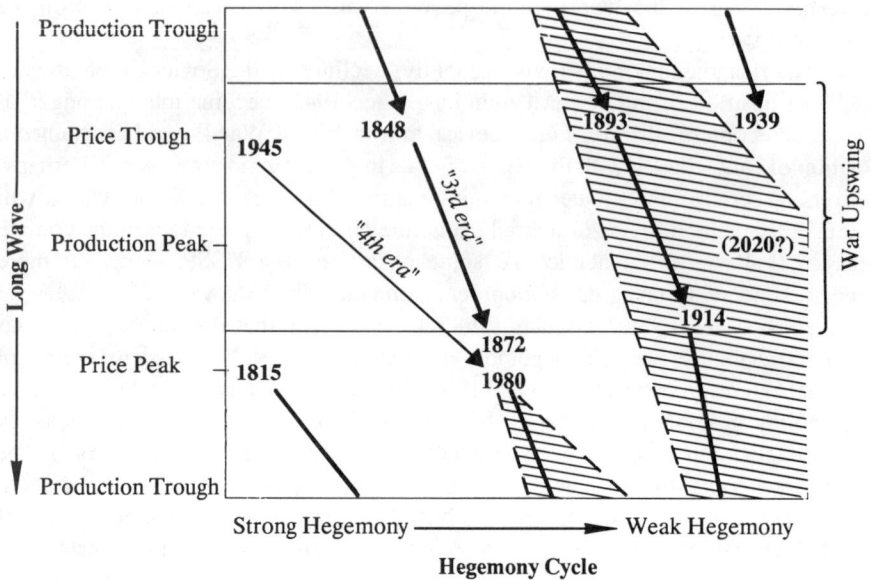

quickly restoring strong hegemony (1945, at left of figure) and ushering in the long 1940–80 price upswing. The erosion of hegemony here seems to have been faster than in the British case, so that the American hegemony of 1980 seems roughly similar to the British hegemony of 1872 (both price peaks). Since 1980 is early in the long wave "war downswing" phase, the danger period for great power war would not be expected for at least two decades.

After 1980, dotted lines indicate a widening region of plausible futures, depending on the continuing rate of hegemonic decline relative to long wave time. The upper dotted line indicates a continuing rapid decline in U.S. hegemony such that hegemonic war might be conceivable rather early in the next war upswing phase (2010?). The lower dotted line shows a slowed rate of decline in which the world system's path might pass through the next war upswing phase without a hegemonic war (as happened under British hegemony in 1848–72).[21] The danger of hegemonic war might then be put off until the next upswing, in the second half of the twenty-first century (by which time the nature of world politics might be very different). A middle path between these diverging possibilities would take us not far from the

21. Perhaps experiencing conventional wars of moderate scale instead. While such wars might be destructive regionally, they would leave intact the basic international power structure, including both superpowers.

Figure 15.6. Clustering of Keohane and Nye's Cases

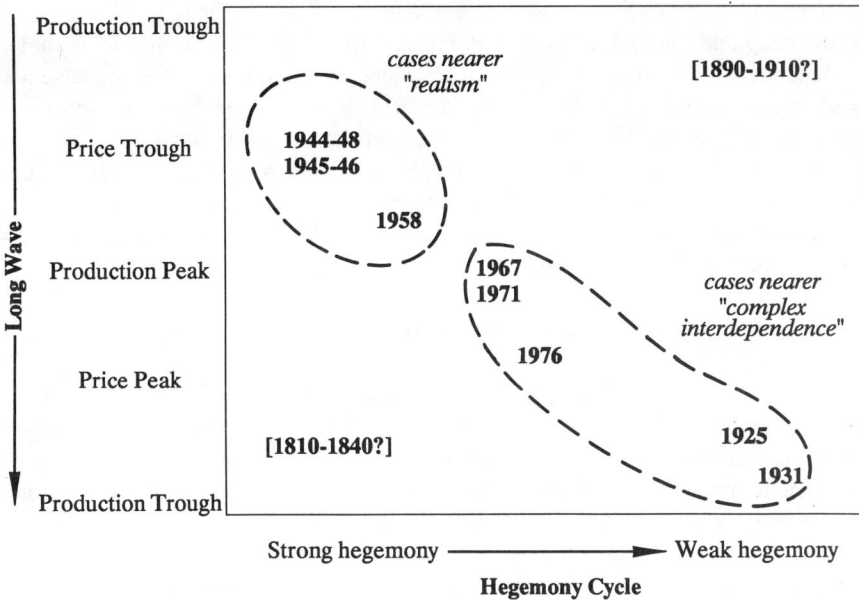

1893–1914 precedent. The danger of hegemonic war would be high, especially late in the next war upswing, around 2020.

In addition to its utility in projecting long cycles into the future, two-dimensional cycle space may also be used as a new framework with which to reconceptualize theories of international relations. For example, Keohane and Nye (1977:28) argue that "realism" is giving way to "complex interdependence" among nations,[22] making "the effects of military force . . . both costly and uncertain."[23] Keohane and Nye see a trend in world politics over the past fifty years, with "the complex interdependence type . . . becoming increasingly relevant" (p. 161). The long cycle perspective suggests a reinterpretation of Keohane and Nye's (p. 161) nine cases of change in international "regimes" concerning money or oceans.[24]

22. As the more relevant ideal type in international relations. See also Rosecrance et al. (1982).

23. While military force is still central to issues of national survival, according to Keohane and Nye (1977:28–29), "employing force on one issue against an independent state with which one has a variety of relationships is likely to rupture mutually profitable relations on other issues. In other words, the use of force often has costly effects on nonsecurity goals." They argue that "the recourse to force seems less likely now than at most times during the century before 1945."

24. Modelski (1981:79) first suggested that a cyclical model "permits the use of both the 'realist' and the 'complex interdependence' [of Keohane and Nye] ideal types to elucidate successive phases of world politics."

Four of the nine cases approximate conditions of "realism," while five are closer to conditions of "complex interdependence," according to Keohane and Nye. As figure 15.6 illustrates, these cases are clustered in terms of both the long wave and hegemony. Conditions of "realism" seem to predominate on the long wave production upswing and in conditions of strong hegemony, while conditions of "complex interdependence" predominate in the long wave production downswing phase and under weaker hegemony.[25] To sort out the effects of the long wave from those of hegemony, one would have to look more closely at the lower-left and upper-right quadrants in the figure, which would mean studying two earlier periods, around 1890–1910 and around 1810–40.[26] In any event, rather than seeing in complex interdependence the downfall of realism, the long cycle perspective suggests a return toward realism in a future phase.

Historical Precedent

The use of long cycles to project possibilities into the future may be strengthened by the use of appropriate historical precedents. In looking toward the future, we all draw precedents from the past by which we interpret events and estimate the probable effects of our actions. In the long cycle perspective, some precedents from the past are more appropriate than others to a particular situation. This is because some past periods structurally resemble the present, occupying a similar position in the cycle space of figure 15.5. The 1870s may have important lessons for the present that could not be gleaned from the 1960s—because while the 1960s are more recent, the 1870s occupy a more comparable position in cycle time (long wave downswing, declining hegemony).

Like future projection, the use of historical precedent is fraught with methodological pitfalls. Historian David Hackett Fischer (1970) includes "false analogy" among eleven common "fallacies" that underlie errors in historical scholarship. The misuses of analogy, according to Fischer (1970:258), can be divided into two groups: drawing inappropriate analogies and applying sound analogies inappropriately.[27] Despite Fischer's warnings, historical analogies do play a major role in political debate and will continue to do so. The long cycle perspective can help to point up

25. This excludes the "pre-1920" ocean regime change, whose timing relative to the long wave is not clear. Inclusion of this case of "realism" in the upper right quadrant (around 1890–1910) would at least weakly imply that the long wave, rather than hegemony, is the factor correlating with the realism-complex interdependence dimension.

26. The period 1890–1910 is particular interesting, since it parallels the period expected around 1990–2010 (see above).

27. "The fallacy of the perfect analogy" arises when a partial resemblance between two entities is extended to imply "an entire and exact correspondence" (p. 247). The "fallacy of prediction by analogy" arises when "analogy is used to anticipate future events—as it so often is, in the absence of anything better" (p. 257). Predictions based on analogies, according to Fischer, are "utterly untestable and inconclusive." He suggests two alternative methods for looking to the future. First is to extrapolate trends (but I find this inadequate in view of cyclical dynamics, see above). Second, theoretical or conditional knowledge ("if-then" propositions) can be used to analyze possible futures.

clearly *inappropriate* analogies and to suggest more relevant historical precedents that might otherwise be overlooked.

The 1893–1914 Precedent

As seen in figure 15.5, the closest historical precedent for the present phase seems to be the period from 1872 to 1893. Both are long wave downswings. Both are phases of low great power war activity following costly wars of containment by the hegemonic power in the previous upswing phase period—Britain in the Crimean War and the United States in the Vietnam War. In both periods, an era of unhampered free trade gives way, as hegemony declines, to greater protectionism.

As for the early decades of the twenty-first century, the 1893–1914 period appears to be most relevant. In chapter 1, I mentioned that the present generation in the West remembers with particular sensitivity the ''lessons of 1939''—that ''appeasement'' leads to war and therefore that armed strength and firmness will deter war.[28] But others feel that 1914 and not 1939 is the more relevant historical case for the present generation. The long cycle perspective makes the 1914 precedent particularly interesting.

Kahler (1979:374) argues for this ''1914 analogy,'' which he finds worthy of reexamination because of ''the lingering strength of the 'lessons' of the 1930s in the United States and our national distance from the events of July 1914.''[29] My projection in two-dimensional cycle time supports a modified version of the 1914 analogy—the buildup to war in 1914 is a useful precedent not for the immediate future but for a period ten to fifty years in the future. My projection lies between that of Modelski, which sees the present phase as analogous to 1848–73,[30] and that of Kahler, which sees the present as analogous to the period just before 1914.

According to Kahler (pp. 375, 381–83), ''the emerging pattern of superpower competition'' at present resembles in certain ways the Anglo-German rivalry after the turn of the century. ''Soviet fears of encirclement'' by the United States and China parallel ''the worst fears instilled in Wilhelmine Germany by the Franco-Russian alliance.'' Present-day reliance on proxies and ''clients'' parallels the pre-1914 pattern ''in which one or another of the Powers [could be] forced into a confrontation by a weaker state.'' And ''exacerbated dependence upon imported oil [has] shaped American strategy in the 'arc of crisis' to the model of classical British strategy in the region.''

But it is in the area of *deterrence* that the 1893–1914 period holds the most interesting precedents for the coming decades. Kahler (pp. 389–94) writes that ''the 1914 analogy points to weaknesses in our dominant mode of thinking about relations

28. For a summary of the conservative argument for the 1930s as the parallel to the 1980s, and for Nazi Germany as parallel to the Soviet Union, see Kartchner (1985).

29. On the 1914 analogy, see also Russett (1981) and Bergesen (1983b).

30. Modelski (1982:114) rejects the 1914 analogy but says that ''we have even less use'' for the 1939 analogy. Based on his dating (see chap. 6), Modelski considers the period since 1973 an upswing in which ''the sources of experience for the decades of the 1980s and '90s are . . . between 1848 and 1873.''

with our adversaries, especially in deterrence theory (an image powerfully shaped by the supposed lessons of the 1930s).'' One big difference between pre-1914 Europe and the present, according to Kahler, is that military forces in the former case "were not viewed as deterrents'' but as instruments for fighting a war that many regarded as inevitable. However, Kahler notes that this difference is now eroding as some officials argue that a limited nuclear war is "winnable.'' "Perhaps the possibility of nuclear war will continue to restrain . . . foreign adventures,'' Kahler argues, but "the 1914 analogy hardly encourages complete reliance upon such restraint.''

Deterrence has a long history. Both the theory of deterrence and its critique were alive and well in the 1893–1914 period. Norman Angell (1914:201) wrote in January 1914: "Mr. Churchill lays it down as an axiom that the way to be sure of peace is to be so much stronger than your enemy that he dare not attack you. One wonders if the Germans will take his advice'' (see also Angell 1910).

Indeed, the escalating costs and destructiveness of war were already being projected as science fiction as early as 1871, when Lord Lytton wrote about the awesome force Vril:

War between the Vril-discoverers ceased, for they brought the art of destruction to such perfection as to annul all superiority in numbers, discipline, or military skill. . . . If army met army, and both had command of this agency, it could be but to the annihilation of each. The age of war was therefore gone (p. 34).

For at least some thinkers in the 1893–1914 period, the rapidly escalating destructiveness of war meant that such a condition already existed. Bloch (1899)[31] stresses what Edwin Mead (in the introduction to the English edition of Bloch's book) calls "the destructiveness of modern warfare, with its frightful new weapons.'' Bloch writes:

The dimensions of modern armaments and the organisation of society have rendered [war's] prosecution an economic impossibility, and, finally, if any attempt were made to demonstrate the inaccuracy of my assertions by putting the matter to a test on a great scale, we should find the inevitable result in a catastrophe which would destroy all existing political organisations. Thus, the great war cannot be made, and any attempt to make it would result in suicide.[32]

Bloch's conclusions are based on a detailed quantitative study of economic and military aspects of modern war in a variety of countries. A great war, Bloch argues, would bog down for years in stalemate, with both sides stuck in their trenches; it

---

31. A founder of "peace research'' before World War I (see Van Den Dungen 1983).

32. Before World War II, as well, a radical deterrence theory surfaced, though only as a minority opinion among mostly civilian rather than military leaders. This theory in its extreme form held that air power had made great war suicidal since "the chief cities of Europe could be destroyed almost completely in the first twenty-four hours of a war'' through bombing and gas attacks (Quigley 1966:664). Quigley argues that this theory, despite being a "farfetched idea,'' "played an important role in persuading the British and French peoples to accept the Munich Agreement.'' The military advocates of "strategic bombing''—long range bombing of industrial and other civilian targets rather than battlefield targets— were "very influential'' in the United States and Britain but not in France, Germany, or Russia, according to Quigley.

would ruin the economies of the contestants and result in loss of life on an unprecedented scale. All of this proved true. Bloch concludes that "war therefore has become impossible, except at the price of suicide" (p. xxxi); so a war cannot occur. This proved false: war occurred even though a number of major actors *did* in fact commit political suicide. Austria-Hungary, Czarist Russia, and Imperial Germany were destroyed, and even the European "winners," France and Britain, lost their positions of power in the world order.

The 1893–1914 precedent also holds interesting lessons about economic interdependence—which is often thought of as a recent phenomenon.[33] Kahler (1979:393) notes that in 1914 "a world characterized by high economic interdependence, unparalleled prosperity, and relative openness still went to war." Today, Kahler argues, economic linkages between the great powers are actually weaker than in 1914, due to constrained East-West trade, restricted migration, and the lack of "a unified international monetary system based upon London." Thus "there is little reason to expect economic interdependence to prove a more serious barrier to the use of force by insecure nation-states than it did before 1914."

As with deterrence, the interdependence argument can be found in the literature of the 1893–1914 period. A September 1913 writer, for example, argues that "peaceful settlement [of international conflicts] is being furthered by the recognition . . . that the world is a unit." International flows of capital, foreign investment, and the international system of credit have created "an economic interweaving and interdependence of the nations that is without parallel in history. . . . The nations have become linked in an interweaving of interests so powerful that the successful functioning of each part depends upon the prosperity of every other part." As a result, the author concludes, "war does not pay."[34] Norman Angell, writing in January 1914, likewise argues that economic interdependence has made war "irrelevant to the end it has in view," since war no longer benefits the winner (p. 197). All of this sounds rather like Keohane and Nye's (1977) view of the 1970s; yet World War I broke out within a year of the above writings.

A final point of interest regarding historical precedent is that, repeatedly, war seems to have occurred in part as a result of preparations to avoid the *last* war. Europe fell into war in 1914 by following the precedent of 1871, which called for a quick offensive breakthrough (see chapter 14). Then in 1939 steps were taken to avoid another 1914, but these only hastened World War II.[35] Since 1945, the great powers have put in place, at staggering cost, the necessary mechanisms to deter another World War II. Each year $435 billion—roughly half of all world military spending—is devoted specifically to "deterring big power war in Europe" (Forsberg, Elias, and Goodman 1985:13).[36]

33. See above discussion of Keohane and Nye (1977).

34. Quoted in Woods and Baltzly (1915:9–13).

35. Both deterrence and appeasement have failed historically. To rely on the 1939 analogy is to risk falling into 1914 again. But to rely on 1914 is to risk falling into another 1939.

36. The other half of world military spending breaks into four roughly equal parts: deterring U.S.-Soviet nuclear and conventional war, deterring big power war in the Far East, permitting large-scale big power intervention in the third world, and deterring or fighting wars within the third world.

To summarize, the long cycle perspective suggests alternative historical precedents with different "lessons" than the most recent precedents found in living memory.

FROM POWER POLITICS
TO COMMON SECURITY

In figure 15.5, above, any estimate of how far American hegemony has declined and how rapidly it will decline can be only rough at best. Yet the general principle based on past experience remains: As hegemony declines, eventually hegemonic war occurs; while the rate of hegemonic decline may vary, hegemony is not restored except through hegemonic war. Thus a major question emerging from the long cycle perspective is, what happens as we approach the right-hand side of the figure, as hegemony weakens? Has the cycle of hegemonic war been broken? Or are forces at work that could break it before its next recurrence?

In the remainder of this chapter I will take up these questions from several angles. First, I will discuss the importance of power politics as an element of continuity in the hegemonic cycle. Then I will consider the potential role of nuclear weapons in changing the historical patterns of war and hegemony. Finally, I will suggest that trends toward a globalization of international politics could lay the basis for a new world order free of hegemonic war.

In the long term (but more like a hundred more years than a thousand, I would guess), a major transition seems to be taking place. The current generation sits atop a great divide between the past ten thousand years, in which war has played a central role in human civilization, and a "postwar" era of the future, marked by at least minimal global political stability.

Power Politics

The recurrence of great power war, in my view, grows out of the underlying practices of international politics in the core of the world system. Those practices are structured around the attempts of nation-states to gain power in the international system (or to prevent others from gaining power) through the use of military force. This aspect of world politics has been quite persistent over the past five centuries and indeed long before that.

The writings of Machiavelli, dating from the beginning of the five centuries under study, are still considered paradigmatic of power politics.[37] Richard Falk argues that Machiavelli best set forth the "modern world picture," which "still dominates the thinking and behavior of virtually every political leader of the world" (Lifton and Falk 1982:240). Although nuclear weapons have changed reality, the Machiavellian

37. Meinecke (1957) and Giddens (1984:350–53) discuss Machiavellianism.

mode of thinking persists, resulting in what Falk calls "a desperate attempt to adapt the technology of mass destruction to the ongoing predominance . . . of the Machiavellian world picture" (p. 241).[38]

The theoretical apologists for power politics are called "realists."[39] Ashley (1985:19) criticizes "realism" for denying the existence of international community, for portraying international relations as an anarchic "space beyond the margins of community." In fact, according to Ashley, there *is* an international community in which national leaders are the members and realism itself is the basis for community. Power-seeking national behavior, and "rituals of power," define this world community and its practice.

Power politics is the predominant set of rules by which international politics is both played and interpreted. Great powers are compelled to adopt realist behavior if they are to survive in a realist environment, so realism reproduces itself. The United States, Soviet Union, and China are the three current great powers that joined the system most recently and from outside the traditional European system. Each was motivated by revolutionary aspirations reaching beyond power politics in the international realm, but each eventually was drawn into playing power politics. In the case of the United States, Woodrow Wilson's idealism went down in flames. The USSR started out with high aspirations in 1917[40] but soon adopted realist behavior little different from other great powers. China, within a few decades of its revolution, became a power balancer, shifting towards the United States against the Soviet Union (its ideological comrade, but also a potentially threatening neighbor).[41] Realism, then, is a code of behavior that both adapts the nation for survival in a "realist" international environment and simultaneously reproduces that environment around itself.

The balance-of-power system of realist international politics has, according to Morgenthau ([1948] 1967:198), prevented world domination for four centuries, but only at the price of recurrent warfare.

In a world whose moving force is the aspiration of sovereign nations for power, peace can be maintained only by two devices. One is . . . the balance of power. The other consists of normative limitations upon that struggle, in the forms of international law, international morality, and world public opinion. . . . Neither of these devices, as they operate today, is likely to keep the struggle for power indefinitely within peaceful bounds (p. 22).

38. Falk argues that the Machiavellian way of thinking obstructs humanity's ability to overcome the nuclear threat and therefore must be removed. He suggests that a new, "holistic" alternative to Machiavellianism may be starting to emerge (p. 242).

39. The power-seeking behavior that underlies realism is summed up by Morgenthau ([1948] 1967: 202): "the desire to attain a maximum of power is universal." International politics are defined in terms of sovereign nations pursuing their own national interests, and power is the ability to influence other nations in order to further one's own interests.

40. Trotsky, on being made foreign minister, said he would issue a few proclamations supporting world revolution and then close up shop.

41. Japan is an unusual case; it has built itself up since 1945 as a world economic power but without commensurate military might. It is not clear, as of this writing, whether Japan will be able to maintain its different path or whether it will be forced back into remilitarization and a return to the rules of power politics.

The long cycle perspective suggests that a balance of power may be only a transitional and unstable phase of the hegemonic cycle. Every balance-of-power system in Europe degenerated into recurring great power wars and eventually hegemonic war. The two centuries after the balance-of-power system was enshrined at Westphalia contained the most regularly recurring war peaks (see chapter 11). Only the revival of strong hegemony after 1815 temporarily dampened the recurrence of great power war. But hegemony itself has always been temporary and has come about only as a result of hegemonic war.

Power politics underlies the long cycles of recurring war in crucial ways. As long as nations try to maximize power by any means, including force, two things will be true. First, economic surplus will continue to be diverted to war, with consequences including the fact that bigger wars will occur in periods of greater economic surplus. Second, changes in relative national power will continue to bring the eventual recurrence of hegemonic war.[42]

Two ultimately contradictory tendencies are at work in global power politics—a tendency toward the recurrence of great power war and a tendency toward the ever-greater destructiveness of war. But great power war cannot continue to recur indefinitely while wars become exponentially more destructive.[43] Thus power politics has brought about its own obsolescence.[44]

Nuclear Deterrence

The existence of nuclear weapons is widely considered to be the most important change in world politics distinguishing the current era from that before 1945. Throughout the previous few centuries, nation-states had developed within borders, forming a "hard shell" against attack; for insular powers (chiefly Britain and the United States), the oceans contributed to secure borders. Nuclear weapons deployed on missiles, however, have eliminated this hard shell and have exposed the strongest military powers, including the most insular ones, to devastating attacks anywhere in their homeland (Dehio [1948] 1962:281).[45] Nuclear weapons made offense much cheaper and defense essentially impossible. Thus only by threatening retaliation can attack be blunted. Each side builds up its forces in order to intimidate the other side from attacking.

42. Hegemonic war could only recur in the current era by "irrational" (even suicidal) acts of political leaders. But the most appropriate historical precedent, World War I, shows that such apparently self-defeating outcomes do occur.

43. Recent research on "nuclear winter" only confirms in the starkest terms that great power war has made itself obsolete.

44. In Modelski's (1978:226) terms, "political innovations" are needed that would allow world leadership to be structured by means other than war. He argues that "we need not conclude that all global systems must inherently be subject to . . . a pattern of events that includes severe global war." Long war cycles are "no more than an explication of the functioning of the global system we have known and experienced over the past few centuries" (p. 235). Alker, Biersteker, and Inoguchi (1985:1) go further and speak of a "transformative decline in the state system itself" marked by a drastic diminishing of "sovereignty."

45. This trend started with airplanes, especially with the strategic bombing in World War II.

Some people think that nuclear weapons have changed the rules of power politics, since it is impossible to use force (except in limited doses) without risking unacceptable retaliation. From my perspective, nuclear war has not done away with power politics but is the culmination of power politics. While nuclear war has made changes in the rules of power politics *necessary,* those changes have not yet come about. We are thus in a curious (and dangerous) transition, waiting for the practice of world politics to catch up with changes in technology.

Nuclear weapons have not replaced but have complemented conventional weapons. Nuclear weapons are used not just to deter nuclear war but to deter all war between great powers (Forsberg 1985). Policymakers, especially in the West, have deliberately avoided a "firebreak" between conventional and nuclear war and instead have integrated forward-based nuclear weapons into all branches of the military. This makes the likelihood high that any great power war (in particular an East-West war in Europe) would lead to nuclear war. And by creating that likelihood, the West uses the threat of nuclear war to deter conventional war.[46]

In theory, this system of extended deterrence minimizes the likelihood of any great power war. But unless the likelihood is zero, the system is flawed—because any great power war would be likely to escalate to nuclear weapons.[47]

The question, then, is whether nuclear deterrence can be relied on to succeed indefinitely, as it seems to have in the past forty years, in preventing great power wars. That is, can the risk of great power war be kept all the way down to zero by means of nuclear deterrence? My answer, which is negative, contains four aspects:

1. Nuclear deterrence has not yet had to face the important test—how it performs in a period of economic upswing coupled with weakened hegemony. It will face that test around 2000–2030. In the first few decades after 1945, American hegemony was extremely strong, and while the great powers remained on a war footing throughout that upswing phase period, no serious challenge to hegemony was possible. In the last ten years, as American hegemony has declined, the long wave has passed into a war downswing phase. Thus the absence of great power war for forty years—which is proudly claimed by advocates of nuclear deterrence—may have little or nothing to do with nuclear deterrence. The period from 1816 to 1852 (nearly forty years) was also free of great power war.

2. Deterrence can fail in theory and has in practice. Deterrence theory rests on the assumption that nation-states will act rationally[48] in avoiding behavior that is self-

46. Such a system of extended deterrence, according to Forsberg (1985), is not likely to move toward "minimal deterrence" because of the fear that, by creating a "firebreak," this would make great power conventional war more likely (and that such a conventional war could in turn jump the firebreak anyway and lead to nuclear war). Thus, Forsberg argues that conventional arms reductions and great power confidence-building measures must be undertaken in parallel with nuclear arms reductions. See also Forsberg, Elias, and Goodman (1985:12–16).

47. Thus deterrence remains unappealing to the average person in need of "security." To quote an American teenager, "When my 11-year-old sister wakes up crying, it doesn't do much good to say, 'Don't worry, Jenny, Reagan is building more bombs, so you don't have to worry about a war' " (*Boston Globe,* June 22, 1983:3).

48. Rationality in the economic sense means acting in a way that maximizes the things one values—action consistent with desired outcomes.

destructive. This assumption is debatable. Levy (1983c) outlines a number of linkages between *misperception* and the outbreak of war. These include misperceptions
of the adversary's capabilities, of the adversary's intentions, or of the likely reactions
of third states whose intervention can critically alter the balance of forces. Jervis
(1976) also stresses the role of misperception in international crises. In addition to
misperception, other psychological influences can distort the rational analysis of the
probable outcomes of alternative actions.[49]

The most relevant historical precedent, the buildup before 1914, culminated with
the failure of deterrence.[50] Nuclear weapons, certainly, are not comparable to the
weaponry of World War I.[51] But the psychology of deterrence was similar—a great
war would lead to very severe costs. In 1914, those costs were miscalculated. It is
true that before World War I, only a minority understood how devastating a great war
would be, while at present a majority of people are aware of the danger.[52] But these
are matters of degree, and, as Kahler (1979) suggests, even these distinctions are
being narrowed currently by strategies that underrate the destructiveness of nuclear
war—war-winning strategies, first-strike force buildups, civilian defense programs,
and/or ''strategic defense'' proposals. Can anyone say confidently that military and
political leaders in the next four decades will accurately estimate the costs of great
power war?

3. Although nuclear war has not occurred, the actual behavior of great powers in
this era has not changed much despite the presence of nuclear weapons. It is power
politics as ususal. Organski and Kugler (1980) analyze the effect of superpower
involvement on the war-or-peace outcomes of international conflicts using data from
the post-1945 period. They ask, ''have the rules governing conflict behavior between
nations been drastically altered since the advent of the nuclear era? Popular credence
argues that they have been largely, if not entirely, changed'' (p. 2). Their analysis
indicates that those rules have *not* changed: ''The tendency to go to war increases as
the likelihood of great-power involvement increases and as the possibility that

49. Jervis, Lebow, and Stein (1985) draw on psychological theory to explain the failures of deterrence
in practice and suggest that nuclear deterrence may actually aggravate the likelihood of war. On the
psychological critique of deterrence as vulnerable to ''misperception,'' see also Van Evera (1985). For a
counterargument to the idea that war resulted from ''miscalculation'' in 1914, see Lynn-Jones (1985).

50. German chancellor Bethmann reportedly was asked, a few days after the outbreak of war in August
1914, why the war had started. ''He threw up his hands and cried 'If I only knew!' '' (quoted in Snyder and
Diesing 1977:549).

51. Consider Bloch's (1899:xviii) statement that ''the possibility of firing half a dozen bullets without
having to stop to reload has transformed the conditions of modern war.''

52. Thomson (1950:212), for instance, writes that ''the careless optimism with which masses of people
were able to contemplate a major European war served only to indicate their ignorance of what it would be
like.'' However, some awareness of the problem was reflected in the popular literature on the horrors of
war that preceded World War I (for example, Lamszus, 1913, on the ''human slaughter-house''.
Increased awareness may not help. Lasswell (1935:248) argues that ''the incessant repetition of the danger
and horror of war strengthens the assumption of inevitability and to this extent preserves the expectation of
violence.'' Lasswell's (1935:247) observation that ''the portrayal of the horrors of war is more dramatic
than ever, yet preparations for war exceed overt preparations for peace'' could be a description of the early
1980s. In fact, it referred to the early 1930s.

nuclear weapons may be used becomes more real. Why, then, is the opposite believed? It can only be from wishful thinking.'' (p. 161). "In short, . . . what peace we have has not been imposed by a nuclear deterrent. . . . Nuclear countries may well fight each other with nuclear weapons one day, should their privileged position or the present international order be threatened'' (p. 216).

4. Finally, the potentials of nuclear proliferation cannot be kept in rein indefinitely in a world governed by power politics. Eventually, more and more nations (and possibly nonnational entities) will obtain nuclear weapons, and this can only blur the current dividing line between conventional wars (raging all over the world) and nuclear wars (limited to great powers and hence more preventable). In the proliferation area, as with the overall prospects for war, the relative success of the past forty years does not necessarily imply continuing success in the next forty years.

Nuclear weapons have not brought about the end of power politics as a paradigm for international relations. As Adams (1985) writes:

The escalation of the power to destroy did not prevent the First World War. Neither did it prevent the Second. It is very unlikely that it will prevent a third. As in the first two cataclysms, it may postpone the catastrophe, while increasing the probability that it will be more nearly total. The problem of contemporary society is how to translate postponement into prevention.

Where, then, should long-term stability be sought in a world where deterrence is not permanently stable?

The Globalization of International Politics

Several trends in the current era have the potential to profoundly alter the dynamic of recurring war. Globalizing influences in international politics—including the advent of strategic intercontinental weapons, the information revolution, and the conquest of space—make both necessary and possible a shift to a new world order based on common security rather than power politics.

The Information Revolution

The information revolution may strongly affect the directions of world politics in the coming decades. Low-cost telecommunications are beginning to tie the planet together in a tightly woven web, laying the basis for the ultimate emergence of global entities that transcend national ones. The emergence of international organizations (including United Nations agencies and many others), of international scientific and technical communities, and of international business networks all point toward a developing pattern of global organization that will be greatly strengthened by continued advances in telecommunications and information processing.

The information revolution has begun to have specific and dramatic effects in the area of military techniques. Kurth (1979:34) suggests that, "Out of a massive telecommunications industry would issue the inventions and innovations for a new kind of weapons systems and military defense, of which existing 'precision-guided munitions,' 'smart bombs,' and 'automated battlefields' are only premonitions.'' Deudney (1983:20) argues that the ''militarization of . . . the electromagnetic spectrum'' has created a ''transparency revolution'' allowing breakthroughs in both intelligence gathering and tactical targeting.[53] Thus, ''Planetary-scale information systems bring the strategic competition between the superpowers to its least stable and most dangerous state. At the same time these systems make planetary-scale security possible for the first time in human history'' (p. 21).

New information technologies may have potentials for revolutionizing conventional warfare in ''peaceful'' ways by allowing new concepts of defense to be realized.[54] Barnaby (1986) argues that new ''smart'' technologies have made tactical military defense much cheaper than offense. For example, a wire-guided shoulder-fired TOW missile costing $15,000 ''has a high probability of destroying a main battle tank costing $3 million or more.'' The TOW missile has a range of nearly four kilometers compared to two kilometers for the tank. Likewise a $250,000 antiship missile using its own radar to home in from up to seventy kilometers away, can destroy a major warship costing hundreds of millions of dollars. Antiaircraft missiles offer similar advantages, as the Afghan rebels have recently shown.

Thus, Barnaby suggests, the fifty thousand Warsaw Pact tanks and twenty thousand NATO tanks, lined up in Europe, are obsolete. Smart antitank missiles will be able to inflict utter devastation on advancing tanks at a relatively low cost in money and people. ''The plain fact is that it is virtually impossible to hide some 60 tons of hot metal on the modern battlefield from the sensors of intelligent missiles.'' NATO's best strategy, according to Barnaby, would be a ''non-provocative defense'' based on a defense zone fifty kilometers deep along the one-thousand-kilometer East-West border. The zone would be saturated with smart weapons having virtually no offensive capabilities but overwhelming defensive capabilities. This kind of approach would both blunt the possibilities for conventional war and allow the West to stop using nuclear weapons to deter conventional war (extended deterrence). The idea of nonprovocative defense, although not yet fully developed, suggests that the information revolution may open up new possibilities for changing the rules of great power war.

Outer Space

The conquest of space will also contribute to the globalization of international politics in the next few decades. The exploration of space has been compared with the ''voyages of discovery'' of the Portuguese sailing ships around 1500. The coming fifty years may see an expansion of the world system comparable to the expansion of

53. The atmosphere, orbital space, and the ocean surface have been ''illuminated'' completely, while the ocean depths remain at least partially opaque, which is fortunate for deterrence because submarines provide a survivable second-strike capability (Deudney 1983:24).

54. These concepts go under the title of ''defensive defense,'' ''non-provocative defense,'' ''alternative defense,'' and the like. Randall Forsberg's ''alternative defense working group'' (at the Institute for Defense and Disarmament Studies in Brookline, Mass.) is working in this field.

the European "world" five centuries ago. The expansion of civilization into space has proceeded at a remarkable pace in the three decades since the first satellite was orbited in the late 1950s.

In the next few decades, the move into space could complement the information revolution. The information revolution provides the microelectronics necessary for control in a space environment, while space provides the location for communication satellites and eventually for producing the silicon crystals that are the building blocks of electronics.

Space has crucial military uses, and this contributes (along with the information revolution) to the globalization of the military system. At present, the military uses of outer space are largely confined to the use of space satellites for surveillance and communications. It is not clear whether orbital space will be used as a base for weapons systems, as the U.S. government currently plans to do, or not. This is, I think, a critical decision that may profoundly affect the character of the dangerous 2000–2030 period. An arms race in space conjures up the worst precedents of the 1893–1914 period—the Anglo-German naval competition and the race for colonies in Africa.

At this writing the U.S. Strategic Defense Initiative ("star wars") program, aimed at developing space weapons, is under fierce debate. It is the central bone of contention between the superpowers (October 1986 Reykjavík summit meeting) and the object of criticism from the mainstream of the U.S. scientific community on grounds of infeasibility and cost (Piel 1986). Nonetheless the budget is growing rapidly. Because of the centrality of this debate to the choices we are making about the 2000–2030 period, I will spend a few pages trying to sum up the structure of the argument as I see it.

First, let us consider the concept of hegemony in space. This would mean that one country had the ability to control space militarily, to destroy any satellite, weapon, or missile that the other side put into (or through) space. In contrast, the hegemonic country's own satellites, weapons, and missiles would have free access to all of space. Orbital space borders on every nation and every city and is just two hundred miles away (and at the top of a strong energy gradient) from any point on earth (Deudney 1983). Thus, as Deudney (1983:17) argues, "effective control of space by one state would lead to planet-wide hegemony."

This was not far from what some researchers into space weapons had in mind. Ten years ago, in the first unclassified article proposing a strategic defense system in space,[55] Hunter (1977:1–8) argued that lasers based in space can ultimately provide "an effective defense against even massive ballistic missile exchanges."[56] But more importantly, "it is easily conceivable that such weapons can be used for tactical

55. Written by Maxwell Hunter of Lockheed after a decade of top-secret research on space-based laser weapons. The 1977 article was intended to stir up debate on a strategic defense system and succeeded in doing so (conversation with author).

56. Apparently the current thinking today is to put the lasers on the ground and reflect them off mirrors in space.

applications''—that is, against tanks, buildings, airplanes, or other targets on the ground. "When lasers are placed in space so that every location on this planet is placed continuously in the target area of a laser battle station,'' wrote Hunter, "then one has a right to expect truly fundamental changes.'' "This would be Pax Americana,'' according to Hunter. And America is uniquely suited to win the race for hegemony in space, in Hunter's opinion:[57]

space forces . . . appear to have basic characteristics which are especially suited to the nature and evolving posture of the United States. We are the strongest nation on earth technically and economically but are having increasing . . . problems with the maintenance of overseas forces and base structures.

But whether or not the United States seizes this opportunity, someone will—so in Hunter's view there is an imperative for the United States to act first: "If we were to do it when the opposition did not, it would give us commanding options compared to the current situation. If the enemy were to do it and we did not, it would totally negate our current strategic posture.'' To use Dehio's terms, true hegemony in space would provide the ultimate insularity—an insularity the United States lost when the Soviet Union deployed long-range nuclear missiles.

The view of star wars as a drive for general hegemony in space (rather than any particular plan of "strategic defense'') seems to be born out by some of the statements of U.S. military leaders in 1982–83:[58]

"We do not have to stretch our imagination very far to see that the nation that controls space may control the world'' (Edward C. Aldridge, Under Secretary of the Air Force).

"We should move into war-fighting capabilities—that is ground-to-space war-fighting capabilities, space-to-space, space-to-ground'' (Gen. Robert T. Marsh, Commander, Air Force Systems Command).

"Space is the new high ground of battle'' (Lt. Gen. Richard C. Henry, recently retired Deputy Commander of Air Force Space Command).

The United States established the Air Force Space Command in 1982 (operations began in 1985) to coordinate the military uses of space. Its commander, Gen. James V. Hartinger, stated that this "means that the Air Force is going operational in space.'' It is U.S. policy to "vigorously pursue'' systems to "project force in and from space'' and to "wage war effectively'' from space.[59] A June 1983 Air Force study calls for "space superiority'' in order to "prevail'' in a conflict on earth. And

57. Defense Advanced Research Projects Agency director Robert Cooper recently testified before Congress that "we are clearly ahead of the Soviets in overall space technology'' (quoted in Center for Defense Information 1983).

58. These quotes and the information in the following paragraph are from Center for Defense Information (1983).

59. *1984–88 Five Year Defense Guidance,* document of the U.S. Department of Defense (Center for Defense Information 1983).

the Air Force Space Master Plan through the year 2000 calls for a move toward "space combat" systems.[60]

If the United States could restore and strengthen its hegemony in this way, wouldn't this be a good thing? Might this not halt the slide toward weakened hegemony that has, in the past, always ended in hegemonic war? This is the essence of the argument in favor of star wars, as I see it. The U.S. proponents want to try to return to strong U.S. hegemony, which would be more stable than the present rough bipolar parity.[61] And the Soviet opposition to the program is essentially an opposition to the restoration of U.S. hegemony.

The question of whether restored U.S. hegemony would be desirable, however, is the wrong question. The point is that renewed U.S. hegemony imposed by military superiority is impossible. It is impossible because the invention of nuclear weapons has permanently changed the nature of great power war. One nuclear weapon can cause utterly unacceptable damage to a country, even a large one. Each side has tens of thousands of nuclear weapons deployed against each other with a large variety of delivery systems.[62] In the event that a strategic defense system were constructed, the opposing side could defeat its purpose at much lower cost by increasing the number and variety of its delivery systems. Nuclear weapons can now be made small enough to fit in the trunk of a car, or on a speedboat or a small plane. Only a tiny fraction of the opposing superpower's nuclear arsenal needs to get through in order to devastate the country. Thus the strategic defense system cannot protect against inevitable catastrophic loss in the event of any all-out war.[63] But hegemony rests on the ability to survive and prevail in an all-out war (which backs up the threat of escalating use of force), and without that ability it is impossible to establish hegemony.[64]

Thus, even if we accept that strengthened U.S. hegemony would be a good thing, that the Soviet Union is a potential challenger to U.S. hegemony, and that a hegemonic challenge would be very bad, it still does not follow that star wars is a good idea. Militarization of space will not restore hegemony. The challenge is to find an alternative to a hegemony imposed by military might.

The move into space may actually help provide that alternative, if the dangers of

60. Spectacular technological failures early in 1986 clearly set back the American drive into space, but their ramifications are not yet clear, except that future shuttle flights in the next few years will be exclusively (rather than just predominantly as planned) devoted to military payloads.

61. Since, from their point of view, the main threat to stability would be a challenge for world domination by the Soviet Union.

62. Only some of these are high-flying ballistic missiles, which a strategic defense system would defend against. Even some of the ballistic missiles would get through, since no one expects the system to work perfectly. The Center for Defense Information (1983) argues that space weapons cannot be defended effectively because "it is impossible to protect military resources fully from the effects of a nuclear explosion in space." With the space weapons of both sides vulnerable, these weapons "increase incentives for a first strike" in order to preserve military and communications capabilities in space.

63. Deudney (1985:272) concludes that space-based defenses cannot "restore the protective insularity that America once enjoyed."

64. The same conditions make it as impossible to successfully challenge and succeed to hegemony as to reestablish hegemony.

militarization of space can be avoided. Space has been a strong area for the creation of international regimes. International cooperation in space has been significant and conflict minimal.[65] Nuclear weapons are currently banned from space by treaty, and "strategic defense" systems are banned under the Anti-Ballistic Missile (ABM) treaty.[66] Furthermore, the sheer size of space may act as a kind of safety valve on superpower conflicts, especially those involving territorial or economic disputes.[67]

One critical benefit of the conquest of space is an intangible one—the new awareness human beings have gained of the oneness of our planet. Only since the 1960s, when the first photographs showed earth as seen from space, has a "global perspective" become tangible. The promising aspects of the information revolution—in terms of connecting humanity in a global network—are enhanced by the move into space, beyond national borders. The global scope of space-based systems could someday strengthen new political structures at the world level.

Ultimately, space may hold potential for human habitation and economic production (O'Neill 1974; 1976, gives the optimistic view). Space has the important advantages of uninterrupted solar energy and a zero-gravity environment, which makes transportation, construction, and materials handling potentially very cheap[68] (fixed gravity environments can be created where desired by the revolution of large structures). Orbital space may be well suited to certain types of industrial and agricultural processes—particularly semiconductor and pharmaceutical manufacturing.[69] Space could become an important energy source, if solar collector satellites in geosynchronous orbit, beaming electricity to cities below, become economically feasible. Eventually food might even be grown in space, where conditions can be controlled and sunlight is plentiful. Someday orbital space colonies may ship food and energy "downstream" to earth in somewhat the manner that the ancient city received its food from peasants upstream (see chapter 1). Space could become the new "periphery" of the world system.

Thus space offers both dangers and opportunities, depending on what path is followed in developing its potentials. If cooperative space regimes become stronger,

---

65. Deudney (1985:290) advocates a strengthened push for peaceful cooperative ventures in space, especially in deep-space pioneering (which would commit both superpowers to a joint program of colonizing the moon, Mars, and nearby asteroids) and in "global habitability and information security" programs. He suggests (1985:278, 283) that "the space movement and the peace movement are natural—even if unrecognized—allies," because "the extensive deployment of weapons in near space will foreclose whatever purely commercial space prospects exist."

66. True, all these treaties and regimes may break down soon, but this cannot be assumed.

67. O'Neill (1974:36) suggests that the extension of "territory" into space may alleviate territorial conflicts on earth. I note that the "scramble for colonies" of the 1890s did not alleviate and may have exacerbated great power tensions. But maybe the problem before 1914 was just that available colonies ran out and the entire world was divided up. In space this would take much longer; geosynchronous orbit alone is many times larger than the earth's surface.

68. Most materials will have to be obtained from the moon or elsewhere off earth, since escaping earth's gravity is very expensive.

69. Silicon and gallium arsenide crystals can be grown with much greater purity and at lower cost in a zero-gravity vacuum environment. Furthermore, turning those crystals into integrated circuits now requires a $100-million fabrication plant, about half the cost of which might eventually be saved by building in space (*Boston Globe*, Mar. 25, 1984:13).

space can be a positive force in changing the traditional rules of international power politics. If, however, the superpowers pursue a race for military hegemony in space, attempting to play out the traditional rules of power politics on an expanded scale, a dangerous period may become even more unstable.

International Regimes

If a global alternative to hegemony is to emerge, new structures at the international and global levels will need to be created. The proliferation of international regimes— tacit or explicit agreements among countries (based on shared norms and rules) governing the operation of the international system—is a hopeful trend in this direction.

Keohane (1984) advocates regimes as an alternative to hegemony. He argues that hegemony is unlikely to be restored soon, since hegemony emerges from global war, which is not an option in the nuclear age. Keohane thus asks, how can we have international cooperation without hegemony? Cooperation is defined as an adjustment process where an inherent harmony of interests is *not* present. International regimes, according to Keohane, can bring about such cooperation by changing the context in which states make self-interested decisions. Regimes help national governments reduce decision costs as well as uncertainty. Thus cooperation can emerge even when self-interested behavior is assumed, in Keohane's view. Regimes *"empower* governments rather than shackling them."

In the current era many international regimes have emerged in areas ranging from security matters and spheres of influence to monetary finances, seabed resources, environmental protection, and outer space. Many functional regimes are organized around the agencies of the United Nations and other international organizations. These regimes and organizational networks can be seen either as transitional forms in moving toward a world government or as prototypes of a new order at the world level that falls short of world "government." In either case, the development of international regimes moves in the direction of providing a stability to world politics that, in the past, only hegemony has provided.

Regimes may offer the United States opportunities to provide world leadership without hegemony. The strategy of actively seeking and promoting global structures to replace hegemony in an orderly way would be a wise move by a declining hegemon. By actively providing "leadership for peace," the United States could ensure itself a major role in shaping a posthegemonic global order in which it would continue to be the most powerful single country. This is a "third way" in distinction from the strategies of seeking renewed military hegemony or withdrawing from world involvement. It is possible to learn from *both* 1914 and 1939.

Toward a New World Order

As the twenty-first century approaches, and we consider the alternative futures that lie before us, we should note the lasting truths that emerge from the historical study of war and economics. Wars cost money. Wars are inflationary. Wars are bad for the economy except in rare cases. These statements apply, though less strongly, to the preparations for war as well as the actual fighting of wars.[70]

The war system is, thus, a monkey on the back of the world's economy, in the sense that the expression is used to describe drug addiction.[71] The world currently spends about $900 billion each year on war and preparations for war (Forsberg, Elias, and Goodman 1985:5). And the security we buy for that sum is precious little, for one simple reason: War and the preparation for war cannot provide security in a globalized, nuclear-armed world. The only meaningful security today is common security (see Palme Commission 1982; Fine et al. 1985). We need to make the transition from a world order based around hegemony, hegemonic rivalry, deterrence, and war to one based on common security at the global level.

In closing, I would stress again the indeterminacy of the future. True, there is no possibility of returning to the past, continuing to live as in the past, or avoiding a transformation of the world system. But the nature of this transformation is not yet determined; it depends on the choices we make. Different futures arise from different assumptions and different strategies.[72] There are an endless number of possible futures, desirable and undesirable.

The transition to a "postwar" world order—be it through global cooperation or global suicide—is inevitable. But how that transition occurs, and where it leads, is up to us to choose. The parting words of Moses come to mind:

I call heaven and earth to witness against you this day, that I have set before you life and death, the blessing and the curse; therefore choose life, that you may live, you and your seed (Deut. 30:19).

70. As I write this, the most recent publication in my hands parallels the most ancient on this point. Lester Thurow (1986) writes that "no defense spending can be justified on economic grounds. . . . The current military buildup is a drain on the future productivity of the American economy." Sun Tzu said much the same about China in 400 B.C.

71. The war system reminds me of a recent insurance advertisement in which King Kong is rampaging through a city, swatting at airplanes and the like. A young woman indignantly shouts at him from high in a skyscraper, "Who's gonna *pay* for this mess?"

72. Revolutionaries foresee the world's transformation into internationalist socialism, ending hegemonic cycles. Liberals dream of its transformation into world government or some other supernational world order, also ending hegemonic cycles. Conservatives can envision its transformation into global empire (the evil empire of their worst fears or a Pax Americana of their dreams), which would also end cycles of hegemony. More dialectically, the world system now holds the potential to transform itself through nuclear war (ending hegemony among other things)—a "negation" of long cycles in the most dialectical sense.

DATA APPENDIXES

APPENDIX A

Data Sources

This appendix describes briefly the source of each economic time series,[1] and any particular considerations relevant to the interpretation of results for that time series. These often include my own subjective judgments as to the accuracy and consistency of the data, based on the notes and explanations of the original authors.

It must be recognized at the outset that the reliability of all such historical economic time series as these (particularly for the earlier centuries) is much lower than for recent decades. Much credence should not be placed in any particular data point in any particular source. I have drawn data from twenty-seven sources in hopes of ensuring at least some high-quality series, balancing the drawbacks of one series against the strengths of others and arriving at an appropriate sample of historical data within the confines of presently available sources.

Given the arbitrary nature of the scaling of variables for purposes of this study, I have rescaled forty-six of the fifty-five series to make them easier to work with computationally. The forty-six series are rescaled (by multiplying through by a constant) so that each series begins at an arbitrary index number of one hundred.[2] The rescaling is merely a practical step and does not affect the substance of the statistical analysis.[3] The nine innovation and invention series are not rescaled because they are actual annual counts of events (innovations or patents), which are meaningful in their original unit scales.

In a few series (mostly individual commodity prices), data for scattered years are missing in the original. In such cases I have made a linear interpolation to estimate those years, reasoning that such an interpolation would only trivially affect the trend of the series based on the existing data points. Such interpolations are noted below in the descriptions of each series.

In several series the original is broken into several time segments that are not entirely compatible—for instance, the scale, the measurement method, or the dimensions of the political unit under study change. In such cases I have "spliced" two or more such subseries together in order to arrive at a single time series. In most such splices, for a certain year the source gives two data points—one ending the first segment in one scale and the other beginning the next segment in another scale. I use the ratio between these as a constant

---

1. War data transformations have been discussed in the text (chap. 8); the war data all come from Levy (1983a).

2. Note that this does not make them comparable as though on the same scale, since each series begins at a different point in time (by which time an earlier series is no longer at 100).

3. In the actual analysis presented in chaps. 9–10, the data were carried to three decimal points. In Appendix B, however, the data are rounded to one decimal point to save space and to better reflect their level of precision.

multiplier, which I apply to the whole first segment in order to join it to the next segment. This type of splice I call a "continuous" splice.

In just a few cases, the splice is more difficult, since the first segment ends in one year and the next segment begins, in a different scale, in the *next* year—a "discontinuous" splice. It is impossible to say what the change between these two years is, and I can only set them equal and then make the splice as above. All splices in the time series are noted in the paragraphs below and are "continuous" unless otherwise noted.

The following paragraphs discuss each series. Fuller information on a series may be found in the original source cited. For each series, a code name of up to eight letters is given.

Price Indexes

BRCNPRI: South English consumer price index, 1495–1954 (Phelps-Brown and Hopkins 1956:193, col. 1). This series, along with BR2WAG, are taken from two 700-year series(!) put together by Phelps-Brown and Hopkins (the years before 1495 were not used). The following years in the 460-year series were interpolated by me: 1563, 1564, and 1575.

BRINPRI: South English industrial price index, 1495–1640 (Doughty 1975:188). Doughty specifically puts forward this series and BRAGPRI as superior alternatives to Phelps-Brown and Hopkins' series (BRCNPRI).

BRAGPRI: South English agricultural price index, 1495–1640 (Doughty 1975:188). See BRINPRI.

SPTEPRI: Spanish (New Castile) textile price index, 1651–1800 (Hamilton 1947:264). Hamilton presents annual price indexes for seven groups of commodities: fruits and nuts, poultry, textiles, animal products, fish, spices, and forest products. I used only the textile and animal product series. No years are missing, but most data points are annotated with superscripts ranging from 1 to 14, for which I found no explanation in the original.

SPANPRI: Spanish (New Castile) animal product prices, 1651–1800 (Hamilton 1947). See SPTEPRI.

BRPRPRI: English producers' goods price index, 1661–1801 (E. Schumpeter 1938:34). Schumpeter's years are given in harvest years, e.g., "1660/61," of which I used the second of the two years. There was a break in the original series at 1696, which I spliced by multiplying the data before that by a constant (1.109). The source also gives a consumer price index, which I did not use.

BRKOPRI: British commodity prices, 1780–1922 (Kondratieff [1928] 1984). Data were taken from the listing given by Van Duijn (1983:75), since the 1984 translation was not yet available.

USKOPRI: U.S. commodity prices, 1791–1922 (Kondratieff [1928] 1984). See BRKOPRI.

BRWPI: British wholesale price index, 1750–1975 (Mitchell 1980:772). Splices in the data set were made at 1790, 1850–51, 1871, 1914, and 1948. A discontinuous splice was made in 1850–51.

FRWPI: French wholesale price index, 1798–1975 (Mitchell 1980:772). Splices were made at 1819–20 (discontinuous), 1913, and 1948.

GEWPI: German wholesale price index, 1792–1918 (Mitchell 1980:772). A splice was made in 1913. I terminated the series after 1918 because of the extreme inflation in Germany after World War I (from 1922 to 1923 alone, prices rose 500-fold, or 50,000 percent), which could not be handled by the methodology of this analysis (and because of the subsequent breakup of Germany).

USWPI: U.S. wholesale price index, 1801–1975 (Fellner 1956:394, for 1801–89; then U.S. Census 1975:199, col. 23, for 1890–1970; then U.S. Census 1983:486, for 1971–75). Fellner cites U.S. government sources.

BEINPRI: Belgian industrial price index, 1822–1913 (Loots 1936:34). Loots gives eleven price indexes in all. I used the "global" index for industrial prices (BEINPRI) and the "total" index for agricultural products (BEAGPRI). Loots also provides detailed price data by commodity, which I did not use.

BEAGPRI: Belgian agricultural price index, 1835–1913 (Loots 1936). See BEINPRI.

Commodity Prices

FRWHPRI: French wheat prices (Paris), 1495–1788 (Baulant 1968:537). 1556, 1557, and 1590 are noted as incomplete years. The series is for top-quality wheat and is the average of four seasonal price levels from 1520 on.

GEWHPRI: German wheat prices (Cologne), 1531–1786 (Ebeling and Irsigler 1976 1: 666). Data were given by harvest year, not calendar year, and I used the first of the two years given. Data are from the *Mittel* (average) column under prices. They also provide annual data on prices of rye, barley, and oats, which I did not use. Elsewhere the source gives very detailed monthly price data (also not used).

GEBDPRI: German bread prices (Cologne), 1658–1772 (Ebeling and Irsigler 1976 2:266). Data are taken from the *"Rechn."* column under *"malterbrot"* (bread). Prices are given in the currency of the Albus, the metal content of which varied over time, as discussed in the source.

NERYPRI: Netherlands prices for Prussian rye sold at the Amsterdam Produce Exchange, 1597–1783 (Posthumus 1964:573). Posthumus compiles overall price indexes for the Netherlands, but only by five-year periods, not annually. He also provides a mass of individual commodity data for the Netherlands but not on a regular enough annual basis to be useful, except in the case of this series, which he compiles separately. Prices are provided monthly, with an annual average for each year; the latter is the source for my series. The designation of the type of rye being recorded varies several times in the period, but with no apparent major effect.

BRMAPRI: English malt prices (Eton College), 1595–1831 (Beveridge 1939:144). Beveridge compiles a large collection of price series from various British sources. I used five. The data are somewhat spotty in places, and these series represent prices for one commodity in one location as kept in one set of records, so these series should be taken less seriously than most of the other price series.

BRHOPRI2: English hops prices (Eton College), 1622–1829 (Beveridge 1939:144, col. "Hops B"). The series was interpolated at 1642–43, 1691, 1693, 1701, 1717, 1753, 1761, 1763, 1765, 1779, 1784, 1802, 1805, 1808, and 1821.

BRWHPRI: English wheat prices (Winchester College), 1630–1817 (Beveridge 1939:81). Data are given for four quarters each year and in an annual figure, which I used.

BRCOPRI2: English coal prices (Eton College), 1653–1830 (Beveridge 1939:145). I interpolated data for the missing years of 1658 and 1664.

BRBDPRI2: English bread prices (Charterhouse), 1694–1800 (Beveridge 1939:208). Quarterly data are also given in the source (not used). I interpolated data for 1709–13.

ITWHPRI: Italian wheat prices (Milan), 1701–1860 (Maddalena 1974:379). Maddalena gives prices for a large variety of commodities, mostly food, of which I have looked at only two.

ITCOPRI: Italian hard coal prices (Milan), 1701–1860 (Maddalena 1974:395). See IT-WHPRI.

SWWHPRI: Swedish wheat prices, 1732–1914 (Jorberg 1972:632). This is an average price across 11–24 regions in a given year. Jorberg, like Maddalena, gives a large number of price series for various commodities, of which I looked at three. Jorberg also lists wage rates in current prices, which I did not use.

SWWDPRI2: Swedish pine wood prices, 1735–1914 (Jorberg 1972:690). This is an average across 1–6 regions from 1732 to 1802, then 24–29 regions through 1875, and 4–5 regions through 1914.

SWIRPRI: Swedish iron ore prices, 1732–1914 (Jorberg 1972:700). The price is an average across 4–5 regions.

Production Indexes

WOIN2PRO: World industrial production, 1740–1850 (Haustein and Neuwirth 1982:76). The authors cite Hoffman as the source. I am skeptical about the quality of Haustein and Neuwirth's data, but nonetheless use several series relating to innovation (see below), and include this world production series as an extension to the time frame covered by Kuczynski (WOINPRO). Haustein and Neuwirth also make indexes for innovation and invention, but it is not clear what they represent, and I did not use them.

WOINPRO: World industrial production, 1850–1975 (Kuczynski 1980:309). Kuczynski provides data on the "world" level. His series are complete, although I am not sure how he arrived at his data for the world as a whole.

WOAGPRO: World agricultural production, 1850–1975 (Kuczynski 1980:309). See WOINPRO.

WOTOPRO: World total production (including mining), 1850–1975 (Kuczynski 1980:310). See WOINPRO.

FRGNP: French real gross national product, 1820–1975 (Maddison 1982). Maddison has spent some years compiling GNP data for a number of countries, and they appear to be among the best estimates currently available.

BRGNP: British real gross national product, 1830–1975 (Mitchell 1980:818). This series comes from Mitchell's compendium of European historical statistics and is of fairly high quality. German GNP data are available but for only 63 years with high enough consistency, so German GNP data were not used. Splices for the British series were made at 1855, 1870, 1913, 1920, 1948, and 1965.

USGNP: U.S. real gross national product, 1889–1970 (U.S. Census 1975:224). The original is expressed in billions of dollars at 1958 prices. Data from 1960 forward include Alaska and Hawaii.

BRINPRO: British industrial production, 1801–1938 (Mitchell 1980:375). The series was spliced at 1855, 1914, and 1920. After 1920 the series covers Great Britain and Northern Ireland. Quality seems to be relatively high. The years 1939–45 were missing in the original, and since these could not reasonably be interpolated I terminated the series in 1938.

FRINPRO: French industrial production, 1815–1913 (Crouzet 1970:96, annexe 8a). The index covers industrial production in seven groups of industries. This series is chosen by Mitchell (1980:375) and appears to be of relatively high quality.

BEINPRO: Belgian industrial production, 1840–1975 (Vandermotten 1980:266). No transformations were needed.

Trade Indicators

SPTRA: Volume of Seville-Atlantic shipping, 1506–1650 (Chaunu 1956 6:334). This series on total tonnage of departing and returning ships in the Seville-Atlantic trade is included in Chaunu's eight-volume study of Seville-Atlantic shipping. Spanish trade with the New World could be particularly important (more so than more general trade indicators), in view of theories that precious metal influx caused long wave price upswings in this period.

BRWHEXP: British net volume of wheat exports, 1700–1775 (Minchinton 1969:63). Minchinton cites a J. Marshall from 1833 as the source. Negative numbers indicate net imports. Flour is included with wheat.

BREXP: English exports in current prices, 1700–1775 (Minchinton 1969). I interpolated data for 1705 and 1712. The series covers exports of produce and manufactures and is the only non-price series I have used that is expressed in current prices (not adjusted for inflation).

WOEXP: Total world exports, 1850–1975 (Kuczynski 1980:310). See WOINPRO. Data are expressed in constant prices.

Innovation Indicators

WOINN5: List of innovations, 1764–1975 (Haustein and Neuwirth 1982:76). See note on data quality under WOIN2PRO. These data are given as a time series listing the number of innovations each year.

WOINN2: List of innovations, 1856–1971 (Van Duijn [1981] 1983:26). These data and the next three innovation indicators are given in the sources as lists of innovations with their respective dates (the dating of each innovation is controversial and varies considerably by source). I converted these lists to time series representing the number of innovations each year. Van Duijn's list covers 13 industrial sectors, for the world as a whole.

WOINN1: List of innovations, 1904–1968 (Clark, Freeman, and Soete 1981:313). The list derives from Jewkes, Sawers, and Stillerman, as dated by Clark, Freeman, and Soete. I created a time series as with WOINN2. Mensch uses the same source but a more restrictive list and dates the innovations differently.

WOINN3: List of product innovations, 1879–1965 (Kleinknecht 1981b:297). Again I created a time series from a list of dates. Kleinknecht distinguishes "product innovations" from "improvement and process innovations," which are less basic. This list includes only the former. The latter comprise WOINN4.

WOINN4: List of improvement innovations, 1859–1969 (Kleinknecht 1981b:297). See WOINN3.

Invention Indicators

BRPAT: Number of British patents, 1738–1935 (Haustein and Neuwirth 1982:76). See note under WOIN2PRO, above.

USPAT: Number of U.S. patents, 1790–1975 (Haustein and Neuwirth, 1982:76). See note under WOIN2PRO, above.

US2PAT: Number of U.S. patents, 1837–1950 (Schmookler 1966:228). This time series, along with USRRPAT, gives the total number of successful patent applications filed each year.

USRRPAT: U.S. patents in building and railroads, 1837–1950 (Schmookler 1966:228). See US2PAT.

Capital Investment

USBLD: U.S. private building volume, 1830–1957 (Schmookler 1966:244, col. 2). Schmookler's data appear to be of relatively good quality throughout. Data are in constant prices.

USRRCAP: U.S. railroad gross capital expenditures, 1870–1950 (Schmookler 1966:233). Data are in constant prices.

Real Wages

BRWAG: Real wages for London, 1700–1787 (Gilboy 1936:140). Gilboy gives data for money wages and for real wages; the latter were used. A parallel series for Lancashire was not used.

BR2WAG: South English real wages, 1736–1954 (Phelps-Brown and Hopkins 1956:193, col. 2). This series is the second of Phelps-Brown and Hopkins's seven-century time series (the first was BRCNPRI). In this series, however, the data from 1495 up until 1736 are missing long stretches of years and were not used. From 1736 on, interpolations were made for missing data in 1774, 1775, 1792–95, 1803–5, 1865, and 1872. Phelps-Brown and Hopkins use their consumer price index (BRCNPRI) to deflate wages in calculating this series.

Data Listing for Fifty-five Economic Time Series and Seven War Series

S. English Consumer Price Index 1495-1954

1450	1500	1550	1600	1650	1700	1750	1800	1850	1900	1950
	105.6	294.4	515.7	942.7	753.9	662.9	1760.7	1088.8	1116.9	3544.9
	120.2	320.2	602.2	791.0	658.4	644.9	1967.4	1079.8	1107.9	4107.9
	137.1	310.1	529.2	728.1	653.9	675.3	1514.6	1098.9	1082.0	4479.8
	128.1	291.0	503.4	650.6	619.1	657.3	1424.7	1275.3	1128.1	4196.6
	120.2	310.1	453.9	610.1	659.6	691.0	1470.8	1421.3	1106.7	4297.8
	115.7	303.4	503.4	596.6	615.7	649.4	1709.0	1431.5	1111.2	
	119.1	415.7	525.8	628.1	655.1	676.4	1633.7	1420.2	1141.6	
	110.1	459.6	504.5	687.6	596.6	823.6	1603.4	1446.1	1158.4	
	112.4	258.4	569.7	725.8	641.6	821.3	1658.4	1337.1	1171.9	
	103.4	286.5	628.1	786.5	783.1	756.2	1819.1	1364.0	1188.8	
	115.7	297.8	565.2	768.5	896.6	722.5	1876.4	1476.4	1116.9	
	109.0	318.0	520.2	728.1	998.9	689.9	1822.5	1462.9	1105.6	
	113.5	298.9	588.8	864.0	716.9	716.9	2062.9	1449.4	1122.5	
	134.8	307.9	616.9	758.4	667.4	736.0	2113.5	1285.4	1147.2	
	132.6	316.9	637.1	738.2	713.5	801.1	1844.9	1348.3	1288.8	
	120.2	325.8	630.3	692.1	725.8	829.2	1648.3	1391.0	1479.8	
	123.6	322.5	631.5	746.1	724.7	839.3	1510.1	1456.2	1856.2	
	124.7	316.9	603.4	648.3	676.4	887.6	1714.6	1512.4	2207.9	
	130.3	315.7	588.8	676.4	646.1	877.5	1719.1	1450.6	2805.6	
	144.9	310.1	555.1	642.7	684.3	805.6	1676.4	1397.8	2532.6	
	153.9	337.1	544.9	648.3	713.5	802.2	1520.2	1394.4	2911.2	
	187.6	297.8	518.0	668.5	678.7	870.8	1337.1	1483.1	2301.1	
	179.8	303.4	587.6	625.8	622.5	964.0	1156.2	1548.3	1878.7	
	152.8	307.9	660.7	657.3	589.9	960.7	1234.8	1614.6	1939.3	
	149.4	420.2	610.1	730.3	661.8	969.7	1340.4	1598.9	1955.1	
	144.9	384.3	600.0	776.4	685.4	915.7	1573.0	1471.9	1919.1	
	149.4	347.2	620.2	732.6	715.7	895.5	1486.5	1539.3	1771.9	
	165.2	407.9	557.3	665.2	669.7	892.1	1389.9	1494.4	1680.9	
	201.1	394.4	523.6	711.2	729.2	928.1	1349.4	1439.3	1668.5	
	178.7	366.3	573.0	689.9	765.2	849.4	1336.0	1359.6	1697.8	
	189.9	384.3	668.5	638.2	673.0	820.2	1287.6	1319.1	1432.6	
	173.0	389.9	766.3	637.1	621.3	853.9	1415.7	1362.9	1287.6	
	201.1	385.4	651.7	674.2	625.8	871.9	1311.2	1280.9	1196.6	
	189.9	364.0	634.8	659.6	611.2	976.4	1231.5	1328.1	1243.8	
	162.9	374.2	686.5	640.4	582.0	982.0	1136.0	1203.4	1232.6	
	147.2	379.8	670.8	731.5	594.4	942.7	1155.1	1152.8	1291.0	
	184.3	395.5	666.3	628.1	605.6	942.7	1282.0	1046.1	1360.7	
	174.2	551.7	697.8	651.7	652.8	937.1	1313.5	1073.0	1432.6	
	155.1	388.8	794.4	619.1	632.6	974.2	1322.5	1067.4	1431.5	
	165.2	397.8	682.0	601.1	614.6	961.8	1419.1	1065.2	1339.4	
	177.5	444.9	613.5	576.4	723.6	978.7	1444.9	1064.0	1768.5	
	185.4	515.7	658.4	553.9	800.0	977.5	1411.2	1121.3	2004.5	
	193.3	415.7	625.8	609.0	709.0	992.1	1304.5	1119.1	2393.3	
	192.1	400.0	621.3	732.6	650.6	1020.2	1157.3	1027.0	2410.1	
100.0	214.6	578.7	644.9	724.7	593.3	1225.8	1212.4	1087.6	2564.0	
105.6	278.7	567.4	639.3	783.1	667.4	1304.5	1260.7	1064.0	2656.2	
113.5	259.6	769.7	749.4	778.7	644.9	1174.2	1412.4	1082.0	2898.9	
107.9	216.9	650.6	865.2	861.8	673.0	1148.3	1241.6	1103.4	3124.7	
111.2	240.4	532.6	922.5	868.5	684.3	1289.9	1162.9	1067.4	3533.7	

S. English Industrial Price Index 1495-1640

1450	1500	1550	1600
	99.1	172.6	276.4
	100.0	177.4	265.1
	95.3	183.0	272.6
	96.2	179.2	270.8
	95.3	180.2	271.7
	92.5	185.8	269.8
	92.5	184.9	280.2
	91.5	188.7	281.1
	94.3	196.2	291.5
	100.0	208.5	291.5
	97.2	219.8	296.2
	95.3	217.0	300.0
	99.1	218.9	296.2
	95.3	224.5	302.8
	99.1	220.8	304.7
	96.2	217.9	298.1
	96.2	216.0	291.5
	99.1	211.3	289.6
	101.9	209.4	284.0
	97.2	217.9	289.6
	105.7	215.1	290.6
	109.4	220.8	290.6
	106.6	226.4	301.9
	107.5	225.5	299.1
	111.3	225.5	286.8
	109.4	222.6	283.0
	110.4	233.0	293.4
	115.1	229.2	304.7
	118.9	225.5	312.3
	117.0	232.1	333.0
	109.4	230.2	326.4
	106.6	231.1	323.6
	107.5	225.5	323.6
	102.8	227.4	321.7
	110.4	235.8	335.8
	104.7	243.4	320.8
	112.3	251.9	331.1
	109.4	250.9	334.0
	113.2	251.9	335.8
	110.4	250.9	332.1
	107.5	251.9	336.8
	111.3	249.1	
	118.9	249.1	
	119.8	251.9	
	125.5	261.3	
100.0	128.3	280.2	
100.9	132.1	288.7	
89.6	139.6	279.2	
90.6	144.3	288.7	
92.5	164.2	273.6	

S. English Agricultural Price Index 1495-1640

1450	1500	1550	1600
	105.0	313.0	597.0
	109.0	284.0	486.0
	109.0	279.0	432.0
	113.0	232.0	423.0
	121.0	290.0	454.0
	110.0	373.0	481.0
	107.0	397.0	462.0
	109.0	243.0	511.0
	106.0	249.0	560.0
	98.0	278.0	555.0
	90.0	296.0	502.0
	101.0	295.0	612.0
	111.0	341.0	640.0
	111.0	338.0	585.0
	115.0	257.0	570.0
	114.0	289.0	685.0
	125.0	280.0	579.0
	136.0	315.0	560.0
	126.0	328.0	535.0
	158.0	279.0	528.0
	169.0	289.0	486.0
	152.0	284.0	566.0
	130.0	332.0	615.0
	117.0	398.0	569.0
	119.0	349.0	580.0
	124.0	333.0	630.0
	147.0	338.0	560.0
	176.0	340.0	513.0
	150.0	346.0	614.0
	150.0	354.0	661.0
	132.0	373.0	783.0
	156.0	378.0	619.0
	162.0	369.0	685.0
	143.0	346.0	682.0
	146.0	326.0	780.0
	168.0	427.0	662.0
	149.0	491.0	714.0
	131.0	353.0	869.0
	131.0	362.0	663.0
	140.0	413.0	587.0
	145.0	507.0	630.0
	159.0	396.0	
	157.0	348.0	
	154.0	379.0	
	182.0	507.0	
100.0	205.0	528.0	
94.0	160.0	691.0	
99.0	162.0	578.0	
110.0	189.0	444.0	
97.0	239.0	467.0	

New Castile Textile Price Index 1651-1800

1650	1700	1750	1800
	116.7	98.4	189.2
100.0	111.3	98.6	
112.2	111.1	116.8	
117.7	117.0	114.5	
118.2	103.2	123.9	
112.0	105.5	115.0	
106.9	105.0	105.3	
111.7	106.4	111.2	
105.0	103.5	115.9	
103.6	99.9	109.9	
101.6	96.0	111.2	
104.8	93.8	112.6	
101.6	105.1	103.4	
114.9	100.1	108.9	
121.6	105.7	108.7	
130.9	109.9	110.0	
127.4	107.9	108.1	
138.4	97.5	113.9	
146.8	99.4	113.0	
140.1	103.2	120.8	
156.5	99.6	108.6	
162.7	94.2	115.5	
165.5	96.4	107.8	
164.8	91.0	116.4	
161.4	99.3	112.0	
158.5	92.5	114.7	
159.4	96.4	117.2	
155.8	99.3	125.0	
148.7	94.5	120.4	
160.4	98.5	125.4	
125.3	93.4	115.9	
104.0	92.9	130.6	
96.2	92.9	122.3	
96.8	92.9	141.6	
96.2	91.7	142.4	
91.8	95.5	148.7	
87.8	92.3	147.7	
96.2	96.6	130.6	
96.1	98.2	135.7	
107.9	97.3	143.3	
107.4	104.8	123.9	
97.7	108.7	138.6	
99.6	110.8	139.2	
100.6	108.8	164.5	
104.2	97.1	183.0	
102.7	95.8	169.3	
119.1	92.8	184.9	
117.8	94.4	191.9	
115.6	94.6	172.1	
117.8	90.9	192.1	

New Castile Animal Product Prices 1651–1800

1650	1700	1750	1800
	79.0	91.5	173.6
100.0	86.6	97.7	
115.2	81.9	97.1	
110.7	83.0	111.7	
103.6	72.5	117.2	
103.1	76.0	125.0	
99.5	79.8	102.3	
90.0	77.2	92.3	
97.6	88.7	94.9	
100.7	94.7	89.0	
94.9	90.4	92.6	
94.9	94.7	91.4	
93.8	92.0	96.7	
109.4	87.6	100.0	
116.8	85.0	105.1	
116.6	100.9	109.2	
116.3	94.7	115.6	
136.4	87.3	111.0	
140.1	86.6	118.9	
147.4	85.4	111.8	
137.6	77.4	112.9	
130.2	79.0	113.1	
132.0	79.9	113.9	
125.8	75.2	106.2	
132.1	85.0	117.4	
130.5	84.3	110.3	
152.4	82.5	113.7	
145.2	84.9	111.2	
148.9	78.1	114.4	
161.6	83.1	116.5	
129.3	77.3	122.9	
94.9	81.1	121.0	
82.8	79.5	123.5	
91.2	82.9	125.2	
87.2	86.3	120.1	
85.0	91.8	128.5	
77.5	93.9	133.1	
73.1	84.9	135.6	
85.4	92.0	137.7	
77.3	96.7	148.0	
76.3	91.4	160.6	
76.4	91.4	146.9	
70.1	96.6	153.6	
71.4	88.5	146.2	
78.2	83.8	148.8	
88.4	78.4	149.0	
89.1	74.0	157.6	
82.3	84.5	172.5	
84.3	85.1	204.1	
80.3	79.0	207.5	

English Producers' Price Index 1661–1801

1650	1700	1750	1800
	93.0	82.7	135.3
	93.9	79.8	152.2
	97.7	76.1	
	97.7	76.1	
	95.8	83.6	
	95.8	85.5	
	92.1	87.4	
	89.2	88.3	
	91.1	94.9	
	93.9	94.9	
	99.6	95.8	
100.0	102.4	94.9	
109.4	92.1	95.8	
101.0	90.2	95.8	
99.0	85.5	94.9	
105.2	80.8	93.0	
112.5	83.6	93.0	
116.7	84.5	93.0	
106.3	85.5	92.1	
95.8	86.4	86.4	
95.8	85.5	88.3	
101.0	83.6	88.3	
94.8	85.5	92.1	
100.0	80.8	93.0	
95.8	81.7	92.1	
92.7	81.7	92.1	
94.8	86.4	94.9	
90.6	91.1	95.8	
88.5	89.2	97.7	
89.6	89.2	103.3	
85.4	92.1	106.1	
82.3	89.2	103.3	
83.3	84.5	112.7	
87.5	80.8	109.9	
86.5	80.8	101.5	
78.1	78.0	100.5	
71.9	77.0	106.1	
74.0	76.1	104.3	
72.9	76.1	106.1	
80.2	81.7	100.5	
92.7	83.6	100.5	
101.0	91.1	100.5	
90.6	91.1	104.3	
92.7	85.5	116.5	
91.7	92.1	111.8	
95.8	76.1	114.6	
105.2	85.5	129.6	
102.4	80.8	132.4	
94.9	83.6	121.2	
95.8	85.5	120.2	

British Commodity Prices 1780–1922

1750	1800	1850	1900
	134.5	73.9	71.8
	142.3	71.8	67.6
	123.9	75.4	66.2
	140.1	91.5	66.2
	137.3	97.9	67.6
	143.7	97.2	69.0
	142.8	97.2	73.9
	141.9	100.7	76.8
	141.0	87.3	70.4
	140.1	90.1	71.1
	140.1	95.1	75.4
	119.0	93.0	76.8
	123.2	97.2	81.7
	131.7	99.3	81.7
	143.0	100.7	81.7
	133.8	97.2	101.4
	119.7	97.9	128.2
	129.6	96.5	164.8
	134.5	95.1	180.3
	123.2	94.4	182.4
	114.8	92.3	181.7
	108.5	96.5	117.6
	105.6	104.9	114.8
	104.2	107.0	
	97.9	97.9	
	109.2	92.3	
	95.1	91.5	
	93.7	90.1	
	89.4	83.8	
	87.3	79.6	
100.0	85.9	84.5	
108.5	88.0	81.7	
109.2	87.3	81.0	
95.1	89.4	78.9	
91.5	89.4	73.2	
88.7	92.3	69.0	
90.8	103.5	66.2	
94.4	94.4	65.5	
90.8	96.5	67.6	
88.0	102.8	69.0	
92.3	100.0	69.0	
91.5	95.1	69.0	
94.4	87.3	65.5	
100.7	79.6	65.5	
99.3	80.3	60.6	
116.9	81.7	59.9	
126.1	85.9	58.5	
130.3	91.5	59.9	
138.0	75.4	61.3	
144.4	71.1	65.5	

U.S. Commodity Prices 1791–1922

1750	1800	1850	1900
	154.1	83.5	75.2
	158.7	86.8	73.6
	130.6	83.5	77.7
	133.9	88.4	79.3
	143.8	91.7	79.3
	147.9	91.7	79.3
	144.6	91.7	82.6
	136.4	90.9	86.8
	133.9	82.6	83.5
	143.8	81.8	90.1
	153.7	81.8	93.4
	148.8	81.8	85.9
	151.2	115.2	91.7
	176.9	103.3	92.6
	219.0	123.1	90.9
	171.9	100.8	93.4
	147.1	137.2	117.4
	148.8	128.9	163.6
	142.1	116.5	179.3
	135.5	114.1	190.9
	109.1	118.2	209.1
	105.0	103.3	136.4
	107.4	106.6	138.0
	102.5	102.5	
	100.8	100.8	
	102.5	95.0	
	98.3	88.4	
	98.3	87.6	
	95.9	84.3	
	95.9	78.5	
	88.4	87.6	
	96.7	85.9	
	96.7	87.6	
	94.2	86.8	
	85.1	81.0	
	95.9	76.0	
	87.6	74.4	
	102.5	75.2	
	99.2	76.9	
	101.7	76.9	
	95.0	75.2	
100.0	102.5	74.4	
105.8	87.6	69.4	
112.4	82.6	71.1	
130.2	83.5	63.6	
147.9	84.3	64.5	
153.7	86.8	62.0	
159.5	86.8	62.0	
157.0	82.6	64.5	
149.6	80.2	69.4	

British Wholesale Price Index 1750–1975

1750	1800	1850	1900	1950
100.0	221.5	107.8	99.2	373.0
94.7	228.8	107.8	95.8	452.3
97.9	181.9	109.0	95.8	466.3
94.7	181.9	132.7	95.8	466.3
94.7	181.9	142.1	96.9	471.0
96.8	199.5	141.0	96.9	484.9
96.8	197.3	141.0	100.4	503.6
114.7	192.1	146.9	105.0	512.9
111.6	211.9	126.8	101.5	498.9
105.3	227.3	131.5	102.7	498.9
103.2	224.4	137.4	107.3	503.6
99.0	212.7	136.2	108.5	512.9
99.0	240.5	141.0	114.2	517.6
105.3	247.9	143.3	115.4	522.2
107.4	225.9	146.9	116.5	540.9
111.6	190.7	141.0	142.4	554.9
112.6	174.5	142.1	184.5	573.5
114.7	193.6	139.8	239.6	573.5
113.7	203.9	137.4	265.5	606.2
104.2	187.7	136.2	293.0	634.2
105.3	168.7	133.9	364.2	666.8
112.6	146.7	133.9	233.1	713.4
123.2	129.1	144.2	187.8	746.1
125.3	143.7	150.0	187.8	890.6
122.1	149.6	145.4	197.5	1221.7
118.9	165.7	139.6	189.4	1412.9
120.0	146.7	136.2	174.8	
113.7	145.2	139.6	168.3	
123.2	140.8	130.4	166.7	
116.8	140.8	123.5	161.9	
115.8	138.6	128.1	142.4	
121.1	139.3	125.8	124.6	
122.1	134.2	126.9	121.4	
135.8	130.5	124.6	121.4	
132.6	126.9	113.1	126.3	
126.3	123.9	106.2	126.3	
125.3	139.3	100.4	134.4	
123.2	137.9	98.1	155.4	
127.4	143.7	100.4	144.1	
123.2	152.5	102.7	145.7	
130.5	150.3	102.7	194.2	
132.0	143.7	106.2	216.9	
129.1	130.5	100.4	226.6	
142.3	117.3	98.1	231.5	
144.5	118.8	92.3	236.3	
168.7	121.7	90.0	241.2	
170.1	126.1	87.7	249.3	
155.5	142.3	88.9	273.6	
158.4	120.3	92.3	312.4	
183.3	108.5	91.2	326.4	

French Wholesale Price Index, 1798-1975

1750	1800	1850	1900	1950
	100.0	64.6	57.6	8227.8
	88.9	63.9	55.3	10548.5
	88.1	69.2	54.6	11075.9
	94.0	80.8	55.8	10548.5
	88.1	86.1	54.6	10337.6
	96.6	89.6	57.0	10337.6
	105.9	90.7	60.4	10759.5
	103.4	87.8	63.4	11392.4
	136.4	79.6	58.8	12763.7
	136.4	79.6	58.8	13291.1
	140.6	83.8	62.8	13713.1
	138.9	82.6	65.7	13924.1
	144.8	82.6	68.6	14346.0
	135.5	83.1	67.4	14873.4
	103.4	82.0	68.6	15084.4
	98.3	76.8	92.8	15295.4
	101.7	78.0	125.1	15611.8
	109.3	76.2	173.5	15611.8
	104.2	76.8	225.9	16139.2
	88.9	75.6	234.1	17510.5
	88.9	77.3	334.9	18670.9
	83.1	80.3	230.1	19831.2
	80.3	83.8	217.9	20991.6
	83.1	83.8	278.5	23734.2
	77.3	76.8	322.9	28481.0
	84.9	75.0	363.2	29324.9
	79.1	75.6	464.1	
	78.0	76.2	407.6	
	75.0	69.7	411.6	
	75.6	68.0	403.6	
	75.6	69.7	351.1	
	72.0	68.0	298.6	
	72.7	66.2	262.3	
	73.2	63.9	250.2	
	74.5	58.8	238.1	
	76.8	57.6	225.9	
	78.5	55.3	262.3	
	73.2	53.5	363.2	
	76.2	55.8	415.7	
	75.6	58.1	435.9	
	78.5	58.1	573.1	
	78.0	57.0	702.2	
	76.2	55.3	819.2	
	70.4	54.6	952.4	
	68.6	50.6	1073.5	
	70.4	49.4	1517.4	
	75.0	47.7	2615.1	
	79.1	48.2	3979.1	
100.0	65.1	50.0	6856.5	
99.2	64.6	54.1	7594.9	

German Wholesale Price Index, 1792-1918

1750	1800	1850	1900
	137.8	72.4	91.8
	136.7	76.5	84.7
	133.7	83.7	82.7
	141.8	93.9	83.7
	138.8	102.0	83.7
	159.2	107.1	87.8
	160.2	107.1	93.9
	151.0	103.1	99.0
	179.6	92.9	91.8
	159.2	90.8	92.9
	134.7	95.9	94.9
	125.5	95.9	95.9
	139.8	95.9	104.1
	122.4	93.9	102.0
	112.2	92.9	107.1
	114.3	90.8	143.3
	126.5	91.8	153.5
	151.0	99.0	181.0
	132.7	99.0	220.1
	105.1	93.9	
	91.8	93.9	
	86.7	102.0	
	85.7	116.3	
	83.7	122.4	
	73.5	114.3	
	77.6	102.0	
	73.5	96.9	
	78.6	92.9	
	79.6	84.7	
	78.6	82.7	
	79.6	88.8	
	83.7	86.7	
	81.6	82.7	
	77.6	81.6	
	77.6	79.6	
	78.6	76.5	
	79.6	73.5	
	75.5	74.5	
	79.6	76.5	
	82.7	83.7	
	81.6	88.3	
	79.6	87.8	
100.0	79.6	81.6	
100.0	79.1	78.6	
103.1	77.6	74.5	
124.5	83.7	73.5	
116.3	89.8	73.5	
110.2	99.0	77.6	
118.4	77.6	80.6	
134.7	71.4	84.7	

U.S. Wholesale Price Index, 1801-1975

1800	1850	1900	1950
	55.7	50.3	142.3
100.0	57.7	49.6	158.5
82.1	55.9	52.9	154.1
84.0	59.4	53.4	152.0
90.8	61.5	53.6	152.4
93.2	61.6	53.9	152.7
91.4	61.6	55.7	157.8
85.9	61.2	58.4	162.3
84.0	55.5	56.4	164.5
83.3	54.6	60.7	164.9
96.3	54.5	63.3	165.1
93.8	54.8	58.3	164.4
95.1	64.1	61.9	164.9
110.6	80.9	62.6	164.4
138.3	103.8	61.2	164.7
108.7	118.1	62.3	168.0
92.6	104.0	76.7	173.6
93.2	93.8	105.4	173.9
91.4	87.4	117.6	178.3
80.2	83.6	124.2	185.2
68.5	77.6	138.5	192.0
65.5	74.1	87.5	198.3
67.3	75.6	86.8	207.2
64.2	74.9	90.3	234.3
63.6	72.5	87.8	278.5
64.2	69.5	92.7	304.2
63.6	64.4	89.8	
64.2	60.4	85.8	
61.1	55.2	87.0	
60.5	52.6	85.4	
58.7	58.2	77.6	
63.0	57.6	65.4	
63.6	59.1	58.4	
63.0	57.8	59.1	
58.7	54.1	67.1	
66.7	50.6	71.8	
74.7	50.1	72.5	
74.1	50.4	77.4	
71.0	51.3	70.4	
74.7	51.3	69.2	
63.6	50.3	70.4	
63.1	50.1	78.4	
58.8	46.8	88.5	
55.3	47.8	92.7	
55.5	43.0	93.2	
56.0	43.8	95.0	
58.0	41.6	108.4	
58.1	41.7	133.1	
55.3	43.5	144.0	
53.8	46.8	136.9	

Belgian Industrial Price Index, 1822-1913

1800	1850	1900
	88.4	100.7
	84.4	97.8
	80.9	95.9
	92.5	97.3
	98.5	98.3
	99.5	100.6
	99.5	109.6
	99.0	108.6
	98.5	105.8
	92.0	105.5
	93.0	110.4
	94.5	106.2
	96.5	110.1
	99.5	112.9
	100.6	
	98.5	
	100.3	
	97.5	
	96.9	
	95.2	
	99.1	
	99.5	
100.0	110.7	
107.5	112.1	
98.0	103.5	
98.5	102.9	
94.5	101.2	
91.0	99.0	
87.4	93.8	
89.4	92.5	
80.9	101.7	
85.9	106.8	
85.4	106.2	
86.4	104.3	
86.4	100.5	
91.5	93.4	
97.5	88.6	
94.5	89.1	
93.5	92.4	
94.5	93.4	
94.0	95.5	
95.0	92.2	
90.5	87.3	
83.4	86.4	
80.9	88.7	
81.4	82.8	
86.9	87.2	
98.5	85.8	
84.9	82.1	
81.9	94.6	

Belgian Agricultural Price Index, 1835-1913

1800	1850	1900
	104.3	101.6
	100.9	100.9
	93.7	99.5
	114.8	95.5
	129.0	101.9
	134.6	103.1
	137.5	109.7
	134.0	114.6
	128.5	116.6
	120.6	103.5
	126.4	108.5
	132.9	117.4
	128.7	122.1
	117.3	119.2
	124.1	
	121.1	
	122.5	
	125.4	
	121.4	
	121.8	
	121.3	
	130.8	
	126.4	
	128.3	
	135.5	
	131.5	
	128.3	
	130.4	
	120.3	
	119.6	
	127.9	
	123.3	
	120.7	
	118.4	
	115.9	
100.0	106.3	
107.0	100.5	
105.9	98.0	
108.1	100.7	
111.8	102.4	
114.1	103.2	
121.3	108.9	
109.4	103.6	
108.2	100.0	
98.0	91.5	
104.3	89.2	
117.6	86.1	
125.0	87.5	
102.3	93.9	
97.1	94.6	

French Wheat Prices (Paris) — 1495–1788

1450	1500	1550	1600	1650	1700	1750
	187.9	715.5	1491.4	5043.1	3793.1	3103.4
	350.0	693.1	1401.7	4353.4	2736.2	3394.8
	363.8	850.0	1358.6	5410.3	2072.4	4267.2
	208.6	665.5	1750.0	3255.2	2165.5	3481.0
	281.0	572.4	1627.6	2575.9	2084.5	3319.0
	282.8	520.7	1455.2	2263.8	2015.5	2553.4
	310.3	755.2	1493.1	2274.1	1663.8	2791.4
	317.2	934.5	1589.7	2187.9	1434.5	3793.1
	269.0	544.8	2101.7	2586.2	2050.0	3255.2
	143.1	646.6	2036.2	2867.2	7075.9	3448.3
	148.3	675.9	1627.6	3103.4	4931.0	3415.5
	162.1	777.6	1746.6	4622.4	3125.9	2741.4
	175.9	1043.1	1715.5	5819.0	3515.5	2769.0
	215.5	1272.4	1589.7	3803.4	4762.1	2737.9
	215.5	681.0	1648.3	3481.0	4925.9	2681.0
	324.1	1120.7	1650.0	2715.5	2769.0	3155.2
	387.9	2005.2	1536.2	2510.3	2289.7	3517.2
	337.9	1222.4	1848.3	2025.9	1837.9	3801.7
	269.0	1381.0	2496.6	1734.5	2129.3	5655.2
	286.2	950.0	1853.4	1691.4	2622.4	5586.2
	291.4	925.9	1643.1	1810.3	4125.9	5006.9
	579.3	1208.6	1815.5	1886.2	2558.6	5767.2
	736.2	1482.8	2251.7	1906.9	2924.1	4862.1
	250.0	2553.4	2446.6	1703.4	4484.5	5086.2
	572.4	2543.1	2069.0	1896.6	4510.3	4579.3
	610.3	1336.2	2020.7	2694.8	4913.8	5086.2
	253.4	1462.1	3146.6	1956.9	4591.4	4300.0
	315.5	1475.9	2839.7	2456.9	3286.2	3998.3
	434.5	1186.2	2112.1	2748.3	2306.9	3869.0
	660.3	1050.0	1929.3	3060.3	2862.1	3513.8
	593.1	1136.2	2258.6	2446.6	2758.6	3308.6
	813.8	1082.8	3610.3	2586.2	3362.1	3577.6
	712.1	1246.6	3270.7	2360.3	2467.2	3437.9
	419.0	1810.3	2370.7	2251.7	2048.3	3470.7
	355.2	1617.2	1934.5	2705.2	2953.4	4569.0
	362.1	1444.8	2015.5	3060.3	2208.6	4289.7
	517.2	2467.2	2274.1	1993.1	2439.7	3556.9
	403.4	3600.0	2246.6	1962.1	2560.3	3815.5
	387.9	1508.6	2108.6	1432.8	3070.7	4137.9
	556.9	1762.1	2031.0	1617.2	3513.8	
	425.9	3750.0	2058.6	1853.4	4419.0	
	432.8	5755.2	2510.3	1858.6	6379.3	
	503.4	3362.1	2456.9	2398.3	3686.2	
	455.2	3212.1	3415.5	4536.2	2208.6	
	648.3	2510.3	3250.0	6013.8	2025.9	
100.0	746.6	2910.3	2193.1	2619.0	2079.3	
129.3	1156.9	3017.2	1939.7	2694.8	2565.5	
129.3	451.7	3156.9	2393.1	2931.0	2677.6	
129.3	467.2	2634.5	2931.0	3663.8	3405.2	
115.5	525.9	1746.6	3384.5	4443.1	3212.1	

German Wheat Prices (Cologne) — 1531–1786

1500	1550	1600	1650	1700	1750
	110.5	391.3	512.4	464.7	515.4
	154.9	357.6	623.5	525.7	477.6
	166.1	320.9	472.4	497.8	429.5
	146.9	360.5	352.0	442.8	462.9
	126.9	349.5	311.0	448.4	490.2
	166.9	318.4	312.9	422.5	363.8
	214.1	321.9	316.4	383.0	506.3
	138.6	330.0	297.1	480.2	592.1
	136.6	337.7	380.1	590.3	648.1
	140.4	337.9	364.0	793.5	719.0
	143.2	332.0	437.7	543.8	636.5
	149.1	414.8	617.5	467.8	700.1
	204.5	365.1	569.3	448.0	647.9
	157.1	288.4	434.9	616.7	498.2
	143.7	281.1	377.1	561.2	611.1
	245.4	323.8	349.5	436.3	514.6
	177.9	415.8	308.0	387.1	508.3
	185.1	398.2	305.8	374.8	649.6
	169.6	316.7	306.5	356.1	650.8
	171.1	262.6	323.5	410.7	508.6
	207.5	260.9	348.7	417.8	832.8
	272.8	332.0	359.5	378.5	718.9
	286.9	418.5	444.2	370.4	757.0
	312.2	452.7	423.0	409.0	687.9
	285.4	478.8	494.3	500.2	729.6
	241.8	602.1	627.8	494.8	620.1
	264.4	544.5	456.5	449.9	518.2
	243.8	409.4	384.9	389.4	559.2
	209.6	489.4	395.0	405.4	525.8
	251.0	523.4	439.9	393.6	439.0
	260.4	510.0	390.4	448.2	571.5
100.0	268.3	451.6	377.7	401.1	561.0
68.0	266.2	467.0	343.1	348.6	569.2
76.4	284.5	492.6	361.0	396.7	623.7
64.2	259.5	550.1	467.9	392.1	676.9
65.9	317.7	609.0	410.2	374.9	609.1
76.1	494.4	624.2	369.8	339.7	
77.3	510.8	647.0	329.5	366.2	
89.0	349.7	541.3	283.1	423.4	
91.8	414.1	448.8	334.6	574.3	
79.5	353.6	410.7	331.4	644.8	
88.2	273.7	482.0	421.6	571.4	
97.9	368.0	617.5	603.3	483.1	
105.7	355.1	529.9	737.6	400.0	
122.5	394.3	508.8	591.2	369.5	
151.6	413.5	422.4	479.0	397.4	
110.5	406.4	335.7	529.7	463.0	
73.8	411.4	368.3	558.8	508.0	
77.7	394.9	478.3	752.4	492.2	
106.7	365.3	579.6	666.9	515.1	

German Bread Prices (Cologne) — 1658–1772

1650	1700	1750
	137.0	173.8
	170.1	179.2
	145.1	166.2
	140.5	150.4
	141.4	170.1
	140.8	136.6
	129.9	201.8
	138.2	207.7
100.0	192.8	172.0
111.1	258.6	194.9
145.8	168.8	195.4
204.2	167.4	256.5
208.5	148.8	224.8
130.5	200.2	159.2
112.5	185.0	202.1
118.8	131.9	196.8
97.4	127.3	142.6
92.4	135.9	162.0
88.9	131.5	177.1
104.3	167.1	
104.4	153.7	
114.8	135.6	
140.3	139.3	
135.9	139.8	
177.3	191.7	
241.2	168.3	
185.7	155.1	
126.1	144.4	
118.1	145.8	
117.8	144.4	
116.9	158.1	
121.7	163.4	
112.7	128.9	
137.0	165.3	
180.5	123.6	
123.2	117.6	
119.4	112.1	
109.2	123.8	
112.5	169.2	
123.6	226.2	
120.6	200.2	
122.5	179.2	
207.7	157.0	
261.1	124.5	
187.1	113.6	
130.6	126.1	
149.1	144.2	
191.4	151.1	
285.4	148.9	
240.8	198.1	

Amsterdam Prices for Prussia Rye — 1597–1783

1550	1600	1650	1700	1750
	80.3	130.4	101.9	59.9
	71.6	140.9	78.6	58.8
	65.1	137.4	65.5	64.9
	73.0	104.3	63.2	59.7
	59.7	71.4	70.0	57.7
	46.2	64.5	61.3	61.7
	40.9	85.6	60.4	80.9
	46.3	85.4	57.0	120.2
	69.9	88.7	68.4	95.1
	71.9	96.1	160.0	70.9
	63.2	104.5	128.9	62.0
	64.3	127.0	92.4	67.1
	74.3	172.7	73.9	80.1
	67.8	123.2	80.6	75.9
	58.7	83.8	94.4	69.1
	52.1	93.5	87.4	73.7
	63.9	80.3	79.1	79.0
	73.3	76.8	70.4	75.6
	63.7	59.0	75.2	78.1
	50.9	47.2	70.5	83.4
	48.4	48.4	71.9	84.9
	49.6	54.8	56.5	129.5
	72.5	74.8	52.5	146.1
	97.3	76.7	56.2	101.9
	109.1	90.5	67.1	84.6
	96.8	124.2	77.7	98.1
	87.5	107.6	76.6	90.1
	89.8	88.1	78.5	71.8
	96.9	70.3	72.3	76.0
	132.1	54.8	66.1	66.9
	163.0	48.7	50.5	70.6
	150.9	50.6	48.0	97.9
	86.7	56.1	51.0	101.2
	71.5	57.8	52.6	92.1
	84.0	69.4	64.8	
	83.8	69.2	60.7	
	72.4	61.5	65.1	
	83.8	50.6	64.2	
	89.4	48.0	61.3	
	79.5	57.1	62.3	
	90.5	60.3	102.3	
	78.5	64.9	104.6	
	67.9	73.2	72.9	
	78.1	112.2	56.7	
	90.4	105.0	54.8	
	75.7	88.4	60.8	
	61.4	86.0	80.5	
100.0	73.3	104.3	87.4	
100.0	93.4	139.6	81.5	
92.9	117.3	175.2	70.5	

English Malt Prices (Eton College) 1595-1831

1550	1600	1650	1700	1750	1800
	110.7	155.4	120.0	135.4	479.4
	101.6	126.2	120.0	144.6	385.9
	72.3	135.4	116.9	141.5	325.4
	67.7	110.8	120.0	147.7	377.3
	84.6	92.3	123.1	141.5	460.4
	100.1	92.3	123.1	135.4	460.4
	84.6	129.2	120.0	163.1	450.0
	89.2	123.1	141.5	184.6	460.4
	130.7	147.7	150.7	166.1	491.5
	113.9	166.2	178.5	145.0	501.9
	83.1	138.5	181.6	148.5	470.8
	110.7	187.7	175.4	142.3	481.2
	120.0	172.3	146.1	176.2	574.6
	120.0	144.6	150.7	194.7	522.7
	120.0	126.2	156.9	179.2	450.0
	126.2	129.2	153.8	185.4	408.5
	96.9	104.6	141.5	185.4	429.2
	92.3	110.7	132.3	185.4	498.4
	90.8	116.9	135.4	176.2	515.7
	89.2	126.2	156.9	154.6	482.9
	80.0	123.1	156.9	166.9	410.2
	92.3	101.6	138.5	185.4	378.1
	137.6	110.7	118.5	205.4	335.8
	126.1	129.2	147.7	213.1	346.2
	101.6	166.1	150.7	213.1	429.2
	116.9	135.4	147.7	210.0	429.2
	109.2	120.0	147.7	185.4	408.5
	87.7	135.4	156.9	179.5	387.7
	87.7	126.2	175.4	173.1	387.7
	132.3	113.9	163.1	170.8	408.5
	186.1	101.6	133.9	189.3	387.7
	135.4	129.2	138.5	189.3	398.1
	118.5	132.3	129.2	224.6	
	147.7	120.0	123.1	250.8	
	136.9	126.2	123.1	244.7	
	129.2	123.1	126.2	244.6	
	138.5	113.9	132.3	232.3	
	226.2	107.7	147.7	226.2	
	158.5	95.4	141.5	221.5	
	127.7	92.3	153.8	216.9	
	136.9	83.1	169.2	221.5	
	124.6	89.2	163.1	247.7	
	120.0	113.9	160.0	236.2	
	132.6	147.7	135.4	275.2	
	145.2	123.1	132.3	278.7	
100.0	132.3	129.2	123.1	292.5	
209.2	143.1	123.1	121.5	264.8	
153.8	189.2	123.1	138.5	257.9	
106.1	184.6	169.3	132.3	271.7	
76.9	200.0	169.3	135.4	351.4	

English Hops Prices (Eton College) 1622-1829

1600	1650	1700	1750	1800
	39.0	36.0	94.9	244.1
	97.4	46.6	81.4	95.6
	61.5	57.2	67.6	104.2
	99.4	54.2	59.2	112.9
	115.5	150.4	50.8	99.5
	113.6	72.0	67.4	114.5
	150.8	90.7	72.7	129.5
	89.1	89.0	76.3	81.4
	88.5	77.3	92.0	111.9
	60.8	150.2	87.5	142.4
	65.4	76.2	76.0	178.7
	53.0	72.9	66.5	156.2
	54.7	114.4	57.1	260.1
	88.2	182.1	97.3	194.3
	64.0	110.2	137.6	204.4
	136.4	177.6	116.5	261.9
	67.8	76.2	95.5	302.4
	67.8	79.7	85.4	259.8
	57.8	83.1	127.1	78.4
	64.2	77.1	107.3	76.8
	57.9	76.9	136.8	59.3
	60.9	59.3	123.9	126.6
100.0	132.6	110.0	172.5	193.8
36.4	94.9	70.0	100.1	119.6
28.5	107.0	203.2	93.2	394.1
32.1	101.5	80.4	92.4	96.0
37.8	70.0	71.8	101.6	102.8
105.3	63.3	71.9	71.5	97.3
135.8	50.4	77.8	57.6	178.7
44.1	32.8	71.2	58.4	216.0
51.7	84.2	169.3	59.1	
58.4	94.9	169.4	63.1	
80.9	68.5	169.5	133.7	
82.3	92.0	173.3	104.0	
79.2	125.9	176.9	105.4	
82.3	93.2	164.6	106.8	
82.9	169.5	115.9	96.2	
68.2	67.5	71.8	199.4	
51.3	36.4	56.5	142.4	
36.3	44.5	99.4	109.4	
62.1	27.1	52.2	105.0	
84.8	34.7	77.8	117.1	
71.1	42.4	77.8	101.7	
57.5	72.2	120.7	195.8	
43.8	102.1	155.2	94.9	
42.6	159.3	82.7	111.9	
34.4	162.8	109.9	125.0	
89.7	178.0	81.9	105.1	
63.4	139.7	86.2	253.2	
166.9	80.5	90.5	379.7	

English Wheat Prices (Winchester) 1630-1817

1600	1650	1700	1750	1800
	100.2	67.7	57.3	308.4
	74.5	51.7	72.5	173.9
	60.2	55.1	71.8	128.2
	46.1	79.9	68.9	118.5
	32.8	55.1	53.9	208.7
	59.3	46.3	63.1	171.3
	60.2	47.8	103.7	179.0
	86.9	55.9	87.5	158.9
	97.2	100.4	64.9	199.4
	96.0	144.4	60.2	247.1
	89.8	93.4	59.4	217.0
	110.8	84.8	59.4	279.3
	69.6	73.2	63.4	266.4
	71.7	101.5	78.8	174.6
	66.0	64.6	82.1	155.8
	63.8	90.5	79.6	143.3
	46.4	79.1	107.2	253.4
	49.8	72.6	106.9	199.4
	70.6	52.0	84.6	
	56.6	65.5	72.7	
	66.5	65.5	90.1	
	57.0	53.6	103.4	
	57.4	59.8	114.1	
	102.8	58.1	102.5	
	96.3	75.1	94.2	
	60.0	79.1	77.6	
	58.8	61.4	84.7	
	96.3	92.2	96.7	
	94.1	91.8	71.9	
	72.3	62.8	71.3	
100.0	77.9	56.0	103.4	
73.6	68.5	47.2	99.8	
72.5	71.0	47.6	107.4	
82.6	67.2	51.3	100.9	
80.2	89.7	64.6	92.3	
77.9	54.4	68.9	82.2	
64.3	64.4	55.9	81.9	
91.4	47.2	53.9	97.1	
63.3	39.4	55.0	100.0	
56.8	60.9	75.6	117.3	
66.5	48.6	104.3	108.7	
61.0	77.2	55.3	87.7	
71.0	95.4	43.4	107.7	
61.0	119.8	37.7	106.3	
52.0	71.8	38.5	131.0	
61.5	112.1	54.5	207.3	
101.5	102.3	58.2	118.9	
113.9	117.8	56.0	134.5	
107.9	115.4	59.4	118.0	
108.7	77.9	55.6	232.6	

English Coal Prices (Eton College) 1653-1830

1650	1700	1750	1800
	99.3	121.6	180.8
	119.5	120.0	186.0
	148.2	120.0	217.9
100.0	133.4	120.0	217.9
100.5	114.6	128.7	217.9
96.6	110.6	147.0	217.9
91.5	112.8	147.0	217.9
92.0	133.7	147.0	217.9
87.6	121.6	150.4	264.3
83.2	119.5	138.5	257.6
80.9	112.8	147.0	246.6
78.1	102.7	149.3	239.9
72.0	108.1	143.6	246.6
80.8	103.6	140.2	261.1
107.9	101.4	144.7	267.6
134.9	101.9	133.4	236.5
105.8	112.1	136.8	220.2
112.1	115.5	135.7	223.1
88.7	113.8	133.4	212.9
89.3	112.1	140.2	205.2
86.6	105.3	151.0	202.7
146.8	103.7	151.4	206.8
151.2	101.9	140.2	206.8
110.3	103.1	140.2	205.1
108.4	101.9	147.0	199.3
102.5	108.7	156.8	197.6
99.7	105.3	162.1	194.2
100.7	105.0	160.5	197.6
92.2	112.4	160.5	190.8
86.9	107.6	161.8	190.8
86.6	118.9	167.2	177.4
85.5	108.8	167.2	
83.3	107.9	156.4	
95.6	106.4	141.9	
96.6	109.8	150.4	
84.6	111.8	151.1	
86.2	111.4	145.3	
87.3	113.2	145.3	
114.3	118.9	145.3	
128.6	131.2	158.8	
118.5	128.4	156.2	
116.7	124.4	157.1	
116.6	116.6	173.7	
109.8	133.4	177.7	
122.9	128.9	195.9	
107.8	128.0	171.0	
105.9	120.6	179.1	
95.9	120.0	180.2	
94.3	120.0	216.2	
90.8	118.2	220.7	

English Bread Prices (Charterhouse) 1694-1800

1650	1700	1750	1800
	82.7	84.0	278.7
	71.3	92.0	
	76.0	97.3	
	100.7	85.3	
	80.7	77.3	
	70.0	86.0	
	71.3	125.3	
	80.7	105.3	
	123.3	86.0	
	116.7	82.0	
	110.0	75.3	
	103.3	83.3	
	96.7	87.3	
	90.0	97.3	
	83.3	114.0	
	94.0	104.0	
	92.0	123.3	
	78.7	126.0	
	68.7	99.3	
	76.0	96.0	
	82.7	111.3	
	75.3	122.7	
	77.3	126.7	
	82.0	121.3	
	94.7	123.3	
	104.0	99.3	
	87.3	108.7	
	110.7	119.3	
	104.0	112.7	
	81.3	105.3	
	76.0	133.3	
	68.0	130.0	
	69.3	135.3	
	80.7	131.3	
	88.7	123.3	
	90.7	110.0	
	92.0	110.7	
	82.0	124.7	
	86.0	132.0	
	108.7	135.3	
	109.3	127.3	
	79.3	116.0	
	70.7	130.7	
	66.0	131.3	
	68.0	164.7	
100.0	68.0	187.7	
124.0	82.7	186.7	
122.7	85.3	139.3	
136.7	82.0	144.0	
127.3	86.0	150.7	
99.3	84.7	242.7	

Italian Wheat Prices (Milan), 1701-1860

1700	1750	1800	1850
	116.0	311.5	153.4
100.0	124.9	357.6	155.3
113.6	132.2	271.5	173.6
100.0	111.1	235.1	213.4
94.4	99.1	224.2	265.9
100.0	104.0	233.4	230.8
117.6	116.5	215.5	245.2
131.8	115.5	160.9	219.8
134.8	103.3	133.6	157.9
158.8	104.9	130.8	179.3
137.9	103.5	188.9	181.9
103.8	94.4	266.6	
96.0	81.2	239.3	
104.2	82.6	182.4	
110.1	104.7	190.6	
100.2	116.5	278.1	
99.3	128.9	336.5	
98.6	140.7	299.5	
98.6	128.7	171.1	
88.9	114.1	142.6	
77.6	117.2	147.5	
77.9	134.4	156.2	
68.9	145.9	140.7	
62.1	174.6	131.3	
53.6	174.1	111.5	
65.2	168.2	121.4	
81.9	116.5	125.2	
82.1	137.2	175.3	
84.9	171.3	178.6	
89.9	151.1	184.9	
84.2	121.2	199.8	
76.0	123.3	186.6	
74.6	156.2	180.7	
104.0	167.3	177.6	
160.5	160.2	156.5	
150.6	145.6	133.9	
117.6	138.8	170.1	
86.4	163.8	232.7	
78.1	148.7	178.4	
86.8	138.1	188.2	
103.3	144.7	189.4	
104.0	116.5	180.2	
107.8	134.8	173.9	
108.5	179.5	179.3	
104.0	182.8	175.8	
101.2	191.3	160.9	
125.6	180.5	186.6	
134.1	177.2	240.5	
147.1	177.4	212.5	
117.2	204.5	195.5	

Italian Hard Coal Prices (Milan), 1701-1860

1700	1750	1800	1850
	113.6	139.0	233.9
100.0	108.5	135.6	227.1
98.3	106.8	135.6	228.8
105.1	111.9	178.0	232.2
98.3	113.6	166.1	232.2
103.4	127.1	155.9	232.2
111.9	110.2	161.0	232.2
105.1	111.9	161.0	232.2
105.1	108.5	166.1	227.1
105.1	110.2	194.9	223.7
103.4	111.9	203.4	220.3
101.7	111.9	203.4	
94.9	110.2	203.4	
100.0	110.2	203.4	
101.7	108.5	203.4	
100.0	111.9	186.4	
103.4	110.2	178.0	
101.7	110.2	178.0	
101.7	108.5	178.0	
100.0	111.9	189.8	
100.0	110.2	235.6	
98.3	110.2	228.8	
98.3	110.2	210.2	
98.3	111.9	205.1	
98.3	110.2	228.8	
103.4	110.2	223.7	
105.1	113.6	186.4	
101.7	115.3	189.8	
96.6	113.6	186.4	
98.3	113.6	186.4	
101.7	110.2	193.2	
101.7	106.8	188.1	
101.7	105.1	186.4	
101.7	111.9	186.4	
98.3	113.6	198.3	
101.7	116.9	205.1	
101.7	118.6	235.6	
103.4	120.3	245.8	
101.7	120.3	249.2	
98.3	118.6	249.2	
106.8	108.5	249.2	
98.3	111.9	249.2	
100.0	115.3	252.5	
96.6	120.3	266.1	
100.0	108.5	257.6	
103.4	105.1	240.7	
106.8	122.0	247.5	
110.2	120.3	249.2	
116.9	125.4	249.2	
120.3	128.8	247.5	

Swedish Wheat Prices, 1732-1914

1700	1750	1800	1850	1900
	135.3	998.5	1544.1	1585.3
	150.0	908.8	1644.1	1570.6
	151.5	811.8	1551.5	1494.1
	133.8	788.2	2214.7	1527.9
	161.8	869.1	1817.6	1582.4
	166.2	850.0	2760.3	1605.9
	216.2	1061.8	2773.5	1604.4
	235.3	1045.6	2251.5	1758.8
	223.5	1242.6	1691.2	1747.1
	173.5	1127.9	1632.4	1788.2
	183.8	1229.4	1935.3	1707.4
	250.0	1539.7	2151.5	1783.8
	377.9	1886.8	1998.5	1751.5
	394.1	1798.5	1654.4	1648.5
	388.2	1613.2	1460.3	2098.5
	377.9	1447.1	1733.8	
	301.5	1648.5	1861.8	
	275.0	1797.1	2705.9	
	261.8	1969.1	2305.9	
	236.8	1713.2	1698.5	
	254.4	1391.2	1773.5	
	377.9	1236.8	2036.8	
	388.2	1226.5	2232.4	
	333.8	1152.9	2410.3	
	297.1	1077.9	1988.2	
	345.6	1058.8	1883.3	
	307.4	1560.3	1985.3	
	298.5	1254.4	2127.9	
	313.2	1083.8	1763.2	
	291.2	1438.2	1866.2	
	294.1	1661.8	1948.5	
	339.7	1769.3	2070.6	
100.0	300.0	1405.9	1850.0	
116.2	383.8	1236.8	1804.4	
110.3	345.6	1395.6	1530.9	
127.9	419.1	1267.6	1385.3	
145.6	433.8	1264.7	1342.6	
107.4	357.4	1383.8	1235.3	
92.6	376.5	1883.8	1558.8	
119.1	458.8	1595.6	1561.8	
148.5	417.6	1648.5	1582.4	
192.6	376.5	1954.4	1783.8	
152.9	436.8	1700.0	1498.5	
154.4	442.6	1364.7	1373.5	
145.6	488.2	1363.2	1148.5	
177.9	486.8	1679.4	1242.6	
186.8	463.2	1733.8	1429.4	
180.9	489.7	1675.0	1680.9	
183.8	552.9	1426.5	1664.7	
186.8	707.4	1498.5	1614.7	

Swedish Pine Wood Prices, 1735-1914

1700	1750	1800	1850	1900
	162.5	512.5	2162.5	3775.0
	187.5	512.5	2162.5	3325.0
	200.0	587.5	2012.5	3000.0
	187.5	525.0	2087.5	3350.0
	187.5	550.0	2212.5	3400.0
	187.5	575.0	2437.5	3600.0
	187.5	587.5	2912.5	3750.0
	162.5	612.5	3050.0	4037.5
	200.0	725.0	2475.0	4475.0
	137.5	987.5	2412.5	4125.0
	200.0	1075.0	2575.0	3862.5
	187.5	1175.0	2687.5	3837.5
	187.5	1250.0	2537.5	4262.5
	212.5	1250.0	2537.5	4750.0
	287.5	1312.5	2500.0	5275.0
	287.5	1225.0	2475.0	
	237.5	1212.5	2525.0	
	200.0	1175.0	2500.0	
	150.0	1137.5	2375.0	
	162.5	1187.5	2237.5	
	175.0	1237.5	2400.0	
	262.5	1287.5	2937.5	
	175.0	1275.0	3312.5	
	225.0	1287.5	4025.0	
	162.5	1325.0	3987.5	
	225.0	1350.0	3887.5	
	337.5	1350.0	3750.0	
	362.5	1412.5	3837.5	
	537.5	1450.0	3400.0	
	537.5	1575.0	3125.0	
	437.5	1575.0	3225.0	
	437.5	1562.5	3475.0	
	412.5	1525.0	3587.5	
	387.5	1625.0	3375.0	
	362.5	1700.0	3300.0	
100.0	362.5	1675.0	3212.5	
100.0	337.5	1662.5	3037.5	
100.0	400.0	1700.0	2812.5	
100.0	387.5	1712.5	2900.0	
112.5	375.0	1737.5	2975.0	
112.5	412.5	1787.5	3150.0	
112.5	362.5	1825.0	3075.0	
112.5	387.5	1887.5	3037.5	
125.0	400.0	1850.0	3037.5	
125.0	437.5	1800.0	3050.0	
162.5	437.5	1812.5	3075.0	
162.5	437.5	1812.5	3087.5	
162.5	487.5	1875.0	3137.5	
125.0	487.5	2000.0	3487.5	
125.0	512.5	2137.5	4087.5	

Swedish Iron Ore Prices, 1732-1914

1700	1750	1800	1850	1900
	119.0	371.4	938.1	1804.8
	138.1	338.1	938.1	1466.7
	138.1	309.5	938.1	1433.3
	138.1	376.2	876.2	1409.5
	138.1	381.0	890.5	1471.4
	138.1	428.6	909.5	1523.8
	138.1	428.6	1109.5	1504.8
	166.7	413.3	1142.9	1471.4
	166.7	433.3	1014.3	1452.4
	166.7	523.8	1000.0	1447.6
	185.7	423.8	1009.5	1490.5
	204.8	500.0	1014.3	1485.7
	204.8	628.6	1014.3	1890.5
	223.8	509.5	1042.9	2119.0
	261.9	552.4	723.8	2152.4
	238.1	576.2	1042.9	
	242.9	638.1	1057.1	
	166.7	671.4	1052.4	
	147.6	676.2	1019.0	
	157.1	690.5	990.5	
	181.0	700.0	1004.8	
	195.2	633.3	1114.3	
	204.8	647.6	1766.7	
	223.8	671.4	2338.1	
	214.3	671.4	1557.1	
	228.6	776.2	1361.9	
	223.8	790.5	1209.5	
	238.1	723.8	1114.3	
	261.9	738.1	1028.6	
	261.9	771.4	985.7	
	252.4	771.4	1200.0	
	247.6	823.8	1190.5	
100.0	247.6	838.1	1171.4	
104.8	257.1	857.1	1166.7	
100.0	257.1	881.0	1166.7	
109.5	257.1	852.4	1161.9	
109.5	257.1	881.0	1028.6	
119.0	257.1	890.5	990.5	
100.0	257.1	890.5	947.6	
100.0	257.1	900.0	976.2	
109.5	271.4	1000.0	1109.5	
109.5	271.4	1000.0	1104.8	
100.0	281.0	1028.6	1095.2	
100.0	290.5	952.4	1081.0	
100.0	338.1	914.3	1042.9	
61.9	342.9	919.0	1038.1	
109.5	342.9	923.8	1076.2	
109.5	347.6	938.1	1185.7	
100.0	352.4	938.1	1442.9	
109.5	381.0	938.1	1642.9	

World Industrial Production (1) 1740-1850

1700	1750	1800	1850
	128.6	357.1	1476.2
	128.6	338.1	
	128.6	357.1	
	133.3	361.9	
	128.6	371.4	
	133.3	381.0	
	119.0	385.7	
	123.8	400.0	
	123.8	381.0	
	119.0	390.5	
	119.0	423.8	
	123.8	447.6	
	123.8	419.0	
	119.0	423.8	
	128.6	428.6	
	128.6	476.2	
	147.6	476.2	
	147.6	476.2	
	142.9	571.4	
	152.4	523.8	
	147.6	523.8	
	147.6	523.8	
	161.9	571.4	
	152.4	619.0	
	142.9	619.0	
	147.6	666.7	
	152.4	619.0	
	157.1	714.3	
	161.9	761.9	
	152.4	714.3	
	152.4	809.5	
	147.6	809.5	
	176.2	761.9	
	171.4	857.1	
	176.2	904.8	
	209.5	952.4	
	219.0	1047.6	
	223.8	952.4	
	219.0	1047.6	
	261.9	1142.9	
100.0	257.1	1142.9	
95.2	261.9	1142.9	
104.8	281.0	1095.2	
100.0	242.9	1142.9	
114.3	252.4	1285.7	
109.5	266.7	1381.0	
114.3	285.7	1381.0	
119.0	261.9	1333.3	
128.6	285.7	1476.2	
114.3	338.1	1476.2	

World Industrial Production (2) 1850-1975

1850	1900	1950
100.0	661.3	2619.4
109.7	687.1	2845.2
119.4	741.9	2912.9
129.0	758.1	3129.0
135.5	761.3	3129.0
141.9	838.7	3500.0
154.8	877.4	3671.0
151.6	903.2	3793.5
151.6	829.0	3693.5
161.3	909.7	4109.7
171.0	974.2	4380.6
171.0	990.3	4538.7
151.6	1077.4	4838.7
164.5	1129.0	5083.9
174.2	1029.0	5500.0
177.4	1061.3	5906.5
203.2	1141.9	6371.0
200.0	1151.6	6464.5
216.1	1083.9	6871.0
225.8	993.5	7380.6
219.4	1051.6	7532.3
238.7	903.2	7683.9
264.5	1106.5	8283.9
261.3	1164.5	9038.7
261.3	1232.3	9112.9
254.8	1332.3	8509.7
264.5	1377.4	
267.7	1467.7	
274.2	1535.5	
280.6	1648.4	
303.2	1445.2	
319.4	1254.8	
341.9	1074.2	
354.8	1209.7	
345.2	1345.2	
341.9	1503.2	
361.3	1693.5	
390.3	1864.5	
406.5	1671.0	
441.9	1954.8	
464.5	2100.0	
471.0	2506.5	
477.4	2925.8	
461.3	3332.3	
477.4	3161.3	
522.6	2190.3	
535.5	1864.5	
561.3	2100.0	
612.9	2258.1	
658.1	2303.2	

World Agricultural Production 1850-1975

1850	1900	1950
100.0	272.4	513.8
100.0	269.0	527.6
103.4	286.2	551.7
103.4	282.8	572.4
103.4	282.8	575.9
106.9	300.0	593.1
110.3	317.2	610.3
110.3	300.0	610.3
113.8	306.9	637.9
117.2	320.7	658.6
117.2	320.7	672.4
117.2	324.1	679.3
110.3	351.7	696.6
106.9	344.8	706.9
113.8	334.5	727.6
124.1	337.9	731.0
127.6	303.4	758.6
127.6	303.4	786.2
131.0	303.4	806.9
131.0	310.3	813.8
144.8	341.4	831.0
141.4	341.4	858.6
148.3	379.3	858.6
148.3	393.1	900.0
144.8	406.9	913.8
158.6	441.4	931.0
158.6	441.4	
165.5	455.2	
169.0	469.0	
172.4	469.0	
182.8	472.4	
169.0	469.0	
193.1	465.5	
186.2	472.4	
200.0	472.4	
203.4	472.4	
200.0	486.2	
196.6	510.3	
210.3	506.9	
220.7	496.6	
203.4	496.6	
227.6	496.6	
217.2	493.1	
224.1	475.9	
217.2	462.1	
248.3	396.6	
251.7	451.7	
241.4	482.8	
269.0	537.9	
258.6	544.8	

World Total Production 1850-1975

1850	1900	1950
100.0	367.1	1011.4
102.7	370.5	1075.2
107.4	396.0	1110.1
109.4	398.0	1173.2
110.7	398.7	1175.2
114.8	430.9	1273.2
120.8	454.4	1327.5
120.1	447.7	1356.4
122.8	435.6	1352.3
127.5	465.8	1459.7
129.5	481.2	1532.9
129.5	487.9	1575.8
120.1	529.5	1657.0
120.8	536.9	1719.5
128.2	503.4	1828.9
136.9	513.4	1920.1
145.0	508.1	2032.2
145.0	511.4	2089.9
151.0	496.6	2198.0
153.0	477.9	2321.5
162.4	518.8	2373.2
164.4	480.5	2428.2
175.8	558.4	2543.6
175.2	586.6	2759.7
172.5	611.4	2806.0
181.9	661.7	2681.9
183.9	671.1	
189.9	704.7	
194.6	730.9	
198.7	758.4	
212.1	714.8	
205.4	664.4	
229.5	618.1	
227.5	653.0	
235.6	685.2	
237.6	722.1	
239.6	778.5	
243.6	838.9	
258.4	791.9	
273.8	845.0	
265.8	879.2	
286.6	965.1	
279.9	1051.0	
281.9	1124.2	
279.9	1076.5	
314.8	813.4	
320.8	793.3	
318.8	871.8	
352.3	952.3	
354.4	965.8	

French Real Gross National Product 1820-1975

1800	1850	1900	1950
	165.3	331.8	597.5
	162.8	320.7	632.2
	171.5	320.7	653.7
	161.6	331.8	669.8
	170.2	347.9	697.9
	168.2	342.6	730.6
	176.0	347.9	774.0
	190.5	353.3	820.2
	200.4	358.7	844.2
	185.1	364.5	871.1
	194.6	364.5	933.5
	187.6	380.6	984.7
	199.6	413.2	1050.8
	209.5	413.2	1106.6
	207.9	390.1	1178.9
	214.1	359.1	1235.1
	214.5	343.8	1299.6
	200.0	333.5	1360.7
	224.8	315.7	1418.6
	234.3	310.7	1517.8
100.0	204.1	338.0	1604.5
107.9	211.6	332.6	1691.3
103.7	227.7	384.7	1791.3
109.5	213.6	405.4	1887.6
114.1	241.7	447.1	1948.8
109.9	252.1	452.1	1952.1
112.4	242.1	457.4	
114.9	247.5	452.1	
115.7	242.6	478.1	
118.6	235.1	519.8	
112.4	249.2	504.1	
113.6	256.6	483.5	
124.4	266.1	462.8	
125.6	252.5	483.5	
124.0	254.5	483.5	
131.4	256.6	467.8	
128.9	259.9	473.1	
134.7	260.7	499.2	
136.4	259.1	499.2	
125.6	263.2	519.8	
143.4	270.7	428.9	
145.0	275.6	340.1	
144.2	283.5	304.1	
146.3	276.4	288.4	
155.0	296.3	252.1	
148.8	290.1	273.6	
145.5	299.2	415.7	
167.4	293.8	452.5	
158.7	309.9	519.8	
164.9	326.0	555.8	

British Real Gross National Product 1830-1975

1800	1850	1900	1950
	150.1	452.4	850.9
	156.2	470.4	874.0
	158.9	473.3	869.6
	165.0	473.5	909.4
	169.5	476.4	944.3
	174.1	486.2	973.6
	180.9	497.8	992.7
	184.8	499.3	1012.6
	186.0	485.3	1017.3
	189.9	501.4	1055.7
	192.8	518.3	1103.1
	202.6	531.8	1141.2
	202.6	531.6	1153.4
	204.5	559.7	1204.6
	207.7	562.9	1274.1
	213.8	611.3	1305.2
	213.5	609.2	1330.6
	216.5	608.7	1364.7
	224.0	597.4	1418.3
	230.9	543.0	1443.4
	248.9	507.3	1477.6
	264.9	482.0	1516.5
	263.1	499.2	1553.5
	263.1	516.5	1688.8
	278.9	532.5	1657.1
	283.0	561.2	1628.1
	286.1	538.1	
	288.5	575.4	
	290.5	584.7	
	285.2	598.7	
100.0	307.0	598.1	
104.5	306.6	567.4	
104.0	311.7	565.7	
104.5	325.3	576.4	
108.8	323.3	614.9	
114.9	322.6	638.8	
119.1	326.1	658.5	
117.4	342.0	683.2	
124.2	347.5	702.9	
145.1	354.4	725.3	
125.9	359.5	821.8	
123.4	371.8	867.2	
120.9	366.2	872.5	
122.7	364.4	887.0	
130.2	383.8	846.3	
137.3	395.4	794.0	
146.3	413.4	789.3	
147.4	414.5	772.6	
149.1	437.7	795.2	
151.6	460.6	817.5	

U.S. Real Gross National Product 1889-1970

1850	1900	1950
	156.6	723.6
	174.5	780.9
	176.2	804.7
	184.9	840.7
	182.7	828.9
	196.1	892.1
	218.9	908.6
	222.4	921.6
	204.1	911.0
	237.9	969.2
	244.6	993.3
	250.9	1012.6
	265.2	1079.0
	267.6	1122.2
	255.8	1183.5
	253.6	1258.2
	273.5	1340.3
	275.4	1375.2
	309.2	1439.1
	298.2	1477.8
	285.1	1471.5
	260.3	
	301.4	
	337.9	
	337.1	
	365.4	
	387.0	
	386.6	
	388.8	
	414.7	
	373.7	
	344.8	
	293.7	
	288.2	
	314.3	
	345.2	
	393.1	
	413.8	
	392.9	
100.0	426.5	
107.3	462.7	
112.2	537.1	
123.0	606.5	
117.1	686.6	
113.8	735.8	
127.5	723.4	
124.8	636.7	
136.7	631.2	
139.7	659.3	
152.3	660.1	

British Industrial Production 1801–1938

1800	1850	1900
	424.3	1523.2
100.0	439.5	1527.0
104.6	454.7	1553.6
107.6	469.8	1521.3
110.7	484.9	1540.3
112.2	500.1	1629.6
115.2	534.3	1698.1
118.2	553.4	1730.5
119.7	542.0	1591.6
122.8	570.5	1603.0
124.3	602.8	1625.9
127.3	602.8	1740.0
128.8	616.1	1785.6
130.3	618.0	1901.6
133.4	665.5	1781.8
136.4	709.3	1819.1
139.4	735.9	1719.7
143.9	692.2	1604.9
148.5	692.2	1552.1
151.5	680.8	1710.4
151.5	764.4	1899.8
166.7	827.2	1548.3
166.7	851.9	1788.9
181.9	861.4	1896.6
181.9	882.3	2105.6
197.0	888.1	2187.9
197.0	903.2	2067.6
197.0	901.3	2384.2
212.2	899.4	2320.8
212.2	867.1	2434.9
227.3	956.5	2330.3
227.3	1017.4	2181.5
242.5	1059.2	2172.0
242.5	1074.4	2314.5
257.6	1034.5	2545.7
257.6	990.7	2742.0
272.8	969.8	2988.9
288.0	1047.8	3166.2
288.0	1108.6	3080.8
303.1	1186.6	
303.1	1203.7	
318.2	1218.9	
333.4	1160.0	
333.4	1140.9	
348.6	1207.5	
363.7	1264.6	
363.7	1357.7	
378.9	1395.8	
394.0	1464.2	
409.2	1523.2	

French Industrial Production 1815–1913

1800	1850	1900
	174.5	353.6
	162.0	352.6
	181.2	345.3
	190.1	368.7
	178.1	348.4
	194.3	388.5
	198.4	396.4
	183.9	413.0
	199.0	405.2
	190.6	432.8
	203.6	422.4
	201.6	462.5
	192.7	532.8
	196.9	520.8
	214.6	
100.0	207.8	
101.6	210.4	
103.6	209.4	
110.9	228.1	
101.6	231.2	
107.8	208.3	
114.1	215.1	
111.5	238.5	
105.2	228.1	
113.5	242.2	
102.6	245.3	
108.3	248.4	
110.9	242.2	
108.9	246.9	
109.4	239.6	
109.4	257.3	
106.2	281.8	
112.0	288.0	
119.3	283.9	
120.3	273.4	
119.8	270.8	
118.0	275.5	
118.7	279.7	
126.0	289.6	
119.3	304.2	
126.6	298.4	
133.3	314.1	
139.1	331.2	
147.4	320.3	
147.9	326.6	
154.7	309.9	
159.4	335.4	
154.7	347.4	
139.1	357.3	
167.7	371.4	

Belgian Industrial Production 1840–1975

1800	1850	1900	1950
	123.5	716.2	1338.2
	135.3	676.5	1500.0
	155.9	705.9	1455.9
	166.2	720.6	1470.6
	175.0	735.3	1544.1
	176.5	750.0	1676.5
	197.1	794.1	1794.1
	194.1	808.8	1823.5
	205.9	779.4	1735.3
	213.2	823.5	1794.1
	226.5	852.9	1941.2
	222.1	897.1	2029.4
	225.0	941.2	2147.1
	230.9	926.5	2308.8
	247.1	705.9	2455.9
	260.3	338.2	2514.7
	282.4	352.9	2558.8
	285.3	279.4	2588.2
	282.4	279.4	2750.0
	314.7	411.8	2985.3
	326.5	720.6	3088.2
	372.1	676.5	3161.8
	398.5	808.8	3323.5
	376.5	911.8	3514.7
	385.3	1014.7	3647.1
	375.0	985.3	3294.1
	366.2	1088.2	
	380.9	1191.2	
	382.4	1294.1	
	366.2	1294.1	
	414.7	1176.5	
	423.5	1088.2	
	461.8	941.2	
	466.2	1000.0	
	457.4	1000.0	
	413.2	1102.9	
	430.9	1176.5	
	469.1	1250.0	
	457.4	1102.9	
	486.8	1176.5	
100.0	560.3	808.8	
94.1	555.9	882.4	
86.8	492.6	750.0	
94.1	575.0	779.4	
95.6	588.2	411.8	
117.6	536.8	514.7	
105.9	605.9	1014.7	
127.9	661.8	1191.2	
108.8	700.0	1279.4	
136.8	708.8	1279.4	

Volume of Seville-Atlantic shipping 1506–1650

1500	1550	1600	1650
	954.4	1498.1	376.0
	905.9	1229.3	
	779.6	1397.3	
	506.3	997.6	
	219.5	736.2	
	754.3	1450.9	
	468.1	1222.4	
	680.2	645.3	
194.1	507.7	1789.6	
135.7	362.2	1452.0	
79.6	645.7	1615.4	
99.7	702.4	1024.7	
158.7	647.8	1372.5	
152.2	605.9	935.7	
225.4	621.1	1099.1	
181.1	846.6	1190.1	
149.6	833.9	1191.1	
267.8	837.6	1283.0	
286.1	751.8	1194.6	
277.6	860.4	1246.8	
317.1	843.7	1186.1	
208.3	694.9	1185.0	
147.8	1178.7	845.9	
170.2	842.3	1075.2	
222.4	1003.7	1492.9	
351.0	773.9	1050.6	
302.7	1065.5	1284.0	
353.1	938.9	1031.9	
216.2	719.0	758.8	
331.0	845.0	919.9	
359.6	886.8	1451.0	
290.9	907.9	573.7	
269.3	903.2	787.3	
305.3	916.5	956.2	
418.0	1285.0	761.7	
465.5	1143.6	984.5	
579.4	1432.3	1115.3	
330.1	958.8	857.3	
392.3	1221.2	529.9	
441.6	1257.0	857.8	
487.3	782.3	675.1	
532.2	862.9	423.0	
574.3	472.6	501.2	
537.3	1328.7	945.4	
347.3	930.8	594.5	
592.3	1193.4	928.2	
572.3	1344.0	882.2	
645.9	899.6	870.6	
724.2	1185.2	534.6	
857.8	945.6	588.3	

British Net Volume of Wheat Exports 1700–1775

1700	1750
100.0	1934.7
200.0	1349.0
183.7	875.5
218.4	612.2
183.7	726.5
195.9	483.7
383.7	210.2
151.0	-265.3
169.4	-22.4
346.9	463.3
28.6	804.1
157.1	902.0
295.9	604.1
359.2	816.3
357.1	810.2
338.8	126.5
153.1	314.3
46.9	-1006.1
146.9	-698.0
261.2	93.9
169.4	153.1
167.3	14.3
365.3	-36.7
322.4	-100.0
502.0	-557.1
416.3	-959.2
289.8	
61.2	
-144.9	
-42.9	
191.8	
265.3	
412.2	
871.4	
1016.3	
312.2	
240.8	
942.9	
1185.7	
571.4	
110.2	
91.8	
598.0	
757.1	
473.5	
663.3	
267.3	
544.9	
1108.2	
1283.7	

English Exports in Current Prices 1700–1775

1700	1750
100.0	218.4
107.0	202.3
83.5	189.7
104.2	201.3
98.3	191.8
104.1	182.5
109.9	199.0
110.6	197.7
116.9	202.1
101.6	232.4
109.0	253.2
94.3	249.1
98.9	216.7
103.5	219.6
128.3	266.0
115.6	233.4
110.8	228.3
124.1	218.9
101.0	223.5
124.1	207.1
106.3	219.1
104.0	258.7
122.0	242.2
124.6	204.7
117.8	231.7
130.7	224.3
115.3	
113.2	
113.2	
109.0	
122.8	
117.2	
130.9	
134.3	
124.6	
136.7	
141.1	
153.7	
161.0	
128.5	
117.8	
138.2	
140.5	
158.4	
124.8	
132.3	
166.0	
155.5	
168.7	
209.4	

Total World Exports 1850–1975

1850	1900	1950
100.0	694.1	1605.9
111.8	705.9	1811.8
111.8	705.9	1788.2
123.5	747.1	1900.0
123.5	770.6	1988.2
123.5	829.4	2158.8
147.1	894.1	2347.1
158.8	905.9	2482.4
158.8	858.8	2411.8
170.6	894.1	2594.1
176.5	941.2	2852.9
176.5	1041.2	2994.1
176.5	1082.4	3164.7
188.2	1117.6	3400.0
200.0	929.4	3741.2
211.8	805.9	4029.4
247.1	847.1	4329.4
247.1	735.3	4523.5
258.8	670.6	5147.1
270.6	770.6	5705.9
258.8	894.1	6200.0
288.2	894.1	6635.3
300.0	970.6	7252.9
311.8	1017.6	8123.5
323.5	1141.2	8617.6
335.3	1217.6	8058.8
347.1	1229.4	
347.1	1364.7	
382.4	1400.0	
400.0	1452.9	
411.8	1329.4	
423.5	1241.2	
447.1	1082.4	
458.8	1094.1	
482.4	1141.2	
482.4	1182.4	
494.1	1217.6	
523.5	1364.7	
523.5	1252.9	
535.3	1252.9	
547.1	1023.5	
547.1	1076.5	
558.8	1188.2	
558.8	1541.2	
594.1	1364.7	
623.5	929.4	
682.4	1105.9	
682.4	1294.1	
694.1	1317.6	
705.9	1388.2	

List of Innovations [Haustein] 1764-1975

1750	1800	1850	1900	1950
	0	0	2	3
	0	0	1	1
	0	2	2	0
	0	0	2	0
	0	1	0	1
	0	0	0	0
	0	4	1	1
	0	0	2	0
	0	0	0	4
	1	1	1	1
	1	0	2	2
	1	1	2	1
	1	0	0	1
	0	1	1	3
1	0	0	2	2
0	0	1	1	0
0	0	2	1	1
0	0	2	0	0
0	0	0	0	3
0	1	1	0	0
0	4	0	1	1
0	0	0	1	2
0	0	1	3	1
0	0	2	2	0
0	2	0	0	0
1	0	1	1	1
0	0	0	1	
0	1	0	1	
0	0	3	1	
0	1	0	1	
1	0	2	1	
1	0	0	0	
0	0	7	1	
0	2	2	0	
0	0	1	3	
0	1	4	7	
0	0	3	2	
0	1	2	1	
0	1	2	1	
0	1	0	3	
0	0	2	1	
0	0	2	1	
0	0	0	1	
1	3	1	2	
0	1	4	1	
1	2	0	2	
0	0	1	0	
0	2	0	1	

List of Innovations [Van Duijn] 1856-1971

1850	1900	1950
	0	3
	1	4
	0	1
	0	2
	0	0
1	1	0
0	0	0
0	0	0
1	0	1
1	2	1
0	0	1
0	0	0
0	4	0
1	0	0
0	0	0
0	0	0
0	1	1
0	0	0
1	3	0
0	0	1
1	0	0
2	0	0
0	2	0
2	2	0
0	1	0
1	0	0
1	0	0
1	0	1
1	1	0
0	4	0
0	0	0
1	2	0
1	2	1
1	3	3
2	3	1
1	1	0
0	3	0
0	1	0
2	0	0
1	0	0
0	2	0
0	0	0
1	5	0
1	0	

List of Innovations [Clark et al] 1904-1968

1900	1950
	2
	2
	2
	1
1	1
0	1
0	0
0	1
0	0
3	1
1	0
1	1
0	1
1	1
0	0
0	0
0	0
1	0
0	0
0	2
2	1
1	0
0	0
2	0
1	2
2	0
1	0
1	1
0	1
1	0
1	3
1	4
2	3
2	1
1	0
1	0
0	2
3	3
2	0
1	0
3	0
0	0
2	0
0	1

List of "Product" Innovations [Kleinknecht] 1879-1965

1850	1900	1950
	0	0
	0	1
	0	0
	0	0
	0	0
0	0	0
0	1	0
0	0	0
0	1	1
0	0	2
0	0	0
0	0	0
0	0	0
0	0	0
0	0	1
0	0	0
0	0	0
0	2	0
0	0	0
0	0	0
0	1	0
0	0	0
0	3	0
0	0	0
0	0	0
0	1	0
0	0	1
0	0	0
0	0	1
0	0	1
0	1	2
0	2	3
0	3	1
0	1	3
0	1	2
0	0	0
0	0	1
0	0	0
0	0	3
0	0	1
0	0	2
0	0	1
0	0	1

List of "Improvement" Innovations [Kleinknecht] 1859-1969

1850	1900	1950
	1	0
	0	0
	0	0
	1	1
	0	1
	0	5
	2	0
	0	0
	0	2
1	1	0
0	0	1
1	1	0
0	0	2
0	?	0
0	0	0
0	0	2
1	0	0
0	0	0
0	0	0
0	0	1
1	1	
0	0	
0	0	
0	0	
0	0	
1	1	
1	0	
1	0	
0	1	
0	0	
0	1	
1	0	
1	2	
2	0	
0	0	
0	0	
0	0	
0	0	
0	0	
0	2	
0	0	
0	1	
1	1	

Number of British Patents 1738-1935

1700	1750	1800	1850	1900
	7.	96.	513.	1204.
	8.	104.	455.	1194.
	7.	107.	469.	1258.
	13.	73.	499.	1380.
	9.	60.	430.	1352.
	12.	95.	467.	1345.
	3.	99.	478.	1378.
	9.	94.	463.	1487.
	14.	95.	446.	1489.
	10.	101.	452.	1378.
	14.	108.	472.	1487.
	9.	115.	467.	1569.
	17.	118.	501.	1446.
	20.	131.	478.	1518.
	18.	96.	463.	1375.
	14.	102.	499.	1047.
	31.	118.	486.	771.
	23.	103.	522.	854.
	23.	132.	569.	988.
	36.	101.	458.	1125.
	30.	97.	549.	1298.
	22.	109.	498.	1618.
	29.	113.	543.	1588.
	29.	138.	633.	1562.
	35.	180.	680.	1541.
	20.	250.	722.	1572.
	29.	141.	710.	1585.
	33.	150.	785.	1612.
	30.	154.	757.	1618.
	37.	130.	757.	1732.
	33.	180.	801.	1899.
	34.	151.	818.	2006.
	39.	147.	854.	1934.
	64.	180.	902.	1515.
	46.	207.	991.	1545.
	61.	231.	895.	1616.
	60.	296.	914.	
	55.	256.	864.	
6.	42.	394.	900.	
3.	43.	411.	974.	
4.	68.	440.	973.	
8.	57.	440.	973.	
6.	85.	371.	1021.	
7.	43.	420.	1055.	
1.	55.	450.	1070.	
4.	51.	572.	1114.	
4.	75.	493.	1140.	
8.	54.	493.	1299.	
11.	77.	388.	1286.	
13.	82.	514.	1295.	

Number of U.S. Patents (1) 1790-1975

1750	1800	1850	1900	1950
	41.	884.	24656.	43039.
	44.	757.	25554.	44326.
	65.	890.	27121.	43616.
	97.	846.	31032.	40467.
	84.	1759.	30259.	33809.
	57.	1892.	29777.	30432.
	63.	2315.	31169.	46816.
	99.	2686.	35860.	42745.
	158.	3467.	32736.	48330.
	203.	4165.	36562.	52408.
	223.	4363.	35130.	47169.
	215.	3040.	32856.	48368.
	238.	3221.	36196.	55691.
	181.	3781.	33915.	45679.
	210.	4638.	39899.	47371.
	173.	6099.	43117.	62854.
	206.	8874.	48892.	68397.
	174.	12301.	40927.	65647.
	222.	12544.	38450.	59101.
	156.	12957.	36795.	67556.
	155.	12157.	37057.	64427.
	168.	11687.	37792.	78314.
	200.	12200.	38361.	74808.
	173.	11616.	38614.	74139.
	228.	12230.	42572.	76274.
	304.	13291.	46432.	71994.
	323.	14172.	44733.	
	331.	12920.	41718.	
	368.	12345.	42326.	
	447.	12133.	45267.	
	544.	12926.	45226.	
	573.	15548.	51756.	
	474.	18135.	53458.	
	586.	21160.	48774.	
	630.	19122.	44419.	
	752.	23282.	40618.	
	702.	21768.	39783.	
	436.	20399.	37683.	
	515.	19552.	38062.	
	404.	23322.	43073.	
3.	458.	25308.	42237.	
33.	490.	22310.	41108.	
11.	488.	22645.	38449.	
20.	494.	22747.	31054.	
22.	478.	19833.	28053.	
12.	475.	20855.	25694.	
44.	566.	21825.	21805.	
51.	495.	22065.	20139.	
28.	584.	20375.	23961.	
44.	988.	23288.	35131.	

Number of U.S. Patents (2)   1837-1950

1800	1850	1900	1950
	883.	24062.	40976.
	752.	26670.	
	885.	29306.	
	844.	29894.	
	1755.	31033.	
	1881.	32772.	
	2302.	33643.	
	2674.	34982.	
	3455.	36476.	
	4160.	39063.	
	4357.	38387.	
	3020.	40860.	
	3214.	41829.	
	3773.	41313.	
	4630.	41105.	
	6088.	40719.	
	8863.	41287.	
	12277.	40993.	
	12526.	34781.	
	12931.	46525.	
	12137.	49681.	
	11659.	53049.	
	12180.	50923.	
	11616.	46569.	
	13102.	46693.	
	13123.	48646.	
	12994.	49348.	
	12317.	52898.	
	12288.	53131.	
	12166.	54435.	
	13198.	54315.	
	15089.	48362.	
	18359.	40639.	
	20059.	34302.	
	20737.	34354.	
	21044.	35248.	
	21325.	37966.	
426.	20786.	39619.	
514.	21053.	40559.	
404.	24022.	38872.	
458.	24190.	36913.	
490.	23907.	31744.	
488.	17900.	27625.	
493.	22618.	27592.	
478.	22433.	32866.	
473.	23741.	41149.	
566.	25520.	49160.	
495.	27693.	45756.	
588.	20569.	41691.	
984.	23615.	40995.	

U.S. Patents in Bldg. & Railroads   1837-1950

1800	1850	1900	1950
	33.	1313.	804.
	39.	1718.	
	45.	2146.	
	29.	2373.	
	75.	2310.	
	61.	2574.	
	61.	2535.	
	70.	2824.	
	167.	2838.	
	182.	2632.	
	141.	2240.	
	95.	2552.	
	98.	2440.	
	110.	2620.	
	140.	2461.	
	195.	2252.	
	278.	2104.	
	470.	1763.	
	453.	1372.	
	505.	1826.	
	454.	1830.	
	424.	2061.	
	517.	2037.	
	620.	1942.	
	666.	1916.	
	595.	2059.	
	625.	2119.	
	491.	2148.	
	468.	2062.	
	523.	2117.	
	669.	1853.	
	813.	1789.	
	1244.	1229.	
	1217.	976.	
	1178.	1050.	
	1266.	1147.	
	1468.	1194.	
15.	1372.	1215.	
18.	1435.	1283.	
14.	1735.	1106.	
28.	2016.	1095.	
20.	1868.	910.	
11.	1720.	624.	
13.	1604.	570.	
10.	1530.	738.	
15.	1398.	787.	
19.	1459.	903.	
22.	1394.	791.	
16.	1052.	771.	
54.	1304.	722.	

U.S. Private Building Volume   1830-1957

1800	1850	1900	1950
	518.1	878.7	2114.5
	565.6	1262.2	1962.8
	649.2	1262.6	1932.3
	697.9	1268.7	2036.6
	676.0	1451.5	2240.7
	640.7	1858.9	2610.3
	675.7	1892.2	2493.9
	639.1	1639.6	2367.7
	419.9	1493.6	
	463.2	2138.5	
	508.0	1905.9	
	344.7	1878.9	
	308.4	2072.5	
	426.6	1704.5	
	231.7	1553.0	
	341.6	874.8	
	476.2	992.7	
	563.2	831.7	
	668.9	606.9	
	737.5	871.2	
	753.5	887.4	
	823.0	942.1	
	659.1	1363.3	
	655.9	1539.8	
	572.3	1706.8	
	590.7	1930.4	
	502.3	2040.2	
	475.3	1981.0	
	424.8	1882.2	
	504.9	1588.7	
100.0	571.2	1077.0	
136.1	682.3	766.4	
210.3	786.8	381.1	
260.0	872.5	309.8	
294.0	941.8	342.5	
317.6	1086.0	478.2	
428.8	1145.1	695.1	
213.8	1203.1	804.7	
184.7	1177.5	731.9	
169.9	1435.8	905.9	
151.5	1612.5	1015.2	
161.5	1434.6	1167.5	
140.0	1506.9	538.4	
127.7	1129.2	271.5	
149.4	1031.0	265.4	
187.0	1336.2	446.4	
266.9	1121.2	1362.2	
343.4	1230.8	1495.3	
353.1	1047.9	1696.5	
411.1	1247.3	1638.3	

U.S. Railroad Gross Capital Expend.   1870-1950

1850	1900	1950
	60.5	87.1
	55.4	
	57.6	
	60.5	
	70.1	
	88.6	
	118.2	
	136.9	
	139.5	
	147.5	
	162.8	
	149.1	
	142.8	
	149.4	
	104.8	
	62.5	
	70.1	
	88.0	
	64.7	
	46.2	
100.0	66.7	
110.8	74.2	
92.9	72.4	
62.9	138.6	
37.8	124.1	
28.2	104.7	
29.7	117.3	
36.5	105.8	
38.0	98.5	
42.3	115.1	
85.5	115.8	
131.5	52.1	
114.9	27.2	
83.3	18.7	
60.6	28.6	
46.5	26.8	
63.5	51.0	
85.3	82.1	
77.8	40.7	
70.9	39.8	
72.0	67.1	
75.8	76.2	
124.9	80.9	
142.4	53.7	
64.9	64.3	
23.7	60.5	
16.3	55.7	
16.7	75.5	
27.7	104.6	
54.2	107.0	

Real Wages for London   1700-1787

1700	1750
100.0	129.0
99.0	120.0
109.0	126.0
110.0	124.0
130.0	128.0
115.0	120.0
127.0	94.0
116.0	100.0
94.0	109.0
82.0	119.0
74.0	122.0
106.0	119.0
112.0	108.0
102.0	110.0
104.0	105.0
109.0	103.0
118.0	98.0
118.0	98.0
118.0	111.0
103.0	112.0
108.0	103.0
121.0	93.0
128.0	89.0
113.0	92.0
111.0	94.0
105.0	92.0
110.0	92.0
104.0	90.0
94.0	96.0
108.0	105.0
122.0	98.0
130.0	98.0
141.0	85.0
128.0	88.0
125.0	95.0
134.0	93.0
125.0	96.0
126.0	95.0
127.0	
108.0	
97.0	
113.0	
120.0	
140.0	
142.0	
126.0	
128.0	
124.0	
118.0	
120.0	

South English Real Wages   1736-1954

1700	1750	1800	1850	1900	1950
	91.9	51.4	113.5	181.1	243.2
	94.6	45.9	114.9	182.4	229.7
	90.5	60.8	113.5	186.5	225.7
	91.9	62.2	106.8	179.7	252.7
	87.8	63.5	95.9	182.4	262.2
	93.2	64.9	95.9	182.4	
	89.2	66.2	95.9	177.0	
	74.3	67.6	94.6	174.3	
	74.3	66.2	102.7	173.0	
	79.7	59.5	100.0	170.3	
	83.8	64.9	91.9	181.1	
	87.8	66.2	97.3	182.4	
	85.1	59.5	97.3	179.7	
	82.4	58.1	110.8	177.0	
	75.7	66.2	105.4	167.6	
	73.0	74.3	108.1	154.1	
	73.0	81.1	110.8	127.0	
	68.9	70.3	106.8	117.6	
	68.9	70.3	110.8	108.1	
	75.7	73.0	116.2	170.3	
	75.7	79.7	116.2	208.1	
	70.3	90.5	109.5	225.7	
	63.5	105.4	110.8	221.6	
	63.5	98.6	113.5	214.9	
	70.3	90.5	113.5	232.4	
	75.7	77.0	124.3	237.8	
	82.4	81.1	118.9	256.8	
	82.4	87.8	121.6	271.6	
	78.4	90.5	127.0	273.0	
	86.5	90.5	133.8	268.9	
	89.2	94.6	137.8	309.5	
	86.5	85.1	133.8	333.8	
	83.8	93.2	141.9	359.5	
	75.7	98.6	137.8	335.1	
	74.3	106.8	151.4	339.2	
	78.4	105.4	158.1	343.2	
100.0	78.4	94.6	174.3	335.1	
93.2	78.4	91.9	170.3	327.0	
95.9	75.7	91.9	170.0	336.5	
98.6	75.7	85.1	171.6	363.5	
83.8	74.3	83.8	171.6	300.0	
75.7	74.3	86.5	162.2	278.4	
85.1	73.0	93.2	162.2	237.8	
93.2	73.0	105.4	185.1	247.3	
104.1	71.6	105.4	171.6	248.6	
102.7	71.6	100.0	174.3	251.4	
90.5	70.3	95.9	178.4	281.1	
94.6	77.0	87.8	175.7	283.8	
90.5	79.7	100.0	171.6	267.6	
89.2	70.3	106.8	189.2	240.5	

War Indicators

ALWAR   Great power battle fatalities from all wars, in 1000s.
GPWAR   Battle fatalities from "great power" wars, in 1000s.
LGWR   Logged GPWAR, +.5 (zeroes remain zero).
GPINT   Intensity (fatal./mill.Eur.pop.) of great power wars.
I1   Incidence of any war involving a great power.
I2   Incidence of war of annual intensity above 100.
I3   Incidence of war of annual intensity above 500.

YEAR	ALWAR	GPWAR	LGWR	GPINT	I1	2	3
1495	2.0	2.0	.8	25.7	1	0	0
1496	4.0	4.0	1.1	59.5	1	0	0
1497	3.5	2.0	.8	29.7	1	0	0
1498	1.5	0.0	0.0	0.0	0	0	0
1499	1.5	0.0	.0	0.0	0	0	0
1500	2.0	0.0	0.0	0.0	0	0	0
1501	4.0	3.0	1.0	44.8	1	0	0
1502	7.0	6.0	1.3	89.7	1	0	0
1503	6.5	6.0	1.3	89.7	1	0	0
1504	3.0	3.0	1.0	44.8	1	0	0
1505	0.0	0.0	0.0	0.0	0	0	0
1506	0.0	0.0	.0	0.0	0	0	0
1507	0.0	0.0	0.0	0.0	0	0	0
1508	5.0	0.0	.0	0.0	0	0	0
1509	5.0	0.0	0.0	0.0	0	0	0
1510	0.0	0.0	.0	0.0	0	0	0
1511	3.0	3.0	1.0	43.5	1	0	0
1512	7.7	7.7	1.4	111.5	1	1	0
1513	10.4	9.4	1.5	136.0	1	1	0
1514	8.4	6.4	1.3	92.5	1	0	0
1515	7.4	6.4	1.3	92.0	1	0	0
1516	3.4	3.4	1.0	49.0	1	0	0
1517	3.4	3.4	1.0	49.0	1	0	0
1518	3.4	3.4	1.0	49.0	1	0	0
1519	1.7	1.7	.7	24.5	1	0	0
1520	0.0	0.0	0.0	0.0	0	0	0
1521	6.4	6.4	1.3	89.9	1	0	0
1522	14.3	12.8	1.6	179.8	1	1	0
1523	14.3	12.8	1.6	179.8	1	1	0
1524	12.8	12.8	1.6	179.8	1	1	0
1525	12.8	12.8	1.6	179.8	1	1	0
1526	12.8	12.8	1.6	179.3	1	1	0
1527	12.8	12.8	1.6	178.8	1	1	0
1528	12.8	12.8	1.6	178.8	1	1	0
1529	9.8	9.8	1.5	137.3	1	1	0
1530	6.8	6.8	1.3	95.8	1	0	0
1531	3.4	3.4	1.0	47.9	1	0	0
1532	5.7	4.7	1.2	64.0	1	0	0
1533	11.3	9.3	1.5	128.0	1	1	0
1534	10.3	9.3	1.5	128.0	1	1	0
1535	4.7	4.7	1.2	64.0	1	0	0
1536	8.0	8.0	1.4	109.5	1	1	0
1537	20.9	20.9	1.8	285.5	1	1	0
1538	17.7	17.7	1.7	242.4	1	1	0
1539	9.7	9.7	1.5	132.9	1	1	0
1540	9.7	9.7	1.5	132.9	1	1	0
1541	9.7	9.7	1.5	132.9	1	1	0
1542	22.3	21.5	1.8	290.1	1	1	0
1543	34.8	33.2	2.0	447.4	1	1	0
1544	25.1	23.5	1.9	316.9	1	1	0
1545	15.3	13.7	1.6	186.4	1	1	0
1546	13.3	11.7	1.6	159.6	1	1	0
1547	6.5	4.8	1.2	66.4	1	0	0
1548	1.6	0.0	0.0	0.0	0	0	0
1549	4.6	3.0	1.0	39.5	1	0	0
1550	3.8	3.0	1.0	39.5	1	0	0
1551	4.4	4.4	1.1	57.8	1	0	0
1552	15.2	15.2	1.7	199.1	1	1	0
1553	21.5	21.5	1.8	282.6	1	1	0
1554	21.5	21.5	1.8	282.6	1	1	0
1555	21.5	21.5	1.8	282.6	1	1	0
1556	19.1	19.1	1.8	250.3	1	1	0
1557	16.7	16.7	1.7	218.0	1	1	0
1558	16.7	16.7	1.7	218.0	1	1	0
1559	18.1	18.1	1.8	235.3	1	1	0
1560	16.5	16.5	1.7	213.7	1	1	0
1561	13.5	13.5	1.6	174.7	1	1	0
1562	10.6	10.6	1.5	137.6	1	1	0
1563	7.8	7.8	1.4	100.5	1	1	0
1564	3.9	3.9	1.1	50.2	1	0	0
1565	4.0	4.0	1.1	51.0	1	0	0
1566	8.0	8.0	1.4	102.0	1	1	0
1567	8.0	8.0	1.4	102.0	1	1	0
1568	4.0	4.0	1.1	51.0	1	0	0
1569	2.2	2.2	.8	27.6	1	0	0
1570	4.4	4.4	1.1	55.3	1	0	0
1571	4.4	4.4	1.1	55.3	1	0	0
1572	4.4	4.4	1.1	55.3	1	0	0
1573	4.4	4.4	1.1	55.3	1	0	0
1574	4.4	4.4	1.1	55.3	1	0	0
1575	4.4	4.4	1.1	55.3	1	0	0
1576	7.8	7.8	1.4	98.1	1	0	0
1577	11.2	11.2	1.5	141.0	1	1	0
1578	11.2	11.2	1.5	141.0	1	1	0
1579	12.2	11.2	1.5	141.0	1	1	0
1580	11.0	9.0	1.5	113.4	1	1	0
1581	7.9	6.9	1.3	85.7	1	0	0
1582	6.9	6.9	1.3	85.7	1	0	0
1583	4.6	3.4	1.0	42.9	1	0	0
1584	2.4	0.0	0.0	0.0	0	0	0
1585	3.7	1.3	.6	15.5	1	0	0
1586	5.0	2.5	.9	30.9	1	0	0
1587	7.0	2.5	.9	30.9	1	0	0
1588	7.0	2.5	.9	30.9	1	0	0
1589	5.8	3.4	1.0	41.8	1	0	0
1590	5.5	4.3	1.1	52.6	1	0	0
1591	4.3	4.3	1.1	52.6	1	0	0
1592	4.3	4.3	1.1	52.6	1	0	0
1593	7.8	7.8	1.4	94.4	1	0	0
1594	11.2	11.2	1.5	136.2	1	1	0
1595	11.2	11.2	1.5	136.2	1	1	0
1596	11.2	11.2	1.5	136.2	1	1	0
1597	11.2	11.2	1.5	136.2	1	1	0
1598	10.3	10.3	1.5	125.3	1	1	0
1599	9.4	9.4	1.5	114.5	1	1	0
1600	10.4	9.4	1.5	114.5	1	1	0
1601	10.4	9.4	1.5	114.5	1	1	0
1602	9.4	9.4	1.5	114.5	1	1	0
1603	9.4	9.4	1.5	114.5	1	1	0
1604	8.2	8.2	1.4	99.0	1	0	0
1605	6.9	6.9	1.3	83.5	1	0	0
1606	3.5	3.5	1.0	41.8	1	0	0
1607	0.0	0.0	0.0	0.0	0	0	0
1608	0.0	0.0	.0	0.0	0	0	0
1609	0.0	0.0	0.0	0.0	0	0	0
1610	1.9	1.9	.8	21.9	1	0	0
1611	3.7	3.7	1.1	43.7	1	0	0
1612	3.7	3.7	1.1	43.7	1	0	0
1613	3.7	3.7	1.1	43.7	1	0	0
1614	1.9	1.9	.8	21.9	1	0	0
1615	1.5	0.0	0.0	0.0	0	0	0
1616	3.0	0.0	.0	0.0	0	0	0
1617	3.1	0.0	0.0	0.0	0	0	0
1618	29.5	24.7	1.9	287.0	1	1	0
1619	52.7	46.4	2.2	539.5	1	1	1
1620	49.7	43.4	2.1	505.0	1	1	1
1621	46.6	43.4	2.1	505.0	1	1	1
1622	43.4	43.4	2.1	505.0	1	1	1
1623	43.4	43.4	2.1	505.0	1	1	1
1624	43.4	43.4	2.1	505.0	1	1	1
1625	51.9	51.9	2.2	595.7	1	1	1
1626	60.4	60.4	2.3	686.4	1	1	1
1627	60.4	60.4	2.3	686.4	1	1	1
1628	60.4	60.4	2.3	686.4	1	1	1
1629	60.4	60.4	2.3	686.4	1	1	1
1630	61.6	61.6	2.3	700.0	1	1	1
1631	62.8	62.8	2.3	713.6	1	1	1
1632	62.8	62.8	2.3	713.6	1	1	1
1633	62.8	62.8	2.3	713.6	1	1	1
1634	62.8	62.8	2.3	713.6	1	1	1
1635	75.7	75.7	2.4	854.2	1	1	1
1636	88.5	88.5	2.4	994.8	1	1	1
1637	88.5	88.5	2.4	994.8	1	1	1
1638	88.5	88.5	2.4	994.8	1	1	1
1639	88.5	88.5	2.4	994.8	1	1	1
1640	88.5	88.5	2.4	994.8	1	1	1
1641	88.5	88.5	2.4	994.8	1	1	1
1642	90.1	88.5	2.4	994.8	1	1	1
1643	91.6	88.5	2.4	994.8	1	1	1
1644	91.6	88.5	2.4	994.8	1	1	1
1645	93.5	88.5	2.4	994.8	1	1	1
1646	95.4	88.5	2.4	994.8	1	1	1
1647	95.4	88.5	2.4	994.8	1	1	1
1648	56.0	49.2	2.2	551.4	1	1	1
1649	16.7	9.8	1.5	107.9	1	1	0
1650	17.7	9.8	1.5	107.9	1	1	0
1651	17.7	9.8	1.5	107.9	1	1	0
1652	21.0	14.2	1.7	154.9	1	1	0
1653	25.4	18.5	1.8	201.9	1	1	0
1654	27.2	20.3	1.8	221.7	1	1	0
1655	24.7	17.8	1.8	194.6	1	1	0
1656	22.9	16.0	1.7	174.4	1	1	0
1657	33.6	26.3	1.9	284.8	1	1	0
1658	41.9	34.1	2.0	368.4	1	1	0
1659	34.5	26.6	1.9	287.6	1	1	0
1660	25.3	17.4	1.7	187.0	1	1	0
1661	22.9	15.6	1.7	167.1	1	1	0
1662	22.4	15.6	1.7	167.1	1	1	0
1663	22.4	15.6	1.7	167.1	1	1	0
1664	12.8	7.8	1.4	83.6	1	0	0
1665	13.3	9.2	1.5	98.0	1	0	0
1666	22.6	18.5	1.8	196.0	1	1	0
1667	14.3	11.2	1.6	119.0	1	1	0
1668	3.5	2.0	.8	21.0	1	0	0
1669	0.0	0.0	0.0	0.0	0	0	0
1670	0.0	0.0	.0	0.0	0	0	0
1671	0.0	0.0	0.0	0.0	0	0	0
1672	29.1	28.5	2.0	298.3	1	1	0
1673	58.2	57.0	2.3	596.7	1	1	1
1674	58.2	57.0	2.3	596.7	1	1	1
1675	58.2	57.0	2.3	596.7	1	1	1
1676	57.6	57.0	2.3	596.7	1	1	1
1677	58.5	57.0	2.3	596.7	1	1	1
1678	31.5	28.5	2.0	298.3	1	1	0
1679	3.0	0.0	0.0	0.0	0	0	0
1680	3.0	0.0	.0	0.0	0	0	0
1681	1.5	0.0	0.0	0.0	0	0	0
1682	11.3	11.3	1.6	116.3	1	1	0
1683	25.1	25.1	1.9	258.1	1	1	0
1684	25.1	25.1	1.9	258.1	1	1	0
1685	22.6	22.6	1.9	232.6	1	1	0
1686	22.6	22.6	1.9	232.6	1	1	0
1687	22.6	22.6	1.9	232.6	1	1	0
1688	60.4	60.4	2.3	618.1	1	1	1
1689	98.1	98.1	2.5	1003.6	1	1	1
1690	98.1	98.1	2.5	1003.6	1	1	1
1691	98.1	98.1	2.5	1003.6	1	1	1
1692	98.1	98.1	2.5	1003.6	1	1	1
1693	98.1	98.1	2.5	1003.6	1	1	1
1694	98.1	98.1	2.5	1003.6	1	1	1
1695	98.1	98.1	2.5	1003.6	1	1	1
1696	98.1	98.1	2.5	1003.6	1	1	1
1697	60.4	60.4	2.3	618.1	1	1	1
1698	22.6	22.6	1.9	232.6	1	1	0
1699	11.3	11.3	1.6	116.3	1	1	0

YEAR	ALWAR	GPWAR	LGWR	GPINT	I1	2	3
1700	1.5	1.5	.7	15.2	1	0	0
1701	55.2	55.2	2.2	550.9	1	1	1
1702	107.3	107.3	2.5	1071.3	1	1	1
1703	107.3	107.3	2.5	1071.3	1	1	1
1704	107.3	107.3	2.5	1071.3	1	1	1
1705	107.3	107.3	2.5	1071.3	1	1	1
1706	107.3	107.3	2.5	1071.3	1	1	1
1707	107.3	107.3	2.5	1071.3	1	1	1
1708	107.3	107.3	2.5	1071.3	1	1	1
1709	107.3	107.3	2.5	1071.3	1	1	1
1710	107.3	107.3	2.5	1071.3	1	1	1
1711	107.3	107.3	2.5	1071.3	1	1	1
1712	107.3	107.3	2.5	1071.3	1	1	1
1713	55.2	55.2	2.2	550.9	1	1	1
1714	3.0	3.0	1.0	30.5	1	0	0
1715	3.0	3.0	1.0	30.5	1	0	0
1716	5.5	3.0	1.0	30.5	1	0	0
1717	8.0	3.0	1.0	30.5	1	0	0
1718	11.8	9.3	1.5	91.7	1	0	0
1719	15.5	15.5	1.7	153.0	1	1	0
1720	9.3	9.3	1.5	91.7	1	0	0
1721	1.5	1.5	.7	15.2	1	0	0
1722	0.0	0.0	0.0	0.0	0	0	0
1723	0.0	0.0	.0	0.0	0	0	0
1724	0.0	0.0	0.0	0.0	0	0	0
1725	0.0	0.0	.0	0.0	0	0	0
1726	2.5	2.5	.9	24.0	1	0	0
1727	5.0	5.0	1.2	48.0	1	0	0
1728	5.0	5.0	1.2	48.0	1	0	0
1729	2.5	2.5	.9	24.0	1	0	0
1730	0.0	0.0	0.0	0.0	0	0	0
1731	0.0	0.0	.0	0.0	0	0	0
1732	0.0	0.0	0.0	0.0	0	0	0
1733	8.8	8.8	1.4	83.6	1	0	0
1734	17.6	17.6	1.7	167.2	1	1	0
1735	17.6	17.6	1.7	167.2	1	1	0
1736	23.9	17.6	1.7	167.2	1	1	0
1737	30.3	17.6	1.7	167.2	1	1	0
1738	21.5	8.8	1.4	83.6	1	0	0
1739	26.3	19.9	1.8	187.7	1	1	0
1740	39.9	39.9	2.1	375.4	1	1	0
1741	42.4	39.9	2.1	375.4	1	1	0
1742	44.9	39.9	2.1	375.4	1	1	0
1743	42.4	39.9	2.1	375.4	1	1	0
1744	39.9	39.9	2.1	375.4	1	1	0
1745	39.9	39.9	2.1	375.4	1	1	0
1746	39.9	39.9	2.1	375.4	1	1	0
1747	39.9	39.9	2.1	375.4	1	1	0
1748	19.9	19.9	1.8	187.7	1	1	0
1749	0.0	0.0	0.0	0.0	0	0	0
1750	0.0	0.0	.0	0.0	0	0	0
1751	0.0	0.0	0.0	0.0	0	0	0
1752	0.0	0.0	.0	0.0	0	0	0
1753	0.0	0.0	0.0	0.0	0	0	0
1754	0.0	0.0	.0	0.0	0	0	0
1755	62.0	62.0	2.3	569.9	1	1	1
1756	124.0	124.0	2.6	1139.7	1	1	1
1757	124.0	124.0	2.6	1139.7	1	1	1
1758	124.0	124.0	2.6	1139.7	1	1	1
1759	124.0	124.0	2.6	1139.7	1	1	1
1760	124.0	124.0	2.6	1139.7	1	1	1
1761	124.0	124.0	2.6	1139.7	1	1	1
1762	124.0	124.0	2.6	1139.7	1	1	1
1763	62.0	62.0	2.3	569.9	1	1	1
1764	0.0	0.0	0.0	0.0	0	0	0
1765	0.0	0.0	.0	0.0	0	0	0
1766	0.0	0.0	0.0	0.0	0	0	0
1767	0.0	0.0	.0	0.0	0	0	0
1768	2.9	0.0	0.0	0.0	0	0	0
1769	5.8	0.0	.0	0.0	0	0	0
1770	5.8	0.0	0.0	0.0	0	0	0
1771	5.8	0.0	.0	0.0	0	0	0
1772	4.1	0.0	0.0	0.0	0	0	0
1773	2.3	0.0	.0	0.0	0	0	0
1774	1.2	0.0	0.0	0.0	0	0	0
1775	0.0	0.0	.0	0.0	0	0	0
1776	0.0	0.0	0.0	0.0	0	0	0
1777	0.0	0.0	.0	0.0	0	0	0
1778	2.8	2.8	1.0	26.8	1	0	0
1779	5.7	5.7	1.3	52.2	1	0	0
1780	5.7	5.7	1.3	50.7	1	0	0
1781	5.7	5.7	1.3	50.7	1	0	0
1782	5.7	5.7	1.3	50.7	1	0	0
1783	5.7	5.7	1.3	50.7	1	0	0
1784	2.8	2.8	1.0	25.3	1	0	0
1785	0.0	0.0	0.0	0.0	0	0	0
1786	0.0	0.0	.0	0.0	0	0	0
1787	19.2	0.0	0.0	0.0	0	0	0
1788	39.2	0.0	.0	0.0	0	0	0
1789	39.9	0.0	0.0	0.0	0	0	0
1790	39.2	0.0	.0	0.0	0	0	0
1791	38.4	0.0	0.0	0.0	0	0	0
1792	52.3	33.2	2.0	290.8	1	1	0
1793	66.3	66.3	2.3	581.6	1	1	1
1794	66.3	66.3	2.3	581.6	1	1	1
1795	66.3	66.3	2.3	581.6	1	1	1
1796	66.3	66.3	2.3	581.6	1	1	1
1797	66.3	66.3	2.3	581.6	1	1	1
1798	66.3	66.3	2.3	581.6	1	1	1
1799	66.3	66.3	2.3	581.6	1	1	1

YEAR	ALWAR	GPWAR	LGWR	GPINT	I1	2	3
1800	66.3	66.3	2.3	581.6	1	1	1
1801	66.3	66.3	2.3	581.6	1	1	1
1802	33.2	33.2	2.0	290.8	1	1	0
1803	77.9	77.9	2.4	671.3	1	1	1
1804	155.7	155.7	2.7	1342.7	1	1	1
1805	155.7	155.7	2.7	1342.7	1	1	1
1806	159.5	155.7	2.7	1342.7	1	1	1
1807	163.2	155.7	2.7	1342.7	1	1	1
1808	166.2	155.7	2.7	1342.7	1	1	1
1809	166.2	155.7	2.7	1342.7	1	1	1
1810	163.2	155.7	2.7	1342.7	1	1	1
1811	163.2	155.7	2.7	1342.7	1	1	1
1812	160.5	155.7	2.7	1342.7	1	1	1
1813	157.7	155.7	2.7	1342.7	1	1	1
1814	156.7	155.7	2.7	1342.7	1	1	1
1815	79.9	77.9	2.4	671.3	1	1	1
1816	0.0	0.0	0.0	0.0	0	0	0
1817	0.0	0.0	.0	0.0	0	0	0
1818	0.0	0.0	0.0	0.0	0	0	0
1819	0.0	0.0	.0	0.0	0	0	0
1820	0.0	0.0	0.0	0.0	0	0	0
1821	0.0	0.0	.0	0.0	0	0	0
1822	0.0	0.0	0.0	0.0	0	0	0
1823	.4	0.0	.0	0.0	0	0	0
1824	0.0	0.0	0.0	0.0	0	0	0
1825	0.0	0.0	.0	0.0	0	0	0
1826	0.0	0.0	0.0	0.0	0	0	0
1827	.2	0.0	.0	0.0	0	0	0
1828	25.0	0.0	0.0	0.0	0	0	0
1829	25.0	0.0	.0	0.0	0	0	0
1830	0.0	0.0	0.0	0.0	0	0	0
1831	0.0	0.0	.0	0.0	0	0	0
1832	0.0	0.0	0.0	0.0	0	0	0
1833	0.0	0.0	.0	0.0	0	0	0
1834	0.0	0.0	0.0	0.0	0	0	0
1835	0.0	0.0	.0	0.0	0	0	0
1836	0.0	0.0	0.0	0.0	0	0	0
1837	0.0	0.0	.0	0.0	0	0	0
1838	0.0	0.0	0.0	0.0	0	0	0
1839	0.0	0.0	.0	0.0	0	0	0
1840	0.0	0.0	0.0	0.0	0	0	0
1841	0.0	0.0	.0	0.0	0	0	0
1842	0.0	0.0	0.0	0.0	0	0	0
1843	0.0	0.0	.0	0.0	0	0	0
1844	0.0	0.0	0.0	0.0	0	0	0
1845	0.0	0.0	.0	0.0	0	0	0
1846	0.0	0.0	0.0	0.0	0	0	0
1847	0.0	0.0	.0	0.0	0	0	0
1848	2.8	0.0	0.0	0.0	0	0	0
1849	5.9	0.0	.0	0.0	0	0	0
1850	0.0	0.0	0.0	0.0	0	0	0
1851	0.0	0.0	.0	0.0	0	0	0
1852	0.0	0.0	0.0	0.0	0	0	0
1853	36.2	36.2	2.1	290.5	1	1	0
1854	72.3	72.3	2.4	581.0	1	1	1
1855	72.3	72.3	2.4	581.0	1	1	1
1856	36.4	36.2	2.1	290.5	1	1	0
1857	.3	0.0	0.0	0.0	0	0	0
1858	0.0	0.0	.0	0.0	0	0	0
1859	20.0	20.0	1.8	159.0	1	1	0
1860	0.0	0.0	0.0	0.0	0	0	0
1861	0.0	0.0	.0	0.0	0	0	0
1862	.8	0.0	0.0	0.0	0	0	0
1863	1.6	0.0	.0	0.0	0	0	0
1864	3.1	0.0	0.0	0.0	0	0	0
1865	1.6	0.0	.0	0.0	0	0	0
1866	35.6	34.0	2.0	270.0	1	1	0
1867	.8	0.0	0.0	0.0	0	0	0
1868	0.0	0.0	.0	0.0	0	0	0
1869	0.0	0.0	0.0	0.0	0	0	0
1870	90.0	90.0	2.5	707.5	1	1	1
1871	90.0	90.0	2.5	707.5	1	1	1
1872	0.0	0.0	0.0	0.0	0	0	0
1873	0.0	0.0	.0	0.0	0	0	0
1874	0.0	0.0	0.0	0.0	0	0	0
1875	0.0	0.0	.0	0.0	0	0	0
1876	0.0	0.0	0.0	0.0	0	0	0
1877	60.0	0.0	.0	0.0	0	0	0
1878	60.0	0.0	0.0	0.0	0	0	0
1879	0.0	0.0	.0	0.0	0	0	0
1880	0.0	0.0	0.0	0.0	0	0	0
1881	0.0	0.0	.0	0.0	0	0	0
1882	0.0	0.0	0.0	0.0	0	0	0
1883	0.0	0.0	.0	0.0	0	0	0
1884	1.0	0.0	0.0	0.0	0	0	0
1885	1.0	0.0	.0	0.0	0	0	0
1886	0.0	0.0	0.0	0.0	0	0	0
1887	0.0	0.0	.0	0.0	0	0	0
1888	0.0	0.0	0.0	0.0	0	0	0
1889	0.0	0.0	.0	0.0	0	0	0
1890	0.0	0.0	0.0	0.0	0	0	0
1891	0.0	0.0	.0	0.0	0	0	0
1892	0.0	0.0	0.0	0.0	0	0	0
1893	0.0	0.0	.0	0.0	0	0	0
1894	0.0	0.0	0.0	0.0	0	0	0
1895	0.0	0.0	.0	0.0	0	0	0
1896	0.0	0.0	0.0	0.0	0	0	0
1897	0.0	0.0	.0	0.0	0	0	0
1898	0.0	0.0	0.0	0.0	0	0	0
1899	0.0	0.0	.0	0.0	0	0	0

YEAR	ALWAR	GPWAR	LGWR	GPINT	I1	2	3
1900	0.0	0.0	0.0	0.0	0	0	0
1901	0.0	0.0	.0	0.0	0	0	0
1902	0.0	0.0	0.0	0.0	0	0	0
1903	0.0	0.0	.0	0.0	0	0	0
1904	22.5	0.0	0.0	0.0	0	0	0
1905	22.5	0.0	.0	0.0	0	0	0
1906	0.0	0.0	0.0	0.0	0	0	0
1907	0.0	0.0	.0	0.0	0	0	0
1908	0.0	0.0	0.0	0.0	0	0	0
1909	0.0	0.0	.0	0.0	0	0	0
1910	0.0	0.0	0.0	0.0	0	0	0
1911	3.0	0.0	.0	0.0	0	0	0
1912	3.0	0.0	0.0	0.0	0	0	0
1913	0.0	0.0	.0	0.0	0	0	0
1914	966.7	966.7	3.5	7202.0	1	1	1
1915	1933.5	1933.5	3.8	14404.0	1	1	1
1916	1933.5	1933.5	3.8	14404.0	1	1	1
1917	1933.5	1933.5	3.8	14404.0	1	1	1
1918	967.6	967.6	3.5	7208.2	1	1	1
1919	1.7	1.7	.7	12.3	1	0	0
1920	1.7	1.7	.7	12.3	1	0	0
1921	.8	.8	.4	6.2	1	0	0
1922	0.0	0.0	0.0	0.0	0	0	0
1923	0.0	0.0	.0	0.0	0	0	0
1924	0.0	0.0	0.0	0.0	0	0	0
1925	0.0	0.0	.0	0.0	0	0	0
1926	0.0	0.0	0.0	0.0	0	0	0
1927	0.0	0.0	.0	0.0	0	0	0
1928	0.0	0.0	0.0	0.0	0	0	0
1929	0.0	0.0	.0	0.0	0	0	0
1930	0.0	0.0	0.0	0.0	0	0	0
1931	2.5	0.0	.0	0.0	0	0	0
1932	5.0	0.0	0.0	0.0	0	0	0
1933	2.5	0.0	.0	0.0	0	0	0
1934	0.0	0.0	0.0	0.0	0	0	0
1935	2.0	0.0	.0	0.0	0	0	0
1936	2.0	0.0	0.0	0.0	0	0	0
1937	31.2	0.0	.0	0.0	0	0	0
1938	62.5	0.0	0.0	0.0	0	0	0
1939	1182.5	1095.0	3.5	7921.4	1	1	1
1940	2245.5	2158.0	3.8	15610.8	1	1	1
1941	2189.2	2158.0	3.8	15610.8	1	1	1
1942	2158.0	2158.0	3.8	15610.8	1	1	1
1943	2158.0	2158.0	3.8	15610.8	1	1	1
1944	2158.0	2158.0	3.8	15610.8	1	1	1
1945	1079.0	1079.0	3.5	7805.4	1	1	1
1946	0.0	0.0	0.0	0.0	0	0	0
1947	0.0	0.0	0.0	0.0	0	0	0
1948	0.0	0.0	0.0	0.0	0	0	0
1949	0.0	0.0	0.0	0.0	0	0	0
1950	159.2	159.2	2.7	1136.8	1	1	1
1951	318.3	318.3	3.0	2273.7	1	1	1
1952	318.3	318.3	3.0	2273.7	1	1	1
1953	159.2	159.2	2.7	1136.8	1	1	1
1954	0.0	0.0	0.0	0.0	0	0	0
1955	0.0	0.0	0.0	0.0	0	0	0
1956	7.0	0.0	0.0	0.0	0	0	0
1957	0.0	0.0	0.0	0.0	0	0	0
1958	0.0	0.0	0.0	0.0	0	0	0
1959	0.0	0.0	0.0	0.0	0	0	0
1960	0.0	0.0	0.0	0.0	0	0	0
1961	0.0	0.0	0.0	0.0	0	0	0
1962	.5	0.0	0.0	0.0	0	0	0
1963	0.0	0.0	0.0	0.0	0	0	0
1964	0.0	0.0	0.0	0.0	0	0	0
1965	3.5	0.0	0.0	0.0	0	0	0
1966	7.0	0.0	0.0	0.0	0	0	0
1967	7.0	0.0	0.0	0.0	0	0	0
1968	7.0	0.0	0.0	0.0	0	0	0
1969	7.0	0.0	0.0	0.0	0	0	0
1970	7.0	0.0	0.0	0.0	0	0	0
1971	7.0	0.0	0.0	0.0	0	0	0
1972	7.0	0.0	0.0	0.0	0	0	0
1973	3.5	0.0	0.0	0.0	0	0	0
1974	0.0	0.0	0.0	0.0	0	0	0
1975	0.0	0.0	0.0	0.0	0	0	0

REFERENCES

Adams, Thomas Boylston. "The Race to War." *Boston Globe,* June 16, 1985, 71.

Adelman, Irma. "Long Cycles—Fact or Artifact?" *American Economic Review* 55, no. 3 (1965): 444–63.

Åkerman, Johan. *Economic Progress and Economic Crises.* London: Macmillan, 1932. Reprint ed., Philadelphia: Porcupine Press, 1979.

———. *Ekonomisk teori.* Vol. 2. Lund: Gleerup, 1944.

Albrecht-Carrié, René. *The Unity of Europe.* London: Secker and Warburg, 1965.

———. *Europe, 1500–1848.* Totowa, N.J.: Littlefield, Adams, 1973.

Aldcroft, Derek Howard, and Richard Rodger. *Bibliography of European Economic and Social History.* Dover, N.H.: Manchester University Press, 1984.

Aldcroft, Derek Howard, and Peter Fearon, eds. *British Economic Fluctuations: 1790–1939.* New York: St. Martin's Press, 1972.

Alexander, Jon. "Cognitive Dominance: The Klingberg and Schlesinger Cycles Explained." Paper presented at the American Political Science Association annual meeting, New Orleans, La., August 1985.

Alker, Hayward R., Jr. "From Political Cybernetics to Global Modeling." In R. C. Merritt and B. M. Russett, eds., *From National Development to Global Community.* London: George Allen & Unwin, Ltd., 1981.

———. "Logic, Dialectics, and Politics." In Alker, ed., *Dialectical Logics for the Political Sciences.* Amsterdam: Rodopi, 1982.

———. "Historical Argumentation and Statistical Inference: Towards More Appropriate Logics for Historical Research." *Historical Methods* 17, no. 3 (1984): 164–73.

Alker, Hayward R., Jr., and Thomas J. Biersteker. "The Dialectics of World Order." *International Studies Quarterly* 28, no. 2 (1984): 121–42.

Alker, Hayward R., Jr., Thomas J. Biersteker, and Takashi Inoguchi. "The Decline of the Superstates: The Rise of a New World Order?" Paper presented at the World Congress of Political Science (IPSA), Paris, July 1985.

Allan, Pierre. "Time and International Politics." Paper presented at the International Studies Association annual meeting, Atlanta, Ga., March 1984.

———. "Social Time." In C. Cioffi-Revilla, R. L. Merritt, and D. A. Zinnes, eds., *Interaction and Communication in Global Politics,* 95–113. Beverly Hills, Calif.: Sage Publications, 1987.

American Economic Association. *Readings in Business Cycle Theory.* Philadelphia: Blakiston Co., 1951.

Amin, Samir. "Toward a Structural Crisis of World Capitalism." *Socialist Revolution* 5 (1975): 9–44.

Amin, S., G. Arrighi, A. Gunder Frank, and I. Wallerstein. *Dynamics of Global Crisis*. New York: Monthly Review Press, 1982.

Anderson, Perry. *Lineages of the Absolutist State*. London: Verso, 1974; reprint ed., 1979.

Anderson, T. W. *The Statistical Analysis of Time Series*. New York: Wiley, 1971.

Angell, Norman. *The Great Illusion*. London: William Heinemann, 1910.

―――. *The Foundations of International Polity*. London: William Heinemann, 1914.

Ashley, Maurice. *The Golden Century: Europe, 1598–1715*. New York: Praeger, 1968.

Ashley, Richard K. *The Political Economy of War and Peace*. London: Frances Pinter, 1980.

―――. "Political Realism and Human Interests." *International Studies Quarterly* 25, no. 2 (1981):204–36.

―――. "The Power of Power Politics: Toward a Critical Social Theory of International Politics." Prepared for inclusion in Terence Ball, ed., *Social and Political Inquiry: Critiques and Alternative Approaches*. Albany, N.Y.: SUNY Press, 1987.

Aston, Trevor, ed. *Crisis in Europe, 1560–1660*. New York: Basic Books, 1965.

Baehrel, René. *Une croissance: La Basse-Provence rurale (fin du XVIe siècle–1789)*. Paris: SEVPEN, 1961.

Baqir, Ghalib M. "The Long Wave Cycles and Re-Industrialization." *International Journal of Social Economics* 8, no. 7 (1981): 117–23.

Barkun, Michael. "Communal Societies as Cyclical Phenomena." *Communal Societies* 4 (1984): 35–48.

Barnaby, Frank. "How the Next War Will Be Fought." *Technology Review* 89 (October 1986): 26–37.

Barr, Kenneth. "Long Waves: A Selective Annotated Bibliography." *Review* (Binghamton, N.Y.) 2, no. 4 (1979):

―――. "Long Waves and the Cotton-Spinning Enterprise, 1789–1849." In Terence K. Hopkins and Immanuel Wallerstein, eds., *Processes of the World-System*, 84–100. Beverly Hills, Calif.: Sage Publications, 1980.

Barraclough, Geoffrey. *An Introduction to Contemporary History*. New York: Penguin Books, 1964.

―――. "The End of an Era." *New York Review of Books* 21, no. 11 (1974): 14–20.

Barraclough, Geoffrey, ed. *The Times Atlas of World History*. Maplewood, N.J. Hammond, 1978.

Baulant, Micheline. "Le prix des grains à Paris de 1431 à 1788." *Annales: Economies, sociétés, civilisations* 23 (1968): 520–40.

Baumgartner, Sverre, and Gottfried Pirhofer. "Das politische Instrumentarium zur Behebung sogenannter Finanzkrisen und Möglichkeiten innovativer Lösungen." *Österreichische Zeitschrift für Politikwissenschaft* (Vienna) 6, no. 3 (1977): 255–63.

Beck, Bernhard. *Lange Wellen wirtschaftlichen Wachstums in der Schweiz, 1814–1913*. Bern: P. Haupt, 1983.

Beck, Paul Allen. "A Socialization Theory of Partisan Realignment." In Richard G. Niemi, ed., *The Politics of Future Citizens*, 199–219. San Francisco: Jossey-Bass, 1974.

Beckman, Robert C. *The Downwave*. New York: E. P. Dutton, 1983.

Beer, Francis. *Peace against War*. San Francisco: W. H. Freeman, 1981.

Berger, Victor L. "A Leading American Socialist's View of the Peace Problem." *Current History* (January 1928): 471.

Bergesen, Albert. "Cycles of Formal Colonial Rule." In Terence K. Hopkins and Immanuel Wallerstein, eds., *Processes of the World-System,* 119–26. (Beverly Hills, Calif.: Sage Publications, 1980.

―――. "Long Economic Cycles and the Size of Industrial Enterprise." In Richard Rubinson, ed., *Dynamics of World Development,* 179–89. Beverly Hills, Calif.: Sage Publications, 1981.

―――. "Economic Crisis and Merger Movements." In Edward Friedman, ed., *Ascent and Decline in the World-System,* 27–39. Beverly Hills, Calif.: Sage Publications, 1982.

―――. "Modeling Long Waves of Crisis in the World-System." In Bergesen, ed., *Crises in the World-System,* 73–92. Beverly Hills, Calif.: Sage Publications, 1983a.

―――. "1914 Again? Another Cycle of Interstate Competition and War." In Pat McGowan and Charles W. Kegley, Jr., eds., *Foreign Policy and the Modern World-System,* 255–73. Beverly Hills, Calif.: Sage Publications, 1983b.

―――. "Cycles of War in the Reproduction of the World Economy." In Paul M. Johnson and William R. Thompson, eds., *Rhythms in Politics and Economics,* 313–32. New York: Praeger, 1985.

Bergesen, Albert, and Ronald Schoenberg. "Long Waves of Colonial Expansion and Contraction, 1415–1969." In Bergesen, ed., *Studies of the Modern World-System.* New York: Academic Press, 1980.

Bergesen, Albert, Roberto M. Fernandez, and Chintamani Sahoo. "America and the Changing Structure of Hegemonic Production." In T. Boswell and A. Bergesen, eds., *America's Changing Role in the World System.* New York: Praeger, 1986.

Bergesen, Albert, ed. *Studies of the Modern World-System.* New York: Academic Press, 1980.

Bernstein, E. M. "War and the Pattern of Business Cycles." *American Economic Review* 30 (1940): 524–35.

Beveridge, Lord. *Prices and Wages in England from the Twelfth to the Nineteenth Century.* Vol. 1. 1939; reprint ed., New York: Augustus M. Kelley, 1966.

Bezy, Fernand. "Les évolutions longues de l'industrie du zinc dans l'ouest européen, 1840–1939." *Bulletin de l'Institut de recherches économiques et sociales* (Louvain) 16, no. 1 (1950): 3–56.

Bieshaar, Hans, and Alfred Kleinknecht. "Kondratieff Long Waves in Aggregate Output?" *Konjunkturpolitik* [Berlin] 30, no. 5 (1984).

Blainey, Geoffrey. "A Theory of Mineral Discovery: Australia in the Nineteenth Century." *Economic History Review* 23, no. 2 (1970): 298–313.

Bloch, Ivan Stanislavovich [Jean de Bloch]. *The Future of War in Its Technical, Economic and Political Relations: Is War Now Impossible?* Boston: Ginn & Co., 1899.

Bogart, Ernest L. *Direct and Indirect Costs of the Great World War.* Oxford: Oxford University Press, 1920.

―――. *War Costs and Their Financing.* New York: D. Appleton, 1921.

Bordo, Michael D., and Anna J. Schwartz. "Money and Prices in the Nineteenth Century: An Old Debate Rejoined." *Journal of Economic History* 40, no. 1 (1980): 61–72.

Bordo, Michael D., and Anna J. Schwartz. "Money and Prices in the Nineteenth Century: Was Thomas Tooke Right?" *Explorations in Economic History* 18, no. 2 (1981): 97–127.

Bornschier, Volker. "World Social Structure in the Long Economic Wave." Paper presented at the International Studies Association annual meeting, Washington, D.C., March 1985.

Bos, Roeland W. J. M. "Long-term Price Fluctuations, Innovations, and Differential

Growth.'' *Proceedings of the Eighth International Economic History Congress* (Budapest, 1982), B3:1.

Bossier, Francis, and Pierre Hugé. ''Une verification empirique de l'existence de cycles longs a partir de données belges.'' *Cahiers économiques de Bruxelles* 23, no. 90 (1981): 253–67.

Bousquet, Nicole. ''Esquisse d'une théorie de l'alternance de périodes de concurrence et d'hegemonie au centre de l'économie-monde capitaliste.'' *Review* 2, no. 4 (1979): 501–18.

———. ''From Hegemony to Competition: Cycles of the Core?'' In Terence K. Hopkins and Immanuel Wallerstein, eds., *Processes of the World-System,* 46–83. Beverly Hills, Calif.: Sage Publications, 1980.

Braudel, Fernand. *The Mediterranean and the Mediterranean World in the Age of Philip II.* 1949; reprint ed., London: Collins, 1972.

———. ''History and the Social Sciences.'' In P. Burke, ed., *Economy and Society in Early Modern Europe: Essays from* Annales, 11–42. New York: Harper and Row, 1972. [1958]

———. *Afterthoughts on Material Civilization and Capitalism.* Baltimore: Johns Hopkins University Press, 1977.

———. ''A Model for the Analysis of the Decline of Italy.'' *Review* 2, no. 4 (1979): 647–62.

———. *On History.* 1969; reprint ed., Chicago: University of Chicago Press, 1980.

———. *The Structures of Everyday Life.* New York: Harper and Row, 1981.

———. *The Perspective of the World.* New York: Harper and Row, 1984.

Braudel, Fernand, and Frank C. Spooner. ''Prices in Europe from 1450 to 1750.'' in E. E. Rich and E. H. Wilson, eds., *The Cambridge Economic History of Europe.* 4:374–486. London: Cambridge University Press, 1967.

Brett, E. A. *International Money and Capitalist Crisis.* Boulder, Colo.: Westview Press, 1983, chap. 4.

Broersma, T. J. *De lange golf in het economisch leven: Empirische en theoretische onderzoekingen.* [Ph.D. diss.] Groningen: VRB, 1978.

Brown, Archie. ''Gorbachev's Policy Innovations.'' *Bulletin of the Atomic Scientists* 41, no. 10 (1985): 18–22.

Bruckman, G. and T. Vasko, eds. *Long Waves, Depression and Innovation.* Proceedings of the IIASA (International Institute for Applied Systems Analysis, Vienna) Workshop in Siena/Florence, October 1983.

Brugmans, I. J. ''Economic Fluctuations in the Netherlands in the Nineteenth Century.'' In F. Crouzet. W. H. Chaloner, and W. M. Stern, eds., *Essays in European Economic History, 1789–1914.* London: Edward Arnold, 1969.

Burke, Peter, ed. *Economy and Society in Early Modern Europe: Essays from* Annales. New York: Harper and Row, 1972.

Burns, Arthur F., and Wesley C. Mitchell. *Measuring Business Cycles.* New York: National Bureau of Economic Research, 1946.

Bushkoff, Leonard. ''Three Confrontations in Asia.'' *Boston Globe,* Apr. 28, 1985, A1.

Business Week, Oct. 11. 1982, 126. ''A Technology Lag that May Stifle Growth.''

The Cambridge Economic History of Europe. Vol. 4. Edited by E. E. Rich and C. H. Wilson. Cambridge: Cambridge University Press, 1967.

Cameron, Rondo. ''The Logistics of European Economic Growth: A Note on Historical Periodization.'' *Journal of European Economic History* 2, no. 1 (1973): 145–48.

Capelle, Stanislas. ''Le volume du commerce extérieur de la Belgique, 1830–1913.'' *Bulletin de l'Institut de recherches économiques* (Louvain) 10, no. 1 (1938): 15–56.

Carnegie Endowment for International Peace. *The Cost of War*. Memoranda Series, no. 2. Washington, D.C.: Carnegie Endowment, 1940.

Caron, François. *An Economic History of Modern France*. New York: Columbia University Press, 1979.

Carr, E. H. *What Is History?* Harmondsworth: Penguin, 1975.

Carus-Wilson, E. M., ed. *Essays in Economic History*, 3 vols. 1954–62; reprint ed., New York: St. Martin's Press, 1966.

Cassel, Gustav. *The Theory of Social Economy*. 1918; rev. ed., New York: Harcourt, Brace & Co., 1932.

Center for Defense Information. "Militarizing the Last Frontier: The Space Weapons Race." *Defense Monitor* 12, no. 5 1983.

Chabert, A. *Essai sur les Mouvements des Prix et des revenus en France de 1798 à 1820*. Paris: Librairie de Médicis, 1945.

Chabert, Alexandre R. E. "More about the Sixteenth-Century Price Revolution." In Peter Burke, ed., *Economy and Society in Early Modern Europe: Essays from* Annales, 47–54. New York: Harper and Row, 1972. [1957]

Chase-Dunn, Christopher, and Richard Rubinson. "Toward a Structural Perspective on the World-System." *Politics and Society* 7, no. 4 (1977): 453–76.

———. "Cycles, Trends and New Departures in World-System Development." In J. W. Meyer and M. T. Hannan, eds., *National Development and the World System: Educational, Economic, and Political Change, 1950–1970*. Chicago: University of Chicago Press, 1979.

Chase-Dunn, Christopher, and Joan Sokolovsky. "Interstate System and Capitalist World-Economy." *International Studies Quarterly* 25, no. 1 (1981): 19–42.

———. "Interstate Systems, World Empires and the Capitalist World-Economy: A Response to Thompson." *International Studies Quarterly* 27, no. 3 (1983): 357–67.

Chaunu, Pierre, and Huguette Chaunu. "The Atlantic Economy and the World Economy." In Peter Earle, ed., *Essays in European Economic History, 1500–1800*. Oxford: Clarendon Press, 1974. [1953]

Chaunu, Huguette, and Pierre Chaunu. *Seville et l'Atlantique (1504–1650)*, 8 vols. Paris: Armand Colin, 1955–60.

Choucri, Nazli, and Robert C. North. *Nations in Conflict: National Growth and International Violence*. San Francisco: W. H. Freeman, 1975.

Cipolla, Carlo M. "The So-called 'Price Revolution': Reflections on 'the Italian situation.'" In Peter Burke, ed., *Economy and Society in Early Modern Europe: Esssays from* Annales, 43–46. New York: Harper and Row 1972. [1955]

———. *Guns, Sails and Empires*. New York: Pantheon Books, 1965.

———. *The Economic History of World Population*. Harmondsworth: Penguin, 1979.

Ciriacy-Wantrup, Siegfried von. *Agrarkrisen und Stockungsspannen zur Frage der langen "Welle" in der wirtschaftlichen Entwicklung*. Berlin: P. Parey, 1936.

Clark, John A. "A Model of Embodied Technical Change and Employment." *Technological Forecasting and Social Change* 16 (1980): 47–65.

Clark, John A., Christopher Freeman, and Luc Soete. "Long Waves, Inventions and Innovations." *Futures* 13, no. 4 (1981): 308–22.

Cleary, M. N., and G. D. Hobbs. "The Fifty Year Cycle: A Look at the Empirical Evidence." In Christopher Freeman, ed., *Long Waves in the World Economy*, 164–82. London: Butterworth, 1983.

Clough, Shepard. *European Economic History: The Economic Development of Western Civilization.* 2d ed. New York: McGraw-Hill, 1968.

Colby, Frank Moore. "War Minds." In *The Colby Essays,* 2:15, New York: Harper & Bros., 1926.

Cole, Arthur Harrison. *Wholesale Commodity Prices in the United States, 1700–1861.* Cambridge, Mass.: Harvard University Press, 1938.

Cole, W. A. "Eighteenth-Century Economic Growth Revisited." *Explorations in Economic History* 10, no. 4 (1973): 327–48.

Cook, Earl. "Energy Sources for the Future." *Futurist* 6, no. 4 (1972): 143–50.

Coombs, R. W. "Innovation, Automation and the Long-Wave Theory." *Futures* 13, no. 5 (1981): 360–70.

Coombs, Rod. "Long Waves and Labor-Process Change." *Review* 7, no. 4 (1984): 675–701.

Crafts, N. F. R. "Gross National Product in Europe, 1870–1910: Some New Estimates. *Explorations in Economic History* 20 (1983): 387–401.

Craig, Gordon A. *The Battle of Koniggratz: Prussia's Victory Over Austria, 1866.* Philadelphia: J. B. Lippincott, 1964.

Craig, Paul P., and Kenneth E. F. Watt. "The Kondratieff Cycle and War: How Close Is the Connection?" *Futurist* 19, no. 2 (1985): 25–28.

Critchley, W. Harriet. "Defining Strategic Value: Problems of Conceptual Clarity and Valid Threat Assessment." *Policy Studies Journal* 8, no. 1 (1979): 28–37.

Cronin, James E. "Theories of Strikes: Why Can't They Explain the British Experience?" *Journal of Social History* 12, no. 2 (1978): 194–220.

———. "Stages, Cycles and Insurgencies: The Economics of Unrest." In Terence K. Hopkins and Immanuel Wallerstein, eds., *Processes of the World-System,* 101–18. Beverly Hills, Calif.: Sage Publications, 1980.

Crouzet, François. "Essai de construction d'un indice annuel de la production industrielle française au XIXᵉ siècle." *Annales: Economies, sociétés, civilisations* 25 (1970): 56–99.

———. "Toward an Export Economy: British Exports during the Industrial Revolution." *Explorations in Economic History* 17 (1980): 48–93.

Davis, Ralph. *English Overseas Trade, 1500–1700.* London: Macmillan, 1973a.

———. *The Rise of the Atlantic Economies.* Ithaca, N.Y.: Cornell University Press, 1973b.

———. *English Merchant Shipping and Anglo-Dutch Rivalry in the Seventeenth Century.* London: HMSO, 1975.

———. *The Industrial Revolution and British Overseas Trade.* Atlantic Highlands, N.J.: Humanities Press, 1979.

Dawson, Sandra, and Mark Rupert. "Hegemony and the Dynamics of Core-Periphery Relations: An Empirical Examination of the Twentieth Century Case." Paper presented at the International Studies Association annual meeting, Washington, D.C., March 1985.

Day, Olive. "War Shocks to European Commerce." *Foreign Affairs* 5 (1927): 633–49.

Day, Richard B. "The Theory of Long Waves: Kondratieff, Trotsky, Mandel." *New Left Review* 99 (1976): 67–82.

Deane, Phyllis, and W. A. Cole. *British Economic Growth, 1688–1959.* 2d ed. Cambridge: Cambridge University Press, 1967.

Dehio, Ludwig. *The Precarious Balance: Four Centuries of the European Power Struggle.* 1948; reprint ed., New York: Vintage Books, 1962.

Delbeke, Jos. "Recent Long-Wave Theories: A Critical Survey." *Futures* 13, no. 4 (1981): 246–57.

———. "Towards an Endogenous Interpretation of the Long Wave: The Case of Belgium, 1830–1930." Discussion paper 82.02, Workshop on Quantitative Economic History, Kath. Univ. te Leuven (Belgium), Centrum voor economische studien, 1982a.

———. "Long Waves and Leading Sectors in the Belgian Industrialization Process: 1831–1913." *Proceedings of the Eighth International Economic History Congress* (Budapest, 1982b), B3:17.

Denis, Anne. *Charles VIII et les Italiens: Histoire et mythe*. Geneva: Droz, 1979.

Denton, Frank H., and Warren Phillips. "Some Patterns in the History of Violence." *Journal of Conflict Resolution* 12, no. 2, (1968): 182.

Deudney, Daniel. "Whole Earth Security: A Geopolitics of Peace." Worldwatch Paper 55 (Washington, D.C.: Worldwatch Institute, July 1983).

———. "Forging Missiles into Spaceships." *World Policy Journal* 2, no. 2 (1985): 271–303.

De Vries, Jan. *Economy of Europe in an Age of Crisis: 1600–1750*. Cambridge: Cambridge University Press, 1976.

Dewey, Edward R. "Evidence of Cyclic Patterns in an Index of International Battles, 600 B.C.–A.D. 1957." *Cycles* (Foundation for the Study of Cycles, Pittsburgh) 21, no. 6, (1970): 121–58.

Dewey, Edward R., and Og Mandino. *Cycles: The Mysterious Forces that Trigger Events*. New York: Hawthorn Books, 1971.

De Wolff, Sam. "Prosperitats- und Depressionsperioden." In O. Jenssen, ed., *Der Lebendige Marxismus*, 13–43. Jena: Thuringer Verlagsanstalt, 1924.

———. *Het economisch getij*. Amsterdam: n.p., 1929.

Dickinson, Frank G. "The Price of War." *Annals of the American Academy of Political and Social Sciences* 175 (1934): 166–74.

———. "An Aftercost of the World War to the United States." *American Economic Review* 30, supplement (1940): 326–39.

Dickson, David. "Technology and Cycles of Boom and Bust." *Science* 219 (1983): 933–36.

Doran, Charles F. *The Politics of Assimilation: Hegemony and Its Aftermath*. Baltimore: Johns Hopkins University Press, 1971.

———. "War and Power Dynamics: Economic Underpinnings." *International Studies Quarterly* 27 (1983): 419–41.

Doran, Charles F., and Wes Parsons. "War and the Cycle of Relative Power." *American Political Science Review* 74, no. 4 (1980): 947–65.

Doughty, Robert A. "Industrial Prices and Inflation in Southern England, 1401–1640." *Explorations in Economic History* 12 (1975): 177–92.

Drucker, Peter F. "Why America's Got So Many Jobs." *Wall Street Journal*, Jan. 24, 1984.

Dupriez, Léon H. *Des mouvements économiques generaux*. Vol. 2: pt. 3. Louvain: Institut de recherches économiques et sociales de l'université de Louvain, 1947.

———. Central Banking Policy and Long Trends in Prices." In *Money, Trade and Economic Growth: In Honor of John Henry Williams*, 243–52. New York: Macmillan, 1951.

———. *Philosophie des conjonctures économiques*. Louvain: Institut de recherches économiques et sociales de l'université de Louvain, 1959.

————. "1945–1971 als Aufschwungsphase eines Kondratiev-Zyklus?" *IFO-Studien* (Munich) 18 (1972).

————. "1974 A Downturn of the Long Wave?" *Banca Nazionale del Lavoro Quarterly Review* 31, no. 126 (1978): 199–210.

Earle, Peter, ed. *Essays in European Economic History, 1500–1800.* Oxford: Clarendon Press, 1974.

Ebeling, Dietrich, and Franz Irsigler. *Getreideumsatz, Getreide-und Brotpreise in Köln, 1368–1797.* Cologne: Böhlau-Verlag, 1976.

Edel, Matthew. "Energy and the Long Swing." *Review of Radical Political Economics* 15, no. 3 (1983): 115–30.

Eelkman, Rooda F. E. "De Kapitaalgoederentheorie als verklaringsgrond voor de Kondratieff-cyclus." *Economisch-statistische berichten* 63 (1978): 1216–20.

Ehrensaft, Philip. "Long Waves in the Transformation of North American Agriculture: A First Statement." *Cornell Journal of Social Relations* 15, no. 1 (1980): 65–83.

Eklund, Klas. "Long Waves in the Development of Capitalism?" *Kyklos* 33, no. 3 (1980): 383–419.

Elder, Robert E., and Jack E. Holmes. "International Economic Long Cycles and American Policy Moods." In Paul M. Johnson and William R. Thompson, eds., *Rhythms in Politics and Economics,* 239–64. New York: Praeger, 1985a.

————. "U.S. Foreign Policy Moods, Institutional Change, and Change in the International Economic System." Paper presented at the American Political Science Association annual meeting, New Orleans, La., August 1985b.

Elliott, J. H. *Europe Divided, 1559–1598.* New York: Harper & Row, 1969.

Erickson, Scott W. "The Transition between Eras: The Long-Wave Cycle." *Futurist* 19, no. 4 (1985): 40–45.

Farrar L. L., Jr. "Cycles of War: Historical Speculations on Future International Violence." *International Interactions* 3, no. 1 (1977): 161–79.

Fellner, William. *Trends and Cycles in Economic Activity.* New York: Henry Holt & Co., 1956.

Fieldhouse, D. K. *Economics and Empire, 1830–1914.* Ithaca, N.Y.: Cornell University Press, 1973.

Fine, Melinda, et al. "The Future in Our Hands: A Call to Common Security." In Joseph Gerson, ed., *The Deadly Connection.* Philadelphia, Pa. New Society Publishers, 1985.

Fischer, David Hackett. *Historians' Fallacies: Toward a Logic of Historical Thought.* New York: Harper & Row, 1970.

Flinn, M. W. "Trends in Real Wages, 1750–1850." *Economic History Review* 27, no. 3 (1974): 395–413.

Floud, Roderick, and Donald McCloskey, eds. *The Economic History of Britain since 1700.* 2 vols. Cambridge: Cambridge University Press, 1981.

Fontvieille, Louis. "Cycles longs et regulation." *Issues: Cahiers de recherche d'économie et politique* 4 (November 1979).

Forrester, Jay W. "Counterintuitive Behavior of Social Systems." *Technology Review* 73, no. 3 (1971).

————. "Business Structure, Economic Cycles, and National Policy." *Futures* 8 (1976): 195–214.

————. "Growth Cycles." *De economist* (Amsterdam) 125 (1977): 525–43.

————. "We're Headed for Another Depression." *Fortune,* Jan. 16, 1978, 145–48.

————. "Innovation and the Economic Long Wave." MIT System Dynamics Group working paper, Dec. 12, 1978. Reprinted in the *McKinsey Quarterly* (New York) (1979): 26–38, and in *Management Review* 68, no. 6 (1979): 16–24.

————. "The Kondratieff Cycle and Changing Economic Conditions." MIT System Dynamics Group working paper, Sept. 16, 1981a.

————. "Innovation and Economic Change." *Futures* 13, no. 4 (1981b): 323–31.

————. Letter to *Business Week,* Nov. 15, 1982, 7.

————. "Economic Conditions Ahead: Understanding the Kondratieff Wave." *Futurist* 19, no. 3 (1985): 16–20.

Forrester, Jay W., Nathaniel J. Mass, and Charles J. Ryan. "The System Dynamics National Model: Understanding Socio-Economic Behavior and Policy Alternatives." *Technological Forecasting and Social Change* 9 (1976): 51–68.

Forrester, Jay W., et al. "An Integrated Approach to the Economic Long Wave." Paper presented at IIASA conference on long waves, Siena/Florence, October 1983; revised February 1984.

Forsberg, Randall. "Parallel Cuts in Nuclear and Conventional Forces." *Bulletin of the Atomic Scientists* 41, no. 7 (1985): 152–56.

Forsberg, Randall, Robert Elias, and Matthew Goodman. "Peace Issues and Strategies." In Institute for Defense and Disarmament Studies, *Peace Resource Book 1986,* 3–33. Cambridge, Mass.: Ballinger, 1985.

Frank, André Gunder. *World Accumulation, 1492–1789.* New York: Monthly Review Press, 1978.

Free, Lloyd A., and Hadley Cantril. *The Political Beliefs of Americans.* New Brunswick, N.J.: Rutgers University Press, 1967.

Free, Lloyd A., and William Watts. "Internationalism Comes of Age . . . Again." *Public Opinion* (April/May 1980): 46–50.

Freeman, Christopher. "The Kondratiev Long Waves, Technical Change, and Unemployment." In *Structural Determinants of Employment and Unemployment,* 2:181–96. Paris: OECD, 1979.

————. "Introduction." *Futures* 13, no. 4 (1981): 239–45.

————. "Long Wave Research at the Science Policy Research Unit, University of Sussex." Typescript, February 1983.

————. "Prometheus Unbound." *Futures* 16, no. 5 (1984): 494–507.

Freeman, Christopher, ed. *Long Waves in the World Economy.* London: Butterworth, 1983.

Freeman, Christopher, ed. *Design, Innovation, and Long Cycles in Economic Development.* New York: St. Martin's Press, 1986.

Freeman, Christopher, John Clark, and Luc Soete. *Unemployment and Technical Innovation.* London: Frances Pinter, 1982.

Freeman, John R. "Granger Causality and the Time Series Analysis of Political Relationships." *American Journal of Political Science* 27, no. 2 (1983): 327–58.

Freeman, John R., and Brian L. Job. "Scientific Forecasts in International Relations: Problems of Definition and Epistemology." *International Studies Quarterly* 23, no. 1 (1979): 113–43.

Friedman, Edward, ed. *Ascent and Decline in the World-System.* Beverly Hills, Calif.: Sage Publications, 1982.

Friedman, Milton. *Capitalism and Freedom.* Chicago: University of Chicago Press, 1962.

Furneaux, Rupert. *The Seven Years' War.* London: Hart-Davis MacGibbon, 1973.

Fusfeld, Daniel R. "The Next Great Depression." *Nebraska Journal of Economics and Business* 18, no. 2 (1979): 3–13.

Futures 12, no. 2 (1980): 166–68. "Innovation: The Springboard for Twenty-five Years of Expansion."

Galtung, Johan. *The True Worlds: A Transnational Perspective.* New York: Free Press, 1980.

Garvey, George. "Kondratieff's Theory of Long Cycles." *Review of Economic Statistics* 25, no. 4 (1943): 203–20.

———. "N. D. Kondratieff." *International Encyclopedia of the Social Sciences,* 8:433–44.

Gayer, Arthur David, W. W. Rostow, and Anna Jacobson Schwartz. *The Growth and Fluctuation of the British Economy, 1790–1850.* New York: Barnes and Noble Books, 1975.

Giarini, Orio, ed. *Cycles, Value and Employment: Responses to the Economic Crisis.* New York: Pergamon Press, 1984.

Giarini, Orio, and Henri Louberge. *The Diminishing Returns of Technology.* New York: Pergamon Press, 1978.

Giddens, Anthony. *The Constitution of Society.* Berkeley: University of California Press, 1984.

Gilboy, Elizabeth W. "The Cost of Living and Real Wages in Eighteenth-Century England." *Review of Economic Statistics* 18, no. 3 (1936): 134–43.

Gilpin, Robert. *War and Change in World Politics.* Cambridge: Cambridge University Press, 1981.

Glamann, Kristof. "European Trade, 1500–1750." In Carlo M. Cipolla, ed., *The Fontana Economic History of Europe.* Vol. 2. Glasgow: Collins, 1974.

Glenday, R. "Long-Period Economic Trends." *Journal of the Royal Statistical Society* 101 (1938): 511–52.

Glismann, Hans H., Horst Rodemer, and Frank Wolter. "Zur Natur der Wachstumsschwäche in der Bundesrepublik Deutschland: Eine empirische Analyse langer Zyklen wirtschaftlicher Entwicklung." *Kieler Diskussionsbeiträge* (Kiel Institut für Weltwirtschaft) 55 (1978).

Glismann, Hans H., Horst Rodemer, and Frank Wolter. "Zur empirischen Analyse langer Zyklen wirtschaftlicher Entwicklung in Deutschland—Datenbasis und Berechnungsmethoden." *Kieler Diskussionsbeiträge* (Kiel Institut für Weltwirtschaft) 72 (1978).

Glismann, Hans H., Horst Rodemer, and Frank Wolter. "Lange Wellen wirtschaftlichen Wachstums, Replik und Weiterführung." *Kieler Diskussionsbeiträge* (Kiel Institut für Weltwirtschaft) 74 (1980).

Glismann, Hans H., Horst Rodemer, and Frank Wolter. "Long Waves in Economic Development: Causes and Empirical Evidence." In Christopher Freeman, ed., *Long Waves in the World Economy,* 135–63. London: Butterworth, 1983.

Goldstein, Joshua S. "Long Waves and War Cycles." M.S. thesis, MIT, 1984a.

———. "War and the Kondratieff Upswing." Paper presented at the International Studies Association annual meeting, Atlanta, Ga., March 1984b.

———. "Long Cycles of Economic Growth and War: Toward a Synthetic Theory." Paper presented at the American Political Science Association annual meeting, Washington, D.C., September 1984c.

———. "Kondratieff Waves as War Cycles." *International Studies Quarterly* 29, no. 4 (1985): 411–44.

———. "Long Waves in Production, War and Inflation: New Empirical Evidence." *Journal of Conflict Resolution* 31, no. 4 (1987).

Gordon, David M. "Up and Down the Long Roller Coaster." In *U.S. Capitalism in Crisis*, 22–34. New York: Economics Education Project of the Union for Radical Political Economics, 1978.

———. "Stages of Accumulation and Long Economic Cycles." In Terrence K. Hopkins and Immanuel Wallerstein, eds., *Processes of the World-System*, 9–45. Beverly Hills, Calif.: Sage Publications, 1980.

———. "The Pulse of Capitalism." Review of *The Long Wave Cycle*, by N. D. Kondratieff. *Atlantic Monthly*, September 1984, 121–24.

Gordon, David M., Richard Edwards, and Michael Reich. *Segmented Work, Divided Workers*. Cambridge: Cambridge University Press, 1982.

Gordon, David M., Thomas E. Weisskopf, and Samuel Bowles. "Long Swings and the Nonreproductive Cycle." *American Economic Review* 73, no. 2 (1983): 152–57.

Goy, Joseph, and Emmanuel Le Roy Ladurie, eds. *Les fluctuations de produit de la dime: Conjoncture decimale et domaniale de la fin du Moyen Age au XVIIIe siècle*. Paris: Mouton, 1972.

Gradish, Stephen F. *The Manning of the British Navy during the Seven Years' War*. London: Royal Historical Society, 1980.

Graham, Alan K., and Peter M. Senge. "A Long-Wave Hypothesis of Innovation." *Technological Forecasting and Social Change* 17 (1980): 283–311.

Granger, C. W. J., and A. O. Hughes. "A New Look at Some Old Data: The Beveridge Wheat Price Series." *Journal of the Royal Statistical Society* (1971): 413–28.

Grenier, Jean-Yves. *"L'Utilisation de l'analyse spectrale pour l'étude des séries de prix dans la France preindustrielle, XVIe–XVIIIe siècles."* *Social Science Information* 23, no. 2 (1984): 427–47.

Grimes, Peter. "Long Waves and International Inequality: A Research Proposal." Paper presented at the International Studies Association annual meeting, Washington, D.C., March 1985.

Hall, P. "The Geography of the Fifth Kondratieff Cycle." *New Society* 55, no. 958 (1981): 535–37.

Hamil, R. "Is the Wave of the Future a Kondratieff?" *Futurist* 13, no. 5 (1979): 381–84.

Hamilton, Earl J. *War and Prices in Spain, 1651–1800*. Cambridge, Mass., Harvard University Press, 1947.

———. "The Role of War in Modern Inflation." *Journal of Economic History* 37, no. 1 (1977): 13–19.

Hanappe, P. "Les 'crises' contemporaines: Vivons-nous un retournement du Kondratieff?" *Metra* 14, no. 4 (1975): 707–21.

Hansen, Alvin H. *Economic Stabilization in an Unbalanced World*. 1932; reprint ed., New York: A M. Kelley, 1971.

———. *Fiscal Policy and Business Cycles*. New York: W. W. Norton, 1941.

Hardin, Garrett. "The Tragedy of the Commons." *Science* 162 (1968): 1243–48.

Harkness, J. P. "A Spectral-Analytical Test of the Long-Swing Hypothesis in Canada." *Review of Economics and Statistics* 50, no. 4 (1968): 429–36.

Hart, Hornell. "Logistic Social Trends." *American Journal of Sociology* 49, no. 4 (1944): 289–301.

Hartman, Raymond S., and David R. Wheeler. "Schumpeterian Waves of Innovation and Infrastructure Development in Great Britain and the United States: The Kondratieff Cycle Revisited." *Research in Economic History* 4 (1979): 37–85.

Haustein, Heinz-Deiter, and Erich Neuwirth. "Long Waves in World Industrial Production, Energy Consumption, Innovations, Inventions, and Patents and Their Identification by Spectral Analysis." *Technological Forecasting and Social Change* 22 (1982): 53–89.

Helphand, Alexander [Parvus]. *Die Handelskrise und die Gewerkschaften.* Munich: M. Ernst, 1901. Repinted in *Die Langen Wellen der Konjunktur,* 7–32. Berlin: Olle & Wolter, 1972.

Hiatt, Fred, and Rick Atkinson. "Arms and America's Fortunes." *Washington Post,* Dec. 1, 1985, A1.

Hirst, Francis W. *The Political Economy of War.* Rev. ed. London: J. M. Dent, 1916.

Hobsbawm, E. J. *Industry and Empire: From 1750 to the Present Day.* Harmondsworth: Penguin-Pelican, 1969.

Hoffman, Walther G. *British Industry, 1700–1950.* Oxford: Basil Blackwell, 1955.

Holmes, Jack E. *The Mood/Interest Theory of American Foreign Policy.* Lexington, Ky.: University of Kentucky Press, 1985.

Holmes, Jack E., and Robert E. Elder, Jr. "A Mood Interpretation of the Legislative/Executive Relationship in American Foreign Policy Formulation." Paper presented at the International Studies Association annual meeting, Washington, D.C., March 1985.

Holsti, Kal. *The Dividing Discipline.* London: Allen and Unwin, 1985.

Hopkins, Terence K., and Immanuel Wallerstein [with the Research Working Group on Cyclical Rhythms and Secular Trends]. "Cyclical Rhythms and Secular Trends of the Capitalist World-Economy: Some Premises, Hypotheses, and Questions." *Review* 2, no. 4 (1979): 483–500. Reprinted in Hopkins and Wallerstein, eds., *World-Systems Analysis: Theory and Methodology,* 104–20. Beverly Hills, Calif.: Sage Publications, 1982.

Hopkins, Terence K., and Immanuel Wallerstein, eds. *World-Systems Analysis: Theory and Methodology.* Beverly Hills, Calif.: Sage Publications, 1982.

Hoskins, Richard Kelly. *War Cycles, Peace Cycles.* Lynchburg, Va.: Virginia Publishing Co., 1985.

Hoszowski, Stanislas. "Central Europe and the Sixteenth- and Seventeenth-Century Price Revolution," in Peter Burke, ed., *Economy and Society in Early Modern Europe: Essays from* Annales, 85–103. New York: Harper and Row, 1972. [1961]

Howard, Michael. *War in European History.* Oxford: Oxford University Press, 1976.

Howarth, David Armine. *The Voyage of the Armada: The Spanish story.* New York: Viking Press, 1981.

Hunter, Maxwell W. "Strategic Dynamics and Space-Laser Weaponry." Typescript. Lockheed Missiles and Space Co., Sunnyvale, Calif.: Oct. 31, 1977.

Huntington, Ellsworth. *The Climatic Factor as Illustrated in Arid America.* Washington, D.C.: Carnegie Institution, 1914.

Huntington, Samuel P. "Generations, Cycles, and Their Role in American Development." In R. J. Samuels, ed., *Political Generations and Political Development,* 9–28. Lexington, Mass.: Lexington Books, 1977.

Hussain, Athar. "Symptomatology of Revolution." Review of *The Second Slump,* by Ernest Mandel. *Economy and Society,* 9, no. 3 (1980): 349–58.

Imbert, Gaston. *Des mouvements de longue durée Kondratieff.* [Ph.D. diss.] Aix-en-Provence: Office universitaire de polycopie, 1956.

———. *Des mouvements de longue Durée Kondratieff.* Aix-en-Provence: La pensée universitaire, 1959.

Irsigler, Franz. "La mercuriale de Cologne (1531–1797): Structure de marche et conjoncture des prix céréaliers." *Annales: Economies, sociétés, civilisations* 33, no. 1 (1978): 93–114.

Irsigler, Franz, and Rainer Metz. "The Statistical Evidence of 'Long Waves' in Pre-Industrial and Industrial Times." *Social Science Information* 23, no. 2 (1984): 381–410.

Isard, Walter. "A Neglected Cycle: The Transport-Building Cycle." *Review of Economic Statistics* 24, no. 4 (1942a): 149–58.

———. "Transport Development and Building Cycles." *Quarterly Journal of Economics* (November 1942b): 90–112.

Isard, Walter, and Caroline Isard. "The Transport-Building Cycle in Urban Development: Chicago." *Review of Economic Statistics* 25, no. 4 (1943): 224–26.

Ischboldin, Boris S. *Genetic Economics.* St. Louis, Mo.: St. Louis University, 1967.

Jervis, Robert. *Perception and Misperception in International Politics.* Princeton, N.J.: Princeton University Press, 1976.

Jervis, Robert, Richard Ned Lebow, and Janice Gross Stein. *Psychology and Deterrence.* Baltimore: Johns Hopkins University Press, 1985.

Jeze, Gaston P. A. *Les dépenses de guerre de la France.* New Haven: Yale University Press, 1926.

Johnson, P. M., and W. R. Thompson, eds. *Rhythms in Politics and Economics.* New York: Praeger, 1985.

Jörberg, Lennart. *A History of Prices in Sweden, 1732–1914.* Vol. 1. Lund: CWK Gleerup, 1972.

Kahler, Miles. "Rumors of War: The 1914 Analogy." *Foreign Affairs* 58 (Winter 1979/80): 374–96.

Kaldor, N. "Structural Causes of the World Economic Recession." *Mondes en développement* 22 (1978): 254–63.

Kalecki, M. "Political Aspects of Full Employment." *Political Quarterly* 14, no. 4 (1943): 331–42.

Kaplan, Herbert H. *Russia and the Outbreak of the Seven Years' War.* Berkeley: University of California Press, 1968.

Kartchner, Kerry M. "Strategic Appeasement: Historical Comparisons between the 1930s and 1980s." Paper presented at the International Studies Association annual meeting, Washington, D.C., March 1985.

Keen, Charles R. *A Note on Kondratieff Cycles in Prewar Japan.* Institute for Research in the Behavioral, Economic and Management Sciences, Institute Paper no. 123. Lafayette, Ind.: Purdue University, 1965.

Kellenbenz, Hermann. *The Rise of the European Economy.* New York: Holmes & Meier Publishers, 1976.

Keohane, Robert O. "The Theory of Hegemonic Stability and Change in International Economic Regimes, 1967–1977." In Ole R. Holsti, Randolph M. Siverson, and Alexander L. George, eds., *Change in the International System.* Boulder, Colo.: Westview Press, 1980.

———. *After Hegemony.* Princeton, N.J.: Princeton University Press, 1984.

Keohane, Robert O., and Joseph S. Nye. *Power and Interdependence: World Politics in Transition.* Boston: Little, Brown, 1977.

Kerhuel, Marie. *Les mouvements de longue Durée des prix*. Ph.D. diss., Université de Rennes, 1935.

Keynes, John Maynard. *The Economic Consequences of the Peace*. New York: Harcourt & Brace, 1920.

———. *The General Theory of Employment, Interest and Money*. 1936; reprint ed., New York: Harcourt Brace Jovanovich, 1964.

Kiernan, V. G. *State and Society in Europe, 1550–1650*. New York: St. Martin's Press, 1980.

Kindleberger, Charles P. *Economic Growth in France and Britain 1851–1950*. Cambridge, Mass.: Harvard University Press, 1964.

———. *Power and Money*. New York: Basic Books, 1970.

———. *The World in Depression, 1929–1939*. Berkeley: University of California Press, 1973.

———. *The Formation of Financial Centers: A Study in Comparative Economic History*. Princeton Studies in International Finance, no. 36. Princeton, N.J.: Princeton University Press, 1974.

King, James C. "The Periodicity of War." Typescript, Causes of War study, University of Chicago, 1935.

Kinser, Samuel. "Annaliste Paradigm? The Geohistorical Structuralism of Fernand Braudel." *American Historical Review* 86, no. 1 (1981): 63–105.

Kissinger, Henry A. *A World Restored*. Boston: Houghton Mifflin, 1973.

Kitwood, T. "A Farewell Wave to the Theory of Long Waves." *Universities Quarterly— Culture, Education and Society* (Oxford) 38, no. 2 (1984): 158–78.

Kleinknecht, Alfred. "Innovation, Accumulation, and Crisis: Waves in Economic Development?" *Review* 4, no. 4 (1981a): 683–711. [German ed. 1979.]

———. "Observations on the Schumpeterian Swarming of Innovations." *Futures* 13, no. 4 (1981b): 293–307.

Klingberg, Frank L. "The Historical Alternation of Moods in American Foreign Policy." *World Politics* 4, no. 2 (1952): 239–73.

———. "Historical Periods, Trends and Cycles in International Relations." *Journal of Conflict Resolution* 14, no. 4 (1970): 505–11.

———. "Cyclical Trends in American Foreign Policy Moods and Their Policy Implications." In Charles W. Kegley and Patrick McGowan eds., *Challenges to America: United States Foreign Policy in the 1980's*. 4:37–55. Beverly Hills, Calif.: Sage Publications, 1979.

———. *Cyclical Trends in American Foreign Policy Moods: The Unfolding of America's World Role*. New York: University Press of America, 1983.

Klingemann, Hans-Dieter, Peter Philip Mohler, and Robert Philip Weber. "Cultural Indicators Based on Content Analysis: A Secondary Analysis of Sorokin's Data on Fluctuations of Systems of Truth." *Quality and Quantity* 16, no. 1 (1982): 1–18.

Kohn, Stanislas, and Alexander F. Meyendorff. *The Cost of the War to Russia*. New Haven: Yale University Press, 1932.

Kolodziej, Edward A. "New Assumptions to Guide the Use and Control of Military Force." *Policy Studies Journal* 8, no. 1 (1979): 17–27.

Kondratieff, N. D. "Die Langen Wellen der Konjunktur." *Archiv für Sozialwissenschaft und Sozialpolitik* (1926). From the Russian version of 1925. Abridged English version: "The Long Waves in Economic Life." *Review of Economic Statistics* 17, no. 6 (1935): 105–15. Complete English version: *Review* 2, no. 4 (1979): 519–62.

————. *The Long Wave Cycle.* 1928; reprint ed., New York: Richardson & Snyder, 1984.

Korpinen, Pekka. *Kriisit Ja Pitkat Syklit* (Crises and Long Cycles). Helsinki: n.p., 1981. English summary: 183–96.

Kruskal, J. B. "An Overview of Sequence Comparison." In D. Sankoff and J. B. Kruskal, eds., *Time Warps, String Edits, and Macromolecules: The Theory and Practice of Sequence Comparison.* Reading, Mass.: Addison-Wesley, 1983.

Kuczynski, Jürgen. *Das Problem der Langen Wellen und die Entwicklung der Industriewarenpreise in den Jahren 1820–1933.* Basel: Philographischer Verlag, 1934.

Kuczynski, Thomas. "Spectral Analysis and Cluster Analysis as Mathematical Methods for the Periodization of Historical Processes . . . Kondratieff Cycles—Appearance or Reality?" *Proceedings of the Seventh International Economic History Congress* (Edinburgh, 1978), 2:79–86.

————. "Have There Been Differences between the Growth Rates in Different Periods of the Development of the Capitalist World Economy since 1850?" In J. M. Clubb and E. K. Scheuch, eds., *Historical Social Research.* Historisch-Sozialwissen-schaftliche Forschungen, Stuttgart, monograph series, no. 6. Stuttgart: Klett-Cotta, 1980.

————. "Leads and Lags in an Escalation Model of Capitalist Development: Kondratieff Cycles Reconsidered." *Proceedings of the Eighth International Economic History Congress* (Budapest, 1982), B3: 27.

Kuhn, Thomas S. *The Structure of Scientific Revolutions.* 2d ed. Chicago: University of Chicago Press, 1970.

Kurth, James R. "American Hegemony: A Thicket of Theories." Paper presented at the Canadian Political Science Association annual meeting, St. Johns, Newfoundland, June 1971.

————. "The Political Consequences of the Product Cycle: Industrial History and Political Outcomes." *International Organization* 33, no. 1 (1979): 1–34.

Kuznets, Simon S. *Secular Movements in Production and Prices.* 1930; reprint ed. New York: Augustus Kelly, 1967.

————. "Schumpeter's Business Cycles." *American Economic Review* 30, no. 2 (1940): 257–71.

Labini, Paolo Sylos. "Le problème des cycles économiques de longue durée." *Economie appliquée* 3 (1950): 481–95.

Lakatos, Imre. "Falsification and the Methodology of Scientific Research Programmes." In Lakatos and Alan Musgrave, eds., *Criticism and the Growth of Knowledge,* 91–196. Cambridge: Cambridge University Press, 1970.

Lamszus, Wilhelm. *The Human Slaughter-House: Scenes from the War That Is Sure to Come.* New York: Frederick A. Stokes Co., 1913.

Landes, David S. "Technological Change and Development in Western Europe, 1750–1914." In E. E. Rich and C. H. Wilson, eds., *The Cambridge Economic History of Europe.* Cambridge: Cambridge University Press, 1966.

Langer, Herbert. *The Thirty Years' War.* Poole: Blandford Press, 1978.

Langer, William L. *European Alliances and Alignments, 1871–1890.* New York: Alfred A. Knopf, 1931.

Langrish, John. "Cycles of Optimism in Design." *Design Studies* 3, no. 3 (1982): 153–56.

Lasswell, Harold. *World Politics and Personal Insecurity.* 1935; reprint eds., New York: Free Press; London: Collier-MacMillan, 1965.

Latham, John. "Food Prices and Industrialization: Some Questions from Indian History." *IDS Bulletin* (Sussex) 9, no. 3 (1978): 17–19.

Lee, J. S. "The Periodic Recurrence of Internecine Wars in China." *China Journal* 14, no. 3 (1931): 111–15; 14, no. 4 (1931): 159–63.

Lenin, V. I. "Imperialism, the Highest Stage of Capitalism" [1917]. In Henry M. Christman, ed., *Essential Works of Lenin,* 177–270. New York: Bantam Books, 1966.

Lenoir, Marcel. *Etudes sur la formation et le mouvement des prix.* Paris: M. Giard, 1913.

Le Roy Ladurie, Emmanuel. "A Long Agrarian Cycle: Languedoc, 1500–1700" [1969]. In Peter Earle ed., *Essays in European Economic History, 1500–1800,* 143–64. Oxford: Clarendon Press, 1974.

———. *The Mind and Method of the Historian.* 1978; reprint ed., Chicago: University of Chicago Press, 1981.

Levy, Jack S. "Alliance Formation and War Behavior: An Analysis of the Great Powers, 1495–1975." *Journal of Conflict Resolution* 25, no. 4 (1981): 581–613.

———. *War in the Modern Great Power System, 1495–1975.* Lexington, Ky.: University Press of Kentucky, 1983a.

———. "World System Analysis: A Great Power Framework." In W. R. Thompson, ed., *Contending Approaches to World System Analysis,* 183–201. Beverly Hills, Calif.: Sage Publications, 1983b.

———. "Misperception and the Causes of War: Theoretical Linkages and Analytical Problems." *World Politics* 36, no. 1 (1983c): 76–99.

———. "Preventive War and the Power Transition." Paper presented at the American Political Science Association annual meeting, Washington, D.C., September 1984.

———. "Theories of General War." *World Politics* 37, no. 3 (1985): 344–74.

Levy, Jack S., and T. Clifton Morgan. "The Frequency and Seriousness of War: An Inverse Relationship?" *Journal of Conflict Resolution* 28, no. 4 (1984): 731–49.

———. "War-Weariness and Other Hypotheses of Addictive Contagion: A National-Level Study." Paper presented at the International Studies Association annual meeting, Washington, D.C., March 1985.

Levy-Pascal, Ehud. *An Analysis of the Cyclical Dynamics of Industrialized Countries.* Washington, D.C.: Central Intelligence Agency [Staff Report PR 76 10009], 1976.

Lewis, W. A. "World Production, Prices and Trade, 1870–1960." *Manchester School of Economic and Social Studies* 20 (1952): 105–38.

———. *Growth and Fluctuations, 1870–1913.* Boston: Allen & Unwin, 1978.

Lifton, Robert Jay, and Richard Falk. *Indefensible Weapons: The Political and Psychological Case against Nuclearism.* New York: Basic Books, 1982.

Loots, François. "Les mouvements fondamentaux des prix de gros en Belgique de 1822 à 1913." *Bulletin de l'Institut des sciences économiques* 8, no. 1 (1936): 23–47.

Lynn-Jones, Sean M. "The 1914 Analogy Reconsidered: Anglo-German Relations, 1911–1914." Paper presented at the Northeastern Political Science Association annual meeting, Philadelphia, November 1985.

Lytton, Lord [Edward Robert] Bulwer. *The Coming Race.* Edinburgh and London: William Blackwood & Sons, 1871.

Macfarlane, Alan. *Witchcraft in Tudor and Stuart England: A Regional and Comparative Study.* New York: Harper & Row, 1970.

Macfie, A. L. "The Outbreak of War and the Trade Cycle." *Economic History* 3 (1938): 89–97.

Macrae, Duncan. "On the Political Business Cycle." In D. A. Hibbs and H. Fassbender, eds., *Contemporary Political Economy,* 169–84. Amsterdam: North-Holland Publishing Co., 1981.

Maddalena, Aldo de. *Prezzi e mercedi a Milano dal 1701 al 1860.* Milano: Banca Commerciale Italiana, 1974.

Maddison, Angus, "Phases of Capitalist Development." *Banca Nazionale Del Lavoro Quarterly Review* 121 (June 1977): 103–37.

———. *Phases of Capitalist Development.* New York: Oxford University Press, 1982.

Mahdavi, K. B. *Technological Innovation: An Efficiency Investigation.* Stockholm: Beckmans, 1972.

Maland, David. *Europe at War, 1600–1650.* Totowa, N.J.: Rowman & Littlefield, 1980.

Mandel, Ernest. *Late Capitalism.* London: New Left Books, 1975.

———. *The Second Slump.* London: New Left Books, 1978.

———. *Long Waves of Capitalist Development.* Cambridge: Cambridge University Press, 1980.

———. "Explaining Long Waves of Capitalist Development." *Futures* 13, no. 4 (1981): 332–38.

Mansfield, Edwin. "Long Waves and Technological Innovation." *American Economic Review* 73, no. 2 (1983): 141–45.

Mao Tsetung. *Quotations from Chairman Mao Tsetung.* Beijing: Foreign Languages Press, 1972.

Marchetti, Cesare. "Recession 1983: Ten More Years To Go?" *Technological Forecasting and Social Change* 24 (1983): 331–42.

Margairaz, Dominique. "Les spécificités régionales des mouvements conjoncturels des prix céréaliers en France, 1756–1870." *Review* 7, no. 4 (1984): 649–73.

Marjolin, Robert. "Mouvements de longue durée, des prix et extraction des metaux precieux." *L'Activité économique* (1937): 119–44.

———. "Rationalité ou irrationalité des mouvements économiques de longue durée." *Annales sociologique,* ser. D, no. 3 (1938).

———. "Long Cycles in Capital Intensity in the French Coal Mining Industry." *Review of Economic Statistics* 23 (1941a): 165–75.

———. *Prix, monnaie et production: Essai sur les mouvements économiques de longue durée.* Paris: Université de Paris, 1941b.

Mass, Nathaniel J. *Economic Cycles: An Analysis of Underlying Causes.* Cambridge, Mass.: Wright-Allen Press, 1975.

Mass, Nathaniel J., and Peter M. Senge. "Reindustrialization: Aiming for the Right Targets." *Technology Review* (August/September 1981): 56–65.

Mattingly, Garrett. *The Defeat of the Spanish Armada.* London: J. Cape, 1962.

Mauro, Frédéric. *L'Expansion européene (1600–1870).* Paris: Presses universitaires de France, 1964.

———. *Le XVIᵉ siècle européen: Aspects économiques.* Paris: Presses Universitaires de France, 1966.

———. *Histoire de l'économie mondiale.* Paris: Editions Sirey, 1971.

McClelland, Peter D. *Causal Explanation and Model Building in History, Economics, and the New Economic History.* Ithaca, N.Y.: Cornell University Press, 1975.

McCloskey, Donald N. *Economic Maturity and Entrepreneurial Decline: British Iron and Steel, 1870–1913.* Cambridge, Mass.: Harvard University Press, 1973.

McEvedy, Colin. *The Penguin Atlas of Modern History (to 1815)*. Harmondsworth: Penguin, 1972.

McGowan, Pat, and Charles W. Kegley, Jr., eds. *Foreign Policy and the Modern World-System*. Beverly Hills, Calif.: Sage Publications, 1983).

McKeown, Timothy J. "Hegemonic Stability Theory and Nineteenth-Century Tariff Levels in Europe." *International Organization* 37, no. 1 (1983): 73–91.

McNeill, William Hardy. *The Pursuit of Power*. Chicago: University of Chicago Press, 1982.

Mefford, Dwain. "Formulating Foreign Policy on the Basis of Historical Analogies: An Application of Developments in Artificial Intelligence." Paper presented at the annual meeting of the International Studies Association, Atlanta, Ga., March 1984.

Mehring, Franz. "The Marxist View: Economic Causation." In Theodore K. Rabb, ed., *The Thiry Years' War*, 9–15. New York: University Press of America, 1981.

Meinecke, Friedrich. *Machiavellism: The Doctrine of Raison d'état and Its Place in Modern History*. New Haven: Yale University Press, 1957.

Melman, Seymour. *Pentagon Capitalism: The Political Economy of War*. New York: McGraw-Hill, 1970.

———. *The Permanent War Economy: American Capitalism in Decline*. New York: Simon & Schuster, 1974.

———. "Swords into Plowshares: Converting from Military to Civilian Production." *Technology Review* 89, no. 1 (1986): 62–71.

Mensch, Gerhard. *Stalemate in Technology: Innovations Overcome the Depression*. Cambridge, Mass.: Ballinger, 1979.

Mensch, Gerhard, Charles Coutinho, and Klaus Kaasch. "Changing Capital Values and the Propensity to Innovate." *Futures* 13, no. 4 (1981): 276–92.

Metcalfe, J. S. "Impulse and Diffusion in the Study of Technical Change." *Futures* 13, no. 5 (1981).

Metz, Rainer. " 'Long Waves' in English and German Economic Historical Series from the Middle of the Sixteenth to the Middle of the Twentieth Century." In Rainer Fremdling and Patrick K. O'Brien, eds., *Productivity in the Economies of Europe*, 175–219. Stuttgart: Klett-Cotta, 1983.

———. "Zur Empirischen Evidenz 'Langer Wellen.' " *Kyklos* 37, no. 2 (1984a): 266–90.

———. "Long Waves in Coinage and Grain Price-Series from the Fifteenth to the Eighteenth Century." *Review* 7, no. 4 (1984b): 599–647.

Midelfort, H. C. Erik. *Witch Hunting in Southwestern Germany, 1562–1684*. Stanford, Calif.: Stanford University Press, 1972.

Midlarsky, Manus I. "A Hierarchical Equilibrium Theory of Systemic War." Paper presented at the International Studies Association annual meeting, Atlanta, Ga., March 1984a.

———. "Some Uniformities in the Origins of Systemic War." Revised version of paper presented at the American Political Science Association annual meeting, Washington, D.C., September 1984b.

———. "Preventing Systemic War: Crisis Decision-Making amidst a Structure of Conflict Relationships." *Journal of Conflict Resolution* 28, no. 4 (1984c): 563–84.

Minchinton, W. E., ed. *The Growth of English Overseas Trade in the Seventeenth and Eighteenth Centuries*. London: Methuen & Co., 1969.

Miskimin, Harry A. *The Economy of Later Renaissance Europe: 1460–1600*. Cambridge: Cambridge University Press, 1977.

Mitchell, B. R. *European Historical Statistics, 1750–1975*. New York: Facts on File, 1980.

Mitchell, B. R., and Phyllis Deane. *Abstract of British Historical Statistics*. Cambridge: Cambridge University Press, 1962.

Mitchell, Wesley Clair. *Business Cycles and Their Causes*. 1913; reprint ed., Berkeley: University of California Press, 1971.

Modelski, George. "The Long Cycle of Global Politics and the Nation-State." *Comparative Studies in Society and History* 20, no. 2 (1978): 214–38.

———. "Long Cycles and United States Strategic Policy." *Policy Studies Journal* 8, no. 1 (1979): 10–17.

———. "Long Cycles, Kondratieffs and Alternating Innovations: Implications for U.S. Foreign Policy." In Charles W. Kegley and Pat McGowan, eds., *The Political Economy of Foreign Policy Behavior*, 63–83. Beverly Hills, Calif.: Sage Publications, 1981.

———. "Long Cycles and the Strategy of U.S. International Economic Policy." In William P. Avery and David P. Rapkin, eds., *America in a Changing World Political Economy*, 97–118. New York: Longman, 1982.

———. "Long Cycles of World Leadership: An Annotated Bibliography." *International Studies Notes* 10, no. 3 (1983): 1–5.

———. "One Long Cycle or a Family of Long Cycles?" Typescript, June 1984a.

———. "Global Wars and World Leadership Selection." Paper presented at the World Peace Science Congress, Rotterdam, June 1984b.

Modelski, George, and Patrick Morgan. "Understanding Global War." Paper presented at the American Political Science Association annual meeting, Washington, D.C., August 1984.

Modelski, George, and William R. Thompson. "Testing Cobweb Models of the Long Cycle of World Leadership." Paper presented at the Peace Science Society (International) North American conference, Philadelphia, November 1981.

Mokyr, Joel, and N. Eugene Savin. "Stagflation in Historical Perspective: The Napoleonic Wars Revisited." *Research in Economic History* 1 (1976): 198–259.

Mols, Roger. "Population in Europe, 1500–1700." In Carlo M. Cipolla, ed., *The Fontana Economic History of Europe*. Vol. 2. Glasgow: Collins, 1974.

Morecroft, J. "System Dynamics: Portraying Bounded Rationality." *Omega* 11 (1983): 131–42.

Morgenthau, Hans. *Politics among Nations: The Struggle for Power and Peace*. 1948; 4th ed. New York: Alfred A. Knopf, 1967.

Morineau, Michel. "D'Amsterdam à Seville: De quelle realité l'histoire des prix est-elle le miroir?" *Annales: Economies, sociétés, civilisations* 23, no. 1 (1968): 178–205.

———. "Juglar, Kitchin, Kondratieff, et Compagnie." *Review* 7, no. 4 (1984): 577–98.

Moyal, J. E. "The Distribution of Wars in Time." *Journal of the Royal Statistical Society* 112 (1949): 446–58.

Namenwirth, J. Zvi. "Wheels of Time and the Interdependence of Value Change in America." *Journal of Interdisciplinary History* 3, no. 4 (1973): 649–83.

Namenwirth, J. Zvi, and Harold D. Lasswell. *The Changing Language of American Values: A Computer Study of Selected Party Platforms*. Beverly Hills, Calif.: Sage Publications, 1970.

Nef, John U. "War and the Early Industrial Revolution." In C. W. Wright, ed., *Economic Problems of War and Its Aftermath*, 1–53. Chicago: University of Chicago Press, 1942.

———. *War and Human Progress*. Cambridge, Mass.: Harvard University Press, 1950.

Newbold, J. T. W. "The Beginnings of the World Crisis, 1873–1896." *Economic History* 11, no. 7 (1932): 437.

Nilsson, Jan-Evert. "Kondratieffcykeln." *Lov og struktur* (Bergen) 17 (1979).

North, D. C. "The Theoretical Tools of the Economic Historian." In Charles P. Kindleberger and Guido di Tella, eds., *Economics in the Long View: Essays in Honor of W. W. Rostow,* 15–26. New York: New York University Press, 1982.

North, Douglass C., and Robert Paul Thomas. *The Rise of the Western World: A New Economic History.* Cambridge: Cambridge University Press, 1973.

North, Robert C., and Richard Lagerstrom. *War and Domination: A Theory of Lateral Pressure.* New York: General Learning Press, 1971.

North, Robert C. "War, Peace and Survival." Typescript. 1985.

Nyilas, József, ed. *Theoretical Problems, Current Structural Changes in the World Economy.* Budapest: Akademiai Kiado, 1976.

Olson, Mancur. *The Logic of Collective Action.* 1965; reprint ed., Cambridge, Mass.: Harvard University Press, 1971.

———. *The Rise and Decline of Nations.* New Haven: Yale University Press, 1982.

O'Neill, Gerard K. "The Colonization of Space." *Physics Today* (September 1974): 32–40.

———. *The High Frontier.* New York: Bantam, 1976.

Onuf, Nicholas Greenwood. "Prometheus Prostrate." *Futures* 16, no. 1 (1984): 47–59.

Organski, A. F. K. *World Politics.* New York: Alfred A. Knopf, 1958.

Organski, A. F. K., and Jacek Kugler. *The War Ledger.* Chicago: University of Chicago Press, 1980.

Paine, Thomas. "Prospects on the Rubicon" [1787]. In *The Writings of Thomas Paine.* Vol. 2. New York: Knickerbocker Press, 1894.

Palme Commission [Independent Commission on Disarmament and Security Issues]. *Common Security: A Programme for Disarmament.* London: Pan Books, 1982.

Pareto, Vilfredo. "Alcuni relazioni fra la stato sociale e la variazoni della prosperita economica." *Rivista italiana di sociologia* (September–December 1931): 501–48.

Parker, Geoffrey. *Europe in Crisis, 1598–1648.* Ithaca, N.Y.: Cornell University Press, 1979.

Parker, Geoffrey, and Lesley M. Smith. "Introduction." In Parker and Smith, eds., *The General Crisis of the Seventeenth Century.* London: Routledge & Kegan Paul, 1978.

Parry, J. H. *The Establishment of the European Hegemony, 1415–1715.* 3d ed. New York: Harper & Row, 1966.

Passerino, C., et al. [Gruppo di Lavoro]. "Il movimento dei prezzi e delle altre quantita economiche secondo la teoria delle fluttuazioni economiche di Nikolai Kondratieff." *Giornale degli economisti e annali di economia* 32, nos. 5–6 (1973): 380–414.

Pennington, D. H. *Seventeenth-Century Europe.* London: Longmans, 1970.

Perez, Carlota. "Structural Change and the Assimilation of New Technologies in the Economic and Social Systems." *Futures* 15, no. 5 (1983): 357–75.

———. "Towards a Comprehensive Theory of Long Waves." Paper presented at the IIASA Meeting on Long Waves, Depression and Innovation, Siena/Florence, October 1983.

Petersen, Ib Damgaard. "The Political Economy of Long Waves." Paper presented at the ECPR Joint Sessions, Göteborg, April 1986.

Petzina, D. " 'Lange Wellen' und 'Wechsellagen': Die derzeitige Diskussion." In D. Petzina and G. van Roon, eds., *Konjunktur, Krise, Gesellschaft.* Stuttgart: Klett-Cotta, 1981.

Pfister, Ulrich, and Christian Suter. "International Financial Relations as Part of the World System." Paper presented at the International Studies Association annual meeting, Washington, D.C., March 1985.

Phelps-Brown, E. H., and Sheila V. Hopkins. "Seven Centuries of Building Wages." In E. M. Carus-Wilson, ed., *Essays in Economic History*. 2:168–78. New York: St. Martin's Press, 1962. [1955]

———. "Seven Centuries of the Prices of Consumables, Compared with Builders' Wage-Rates." In E. M. Carus-Wilson, ed., *Essays in Economic History*. 2:179–96. New York: St. Martin's Press, 1962. [1956]

Phelps-Brown, Henry. "A Non-monetarist View of the Pay Explosion." *Three Banks Review* 105 (1975): 3–24.

Piatier, André. "Innovation, Information and Long-term Growth." *Futures* 13, no. 5 (1981): 371–82.

Piel, Gerard. "Natural Philosophy in the Constitution." *Science* 234 (1986): 1056.

Pigou, Arthur Cecil. *The Political Economy of War*. London: Macmillan, 1940.

Pirages, Dennis. "Long Waves, Cycles and the Contemporary Economic Problem." Paper presented at the International Studies Association convention, Atlanta, Ga., March 1984.

Polišenský, J. V. *War and Society in Europe, 1618–1648*. Cambridge: Cambridge University Press, 1978.

———. "Social and Economic Change and the European-Wide War." In Theodore K. Rabb, ed., *The Thirty Years' War*, 57–69. New York: University Press of America, 1981.

Pomian, Krzysztof. "The Secular Evolution of the Concept of Cycles." *Review* 2, no. 4 (1979): 563–646.

Pope, David. "Rostow's Kondratieff Cycle in Australia." Working Papers in Economic History, Australian National University, Canberra, 1983.

Popper, Karl R. *The Poverty of Historicism*. 1957; reprint ed., New York: Harper & Row, 1964.

Posthumus, N. W. *Inquiry into the History of Prices in Holland*. 2 vols. Leyden: E. J. Brill, 1964.

[Edition Prinkipo.] *Die Langen Wellen der Konjunktur*. Berlin: Olle & Wolter, 1972.

Pruden, Henry O. "The Kondratieff Wave." *Journal of Marketing* 42, no. 2 (1978): 63–70.

Quigley, Carroll. *Tragedy and Hope: A History of the World in Our Time*. New York: Macmillan, 1966.

Rabb, Theodore K. "The Effects of the Thirty Years' War on the German Economy." *Journal of Modern History* 35 (1962): 40–51.

———. *The Struggle for Stability in Early Modern Europe*. New York: Oxford University Press, 1975.

———. "Preface." In Rabb, ed., *The Thirty Years' War*. New York: University Press of America, 1981a.

———. "The Economic Effects of the War Reviewed." In Rabb, ed., *The Thirty Years' War*, 69–79. New York: University Press of America, 1981b.

Rand, Benjamin. *Economic History since 1763*. New York: McGraw-Hill, 1911.

Rapkin, David P. "World Leadership, Hegemony, and Kindred Matters." Paper presented at the American Political Science Association annual meeting, Washington, D.C., September 1984.

Rasler, Karen A., and William R. Thompson. "Global Wars, Public Debts, and the Long Cycle." *World Politics* 35, no. 4 (1983): 489–516.

———. "War Making and State Making: Governmental Expenditures, Tax Revenues, and Global Wars." *American Political Science Review* 79, no. 2 (1985a): 491–507.

———. "War and the Economic Growth of Major Powers." *American Journal of Political Science* 29, no. 3 (1985b): 513–538.

Ray, George F. "Innovation in the Long Cycle." *Lloyds Bank Review* 135 (January 1980a): 14–28.

———. "Innovation as the Source of Long Term Economic Growth." *Long Range Planning* 13, no. 1 (1980b): 9–19.

———. "Energy and the Long Cycles." *Energy Economics* 5, no. 1 (1983a): 3–8.

———. "Innovation and Long-Term Growth." In Christopher Freeman, ed., *Long Waves in the World Economy*, 183–94. London: Butterworth, 1983b.

Raymond, Gregory A., and Charles W. Kegley. "Long Cycles and Internationalized Civil War." Paper presented at the International Studies Association annual meeting, Washington, D.C., March 1985.

Reijnders, Jan. "Perspectivistic Distortion: A Note on Some Fundamental Problems Concerning the Approximation of Trends and Trend-Cycles." *Social Science Information* 23, no. 2 (1984): 411–26.

Richardson, Lewis F. *Statistics of Deadly Quarrels*. Pittsburgh, Pa.: Boxwood Press, 1960.

Rist, Charles. "Quelques observations sur les relations entre la vitesse d'accroissement de la production de l'or et les mouvements des prix." *Revue d'économie politique* 52, no. 5 (1938): 1314–24.

Romano, Ruggiero. "Between the Sixteenth and Seventeenth Centuries: The Economic Crisis of 1619–22." In Geoffrey Parker and Lesley M. Smith, eds., *The General Crisis of the Seventeenth Century*. London: Routledge & Kegan Paul, 1978.

Rose, Albert. "Wars, Innovations and Long Cycles." *American Economic Review* 31 (1941): 105–7.

Rosecrance, Richard, et al. "Whither Interdependence." In R. Maghroori and B. Ramberg, eds., *Globalism versus Realism: International Relations' Third Debate*, 125–69. Boulder, Colo.: Westview Press, 1982.

Rosenberg, Nathan, and Claudio R. Frischtak. "Long Waves and Economic Growth: A Critical Appraisal." *American Economic Review* 73, no. 2 (1983): 146–51.

———. "Technological Innovation and Long Waves." *Cambridge Journal of Economics* 8, no. 1 (1984): 7–24.

Rostow, W. W. *British Economy of the Nineteenth Century*. Oxford: Clarendon Press, 1948.

———. *The Process of Economic Growth*. New York: W. W. Norton, 1962.

———. "Kondratieff, Schumpeter and Kuznets: Trend Periods Revisited." *Journal of Economic History* 25, no. 4 (1975a): 719–53.

———. "The Developing World in the Fifth Kondratieff Upswing." *Annals of the American Academy of Political and Social Science* 420 (July 1975b): 111.

———. *How It All Began: Origins of the Modern Economy*. New York: McGraw-Hill, 1975c.

———. *The World Economy: History and Prospect*. Austin, Tex.: University of Texas Press, 1978.

———. Letter to *Lloyds Bank Review* 133 (July 1979): 53.

———. "A Policy for the Fifth Kondratieff Upswing." Typescript, Austin, Tex., 1978.

———. "Cycles in the Fifth Kondratieff Upswing." In *The Business Cycle and Public Policy, 1929–80: A Compendium of Papers Submitted to the Joint Economic Committee, Congress of the United States*. Washington, D.C.: U.S. Government Printing Office, 1980.

Rostow, W. W., and Michael Kennedy. "A Simple Model of the Kondratiev Cycle." *Research in Economic History* 4 (1979): 1–36.

Rothbarth, E. "Review of Schumpeter's Business Cycles." *Economic Journal* (London) 52 no. 206–7 (1942):223–29.

Ruggie, John Gerard. "Social Time and International Policy: Conceptualizing Global Population and Resource Issues." Paper presented at the International Studies Association annual meeting, Washington, D.C., March 1985.

Rupert, Mark E., and David P. Rapkin. "The Erosion of U.S. Hegemonic Leadership Capabilities." In Paul M. Johnson and William R. Thompson, eds., *Rhythms in Politics and Economics*. New York: Praeger, 1985.

Russett, Bruce. "Security and the Resources Scramble: Will 1984 Be like 1914?" *International Affairs* (Winter 1981/82): 42–58.

———. "Prosperity and Peace." *International Studies Quarterly* 27, no. 4 (1983): 381–87.

———. "The Mysterious Case of Vanishing Hegemony." *International Organization* 39, no. 2 (1985): 207–31.

Salvati, Michele. "Political Business Cycles and Long Waves in Industrial Relations: Notes on Kalecki and Phelps Brown." In Christopher Freeman, ed., *Long Waves in the World Economy*, 202–24. London: Butterworth 1983. [1981]

Sau, Ranjit. "Economic Crisis and Economic Theory." *Economic and Political Weekly* (Bombay) 17 (1982): 573–88.

Schlesinger, Arthur M. "Tides of American Politics." Yale Review 29, no. 2 (1939): 217–30.

Schlesinger, Arthur M., Jr. *The Cycles of American History*. Boston: Houghton Mifflin, 1986.

Schmookler, Jacob. *Invention and Economic Growth*. Cambridge, Mass.: Harvard University Press, 1966.

Schneider, William. "Elite and Public Opinion: The Alliance's New Fissure?" *Public Opinion* (February/March 1983): 5–8, 51.

Schouten, D. B. J. "Comment on Van Der Zwan's Paper." In S. K. Kuipers and G. J. Lanjouw, eds., *Prospects of Economic Growth*. Oxford: North-Holland, 1980: 235–37.

Schulte, Heinrich. *Statistische-methodische Untersuchungen zum Problem langer Wellen*. Schriften zur Wirtschaftswissenshaftlichen Forschung, no. 135. Meisenheim am Hain: A/VVA, 1981.

Schumpeter, Elizabeth Boody. "English Prices and Public Finance, 1660–1822." *Review of Economic Statistics* 20 (1938): 21–37.

Schumpeter, Joseph A. "Depressions: Can We Learn from Past Experiences?" In Schumpeter, *The Economics of the Recovery Program*, 3–21. New York: McGraw-Hill, 1934. Reprinted in Schumpeter, *Essays of J. A. Schumpeter*, 108–17. Cambridge, Mass.: Addison-Wesley, 1951.

———. *Business Cycles*. New York: McGraw-Hill, 1939.

Screpanti, Ernesto. "Long Economic Cycles and Recurring Proletarian Insurgencies." *Review* 7, no. 2 (1984): 509–48.

Seaton, Albert. *The Austro-Hungarian Army of the Seven Years' War*. Osprey Publishing, Ltd., 1973.

Šećerov, Slavko. *Economic Phenomena before and after War: A Statistical Theory of Modern Wars*. London: Routledge & Kegan Paul; New York: Dutton, 1919).

Seligman, Edwin R. A. "The Cost of the War and How It Was Met." *American Economic Review* 9 (1919): 739–70.

Sella, Domenico. "European Industries, 1500–1700." In Carlo M. Cipolla, ed., *The Fontana Economic History of Europe*. Vol. 2. Glasgow: Collins, 1974.

Senge, Peter M. "The Economic Long Wave: A Survey of Evidence." MIT System Dynamics Group working paper, April 1982.

Senghaas, D. "The Cycles of War and Peace." *Bulletin of Peace Proposals* 14, no. 2 (1983): 119–24.

Shaikh, A. "An Introduction to the History of Crisis Theories." In [Union for Radical Political Economics], *U.S. Capitalism in Crisis*, 219–41. New York: URPE, 1978.

Shuman, James B., and David Rosenau. *The Kondratieff Wave*. New York: World Publishers, 1972.

Silberling, Norman J. *The Dynamics of Business: An Analysis of Trends, Cycles, and Time Relationships in American Economic Activity since 1700 and Their Bearing upon Governmental and Business Policy*. New York: McGraw-Hill, 1943.

Silberner, Edmund. *La guerre dans la pensée économique du XVIe au XVIIIe siècle*. Paris: Librairie du recueil Sirey, 1939.

———. *The Problem of War in Nineteenth-Century Economic Thought*. Princeton, N.J.: Princeton University Press, 1946.

Silk, Leonard. "Fifty-Year Cycle: Real or myth?" *New York Times,* June 1, 1978, D2.

Simiand, François. *Les fluctuations économiques à longue période et la crise mondiale*. Paris: Librairie Felix Alcau, 1932a.

———. *Recherches anciennes et nouvelles sur le mouvement général des prix de XVIe au XIXe siècle*. Paris: Domat Montchrestien, 1932b.

Singer, J. David. "The Level-of-Analysis Problem in International Relations." *World Politics* 14, no. 1 (1961): 77–92.

———. "Accounting for International War: The State of the Discipline." *Journal of Peace Research* 18 (1981): 1–18.

Singer, J. David, and Thomas Cusack. "Periodicity, Inexorability, and Steersmanship in International War." In Richard L. Merritt and Bruce M. Russett, eds., *From National Development to Global Community*, 404–22. London: George Allen & Unwin, Ltd., 1981.

Singer, J. David, and Melvin Small. *The Wages of War, 1816–1965*. New York: John Wiley, 1972.

Slutsky, E. "The Summation of Random Causes as the Source of Cyclic Processes." *Econometrica* 5 (1937): 105–46.

Small, Melvin, and J. David Singer. *Resort to Arms: International and Civil Wars, 1816–1980*. Beverly Hills, Calif.: Sage Publications, 1982.

Snyder, Carl. "On the Structure and Inertia of Prices." *American Economic Review* 24, no. 2 (1934): 187–207.

Snyder, Glenn H., and Paul Diesing. *Conflict among Nations*. Princeton, N.J.: Princeton University Press, 1977.

Soper, John C. *The Long Swing in Historical Perspective [1971]*. New York: Arno Press, 1978.

Sorokin, Pitirim A. *Social and Cultural Dynamics*. Vol. 3: *Fluctuations of Social Relationships, War, and Revolution*. New York: American Book Company, 1937.

———. *Social Change and Cultural Dynamics*. Boston: Porter Sargent, 1957.

Spiethoff, A. "Krisen." *Handwörterbuch der Staatswissenschaften* 6 (1925): 8–91.

Spree, Reinhard. " 'Lange Wellen' des Wirtschaftswachstums." In W. H. Schröder and R. Spree, eds., *Historische Konjunkturforschung*, 304–15. Vol. 2 of *Historische-sozial-wissenschaftliche Forschungen*. Stuttgart: Klett-Cotta, 1980.

Steinberg, S. H. *The Thirty Years' War and the Conflict for European hegemony, 1600–1660*. New York: W. W. Norton, 1966.

Sterman, John D. "A Simple Model of the Economic Long Wave." MIT System Dynamics Group working paper D–3410, March 1983a.

———. Letter to *Science* 219 (1983b): 1276.

———. "An Integrated Theory of the Economic Long Wave." *Futures* 17, no. 2 (1985): 104–31.

Sterman, John D. "The Economic Long Wave: Theory and Evidence." *System Dynamics Review* 2, no. 2 (1986): 87–125.

Sterman, John D., and Dennis Meadows. "Strategem-2: A Micro-Computer Simulation Game of the Kondratiev Cycle." Sloan School of Management working paper WP–1623–85, MIT, 1985.

Stetson, Harlan T. *Sunspots in Action*. New York: Ronald Press, 1947.

Stoken, D. "What the Long Term Cycle Tells Us about the 1980s: The Kondratieff Cycle and Its Effects on Social-Psychology." *Futurist* 14, no. 1 (1980): 14.

Strickland, Julie Z. "Long Cycles, Lateral Pressure, and World War I: An Integration of Systemic and Nation-State Level Explanations." Paper presented at International Studies Association—West, San Diego, Calif., March 1982.

Sun Tzu. *The Art of War*. Trans. Samuel B. Griffith. New York: Oxford University Press, 1963.

Taagepera, Rein. "Size and Duration of Empires: Growth-Decline Curves, 3000 to 600 B.C." *Social Science Research* 7 (1978): 180–96.

———. "Size and Duration of Empires: Growth-Decline Curves, 600 B.C. to 600 A.D." *Social Science History* 3, no. 3 (1979): 115.

Taylor, A. J. P. *The Struggle for Mastery in Europe, 1848–1918*. Oxford: Clarendon Press, 1954.

———. *The Origins of the Second World War* [1961]. New York: Atheneum, 1966.

Taylor, F. L. *The Art of War in Italy, 1494–1529*. 1921; reprint ed., Westport, Conn.: Greenwood Press, 1973.

Thomas, Brinley. "The Rhythm of Growth in the Atlantic Economy of the Eighteenth Century." *Research in Economic History* 3 (1978): 1–46.

Thomas, Kenneth P., and Robert A. Denemark. "The Brenner-Wallerstein Debate: A Preliminary Assessment." Paper presented at the American Political Science Association annual meeting, New Orleans, La., August 1985.

Thompson, William R. "Phases of the Business Cycle and the Outbreak of War." *International Studies Quarterly* 26, no. 2 (1982): 301–11.

———. "Uneven Economic Growth, Systemic Challenges, and Global Wars." *International Studies Quarterly* 27, no. 3 (1983a): 341–55.

———. "World Wars, Global Wars, and the Cool Hand Luke Syndrome." *International Studies Quarterly* 27, no. 3 (1983b): 369–74.

———. "Cycles, Capabilities, and War." In Thompson, ed., *Contending Approaches to World System Analysis*. Beverly Hills, Calif.: Sage Publications, 1983c.

———. "The World-Economy, the Long-Cycle, and the Question of World-System Time." In Pat McGowan and Charles K. Kegley, eds., *Foreign Policy and the Modern World-System*, 35–62. Beverly Hills, Calif.: Sage Publications, 1983d.

———. Global War and the Dissynchronization of Hegemonic Power, Kondratieffs, and

Long Cycles.'' Paper presented at the American Political Science Association annual meeting, Washington, D.C., September 1984.

———. ''Cycles of General, Hegemonic, and Global War and the Periodicity Question.'' In Michael D. Ward and Urs Luterbacher, eds., *Dynamic Models of International Conflict*, 462–88. Boulder, Colo.: Lynne Reinner, 1985a.

———. ''Polarity, the Long Cycle, and Global Power Warfare.'' Paper presented at the American Political Science Association annual meeting, New Orleans, La., August 1985b.

Thompson, William R., and L. Gary Zuk. ''War, Inflation, and the Kondratieff Long Wave.'' *Journal of Conflict Resolution* 26, no. 4 (1982): 621–44.

Thompson, William R., ed. *Contending Approaches to World System Analysis*. Beverly Hills, Calif.: Sage Publications, 1983.

Thomson, David. *England in the Nineteenth Century*. 1950; rev. ed. Harmondsworth: Penguin 1978.

Thurow, Lester C. ''The Economic Case against Star Wars.'' *Technology Review* 89, no. 2 (1986): 11.

Tilly, Charles. ''Reflections on the History of European State-Making.'' In Tilly, ed., *The Formation of National States in Western Europe*. Princeton, N.J.: Princeton University Press, 1975.

———. *As Sociology Meets History*. New York: Academic Press, 1981.

Tinbergen, Jan. ''Kondratiev Cycles and So-Called Long Waves: The Early Research.'' *Futures* 13, no. 4 (1981): 258–63.

Tinbergen, Jan, and J. J. Polak. *The Dynamics of Business Cycles*. 1942; reprint ed., Chicago: University of Chicago Press, 1950.

Toynbee, Arnold J. *A Study of History*, Vol. 9. London: Oxford University Press, 1954.

Trevor-Roper, H. R. *The Crisis of the Seventeenth Century*. New York: Harper & Row, 1956.

Trotsky, Leon. Speech on long waves, in *Proceedings of the Third Communist International* (June–July 1921): 22.

———. *The First Five Years of the Communist International*. New York: Monad Press, 1972.

———. ''The Curve of Capitalist Development'' [1923]. In Trotsky, *Problems of Everyday Life*, 273–80. New York: Monad Press, 1973.

Tylecote, Andrew. ''Towards an Explanation of the Long Wave, 1780–2000.'' *Review* 7, no. 4 (1984): 703–17.

U.S. Bureau of the Census. *Statistical Abstract of the United States, 1984*. Washington, D.C., 1983.

———. *Historical Statistics of the United States, Colonial Times to 1970*. Washington, D.C., 1975).

Valley Camp Coal Company. *Five Centuries of War, Peace and Wheat Prices*. Cleveland, Ohio: Century Press, 1942.

Van Den Dungen, Peter. ''Jean De Bloch: A Nineteenth Century Peace Researcher.'' *Peace Research* (Brandon, Manitoba) 15, no. 3 (1983): 21–27.

Vanderlip, Frank A. ''The Cost of the Spanish American War.'' *McClure's Magazine* 11 (1898): 553–58.

Vandermotten, Christian. ''Tendences longues de l'évolution de la production, de l'emploi et de la productivité industriels en Belgique: 1840–1978.'' *Cahiers économiques de Bruxelles* 22 no. 86 (1980): 261–301.

Van Der Wee, Herman. ''European Historical Statistics and Economic Growth.'' *Explorations in Economic History* 13 (1976): 347–51.

Van der Zwan, A. ''On the Assessment of the Kondratieff Cycle and Related Issues.'' In S. K.

Kuipers and G. J. Lanjouw, eds., *Prospects of Economic Growth*, 183–222. Oxford: North-Holland, 1980.

Van Dillen, J. G. "Economic Fluctuations and Trade in the Netherlands, 1650–1750" In Peter Earle, ed., *Essays in European Economic History, 1500–1800*, 199–211. Oxford: Clarendon Press, 1974.

Van Duijn, J. J. "The Long Wave in Economic Life." *De Economist* (Amsterdam) 125, no. 4 (1979): 544–76.

———. "Comment on Van Der Zwan's Paper." In S. K. Kuipers and G. J. Lanjouw, eds., *Prospects of Economic Growth*, 223–33. Oxford: North-Holland, 1980.

———. "Fluctuations in Innovations over Time." *Futures* 13, no. 4 (1981): 264–75.

———. *The Long Wave in Economic Life*. 1979; reprint ed., Boston: Allen and Unwin, 1983.

Van Evera, Stephen. "Why Cooperation Failed in 1914." *World Politics* 38, no. 1 (1985): 80–117.

Van Ewijk, Casper. "The Long Wave: A real phenomenon." *De Economist* (Amsterdam) 129, no. 3 (1981): 324–72.

———. "A Spectral Analysis of the Kondratieff Cycle." *Kyklos* 35, no. 3 (1982): 468–99.

Van Gelderen, J. [J. Fedder pseudo.] "Springvloed: Beschouwingen over industrieele ontwikkeling en prijsbeweging" (Spring Tides of Industrial Development and Price Movements). *De nieuwe tijd* 18 (1913).

Van Paridon, C. W. A. M. "Onderzoek naar de lange golf in het economisch leven." *Maandschrift Economie* 43 (1979): 227–39, 280–98.

Van Roon, Gerrit. "Historians and Long Waves." *Futures* 13, no. 5 (1981): 383–88.

Väyrynen, Raimo. "Economic Fluctuations, Technological Innovations and the Arms Race in a Historical Perspective." *Cooperation and Conflict* 18, no. 3 (1983a): 135–59.

———. "Economic Cycles, Power Transitions, Political Management and Wars between Major Powers." *International Studies Quarterly* 27, no. 4 (1983b): 389–418.

Verlinden, C., J. Craeybeckx, and E. Scholliers. "Price and Wage Movements in Belgium in the Sixteenth Century." In Peter Burke, ed., *Economy and Society in Early Modern Europe: Essays from* Annales, 55–84. New York: Harper & Row, 1972. [1955]

Volland, Craig S. "The Passing of the Hydrocarbon Era: New Technologies Key to Economic Revival, Says Kondratieff Long-Wave Theory." *High Technology* (January 1983): 74–76.

Volland, Craig S. "Kondratieff's Long-Wave Cycle." *Futurist* 19, no. 1 (1985): 26–28.

Von Tunzelmann, G. N. "Trends in Real Wages, 1750–1850, Revisited." *Economic History Review* 32, no. 1 (1979): 33–49.

Wagemann, Ernst. *Struktur und Rhythmus der Weltwirtschaft: Grundlagen einer weltwirtschaftlichen Konjunkturlehre*. Berlin: Reimar Hobburg, 1931.

Wallerstein, Immanuel. *The Modern World-System*. Vol. 1: *Capitalist Agriculture and the Origins of the European World-Economy in the Sixteenth Century*. New York: Academic Press, 1974.

———. "World-System Analysis: Theoretical and Interpretive Issues." In Barbara Hockey Kaplan, ed., *Social Change in the Capitalist World Economy*, 219–35. Beverly Hills, Calif.: Sage Publications, 1978.

———. "Kondratieff Up or Kondratieff Down?" *Review* 2, no. 4 (1979): 663–73.

———. *The Modern World-System*. Vol. 2: *Mercantilism and the Consolidation of the European World-Economy 1600–1750*. New York: Academic Press, 1980.

———. "The Three Instances of Hegemony in the History of the Capitalist World-Economy." *International Journal of Comparative Sociology* 24, no. 1–2 (1983): 100–108.

———. "Long Waves as Capitalist Process." *Review* 7, no. 4 (1984a): 559–75.

———. "Economic Cycles and Socialist Policies." *Futures* 16, no. 6 (1984b): 579–85.

Wallerstein, Immanuel, ed. *The Politics of the World-Economy*. Cambridge: Cambridge University Press, 1984.

Waltz, Kenneth. *Man, the State and War*. New York: Columbia University Press, 1959.

———. *Theory of International Politics*. Reading, Mass.: Addison-Wesley, 1979.

Ward, Benjamin. *The Ideal Worlds of Economics: Liberal, Radical and Conservative Economic World Views*. New York: Basic Books, 1979. [Later released as 3 vols., page numbers of which are cited as 1979a, b, or c.]

Warren, Robert. "War Financing and Its Economic Effects." *Proceedings of the Academy of Political Sciences* 18 (January 1940): 447–54.

Warsh, David. *The Idea of Economic Complexity*. New York: Viking Press, 1984.

Weber, Robert Philip. "Society and Economy in the Western World System." *Social Forces* 59, no. 4 (1981): 1130–48.

———. "Cyclical Theories of Crisis in the World System." In Albert Bergesen, ed., *Crises in the World-System*, 37–55. Beverly Hills, Calif.: Sage Publications, 1983.

Wedgwood, C. V. "The Futile and Meaningless War." In Theodore K. Rabb, ed., *The Thirty Years' War,* 15–32. 1938; reprint ed., New York: University Press of America, 1981.

Weinstock, Ulrich. *Das Problem der Kondratieff-Zyklen*. Berlin: Duncker & Humblot, 1964.

Wheeler, Hugh G. "Effects of War on Industrial Growth." *Society* 12 (1975): 48–52.

———. "Postwar Industrial Growth." In J. David Singer, ed., *The Correlates of War II: Testing Some Realpolitik Models,* 258–84. New York: Free Press, 1980.

Wheeler, Raymond Holder. "The Effect of Climate on Human Behavior in History." *Transactions of the Kansas Academy of Science* 46 (1943): 22.

Wicksell, Knut. *Interest and Prices: A Study of the Causes Regulating the Value of Money* 1898; reprint ed., New York: Augustus Kelley, 1965.

Wight, Martin. *Systems of States*. Leicester: Leicester University Press, 1977.

Willoughby, John A. "The Lenin-Kautsky Unity-Rivalry Debate." *Review of Radical Political Economics* 11 (Winter 1979): 91–101.

Wilson, Charles. *The Transformation of Europe, 1558–1648*. Berkeley: University of California Press, 1976.

Wilson, Charles, and Geoffrey Parker, eds. *An Introduction to the Sources of European Economic History, 1500–1800*. Ithaca, N.Y.: Cornell University Press, 1977.

Woods, Frederick Adams, and Alexander Baltzly. *Is War Diminishing?* Boston: Houghton Mifflin Co., 1915.

Woytinsky, W. "Das Rätsel der langen Wellen." *Schmoller's Jahrbuch* 55 (1931).

Wright, Chester W., ed. *Economic Problems of War and Its Aftermath*. Chicago: University of Chicago Press, 1942.

Wright, Quincy. *A Study of War*. 1942; reprint ed., Chicago: University of Chicago Press, 1965.

Zambell, Richard G. *Hyperinflation or Depression?* West Palm Beach, Fla.: Weiss Research, 1984.

Zeeuw, J. W. de. *Peat and the Dutch Golden Age: The Historical Meaning of Energy-Attainability*. Wageningen: Afdeling agrarische geschiedenis landbouwhogeschool, 1978.

INDEX

Aboukir, battle of (*1798*), 114*n*

Adduction, 2, 12, 179, 281, 350

Africa, 127, 290, 293, 300, 334, 371

Agriculture, 341; effects of war on, 34*n*, 268*n*, 339; in long wave, 54, 56*n*, 87, 91, 96*n*, 169, 195, 200, 206, 211, 213, 215; in preindustrial economies, 60*n*, 327

Airplanes. *See* Military forces, air; Transportation

Alliances, 102, 119. *See also* Hegemonic war, coalitions in

American Revolution, 104*n*, 128

Amsterdam, 79*n*, 201, 202, 207, 208; as financial center, 128, 302, 314, 315

Analogy. *See* Historical analogy

Anglo-German arms race, 336–37, 345, 361, 371

Anti-Semitism, 61, 262, 264

Antwerp, Belgium, 127, 296, 301, 304

Armada, war of Spanish (*1588*), 113, 116, 127, 306

Arms sector, 42, 102, 264*n*

Artillery. *See* Military forces

Asia trade, 112, 113, 127, 128, 290, 293, 300, 314, 315, 316, 318, 319

Austria, 286, 290, 296; and war, 114*n*, 255, 294, 309–13; economy of, 293, 301

Austro-Prussian War (*1866*), 101*n*, 334, 338

Auto-Correlation Function, 194, 244

Balance of power, 12, 119, 120, 123, 146*n*, 294*n*, 334, 366; system, 102, 115, 128, 287, 313, 365

Baltic trade, 128, 292–93, 298–300, 307, 314, 315, 316, 319

Bankruptcies, 262, 284, 302, 306, 357*n*

Base dating scheme. *See* Long wave base dating scheme

Belgium, 308*n*, 314*n*; long waves in, 54, 69, 72, 90, 91, 97, 200, 208, 213, 214, 303–4

Bethmann, Chancellor, of Germany, 368*n*

Biogenetics, 62, 353

Box-Tiao analysis, 103, 268, 270

Breitenfeld, Battle of (*1631*), 323

Bretton Woods, 138

Britain. *See* Great Britain

Business cycles (Juglar), 7*n*, 21*n*, 32*n*, 44*n*, 53, 54, 56, 66, 75, 83, 85, 88–89, 90, 97, 184; political, 7*n*, 47

Cannon. *See* Military forces, artillery

Capabilities. *See* National capabilities

Capital investment, 44*n*, 180–81, 189*n*, 327, 363, 384; role in long wave, 25–27, 43, 45, 46, 47, 52, 56, 58–59, 64–65, 78, 81*n*, 91, 96, 164, 167, 227–28, 231–33, 256–57, 258–59, 274, 276; affected by war, 33, 34*n*, 35, 37, 268, 269, 276, 278, 339

Capital investment school, 14, 24, 25, 40, 47–50, 55, 148–49, 167*n*, 278

Capitalism, 27–31, 34, 42*n*, 60, 61, 155, 159, 286; as basis of world-system, 12, 126, 133, 150, 165*n*; crises, role in long wave, 27–31, 42, 45, 47, 134, 158, 168; "universal" crises in, 30, 44; stability of, 30, 39, 44, 45, 282. *See also* Property rights

Capitalist crisis school, 14, 24, 25, 40, 59, 87–88, 91, 148, 167*n*, 278. *See also* Marxism

Caribbean Sea, 319, 324

Cateau-Cambresis, Treaty of (*1559*), 288, 306

Champagne fairs, 292–93

Charles V of Austria, 112, 113, 305, 306, 346*n*

Charles VIII of France, 296, 305

China, 11, 31*n*, 118, 347, 351, 352*n*, 361, 365

Civil War, U.S., 34, 36, 273*n*, 347

Class struggle, 24, 42–43, 44–46, 133, 134*n*, 168, 181*n*, 230–31, 233, 273–74, 278, 303–4, 331–32; inequality, 47, 56*n*, 133, 134*n*, 268*n*, 278

Coal, 83, 129, 201, 207, 298, 300, 319, 328, 331

Cold war, 42, 152, 342, 344, 345, 351, 352, 356–57; SALT agreements, 288, 355–56

Cologne, 74, 200–201